GREAT NECK LIBRARY

FRANCE
PAU
TOULOUSE
MONTPELLIER
PERPIGNAN
Garonne

Vielha
Parc Nacional d'Aigüestortes ★★
★★★ **PIRINEOS CATALANES**
ANDORRA ★★
Puigcerdà
El Port de Llança
SANT PERE DE RODES ★★★
★ **Figueres**
★★ **Besalú**
Cadaqués ★★
★★ **Girona**
Empúries ★★
Lleida ★
COSTA BRAVA ★★★
★★★ **POBLET**
★★ **Montblanc**
BARCELONA ★★★
Sitges ★★
★★★ **Port Aventura** **Tarragona** ★★
Costa Daurada ★★

MEDITERRANEAN SPAIN
MAR
MEDITERRANEO
Peñíscola

MEDITERRANEAN COAST

VALENCIA ★★★
P. Natural de la Albufera
Cullera
Gandia
Alcoi / Alcoy
Xàbia ★
Guadalest ★
Calp
Altea
Xixona
Benidorm
ALACANT / ALICANTE ★★
Costa Blanca ★

IBIZA   ISLAS   BALEARES

1	Galicia (1050 km)
2	Around the Montes de Cantabria (800 km)
3	Basque Country, Rioja and Navarra (700 km)
4	Catalunya (1000 km)
5	Castilla y León (750 km)
6	Zaragoza, Soria, Guadalajara and Teruel (900 km)
7	Around Madrid (700 km)
8	Extremadura and the Peña de Francia (800 km)
9	Castilla–La Mancha (850 km)
10	The Levant region (750 km)
11	Córdoba, Sevilla, Cádiz and Málaga (900 km)
12	Granada, Almería and Jaén (850 km)

Old Toledo by the Tajo with the cathedral (left) and the Alcázar (right)
© Bertrand Gardel/hemis.fr

THEGREENGUIDE
Spain

How to...

Planning
Your Trip

Introducing
Spain

Discovering
Spain

Welcome
to Spain

If this is your first trip to Spain, welcome to a land that boasts many different
cultures and languages, virtually every kind of landscape, a wealth of heritage
and history, world-renowned cuisine and quality wines. Whether you opt for
beach or mountains, city or countryside, Spain consistently delivers.

Returning visitors will note with delight how Spain's towns and cities have
reinvented themselves to keep up with the times while preserving their heritage.
Travelling the country is easier than ever, whether by train, road or plane. Resorts
offer new cultural attractions and personalized experiences, too. Meanwhile,
reassuringly, large swaths of wild Spain – mountains, marshland, forests and
rolling olive groves – remain ripe for exploration.

Since the financial crisis of 2008, Spain has faced great economic hardships, and
visitors to the Costa del Sol (for example) may notice the oversupply
of holiday housing and speculative building. Locally owned hotels and
restaurants were hit hardest, so seek them out, when possible, over big brands.
The silver lining for travellers is that the real cost of many Spanish holidays is low
compared to other European destinations, despite the country being the classic,
unparalleled travel destination it always has been.

Eivissa, Ibiza © Tono Balaguer/age fotostock

Green Guides - Discover the Destination

Main sections

PLANNING YOUR TRIP
The blue-tabbed section gives you **ideas for your trip** and **practical information.**

INTRODUCTION
The orange-tabbed section explores **Nature, History, Art and Culture** and the **Region Today.**

DISCOVERING
The green-tabbed section features Principal Sights by region, **Sights, Walking Tours, Excursions,** and **Driving Tours.**

Region intros

At the start of each region in the Discovering section is a brief introduction. Accompanied by the region maps, these provide an overview of the main tourism areas and their background.

Region maps

Star ratings

Michelin has given star ratings for more than 100 years. If you're pressed for time, we recommend you visit the three- or two-star sights first:

★★★ Worth a special journey

★★ Worth a detour

★ Interesting

Tours

We've selected driving and walking tours that show you the best of each town or region. Step-by-step directions are accompanied by detailed maps with marked routes. Selected addresses give you options for accommodation and dining en route.

Addresses

We've selected the best hotels, restaurants, cafés, shops, nightlife and entertainment to fit all budgets. See the Legend on the cover flap for an explanation of the price categories. See the back of the guide for an index of where to find hotels and restaurants.

Other reading

+ Green Guide Portugal
+ Must Sees Andalucia
+ Must Sees Barcelona
+ National Map
  Spain, Portugal
+ Road Atlas
  Spain & Portugal

Planning Your Trip

Introducing Spain

Discovering Spain

Regions of Spain

Central Spain (pp114-227)

The central tableland's rare grandeur and sense of history is best felt in its Medieval court and cathedral cities such as **Segovia**, **Ávila**, **Salamanca**, **Burgos**, **Valladolid** and **Toledo**. Journeys between them take you across light-soaked plains where castles, often dramatically rearing up above them, are a reminder of Castilla's embattled past. Yet the landscapes here can also be unexpected. **La Mancha**'s flatlands – home to Don Quixote – contrast with **Soria**'s soft green river valleys, **Extremadura**'s boulder-strewn hills and the high, rocky sierras north and west of Madrid. City sights allow you to travel back in time. **Mérida**, for example, preserves classical Roman monuments. But elsewhere, above all in **Madrid**, the country's political and business capital, there is a taste for vibrant modernity. Its hectic nightlife and shopping culture are as much part of any visit to the city as the time spent lingering in its splendid art galleries and museums.

Atlantic Spain (pp228-319)

Atlantic Spain's shoreline stretches from France west to the deeply indented Galician coastline, then south to the Portuguese border. Rough seas break onto rocks, beaches and the coastal promenades of fishing villages, resorts and cities such as **Donostia-San Sebastián**, **Bilbao**, **Santander**, **A Coruña** and **Vigo**. Behind the coast lie verdant mountains and valleys in the **Basque Country**, **Cantabria**, **Asturias** and **Galicia** where traditional farming life survives along with local languages and dialects. Further inland in **Navarra** and **La Rioja** are historic vineyards, many now boasting state-of-the-art wineries such as Bodegas Ysios and museums in Briones and Elciego. The Medieval **Camino de Santiago** pilgrimage route, still walked today, is a popular way to explore all these northern regions. Monasteries, hermitages and hostels lie on its path. So, too, do cities such as **Santiago de Compostela**, its end point, and **Pamplona**, world-famous for its (controversial) bull-running. Bilbao, with its spectacular Guggenheim Museum, and the gourmet mecca of Donostia-San Sebastián catch the eye of more visitors than ever.

Praia das Catedrais, Rías Altas, Galicia, Atlantic Spain
© j-wildman/iStockphoto.com

Cadaqués, Costa Brava, Mediterranean Spain
© KarSol/iStockphoto.com

Mediterranean Spain (pp320-469)

Spain's eastern Mediterranean coast and the Balearic Islands are famed for their beaches. **Benidorm**'s are the most crowded, but there is variety to satisfy all tastes: the **Costa Brava** offers coves; **Murcia** has fine scuba-diving waters; and **Menorca** boasts spectacular long sands. Inland, **Aragón**'s desolate mountains and flatlands, bisected by the giant River Ebro, and the hill country of **Catalunya** and **Valencia** are vast areas of unspoilt beauty. Their historic cities stand out for their regional architectural styles. Highlights include **Zaragoza**'s Mudéjar architecture, **Tarragona**'s Roman monuments, **Girona**'s Gothic cathedral, Murcia's Baroque splendour, **Palma de Mallorca**'s old town and Valencia's medieval quarter and striking **Ciudad de las Artes y las Ciencias**, Europe's largest cultural centre. Yet it is the port city of **Barcelona** that receives the bulk of tourists, thanks to its museums, arts scene, football, nightlife and restaurants. Rural escapes to wine country, tiny villages and parks in the mountainous interior are an antidote to the nerve-jangling bustle of urban sightseeing.

Andalucía and the Canary Islands (pp470-579)

Andalucía's coastline is the most heavily developed in the Iberian peninsula. The resorts and golf courses of the **Costa del Sol** can stretch miles inland. But away from the coast sit three unmissable cities – **Granada**, **Sevilla** and **Córdoba** – with architectural wonders dating from Islamic al-Andalus. The *pueblos blancos* (white villages), which cling to rocky clifftops, and the ports of **Almería**, **Cádiz** and **Huelva** are the epitome of Andalusian charm. Tourists are rediscovering **Málaga**, the once-scruffy port city on the Costa del Sol that's an emerging cultural capital. They never left the **Canary Islands**, the volcanic archipelago off the Moroccan coast famous for its balmy year-round climate and family-friendly resorts.

Each island is a world apart. **El Hierro** and **La Gomera** offer unbridled nature, while **La Palma** preserves old-fashioned colonial elegance. **Gran Canaria**, **Tenerife** and, to a lesser extent, **Lanzarote** are cosmopolitan centres laden with characterless resorts, but they boast plenty of hidden, locals-only corners if you know where to look.

Roman bridge over the Guadalquivir and the Mezquita, Córdoba, Andalucía
© carmengabriela/iStockphoto.com

Planning
Your Trip

Camino de Santiago through the vineyards near, Ventosa, La Rioja
©Daniel Acevedo/age fotostock

Planning Your Trip

Plaza de España, Sevilla
© Jon Arnold Images/ hemis.fr

Inspiration

WHAT'S HOT

– A neglected port city no longer, **Málaga** (p488) has become the unofficial cultural capital of southern Spain, thanks to new outposts of the Centre Pompidou and State Russian Museum, plus the independently owned Ifergan Collection, which opened in 2018 and houses an unparalleled variety of Phoenician artifacts.

– After a decade of construction, Spain's fast train (AVE) now calls at **Granada**, shaving two hours off of journeys from Madrid and putting the Alhambra and the ski slopes of the **Sierra Nevada** (p483) at your fingertips.

– Up north, the UFO-like Centro Botín has put the seaside city of **Santander** on the contemporary art map with its internationally acclaimed exhibitions, while in the Basque Country, the Chillida-Leku sculpture museum (**San Sebastián**) reopened in 2019 after an eight-year hiatus and revamp.

– Move over, fine-dining restaurants: In **Madrid**, the most intriguing dishes (think Peruvian tapas or Spanish-Japanese tasting menus) are often found in traditional markets like the Mercado de Vallehermoso.

Centre Pompidou Málaga, designed by Javier Pérez de la Fuente y Juan Antonio Marín Malavé
© Málaga City Council/Turespaña

Spain's Cities

I t's a tough choice: the museums of Madrid, or the bars and beaches of Barcelona? Sizzling Seville, or vibrant Valencia? It's easily resolved – spend a long weekend in each!

MADRID 🔊 See p119

Madrid's city centre may lack the old-world charm of many of Spain's major cities, but its electric street life, best seen during the paseo when Madrileños cram the promenades and tapas bars around the back streets of Plaza Mayor and Plaza Santa Ana, wins over most visitors. Art is the city's biggest cultural treasure, and the so-called Golden Triangle – the Prado, Thyssen-Bornemisza and Centro Reina Sofía – is a bucket-list destination for art lovers the world over.

BARCELONA 🔊 See p325

Historic cobbled streets oozing medieval atmosphere; a superb sandy beach just yards away from the famous Las Ramblas; vibrant nightlife; world-class museums and galleries; shops, bars and markets where local character rises above international fashion – Barcelona really does have it all. The jewel in the crown, however, (unless you're a football fan) is the legacy of Gaudí; don't leave without exploring landmarks like Casa Milà, Casa Batlló or la Sagrada Familia, scheduled to be finished in 2026.

Roof terrace of Círculo de Bellas Artes, Madrid

© Facto Foto/age fotostock

Casco Viejo, Bilbao
© Jon Arnold Images/hemis.fr

SEVILLA
♢See p520

Beyond the Alcázar, a stunning Moorish fortress, and the cathedral, with its unmistakable Giralda bell tower, Sevilla's Barrio de Santa Cruz is filled with romantic corners and locals-only bars and taverns. Triana, the old Romani and fishermen's quarter across the Guadalquivir, has ceramic shops, flamenco haunts and riverside restaurants, while the Barrio de la Macarena (for its produce market), the Museo de Bellas Artes and the Convento de Santa Paula complete the list of must-see sites.

VALENCIA
♢See p424

The Ciutat de les Arts i les Ciències, with its Caltrava-designed space-age structures, represents Valencia's forward-looking gaze, but the city's most iconic architecture – such as the Gothic La Lonja and Modernist Mercat Central – are a reminder of its rich past. Don't miss exploring the Ciutat Vella (old town) and trendy Ruzafa district, stopping at key landmarks like the Palau de la Generalitat, Palacio del Marquès de Dos Aguas and the Estació del Nord railway station.

TOURIST OFFICES
www.spain.info

London
1st Floor, 100 George Street
W1U 8NU
☎020 731 72011

New York
60 East 42nd Street - Suite 5300
New York, NY 10165-0039
☎212 265 8822

Chicago
333 North Michigan Avenue,
Suite 2800
Chicago, IL 60601
☎312 642 1992

Los Angeles
8383 Wilshire Blvd, Suite 960
Beverly Hills, CA 90211
☎323 658 7195

Miami
2655 Le Jeune Rd, Suite 605
Coral Gables, FL 33134
☎305 476 1966

Toronto
2 Bloor St West, Suite 3402
Toronto, Ontario M4W 3E2
☎416 961 3131

BILBAO
♢See p256

Frank Gehry's Guggenheim Bilbao may have put this industrial city on the tourism circuit, but don't overlook the equally worthy Museo de Bellas Artes with its 10,000-some works spanning nine centuries. The Casco Viejo, or old town, brims with Belle Époque buildings and boasts a lively pintxo (Basque tapas) scene. Other recommended sights include the Euskal Museoa (Basque Museum) and 19C Ensanche neighborhood with its Philippe Starck-designed Azkuna Zentroa cultural centre, housed in a defunct wine warehouse.

The Coast

When you visit Spain's coastal areas is almost as important as *where* you visit, so take the weather, crowds, and prices into account when planning your holiday.

MEDITERRANEAN COAST
See p322

Spain has thousands of miles of idyllic coastline, but the Mediterranean, with its placid, warm waters and talc-fine sand, has long lured Spanish and foreign visitors by the millions.

Costa Brava – The rugged and indented **Costa Brava**, or Wild Coast, with its charming coves and lively resorts, extends from the north of Barcelona to the French border.

Levante – The **Levante** coast, characterised by long sandy beaches and built-up resorts such as Benidorm, Cullera and Gandía, is as popular as ever. This area is also favoured by Spanish families, with lots of second homes here.

Costa del Sol – The **Costa del Sol**, in particular the stretch between Málaga and Estepona, is a succession of luxury developments and golf courses. Marbella is the leading resort here, reinforced by its international jet-set reputation. The remainder of the Andalucían coast is generally quieter, attracting Spanish visitors.

Balearic Islands – The **Balearic Islands** are one of the country's most popular tourist destinations. Of the three main islands, Mallorca and Ibiza attract large numbers of Spanish and foreign visitors, who come here to enjoy their magnificent landscapes and beaches and lively nightlife. Menorca and Formentera's resorts are quieter and offer a more relaxed, nature-focussed holiday.

ATLANTIC COAST
See p230

Spain's North Atlantic coast stretches from the Basque Country in the east to Galicia in the west. Its main resorts, San Sebastián, A Coruña and Santander, are frequented by domestic

Garachico, Tenerife

© RossHelen/iStockphoto.com

visitors, who come for the surfable waves, scenic beaches and pristine seafood. With a few exceptions, the coast of northern Spain has escaped the frenetic development of the Mediterranean and as such preserves its natural beauty and traditional architecture. Most foreigners have yet to discover the **Costa de la Luz** (Coast of Light) stretching from the southernmost tip of Spain to the Portuguese border; it takes in some of the country's finest beaches plus charming family resorts, Roman ruins and vibrant cities like Cádiz, said to be Europe's oldest metropolis.

CANARY ISLANDS
See p552

The archipelago floods with sun-seeking Northern Europeans each winter, but those who venture beyond the pool deck are rewarded with otherworldly landscapes, Caribbean-influenced cuisine, and pulsing local culture. Southern Gran Canaria and Tenerife are lined with big-box resorts, but inland and on the smaller islands, untouched natural beauty abounds.

National Parks

S pain is the bridge between Europe and Africa, and its small footprint belies a dizzying variety of landscapes and ecosystems including salt marshes, conifer forests, high mountains, Mediterranean woodland and the only true desert on the continent. The country's 15 national parks, of which five belong to its islands, are of invaluable ecological import, and protections such as visitor quotas and hunting and fishing bans are in place to preserve their precious flora and fauna. Even today, wilderness still abounds on the Iberian Peninsula; for hikers and nature lovers, there may be no better place in Europe to truly get away from it all.

MOUNTAIN PARKS

Parque Nacional de los Picos de Europa &p277

The country's first national park was the Parque de Montaña de Covadonga, established in 1918. In 1995, this protected area was significantly extended (from 16 925ha/41 822 acres to 64 600ha/ 159 626 acres) and became known as the **Parque Nacional de los Picos de Europa**. This magnificent area, spread over three massifs, is characterised by lush, misty landscapes of glacial *cirque* lakes; wildflower meadows; and extensive forests of beech, chestnut and oak peppered with wild olive, fig and terebinth trees.

In terms of fauna, critters to keep an eye out for include chamois, mountain cats, polecats, foxes, otters, squirrels, eagles and some of the last brown bear colonies in Spain. The park is also home to a staggering 137 butterfly species, some of which occur nowhere else on earth.

Parque Nacional de Ordesa y Monte Perdido &p417

The **Parque Nacional de Ordesa y Monte Perdido**, at the heart of the Pyrenees in the province of Huesca, takes in 15 608ha/38 567 acres and four valleys with landscapes distinguished by rivers, waterfalls, and rocky peaks flanked by mountain pine, beech and fir. Notable tenants range from wild boars to bearded vultures to chamois; sadly, the last Pyrenean ibex (once a hallmark of the park) perished in 2000 .

Parc Nacional d'Aigüestortes i Estany de Sant Maurici &p386

You'd be hard-pressed to find a more idyllic mountain area in Europe than the **Parc Nacional d'Aigüestortes i Estany de Sant Maurici** covering 14 119ha/34 889 acres in the province of Lleida, in the Catalan Pyrenees. Crystalline lakes, dense evergreen forests, and flower-carpeted meadows are the defining features of this alpine eden populated by mountain goats, stoats, pine martens, dormice, golden eagles, capercaillie and grouse.

Sierra Nevada &p483

The **Sierra Nevada** (90 000ha/222 390 acres) is a mountain park with several summits over 3 000m/9 840ft, including Mulhacén, the highest peak

Parc Nacional d'Aigüestortes i Estany de Sant Maurici

© Lucas Vallecillos/age fotostock

on mainland Spain at 3 479m/11 413ft. The variety of the park's flora and fauna is particularly striking in the alpine zone (above 2 600m/8 500ft), where more than 40 endemic herbs thrive and birds associated with northern climes – such as crossbill or greenfinch – are unexpected visitors.

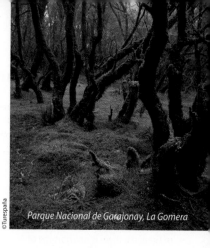
Parque Nacional de Garajonay, La Gomera
©Turespaña

Parque Nacional de Sierra de Guadarrama &p145

The **Parque Nacional de Sierra de Guadarrama** (33 960 ha/83 917 acres), located to the north of Madrid in Castilla y Léon, was established in 2013 and is the country's newest national park. Its landscape is dominated by rocky summits and pine forests boasting exceptional biodiversity. Wolves have made a comeback in the last decade with five packs prowling the area in 2019.

Parque Nacional Monfragüe &p218

The **Parque Nacional Monfragüe** (18 118ha/44 770 acres) runs westward along the River Tagus in Extremadura through holm oak *dehesas* and mountainous ridges. It contains rare mammals like lynxes and genets and some 20 species of birds of pray .

FLATLANDS & WETLANDS
Parque Nacional de Cabañero &p203

The **Parque Nacional de Cabañeros** occupies a flatland tucked between the rocky Montes de Toledo. Covering 40 856ha/100 957 acres, it's primarily Mediterranean forest, abundant with deer, wild boar and birds of prey.

Tablas de Daimiel &p206

The **Tablas de Daimiel**, in the province of Ciudad Real, is the smallest of Spain's national parks with an area of 1 928ha/4 764 acres. Here, the flooding of the Cigüela and Guadiana rivers creates wetlands that are colonised by various species of birds

including migratory herons, egrets and red-crested pollards and wintering pintails and shovelers. The park almost disappeared altogether due to agricultural mismanagement, but after a slap on the wrist by the European Commission and concerted efforts by environmentalists, the aquifers have bounced back some 20m/66ft since their nadir in 2009; lost bird populations have also returned.

Parque Nacional de Doñana &p535

The wealth of species in the **Parque Nacional de Doñana** (50 720ha/125 329 acres) is the result of its three distinct habitats: coastal dunes, salt marshes and former hunting grounds, or *cotos*. A stone's throw from Africa, its wetlands are a key waypoint for migratory birds. Rare animals such as the Iberian lynx and the imperial eagle are occasionally sighted here as well.

Parks On The Spanish Islands &p297, 450, 552, 570, 574, 578

The **Parque Nacional Marítimo-Terrestre de Las Islas Atlánticas de Galicia** comprises the four archipelagos of Cíes, Ons, Sálvora and Cortegada, off the coast of Pontevedra. The tiny **Cabrera Archipelago**, in the Balearics, is an untouched Mediterranean paradise, while the Canaries are home to the **Parque Nacional del Teide**, on Tenerife; the **Caldera de Taburiente**, on La Palma; **Timanfaya**, on Lanzarote; and **Garajonay**, on La Gomera.

The Great Outdoors

Spain's varied climate and landscapes make it possible to enjoy almost every sport and outdoor pursuit imaginable. Whatever experience you're after, you'll find ample offerings and experts to help you up your game.

CYCLING

Spain offers a plethora of **famous cycling routes** in the mountains and on flatter terrain. From the Pyrenees to the Picos de Europa to the Alpujarras of Granada, there is no shortage of scenic highland riding for the fit and ambitious. The **three-nation loop** through Spain, Andorra and France – beginning and ending in La Seu d'Urgell – is a physical challenge with stunning Pyrenean scenery.

For flatland cycling, the Delta del Ebro south of Tarragona (⏱see p390) and the Cerdanya Valley (⏱see p376) in the Pyrenees north of Barcelona have a remarkably level network of roads for easy riding. Cycling the Basque coast along the old corniche road along the Bay of Biscay (⏱see p253) is a perfect way to see fishing villages and rural farmhouses that motorists miss. The **Vía de la Plata** route from Sevilla to Santiago de Compostela (⏱see p290) is a favourite long-distance cycling journey, while the Baix Empordà region (⏱see p364) in northern Catalunya has 19 bike routes through some of the Costa Brava's most picturesque and often overlooked inland villages. Lanzarote (⏱see p568) is the most popular Canary Island for recreational cycling, thanks to its well-paved roads and volcanic landscape. Spain also has 2 200km/1 367mi of abandoned railway lines that have been converted to **Vías Verdes** (green paths). Check www.viasverdes.com for itineraries.

FISHING

Spain's 76 000km/47 235mi of river courses provide a wealth of options for freshwater fishing enthusiasts, although seasons can vary from one region to another. Fishing permits are issued by the Environment Agency (**Ministerio de Agricultura, Alimentación y Medio Ambiente; www.magrama.gob.es**) in the relevant autonomous community. For further information on sea and freshwater fishing, contact the **Federación Española de Pesca y Casting (Calle Navas de Tolosa 3, 1°, 28013 Madrid; ℘915 32 83 53; www.fepyc.es)**.

GOLF

There are over 400 golf courses across the country, a number that is steadily growing, particularly in coastal areas. For further information, contact the **Real Federación Española de Golf (Calle Arroyo del Monte 5, 28035 Madrid; ℘915 55 26 82; www.rfegolf. es)**. A map of golf courses is also available from most tourist offices.

HIKING AND MOUNTAINEERING

Hiking is one of Spain's main attractions. For information on hiking routes and paths, as well as mountaineering, contact the **Spanish Mountaineering Federation (Federación Española de Deportes de Montaña y Escalada, Carrer de Floridablanca 84, 08015 Barcelona; ℘934 26 42 67; www.fedme.es). Long-distance hiking trails** (designated GR for **Gran Recorrido**) vein all of peninsular Spain and the Balearic (⏱see p450) and Canary Islands (⏱see p552). The GR11 is the six-to-seven-week trans-Pyrenean trail that begins at Cabo Higuer west of Hondarribia (⏱see p254) and ends at Cap de Creus (⏱see p362), the Iberian Peninsula's easternmost point just north of Cadaqués. The GR11 intersects with the HRP (Haute Randonnée Pyrénéenne) which follows the Pyrenean crest (⏱see p374, 419) on either side of the France-Spain border.

© Alfred Abad/age fotostock

Hiking in the Vall de Núria, Pirineos Catalanes

Other famous hikes include the **Alberes Mountains** (☝see p374) walk from Puig Neulós above the Le Perthus French border crossing to Banyuls-sur-Mer (one day) or Cap de Creus (two days). The climb from Núria (☝see p376) to the Coll de Núria followed by the traverse east over the Sierra de Catllar to the refuge at Ulldeter affords panoramic views north and south from the crest of the Pyrenees. The **Parc Nacional d'Aigüestortes i Estany de Sant Maurici** (☝see p386) is a hiker hotspot between late May and September. **Parque Nacional de Ordesa y Monte Perdido** (☝see p417) has a good day trip up to the Cola de Caballo waterfall and back or with an overnight up at the Refugio de Góriz overlooking Spain's 'Grand Canyon'.

HORSE RIDING

Activities for riders both novice and experienced range from short excursions to lessons in the ring to multiday treks. Whether you're drawn to the lush forests of Asturias or the parched peaks of Andalucía, there's no shortage of tour companies, equestrian activities and even horse-themed hotels. For further information, contact local tourist boards or the **Spanish Horse Riding Federation (Federación Hípica Española; calle Monte Esquinza 28, 3º, 28010 Madrid; ☎914 36 42 00; www.rfhe.com**

USEFUL WEBSITES

www.spain.info – The official site of the Spanish Tourist Board, providing comprehensive information on all aspects of the country, including transport, accommodation, sport and leisure activities.

www.spain.info/en_GB – The Spanish Tourist Board's site for visitors from the UK.

www.spain.info/en_US – The Spanish Tourist Board's site for visitors from the US.

www.spain.info/en_CA – The Spanish Tourist Board's site for Canadian visitors.

www.fco.gov.uk – The British Government's Foreign and Commonwealth Office website.

www.state.gov – American visitors may check the US State Department website for travel advice.

www.international.gc.ca – Website of Foreign Affairs Canada with relevant travel updates.

www.tourspain.es – The business-to-business site of the Spanish Tourist Board is useful for travel professionals.

Sailboats in Ría de Vigo viewed from Baiona, Galicia

© Javier Larrea/age fotostock

HUNTING

Spain's forests, plains and mountains are hunting grounds where you can find big game including boar, red stag, roe deer, ibex, wild goat and moufflon, and smaller prey such as partridge, pheasant, woodcock, rabbit, hare, quail and duck.

The season generally runs from September to February, although this varies by region and species. Hunting and firearm permits are issued by autonomous community governments. For further information, contact the **Royal Spanish Hunting Federation (Real Federación Española de Caza; Calle de Francos Rodríguez 70, 28039 Madrid; 913 11 14 11; www.fmcaza.es)**.

SAILING

The waters of the Mediterranean (see p320) and Atlantic (see p228) are one of Spain's major attractions. As a result, hundreds of sailing clubs and pleasure marinas have been established along the coastlines. A good resource for recreational sailors is the **Royal Sailing Federation (Real Federación de Vela, Calle Luis de Salazar 9, 28002 Madrid; 915 19 50 08; www.rfev.es)**.

SCUBA DIVING

Spain, particularly the Mediterranean coast, (see p320), appeals to scuba divers of all skill levels, thanks to the development of diving sites such as the Cabo de Gata in Almería, the Islas Medes on the Costa Brava, and resorts in the Balearic and Canary islands. For further information, contact the **Spanish Scuba Diving Federation (Federación Española de Actividades Subacuáticas; Carrer Aragó 517, 08013 Barcelona; www.fedas.es)**.

WINTER SPORTS

There are 33 ski resorts in Spain including 18 in the Pyrenees (see p374, 419), six in the Cordillera Cantábrica (see p109), four in the Sistema Central (see p162), three in the Sistema Ibérica (see p277), two in the Sistema Penibético (near Granada, see p483) and an indoor ski slope in Madrid. Information on these is available via the **Federación Española de Deportes de Invierno (Avenida de los Madroños 36, 28043 Madrid; 913 76 99 30; www.rfedi. es)**, or from **ATUDEM (Asociación Turística de Estaciones de Esquí y Montaña, Avda. Diagona 652 Edificio A Bajos, Barcelona; 932 05 82 95; www.atudem.es)**.

UNESCO World Heritage Sites

Spain has 48 UNESCO World Heritage Sites, defined as monuments with unique historical, artistic or scientific features; groups of buildings; or combined works of man and nature of exceptional beauty. 2019 saw the addition of Gran Canaria's Risco Caído, a craggy mountain area with remnants of of pre-Hispanic culture. UNESCO also compiles a Representative List of Intangible Cultural Heritage that includes such Spanish customs as the Mystery Plays of Elche, Catalan human towers (Castells) and flamenco.

CENTRAL SPAIN

Madrid and Around p118
Alcalá de Henares: University and historic quarter.
Aranjuez: Cultural landscape.
El Escorial: Monastery.

Castilla-León: Ávila, Salamanca & Zamora p158
Ávila: Old town and extra-muros churches.
Salamanca: Old town.

Castilla-León: Segovia, Valladolid & Soria p176
Segovia: Old town; aqueduct.
Sevilla: Cathedral; Alcázar; Archivo de Indias.

Castilla-La Mancha p192
Cuenca: Historic fortified town.
Toledo: Historic city.

Extremadura p216
Cáceres: Old town.
Guadalupe: Monasterio Real de Santa María.
Mérida: Archaeological site.

ATLANTIC SPAIN

El País Vasco and La Rioja p250
San Millán de la Cogolla: Monasterio de Yuso; Monasterio de Suso.

Cantabria and Asturias p270
Oviedo: Monuments in the city; kingdom of Asturias.

Galicia p289
Lugo: Roman walls.
Santiago de Compostela: Old town; Camino de Santiago; Cathedral.

Castilla-León: Burgos, León and Palencia p307
Atapuerca (Burgos): Prehistoric remains.
Burgos: Cathedral.

MEDITERANEAN SPAIN

Barcelona and Around p324
Barcelona: Parc Güell; Palau Güell; Casa Milà; Casa Vicens; Casa Batlló; Palau de la Música Catalana; Hospital de Sant Pau; Colònia Güell Crypt.

Northern Catalunya and Principat d'Andorra p353
Vall de Boí (Lleida): Romanesque churches.

Tarragona and Southern Catalunya p390
Poblet: Monastery.
Tarragona: Roman town (Tarraco).

Aragón p403
Teruel: Mudéjar architecture.

La Comunitat Valenciana & La Región de murcia p423
Elx/Elche: El Palmeral palm grove.
Valencia: La Lonja de la Seda.

The Balearic Islands p450
Ibiza: Biodiversity and culture.

ANDALUCÍA AND THE CANARY ISLANDS

Southern Andalucía p474
Granada: Alhambra; Generalife; Albaicín.
Antequera: ancient dolmens.

Northern Andalucía p503
Córdoba: Historic centre; Medina Azahara; Mosque-Cathedral.
Úbeda & Baeza: Renaissance monumental ensembles.

Western Andalucia p519
Doñana: National Park.

The Canary Islands p552
Gran Canaria: Risco Caído
La Gomera: Garajonay National Park.
Tenerife: San Cristóbal de la Laguna; Parque Nacional del Teide.

Michelin Driving Tours

⟳ **See the driving tours map on the inside front cover. Purchase Michelin maps 571, 572, 574, 577 and 578 to make the most of these tours.**

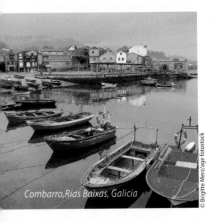

Combarro, Rías Baixas, Galicia

1 GALICIA

Round trip of 1 031km/644mi from A Coruña/La Coruña – Galicia, in Spain's northwest, takes in misty medieval towns, clover-green landscapes, craggy coastline and characterful off-the-radar villages with down-home seafood restaurants. After visiting **A Coruña/La Coruña**, with its old quarter and stately seafront promenade, head south to **Santiago de Compostela** to marvel at Spain's most iconic cathedral, whose Baroque façade was restored in 2019 . The tour runs along the **Rías Baixas/Rías Bajas** via **Pontevedra** to the mouth of the Miño, which forms a natural border with Portugal. Along this stretch of coastline, with the scenic fishing village of **Combarro** and the summer resort of **Baiona**, the sea has created a series of beautiful inlets. Follow the Miño as far as historic **Tui** and take the motorway to **Ourense**. Continue along the **Gargantas del Sil** into the province of León via Ponferrada, the gateway town to the ancient **Las Médulas** gold mines. Looping back into Galicia, stop in **Lugo**, hemmed in by Roman walls, and drive north to the coast, winding through the **Rías Altas** before returning to A Coruña/La Coruña.

2 AROUND THE MONTES DE CANTABRIA

Round trip of 764km/477mi from Santander – Depart west from **Santander** to medieval **Santillana del Mar**, and visit the replica of the **Cuevas de Altamira**. Continue to the picturesque port of **Comillas** and on to the seaside resort of **San Vicente de la Barquera**. From here, ascend into the mountains and the **Parque Nacional de los Picos de Europa;**, making sure to pause at the **Mirador del Fito** to marvel at the towering mountainscape. Drive along the **Costa Verde** to scrappy Gijón with its lively urban beach, then south to **Oviedo** for a dose of culture and outstanding architecture. Continue inland to noble **León**, then east across the Meseta towards Burgos along the Camino de Santiago. Visit Villalcázar de Sirga, Carrión de los Condes and **Frómista** en route. Explore the magnificent religious sites in **Burgos** before driving on to Aguilar de Campoo and Reinosa, at the foot of the Montes Cantábricos. From here, make an excursion to

Parque Nacional de los Picos de Europa

the **Pico de Tres Mares**, or return to Santander, stopping at **Puente Viesgo** to admire the wall paintings in the Cueva del Castillo.

3 THE BASQUE COUNTRY, RIOJA AND NAVARRA

Round trip of 696km/435mi from Bilbao – This tour combines stunning coastline dotted with picturesque villages, the delightful inland landscapes of northern Spain and the Camino de Santiago pilgrimage route as well as charming towns and cities renowned for their gastronomy. Start at the Guggenheim Bilbao and follow the **Costa Vasca** eastwards through quaint fishing villages to **Donostia-San Sebastián**, set on one of Spain's finest bays. From here, continue to **Hondarribia**, a fishing port with colorful houses and an attractive old quarter, pausing in **Getaria** for a seaside meal. The **Valle del Bidasoa** provides the backdrop as you head inland to **Pamplona**, whose medieval old town is built around an imposing cathedral; the city is synonymous with the annual running of the bulls. Then venture deeper into Navarra, past monasteries and important staging-posts on the **Camino de Santiago** (**Leyre**, **La Oliva**, **Sangüesa/Zangoza** and **Puente la Reina**) and historic towns such as Sos del Rey Católico and Olite/Erriberri, before reaching **Estella**, one of the most important stops along the famous pilgrimage route. After visiting the nearby Monasterio de Irache, the Camino continues to Logroño, the modern, urban capital of La Rioja, and beyond to the vineyards for which this region is renowned. Key stops on this section are the quiet medieval towns of **Nájera** and **Santo Domingo de la Calzada**. Before returning to the Basque Country via its capital, **Vitoria-Gasteiz**, with its underrated old quarter and several museums of interest, visit Haro and the Museo del Vino de La Rioja. Loop back to Bilbao via the motorway.

Hondarribia, Costa Vasca

4 CATALUNYA

Round trip of 1 020km/637mi from Barcelona – This Catalunya road trip is characterised by Pyrenean peaks, serene coves, long sandy beaches, picturesque villages, exquisite Romanesque churches, impressive monasteries and towns and cities overflowing with history. Once you've had your fill of **Barcelona**, strike out for the **Costa Brava** and the Ancient Roman colony of **Empúries**; then, venture on to postcard-perfect **Cadaqués**, the **Monestir de Sant Pere de Rodes** and El Port de Llançà. Head inland to **Figueres**, home of the Dalí Theatre and Museum, then to **Girona** with vestiges of its Roman, Jewish, Moorish and Christian past. From here, drive up the **Pirineos Catalanes** through dramatic valleys and the mountain villages of **Besalú**, Camprodón, Ripoll and Puigcerdà. From Puigcerdà, head west through the **Cerdanya Valley** and **La Seu d'Urgell** with its 12C cathedral before setting off into the Noguera Ribagorçana valley and the **Parc Nacional d'Aigüestortes**. Continue north through the Val d'Aran to reach **Lleida/Lérida**. The journey back to the sea passes **Poblet**, the most famous Cistercian monastery in Spain, and the walled town of **Montblanc**. In the nearby city of **Tarragona**, explore one of Europe's best-preserved Roman amphitheatres before heading back to Barcelona. The final leg of the tour runs past the LGBTQ-friendly resort of **Sitges**, .

Castillo de Coca, Castilla y León

© Marcelino Ramírez/age fotostock

5 CASTILLA Y LEÓN

Round trip of 756km/472mi from Salamanca – Sandstone towns, centuries-old churches, and lofty castles dominate this tour of old Castile. After touring **Salamanca**, one of Europe's first university towns, head north to **Zamora** to admire the cathedral. The road east to Valladolid passes through **Toro** and Tordesillas. In **Valladolid**, renowned for its Isabelline art, visit the National Sculpture Museum and bustling Mercado del Val. Pass golden wheat fields en route to **Palencia**, with its magnificent catedral, via Medina de Rioseco. Heading east into Burgos province, the itinerary takes in charming small towns and villages such as Lerma and **Covarrubias**. One of the highlights of this tour is the **Monasterio de Santo Domingo de Silos**; its cloisters are a triumph in Romanesque art. From here, the itinerary heads south, skirting along the banks of the Duero, to visit a series of castles – the ruined fortress at **Peñaranda de Duero**, the impressive castle at **Peñafiel**, **Cuéllar** and the more unusual Mudéjar castillo at **Coca**. Continue on to **Segovia**, famous for its aqueduct and fairytale castle, then to **Ávila**, a city of convents and churches encircled by crenellated medieval walls. Before completing your circuit, stop in the small town of Alba de Tormes.

6 ZARAGOZA, SORIA, GUADALAJARA AND TERUEL

Round trip of 869km/543mi from Zaragoza – This tour passes through rugged mountain landscapes, villages crowned by old castles and towns that transport you back in time. From **Zaragoza**, hop over to Navarra to visit **Tudela** with its striking Mudéjar architecture and renowned restaurants. Then head to Tarazona, famous for its old quarter and cathedral, and beyond to the **Monasterio de Veruela**. Continue to the quietly regal **Soria**, with its impressive churches, and veer southwest, via Calatañazor – a clifftop village protected by a stone castle – to **Burgo de Osma**, another fairy-tale town with a lively central square. Make your next stop Berlanga de Duero, followed by San Baudelio de Berlanga, a hermitage with an 11C Mozarabic chapel. Once past Atienza, continue to historic **Sigüenza** with its fortified cathedral and castle (now a Parador). Take the fast highway east, along the banks of the Jalón, crossing the river briefly to visit the splendid Cistercian/Renaissance **Monasterio de Santa María de Huerta**. After passing Ateca, make your way south to the **Monasterio de Piedra** and walk to its idyllic waterfall. The tour continues via Molina de Aragón, with another castle, before entering the **Sierra de Albarracín** and the terracotta-roofed village of the same name. Beyond it lies **Teruel**, a high-altitude town brimming with jewels of Mudéjar architecture. Head north to the walled town of **Daroca** before joining the motorway back to Zaragoza.

7 AROUND MADRID

Round trip of 689km/431mi from Madrid – The area around the Spanish capital is home to several towns of major import, a number of royal palaces and the scenic Sierra de Gredos and Sierra de Guadarrama ranges. From **Madrid**, drive to **Alcalá de Henares**, where the major attractions are the centuries-old university buildings. From here, drive to **Chinchón** to unwind in one of the country's prettiest main squares, and then to **Aranjuez**, popular for its palace and gardens on the bank

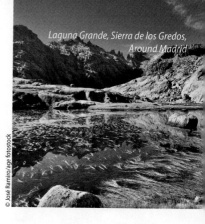

Laguna Grande, Sierra de los Gredos, Around Madrid

of the Tagus. Dive into Castile's pre-Columbian Christian, Jewish and Islamic past in nearby **Toledo**, the old capital, before heading west to Talavera de la Reina, famous for its ceramics, and on to **Sierra de Gredos**, which houses the dripstone-packed **Cuevas del Águila**. The closest city is Ávila, filled with churches and convents. Head east to **El Escorial**, Philip II's immense monastery. En-route to Segovia, keep an eye out for the massive cross looming over the **Valle de los Caídos**, Franco's pharaonic tomb built by his political prisoners. In **Segovia**, admire the soaring 2 000-year-old Roman aqueduct, Romanesque churches and storybook Alcázar. Close by are the palace and fanciful gardens of **La Granja de San Ildefonso**. Return to the mountains, cross the Navacerrada Pass and take the valley road to the **Monasterio de El Paular**. Continue on through the Navafría Pass before descending to **Pedraza de la Sierra**, a seigniorial town full of charm. On your way back to the motorway to Madrid, pause in Sepúlveda, a tranquil old town set above a deep gorge of the River Duratón.

8 EXTREMADURA AND THE PEÑA DE FRANCIA

Round trip of 780km/487mi from Plasencia – This tour focuses on Extremadura's strong links with the Romans, the Conquistadores and Emperor Charles V.

The tour starts beyond **Plasencia** in the verdant Valle de La Vera, home to the arcaded **Monasterio de Yuste** and 15C castle in Jarandilla de la Vera (now a Parador). Exit the valley via the country road that crosses the Valdecañas Reservoir, and you'll arrive in the village of **Guadalupe**, huddled around its uncannily grand monastery. Visit the shrine, then continue west to the monumental town of **Trujillo**, the birthplace of conquistadors like Pizarro and Orellana. From Trujillo, veer southwest by fast highway to **Mérida** to admire the city's Roman remains and the Museo Nacional de Arte Romano, which bears witness to Mérida's importance during this period. An hour's drive north lies **Cáceres**, whose entire old town – presided over by a healthy stork colony – is protected by UNESCO (scenes of Game of Thrones were shot here). The next stop is **Alcántara**, with points of interest including the San Benito monastery and an exceptional Roman bridge spanning the Tagus. Head northeast to Coria to visit its cathedral, and then into the province of Salamanca, to **Ciudad Rodrigo**, a pleasant town with several buildings of interest hidden behind its walls. The tour ends with a visit to the **Peña de Francia**, a crag rising to 1 723m/5 655ft, and the Sierra de Béjar, with its typical mountain village of the same name. In spring, tack on an excursion to the **Valle del Jerte**, which erupts in pink cherry and almond blossoms.

Teatro Romano, Mérida, Extremadura

Xàtiva castle, La Comunitat Valenciana

© Barbara Boensch/Boensch/imageBROKER/age fotostock

9 LANDS OF LA MANCHA

Round trip of 849km/531mi from Cuenca – Despite what some Spaniards might tell you, Castile-La Mancha is far more than an endless expanse of cereal crops, olive groves and vines: It takes in mountains, marshland, rivers and some of the most scenic villages in Spain.
Cuenca, spectacularly positioned between the ravines of the Júcar and Huécar, is an ideal jumping-off point. Begin by driving through the **Sierra de Cuenca**, famous for the **Ciudad Encantada** with its unusual stone formations. After looping back to Cuenca, venture southwest to the flat landscapes surrounding **Belmonte**, whose castle and collegiate church rise above the plains, and **Campo de Criptana**, a white-and-blue Manchegan village fringed by windmills. After passing through Alcázar de San Juan, continue to **Consuegra**; its castle and windmills on a hill are perhaps the region's most iconic sight; then, head south to the wetlands of the **Parque Nacional de las Tablas de Daimiel**. The next stop is **Almagro**, with terrific tapas bars on its medieval square. Due east lies **Villanueva de los Infantes**, then **Alcaraz**, with its buzzy *plaza*. Albacete, farther east, is worth a stop for its provincial museum. An hour's drive north you'll find **Alarcón**, towering over the River Júcar with an imposing medieval castle (now a Parador); continue north and you're back to square one in Cuenca.

10 THE LEVANTE REGION

Round trip of 715km/447mi from Valencia – This tour runs along the coast and inland through the provinces of Valencia, Alicante and Murcia. Ideal for beach-goers, it encompasses sandy coastline, charming villages and towns and fascinating art and architecture. Departing from **Valencia**, trace the coast to El Saler and luxuriate on its long beaches. Restaurants lining the nearby **Parque Natural de la Albufera** are famous for their rice dishes. Skip the over-developed resorts of Cullera, Platja/Playa de Gandía and Dénia for **Xàbia/Jávea** with its cobblestone old quarter. Don't miss the stunning sea views from nearby Cabo de la Nao, Calpe and the mighty Penyal d'Ifac rock. **Altea**, to the south, is one of the area's most attractive coastal towns with steep narrow streets that empty out onto quaint *plaças*. Bypass the skyscrapers of Benidorm, perhaps halting at **Terra Mítica** theme park, before burrowing inland through the mountains to **Guadalest**, in a spectacular location on a rocky ridge and **Alcoy**, which occupies a fertile river valley. In **Xixona**, stock up on nougat, a local specialty. Back on the coast, **Alicante is** a busy provincial capital that sits under the gaze of Castillo de Santa Bárbara. Driving south, past Guardamar del Segura and Torrevieja, you'll reach the shallow lagoon of Mar Menor and to Cartagena. Next up is the town of **Murcia**, whose main sights are its 15C cathedral and Museo Salzillo, dedicated to the 18C sculptor. Continue northeast to **Orihuela**, a tranquil town with attractive churches, and then to **Elx/Elche**, famous for its palm grove. From here the itinerary heads further inland, by dual carriageway, to Villena, protected by its imposing castle. The final stop on this driving tour is **Xàtiva**, "the town of a thousand fountains" and birthplace of two popes. Situated on a fertile plain, the town has preserved a umber of buildings of considerable architectural interest.

1 1 CÓRDOBA, SEVILLA, CÁDIZ AND MÁLAGA

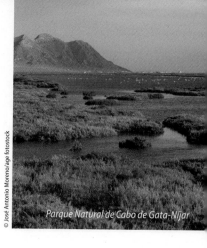

© José Antonio Moreno/age fotostock

Parque Natural de Cabo de Gata-Níjar

Round trip of 890km/556mi from Córdoba – This tour takes in some of the finest cities of inland Andalucía, delightful whitewashed villages (**Pueblos Blancos**) in the provinces of Cádiz and Málaga, and the famous Costa del Sol resorts.

Córdoba, where this tour begins, is one of Spain's most stunning cities, with ancient monuments, whitewashed streets and a history influenced by Christians, Muslims and Jews. Head west to **Écija**, the 'frying pan of Andalucía', a town of churches, convents, palaces and bell towers. West is **Sevilla**, an enchanting city filled with tapas bars and historic sites that merits several days' exploration. Next, head towards the Atlantic, pausing in scruffy **Jerez de la Frontera**, famous for its horses, sherry bodegas and annual *feria* (horse fair), before arriving in **Cádiz**. This provincial capital and port is one of Spain's best-kept secrets with its 18C architecture, historic squares, impressive monuments and superb beaches. Founded by the Phoenicians in 1104 BC, Cádiz is arguably the oldest city in Europe. South, Chiclana de la Frontera is the closest town to the unspoilt Playa de la Barrosa. From here, drive inland to **Medina Sidonia**, one of the oldest towns in Europe, its medieval quarter perched high above the surrounding plains. The white-washed town of **Arcos de la Frontera** has an even more dramatic location, on a ridge above a gorge.

Beyond it is whitewashed **Ronda**, straddling two cliffs, synonymous with bullfighting. From here, wind through stunning mountain scenery down to the coast with the **Rock of Gibraltar** ever looming on the horizon. After arriving at the **Costa del Sol**'s most famous resorts (**Estepona, Marbella,** Fuengirola, Benalmádena…), continue east to the art and culture hotspot of **Málaga**; then, take the fast highway to **Antequera** and **Estepa**. The hilltop town of **Osuna**, the final leg of the journey, is a stately stunner with numerous palaces and noble mansions. From Osuna, return to Córdoba.

1 2 GRANADA, ALMERÍA AND JAÉN

Round trip of 835km/522mi from Granada – This tour of eastern Andalucía combines deserted beaches, gasp-worthy mountain scenery, dense olive groves, and historic towns and cities with outstanding artistic heritage.

After exploring the world-famous Alhambra and city of **Granada,** cross the **Alpujarras** mountains – via the spectacular Pueblos Blancos – to **Almería**, presided over by a Moorish fortress. Continue through the **Parque Natural de Cabo de Gata-Níjar,** along the Almerian coast, a paradise of clear blue skies, sand dunes, wild beaches and Africa-like desert landscapes. Pause to explore hilltop **Mojácar**; then, follow the highway north to Vélez Blanco. A cross-country route leads to Pontones at the heart of the **Parque Natural de las Sierras de Cazorla, Segura y las Villas**, with its impressive mountain landscapes cut by deep ravines, rivers and streams. Push on to **Úbeda** and **Baeza**, two monumental Renaissance towns.

A sea of olive groves lies between here and **Jaén**, Spain's unofficial olive oil capital, at the foot of the Cerro de Santa Catalina, where an imposing Arab fortress, a sumptuous cathedral and historic Arab baths await.

Ciudad del Vino, Marqués de Riscal, Elciego, La Rioja

© Marqués de Riscal

Wine Tours

Wineries in traditional viticultural areas like La Rioja, Penedès, Priorat and the Rías Baixas in Galicia generally offer vineyard and winery tours and tastings. Several bodegas are worth visiting for their envelope-pushing architecture alone.

⚭CASTILLA LEÓN
In Ribera de Duero, northwest of Madrid, legendary wineries such as Vega Sicilia, Pingus and Abadía Retuerta are magnets for oenophiles.

⚭BASQUE COUNTRY AND LA RIOJA
Frank Gehry's wine spa at **Marqués de Riscal** in Elciego exists at the intersection of hospitality, architecture and oenology and is a bucket-list destination for any wine lover, but there are other bodegas worth visiting such as **Bodegas Ysios** in Laguardia, designed by Santiago Calatrava, and **Marqués de Murrieta** in Logroño, a Rioja icon since 1852. Smaller bodegas specializing in natural wine, such as **Hontza** and **Juan Carlos Sancha**, offer more intimate, less corporate tastings .

⚭TARRAGONA AND SOUTHERN CATALUNYA
Álvaro Palacios in Gratallops, Priorat, south of Barcelona, offers DIY grape harvest experiences in addition to standard tastings and tours.

Conde de los Andes celler, La Rioja, Cellar Tours

© Cellar Tastings

⚭ANDALUCÍA
Learn how the current 'it-beverage' has been made for centuries at historic bodegas in and around Jerez, Puerto de Santa María and Sanlúcar de Barrameda like **Tío Pepe** and **Lustau**.

TOUR OPERATORS
Cellar Tours (www.cellartours.com/ spain) runs high-end, niche wine itineraries, while broader 'food tour' companies like **Epicurean Ways (www.epicureanways.com)** and **Devour Tours (www.devourspain. com)** offer more affordable group or individual wine-centric itineraries, often with a culinary component..

Spas

With the rise of 'slow' travel, unplugged retreats, and ecotourism, spas and wellness centers are garnering fresh interest. Incorporating relaxation into your Spanish travel itinerary ensures that you won't burn out hopping from place to place. Some spas and resorts are about hedonistic pampering, pure and simple, while others allay aches and with their mineral-rich waters. Many have wellness and nutrition specialists on site.

Generally speaking, spa complexes are found in areas of outstanding beauty where visitors and patients are also able to enjoy the surrounding nature and leisure facilities available. Spain boasts an ever-increasing number of spa resorts that draw on both new research and ancient traditions passed down from the Greeks, Romans and Moors. For information on the treatments and facilities available at individual spas, contact the **National Spa Resort Association (Asociación Nacional de Balnearios, Calle Rodríguez San Pedro 56, 3º, 28015 Madrid; ☏902 11 76 22; www.balnearios.org)**.

Activities for Kids

Many attractions offer discounted fees for children. The following are just a few examples of places that will guarantee a fun day out for children and parents alike. In this guide, **sights of particular interest to children** are indicated with a KIDS symbol (👫).

THEME PARKS

The country's best-known theme parks are **Port Aventura** (👶see p401, **near Salou; www.portaventuraworld.com**), **Terra Mítica** (👶see p445, **Benidorm; www.terramiticapark.com**), **Isla Mágica** (👶see p527, **Sevilla; www.islamagica.es**) and **Warner Bros. Park** (👶see p144, **on the outskirts of Madrid; www.parquewarner.com**).

WILDLIFE PARKS

Wildlife parks, such as the **Parque de la Naturaleza de Cabárceno** (👶see p273, **near Santander; www.parquedecabarceno.com**); zoos and aquariums (Barcelona (👶see p324), Madrid (👶see p119), Benidorm (👶see p444), Donostia-San Sebastián (👶see p251), and O Grove (👶see p296), in Galicia), continue to be popular with youngsters of all ages, as do the bird and animal parks in the Canary Islands, including **Loro Parque (www.loroparque.com)** on Tenerife (👶see p558) and Oasis Park (www.fuerteventuraoasispark.com) on Fuerteventura (👶see p573).

WATER PARKS

The Spanish coastline boasts numerous **water parks** that are invariably full throughout the summer. **Interactive science museums**, such as those in Valencia (👶see p432), Granada (👶see p482), Burgos (👶see p310) and A Coruña (👶see p304), offer an interesting and educational alternative to the leisure options above, as does a visit to the **Parque Minero de Riotinto** (👶see p529, **near Huelva; www.parquemineroderiotinto.com**), where visitors are transported by train into the depths of a mine.

Near Almería (👶see p487), **Oasys**/Mini Hollywood; www.oasysparquetematico.com, is where many of the early Spaghetti Westerns were part filmed.

What to Buy & Where to Shop

Spain has a rich tradition of **arts and crafts** reflecting regional traditions as well as the those of the civilisations – Iberian, Roman, Visigothic and Muslim – that preceded them. Traditional wares such as pottery, knives, baskets, and textiles are produced countrywide. Seek out these products at local markets, boutiques and art studios – not at souvenir shops .

POTTERY AND CERAMICS
Castilla (p158, 176, 307)
In Castilla, traditional pottery is plain and utilitarian. Kitchen utensils, jars and water pitchers are common finds. The crockery used in Castilian farmhouses and rustic B&Bs – clay *cazuelas*, soup tureens and glazed earthenware bowls (*barro cocido*) – can be purchased at flea markets and craft and antique shops. Many of the hallmarks of Castilian ceramics – metal lustre, *cuerda seca*, decorative motifs – were adopted from the Moors.

Toledo (p193)
There are two pottery centres in Toledo province, **Talavera de la Reina**, famous for its ceramics in blue, green, yellow, orange and black, and that of **El Puente del Arzobispo**, distinguished by nature scenes and green accents.

Catalunya (p324, 353, 390)
Pottery from **La Bisbal d'Empordà** in Catalunya has a yellow background with green decorative motifs. The Mudéjar tradition is evident in Aragón

and the Levante region where blue and white pottery is made in **Muel**, green and purple ceramics in **Teruel** and lustreware in **Manises** (in the province of Valencia). Most of the figurines used as decoration for cribs at Christmas are produced in **Murcia**.

Andalucía (p474, 503, 519)
Spain's richest pottery region is Andalucía with famed factories in **Granada** (known for pieces with thick green and blue strokes), **Guadix** (red crockery), **Triana** in Sevilla (polychrome animal figures), **Úbeda**, **Andújar** (cobalt blue patterns) and **Vera** (white with undulating shapes).

Galicia (p289)
In Galicia, porcelain and earthenware goods with contemporary shapes and designs have been factory-made since 1806 at the **Sargadelos** centre in A Coruña province, but there is also a craft industry at **Niñodaguia** in Ourense (where the yellow glaze only partially covers the pottery) and at **Bruño** (where yellow motifs pop against a dark brown background).

Talavera ceramics © Turespaña

Balearic Islands (p450)

Xiurels, whistles decorated in red and green from the Balearic Islands, make terrific souvenirs.

LACE, WOVEN AND EMBROIDERED GOODS

Blankets and carpets

The textile industry first prospered in Islamic Spain. Several workshops still thrive today. Brightly coloured blankets and carpets are woven in the Alpujarras region (p484); La Rioja (p265); in and around Grazalema, Cádiz (p541); and at Níjar near Almería (p487, where *tela de trapo* carpets are made from strips of cloth). Historically, blankets from Zamora (p173), Palencia (p315) and Salamanca (p163) were prized across Spain for their quality.

Silk and lace

The village of **El Paso**, on the island of La Palma (p576) in the Canary Islands, is the only place in Spain that still produces silk fabrics. In some villages of Ciudad Real province (p206), particularly in **Almagro**), you might still spot the odd female lacemaker at work in her doorway with bobbins and needles. Lacework from **Camariñas** in Galicia (p304) was once widely known. The most ubiquitous – though still endangered – traditional craft is embroidery, taught in the family, and the best examples hail from Toledo province (p193, particularly **Lagartera** and **Oropesa**). Embroidery remains

relevant thanks to its use in two quintessential Spanish traditions: first, to adorn the *pasos* (elaborate religious floats) during Holy Week, and second, in the bullfighter costume called traje de luces.

METALWORK

Iron and copper

Iron forging, an ancient practice in Spain, has produced outstanding works of art such as the wrought-iron grilles and screens that adorn many churches. Blacksmiths continue to make the grilles for doors and windows in the south of Spain (see La Mancha p192, Extremadura p216, Andalucía p474, 503, 519). **Guadalupe**, in Extremadura (p223), is an important centre for copper production (boilers, braziers, etc.).

Weapons

Damascene weapons (steel inlaid with gold, silver and copper) are still produced in **Eibar** (País Vasco, p250) and **Toledo** (p193) with little variation from the ancient Islamic method. The best switchblades and knives in Spain are produced in **Albacete** (p208), Las Palmas de Gran Canaria (p561) and Taramundi (p270, Asturias).

Gold and silver

Gold- and silver-smithing were developed in antiquity and have retained some traditional methods. One example is filigree, ornamentation

(soldered, intertwined gold and silver threads) crafted in **Córdoba** (p504) and **Toledo** (p193). Salamanca (p163), Cáceres (p219) and Ciudad Rodrigo (p169) specialise in gold jewellery. **Santiago de Compostela** (p290) is the world's leading centre for black amber ornaments.

BASKETWORK

Basket-making has endured into the 21st century, particularly along the Mediterranean coast (p320) and on the Balearic Islands (p450).
The forms and material vary from region to region. Baskets, hats and mats are fashioned out of reeds, willow, **esparto** grass, strips of olive-wood and birch and chestnut bark, while furniture may be made of rush or wicker. Willow is often used in Andalucía (p474, 503, 519) and in the Levante (p32), hazel and chestnut are favored in Galicia and Asturias (p289, 270), and straw and esparto grass are typical on the island of Ibiza (p466). Keep an eye out for antique hand-woven esperto baskets and *esteras* (round mats) at flea markets – they're pleasing to the eye and virtually indestructible.

LEATHERWORK
Tradition
Leather-making has been an important trade, especially in Andalucía (p474, 503, 519), since Islamic times and has largely become industrialised. The town of **Ubrique** (Cádiz province) is the leading producer of leatherwork in Spain, followed by the Alicante area (p440) and the Balearic Islands (p450). The production of famous **Córdoba** (p504) leather, including embossed polychrome leatherwork, continues.

Horses and Hunting
Find workshops specialising in horse tack and hunting in Andalucía (p470), Jerez de la Frontera, Alcalá de los Gazules, Villamartín, Almodóvar del Río and Zalamea la Real).

Wine
Spanish wineskin containers (*botas*) are made in the provinces of Bilbao (p256), Pamplona (p233) and Burgos (p308) and in other wine-growing areas. 'ZZZ' is the brand to buy up north, while the wineskins produced in Valverde del Camino (p533, Huelva) are the go-to down south.

Baskets and tapestries, Pampaneira, Las Alpujarras

© C. Sanchez Pereyra/Photographer's Choice RF/Getty Images

Biarritz, France

© NJS Photos/age fotostock

Over the Border

I f you're staying close to Spain's national borders, you may wish to consider a day trip into **southwest France** or **Portugal** to visit a number of sights of interest within easy distance. The Green Guide collection covers these areas (Atlantic Coast; Languedoc Roussillon Tarn Gorges; and Portugal), in addition to the Michelin Guide France, the Michelin Guide España & Portugal, and a comprehensive range of maps and plans to enhance your touring itineraries.

FRANCE

⚅**Michelin Green Guide France.**
Across the border from the province of **Gipuzkoa**, the Basque Country of France boasts some of the country's most picturesque and best-known resorts such as Saint-Jean-de-Luz, Biarritz and Bayonne. If you visit Hondarribia, why not take the 10-minute ferry across to Hendaye, France, for a change of scenery (and an éclair or two)?
Less than 30km/18.6mi from **Roncesvalles** (Navarra) is St-Jean-Pied-de-Port, a staging-post on the Camino de Santiago. Various passes in the **Pirineos Aragoneses,** such as Somport and Portalet, connect to the Parc National des Pyrénées, a protected area within the French Pyrenees. The **Pirineos Catalanes** abut equally impressive landscapes on the French side along the Vall d'Aran and, farther east, in the Cerdanya Valley, which straddles France and Spain. From **Cerbère** (Girona), the coastal road snakes north to the delightful village of Collioure, cradle of the Fauvistes, where poet Antonio Machado died, and then inland to Perpignan, capital of French Catalunya.

PORTUGAL

⚅**Michelin Green Guide Portugal.**
Opposite the Galician town of **Tui/Tuy,** and linked by a bridge designed by Gustave Eiffel over the River Miño, stands Valença do Minho, whose Monte do Faro rewards you with fine views after a quick climb.
To the south lies **Puebla de Sanabria** (Zamora province), with a quaint old town, and the historic Portuguese city of Braganza. From **Ciudad Rodrigo** you may wish to explore the fortified town of Almeida.
From **Cáceres**, the N 521 runs west into Portugal and the attractive mountain landscapes of the Serra de São Mamede, which takes in the fortified town of Marvão and Castelo de Vide.
The walled Portuguese town of Elvas sits across the border from **Badajoz** with Estremoz and its attractive old quarter some 50km/31mi farther west. **Ayamonte**, the closest town to Portugal in southern Spain, is the starting point from which to explore the summer playground of the Eastern Algarve, sought out for its long beaches, lively resorts and characterful fishing villages.

Festivals & Events

Spain's festivals almost always involve Spanish 'street food', like blistered sausages and mounds of paella, and an endless stream of beer, wine and mixed drinks. Dates and times may vary slightly, so check with the relevant local tourist office for an official calendar of events. In summer, practically every small town and village hosts a fiesta in honour of its patron saint.

JANUARY

5 JANUARY
Three Kings Day
Sitges (www.visitsitges.com)

20 JANUARY
San Sebastián Day:
La Tamborrada San Sebastián
(www.sansebastianturismoa.eus)

FEBRUARY

AROUND 10 FEBRUARY
Vella Terra Natural Wine Fair
Barcelona (www.vellaterra.com)

MARCH

WEEK BEFORE ASH WEDNESDAY
Carnival Cádiz
(wwwcarnavaldecadiz.com),
Santa Cruz de Tenerife (www.
elcorazondetenerife.com), Las
Palmas (www.lpacarnaval.com)

3RD SATURDAY OF LENT
Magdalena Festival Castellón de la
Plana (www.castellonturismo.com)

15–19 MARCH
Las Falles festival Valencia (www.
visitvalencia.com)

3RD WEEKEND IN MARCH
Barcelona-Sitges Vintage Car Rally
(www.rallybarcelonasitges.com)

HOLY WEEK
Processions Cartagena, Cuenca,
Málaga, Sevilla, Valladolid, Zamora

APRIL

TWO WEEKS AFTER HOLY WEEK
April Fair Sevilla (http://feriade
sevilla.andalunet.com)

24–27 APRIL
St George's Festival:
'Moors and Christians' Alcoy/Alcoi
(www.alcoyturismo.com)

LAST SUNDAY IN APRIL
Romería (pilgrimage) to the
Virgen de la Cabeza Andújar
(www.turismoandujar.com)

LATE APRIL–EARLY MAY
Horse Fair Jerez de la Frontera
(www.jerez.es)
Las Cruces Festival Córdoba
(www.turismodecordoba.org)

MAY

AROUND 15 MAY
San Isidro Festival Madrid
(www.sanisidro.madrid.es)

WHITSUN
Pilgrimage to the Nuestra Señora
del Rocío shrine El Rocío (www.
andalucia.com/festival/rocio.htm)
La Caballada Festival Atienza
(www.turismoatienza.es)

JUNE

2ND SUNDAY AFTER WHITSUN
Corpus Christi celebration with
flower carpets Puenteareas
(www.ponteareas.gal). Sitges
(www.visitsitges.com). Toledo
(www.turismo.toledo.es)

20–24 JUNE
'Fogueres' St John's Festival Alicante
(www.hogueras.es)
Festas de Sant Joan/Midsummer's
Day Festival Ciutadella (www.
ajciutadella.org)

JULY

1ST SATURDAY IN JULY
A Rapa das Bestas festival A Estrada
(www.rapadasbestas.gal)

1ST WEEKEND IN JULY
LGBTQ Pride protest/parade Madrid
(www.madridorgullo.com)

APRIL: Moros y Cristianos festival, Alcoy/Alcoi

6–14 JULY
San Fermín Festival, the running of the bulls Pamplona
(www.sanfermin.com)

AUGUST

1ST SATURDAY IN AUGUST
Kayak races on the River Sella Arriondas y Ribadesella (www.
descensodelsella.es)

14–15 AUGUST
Elx/Elche Mystery Play Elx/Elche
(www.misteridelx.com)

LAST WEDNESDAY IN AUGUST
La Tomatina Buñol
(www.latomatina.info)

SEPTEMBER

7–17 SEPTEMBER
Fair (Feria) Albacete (www.
feriadealbacete.net)

21 SEPTEMBER
St Matthew's Festival Oviedo
(www.ayto-oviedo.es)

20–26 SEPTEMBER
Rioja Wine Harvest Festival Logroño
(www.logroño.es)

24 SEPTEMBER
La Mercè festival Barcelona
(www.barcelona.cat)

OCTOBER

WEEK OF 12 OCTOBER
Pilar Festival Zaragoza
(www.zaragoza.es)

MUSIC, THEATRE AND FILM

HOLY WEEK
Sacred Music Festival Cuenca
(www.smrcuenca.es)

LATE MAY–EARLY JUNE
Primavera Sound Barcelona (www.
primaverasound.es)

SECOND WEEKEND IN JUNE
Paraíso electronic music festival
Madrid (www.paraisofestival.com)

LATE JUNE–MID-JULY
International Music & Dance Festival
Granada (www.granadafestival.org)

MID-JULY
Jazz Festival Vitoria (www.jazz
vitoria.com)

LAST WEEK OF JULY
Jazz Festival Donostia-San Sebastián
(www.heinekenjazzaldia.com)

JULY–LATE AUGUST
Classical Theatre Festival Mérida
(www.festivaldemerida.es)
Castell de Perelada Festival Peralada
(www.festivalperalada.com)

LATE SEPTEMBER
**San Sebastián International Film
Festival** Donostia-San Sebastián
(www.sansebastianfestival.com)

MID-OCTOBER
**International Fantastic Film
Festival of Catalonia** Sitges (www.
sitgesfilmfestival.com)

LAST WEEK IN OCTOBER
Seminci (International Film Week)
Valladolid (www.seminci.es)

Practical Info

TOP TIPS

Best time to go: Late spring and late summer; try to avoid school holidays
Best way around: High-speed train (AVE) in the country; on foot in town
Best for sightseeing: Any time but August; Mondays; mid-afternoons
Most authentic accommodation: Family-run hotels and *casas rurales*
Need to know: A few words of Spanish go a long way and are indispensable in the countryside (see Useful Words and Phrases p604)
Need to taste: Tapas, pintxos, seafood, cider, local wines and cava

TEMPERATURE CHART (ºC)

Maximum temperatures in black. Minimum temperatures in red.

Month	Jan	Feb	Mar	Apr	May	Jun	Jul	Aug	Sep	Oct	Nov	Dec
Barcelona	6	7	9	11	14	18	21	21	19	15	11	7
	9	11	15	18	21	27	31	30	26	19	13	9
Madrid	1	2	5	7	10	14	17	17	14	9	5	2
	12	12	15	15	17	20	22	22	21	18	15	12
Santander	7	6	8	9	11	14	16	16	15	12	9	7
	15	17	20	23	26	32	36	36	32	26	20	16
Sevilla	6	6	9	11	13	17	20	20	18	14	10	7
	15	16	8	20	23	26	29	29	27	23	19	16
Valencia	5	6	8	10	13	16	19	20	17	13	9	6

Before You Go

WHEN TO GO
SEASONS

The best seasons to visit Spain are spring and autumn, when temperatures across the country are generally pleasant.

Spring is an ideal time to explore Extremadura, Castilla-La Mancha and Andalucía, which invariably bake in the summer heat. Late spring makes for fine holidays along the Mediterranean coast and in the Balearic Islands, as the sea is warm and the crowds sparse.

In **summer**, the country's northern coast springs back to life with sunnier days that invite sightseeing and relaxing on the beach – without the oppressive heat of central and southern Spain.

This time of year is also best for discovering the alpine villages and landscapes of the Pyrenees, Picos de Europa, Sierra de Gredos, Sierra de Guadarrama and Sierra Nevada.

Autumn sees a welcome lull in tourism across Spain, except for in winemaking regions like La Rioja, where harvest festivities unfold.

In **winter**, skiing enthusiasts head for the Pyrenees or Sierra Nevada, while other holidaymakers make a beeline to the Canaries to flee the chill. For up-to-date weather information on **weather**, visit the Meteorological Office portal at www.aemet.es.

WHAT TO PACK

Spain is blessed with bountiful sunshine and warmer weather than most other European countries, so pack plenty of breathable garments and sunblock. Travellers visiting in winter – and those heading to the mountains – shouldn't underestimate how cold it gets at night, particularly inland. If the north of Spain is on your itinerary, bring

PUBLIC HOLIDAYS	
1 January	New Year's Day
6 January	Three Kings' Day
2nd day before Easter	Good Friday
1 May	Labour Day
15 August	Assumption Day
12 October	Hispanic Day
1 November	All Saints Day
6 December	Constitution Day
8 December	Immaculate Conception
25 December	Christmas Day

rainwear and a lightweight jacket. Overall, Spain more formal than you might expect in the clothing department; smart attire and dress shoes are a must in most fine-dining restaurants and posh nightclubs.

GETTING THERE
BY PLANE

A number of domestic and international airlines operate direct routes to airports across Spain. These include, but are not limited to:

Iberia: ℘0203 684 3774; within the US and Canada ℘800 772 4642. www.iberia.com.

British Airways: ℘0344 493 0787; within the US and Canada ℘800 247 9297. www.ba.com.

Aer Lingus: ℘3531 886 8505. www.aerlingus.com.

Low-cost airlines (online booking only) also service Spanish cities from the UK and mainland Europe; these include:

EasyJet www.easyjet.com
Norwegian www.norwegian.com
Ryanair www.ryanair.com
Vueling www.vueling.com

Charter flights also connect the UK to Spanish cities, commonly those on the Mediterranean coast and in the Balearic and Canary islands.

BY SHIP

Brittany Ferries operates the only maritime service to northern Spain from the UK. Boats depart from Plymouth (20hr journey time) and from Portsmouth to Santander (24hr journey).

There is also a service from Portsmouth to Bllbao; for reservations, contact: **Brittany Ferries:** ✆0330 159 7000 (UK); ✆902 108 147 (Bilbao and Santander). www.brittany-ferries.com.

BY TRAIN

Eurostar (✆03432 186 186; www.eurostar.com) operates high-speed passenger trains from the UK to Paris, where you can catch a direct six-hour train to Barcelona and continue on to Madrid or other parts of Spain. There are also trains to Barcelona and Madrid from a handful of French cities, including Lyons, Marseilles and Toulouse, which stop at Figueres and Girona. Services from Paris, as well as train tickets within Spain, can be booked through the Spanish State Railway Network's (RENFE). UK agent, SpainRail: ✆0203 137 4464; www.spainrail.com. Alternatively, book via the official **RENFE** website at www.renfe.com.

From Portugal, a daily overnight service connects Lisbon with Madrid. The Sud Express train hotel between Paris and Lisbon calls at Irún on the French-Spanish border, Burgos, Valladolid, Salamanca and Coimbra.

BY COACH/BUS

Regular long-distance bus services operate from London to all major towns and cities in Spain. For information, contact:
Eurolines UK: ✆08717 818 181. www.eurolines.eu.
Busabout (✆08082 811 114; **www.busabout.com**) offers one-and

DISCOUNTS

Consult the **Instituto de la Juventud** (Calle de José Ortega y Gasset 71, 28006 Madrid; ✆91 782 76 00; www.injuve.es) for links to youth-orientated travel services. The organisation can arrange hostel stays, low-cost transportation and language study. There are offices in other major cities. The European Youth Card (www.eyca.org), issued by student organisations in 36 countries, entitles everyone 30 and under to discounts on travel, cultural events, accommodation, etc. In Spain, some 50 000 outlets participate in the scheme.

Student IDs often provide hefty discounts at museums, historical sites, cinemas and more. **Senior citizens** aged 65 and over qualify for significant price reductions on transport, entrance fees to monuments and events and shows (ID required). Many museums offer half-price or free entry to visitors of all ages during certain hours.

A number of tourist offices offer "passport" cards with discounts on attractions, transport, dining, etc., but check the fine print: These are sometimes not worth the price.

two-week tours combining cities like Madrid, Toledo, Granada, Sevilla and Portugal. They also cover popular fiestas.
Avanza (✆912 722 832; www.avanzabus.com) and **ALSA** (✆902 422 242; www.alsa.com) are the primary bus companies for journeys within Spain

DOCUMENTS

Visitors must be in possession of a valid **passport**. Holders of British, Irish and US passports do not need a visa for a visit of up to 90 days. Visitors from some Commonwealth countries or those planning to stay longer than 90 days should enquire about visa requirements at their local Spanish consulate.

US citizens may reference the International Travel Information for Spain online (http://travel.state.gov) for general information on visa requirements, customs regulations, medical care, etc.

CUSTOMS REGULATIONS

In the UK, **HM Revenue and Customs** (www.hmrc.gov.uk/customs) dictates customs regulations and duty-free allowances.

US Customs and Border Protection (www.cbp.gov/travel; ☎877 227-5511) offers free publication **Know Before You Go** for download.

HEALTH

British and Irish citizens should apply for the European Health Insurance Card (UK: ☎0300 3301350; www.ehic.org.uk or at a post office; Ireland: www.ehic.ie or at a local health office) to ensure free or reduced-cost treatment in the EU. All visitors should consider **insurance** for medical expenses, lost luggage, theft, etc.

Pets (cats and dogs) – A general health certificate and proof of rabies vaccination should be obtained from your local vet before departure.

♿ ACCESSIBILITY

Information on facilities for disabled travellers within Spain is available via **Polibea**, Ronda de la Avutarda 3, 28043 Madrid. ☎917 59 53 72. www.polibea.com. You can also visit the 'Accessible Tourism' page on the tourist board's website, www.spain.info (type 'disabled' into Search); alternatively book a personalized itinerary with **Accessible Spain**, Pujades 152, 3–1, 08005 Barcelona. www.accessiblespaintravel.com.

On Arrival

GETTING AROUND
BY PLANE

Spain has 48 commercial airports including 12 on the islands. Information on any of these is available from **AENA** (Aeropuertos Españoles y Navegación Aérea): ☎902 40 47 04. www.aena.es. The largest airports in the country are as follows: Madrid-Barajas, Barcelona, Palma de Mallorca, Málaga, Alicante, Tenerife South, Gran Canaria, Ibiza and Lanzarote.

Major Airline companies

Iberia: ☎901 111 500 (information and bookings). www.iberia.com.
Air Europa: ☎08714 230 717. www.aireuropa.com.

BY SHIP

Several ferry companies operate services between the mainland and the Balearics, Canaries, Italy and North Africa including:
Trasmediterránea ☎902 454 645. www.trasmediterranea.es.

Routes: Valencia to the Balearics; Barcelona to the Balearics; inter-Balearic Island services; Cádiz to the Canary Islands; inter-Canary Island services; Algeciras to Tanger and Ceuta; Almería to Orán, Melilla, Nador & Ghazaouet; Málaga to Melilla.

Baleària – Baleària (☎902 160 180. www.balearia.com) operates the following routes: Barcelona to the Balearics; Algeciras to Ceuta and Tangier; Dénia to the Balearics; Valencia to the Balearics; inter-Balearic Island services.

BY TRAIN

RENFE (☎912 320 320; www.renfe.com) the one-stop shop for tickets including for **AVE** (Alta Velocidad Española), high-speed trains that run from Madrid to: Sevilla (2hr 20min), Córdoba (1hr 40min), Granada (3hr 5min), León (1hr 55min), Valladolid (1hr), Barcelona (2hr 45min), Valencia (1hr 38 min), Albacete (1hr 20min), Huesca (2hr 5 min), Alicante (2hr 12min), Málaga (2hr 20min); from Barcelona to: Sevilla (5hr 30min), Málaga (5hr 50min) and Granada (6hr 30min) and from Valencia to: Sevilla (3hr 50min). International AVE/TGV routes connect Barcelona to Marseille (4hr 30min), Toulouse (4hr 40 min), Lyon (5hr 40 min), and Paris (7hr).

"Green" stations – Nine railway stations are designated **estaciones verdes** for their location near nature reserves and other outdoor attractions. More information is available on www.spain.info (search 'estaciones verdes').

Tourist Trains
RENFE Trenes Turísticos
(☎912 555 912; www.renfe.com) is the umbrella company and vendor of the following experiences:

El Transcantábrico Gran Lujo – This luxury narrow-gauge (*feve*) train journeys from Donostia-San Sebastián to Santiago de Compostela via the shores of the Bay of Biscay. The trip lasts eight days and combines rail and bus travel. The service operates from April to October. From €5150.

El Tren Al-Andalus – Despite its name, this luxury palace on wheels is not confined to Andalucía. Beyond the classic seven-day tour departing from Sevilla – with stops in Cordóba, Granada, Ronda and more – it also runs an Extremaduran itinerary from Sevilla to Madrid. From €3030.

El Expreso de la Robla – Originally a coal carrier line from Bilbao to León, this locomotive now makes the journey there and back in four days, offering lush mountain scenery and old-world railroad luxury along the way. There is also a four-day coastal tour from Bilbao to Oviedo via Santander. From €875.

El Tren de la Fresa – The 'Strawberry Train' operates vintage carriages between Madrid and Aranjuez (50min) on select dates from April to October. Kid-friendly itineraries are available. From €30 ☎915 068 342.

BY METRO/TRAM

Cities that have a metro, light rail or tram network include Alicante, Barcelona, Bilbao, Granada, Madrid, Murcia, Palma de Mallorca, Santa Cruz de Tenerife, Sevilla, Valencia, Vitoria-Gasteiz and Zaragoza. Though usually reliable, public transport may be affected by strikes and construction, so budget extra time in case a plan B is needed.

BY COACH/BUS

The Spanish bus network is a comfortable and inexpensive – if poky – way to travel. Numerous companies offer local and long-distance services. Routes, timetables and prices are available online and at bus stations and tourist offices.

Alsa – Far-reaching routes across the country, particularly in the northwest, centre, and along the Mediterranean. www.alsa.es.

Avanzabus – Madrid-based company providing nationwide services. www.avanzabus.com.

BY RIDESHARE

Travellers who care about their carbon footprint – and those on a budget – should consider **Blablacar**, Europe's premier ridesharing service. Download the app, select the journey that fits your schedule and pay via credit card. Rideshares are typically faster than buses and are a great way to meet locals. Rates remain low as Blablacar drivers are prohibited from making a profit (what you pay goes toward petrol and tolls). www.blablacar.com.

BY CAR
Road Network

Spain has over 343 000km/213 130mi of roads, including 9 000km/5 592mi of highways. Speed limits for all vehicles are as follows: 120kph/74mph on expressways and divided highways, 100kph/62mph on roads with a hard shoulder of at least 1.5m/5ft, 90kph/56mph on roads without a shoulder and 50kph/31mph in populated areas.

Tolls

Tolls apply on some highways; skirt them by marking 'avoid tolls' in your navigation app of choice. On Michelin maps, tolls are indicated by kilometre markers in red; toll-free sections are marked in blue. Credit card payments are accepted.

Documents

Most motorists need only have a driving licence from their country of origin and valid papers (vehicle documentation and insurance) to drive in Spain. US drivers must obtain an International Driver's Permit. Learn more at the AA (www.theaa.com) or RAC (www.rac.co.uk) in the UK and via AAA (www.aaa.com) in the US.

Driving Regulations

The minimum driving age is 18. Traffic drives on the right.

All passengers must wear **seat belts**, and all motorcyclists must wear helmets. Motorists must carry two red warning triangles, reflective vests, a spare tyre, first-aid kit and headlamp beam deflectors; rental agencies will provide these items. Beware of traffic bans and limited-access zones, particularly in Madrid and Barcelona, where restrictions went into effect in 2019 and January 2020, respectively .

It is illegal to use a handheld **cell/mobile phone** when driving. Those caught are often forced to pay heavy on-the-spot fines.

Insurance

Motorists entering Spain in their own vehicles should double-check that their insurance policy covers overseas travel. **Accident** and **breakdown** coverage are recommended. Motoring organisations (e.g., AA, RAC, AAA) can help break down any fine print. Members of the AA or AAA should enquire about applicable benefits.

To drive a car that is not your own, you must be accompanied by the owner or carry a signed note consenting that you may drive the vehicle.

Road Information

The **National Traffic Agency** (Dirección General de Tráfico) can provide information (Spanish only) on road conditions, driving itineraries, regulations, etc. ✆011 for traffic conditions. www.dgt.es.

Maps And Plans

Michelin's España & Portugal spiral **road atlas** and general **road maps** are up-to-date and intuitive; find them in the **Maps and Plans** section at the back of this guide.

Motoring Organisations

RACE (Royal Automobile Club of Spain) ℘900 100 992; 91 594 93 94 (roadside assistance). www.race.es. **RACC** (Royal Automobile Club of Catalunya) ℘902 357 357) and 902 242 242. (roadside assistance). www.racc.es.

Car Hire

All major car hire companies have branches in Spain. Cars can be hired online or at airports, train stations, and rental centers in all large towns and cities:
Avis ℘902 18 08 54. www.avis.es. **Europcar** ℘902 50 30 10. www.europcar.es.
Hertz ℘91 749 90 69. www.hertz.es. **Sixt** ℘91 871 180 192 www.sixt.es.

Although the legal driving age in Spain is 18, most companies will only rent vehicles to drivers over 21.

PLACES TO STAY AND EAT

Hotel and restaurant recommendations, which have been painstakingly selected for their location, comfort, quality, value or all of the above, are located in the Addresses section of each locale within the Discover Spain portion of this guide. For coin–price equivalents and descriptions of all symbols used in Addresses, see the Legend on the cover flap.
We have also made a conscious effort to cover all budgets, although certain regions (for example the Costa Brava, Costa del Sol and the Balearic Islands) are notoriously expensive in peak season. Madrid and Barcelona are on par with other Southern European cities, price wise.

Restaurants generally serve lunch from 1.30pm to 3.30pm and dinner from 9pm to 11pm.

STAY

This guide lists a selection of hotels, resorts, **hostales** and **pensiones** based on the price of a double room in high season (excluding breakfast and VAT, unless otherwise indicated). The difference in rates between high and low season can be significant, particularly on the coast and islands, so be sure to have a written record of any price you were offered at the time of booking.

Paradores

Almost all of these state-owned luxury hotels are in restored historic monuments (castles, palaces, monasteries, etc.) in privileged locations. For more information, contact **Paradores de Turismo de España (**Calle José Abascal 2-4, 28003 Madrid; ℘902 54 79 79; www.parador.es). The official UK representative is **Keytel International** (The Foundry, 156 Blackfriars Road, London SE1 8EN; ℘0800 160 1013; www.keytel. co.uk). Weekend offers are often available, in addition to a five-night "go as you please" accommodation card. In the US, contact **PTB Hotels** (℘1 800 634 1188; www.petrabax. com) with any questions.

Rural accommodation

More and more visitors to Spain are seeking out rural and 'agri-tourism' destinations. Most autonomous communities publish a practical guide listing resources for rural accommodation including rooms in private houses, hostels for groups, entire houses for rent and farm campsites. Contact tourist offices listed within the Principal Sights for further details, or consult listings on www.booking.com.

Campsites

Camping regulations vary greatly from region to region. The Secretaría General de Turismo publishes an annual campsite guide. Further details on camping and caravanning are supplied by the Federación Española de Campings (Calle Orense 32, entreplanta, 28020 Madrid; 618 54 89 43; www.fedcamping.com). Book in advance for popular resorts during summer.

Hostels

Spain's newest hostels bear little resemblance to the grungy, bare-bones *albergues* of yore: Cities like Madrid and Barcelona now boast 'designer' options that hit the sweet spot between value, style and comfort. Bilbao unveiled a futuristic capsule hotel – the only of its kind in Spain– in 2019.

Spain's 300-plus registered youth hostels are open to travellers with a virtual **international card**, which can be purchased and downloaded online via the **Spanish Youth Hostel Network** (Red Española de Albergues Juveniles, C/Marqués de Riscal 16, 28010 Madrid; 91 30 84 675; www.reaj.com).

Special offers

Hotels catering to business travellers often offer reduced rates at weekends, while those with a more tourist-heavy crowd have occasional deals on weekdays. Chains and agencies with regular special offers include:

NH Hoteles 916 008 146. www.nh-hoteles.es. Discounts are available via NH Rewards scheme.

Viajes El Corte Inglés 915 415 807 (Madrid office). www.elcorteingles.com.

Halcón Viajes 900 802 020. (information and reservations) www.halconviajes.com.

Hoteles Meliá 912 764 747. www.melia.com. Discounts and special weekend offers available via the Meliá Rewards card.

Don't forget the Michelin Guide
The red-cover **MICHELIN GUIDE ESPAÑA & PORTUGAL** is revised annually and is an indispensable complement to this guide with additional information on hotels and restaurants including category, price, degree of comfort and setting.

EAT

The restaurants listed in the Addresses in this guide have been chosen for their food and wine quality, surroundings, ambience, typical dishes or unusual character. Coin symbols (see the Legend on the cover flap) correspond to average cost of a meal and are given as a guideline only.

Tapas

You can't leave Spain without partaking in one of its favourite pastimes, tapas (**pintxos** in northern Spain). To that end we have included a list of top spots to enjoy an aperitif or light meal throughout the day and late into the evening.In Madrid, central Spain, and the south, bars often serve a complimentary tapa with each drink, alcoholic or not; Granada is known for its gargantuan free tapas that can easily become a meal. In the north, tapas (and Basque pintxos) are generally more elaborate and are charged separately.Always ask the bartender about portion size so you don't over- or under-order.

Practical A–Z

BUSINESS HOURS

Traditional shops usually open 10am–2pm and 5–8.30pm, while large stores and international brands are often open through lunch. Most shops close Sundays, restaurants close Sunday dinner, and some close on Saturday afternoons.

ELECTRICITY

220V AC (some establishments may still be 110V). Plugs are 2-pin.

EMBASSIES AND CONSULATES

US Embassy & Consulate
Calle de Serrano 75, 28006 **Madrid**
℘91 587 22 00. http://es.
usembassy.gov.
US Consulate
Paseo Reina Elisenda de
Montcada 23, 08034 **Barcelona**
℘93 280 22 27
Australian Embassy
Torre Espacio, Paseo de la
Castellana, 259D, Planta 24,
28046 Madrid
℘913 53 66 00
www.spain.embassy.gov.au
**British Embassy &
Consulate-General**
Torre Espacio, Paseo de la
Castellana, 259D, 28046 Madrid
℘917 146 300
www.gov.uk/world/spain
British Consular Offices
**Alicante, Barcelona, Ibiza, Las
Palmas, Málaga, Palma de Mallorca
and Santa Cruz de Tenerife.**
www.gov.uk/world/spain
Canadian Embassy
Torre Espacio, Paseo de la
Castellana, 259D, 28046 Madrid
℘913 82 84 00
www.espana.gc.ca
Canadian Consulate
Barcelona ℘932 70 36 14
Málaga ℘952 22 33 46

Embassy of Ireland
Ireland House, Paseo de la
Castellana 46, 4ª
28046 Madrid
℘914 36 40 93
www.dfa.ie/irish-embassy/spain
Honorary Irish Consulates
www.dfa.ie
Alicante ℘965 10 74 85
Barcelona ℘934 91 50 21
Bilbao ℘944 23 04 14
El Ferrol (La Coruña)
℘981 351 480
Lanzarote ℘928 81 52 62
Las Palmas, Gran Canaria
℘928 29 77 28
Fuengirola (Málaga)
℘952 47 51 08
Palma de Mallorca ℘971 71 92 44
Sevilla ℘954 69 06 89
Santa Cruz de Tenerife
℘922 24 56 71

EMERGENCIES

℘112 connects with all emergency services in Spain.
- **Police:** ℘091 (nat.), 092 (loc.)
- **Medical emergencies:** ℘061
- **Fire:** ℘080
- **Civil Guard:** ℘062
- **Mossos d'Esquadra (Catalan police):** ℘088
- **Directory Enquiries:** ℘11818
- **International Directory Enquiries:** ℘11825

MAIL/POST

Post offices (**correos**; www.correos.
es) are usually open Mon–Fri from
8.30am (closing times vary) and Sat
9.30am–1pm. Stamps (**sellos**) can
also be purchased at tobacconists
(**estancos**).

NEWSPAPERS

El País is Spain's left-leaning
'newspaper of record'. Barcelona's
La Vanguardia is a respected daily
distributed nationwide. **El Mundo**

has a conservative slant and solid culture section. **El Periódico de Catalunya** is a liberal Barcelona daily published in Spanish and Catalan. **ABC** is a monarchist, nationalist Madrid daily; its counterparts might be **Público** and **eldiario.es**, progressive online journals. Regional newspapers offer up-to-date info about local businesses and events. Free newspapers such as **20 Minutos** and **Que!**, distributed in the metro, are informative if sensationalist. English, French and German media are often vailable at kiosks in cities and beach resorts.

PHARMACIES

Spanish pharmacies are marked by large illuminated green crosses on the street. Every neighourhood has a *farmacia de guardia* open around the clock. Lists of all-night and weekend pharmacies are published in the windows of all pharmacies.

SIGHTSEEING

Opening times and entrance fees for monuments, museums, churches, etc. are included in the **Discovering Spain** section of this guide. This information is given as a guideline only, as times and prices are liable to change without prior warning.

Prices shown are for individual visitors and do not take into account discounts for groups, who may also benefit from private visits. As many monuments require frequent maintenance and restoration, it is advisable to phone ahead to avoid disappointment. Information for churches is only given if the interior contains a sight of particular interest with specific opening times or if an entrance fee is payable. In general, religious buildings should not be visited during services, although some only open for Mass, in which case visitors

should show appropriate respect (i.e., modest dress, silence, no flash photography).

SMOKING

The Spanish anti-smoking law put into effect in 2011 bans smoking in all indoor spaces including on public transport, and at airports (though many of the latter have smoking lounges).

TELEPHONES

A 2017 law lifted all roaming charges within the EU for those with European SIM cards; ask your mobile provider about your specific data allowances abroad. Non-Spanish mobile phones usually require 00-34 before the nine-digit number. For **international calls** from Spain, dial 00, then dial the country code (44 for the UK, 353 for Ireland, 1 for the US and Canada), followed by the area code (minus the first 0 of the STD code when dialling the UK), and then the number.

For calls **within Spain**, dial the full 9-digit number of the person you are calling. When calling Spain **from abroad**, dial the international access code, followed by 34, then the full 9-digit number. For more information, call ✆1004 (in Spain) or visit www.telefonica.com.

TIME

Peninsular Spain is 1hr ahead of GMT. Daylight saving time runs from the last Sunday in March to the last Sunday in October.

TIPPING

Restaurants usually include both taxes and service in prices; when in doubt, ask. It is customary to leave an additional cash tip of 5–10 per cent. Tip porters 1€ per bag for assistance, and chambermaids 1€ per day. Guides may be tipped at your discretion.

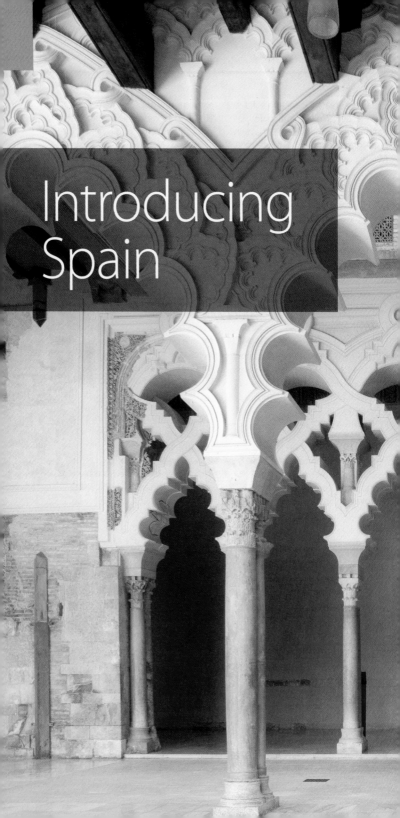

Introducing
Spain

Palacio de la Aljafería, Zaragoza
© Hervé Hughes/hemis.fr

Features

Castell in front of the cathedral,
Santa Tecla Festival, Tarragona, Catalunya
© Lucas Vallecillos/age fotostock

Spain Today

Spain goes to show that countries can change profoundly in mere decades: from Francoist dictatorship to free society, from economic backwater to dynamic financial hub and from a homogeneous, conservative populace to a diverse one enriched by immigrants. Like elsewhere in Europe, recently Spain has seen a worrying resurgence of neofascism and far-right politics, but don't let the headlines fool you: The country remains one of the most tolerant on earth; it bears reminding that Spain was the third nation in the world to legalise same-sex marriage, in 2005.

Today, Spain is a nation of thrilling contrasts – of tapas bars and African lunch counters, of Holy Week processions and Pride parades, of coiffed *señoras* and tatted-up punks and of soulful flamenco shows and fist-pumping DJ sets. In other words, there's something for everyone here – and no better time to visit.

» A Way of Life   p57
» Fiestas, Folklore and Culture   p60
» Spanish Cuisine   p64

A Way of Life

When foreigners conjure up an image of Spain, they may envision sangría-filled evenings, daily siestas, bustling cobblestone squares and leisurely lunches savoured to the soundtrack of Paco de Lucía. You'll no doubt come into contact with some of these age-old tropes when travelling here, but 21C Spain is far too cosmopolitan, complex and diverse to paint with such broad brushstrokes. Even so, there's no denying that Spain has rhythms and quirks all its own – and an infectious *alegría* that will make you want to return again and again. The country may be a patchwork quilt of different cultures, languages and traditions, but wherever you wind up, you'll notice certain common themes.

STREET LIFE

The sunny climate enjoyed by most parts of the country has imbued Spanish society with electric street life. The *paseo*, or evening stroll, embodies Spaniards' love for *la Calle* and for the social mingling that comes with it. More inclined to meet in bars, cafés and parks than at one another's houses or apartments, Spaniards – more than most Europeans and Americans – relish any opportunity to be out among the bustling masses. This affection for going out as a group, for meeting friends over unhurried dinners or tapas or drinks, is second nature to the Spanish, irrespective of age or social standing. Ask a local for a bar recommendation, and you might wind up sharing a bottle of wine with him or her at the corner *taberna*.

SPANISH TIME

The combination of extreme summer heat and being in the 'wrong' time zone – Franco redrew it in 1942 to align with Nazi Germany's – makes Spain's rhythms quite peculiar to outsiders. Lunch is generally eaten at 2pm or 3pm, and dinner is rarely taken before 9; the mid-morning **almuerzo** and mid-afternoon **merienda** 'snacktimes' tide Spaniards over between meals. Spain is a country of night owls: It's not uncommon to see children playing in the street at 11pm. Partiers should note that most nightclubs peak around 4am and close at 6.

TAPAS

Nobody should leave Spain without partaking in one of its mot glorious gastronomic pastimes, taPo. Initially, tapas were simple canapés used to cover ('tapar') one's glass to keep it free of bugs and debris. Over the centuries, they became synonymous with the *aperitivo*, or pre-meal snack, and were enjoyed standing up in neighborhood bars and taverns across Spain, particularly in Madrid and the south. Today, however, tapas often *are* the meal, shared among friends.

'Tapa' is an increasingly vague term: It used to mean, say, a handful of olives here or some bread topped with chorizo there; these days, it seemingly applies to everything under the sun, from a hunk of aged manchego cheese to tweezed-and-foamed concoctions that look like they belong in a museum. In general, a tapa is a small, individal portion, while a *media ración* or *ración* (half-portion or full portion) is more apt for sharing. Tapas are Called *pintxos* in the Basque Country, and these range widely in size. Traditional tapa sidekicks include draught beer *(una caña),* non-alcoholic beer *(una cerveza sin alcohol),* red and white wine and, in southern Spain, a glass of dry sherry *(una copa de fino).* Dishes like Spanish omelette *(tortilla de patata),* garlic prawns *(gambas al ajillo)* and Iberian ham *(jamón ibérico)* are ubiquitous across Spain, but every locale has its specialities worth seeking out.

Plaza del Obispo in front of the cathedral, Málaga

BARS

There are tens of thousands of bars, bodegas, and *tabernas* in Spain, including in the smallest and most remote hamlets. They're integral to the country's social fabric, particularly in rural communities and tight-knit neighborhoods. Locals flock to bars and taverns in their free time – especially during football matches. Come early evening, you may come across locals playing cards or indulging in a game of dominoes over coffee or something stronger.

The mornings are busy in bars as well, with regulars stopping in for a pastry and coffee or slice of Spanish omelette (*pincho de tortilla*). Smoking is banned in bars, though many establishments have heated outdoor seating areas with ashtrays.

TERRACES

With the onset of fine weather, terraces spring up across Spain – outside restaurants, cafés, bars and ice-cream parlours, on pavements and patios and in gardens and narrow alleyways. It is pleasant at any time of day to take the weight off your feet for a short while and watch the world go by in front of your table. There is usually a nominal fee for terrace service.

Many of the most crowded bars and clubs provide outdoor terraces for their customers till the early hours of the morning in summer. In winter they often open only at midday in good weather.

Do not set your mobile phone down on the tabletop or hang your purse on the back of your chair when dining outdoors, particularly in busy areas; these are open invitations for thieves.

BEACH BARS

These typical features of resorts along the Spanish coast come in various guises, ranging from the cheap and cheerful to the expensive and luxurious. These *chiringuitos*, as they are known, are a fine place to enjoy a drink or have a meal wearing only one's swim suit. To meet new health and safety requirements, many have turned into to drinks-only establishments.

NIGHTLIFE

One of the things that sticks with travellers most about Spaint is its pulsatingnightlife. The choice of venues is overwhelming with something to suit every budget and taste: cafés for cosy cocktails among friends; multi-storey nightclubs blaring electro-pop and hip-hop; live-music venues of all sizes; and secret after-parties and speakeasies. Friday and Saturday are the main party nights, but in cities and larger towns, there's almost always something going on late into the evening on weeknights as well. Traffic jams at three or four in the morning are not uncommon! Be sure to carry a government-issued ID as some nightclubs have a strict door. Many have dress codes (inquire ahead).

THE SIESTA

Although ever-increasing work hours and longer commutes prevent most Spaniards from perpetuating this healthy custom on a day-to-day basis, most will make sure that they take a restorative siesta on weekends and when they're on holiday. The few lucky ducks (generally, owners of mom-and-pop shops) whose work schedule allows the traditional three hours off from 2–5pm, will go home for lunch and a short sleep before returning to work to finish out the day.

THE FAMILY

The face of the Spanish family is changing with the times as the new generation redefines the social and gender norms inherited from generations past. As a whole, Spaniards are having fewer children, getting married later (if at all) and, in many cases, not sticking around their hometowns . Yet, in line with other Latin countries, family remains the bedrock of many Spaniards' lives. Extended families often meet on weekends for leisurely lunches, and it's not uncommon to see four generations sat around one table.

BULLFIGHTING

Before FIFA, Spain had bullfighting. Locals would flock to neighbourhood taverns to chat about their favourite matadors. They'd attend weekend *corridas* in jam-packed stadiums and devour newspaper articles about fancy manoeuvres and fatal blunders.

But now more than ever, people are calling into question the merits of a tradition that hinges on the torture and inevitable slaughter of animals.

Ask a Spaniard what he or she thinks of bullfighting, and you're likely to get a visceral, impassioned earful: Those in favor argue that bullfighting is a vital part of Spain's identity, while detractors posit that it is animal cruelty, pure and simple.

Bullfighting remains legal in every autonomous community except for the Canary Islands.

Chiringuito on Platja de Sant Sebastià, Barceloneta, Barcelona

© Bertrand Gardel/hemis.fr

Fiestas, Folklore and Culture

Spain keeps its age-old traditions alive through its fervently celebrated fiestas and cultural events, which range from food festivals to horse fairs to flamenco concerts. Don't miss the opportunity to get in on the action and celebrate like a local – you'll likely learn some fascinating history and sample some delectable Spanish street food along the way.

FIESTAS AND TRADITIONS

Fiestas across Spain draw huge crowds and often have a sense of ceremony and theatre. They are extraordinarily diverse. A calendar of major festivals can be found in the Planning Your Trip section of this guide.

Major festivals

To a greater or lesser degree, every Spanish town and city celebrates one main festival every year, normally in honour of its patron saint. These celebrations, many of which take place over the summer months, attract the entire local population, as well as inhabitants from outlying villages and rural areas. Typical events vary from one region to the next: they may include religious celebrations and processions, floral offerings, fireworks or bullfights and bull-running. Many people attend just to indulge in animated discussions with friends until the early hours, or to enjoy rides on the fairground attractions, or to eat and drink together, often on the street. The most important festivals in Spain include:

San Fermín (Pamplona), held in honour of St Fermín (7 July), starts on 6 July with the setting-off of a huge firework rocket, or *chupinazo*.
The city is the backdrop for a non-stop week-long party that climaxes with the morning running of the bulls *(encierros)* and early-evening bullfights. Festivities end at midnight on 14 July with the candlelit singing of *Pobre de Mí* (Poor Me).
Falles de Valencia, held in March in honour of San José, are renowned for bonfire sculptures and gunpowder bangs. *La despertà* (the wake-up call) begins at 8am with a heady mix of brass

bands and firecrackers. It culminates in the *Nit del foc* (Night of Fire) when the impressive *ninots* (bonfire sculptures) dotted around the city are set ablaze.

Andalucían fairs

Sevilla's *Feria de Abril* (April Fair) is the most famous of these spring and early summer festivals held in Andalucían cities. They are renowned for their exciting atmosphere, colourful costumes and spontaneous dancing of sevillanas. Heaps of tapas are consumed, washed down with chilled dry sherry *(fino)* such as *manzanilla*. The streets of the fairground area are a mass of colour as Andalucíans parade on foot and horseback dressed in long flounced flamenco dresses or horseriding suits.

Romerías

Romerías (pilgrimages) are an important aspect of religious life in Spain.
Although each has its own specific characteristics, the basic principle is the same: an annual pilgrimage on foot, and occasionally on horseback, to a hermitage or shrine to venerate a statue. Usually, this peregrination will also include a procession, music, dancing and a festive open-air meal.
The pilgrimage to El Rocío (Almonte, Huelva) is the largest and most deeply felt *romería* in the whole of Spain, attracting around one million pilgrims every year. Another pilgrimage of note is the St. John of the Mountain Festival in Miranda de Ebro dating to the 14C .

Semana Santa

Holy Week processions display Spain's deep Christian heritage. Villages, towns and cities around the country partici-

Tablao El Cardenal, Córdoba

© René Mattes/hemis.fr

FLAMENCO

Flamenco – a form of song, music and dance that to many is a way of life – is one of Spain's most vibrant cultural expressions. The 'deep song', or *cante jondo*, as it was Called, took shape toward the end of the 18C in the Romani quarters of such southern cities as Cádiz and Jerez. At that time its dance, or *baile*, often remained behind closed doors in tight-knit communities. Flamenco guitar, or *toque*, then strikingly simple, evolved in the last century and change to acquire great technical complexity. The three are closely intertwined in live performance around flamenco's palpable emotions of joy, hardship and tragedy.

You can see flamenco as a stage show, as a recital in a classical auditorium or as an acoustic session in a small club. Sadly, gone are the days when tourists could stumble upon underground, locals-only flamenco parties. Aficionados shouldn't miss major events on the flamenco calendar: Seville's Bienal gives a sampling of pure and fusion flamenco; Jerez's spring festival is all about dance; Murcia's Festival Nacional de Cante de las Minas, spotlighting miners' flamenco, includes youth talent shows and gala performances by local and national stars.

Flounced dresses, castanets and fans are hallmarks of flamenco, but don't be surprised if a show is contemporary in its aesthetics. Today's artists, keen to shrug off stereotypes, especially since flamenco won UNESCO World Heritage status, are often experimental. Accordingly, the National Flamenco Centre in Jerez's old town is housed in a radically modern building.

© JTB Photo/UIG/age fotostock

Venta El Gallo, Sacromonte, Granada

pate in these expressions of sombre feeling, which see thousands of people taking to the streets to accompany the passion of Christ and the pain of his mother. Semana Santa tends to be a more austere affair in Castilla and more festive one in Andalucía. The craftsmanship of the statues (often works of art in their own right), solemnity of the marchers, and scenic settings where thy unfold create an atmosphere sure to move believers and non-believers alike. Although Holy Week in Sevilla is the most famous, the processions in Valladolid, Málaga, Zamora, Cuenca and Lorca are also worthy of particular note.

Carnival

Carnaval celebrations are extravagant and irreverent affairs. They often involve many months of rehearsing and making costumes. They remain liveliest on the periphery of Spain, where Franco's 40-year ban on Carnival was blissfully flouted. In the Canaries, particularly on Tenerife, Carnival is an important aspect of island tradition, involving a procession of floats and the election of the Carnival queen. Carnival in Las Palmas is particularly famous for its Drag Queen Gala. Carnival in Cádiz is full of humour and music, while Galician Carnival is famous for its folk costumes.

Christmas

The Christmas period (*Navidades*) in Spain is traditionally a time for family celebration. The Christmas tree and crib are essential decorative features; families congregate for dinner on Christmas Eve and/or on Christmas Day, depending on the local custom. Perhaps even more important than Christmas is the procession of the Kings on the eve of Epiphany: the Three Wise Men and their pages ride through the streets of towns and cities on 5 January, handing out sweets to excited children lining their path.

Bullfighting festivals

It is impossible to broach the subject of fiestas without mentioning bullfighting (see A Way of Life, 'Bullfighting', p59).

Despite modern protests, bullfighting festivals remain undeniably relevant to modern Spanish culture, barring the Canary Islands, where bullfighting is illegal, and in Catalunya and the Balearic Islands, whose regional governments have effectively banned the practice.

Travellers keen to see a bullfight in person should read up on the various moves and stages of the contest to fully appreciate the spectacle; many first-timers are unprepared for its gut-churning violence.

The bullfighting season runs from spring to autumn, and the most important festivals are in Sevilla, held during the April Fair; in Pamplona, during San Fermín in July; and in Madrid, during the San Isidro festival in May.

REGIONAL DANCES AND TRADITIONS

Aragón

Festivals and parties are often rung in with a **jota**, a bounding, leaping dance in which couples hop and whirl to the tunes of a *rondalla* (group of stringed instruments), stopping only for the occasional brief singing of a *copla*.

Castilla and Extremadura

Traditional dances in these rugged, storied regions include the *seguidilla*, originating from La Mancha region, and the *paloteo*, also known as the *danza de palos*, accompanied by flute, tambourine, bass drum (*caja*) and the most typical of Castilian instruments, the reed-pipe (*dulzaina*). Costumes may be richly embroidered with precious stones and silk thread.

Catalunya and the Comunidad Valenciana

The *sardana* dance is still very popular in Catalunya where it is performed in a circle in main squares on Sundays. Inscribed on UNESCO's List of the Intangible Cultural Heritage of Humanity, **Castells** are human towers that may be seen in festivals at El Vendrell and Valls. In the Levante, the baroque local costume notable for its colour and intricate embroidery is donned during festivals. Valencia's **Falles** in March bring regular city life to a stop; Alicante's **Fogueres** in June rival them on a smaller scale. **La Tomatina**, which takes place in the Valencian town of Buñol every August, is a brief, messy food fight involving tonnes of over-ripe tomatoes. Lastly, the **Moros y Cristianos** festivals give a theatrical costumed replay of the confrontations between Moors and Christians during the so-called Reconquista. Those of Alcoy (April) are the best known, but there are others around Alicante province. –

Galicia, Asturias and Cantabria

Romerías in Asturias and Galicia are often accompanied by the shrill tones of the **gaita**, a type of bagpipe, and sometimes by drums and castanets. The *gaita* is played during events in honour of cowherds, shepherds, sailors and other traditional occupations in these rural coastal regions. It is also part of all celebrations of Celtic music, which are held here during the summer. The most typical festivals are those held in summer for *vaqueiros*, or cowherds, in Aristébano and others for shepherds near the Lago de Enol. Common dances in Galicia include the *muñeir;* or dance of the miller's wife; the sword dance, performed only by men; and the *redondela*. A local form of bowling (*bolos*) is a very popular game, supposedly brought to the region by pilgrims on the Camino de Santiago.

Murcia

Flamenco flourishes in Murcia as does improvised rhyming poetry, or *trovos*. Cuban-influenced songs, Called *habaneras*, are celebrated in an annual festival in Torrevieja. Murcia city hosts the International Festival of Mediterranean Folklore.

Basque Country and Navarra

The **Basque Country** and Navarra have preserved many of their distinct traditions. Men dressed in white with red sashes and berets dance in a ring accompanied by **zortzikos** (songs), a **txistu** (flute) and a *tamboril*. The most solemn dance, the *aurresku*, is a chain dance performed by men after Mass on Sundays. The **espata-dantza**, or sword dance, recalls warrior times while others, like the spinners' dance or another in which brooms are used, represent daily tasks. The Basques, particularly Basque men, relish age-old contests such as tug-of-war, trunk cutting, stone lifting and pole throwing. But the most popular Basque sport is *pelota*, played in different ways: with a **chistera**, or wickerwork scoop; with the similar **cesta punta** in an enclosed three-walled court (*jai alai*); with a wooden bat, or *pala;* or simply with the palm of one's hand, **a mano**. Lucky travellers might catch a glimpse of *rebote*, considered the finest form, played on a large open court. The main competitive event of the year for enthusiasts is the Manomanista championship (April–May).

Balearic Islands

Mallorca's traditional dances include the *copeo*, the *jota*, the *mateixes* and the *bolero*. Dances and festivals are accompanied by a *xeremía* (local bagpipes) and a tambourine. In Menorca a festival that dates back to medieval times and calls for about 100 horsemen in elegant costumes is held at Ciutadella (The Feast of St John or *Sant Joan*, on 23–24 June). Popular dances in Ibiza have a poetical accompaniment.

Canary Islands

The folklore of the Canaries shows influences from the Spanish mainland, Portugal and South America, which in turn have become intertwined with local traditions. The **isa**, **malagueña**, *folía* and *tajaraste* are the best-known types of dance. The *salto del pastor* (shepherd's leap), a vaulting sport, and *lucha del garrote*, Canarian wrestling, are traditional athletic activities throughout the islands. On La Gomera there is a revival of the *silbo*, or whistling language, once used by shepherds to communicate between that island's abrupt valleys .

Spanish Cuisine

Spanish food varies enormously from region to region, but a few dishes are served throughout the country including garlic soup, *cocido* (a catch-all term fo meat-and-legume stews), Spanish potato omelette and cured pork products like *serrano* ham and chorizo sausage. Fish and seafood are outstanding everywhere, even inland, thanks to daily deliveries from the coast. No description of Spanish food would be complete without a mention of tapas (see p57). A selection of tapas makes for a delightfully varied lunch or supper accompanied by a glass of house wine (*vino de la casa*) or draught beer (*caña*).

REGIONAL CUISINES

Galicia

Galicia's cuisine owes its simplicity to the quality of its **seafood** such as hake, scallops *(vieiras)*, goose barnacles *(percebes)*, king prawns *(langostinos)* and Norway lobsters *(cigalas)*.

There is also **caldo gallego**, a green soup, **lacón con grelos** (boiled ham with turnip tops) and **pulpo a la gallega** (Galician-style octopus), boiled in copper cauldrons.

Empanadas (flat savoury pies), baked in Galicia since at least the 7C, make fine picnic fare. Desserts include *tarta de Santiago* (almond cake), and sugared *filloas* (crêpes). All of the above may be accompanied by Ribeiro, Albariño or Godello wines.

Asturias and Cantabria

Fish and seafood are mainstays here, but gourmands also rave about the mountain cheeses such as blue-veined Cabrales, aged in damp mountain caves. A casserole Called **fabada**, made with local white beans, pork, bacon and smoked sausages, is Spain's answer to cassoulet. The top-grade dairy in the regions sets Cantabrian cheesecake and Asturian rice pudding a echelon above other regions' renditions. In Asturias it is fun to eat in the ciderhouses close to the apple orchards.

Basque Country

Most Spaniards agree that the country's best cooking is found in the **Basque Country.** Here, the traditional and avant-garde intermingle in cities like Donostia-San Sebastián and Bilbao. Aged beef, salt cod, anchovies, sheep's cheeses and farm-fresh vegetables loom large on menus. *Chipirones en su tinta*, baby squid cloaked in ink sauce, and *marmitako*, a fish soup, sing alongside txakoli, the tart local white.

Navarra and La Rioja

Navarra and La Rioja are synonymous with wild game, seasonal vegetables and world-class wines, especially reds. Partridge, salt cod and charred red peppers compete with trout and chorizo for pride of place on local menus. In Navarra, pungent Roncal cheese is made in the valleys from ewe's milk.

Aragón

Aragón is the land of **chilindrón**, a stew made with meat or poultry and peppers, and of **ternasco** (baby roast kid or lamb). These may be followed by preserved peaches or wine-poached pears and washed down with the region's up-and-coming wines from Cariñena, Somontano or Borja.

Catalunya

Look out for *pa amb tomaquet* (garlic- and tomato-rubbed toast) and Mediterranean fish dishes with a variety of sauces such as *allioli* (crushed garlic and olive oil) and *samfaina* (tomatoes, peppers and aubergines). Fresh **Butifarra** and dry-cured *fuet* are popular pork sausages. The most widespread dessert is **crema catalana**, akin to crème brûlée. Catalunya's wines include sparkling white *Cava* and bold, meaty reds from Priorat and Montsant.

Castilla and Extremadura

Spain's most rugged, inland regions are known for their meat-heavy comfort food like roast lamb (**cordero asado**), suckling pig (**cochinillo**) and **cocido**, all of which may be accompanied by a light, fresh Valdepeñas red. Other wines include tropical, easy-drinking whites from Rueda and gutsy, high-octane reds from Toro and Ribera del Duero.

Both areas are also famed for their ewe's milk cheeses, especially manchego, often paired with *membrillo*, or quince jam. A favourite confection is Toledo marzipan *(mazapán)*.

Castilla and Extremadura contain most of the grazing pasture for black-footed pigs and churn out exquisite cured hams. Those from Guijuelo (Salamanca) and Montánchez (Cáceres) are famous.

Levante

The freshwater lake of l'Albufera just outside Valencia is said to be the birthplace of **paella**. The classic Valencian rendition is prepared with rabbit and green beans, though seafood is often thrown in as well. Farther south at Jijona, **turrón**, a soft or hard almond and honey nougat, is made. Ice creams

and iced drinks, such as *horchata de chufa*, made from tiger-nuts, water and sugar, are also popular.

Balearic Islands

Soups are specialities in the Balearics; Mallorca's classic *sopa* has bread, leeks and garlic, while other soups are made with fish. **Tumbet** is a Mediterranean vegetable casserole and **sobrasada**, a soft lean spreading sausage. **Cocas**, a little like pizzas, and **ensaimadas**, light spiral rolls, make delicious desserts or breakfasts.

The Canary islands

Canarian specialities include **papas arrugadas**, small wrinkly potatoes with a dry, salty coating, served with green or red *mojo* or dipping sauce.

Stoneground flour made from roasted maize, Called *gofio*, is added to many foods. The Canary Islands are also known for Shakespearian sack wine, made from malvasia grapes.

Andalucía

The best-known dish is **gazpacho**, a cold tomato soup made with oil and vinegar, but *Andaluces* also love wine-braised meats and seafood flash fried in olive oil. Pigs are reared in the Sierra Nevada and Sierra de Aracena for making exquisite hams. Among local desserts, *tocino de cielo* custards and convent sweets are worth searching out. The region is well known for its **Jerez** or sherry wines, the classic southern sidekick to taPo.

NEW SPANISH WINES

By now you probably know your Rioja from your Ribera del Duero and your Rueda from your Albariño, but Spain boasts an infinite spectrum of wines beyond its storied standbys. Little-known indigenous grapes (e.g., albillo, caíño, albarín, airén) are gaining traction, and a new generation of winemakers is experimenting with natural, organic and biodynamic methods. The best Spanish wines often bear regional appellations – *denominaciones de origen* (DO) – identifying the place of production. Winemaking areas currently turning sommeliers' heads include Bierzo (Castilla y León), Montsant (Catalunya), Ribeira Sacra (Galicia), Somontano (Castilla y León) and Utiel-Requena (Valencia).

Spanish History

Spain's history is as fascinating as it is complex, spanning periods of peace and war, unity and division and acceptance and intolerance. The Phoenicians, Celts, Romans, Visigoths and Moors played key roles in shaping the physical and cultural landscape of modern Spain. From the flourishing of the sciences in Al-Andalus to the Golden Age of art and literature to the brutal colonisation of Latin America to the Spanish Civil War and the post-Franco era, Spain has left its mark on the world in countless ways.

Today, as Spain grapples with the Catalan independence movement, the aftermath of the 15-M anti-austerity protests and new calls to exhume Franco's body from the Valle de los Caídos basilica, Spain's history is more relevant –and perhaps more hotly debated – than ever.

» Key Events   p67

THE CHRISTIAN RECONQUEST OF THE IBERIAN PENINSULA

Recovered territory

Kingdom of Asturias C.750

C. 850

C. 1040

C. 1150

C. 1270

Between 1270 & 1492

Christian victories   Muslim victories   Muslim strongholds

Key Events

This timeline encompasses important dates, events, people and the political and cultural shifts from Antiquity to the 21C and includes everything from the Conquistadors to the Armada to the Civil War and Benidorm's tourist boom. It is by no means exhaustive.

ANTIQUITY TO THE VISIGOTHIC KINGDOM

11–5C	**Phoenician** and **Greek** trading posts go up on the eastern and southern coasts of the Iberian Peninsula, inhabited by **Iberians** and **Tartessians,** respectively. In the 9C BC, the Central European **Celts** settle in the west and on the Meseta, intermingling with the Iberians (forming **Celtiberians**).
3–2C	The **Carthaginians** take over the southeast after conquering the Greeks and Tartessians. The capture of Sagunto by Hannibal leads to the Second Punic War (218–201 BC). Rome expels the Carthaginians and begins the conquest of the peninsula (with resistance at **Numancia**).
1C	Cantabria and Asturias are finally pacified in AD 19. By now, the Iberian Peninsula is referred to as Hispania by the Romans.
	Christianity reaches Hispania and begins to spread.
5C–6C	Early Suevi (**Swabian**) and **Vandal** invasions are followed by those of the **Visigoths** (456), who establish a powerful monarchy with Toledo as capital. The peninsula unites under King Leovigild (569–86).

MUSLIM SPAIN AND THE RECONQUISTA

8C	The Visigothic Kingdom sees an intensification of raids by Arab-Berber tribes. The **Battle of Guadalete** (711–18) and Pelayo's victory at **Covadonga** in 718 mark the beginning of the so-called Reconquista, a protracted period of conflict and peace between (and within) Islamic and Christian factions lasting eight centuries.
	Abd al-Rahman I breaks with Damascus and forms a *de facto* independent emirate at Córdoba in 756.
9C	Settlement of uninhabited lands in north by Christians.
10C	Golden age of the emirate of Córdoba, which is raised to the status of a caliphate (1031) by **Abd ar-Rahman III**. A period of great prosperity ensues during which the expansion of Christian kingdoms is checked. Fortresses are built in the north along the Duero river.

11-12C	So-called Christian Spain by 1100 includes the Kingdoms of León, Castilla and Navarra and the County of Barcelona and Valencia. The Caliphate of Córdoba disintegrates into about 20 **taifa city-kingdoms** (1031). Alfonso VI of Castilla conquers Toledo (1085), and the area around the Tajo river is resettled by Christians. The *taifa* kings call upon the **Almoravids** (Saharan Muslims) for assistance and in a short time the tribe overruns a large part of Spain. Pilgrims begin to tread the Camino de Santiago. **El Cid** conquers Valencia (1094).

EL CID

Rodrigo Díaz de Vivar was born to a noble family around 1040 in Vivar, near Burgos. He served under two kings in the Reconquista, during which time he earned the title of 'El Campeador' for his perspicacity and leadership. Untamable, he was exiled by King Alfonso VI in 1079 for insubordination, but a bloody defeat of Christian troops at the Battle of Sagrajas (1086) prompted the king to take El Cid back. El Cid then raised an army and beseiged Valencia, finally conquering the city in May 1094 and effectively turning it into his own fiefdom (despite officially ruling in the name of King Alfonso). El Cid, a national icon to the present day, has inspired everything from epic poems ('The Song of the Cid') to Hollywood films (*El Cid*, 1961, starring Charlton Heston). His grave is the centrepiece of Burgos Cathedral. Tizona, his legendary sword, can be found at the Museo de Burgos (ℂsee p310).

12C	Islamic dissension within second wave of *taifa* kingdoms assists the Reconquista, especially in the Ebro Valley (Zaragoza is taken in 1118, Tortosa in 1148 and Lleida in 1149), but after Yakub al-Mansur's victory in Alarcos (1195), the **Almohads** (who routed the Almoravids) recover Extremadura and check Christian expansion toward the Guadiana and Guadalquivir rivers. Sevilla, with Córdoba under its control, enjoys great prosperity.
	Great military orders are founded (Calatrava, Alcántara and Santiago).
	Dynastic union of Kingdom of Aragón and County of Barcelona creates Crown of Aragón (1137).
13C	The *taifa* kingdoms begin to unravel with the **Battle of Las Navas de Tolosa** (1212). Islamic influence is reduced to the Nasrid Kingdom of Granada (modern provinces of Málaga, Granada and Almería), which holds out until its capture in 1492.
	Castilla and León unified under St Ferdinand III (1230).
	The crown of Aragón, under James I the Conqueror (1213–76), gains control over considerable territory in the Mediterranean.

THE CATHOLIC MONARCHS (1474–1516)
AND UNIFICATION

1474	Isabella, wife of Ferdinand, succeeds her brother Henry IV to the throne of Castilla. She contends with opposition from the supporters of her niece Juana la Beltraneja until 1479.
1478–79	The court of the **Inquisition** is instituted by a special Papal Bull and **Tómas de Torquemada** is later appointed Inquisitor-General. The court, a political and religious institution directed against Jews, Moors and, later, Protestants, survives until the 19C. Ferdinand becomes King of Aragón in 1479 and the Iberian Peninsula is united under Isabella and Ferdinand. The country of Spain, as we know it, is born
1492	Fall of Granada marks the end of the so-called Reconquista. Expulsion of Jews.
12 Oct 1492	Christopher Columbus lands in the Americas.

1492

Everything changed in 1492. That year, after some 800 years of Islamic rule, the period that would (much) later be termed the Reconquista ended with the fall of Granada on 2 January. This was also the year that the Jews were expelled from Spain, the year Spaniard Roderic de Borja (Borgia) became Pope Alexander VI and the year Christopher Columbus landed in the Americas.

Christopher Columbus (Cristóbal Colón) (1451–1506) and the discovery of America – Born in Genoa, the son of a weaver, Columbus began his seafaring career young. He travelled to Lisbon in 1476, where he developed a passion for map-making upon discovering Ptolemy's *Geography* and Pierre d'Ailly's *Imago Mundi*. Convinced that the Indies could be reached by sailing west, he submitted a navigation plan to João II of Portugal and to the Kings of France and England. Ultimately he gained the support of the Duke of Medinaceli and that of the Prior of the Monasterio de La Rábida, Ximenes de Cisneros, who was Isabel the Catholic's confessor. The Catholic Monarchs agreed to finance his expedition and, if he was successful, to bestow upon him the title of Admiral of the Ocean Sea and the viceroyship of any lands discovered.

On 3 August 1492, heading a fleet of three caravels (the *Santa María*, under his command, and the *Pinta* and the *Niña*, captained by the Pinzón brothers), he sailed from Palos de la Frontera. On 12 October, after a difficult crossing, San Salvador (Bahamas) came into sight; a short time later Hispaniola (Haiti) and Cuba were discovered by the Europeans. On his return to Spain on 15 March 1493, Columbus was given a triumphant welcome and the means with which to organise new expeditions. This marked the beginning of the Spanish and European colonisation of the Western Hemisphere.

1494	The **Treaty of Tordesillas** divides much of the Western Hemisphere between Spain and Portugal.
1496	Joanna (Juana), daughter of the Catholic Monarchs, marries Philip the Handsome (Felipe el Hermoso), son of Holy Roman Emperor Maximilian I of the Habsburgs.

1504	Death of Isabella. The kingdom is inherited by her daughter, Joanna (Juana la Loca), but Ferdinand governs as regent until Joanna's son Charles (1500–1558), future Emperor Charles V, comes of age to rule as Charles I.
1512	The Duke of Alba conquers Navarra, bringing territorial unity to Spain.

THE HABSBURGS (1516–1700) AND AMERICA

1516	**The apogee: Charles I** (1516–56) and **Philip II** (1556–98). On the death of Ferdinand, his grandson becomes Charles I (Carlos I) of Spain. Through his mother, Charles inherits Spain, Naples, Sicily, Sardinia and American territories. Cardinal Cisneros governs until the new king arrives for the first time in Spain in 1517.
1519	On the death of Maximilian of Austria, Charles I is elected Holy Roman Emperor under the name of **Charles V** (Carlos V). He inherits Germany, Austria, the Franche-Comté and the Low Countries.
1520–22	The Spanish, incensed by Charles V's largely Flemish court of advisers and the increasing number of taxes, rise up in arms. The emperor quells **Comuneros** and **Germanías** revolts.
1521–56	Charles V wages five wars against France in order to secure complete control of Europe. In the first four he conquers Francis I (imprisoned at Pavia in 1525) and in the fifth he routs the new French king, Henri II, and captures Milan.
	The Conquistadores move across America. **Vasco Núñez de Balboa** 'discovers' the Pacific; **Hernan Cortés** seizes Mexico in 1521; **Francisco Pizarro** and **Diego de Almagro** subdue Peru in 1533; **Francisco Coronado** explores the Colourado river in 1535; **Hernando de Soto** takes possession of Florida in 1539; and **Pedro de Valdivia** founds Santiago de Chile in 1541.
1555	Charles V signs the Peace of Augsburg with the Protestants in Germany after failing to suppress the Reformation.
1556	Charles V abdicates in favour of his son and retires to a monastery in Yuste. **Philip II** becomes king, inheriting Spain and its colonies, the kingdom of Naples, Milan, the Low Countries and the Franche-Comté, but not Germany and Austria, which are left by Charles to his brother Ferdinand I of Austria. Philip II turns his attention to Spain and the defence of Catholicism. He chooses Madrid as his *de facto* capital in 1561. Spain goes through a serious economic crisis.

THE EMPIRE OF CHARLES V

- Burgundian inheritance
- Spanish inheritance
- Austrian inheritance
- Charles V's conquests
- Other possessions
- – – – The Holy Roman Empire

1568–70	Revolt of the **Moriscos** (Muslims who converted to Christianity) in Granada.
1571	The Turks are defeated in the **Battle of Lepanto** by a fleet of ships sent by the Pope, the Venetians and the Spanish under the command of **Don John of Austria**, the king's natural brother. The victory seals Spain's command of the Mediterranean.
1580	The King of Portugal dies without an heir. Philip II asserts his rights, invades Portugal and is proclaimed king in 1581.
1588	Philip II sends the **Invincible Armada** against Protestant England, which supports the Low Countries. The destruction of the fleet marks the end of Spain as a sea power.
1598	Philip II dies, leaving a vast kingdom which, in spite of huge wealth from the Americas, is crippled by debt after 70 years of almost incessant war and monumental building projects like El Escorial.
1598–1621	**The decline** – The last Habsburgs, **Philip III** (Felipe III, 1598–1621), **Philip IV** (Felipe IV, 1621–65) and **Charles II** (Carlos II, 1665–1700), struggle to maintain the kingdom. Paradoxically, Spain enjoys its **Golden Age** of art and culture. Philip III entrusts the affairs of state to the **Duke of Lerma**, who advises him to expel the Moriscos in 1609. By 1614, 300,000 Moriscos have left Spain, with disastrous consequences for agriculture.

1640	Under Philip IV (Felipe IV), the Count-Duke of Olivares adopts a policy of decentralisation which spurs Catalunya and Portugal to rebellion. The Portuguese proclaim the Duke of Braganza King John IV, but their independence is not recognised until 1668.
1618–48	Spain wastes vital resources in the **Thirty Years' War**, and in spite of victory at Breda (1624), the defeat in the Netherlands at Rocroi (1643) signals the end of Spain as a major European power. The **Treaty of Westphalia** gives the Netherlands independence.
1659	The **Treaty of the Pyrenees** ends war with France.
1665	Charles II, the final Habsburg monarch, of poor health, comes to the throne.
1667–97	Spain loses strongholds in Flanders to France during the **War of Devolution** (1667–68). The Dutch Wars (1672–78) end with the **Treaty of Nijmegen**. The **Treaty of Ryswick** (1697) concludes the war waged by the Confederation of Augsburg (Spain is a member) against France (1688–97).

THE BOURBONS, NAPOLEON AND WAR OF INDEPENDENCE (1808–14)

1700	Charles II dies without issue. He wills the crown to Philip, Duke of Anjou, grandson of his sister María Teresa and Louis XIV. Emperor Leopold, who had renounced his rights to the Spanish throne in favour of his son, the Archduke Charles of Austria, is displeased.
1702–14	**War of the Spanish Succession** – England, the Netherlands, Denmark and Germany support the Archduke of Austria against France and Philip of Anjou. Catalan, Valencian and Aragonese cities side with the Archduke and war spreads throughout Spain (1705). By the **Treaty of Utrecht (1713), ending the war**, Spain cedes Gibraltar and Menorca (taken by the English) and many Italian territories to Austria. **Philip V** (Felipe V) is proclaimed King of Spain (1683–1746).
1759–88	The reign of **Charles III** (Carlos III), an enlightened despot, is the most brilliant of the Bourbon dynasty. He is assisted by competent ministers (Floridablanca and Aranda) who draw up important economic reforms. He expels the Jesuits from Spain and its empire in 1767.
1788	**Charles IV** (Carlos IV) succeeds to the throne. The country is largely governed by his wife María Luisa and her favourite bodyguard, Manuel Godoy.
1793	Louis XVI dies and, Spain declares war on France (then in the throes of the Revolution).

1796–1805	Spain signs an alliance with the French Directorate against England (Second **Treaty of San Ildefonso**, 1796). **Napoleon** enters Spain with his troops on the pretext that he is going to attack Portugal. The renewed offensive against England in 1804 ends disastrously with the **Battle of Trafalgar** the following year.
1805–08	Napoleon takes advantage of the disagreement between Charles IV and his son Ferdinand to engineer Charles IV's abdication.
2 May 1808	The Madrid uprising against French troops marks the beginning of the **War of Independence** (aka the **Peninsular War**), which lasts until Napoleon is exiled by Wellington in 1814.
	During the war Napoleon's brother, Joseph, rules Spain while provincial Juntas defend Ferdinand VII's rights, supported by British and Portuguese forces. Battles at Bailén (1808), Madrid, Zaragoza and Girona.
1812	The French are routed by Wellington in the Arapiles Valley; King Joseph flees from Madrid. Valencia is taken by the French General Suchet.
	Spanish patriots convene the **Cortes** (parliament) and draw up the liberal **Constitution of Cádiz**, one of the first constitutions in the world.
1813–14	Anglo-Spanish forces expel Napoleon after successive victories.
	Ferdinand VII (Fernando VII) returns to Spain, repeals the Constitution of Cádiz and so reigns as an absolute monarch until 1820. Meanwhile, the Latin American colonies struggle for independence.

THE DISTURBANCES OF THE 19C

1820–23	The liberals oppose the king's absolute rule but their uprisings are all severely quelled. The 1812 constitution is reinstated after a liberal revolt led by **General Riego** in Cádiz in 1820, but only for three years.
	In 1823 Ferdinand VII appeals to Europe for assistance and 100 000 Frenchmen are sent in the name of St Louis to re-establish absolute rule, which lasts until 1833.
1833–39	On the death of his brother Ferdinand VII, Don Carlos disputes the right to the throne of his niece Isabel II, daughter of the late king and **Queen María Cristina**. She comes to the throne. The traditionalist **Carlists** fight Isabel's supporters, who win the **First Carlist War** (Convention of Vergara 1839). In 1835, the new prime minister **Mendizábel** has a series of decrees passed which approve sale of church and religious orders' lands *(desamortización)*.

1840	A revolutionary junta forces the regent María Cristina into exile. She is replaced by General Espartero.
1843–68	Queen Isabel II comes of age. The **Narváez** moderate uprising forces Espartero to flee. A new constitution is drawn up in 1845. The **Second Carlist War** (1847–49) ends in victory for Isabel II but her reign is troubled by uprisings on behalf of progressives and moderates, one of which, the 1868 revolt led by General Prim, puts an end to her reign. Isabel leaves for France and General Serrano is appointed leader of the provisional government.
1869	The Cortes passes a progressive constitution with universal male suffrage and a monarchy. Amadeo of Savoy is elected king.
1873	**The Third Carlist War** (1872–76). Unable to keep the peace, the king abdicates. The National Assembly proclaims the **First Spanish Republic**.
1874	Brigadier Martínez Campos leads a revolt. The head of the government, Cánovas de Castillo, proclaims Isabel's son **Alfonso XII** King of Spain. The Bourbon Restoration and 1876 constitution open a long period of peace.
1885	Death of Alfonso XII (at 28). His widow, María Cristina (who is expecting), becomes regent.
1898	Uprisings in Cuba and the Philippines weaken Spain. The United States gets in on the imperialist action and occupies Puerto Rico and the Philippines, marking the **end of the Spanish Empire**.
1902	**Alfonso XIII** (born after the death of his father Alfonso XII) assumes the throne at 16.

THE LEAD-UP TO THE SPANISH CIVIL WAR (1910–36)

1910	The **Confederación Nacional del Trabajo (CNT)**, an anarcho-syndicalist confederation, is founded in Barcelona, strengthening the labour movement.
1914–19	Spain remains neutral throughout the **First World War**. CNT holds **La Canadiense strike** in Catalunya in 1919; a success, it lasts 44 days and results in the first law enshrining the eight-hour workday.
1921	Insurrection in Morocco; General Sanjurjo occupies the north (1927).
1923	General **Miguel Primo de Rivera** tears up the 1876 constitution and establishes a military dictatorship with the king's approval. Order and economic growth are restored, but opposition increases among the working classes.
1930	Hostile masses force Primo de Rivera into exile.
1931	April municipal elections bring victory to the Republicans in Catalunya, Basque Country, La Rioja and the Aragonese province of Huesca. The king

abdicates. The Second Republic is proclaimed and Generalitat of Catalunya created.

Jun 1931
A constituent Cortes is elected with a socialist Republican majority; a Constitution is promulgated in December.
Agrarian reforms, such as compulsory purchase of large properties, meet strong right-wing opposition.

1933
The **Falange Party**, which opposes regional separation, is founded by **José Antonio Primo de Rivera**, son of the dictator. The right wins general elections.

Oct 1934
Catalunya proclaims its autonomy. Miners in Asturias spark a revolt against the government and are brutally repressed.

Feb 1936
The **Popular Front** wins general elections and in May Azaña becomes President of the Republic.

THE CIVIL WAR (1936–39)

1936
The **Melilla uprising** triggers the **Civil War**.
The army takes control and puts an end to the Second Republic.

Nationalist troops based in Morocco and led by General **Franco** cross the Straits of Gibraltar and make their way to Toledo, which is taken at the end of September. Franco is proclaimed Generalísimo of the armed forces and Head of State in Burgos. Nationalists lead an unsuccessful attack against Madrid.

While Madrid, Catalunya and Valencia remain faithful to the Republicans, the poorer agricultural regions – Andalucía, Castilla and Galicia – are brutally overtaken by the Nationalists. Republicans are weakened by infighting among the CNT, the Communist PCE and the Marxist POUM but get a leg-up from the International Brigades. Poet and playwright **Federico García Lorca** is killed by the Nationalists; his body was never recovered.

1937
Franco's campaign of terror rages on. Industrial towns in the north are taken by Nationalists in the summer (on 26 April, Gernika is bombed by German planes). The Republican government is moved to Barcelona in November.
In the battle of Teruel in December, the Republicans try to breach the Nationalist front in Aragón to ease the chokehold Catalunya. Teruel is taken by the Republicans but recaptured by the Nationalists soon after. Franco's forces kill intellectuals, hold book-burnings and fire approximately 40 000 educators.

1938
The Nationalist army reaches the Mediterranean, dividing Republican territory into two parts.
The **Battle of the Ebro** lasts from July to November: Franco launches an offensive against Catalunya, which falls in February 1939.

| 1 Apr 1939 | The Spanish Civil War ends with the capture of Madrid. Across Spain, thousands of corpses fester in crude graves; most have still not been unearthed. |

THE FRANCO ERA

1939–49	Spain is a monarchy with Franco as regent and Head of State. He declares neutrality in the **Second World War**, despite allowing the SS to carry out military tests in Spanish territory, building a submarine base at Hitler's behest and and refusing the reentry of 40 000 Sephardic Jews, who would die at Buchenwald. UN declares diplomatic boycott of Spain (1946).
1952–59	Spain opens up, slightly: It joins UNESCO (1952) and is readmitted to the United Nations (1955); Spanish entry visas abolished in 1959.
1960	500% increase in visitor arrivals in Spain. The *boom turístico* begins and brings a degree of prosperity to what remains, largely, a pariah state.
1964	The Spanish national football team wins the European Championship.
1969	Prince Juan Carlos is named as Franco's successor.
20 Dec 1973	Prime Minister Carrero Blanco is assassinated.
20 Nov 1975	Death of Franco; **Juan Carlos I** becomes King.

DEMOCRACY

1977	General elections – **Adolfo Suárez** is elected prime minister.
1978	A new constitution is passed by referendum. Statutes of autonomy are approved for Catalunya, the Basque Country (Euskadi) and Galicia.
1981–82	Suárez resigns. An attempted military coup takes place on 23 February 1981. **Felipe González** (Socialist Party) becomes prime minister.
1 Jan 1986	Spain joins the **European Economic Community**.
1992	Barcelona hosts the **Olympics**. The event is used to gentrify parts of the city, reclaim the port area and improve infrastructure. Sevilla hosts Expo and also boosts its visitor credentials.
1996	**José María Aznar** (People's Party) becomes prime minister.
1997	The Guggenheim Museum Bilbao opens.
2000	Santiago de Compostela is European Capital of Culture.
2002	Spain adopts the **Euro**.
11 Mar 2004	The **Madrid train bombings** by an al-Qaeda terrorist cell leave 193 dead and 2 050 injured.

14 Mar 2004	**José Luis Rodríguez Zapatero** (Socialist Party) becomes prime minister.
22 May 2004	The Prince of Asturias, Felipe, heir to the Spanish crown, marries Letizia Ortiz Rocasolano, a journalist.
2008	Prime Minister Zapatero is reelected. The property bubble bursts and the economy begins heading into recession (confirmed Feb 2009). The Spanish national football team claims its first major title in 44 years by winning the European Championship.
Jul 2010	Spain solidifies its football prowess by winning the World Cup. Rafael Nadal wins Wimbledon to beocome the world's number one tennis player.
2010	Unemployment is the highest in the EU at over 20%.
15 May 2011	Millions of anti-austerity demonstrators fill the streets across Spain, founding the 15-M movement.
Dec 2011	A new conservative government headed by Mariano Rajoy (People's Party) takes office and announces fresh austerity measures to slash public spending by €16.5bn euros.
Jun 2012	Spain formally requests Eurozone Financial Stability funds to bail out its struggling bank sector.
Jul 2012	The Spanish football team becomes the first team to ever retain the European Championship.
Apr 2014	Unemployment climbs to 26%, with youth (under-25s) unemployment approaching a staggering 56%. Both statistics are the highest in the Eurozone.
Jun 2014	King Juan Carlos abdicates in the midst of an embezzlement scandal and his son, Felipe, becomes the new monarch, King Felipe VI.
Sept 2015	Separatist parties win the majority of seats in the Catalonian parliament elections.
1 Oct 2017	Catalunya holds an independence referendum, in defiance of the Constitutional Court. In an attempt to stop voting, PM Rajoy dispatches the National Police and Civil Guard, which use excessive force, further polarising the fraught political climate.
27–28 Oct 2017	Catalan parliament votes to unilaterally declare independence; direct rule is enforced in Catalunya from Madrid; pro-independence leaders flee to Belgium.
2018	Spain receives 82.8 million foreign tourists, making it the second-most visited country in the world.
2 May 2018	Basque separatist group ETA officially disbands.
1 June 2018	PM Rajoy is ousted in a no-confidence vote; Pedro Sánchez (Socialist Party) is automatically installed.
11 June 2018	Judge upholds prison sentence for Iñaki Urdangarin, the king's brother-in-law, over a €7 million embezzlement scandal. His wife, Princess Cristina, is fined for her involvement.
28 Apr 2019	Pedro Sánchez wins the popular vote in the national election but falls short of an absolute majority.

Spanish Art and Culture

Spain contains a treasure trove of artistic and architectural marvels ranging from snug Romanesque chapels, lofty Gothic cathedrals and exuberant Baroque churches to awe-inspiring Hispano-Arab monuments, imposing castles, instantly recognizable paintings and gorgeous sculptures and tapestries.

Trascoro by Bartolomé Ordóñez,
Barcelona Cathedral
© Yann Guichaoua/Travel Pictures

Prehistory to the Muslim Conquest

The earliest inhabitants of the Iberian Peninsula probably walked from Africa, across the landbridge that once ran across the Strait of Gibraltar. Cave paintings show that deer, bison and wild horses arrived with them.

PREHISTORIC ART

Prehistoric inhabitants of the Iberian Peninsula left some outstanding examples of their art. The oldest European hominid settlements are at Atapuerca, in Burgos (850–780,000 BC) but the earliest cave paintings are Upper Palaeolithic (40 000–10 000 BC) in Cantabria (Altamira and Puente Viesgo), Asturias (El Pindal, Ribadesella and San Román) and the Levante (Cogull and Alpera). Megalithic monuments like the famous Antequera dolmens were erected during the Neolithic Era (7500–2500 BC), or New Stone Age, while in the Balearic Islands, stone monuments known as **talaiots** and *navetas* were built by a Bronze Age people (2500–1000 BC).

FIRST MILLENNIUM BC

The Iberians produced fine sculpture and gold and silver treasures (e.g., from Villena, on display in the town museum, and from Carambolo, in Sevilla's Museo Arqueológico). Some of their handiwork, such as the Córdoba lions, the Guisando bulls and – in the Museo Arqueológico in Madrid – the *Dama de Baza* and the *Dama de Elche*, influenced 20C art. Around the same time, the Phoenicians were burying sarcophagi in Cádiz, the Punics were making sculptural art in Ibiza and Cartagena and the Greeks were decorating amphorae in Empúries.

ROMAN SPAIN (1C BC–5C AD)

Besides roads, bridges, aqueducts, towns and monuments, Roman legacies include the Theatre of Mérida, the ancient towns of Itálica and Empúries, the Aqueduct of Segovia, the Circus of Tarragona and the Forum of Alcalà de Henares.

THE VISIGOTHS (6C–8C)

Christian **Visigoths** built small stone churches (Quintanilla de las Viñas, San Pedro de la Nave) adorned with friezes carved in geometric patterns with plant motifs. The apsidal plan was square and the arches were often horseshoe-shaped. The Visigoths were outstanding gold- and silversmiths who made sumptuous jewellery in the Byzantine and Germanic traditions. Gold votive crowns (Guarrazar treasure in Toledo), fibulae and belt buckles adorned with precious stones, or *cloisonné* enamel, were presented to churches or placed in the tombs of the great.

Dama de Elche, Museo Arqueológico Nacional, Madrid

© Paul Gordon/age fotostock

Hispano-Arabic style (8–15C)

The three major periods of Hispano-Arabic architecture correspond to the reigns of successive dynasties over the Muslim-held territories in the Peninsula. Each left a spectacular legacy.

CALIPHATE OR CÓRDOBA ARCHITECTURE (8C–11C)

This period is characterised by three types of building: **mosques**, built to a simple plan consisting of a minaret, a courtyard with a pool for ritual ablutions and a square prayer room with a mihrab (niche facing Mecca); **alcázares** (palaces), built around attractive patios and surrounded by gardens and fountains; and **alcazabas** (castle fortresses), built on high ground and surrounded by several walls crowned with pointed merlons – one of the best examples of these can be found in Málaga. The most famous monuments from this period are in Córdoba (the Mezquita and the Medina Azahara palace, declared a UNESCO World Heritage site in 2018) and in Toledo (Cristo de la Luz). Beyond the ubiquitous horseshoe arch – that greatest hit of Moorish architecture – other design touches developed during this time period include ornamental brickwork in relief, cupolas supported on ribs, turned modillions, arches with alternating white stone and red-brick voussoirs, **multifoil arches** (&see illustration) and doors surmounted with blind arcades. These features would later become popular in Mudéjar and Romanesque churches. The Umayyads brought a taste for profuse decoration from Syria. As the Koran forbids the representation of human or animal forms, Muslim decoration is based on calligraphy (Cufic inscriptions running along walls), geometric patterns (polygons and stars made of ornamental brickwork and marble) and plant motifs (flowerets and interlacing palm leaves).

ALMOHAD OR SEVILLA ARCHITECTURE (12C–13C)

The religious puritanism of the **Almohad dynasty**, of which **Sevilla** was the capital, was expressed in architecture by a refined, though sometimes rather austere, simplicity. One of the characteristics of the style consisted of brickwork highlighted by wide bands of decoration in relief, without exces-

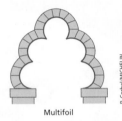

Multifoil

R. Corbel/MICHELIN

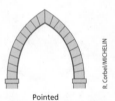

Pointed

R. Corbel/MICHELIN

THE DECORATIVE ARTS

Extremely rich and varied decorative artefacts from the Almohad period include geometric wood strapwork, brocades, weapons, ceramics with *esgrafiado* decoration and small ivory chests.

GRANADA – La Alhambra (14C)

Mocárabes:
decorative motifs of
Muslim architecture
formed by
assembled prisms
ending in concave
surfaces. Used to
adorn vaults, arches
and cornices

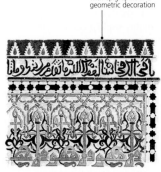

A panel of **azulejos**
with epigraphic and
geometric decoration

H. Choimet/MICHELIN

sive ornamentation (the Giralda tower in Sevilla is a good example).

The style was later used in the Mudéjar architecture of Aragón. Other features that emerged at this time include *artesonado* ceilings and *azulejos*. Arches of alternate brick and stonework disappeared, the horseshoe arch became **pointed** and the multifoil arch was bordered by a curvilinear festoon (ornament like a garland) as in the Aljafería in Zaragoza. Calligraphic decoration included cursive (flowing) as well as Cufic script to which floral motifs were added to fill the spaces between vertical lines.

NASRID OR GRANADA ARCHITECTURE (14C–15C)

This period of high sophistication, of which the **Alhambra** in Granada (&see *illustration*) is the masterpiece, centred on stucco and ceramic decorative elements as opposed to architecture. Door and window frames became focal points for every room's design, and the spaces between them were filled by perfectly proportioned panels. Simul-

taneously, certain motifs were simplified; for example, the stilted round arch became widespread.

MUDÉJAR ARCHITECTURE

This is the name given to work carried out in the Islamic style, usually by Muslim artisans, for Christian clients. It was fashionable from the 11C to the 15C, throughout the period that later historians would call the Reconquista, though some features, like *artesonado* ceilings, continued as decorative themes in the ensuing centuries.

Court Mudéjar, the subgenre developed by Muslim artists (in buildings ordered by Peter the Cruel in Tordesillas and Sevilla, and in synagogues in Toledo), was an extension of the Almohad or contemporary Nasrid style.

Popular Mudéjar, on the other hand, was produced by local Muslim workshops and reflects marked regional taste: Walls were decorated with blind arcades in Castilla (Arévalo, Sahagún and Toledo), and belfries were faced with *azulejos* (&see *illustration*) and geometric strapwork in Aragón.

81

Pre-Romanesque and Romanesque (8–13C)

Thanks to a number of influences, not least the Reconquista and the establishment of the Camino de Santiago, Spain is blessed with some of Europe's finest surviving Romanesque art and architecture.

ASTURIAN ARCHITECTURE

A highly sophisticated style of court architecture, characterised by sweeps of ascending lines, developed in the small kingdom of Asturias between the 8C and 10C.

Asturian churches (Naranco, Santa Cristina de Lena) followed the precepts of the Latin basilica in their rectangular plan with a narthex, a nave and two aisles separated by **semicircular arches** (*see illustration*), a vast transept and an east end divided into three.

Decoration inside consisted of frescoes and borrowings from the East including motifs (strapwork, rosettes and monsters; *see illustration*) carved on **capitals** and ornamental openwork around windows. Gold- and silversmiths in the 9C and 10C produced rich treasures, many of which are on display in the Cámara Santa in Oviedo Cathedral.

MOZARABIC STYLE

This term is given to work carried out by Christians living under Arab rule after the Moorish invasion of 711. Churches built in this style, especially in Castilla (San Miguel de Escalada, San Millán de la Cogolla), brought back Visigothic styles enriched by Moorish features such as ribbed cupolas and turned modillions.

Illuminated manuscripts provide the earliest-known examples of Spanish medieval painting (10C). They were executed in the 10C and 11C by Mozarabic monks and have Moorish features such as horseshoe arches and Arab costumes. They portray St John's Commentary on the Apocalypse written in the 8C by the monk **Beatus de Liébana**.

CATALUNYA, HOME OF THE ROMANESQUE

Catalunya had intimate links with Italy and France and consequently developed an architectural style strongly influenced by Lombardy from the 11C to the 13C. This evolved in the Pyrenean valleys, isolated from the more travelled pilgrim and trade routes. Sober little churches were often completed by a separate bell tower decorated with Lombard bands. Interior walls in the 11C and 12C were only embellished with frescoes that, in spite of their borrowings from Byzantine mosaics (heavy black outlines, rigid postures, and themes like Christ in Glory portrayed within a mandorla), proved by their realistic and expressive details to be typically Spanish. Wooden altar fronts, painted in bright colours, followed the same themes and layout.

THE PILGRIM ROUTES

Northwest Spain became markedly cosmopolitan during the reign of Sancho the Great, in the early 11C. Cistercian abbeys were founded and French merchants settled freely in towns such as Estella, Sangüesa and Pamplona. Meanwhile, the surge of pilgrims from France and elsewhere in Europe to Com-

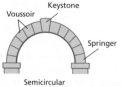

Keystone

Voussoir

Springer

Semicircular

R. Corbel/MICHELIN

Romanesque

SANTIAGO DE COMPOSTELA – Cathedral: Interior (11C-13C)

Santiago cathedral is a typical example of a Spanish pilgrimage church and shows clear French influence.

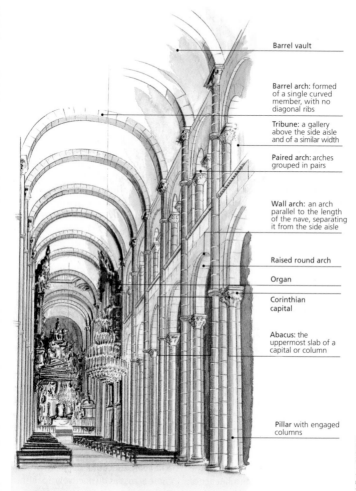

Barrel vault

Barrel arch: formed of a single curved member, with no diagonal ribs

Tribune: a gallery above the side aisle and of a similar width

Paired arch: arches grouped in pairs

Wall arch: an arch parallel to the length of the nave, separating it from the side aisle

Raised round arch

Organ

Corinthian capital

Abacus: the uppermost slab of a capital or column

Pillar with engaged columns

H. Choimet/MICHELIN

postela brought about the construction of a multitude of French-influenced religious buildings, most notably the Cathedral of Santiago de Compostela. In Aragón, Romanesque art was particularly evident in sculpture. In the early 12C, a reform of the **Cistercian Order** with emphasis on austerity brought an important change to architecture. The transitional style that heralded the Gothic (intersecting ribbed vaulting, squared apses) was introduced and the profusion of Romanesque decoration disappeared, as may be seen in the monasteries of Poblet, Santes Creus, La Oliva and Santa María de Huerta.

Gothic Period (from the 13C)

Many of Spain's most impressive buildings – from mighty cathedrals to churches to monasteries to trade exchanges – are from this period and remain atmospheric reminders of the country's erstwhile glory.

THE EARLY STAGES

French Gothic architecture made little headway in Spain, except in Navarra, where a French dynasty ruled from 1234.

The first true Gothic buildings (Roncesvalles church, Cuenca and Sigüenza cathedrals) were constructed in the 13C. Bishops in the main population centres of Castilla – León (&see illustration), Burgos and Toledo – sent abroad for cathedral plans, artists and masons. An original style of church, with no transept, a single nave (aisles, if there were any, would be as high as the nave) and pointed stone arches or a wooden roof resting on diaphragm arches, developed in **Valencia**, **Catalunya** and the **Balearic Islands**. The unadorned walls enclosed a large, homogeneous space in which there was little carved decoration, a departure from previous traditions that bestowed an understated elegance.

Civil architecture followed the same pattern and mirrored churches' geometrical sense of space. A prime example is the the *lonjas,* or commodity exchanges, of Barcelona, Palma, Valencia and Zaragoza.

THE GOTHIC STYLE DEVELOPS

In 14C and 15C Castilla, the influence of artists from the north, such as **Johan of Cologne** and **Hanequin of Brussels**, ushered in a style approaching Flamboyant Gothic. As it adapted to Spain, the style split into two schools: In one, decoration proliferated to produce the florid Isabelline style; in the other, structures were more geometric and streamlined. The latter remained in favour until the mid-16C (Segovia and **Salamanca**, &see illustration).

THE LAST OF THE GOTHIC CATHEDRALS

Cathedrals across Spain became ever more vast, culminating in Sevilla with the construction of what remains the largest Gothic cathedral on earth. Aisles almost as large as the nave increased the volume of these buildings, while pillars, though massive, vaulted the interiors so high that they seemed airy. A new plan emerged in which the old crescendo of radiating chapels, ambulatory, chancel and transept was superseded by a plain rectangle. Gothic decoration was concentrated around doors, on pinnacles and in elaborate star vaulting, a style echoed in some Andalucían cathedrals.

PAINTING

Artists in the Gothic era worked on polyptyches and altarpieces that sometimes reached a height of more than 15m/49ft. The Primitives, who customarily painted on gold backgrounds, were influenced by the Italians (soft contours), the French and the Flemish (rich fabrics with broken folds and painstaking detail). Nonetheless, as they strove for expressive naturalism and lively anecdotal detail, their work came across as distinctively Spanish.

There was intense artistic activity in the states attached to the Crown of Aragón, especially in Catalunya. The Vic, Barcelona and Valencia museums contain works by **Jaume Ferrer Bassá** (1285–1348), who was influenced by the Sienese **Duccio**, his successor **Ramón Destorrents** (1346–91) and the **Serra** brothers, Destorrents's pupils. Other famous artists of this period were **Luis Borrassá** (c. 1360–c. 1425), renowned

Gothic

LEÓN – Cathedral: side façade (13C-14C)

In Gothic architecture, light was considered the essence of beauty and the symbol of truth. León cathedral is the brightest and most delicate of all the major Spanish cathedrals and is viewed as the best example of this concept. The beauty and magnificence of its stained glass attracts the admiration of its many thousands of visitors every year. French influence is clearly evident in its ground plan (Reims) and sculptures (Chartres).

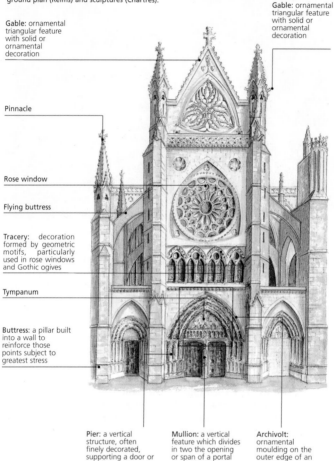

Gable: ornamental triangular feature with solid or ornamental decoration

Gable: ornamental triangular feature with solid or ornamental decoration

Pinnacle

Rose window

Flying buttress

Tracery: decoration formed by geometric motifs, particularly used in rose windows and Gothic ogives

Tympanum

Buttress: a pillar built into a wall to reinforce those points subject to greatest stress

Pier: a vertical structure, often finely decorated, supporting a door or a wall

Mullion: a vertical feature which divides in two the opening or span of a portal or window

Archivolt: ornamental moulding on the outer edge of an arch

H. Choimet/MICHELIN

for his Italianate expressiveness; **Bernat Martorell**, a Flemish-influenced master of landscapes; **Jaume Huguet** (1412–92), considered to be the leader of the Catalan School; and **Luis Dalmau** and **Bartolomé Bermejo** (c. 1440–c. 1498), both influenced by Van Eyck, who accompanied a mission sent to Spain by the Duke of Burgundy.

In Castilla, French influence predominated in the 14C and Italian in the 15C until about 1450, when Flemish artists like **Roger van der Weyden** arrived. By the end of the 15C, **Fernando Gallego** (c.1440-1507) had become the main figure in the Hispano-Flemish movement, to which the masterful Renaissance painter **Juan de Flandes** belongs.

Sculpture

Gothic sculpture, like architecture, became more refined over time. Relief

Detail, Nativity and Saint John the Evangelist *(1407-1411) by Guerau Gener and Lluís Borrassà, Museu Nacional d'Art de Catalunya, Barcelona*

was more accentuated than in Romanesque carving, postures more natural and details more meticulous. Decoration grew increasingly abundant as the 15C progressed, and faces became so individualised that recumbent funerary statues clearly resembled the deceased. Statues were surmounted by an openwork canopy, while door frames, cornices and capitals were decorated with friezes of intricate plant motifs. After being enriched by French influence in the 13C and 14C and Flemish in the 15C, Spanish sculpture came into its own, distinct style, the **Isabelline**. Early Isabelline portals showed a French influence. Tombs were at first sarcophagi decorated with coats of arms, sometimes adorned with a recumbent statue with a peaceful mien and clasped hands. Later, sculptors paid more attention to the costume of the deceased: Carvers transformed crude slabs of marble into rich brocades and flowing silks. In the 15C, sculptors produced lifelike figures in natural positions – kneeling, for instance, or lying nonchalantly on their side like the *Sepulcro de Doncel* in Sigüenza Cathedral.

Altarpieces comprised a predella, or plinth, topped with several levels of panels and finally by a carved openwork canopy. Choir stalls were adorned with biblical and historical scenes or carved to resemble delicate stone tracery.

The Isabelline style

At the end of the 15C, the prestige surrounding the royal couple and the grandees in the reign of Isabel the Catholic (1474–1504) laid the groundwork for the emergence of an aspirational new style distinguished by exuberant decoration. Entire facades of civil and religious buildings were blanketed with flamboyant ornamentation.

Design elements included supple free arcs, lace-like carvings, heraldic and geomorphic motifs and every other fantastical form that imagination could devise. The diversity of inspiration was largely due to foreign artists: **Simon of Cologne** (son of Johan; San Pablo church in Valladolid, Capilla del Condestable in Burgos), **Juan Guas** (son of the Frenchman Pierre; San Juan de los Reyes in Toledo), and **Enrique Egas** (nephew of Hanequin of Brussels; Capilla Real in Granada).

Renaissance (16C)

I n the 16C, at the dawn of its Golden Age, Spain was determined to develop its own national character and so created a style in which Italian influence became acceptable only when Hispanicised.

ARCHITECTURE

Plateresque was the name given to the early Renaissance style because of its flowy and lavish decoration reminiscent of silverwork (*platero*: silversmith).

Although similar to the Isabelline style in its profusion of carved forms extending over entire facades, its signature rounded arches and ornamental themes (grotesques, foliage, pilasters, medallions and cornices) were Italian. The Plateresque style was brought to a climax in **Salamanca** in the **facade of the Universidad** (*see illustration*) and that of the Convento de San Esteban. Among architects of the time

were **Rodrigo Gil de Hontañón**, who worked at Salamanca (Palacios de Monterrey and Fonseca) and at Alcalá de Henares (university facade), and **Diego de Siloé**, the main architect in Burgos (Escalera de la Coronería). Together with **Alonso de Covarrubias** (1488–1570), who worked mainly in Toledo (Alcázar and Capilla de los Reyes Nuevos in the cathedral), Diego de Siloé marked the transition from the Plateresque style to the Classical Renaissance. **Andrés de Vandelvira** (1509–75) was the leading architect of the Andalucían Renaissance (Jaén Cathedral). His work introduced the

Renaissance

TOLEDO - Hospital Tavera: patio (16C)

The sense of proportion, visible on both the ground and first floors surrounding the double patio of this hospital, is a typical feature of pure Renaissance style.

87

austerity that was to characterise the works of the last quarter of the century. The Renaissance style drew upon Italian models and adopted features from classical architecture such as rounded arches, columns, entablatures and pediments. Decoration took a back seat to architectonic perfection. **Pedro Machuca** (c. 1490–1550), who studied under Michelangelo, designed the palace of Charles V in Granada, embodying this Italianate sensibility. Another important figure, **Bartolomé Bustamante** (1500–70), built the **Hospital de Tavera** in **Toledo** (see illustration), while Genovese architect **Michele Carlone** (1468–1519) constructed the **Calahorra Castle**, in Granada province, using Italian materials .

The greatest figure of Spanish Classicism was **Juan de Herrera** (1530–93), known for combining grandeur and austerity. He was the favourite architect of Philip II, who saw in his work the sobriety that suited the Counter-Reformation and, in 1567, entrusted him with the task of continuing work on El Escorial, his greatest achievement.

SCULPTURE

Sculpture in Spain peaked during the Renaissance. In the 16C, choir stalls, mausoleums and **altarpieces** (also known as **retables**) were painstakingly carved alabaster and wood. These were painted using the *estofado* technique, in which gold leaf is layered beneath paint or dye, which gets delicately scored to produce gold highlights. Carved altarpiece (*retablo*) panels were framed by Corinthian architraves (epistyles) and pilasters.

The sculptures of **Damián Forment** (c. 1480–1540), who worked mainly in Aragón, belong to the transition period between Gothic and Renaissance styles. Burgundian **Felipe Vigarny** (c. 1475–1542) and Burgos native **Diego de Siloé** worked in tandem on Burgos Cathedral. **Bartolomé Ordóñez** (c. 1480–1520) studied in Naples and carved the *trascoro* (choir screen) in **Barcelona Cathe-**

Plateresque

SALAMANCA – University: façade (16C)

Although the exuberant decoration used to cover the entire façade is somewhat Gothic in style, the motifs used are Classical.

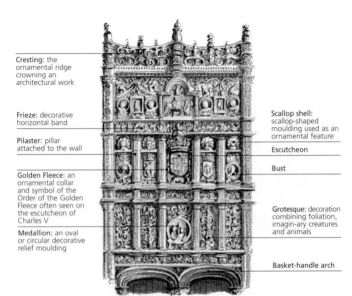

Cresting: the ornamental ridge crowning an architectural work

Frieze: decorative horizontal band

Pilaster: pillar attached to the wall

Golden Fleece: an ornamental collar and symbol of the Order of the Golden Fleece often seen on the escutcheon of Charles V

Medallion: an oval or circular decorative relief moulding

Scallop shell: scallop-shaped moulding used as an ornamental feature

Escutcheon

Bust

Grotesque: decoration combining foliation, imagin-ary creatures and animals

Basket-handle arch

H. Choimet/MICHELIN

dral and the mausoleums of Joanna the Mad, Philip the Handsome (Capilla Real in Granada) and Cardinal Cisneros (Alcalá de Henares).

The epicentre of the Renaissance School moved from Burgos to Valladolid in the mid-16C, by which time Spain had absorbed foreign influences and its two greatest Renaissance sculptors had emerged. The first, **Alonso Berruguete** (c. 1488–1561), who studied in Italy under Michelangelo, had a style that drew closely on the Florentine Renaissance. He sought strength of expression over empirical beauty, and his tormented, fiery human forms remain deeply disturbing today (don't miss *San Sebastián* in the Museo de Valladolid). The second, **Juan de Juni** (c. 1507–77), a Frenchman who settled in Valladolid, was also influenced by Michelangelo and founded the Catalan School of sculpture. His statues, recognisable for the fullness of their forms, anticipate the Baroque style through dramatic sorrowful postures. Many of his works, such as the famous *Virgen de los Siete Cuchillos* (Virgin of the Seven Knives) in the Iglesia de las Angustias in Valladolid and the Entombments in the Museo de Valladolid and Segovia Cathedral, were subsequently copied.

Most of the finely worked wrought-iron grilles closing off chapels and *coros* (chancels) were carved in the 15C and 16C. Enrique, Antonio and Juan **Arfe** stand out in the field of gold- and silversmithing. They made the monstrances of Toledo, Santiago de Compostela and Sevilla Cathedrals, respectively.

PAINTING

Drawing from the Italian Renaissance, Spanish painting in the 16C showed a mastery of perspective, a taste for clarity of composition and glorification of the human body. These features found their way into Spanish painting mainly through the Valencian School, which had close ties to Italian artists and patrons. **Fernando Yáñez de la Almedina** and **Hernando Llanos** introduced the style of Leonardo da Vinci, while **Vicente Macip** and his son **Joan de Joanes** further developed the Valencian Renaissance style.

In Sevilla, **Alejo Fernández** painted the famous *Virgin of the Navigators* in the Alcázar. In Castilla, the great master of the late 15C was **Pedro Berruguete** (c. 1450–1503), whose markedly personal style draws on a number of artistic influences. His successor, **Juan de Borgoña**, specialised in landscape, architecture and decorative motifs. Another artist, **Pedro de Campaña** from Brussels, used the *chiaroscuro* (marked contrasts between light and shadow) technique to dramatic effect, while **Luis de Morales** (c. 1520–86), a Mannerist, gave his religious work a human, emotional dimension that resonated with the elite and common folk alike.

At the end of the 16C, Philip II sent for a great many Italian or Italian-trained artists to paint at the royal grounds of El Escorial. During his reign he introduced portrait painting under the Dutchman **Antonio Moro** (c. 1519–c. 1576), his cohort **Alonso Sánchez Coello** (1531–88) and **Juan Pantoja de la Cruz** (1553–1608). **El Greco** (1541–1614), on the other hand, was scorned for his unconventional artworks bearing distorted, almost Expressionist-like forms, and settled in Toledo.

© DEA/G DAGLI ORTI/age fotostock

Detail, Virgin of the Navigators *(1531–36) by Alejo Fernández, Real Alcázar, Sevilla*

Baroque Period (17–18C)

S panish art reached its apogee in the mid-17C. Art from the Baroque Period echoed the religious fervour of the Counter-Reformation and blossomed in Andalucía, then flush with riches plundered in the Americas.

ARCHITECTURE

Architects in the early 17C were still under the influence of 16C Classicism and the Herreran style, to which they added decorative details. Public buildings proliferated and many continued to be built throughout the Baroque period; these include the Plaza Mayor in Madrid, by **Juan Gómez de Mora**, erected shortly before the *ayuntamiento* (town hall), and the present Ministerio de Asuntos Exteriores (Ministry of Foreign Affairs) building, by **Juan Bautista Crescenzi**, who also designed the Panteón de Reyes at El Escorial.

Church architecture shed the yoke of Classicism. A new style of Jesuit church, with a cruciform plan and a large transept that served to light up altarpieces, began to emerge; Madrid has several examples including the Iglesia de San Isidro, built by Jesuits **Pedro Sánchez** and **Francisco Bautista**, and the Real Convento de la Encarnación, by **Juan Gómez de Mora**. By the middle of the 17C, architects were less rigid, changing plans and facades, breaking up entablatures and elaborating pediments. An example of this Italian Baroque style is Madrid's Iglesia Pontificia de San Miguel (18C).

Baroque

MADRID – Museo Municipal (Antiguo Hospicio): portal (18C)

The Baroque retable or altarpiece, which reached new architectural heights in Spain, was occasionally created on the façade of a building, rather than inside it.

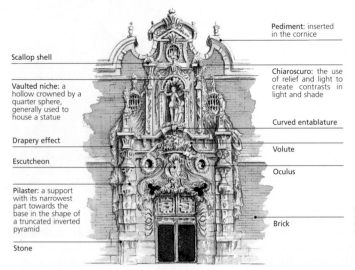

Pediment: inserted in the cornice

Scallop shell

Chiaroscuro: the use of relief and light to create contrasts in light and shade

Vaulted niche: a hollow crowned by a quarter sphere, generally used to house a statue

Curved entablature

Drapery effect

Volute

Escutcheon

Oculus

Pilaster: a support with its narrowest part towards the base in the shape of a truncated inverted pyramid

Brick

Stone

H. Choimet/MICHELIN

A new feature, the **camarín**, was introduced: at first simply a passage behind the high altar, it evolved into a highly ornate chapel.

Decoration of this kind may be seen in Zaragoza's Basílica de Nuestra Señora del Pilar designed by **Francisco Herrera el Mozo** (1622–85). The Clerecía in Salamanca is a magnificent Baroque creation with a patio that anticipates the bold and abundant decoration of the Churrigueresque style.

CHURRIGUERESQUE STYLE

In this style, named after the Churriguera family of architects (late 17C), buildings were erected as mere vehicles for dense, over-the-top ornamentation. The style is typified by the use of *salomónicas*, barley sugar columns entwined with vines, and *estípites*, pilasters arranged in an inverse pyramid.

Early examples of this extravagance, such as the altarpiece of the Convento de San Esteban in Salamanca and the palace in Nuevo Baztán near Madrid, were by **José de Churriguera** (1665–1725), the style's namesake instigator. His brothers **Joaquín** (1674–1724) and, especially, **Alberto** (1676–1750), who designed the Plaza Mayor in Salamanca (perhaps the most stunning square in Spain), took greater liberties in their work.

Pedro de Ribera (1681–1742), a Castilian architect who worked mainly in Madrid, surpassed the Churriguera brothers in decorative delirium.

The other great Castilian, **Narciso Tomé**, is remembered for the facade of the Universidad de Valladolid (1715) and the *Transparente* in Toledo Cathedral (1721–32).

REGIONAL VARIATIONS

The popularity of the Baroque spread like wildfire yet differed from province to province. In **Galicia**, where the hardness of the granite precluded delicate carving, Baroque took the form of softer lines and decorative mouldings. The best example of this variation is by **Fernando de Casas Novoa**, author of the Obradoiro facade of Santiago de Compostela Cathedral (1750).

In **Andalucía**, Baroque attained its utmost splendour, especially in decoration. Undulating surfaces characterised the facades of palaces (Écija), cathedrals (Guadix) and the doorways of countless churches and mansions (Jerez) in the 18C. Sculptor and painter **Alonso Cano** was the founder of Andalucían Baroque and designed the facade of Granada Cathedral, but the style's major exponent was **Vicente Acero**, who worked on the facade of Guadix Cathedral (1714–20), designed Cádiz Cathedral and built the tobacco factory in Sevilla. Mention should also be made of **Leonardo de Figueroa** (1650–1730) for the Palacio de San Telmo in Sevilla and **Francisco Hurtado** (1669–1725) and **Luis de Arévalo** for La Cartuja in Granada; Hurtado worked on the monastery's tabernacle and Arévalo on the sacristy, the most exuberant Baroque works in Andalucía.

In the **Levante**, Baroque artists used polychrome tiles to decorate church cupolas and spires like that of Santa Catalina in Valencia. In the same town, the Palacio del Marqués de Dos Aguas, by **Luis Domingo** and **Ignacio Vergara**, is reminiscent of facades by Ribera. The cathedral in Murcia has an impressive facade by **Jaime Bort y Meliá**.

THE GOLDEN AGE OF SPANISH PAINTING

The rejection of the previous century's Mannerism and the adoption of Naturalism led to Spain's Golden Age of Painting. Its impetus was Caravaggio's tenebrism – powerful contrasts of light and shade – and his stern realism. Painters took up portraiture and still life *(bodegón)*, while allegories on the theme of *vanitas* (still-life paintings showing the ephemerality of life) reflected a philosophical purpose by juxtaposing everyday objects with symbols of decay. Among 17C artists were two from the Valencian School – **Francisco Ribalta** (1565–1628), who introduced tenebrism into Spain, and

Detail, St Hugh and Carthusian Monks at Table *(c.1655) by Francisco de Zurbarán, Museo de Bellas Artes, Sevilla*

José de Ribera (1591–1652), known for his forceful realism.

Some of the greatest Baroque artists worked in Andalucía. One was **Francisco de Zurbarán** (1598–1664), master of the Sevilla School; light in his paintings springs from within the subjects themselves. Other artists included **Bartolomé Esteban Murillo** (1617–82), who painted intimate, mystical scenes, and **Valdés de Valdés Leal** whose realism challenged earthly vanities. **Alonso Cano** (1601–67), architect, painter and sculptor, settled in Granada and painted delicate figures of the Virgin.

The Castilian painters **Vicente Carducho** (c. 1576–1638) and portraitists **Juan Carreño de Miranda** (1614–85) and **Claudio Coello** (1642–93), while excellent, nonetheless pale beside **Diego Velázquez** (1599–1660), whose perspective, composition, sense of depth, technique and psychology are recognised as those of a universal master. Velázquez would influence generations of painters (Goya, for starters) in Spain and beyond.

Sculpture

Spanish Baroque sculpture was naturalistic and intensely emotive. Wood was the most common medium, and while altarpieces continued to be carved, *pasos* or statues made for Semana Santa processions proved a great novelty.

The two major schools of Baroque sculpture were in Castilla and Andalucía. **Gregorio Hernández**, Juni's successor, worked in Valladolid, the Castilian centre. His style was more natural than that of his master, and his *Christ Recumbent* for the Convento de Capuchinos in El Pardo was widely copied. Sevilla and Granada were the main centres for the Andalucían School.

Juan Martínez Montañés (1568–1649) settled in Sevilla and worked exclusively in wood, carving numerous pasos and various altarpieces. **Alonso Cano** became famous for the grace and femininity of his Immaculate Conceptions, and his best-known disciple, **Pedro de Mena (1628–88)**, produced sculptures of phenomenal dramatic tension, a departure from his master's understated style. The statue of Mary Magdalene (Museo Nacional de Escultura Policromada, Valladolid), St Francis (Toledo Cathedral) and the *Dolorosa* (Monasterio de las Descalzas Reales, Madrid) epitomise his work.

The 18C saw the rise to prominence of the great Murcian, **Francisco Salzillo** (1707–83), whose dramatic sculptures were inspired by Italian Baroque.

Churrigueresque excess in sculpture took the form of immense altarpieces, often so hefty they required architects to install them. Statues were smothered in decoration and lost in gilding and stucco.

Bourbons (18–19C)

S pain's Catholic imperialism was succeeded by 'enlightened' Bourbon despotism. In this period, art and expression were regulated by officials like the Academia de Bellas Artes de San Fernando.

ARCHITECTURE

During the first half of the century, architecture still bore the stamp of Spanish Baroque, itself influenced at the time by French Rococo. The king and queen had palaces built in a moderate Baroque style (El Pardo, Riofrío, La Granja and Aranjuez) and began work on Madrid's Palacio Real, modelled on Versailles. These buildings sought to meld French Classical harmony with Italian grace; as such, most of the work was entrusted to Italian architects, who generally respected the traditional Spanish quadrangular plan of *alcázares*. The vast gardens generally had a French design.

Excavations of Pompeii and Herculaneum contributed to the emergence of a new, **Neoclassical** style that flourished between the second half of the 18C and 19C. It repudiated Baroque excess and aspired to Hellenistic beauty and Classical geometry and clean lines. The Kings of Spain, Charles III in particular, embellished the capital by building fountains (Cibeles, Neptune) and gates (Alcalá and Toledo) and by planting botanic gardens.

The first Spanish Neoclassical architect, **Ventura Rodríguez** (1717–85), who ironically apprenticed in Italian Baroque, quickly developed an academic style. His works include the facade of Pamplona Cathedral, the Paseo del Prado in Madrid and the Basílica de Nuestra Señora del Pilar in Zaragoza. **Francesco Sabatini** (1722–97), whose style developed along similar lines, designed the Puerta de Alcalá and the eponymous gardens in Madrid.

The leading architect was **Juan de Villanueva** (1739–1811), schooled in Classical principles during a stay in Rome.

He designed the **Museo del Prado**. Two notable town planners emerged during the 19C: **Ildefonso Cerdá** (1815–76) in Barcelona and **Arturo Soria** (1844–1920) in Madrid.

PAINTING

Bourbon monarchs took pains to attract the greatest painters to court and grant them official positions. In 1752 Ferdinand VI founded the Academia de Bellas Artes de San Fernando, where it was intended that students learn classical painting techniques and study the Italian masters. Leading artists of the time were **Anton Raphael Mengs** (1728–79), from Bohemia, and **Gianbattista Tiepolo** (1696–1770), from Venice, both of whom decorated the Palacio Real. There was also **Francisco Bayeu** (1734–95) from Aragón, who painted a great many tapestry cartoons. His brother-in-law was the visionary **Francisco de Goya** (1746–1828), whose work, much of which may be seen in the Prado, Madrid, would define the century.

Painters working in the post-Goya period did not follow in the master's

Detail, The Third of May *(1814) by Francisco de Goya, Museo Nacional del Prado*

© Imagestate/Tips Images

Neo-Classical

MADRID - Observatorio Astronómico (18C)

This small building designed by Juan de Villanueva is a model of simplicity and purity which shows clear Palladian influence in its proportions and design.

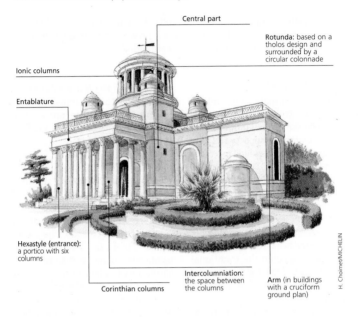

Central part

Rotunda: based on a tholos design and surrounded by a circular colonnade

Ionic columns

Entablature

Hexastyle (entrance): a portico with six columns

Intercolumniation: the space between the columns

Corinthian columns

Arm (in buildings with a cruciform ground plan)

H. Choimet/MICHELIN

footsteps as academic Neoclassicism and Romanticism gained favour. Goya's legacy was not fully appreciated until the end of the 19C. The following Romantic artists from this period stand out: **Federico de Madrazo**, who channeled official taste in royal portraits and historical scenes; **Vicente Esquivel**, portrait-painter; and **Leonardo Alenza** and **Eugenio Lucas Velázquez**, spokesmen for **Costumbrismo**, which had attained full status as a genre. (This was a style of painting illustrating scenes of everyday life that gradually developed from the simply anecdotal to the transcendental in its search for the Spanish soul.) Historical themes became very popular in the 19C with works by **José Casado del Alisal**, **Eduardo Rosales** and **Mariano Fortuny**. Impressionist features began to appear in naturalist paintings by **Ramón Martí Alsina** and in post-Romantic landscapes by **Carlos de Haes**. The style secured a definitive hold in the works of **Narciso Oller; Ignacio Pinazo Camarlench;** the

best Valencian Impressionist, **Darío de Regoyos;** and **Joaquín Sorolla**, who specialised in light-filled folk scenes, portraits and regional subjects.

The Basque artist **Ignacio Zuloaga** (1870–1945) expressed his love for Spain in brightly coloured scenes of the quotidien at a time when Impressionism was sweeping Europe.

The Decorative Arts

Factories were built under the Bourbons to produce decorative material for their palaces. In 1760, Charles III founded the Buen Retiro works, where ceramics for the famous Salones de Porcelana in the royal palaces of Aranjuez and Madrid were made. The factory was destroyed during the Napoleonic invasion.

In 1720, Philip V opened the Real Fábrica de Tapices de Santa Bárbara (in Madrid), the equivalent of the French Gobelins factory in Paris. Some of the tapestries depicted Don Quixote while others illustrated scenes of everyday life based on preparatory cartoons by Bayeu and Goya.

20C Creativity

Picasso, Dalí and Gaudí, controversial and often snubbed in their day, are now celebrated the world over. They belong to a game-changing generation of artists whose influence would reverberate into the 21C.

FROM MODERNISM TO SURREALISM

The artistic lull that Spain experienced at the end of the 19C was interrupted by a vast cultural movement in Catalunya known as *Modernisme*. Its greatest relics are the mind-bending architectural masterpieces by **Antoni Gaudí, Lluís Domènech i Montaner** and **Josep Maria Jujol**.

Painting was varied and prolific. The following are worth nothing among the many artists of the time: **Ramón Casas**, the best Spanish Impressionist, whose works are suffused with of grey melancholy; **Santiago Rusiñol; Isidro Nonell**, instigator of **Spanish Expressionism**; and **Pablo Picasso** (1881–1973), whose works from his various periods one could spend a lifetime studying.

In the 1920s a movement began to emerge that was influenced by Cubism and, more particularly, by **Surrealism**. Its sculptors were **Ángel Ferrant, Victorio Macho, Alberto Sánchez Pérez** and **Julio González**. Painters included **Daniel Vázquez Díaz**, Juan Gris, Joan Miró and Salvador Dalí. **Juan Gris** (1887–1927), the most faithful analytical Cubist, worked in Paris. The works of **Joan Miró** (1893–1983), champion of Surrealism, are characterised by childlike spontaneity. **Salvador Dalí** (1904–89), a quasi-Surrealist, dreamed up his own creative method, which he Called the paranoic critical. Some of his best paintings explore the subconscious and the dream world.

Post-war art

Art suffered during and following the Civil War. Many visionaries, including Picasso, went into exile. Official taste in architecture favoured the ostentatious, triumphalist and monumental. The most striking specimen of the era is Valle de los Caídos. Innovation didn't completely flounder in post-war Spain; architect **Miguel Fisac** is a case in point. In 1950, a new style based on functional criteria emerged. Examples abound in Barcelona (the Vanguardia building by **Oriol Bohigas** and **José María Martorell**) and in Madrid (the Torres Blancas, or White Towers by **Francisco Javier Sáenz de Oíza**). Post-war paintings of **José Gutiérrez Solana** are full of anguish; the landscape painters **Benjamín Palencia** and **Rafael Zabaleta** added levity to an otherwise difficult period.

Avant-Garde painters gained a foothold after the war. The first post-war Surrealists were Called the **Dau al Set** with **Antoni Tàpies** being one of its major proponents.

Contemporary Art

In the 1950s two abstract groups were formed: the **El Paso** group with **Antonio Saura, Manolo Millares** and **Rafael Canogar** and the **Equipo 57** with **Eusebio Sempere, Ángel Duarte, Agustín Ibarrola, Juan Serrano** and **José Duarte**. The movement's sculptors included Basque artists **Jorge Oteiza** and **Eduardo Chillida**. Other internationally acclaimed figures with influence to this day are painter Miquel Barceló, artist Ángela de la Cruz and the late sculptor Juan Muñoz.

The works of deceased Lanzarote artist **César Manrique** continue to enthrall island visitors. Space-age structures by **Santiago Calatrava** dot Spain from La Rioja to Valencia. Graffiti is perhaps Spain's buzziest art frontier with names to watch including Aryz, Pejac and Sr X.

Modernism

BARCELONA –Casa Batlló (Antoni Gaudí: 1905-07)

Modernism is a colourful, decorative and sensual style which recreates organic forms in a world dominated by curves and reverse curves.

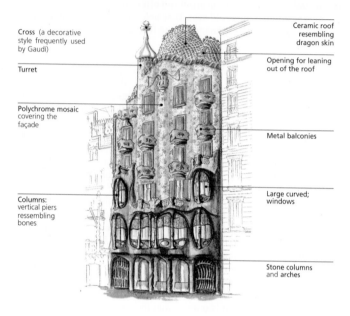

Cross (a decorative style frequently used by Gaudí)

Turret

Polychrome mosaic covering the façade

Columns: vertical piers resembling bones

Ceramic roof resembling dragon skin

Opening for leaning out of the roof

Metal balconies

Large curved; windows

Stone columns and arches

Mediterranean Rationalist

BARCELONA – Fundació Joan Miró (JL Sert: 1972-75)

The building consists of a series of interrelated architectural features and open spaces in which natural light plays a fundamental role.

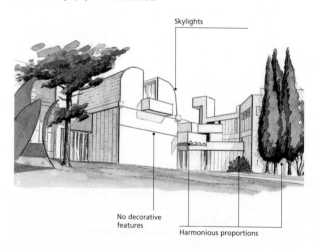

Skylights

No decorative features

Harmonious proportions

A–Z of Architectural Terms

Everything you always wanted to know about architectural terms but were too afraid to ask.

Words in italics are Spanish.

Ajimez paired window or opening separated by a central column.

Alfarje wooden ceiling, usually decorated, consisting of a board resting on cross-beams (a feature of the Mudéjar style).

Alfiz rectangular surround to a horseshoe-shaped arch in Muslim architecture.

Alicatado section of wall or other surface covered with sheets of ceramic tiles *(azulejos)* cut to form geometric patterns. Frequently used to decorate dados (a Mudéjar feature).

Alhondiga (*almúdin*) granary or food store, often Muslim in origin, but preserved after the so-called Reconquista.

Horseshoe (Moorish)

R. Corbel/MICHELIN

Aljibe Arab word for cistern.

Altarpiece (also retable). Decorative screen above and behind the altar.

Apse far end of a church housing the high altar; can be semicircular, polygonal or horseshoe-shaped.

Apsidal or radiating chapel small chapel opening from the apse.

Arch (⏚ *see illustrations.*)

Archivolt ornamental moulding on the outer edge of an arch.

Barrel

R. Corbel/MICHELIN

Artesonado marquetry ceiling in which raised fillets outline honeycomb-like cells in the shape of stars. This decoration, which first appeared under the Almohads, was popular throughout the country, including Christian Spain, in the 15C and 16C.

Ataurique decorative plant motif on plaster or brick which was developed as a feature of the Caliphate style and was subsequently adopted by the Mudéjar.

Azulejos glazed, patterned, ceramic tiles.

Barrel vaulting vault with a semicircular cross-section. (⏚ *see illustrations.*)

Cabecera the east or apsidal end of a church.

Caliphate the architectural style developed in Córdoba under the Caliphate (8C–11C) of which the finest example is the mosque in that city.

Camarín a small chapel on the first floor behind the altarpiece or retable. It is plushly decorated and very often contains a lavishly costumed statue of the Virgin Mary.

Capilla mayor the area of the high altar containing the *retablo mayor* (monumental altarpiece), which often rises to the roof.

Coro a chancel in Spanish canonical churches often built in the middle of the nave. It contains the **stalls** *(sillería)* used by members of religious orders. When placed in a tribune or gallery it is known as the *coro alto*.

Churrigueresque in the style of the Churrigueras, an 18C family of architects. Richly ornate Baroque decoration.

Crucero transept. The part of a church at right angles to the nave which gives the church a cross shape.

Estípite pilaster in the shape of a truncated inverted pyramid.

Gargoyle projecting roof gutter normally carved in the shape of a grotesque animal.

Girola (also *deambulatorio*) ambulatory. An extension to the aisles forming a gallery around the chancel and the altar.

Arches

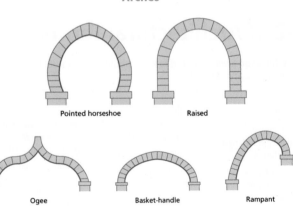

Pointed horseshoe   Raised

Ogee   Basket-handle   Rampant

Vaults

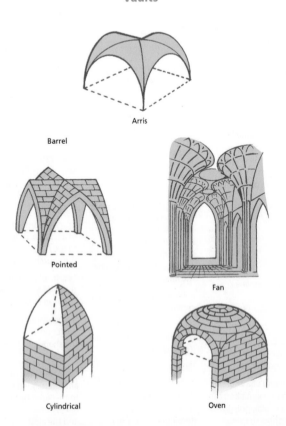

Arris

Barrel

Pointed

Fan

Cylindrical   Oven

R. Corbel/MICHELIN

Tympanum

Groined vaulting vault showing lines of intersection of two vaults or arches (usually pointed).

Grotesque typical Renaissance decoration combining vegetation, imaginary beings and animals.

Kiblah sacred wall of a mosque from which the mihrab is hollowed, facing toward Mecca.

Lacería geometric decoration formed by intersecting straight lines making star-shaped and polygonal figures. Characteristic of Moorish architecture.

Lombard bands decorative pilaster strips typical of Romanesque architecture in Lombardy.

Lonja commodity exchange building.

Mihrab richly decorated prayer-niche in the sacred wall (kiblah) in a mosque.

Minaret tower of the mosque (*mezquita*), from which the muezzin calls the faithful to prayer.

Minbar pulpit in a mosque.

Mocárabes decorative prismatic motifs of Muslim architecture. They resemble stalactites or pendants and adorn vaults and cornices.

Mozarabic the work of Christians living under Arab rule after the Moorish invasion of 711. On being persecuted in the 9C, they sought refuge in Christian areas bringing with them Moorish artistic traditions.

Mudéjar the work of Muslims living in Christian territory following the so-called Reconquista (13C–14C).

Mullion slender column or pillar dividing an opening in a door or window.

Naveta megalithic monument found in the Balearic Islands, which has a pyramidal shape with a rectangular base.

Plateresque term derived from *platero* (i.e. silversmith); used to describe the early style of the Renaissance characterised by finely carved decoration.

Predella the lower part of an altarpiece.

Presbiterio the space in front of the altar (the presbytery is known as the *casa del cura*).

Púlpito pulpit.

Sagrario chapel containing the Holy Sacrament. May sometimes be a separate church.

Sebka type of brick decoration developed under the Almohads consisting of an apparently endless series of small arches forming a network.

Seo cathedral.

Sillería the stalls.

Soportales porticoes of wood or stone pillars supporting the first floor of houses. They form an open gallery around the plaza mayor of towns and villages.

Star vault vault with a square or polygonal plan formed by several intersecting arches.

Stucco type of moulding mix consisting mainly of plaster, used for coating surfaces. It plays a fundamental role in wall decoration in Hispano-Muslim architecture.

Talayot: megalithic monument found in the Balearic Islands, which takes the form of a truncated cone of stones.

Taula (*mesa* in the Mallorcan language) megalithic monument found in the Balearic Islands consisting of a monolithic horizontal stone block placed on top of a vertical stone block.

Trasaltar back wall of the *capilla mayor* in front of which there are frequently sculptures or tombs.

Trascoro the wall, often carved and decorated, which encloses the *coro*.

Triforium arcade above the side aisles which opens onto the central nave of a church.

Tympanum inner surface of a pediment. This often ornamented space is bounded by the archivolt and the lintel of the doors of churches.

Venera scallop-shaped moulding frequently used as an ornamental feature. It is the symbol of pilgrimages to Santiago de Compostela.

Yesería plasterwork used in sculptured decoration.

Spanish Gardens

The gardens of Spain reflect the country's rich heritage and show an enviable ability to adapt to a varied climate. Though Spanish landscape gardening inherited many of its traditions from within Europe, it benefited most from the Moors, who introduced exotic plants, new irrigation techniques and a sense of spacial and aesthetic balance.

GENERALIFE (14C), GRANADA

The Generalife is the Moorish garden par excellence. Its hill-top position makes it a fantastic lookout, but within it you'll find the intimate, sensual character and evocation of paradise typical of Islamic gardens.

Despite questionable alterations over the centuries, it remains a harmonious feast for the senses. Nothing has been left to chance: the colour of the plants and flowers, their aromas and and the omnipresence of water combine to create a heavenly ambience. The Generalife is laid out on several levels to ensure that the trees in one garden do not interfere with the views from another. In fact, the garden is best considered as a series of landscaped areas and enclosures, each with its own individuality within the overall design. The architecture and vegetation complement each other and glimmer in the fountains and water channels around every corner.

LA GRANJA (18C), SEGOVIA

These magnificent Baroque palace gardens bring to mind those of Versailles, where Philip V spent his childhood. He was to make **La Granja** his personal retreat. While it lacks Versailles' grandiose perspectives, it gains in its backdrop of dramatic mountains, whose snows feed its burbling fountains. The rigidity of the French garden is lost here as there is no clear central axis; instead, La Granja consists of a succession of zones, each with a certain independence, recalling Moorish tastes.

Although the French gardeners that Philip V invited south brought with them a variety of species, they were able to adapt them perfectly to the local landscape in the palace's nurseries. Elaborate sculptures scattered in

La Granja de San Ildefonso, Segovia

small squares and along avenues add a theatrical touch. The gardens are at their sumptuous prime when the fountains are switched on for selected days in spring and early summer.

PAZO DE OCA (18–19C), LA ESTRADA, A CORUÑA

A *pazo* is a Baroque-style manor typical of Galicia comprising a recreational garden, a kitchen garden and cultivated farmland. The garden of the Pazo de Oca ('Goose Manor') is the oldest in Galicia and a quintessential example of the genre. The damp climate allows vegetation to grow on rocks, creating a dialogue between man-made architecture and natural features. Water plays a vital role, appearing in basins or fountains and trickling through the garden. The most romantic area is hidden behind a parterre and has two ponds and a delightful footbridge flanked by with benches. The lower pond contains the *pazo*'s most representative and famous feature: the stone 'boat', with its two petrified sailors, planted with hydrangeas.

JARDINS DE MONFORT (19C), VALENCIA

The River Turia's ribbon of green parkland running through Valencia's city centre links three older gardens: the Jardins del Reial, which date to Islamic times; the Jardí Botànic, founded in 1567; and the Jardins de Montfort, the smallest but perhaps most striking of the three.

When the Marqués de San Juan, an ennobled businessman, created this romantic garden in the 1860s, it lay between orchards and rural palaces. Today, protected by its sturdy brick walls, it remains an ingenious oasis with a microclimate that fosters flowering plants and aromatics year round. Beyond a small pavilion, a waist-high labyrinth of trimmed hedges is decorated by Italian marble statues and a graceful fountain. From here a bougainvillea bower leads to a larger informal area shaded by olive and orange trees, and a fragrant rose garden and oriental

© Vladislav Zolotov/iStockphoto.com

Marimurtra, Blanes

bamboo pond. As in other great Spanish gardens, you are never far from the sound of splashing water.

MARIMURTRA (20C), BLANES, GIRONA

Carlos Faust, the German impresario who settled on the Costa Brava, created this botanical garden in 1921 for research purposes and to preserve plants threatened with extinction. Sandwiched between the sea and the mountains, it offers visitors 180-degree views of the coast. Today Marimurtra is a fine example of a contemporary Mediterranean garden, although if you look close, you can spot species from every continent. There's a cactus garden, an impressive aquatic garden, and a catalogued collection of medicinal, toxic and aromatic plants. The only architectural feature, which has a purely decorative function, is the small temple built at the end of the steps running down to the sea.

PALMETUM (21C), SANTA CRUZ DE TENERIFE, CANARY ISLANDS

What was once Santa Cruz de Tenerife's municipal dump has been transformed into 30 acres/12ha of rolling palm groves. Overlooking the Atlantic, the gardens boast the most diverse collection of palm treas on earth with nearly 600 species on display. Converting mounds of refuse into a paradisiacal public park was no small feat; it took a team of architects, botanists and gardeners 19 years to complete it. Palmetum opened to the public in 2014 and has been a popular site on the Canarian tourist circuit since.

Spanish Music

Alongside its folk music, Spain has developed an extraordinarily rich musical repertory since the Middle Ages marked by a large number of influences including Visigothic, Arabic, Mozarabic and French.

CHANTS TO CHARTS

Polyphonic chants were studied in the 11C and the oldest known piece for three voices, the *Codex calixtinus*, was composed at Santiago de Compostela c.1140. During the so-called Reconquista, the church encouraged musical creativity by liturgical chants and plays such as the *Elche Mystery,* still performed today. At the end of the 15C, the dramatist **Juan de la Encina** composed secular song,but music, like the other arts, blossomed in Spain in the second half of the 16C under the encouragement of the early Habsburgs. **Tomás Luis de Victoria** (1548–1611) was one of the most famous composers of polyphonic devotional pieces, while among his contemporaries, **Francisco de Salinas** and **Fernando de las Infantas** were learned musicologists. **Cristóbal de Morales** and **Francisco Guerrero** emerged as religious composers. As for instruments, the organ became the centre of sacred music, while a favourite for profane airs was the *vihuela*, a guitar with six double strings, soon replaced by the lute and, later, the five-string Spanish guitar. In 1629, **Lope de Vega** wrote the text for the first Spanish opera. **Pedro Calderón de la Barca** is credited with creating the **zarzuela**, a musical play with spoken passages, songs and dances, which, since the 19C, has based its plot and music on popular themes.

In the 19C, the Catalan **Felipe Pedrell** elevated music on the Iberian Peninsula by combining traditional melodies with classical genres. In the early 19C, while works by French composers (Ravel's *Bolero*, Bizet's *Carmen*, Lalo's *Symphonie Espagnole…*) bore a pronounced Hispanic stamp, Spanish composers turned to national folklore and traditional themes: **Isaac Albéniz** (1860–1909) wrote *Iberia*, **Enrique Granados** (1867–1916) became famous for his *Goyescas* and **Joaquín Turina** (1882–1949) for his *Sevilla Symphony*. This vein led to works by **Manuel de Falla** (1876–1946) including *Nights in the Gardens of Spain*, *El Amor Brujo* and *The Three-Cornered Hat*.

Among the best-known contemporary classical guitar players, **Andrés Segovia** (1893–1987); **Joaquín Rodrigo** (1901–99), famous for his *Concierto de Aranjuez*; and **Narciso Yepes** (1927–97) have shown that this most Spanish of instruments can interpret a wide variety of music. Equally, **flamenco** giants like **Paco de Lucía, Camarón de la Isla,** Tomatito and Enrique Morente challenged the tenets of traditional flamenco by incorporating jazz, North African and even heavy metal music. Another Spaniard, **Pablo Casals** (1876–1973), was possibly the greatest cellist of all time. Spain holds a leading position in the world of opera with singers such as **Victoria de los Ángeles** (1923–2005), **Montserrat Caballé** (1933–2018), **Plácido Domingo**, **Alfredo Kraus** (1927–99) and **José Carreras**.

Today's influential musicians range from chart-topping pop stars like **Enrique Iglesias**, **Pablo Alborán** and Rozalén to flamenco fusion sensation **Rosalía** to reggaeton and trap artists Juan Magan, **C. Tangana** and Bad Gyal. Latin American trap and reggaeton are currently all the rage in nightclubs with favourite artists including Ozuna, **J Balvin, Bad Bunny** and Maluma. These and many international artists headline of Spain's top music festivals such as Benicàssim (near Valencia), **Sónar** (Barcelona), Dreambeach (near Almería), Bilbao BBK Live and Paraíso (Madrid).

Spanish Literature

Knights, Don Juans, mystics and rogues occupy a hallowed place in the Spanish canon. Traditionalists say the country's literature peaked in the 16C–17C, but in reality, Spain has never stopped being a literary powerhouse.

BEGINNINGS

Roman Spain produced great Latin authors such as **Seneca the Elder**, his son **Seneca the Younger** and the poets **Martial** and **Lucan**. In the 8C, the monk **Beatus** wrote the Commentary on the Apocalypse, which gave rise to the illuminated beatus manuscripts. Arab writers, especially poets like **Ibn Hani** and Ibn Abdun, won renown during the early Islamic period.

THE MIDDLE AGES

Some of the Middle Ages' greatest minds, such as **Avicenna,** the father of modern medicine, and **Maimonides**, the revered Jewish philosopher, came from Al Andalus, or Islamic Spain. The works of Aristotle and other Classical philosophers, forgotten for centuries, were rediscovered by the Moors. Simultaneously the first texts written in Old Castilian began to emerge such as the 12C *El Cantar del Mío Cid*, an epic poem chronicling the adventures of the fearless knight. In the 13C, the monk **Gonzalo de Berceo**, drawing on religious themes, won renown through his works of *Mester de Clerecía*. **Alfonso X the Wise**, an erudite king who wrote poetry in Galician, decreed that Castilian supplant Latin as the official language, an act subsequently repeated in other kingdoms across the Peninsula. In the 14C, **Juan Ruiz, Archpriest of Hita** wrote the famed satirical verse work *El Libro de Buen Amor*, the forerunner to picaresque novels.

THE RENAISSANCE

In the 15C, lyric poetry flourished under Italian influence with poets such as **Jorge Manrique** and the **Marquis of Santillana**. **Romanceros**, collections of ballads in an epic or popular vein, perpetuated the medieval style until the 16C when *Amadís de Gaula* (1508) redefined notions of romance and chivalry. In 1499, *La Celestina*, a novel of passion by **Fernando de Rojas**, anticipated modern drama in a subtle, well-observed tragicomic intrigue.

THE GOLDEN AGE (SIGLO DE ORO)

Spain arguably enjoyed its greatest literary flowering under the Habsburgs (1516–1700), thanks to lyric poets such as **Garcilaso de la Vega**, mystic verse poet **Fray Luis de León** and, above all, **Luis de Góngora y Argote** (1561–1627) whose *sui generis* style earned him his own genre, Gongorism.

The **picaresque** novel, however, was the genre favoured by Spanish writers at the time. The first to appear, in 1554, was *Lazarillo de Tormes*, the anonymous – and truly hilarious – tale of an astute rogue (*pícaro*) who casts a sardonic eye on society and its shortcomings.

There followed **Mateo Alemán**'s *Guzmán de Alfarache*, with its brisk style and colourful vocabulary, and *La Vida del Buscón*, an example of the varied talents of **Francisco de Quevedo** (1580–1645), essayist, poet and satirist. The preeminent genius of the Golden Age, however, was **Miguel de Cervantes** (1547–1616), author of **Don Quixote** (1605), the world's bestselling novel. Dramatists proliferated, among them **Lope de Vega** (1562–1635), who reimagined drama for popular audiences; he wrote more than 1 000 plays, including *Fuenteovejuna*, and Europe's first manifesto on modern theatre. His successor, **Calderón de la Barca** (1600–81), wrote historical and philo-

A LIFE LESS ORDINARY

Miguel de Cervantes Saavedra was born in poverty in Alcalá de Henares in 1547, yet he went on to lead a life of adventure. From being a valet in Renaissance Rome, Cervantes would later fight against the Ottomans in the Battle of Lepanto (1571). He spent five years as a slave in Algiers before returning to Madrid as a purveyor and tax collector for the Spanish Armada. While being imprisoned for debts in La Mancha, it is said that he had the idea for his famous literary work, **Don Quixote de La Mancha**, *(vol I 1605, vol II 1615)*, one of the greatest novels of all time. He died in 1616.

sophical plays (*El Alcalde de Zalamea* or *The Mayor of Zalamea*) that reflected the mood of Spain in the 17C. **Tirso de Molina** (1579–1648) left his interpretation of Don Juan for posterity while **Guillén de Castro** wrote *Las Mocedades del Cid (Youthful Adventures of the Cid)*. Mention should be made of works on the conquest of America by chroniclers **Cortés** and **Bartolomé de las Casas** among others. Finally, the moralist **Fray Luis de Granada** and the mystics **Santa Teresa de Ávila** (1515–82) and **San Juan de la Cruz** (St John of the Cross) (1542–91) wrote inspiring theological works.

18C AND 19C

The Enlightenment found expression in the works of essayists such as **Benito Jerónimo Feijoo**, a monk, and **Jovellanos**, while elegance dominated the plays of **Moratín**. The great romantic poet of the 19C was **Bécquer** (1836–70) from Sevilla, while **Larra** was the main social satirist and **Menéndez Pelayo** the preeminent literary critic of his day. Realism was introduced to the Spanish novel by **Alarcón** (*The Three-Cornered Hat*) and **Pereda** (*Peñas Arriba*), who homed in on regional themes. By the end of the 19C, the best realist was **Pérez Galdós**, whose prolific, lively work (*National Episodes*) stands out for its exploration of human sympathy.

20C

A group of intellectuals known as the Generation of '98, saddened by Spain's rapid decadence, produced writing with a new moral spirit as reflected in the work of essayists such as **Miguel de Unamuno** (1864–1936), author of *El Sentimiento Trágico de la Vida (The Tragic Sense of Life)* and **Azorín**, philologist **Menéndez Pidal**, novelist **Pío Baroja** and the radical aestheticist **Valle Inclán**. Among their contemporaries were **Jacinto Benavente** (1922 Nobel Prize for literature winner), who explored social class in his dramas, and bestselling Valencian author **Blasco Ibañez**. Great poets began to surface including **Juan Ramón Jiménez** (Nobel Prize 1956), who expressed his feelings through simple unadorned prose poems (*Platero y Yo*); **Antonio Machado** (1875–1939), the bard of Castilla; and **Rafael Alberti**. **Federico García Lorca** (1898–1936), a peerless poet and dramatist (*Bodas de Sangre*) for his time, anticipated magical realism in his rich use of symbol and metaphor. His oeuvre is, perhaps, the most fascinating reflection of a fraught era in Spain that **José Ortega y Gasset** (1883–1955), essayist and philosopher, also spent his life trying to understand.

POST-WAR TO PRESENT

Despite the brain drain resulting from the Civil War, during which Franco's troops purposefully killed dozens of intellectuals, writing rose from the ashes with works by essayists (**Américo Castro**, in exile), playwrights (**Alfonso Sastre**) and novelists such as **Miguel Delibes**, **Ramón Sender** and **Camilo José Cela** (*La Familia de Pascual Duarte*), who won the Nobel Prize for Literature in 1989.

The contemporary era in Spain has produced a flurry of phenomenal, best-stlling authors like **Almudena Grandes**, **Javier Marías, Arturo Pérez-Reverte** and **Carlos Ruiz Zafón**, whose *Shadow of the Wind* (2001) has sold more than 15 million copies.

SPAIN IN WRITING

BIOGRAPHY

Juan Carlos: Steering Spain from Dictatorship to Democracy – Paul Preston (2010). A study of the man who ruled Spain from 1975 until his abdication in 2014.

Reinventing Food – Colman Andrews (2010). The biography of El Bulli chef Ferran Adrià.

REFERENCE

The New Spaniards – John Hooper (2006). An authoritative book on modern Spanish culture by a foreign correspondent.

HISTORY

Collectives in the Spanish Revolution – Gaston Leval (1972). A chronicle of Spain's potent workers' movements up to the Civil War.

The Basque History of the World – Mark Kurlansky (1999). A concise, fascinating history of Europe's oldest culture.

Ghosts of Spain – Giles Tremlett (2012). A journalist tours the country to explore the darker episodes of Spain's history.

Homage to Catalonia – George Orwell (1938). A look at the Spanish Civil War from the Republican side depicting the Communist purges that engulfed Barcelona in 1937.

Spain – William Chislett (2013). An engaging overview of history from Islamic Spain to the present.

FICTION

Don Quixote de La Mancha – Miguel de Cervantes (1605; 2015). Spain's timeless national novel.

The Cathedral of the Sea – Ildefonso Falcones (2009). A *Pillars of the Earth*-like historical novel about the construction of Barcelona's Santa María del Mar basilica.

The Sun Also Rises – Ernest Hemingway (1926). The Lost Generation takes on Pamplona's San Fermín festival.

For Whom the Bell Tolls – Ernest Hemingway (1938). Hemingway's story of a young American idealist fighting for the Republic in the Spanish Civil War.

Southern Seas – Manuel Vázquez Montalbán (1979). A favourite of the Pepe Carvalho series involving murder, lust and nouvelle cuisine, set in Barcelona.

The Shadow of the Wind – Carlos Ruiz Zafón (2001). Contemporary allegory of post-Civil War Barcelona infused with Latin American magical realism.

TRAVEL

Death in the Afternoon – Ernest Hemingway (1932). A terse take on bullfighting, tradition and the Spanish soul.

Driving over Lemons – Chris Stewart (1999). The first in a trilogy about expat life in rural Granada.

Duende – Jason Webster (2004). A young Anglo-American man's journey into the world of flamenco.

South from Granada – Gerald Brenan (1957; 2008). A literary and folkloric account of Spain in the last century.

Spain – Jan Morris (1970). The Morris take on Spain: history, encounters and pleasures.

Walking to Santiago – Ryan Tandler (2017). A modern guide to the famous pilgrimage route.

ART

The Shameful Life of Salvador Dalí – Ian Gibson (1998). A portrait of a tortured soul.

Picasso – Patrick O'Brian (1976). A moving, non-academic biography that captures the artist's character. .

Spanish Cinema and Stage

Over the centuries, Spain has produced countless thespians and playwrights of world renown. In the 20C and 21C, film directors such as Luis Buñuel, Luis Berlanguer and Pedro Almodóvar have drawn the country international renown.

PERFORMING ARTS

Opera, disliked by Franco, has made a comeback in Madrid's Teatro Real and Barcelona's historic Liceu. The revival of theatre is wider, with Catalunya's tradition of comedy joined by notable new work from Andalucía and Madrid.

CINEMA

Spanish cinema dates back to a short film in 1897 that shows people leaving the Basílica de Nuestra Señora del Pilar in Zaragoza after Mass. Studios for silent movies were later set up in Barcelona. In the 1920s, several Surrealists tried their hand at the new art form. Among them were **Dalí** and, above all, **Luis Buñuel**, the master of Spanish cinema who made Un Chien Andalou (An Andalucían Dog) in 1928 and Âge d'Or (The Golden Age) in 1930.

When talking films appeared in the 1930s, Spain was in the throes of a political and economic crisis. Studios lacked the means to procure the necessary equipment, and production was limited.

At the end of the 1930s, when films like Sor Angélica (Sister Angelica) by **Francisco Gargallo** tended to address religious themes (Franco's doing), Juan Piqueras launched a magazine Called Nuestro Cinema, which was strongly influenced by Russian ideas, as a counterweight. It gave star billing to films such as Las Hurdes (Land Without Bread) by Buñuel (1932), which depicted poverty in rural Spain.

In the decades following the Civil War, non-Spanish films were banned or heavily censored. Cinema became a vehicle for Francoist ideology with religious themes, tradition and devotion front and centre. But there were exceptions such as the humourous Marcelino Pan y Vino (The Miracle of Marcelino) by Ladislao Vajda (1955). Other flicks that have stood the test of time include Juan Antonio Bardem's Muerte de un Ciclista (Death of a Cyclist) and **Luis García Berlanga**'s Bienvenido Mister Marshall (Welcome Mr Marshall, 1953) and El Verdugo (The Executioner, 1963).

The 1960s saw a period of renewal with the emergence of directors like **Carlos Saura**, whose first film, Los Golfos (The Delinquents), came out in 1960. Saura's Ana y los Lobos (Anna and the Wolves, 1973) was also poular. The 70s and 80s ushered in new talent with notable films including El Espíritu de la Colmena (The Spirit of the Beehive, 1973) and El Sur (The South, 1983), by **Víctor Erice**; La Colmena (The Beehive, 1982), by **Mario Camus**; and politically charged films like **Manuel Gutiérrez Aragón**'s La Mitad del Cielo (Half of Heaven, 1986) illustrating the changes democracy brought to Franco's Spain.

But Spanish cinema had never seen anyone quite like **Pedro Almodóvar,** whose films, which sprung on the scene in the late 80s, would explore the complexities and existential dilemmas of modern Spain, often with a streak of dark comedy. Spain's most lauded director to this day, he has won over critics and audiences around the world. Mujeres al Borde de un Ataque de Nervios (Women on the Verge of a Nervous Breakdown, 1988), Volver (2006) and La Piel Que Habito (The Skin I Live In, 2011) are three of his best. His latest release, Dolor y Gloria (Pain and Glory, 2019), is essentially autobiographical and has been met with rather mixed reviews.

SPAIN ON FILM

Un Chien Andalou (An Andalucían Dog; 1929). A graphic, intentionally nonsensical surrealist masterpiece by Luis Buñuel and Salvador Dalí.

Las Hurdes (Land Without Bread, 1933). Buñuel charts the hard lives of Extremaduran peasants.

Surcos (Furrows; 1951). A neo-realist drama by José Antonio Nieves Conde about the disintegration of a family unit in Franco's Madrid.

La Caza (The Hunt; 1966). A thriller by Carlos Saura about war veterans whose reunion turns to violence.

Cría Cuervos (Raise Ravens; 1976). A symbolic criticism of the Franco regime by Saura, with a haunting soundtrack by Jeanette.

Mujeres al Borde de un Ataque de Nervios (Women on the Verge of a Nervous Breakdown; 1988). Pedro Almodóvar's feminist comedy, marking his international breakthrough.

Jamón, Jamón (Ham, Ham; 1992). Bigas Luna's satire on Iberian machismo starring Penélope Cruz and Javier Bardem.

Los Amantes del Círculo Polar (The Lovers of the Arctic Circle; 1998). An homage to love and fate by Julio Medem.

Land and Freedom (1995). A Liverpudlian's experience of fighting for the Republic in the Civil War, with a narrative comparable to Orwell's Homage to Catalonia.

Hable con Ella (Talk to Her; 2002). An Oscar winner by Almodóvar about two men and their devotion to the comatose women who they love.

Mar Adentro (The Sea Inside; 2004). Amenábar's Oscar-winning biopic about Ramón Sampedro and his struggle with disability.

El Laberinto del Fauno (Pan's Labyrinth; 2006). The horrors of post-Civil War Spain, and a young girl embracing her fantasy world, sumptuously brought to life by Guillermo del Toro.

Biutiful (2010). Directed by México's Alejandro González Iñárritu, starring Javier Bardem, and set in Barcelona, this chronicle of a man in free-fall is a portrait of Barcelona's gritty underbelly and the flip side of Woody Allen's Vicky Cristina Barcelona (2008).

Agnosia (2010). Eugenio Mira's psychological and romantic thriller about a woman suffering from agnosia (the inability to recognize faces) is set in an opulent late 19C Barcelona.

Pa Negre (Pan Negro or Black Bread; 2010). Beautifully filmed post-Spanish Civil War drama by Agustí Villaronga about a young boy drawn into the lives and lies of the adults around him, and the ideological purges of post-Civil War Spain.

Balada Triste de Trompeta (Sad Trumpet Ballad; 2010). Alex de la Iglesia's drama about two 1973 circus clowns fighting for the love of a dancer is borderline surreal but riveting.

La piel que habito (The Skin I Live In; 2011). Almodóvar's dark, multi-award winning thriller casts Antonio Banderas as a troubled plastic surgeon who creates an indestructible synthetic skin for a mysterious woman.

Loreak (Flowers; 2014). The first Basque-language film to be entered by Spain for Best Foreign Language Film in the 2016 Academy Awards.

La Isla Mínima (Marshland; 2014). A 1980 murder mystery directed by Alberto Rodríguez set in rural Andalucía that won 10 Goya Awards.

Nature

Few countries in the world boast such diversity in climate, wildlife and scenery as Spain. Bridging Europe and Africa, the country brims with natural attractions ranging from sandy beaches, sheltered coves and craggy cliffs to soaring mountains, placid marshland and lunar lavascapes.

The centre of Spain, known as the Meseta, is marked by seemingly endless expanses of flat, dry terrain, but there are diamonds in the rough if you know where to look.

» Spain's Landscapes p109
» Spain's Climate p110

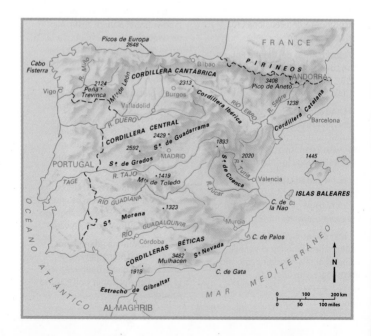

Spain's Landscapes

S uch is Spain's varied topography that in Granada you can drive in the morning to ski on the snowy slopes of the Sierra Nevada, then drive down to the baked Mediterranean coast to waterski in the afternoon.

RELIEF

The dominant feature of the peninsula is the immense plateau at its centre. This is the **Meseta**, a Hercynian platform between 600m/1 968ft and 1 000m/3 281ft high. It tilts slightly westwards and is surrounded by long mountain ranges that form barriers between the central plateau and the coastal regions. These peripheral ranges – the **Cordillera Cantábrica** in the northwest (an extension of the Pyrenees), the **Cordillera Ibérica** in the northeast and the **Sierra Morena** in the south – were caused by Alpine folding.

Other mountains rising here and there from the Meseta are folds of the original, ancient massif. They include the **Sierras de Somosierra, Guadarrama** and **Gredos**; the **Peña de Francia;** and the **Montes de Toledo**.

The highest massifs in Spain, the **Pyrenees** (Pirineos) in the north and the **Sierras Béticas**, including the **Sierra Nevada**, in the south, are on the country's outer edge, as are Spain's greatest valleys, those of the Ebro and Guadalquivir rivers.

The average altitude in Spain is a whopping 650m/2 100ft above sea level, and one sixth of the terrain rises to more than 1 000m/3 300ft. The highest peak on the Spanish mainland is Mulhacén (3 422m/11 427ft) in the Sierra Nevada. Mount Teide, in Tenerife, Canary Islands, is Spain's highest summit with a height of 3 718m/12 195ft.

BEACHES

Surrounded on nearly all sides by water, Spain is a veritable paradise for beach-goers. The country's coastline of around 5 000mi/8 000km has something for everyone: There are family-friendly resorts (Gandía and Benidorm), virgin beaches (Costa de la Luz and Bolonia), rocky sheltered coves (Galicia, Asturias and the Costa Brava) and endless dunes (Fuerteventura and Maspalomas).

Snow-capped mountains of the Parque Nacional de Sierra Nevada and almond trees in bloom in February, Jerez del Marquesado, Granada Provice

© Jean Heintz/hemis.fr

Spain's Climate

Though much of Spain enjoys 300 days of sunshine a year, you may need a raincoat (or snow shoes!) depending on your destination: Spain's great diversity of climates and landscapes means you'll never tire of visiting.

UNDER THE SUN

The **Meseta** accounts for 40% of the surface area of Iberia and includes Castilla y León, Castilla–La Mancha, Madrid and Extremadura. It has a continental climate with extremes of temperature ranging from scorching hot in summer to freezing cold in winter. These excesses are combined with modest and irregular rainfall to form an arid landscape that complements the seemingly infinite horizons in this part of Spain. The massif of the adjoining Pyrenees has a colder alpine climate; the lowest temperatures ever reached in Spain, -32°C/-26°F, were recorded here. This climate is also prevalent in the Sierra Nevada in Andalucía.

The northern coast, which runs from **Galicia** to the **Basque Country**, is nicknamed **España verde** (Green Spain) due to its mild and very humid climate, with rainfall being much higher than in the heartlands of northern Europe. This is in stark contrast to the stereotypical image of Spain as a dry, sunny country. **The Levante** has a Mediterranean climate with rainfall being restricted mainly to autumn and spring; a temperate climate in the winter gives way to high temperatures between June and August. The moist heat is tempered by the Levante, the cool wind for which this eastern coast, from Almería in the south to Catalunya in the north, is named.

Europe's only true desert is in Tabernas municipality, **Almería,** in southeastern Andalucía. The remaining coastline of **Andalucía** has a mild and sunny climate tempered by Levante and Poniente winds. Head inland during the summer months and risk being cooked alive: In 2017, temperatures in Córdoba province soared to 47.3 °C (117.1 °F), the highest on record.

The climate of the **Balearic Islands** (Mallorca, Menorca, Ibiza, Formentera) in the Mediterranean Sea is characterised by mild and tempestuous winters and hot and sunny summers.

The **Canary Islands** (Tenerife, Gran Canaria, Lanzarote, Fuerteventura, La Palma, La Gomera, El Hierro, *see Discovering the Canary Islands*) enjoy a subtropical climate, due to their latitude in the Atlantic Ocean. They are well known for their year-round pleasant temperatures and low rainfall, making them a haven for winter sun-seekers. Even here, however, there are significant climate differences between the coast and inland.

THE CLIMATE CRISIS

Experts warn that 80% of Spain may be desertified by the end of the century. Drought has been exacerbated by irresponsible agriculture and coastal tourism: Golf courses greedily drink thousands of gallons to remain lush year-round, while hotel laundries and swimming pools further deplete valuable water resources.

Desalination plants are likely to multiply to meet demand – like wind-farms, which produced a laudable 23% of the country's energy in 2018 – but even still, drinking water shortages are likely in the coming decades.

Sea-level rise will hit coastal cities – such as Donostia-San Sebastián, Barcelona and Valencia – hardest.

Spain has already lost 80% of its glaciers, and those in the Pyrenees are on track to melt by 2050.

Discovering
Spain

Procession of the pilgrims of El Rocío during the Whitsun weekend, Andalucía
© Kaos/Sime/Photononstop

Central Spain

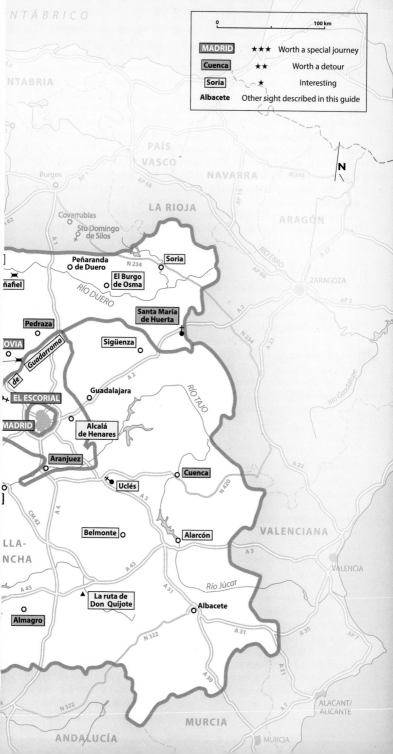

Central Spain

MADRID	★★★	Worth a special journey
Cuenca	★★	Worth a detour
Soria	★	Interesting
Albacete		Other sight described in this guide

0   100 km

NTÁBRICO

NTABRIA

PAÍS VASCO

NAVARRA

LA RIOJA

ARAGÓN

Burgos

Covarrubias

Sto Domingo de Silos

RÍO EBRO

ZARAGOZA

Peñaranda de Duero

Soria

ñafiel

El Burgo de Osma

RÍO DUERO

Santa María de Huerta

Pedraza

OVIA

de Guadarrama

Sigüenza

N 234

A 2

RÍO TAJO

Guadalajara

EL ESCORIAL

MADRID

Alcalá de Henares

Aranjuez

Cuenca

Uclés

A 3

RÍO JÚCAR

Belmonte

Alarcón

VALENCIANA

VALENCIA

A 3

LLA-NCHA

A 4

A 43

La ruta de Don Quijote

A 31

Albacete

Almagro

N 322

A 31

A 35

AP 7

ALACANT/ ALICANTE

MURCIA

ANDALUCÍA

MURCIA

N

Madrid and around

Set on on the arid tableland known as the *meseta*, Madrid stands at the geographical heart of Spain. Its central location contributed to Philip II's decision to settle his court here; so, too, did its healthy climate, riverside position and stunning mountain backdrop. It is one of the most boisterous cities in Europe with packed bars, buzzing late-night crowds and unmatched street life. Art-wise, it competes with London and Paris with its dozens of museums. Madrid is Europe's hottest capital with August temperatures soaring above 40°C (10°F) despite the fact that it's also the continent's highest, clocking in at over 640m/2 100ft above sea level. Happily, it still doesn't see the dense tourist hordes (or steep prices) of Barcelona thanks to its landlocked location. Like Berlin or Brussels, Madrid is an inexhaustible city that takes time to get to know – even if you can tackle its main sights in a few days. But those who stick around will no doubt fall in love with this open-hearted, multicultural city that's oozes history and innovation in equal measure. Scenesters, foodies and clubbers appreciate Madrid as much as the museum mavens who relish its stunning art collections.

Highlights

1. Nibbling tapas in and around the 17C **Plaza Mayor** (p123)
2. Enjoying dinner and a night out around **Plaza de Santa Ana** (p136)
3. Gazing in wonder at the **Prado's** Spanish **art collection** (p139)
4. Seeing Picasso's Guernica in the **Museo de Arte Reina Sofía** (p143)
5. Strolling in the palace river gardens of **Aranjuez** (p152)

Paseo del Prado

This stately avenue, lined by plane trees, is home to the Prado museum, which houses the Spanish royal collection of classical paintings including Velázquez's *Las Meninas*. Since the Paseo was laid out in the 18C it has attracted a host of other museums, galleries and art centres, including the famous Museo Thyssen-Bornemisza and the Reina Sofía contemporary art museum where Picasso's *Guernica* hangs. Such is the richness of these and other art collections that many art-loving visitors choose to spend most of their days here, taking breaks in the green Retiro Park or Royal Botanical Garden nearby. At the Paseo's southern end, Atocha station is a central junction for the high-speed AVE train network.

Habsburg Madrid

Centring on the Plaza Mayor, the old town (aka Barrio de los Austrias) combines narrow alleyways with squares, churches, convents and monasteries, plus traditional and modern shops and a host of places to eat and drink. The grandiose 2 800-room Royal Palace, built over earlier Habsburg palaces and an Islamic *alcázar*, merits a few hours' exploration. An evening stroll around Los Austrias's winding streets is a fine way to imagine the city's erstwhile opulence.

Centro

The popular quarters around the wide arterial avenues of Alcalá and the newly refurbished Gran Vía are a mosaic of bustling pedestrianised shopping streets and quaint residential areas. Many of the city's hotels, theatres and cinemas are here, and this is also the epicentre of its famed nightlife.

Day trips and excursions

An hour's drive or train ride from the city centre plops you in El Escorial, a medieval town with a 16C palatial complex containing a palace, church, monastery, mausoleum and museum, or in Alcalá de Henares, Cervantes' birthplace with a UNESCO-protected old town. Romantics and music lovers shouldn't miss the palace of Aranjuez for its gardens that inspired Rodrigo's haunting guitar concerto, while those with more time on their hands may opt to visit Toledo, Castilla's old capital and El Greco's birthplace, or Segovia, famed for its Roman aqueduct.

Madrid★★★

Madrid is one of Europe's liveliest and most extroverted cities, with wide avenues, attractive parks and a general *alegría* or joie de vivre. It became the capital fairly late in the game by Spanish standards, in the 16C, when Spain ruled a vast empire. Its monuments date primarily to the 17C, 18C and 19C. The city is world-famous for its exceptional wealth of paintings.

MADRID TODAY

Madrid is Spain's judicial, political and business capital as well as its cultural – and multicultural – epicentre.

Return travellers may not recognise new architectural marvels like the **Caixa Forum** art and exhibition centre, designed by Jacques Herzog and Pierre de Meuron; the **Banco de Bilbao-Vizcaya** in the **AZCA centre**; the 250 m/820 ft highrise **Cuatro Torres**; and the **Ciudad de Justicia** (City of Justice) complex.

A BIT OF HISTORY

Madrid owes its name to the 9C fortress (*alcázar*) of Majerit. In 1085 it was captured by Alfonso VI, who purportedly discovered a statue of the Virgin by a granary (*almudín*). He converted the mosque into a church dedicated to the Virgin of the Almudena, who was declared the city's patron. Emperor Charles V rebuilt the Muslim *alcázar*, and in 1561 his son Philip II moved the court from Toledo to Madrid.

The town grew dramatically in Spain's Golden Age (16C). King Philip IV gave court patronage to artists like **Velázquez** and **Murillo** and writers like Lope de Vega, Quevedo and Calderón. Madrid underwent its greatest transformations in the 18C under the Bourbons. Philip V built a royal palace, and Charles III constructed the Paseo del Prado and Puerta de Alcalá, examples of Neoclassical town planning. The 19C began with French occupation and the Madrid rebellion of May 1808 and its

▶ **Population:** 3 141 991.

◔ **Michelin Map:** 575 or 576 K 18–19 (town plan).

🚹 **Info:** Plaza Mayor 27; Plaza de Neptuno; Plaza de Cibeles 1; Ronda de Atocha; Plaza de Callao; Faro de Moncloa Tourist Info Point: Avendia Arco de la Victoria 2; Aeropuerto de Barajas (T2, lounges 5 and 6; T4, lounges 10 and 11). Tourist information: 🖉91 578 78 10. www.esmadrid.com; www.turismomadrid.es.

◖ **Location:** Europe's highest capital (646m/ 2 119ft), at the centre of the Iberian Peninsula, with a dry climate: hot summers and cold, sunny winters.

🅿 **Parking:** It's best to park for the duration and use the excellent Metro.

⊛ **Don't Miss:** The Prado, Plaza Mayor, bars in Plaza Santa Ana, Museo Colecciones Reales.

🕓 **Timing:** Start with the art museums, and take a siesta in order to enjoy Madrid's late-hours dining and bars.

👪 **Kids:** Faunia, Parque de Atracciones de Madrid, Parque Warner Madrid, Zoo-aquarium, and Aquópolis.

brutal repression. In 1857 the remaining ramparts were demolished and a vast expansion plan (*ensanche*) gave rise to the districts of Chamberí, Salamanca and Moncloa. At the beginning of the 20C, architecture was French-inspired, as in the Ritz (under construction as of September 2019) and Palace hotels; the neo-Mudéjar style was also popular, as evidneced by the bullring at Las Ventas. **Gran Vía** linked Madrid's new districts in 1910. Since then its footprint has only expanded, largely thanks to the metro underground and train system.

GETTING FROM A TO B

Airport – Madrid-Barajas airport is located northeast of the city, 13km/8mi from downtown.

The Línea Exprés bus operates between the airport's four terminals and city centre, ending at Atocha Station (€5). www.emtmadrid.es. Departures every 15–20 mins (35 mins at night; night buses terminate in Plaza de Cibeles).

🚇 **Metro line no. 8** connects the airport with the city. It's a 15-minute journey from Nuevos Ministerios to all terminals. A modern suburban train line (Cercanías) connects Terminal 4 with several key locations in Madrid: Chamartin, Nuevos Ministerios, Atocha and Principe Pío.

Airport information: 🖉902 40 47 04; www.aeropuertomadrid-barajas.com. Info-Iberia and bookings: 🖉901 111 500.

🚃 **RENFE (Spanish State Railways)** – The city's main railway stations are Atocha (Pl. del Emperador Carlos V and Glorieta Carlos V) and Chamartín (Agustín de Foxa). For information and reservations, visit *www.renfe.com*. AVE high-speed trains depart from Atocha, taking just 2hr20min to reach Sevilla via Córdoba (1hr40min); Barcelona (2hr45min) via Zaragoza (1hr15min); Toledo (30min); Albacete (1hr20min); Málaga (2hr20min); Valencia (1hr38min); Alicante (2hr12min); Valladolid (1hr); León (1hr55min); Huesca (2hr5min); and – since 2019 – Granada (3hr5min). Madrid has a good suburban train network (**Cercanías**) with routes to El Escorial, the Sierra de Guadarrama, Alcalá de Henares and Aranjuez.

🚌 **Inter-city buses** – Most inter-city buses depart from the Estación Sur (Méndez Álvaro 83; 🖉902 996 666; www.estacionautobusesmadrid.com).

Car hire – All the familiar names are located at Barajas airport and Atocha and Chamartín railway stations. Pepecar (🖉807 414 243, www.pepecar.com) offers good-value car hire with a wide range of models and pick-up points, including the airport.

Taxis – Madrid has a large fleet of registered taxis (white with a red diagonal stripe). The green light indicates that the taxi is for hire; registered taxis may also be hailed via the Free Now app, which has a fixed-price option. Ride-hail apps **Uber** and **Cabify** operate in the city, and premium service UberONE added 50 Teslas to its fleet in 2017.

🚌 **Local buses** – For information, call 🖉914 068 810. Passengers should beware of pickpockets. Generally buses operate between 6am and 11.30pm. Night buses operate from 11.30pm onwards, with most departing from Plaza de Cibeles. In addition to single tickets (*un sencillo*; €1.50), passengers can purchase a ten-trip ticket (*un bono de 10 viajes*; €18.30) or a 1–7 day unlimited ticket (*abono turístico*; €8.40–€35.40), both valid on both metro and bus networks. Bicycles and pets may be taken on the metro on weekends and at limited times on weekdays.

🚇 **Metro** – Metro stations are shown on the maps in this guide (🖉902 44 44 03, www.metromadrid.es/en). The metro system is the fastest way to get around the city. It operates from 6am to 1.30am. 🙂Passengers should beware of pickpockets.

🚲 **Bicycle-share** – The Bicimad network has 208 docks with electric bicycles distributed across the city centre. Few designated bike lanes means you are often riding in busy traffic (www.bicimad.com; €2 for up to one hour).

SIGHTSEEING

The **Guía del Ocio** (www.guiadelocio.com/madrid) is a weekly guide containing a list of every cultural event and show in the city. It can be purchased at newspaper stands.

Madrid City Tours – The iconic red double-decker bus offers two circular routes around the city (historic

Madrid, modern Madrid). Tickets, which can be purchased on board, in some hotels, at newspaper kiosks and online are valid for one or two days during which passengers can hop on and off both routes. Services operate 10am–6pm in low season, 9am–10pm in high season. The 37 stops include the Paseo del Prado, Plaza Colón, Gran Vía, Palacio Real and Puerta del Sol. For information and prices, see www.madridcitytour.es.

Bike tours – BravoBike (Juan Alvarez Mendízábal, 19; ☎917 582 945, www.bravobike.com) run cycle tours in and out of Madrid, from €15 and also rent bikes.

DISTRICTS

Madrid is a highly walkable city. On a stroll through its streets and squares, you'll discover a variety of neighbourhoods, aka *barrios* or *distritos*, each with its own character and key sites.

Centro – This historic district is made up of several areas and has a reputation for being noisy and packed with tourists, though visitors who meander are often surprised by its quieter corners. It includes **Sol-Callao**, the commercial shopping area par excellence with a sprawling pedestrianised precinct (Preciados district), and **Fuencarral** street, known for vintage and high-end boutiques . A number of cinemas are also located in this area.

Barrio de los Austrias – Madrid's oldest district is wedged between Calles Mayor, Bailén, Toledo, Las Cavas and the Plaza de la Cebada. Its origins are Islamic, and it still retains evocatively named streets from medieval times and Mudéjar towers. It's a classic, if touristy, area for dining. On Sundays, the famous **Rastro** flea market (✆see Calle de Toledo) starts near here, on Ribera de Curtidores.

Lavapiés – This rough-and-ready district runs north from Plaza de Lavapiés to Calle Atocha through steep streets lined with houses dating to the 17C. Despite recent waves of gentrification, it's persevered as a largely tourist-free melting pot with a mix of locals and immigrants from every corner of the globe. Artists and alternative types flock here.

Barrio de las Letras – The neighbourhood bisected by Calle de las Huertas was Spain's literary nerve centre in the 17C. Today it's largely pedestrianised and packed with upmarket bars and restaurants. Come sundown, its taverns, *coctelerías* and nightclubs draw a well-heeled over-30 crowd.

Malasaña – Previously Called Maravillas, Malasaña is a tangle of cobblestone streets roughly bounded by the Bilbao and San Bernardo metro stops in the north and the Gran Vía thoroughfare in the south. Activity centres around Plaza del Dos de Mayo. Mornings in this trendy 19C *barrio* are quiet and full of local character, but evenings are defined by the legions of twentysomethings who pack into its dive bars, many of which are holdouts from the 1980s Movida era. The district also has some tranquil cafés and restaurants.

Alonso Martínez – The average age and financial standing of this district's denizens is higher than in neighbouring Bilbao and Chueca, as evidenced by the posh bars, restaurants and shops patronised by the city's nouveau riche.

Chueca – Just east of Malasaña, Chueca is Madrid's main 'gayborhood' and centre of Pride festivities, but it's also popular for its sophisticated boutiques, design shops and galleries.

Salamanca – In the 19C the Marquis of Salamanca designed this wide-avenued, aristocratic residential area above Retiro park according to a gridiron plan. Top high-end fashion boutiques (on Serrano and Ortega y Gasset streets) and an impressive collection of stores selling luxury goods can be found here.

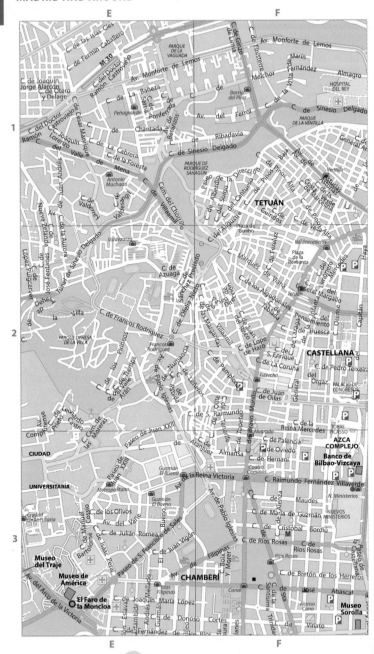

🐾 WALKING TOUR

1 OLD MADRID (CENTRO)★

⏱ See map of walking tour p126–127.
🕐 Try to visit early, or late in the afternoon when the churches are open.

Narrow streets, timeworn churches, tree-shaded squares, and 17C palaces and mansions with wrought-iron balconies characterise this must-see barrio at the historic centre of the city.

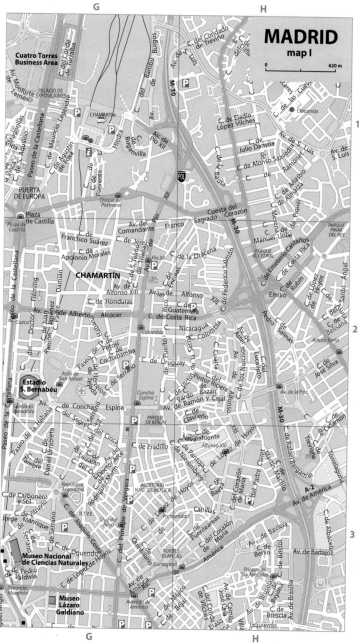

Plaza Mayor★★

Ⓜ Sol.

The square built by Juan Gómez de Mora in 1619 is the heart of **Habsburg Madrid**. On the north side, the **Casa de la Panadería** (a former bakery, now a tourism centre) was reconstructed by Donoso in 1672. The plaza was once the site of **autos de fe**, executions, bullfights and coronations.

A stamp and coin market is held on Sunday mornings and holidays (9am–2pm),

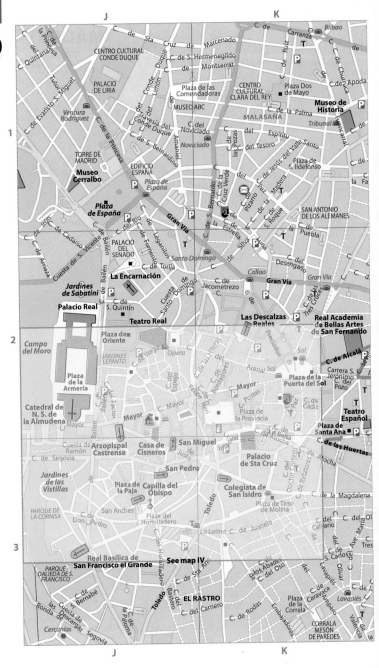

while at Christmas, stalls sell decorations. Shops around the square retain a yesteryear look.

Pass through the **Arco de Cuchilleros** (pl. Mayor 9) into the street fronted

by old houses with convex facades. The **Cava de San Miguel** provides a rear view of the houses on the square. This area is crowded with small restaurants (*mesones*) and bars (*tavernas*).

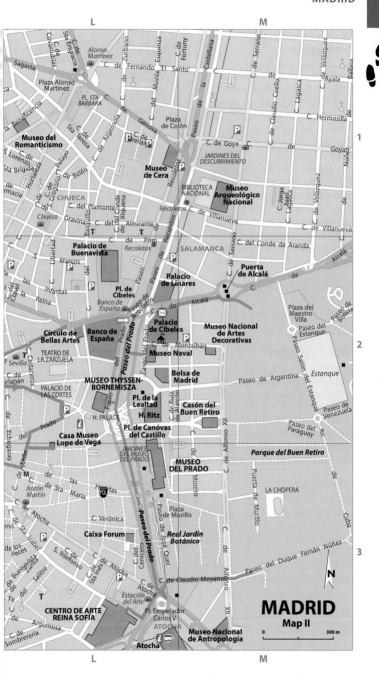

Mercado de San Miguel, an indoor early 20C market, is now an elegant (if overpriced) food emporium (open from 10am until 2am; www.mercado desanmiguel.es) set in an iron frame.

▶ Take Conde de Miranda. Cross Plaza del Conde de Barajas and Gómez de Mora to Plaza de San Justo or Puerta Cerrada, a city gate. Continue right on San Justo.

Basílica Pontificia de San Miguel★

C. de San Justo 4. 🚇 Tirso de Molina or Ópera. Open daily 1 Jul–10 Sept 9.45am–1.15pm, 6–9.15pm, public hols 9.45am–1.30pm, 6.30–9.15pm; 10 Sep–30 Jun 9.45am–1.30pm, 5.30–9.15pm; public hols 9.45am–2.15pm, 6–9.15pm. 📞915 48 40 11. www.bsmiguel.es.

This basilica by Bonavia is a rare Spanish church in that it is inspired by 18C Italian Baroque. Its convex facade, designed as an interplay of inward and outward curves, is adorned with fine statues. The interior is graceful and elegant with an oval cupola, intersecting vaulting, flowing cornices and abundant stuccowork.

▶ Follow Puñonrostro and del Codo to Plaza de la Villa.

Plaza de la Villa★

🚇 Ópera.

Buildings around the square include the **Casa de la Villa** (town hall), built by Gómez de Mora in 1617; the **Torre de los Lujanes** (Luján Tower), a rare example of 15C civil architecture; and the 16C **Casa de Cisneros**, connected to a city-hall offshoot by an arch.

Calle Mayor

🚇 Ópera.

The name, 'Main Street', gives an indication of its importance. At no. 61 is the narrow house of 17C playright **Pedro Calderón de la Barca.**

The Antigua Farmacia de la Reina Madre (Queen Mother's Pharmacy) at no. 59, founded in 1576, previously an alchemist, keeps a collection of chemist's jars and pots. The **Instituto Italiano de Cultura** (no. 86) occupies a 17C palace. The Palacio Uceda opposite, from the same period, is now the military headquarters of the **Capitanía General** (Captaincy General). In front of the **Iglesia Arzobispal Castrense** (17C–18C), a monument that commemorates an attack on Alfonso XIII and Victoria Eugenia in 1906. In the nearby Calle de

MADRID
Map III
0 — 90 m

N

Palacio Real

Campo del Moro

Plaza de la Armería

Catedral de N. S. de la Almudena

Vega — C. Mayor

P. Ciudad de Plasencia

Cuesta de la Vega

Capitan Genera

PARQUE DE ATENAS

PARQUE DE LA CUESTA DE LA VEGA

C. de Segovia — C. de Segovia

Segovia

Jardines de las Vistillas

C. de Mazareido

C. de Moreno Nieto

PARQUE DE LA CORNISA

Travesía de las Vistillas

Ronda

C. de Algeciras

Paseo Imperial

Real Basílica de San Francisco el Grande

N

San Nicolás is the Mudéjar tower of San Nicolás de los Servita.

▶ Take del Sacramento to Plazuela del Cordón; go south on Cordón then continue to Segovia.

Across the street rises the 14C Mudéjar tower of the **Iglesia de San Pedro el Viejo** (Church of St Peter), a rare example of the Mudéjar style in Madrid.

▶ Go along Príncipe Anglona.

Plaza de la Paja

This predates the Plaza Mayor as a commercial centre in the Middle Ages. The Palacio Vargas obscures the Gothic **Capilla del Obispo**, a 16C chapel. In Plaza de los Carros, the Capilla de San Isidro (chapel) is part of the 17C Iglesia de San Andrés, built in honour of Madrid's patron saint, San Isidro.

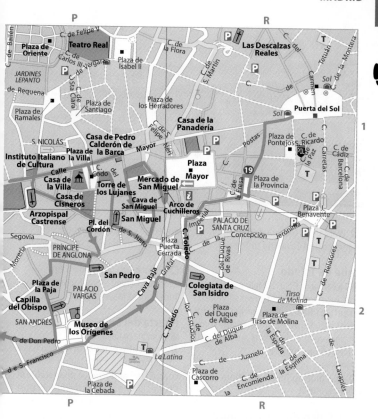

The **Museo de San Isidro, Los Orígenes de Madrid** (Pl. San Andrés 2; ⬤Latina; open Tue–Sun & hols 10am–8pm, 16 June-15 Sept open Tues-Sun 10am-7pm; closed 1 Jan, 1 May, 24, 25 and 31 Dec; ℘913 66 74 15; www.madrid.es/museosanisidro), a museum containing a stone well and a fine Renaissance patio, is next to this complex of religious buildings. There is also an exhibit on Madrid from prehistory to the 16C installation of the Royal Court.

◗ Cross Bailén and take the first street on the right.

Jardines de las Vistillas (Vistillas Gardens)

⬤La Latina.

There are **views** to the west, especially at sundown, of the Sierra de Guadarrama, Casa de Campo, the Catedral de la Almudena and the viaduct.

Basílica de San Francisco el Grande

C. de San Buenaventura 1. ⬤La Latina. Open Tue–Sat 10.30am–12.30pm, 4–6pm; Jul and Aug Tue–Sun 10.30am–12.30pm, 5–7pm. €5. ℘913 65 38 00.

The church's vast Neoclassical facade is by Sabatini; the circular edifice itself, with six radial chapels and a large dome, is by Francisco Cabezas. The latter is the largest in Spain and the fourth-largest in Europe. Walls and ceilings have 19C frescoes and paintings (18C in the chapels of St Anthony and St Bernardino). The Capilla de San Bernardino holds an early **Goya** of St Bernardino of Siena preaching before the King of Aragón (1781). Plateresque **stalls★** from the Monasterio de El Parral outside Segovia are in the chancel.

16C **stalls★** in the sacristy and chapter house are from the Cartuja de El Paular, a Carthusian monastery near Segovia.

Plaza Mayor

© benedek/iStockphoto.com

▶ Walk along Carrera de San Francisco and Cava Alta to Toledo.

Calle de Toledo
🚇 La Latina or Tirso de Molina.
This is one of the old town's liveliest streets. **El Rastro** flea market is held here (open Sun & public hols 9am–3pm; 👁 beware of pickpockets and inflated prices; always haggle!).

▶ Continue up Toledo for about 200m/656ft.

Real Colegiata de San Isidro
C. de Toledo 37. 🚇 La Latina or Tirso de Molina. Open daily 7.30am–1pm, 6–9pm. 📞913 69 20 37.
Formerly the church of the Imperial College of the Company of Jesus (1622), it was the cathedral of Madrid from 1885 until 1993 and contains the relics of Madrid's patron saint, San Isidro.

▶ Head north on Toledo then continue NE and along Esparteros. Turn right at Mayor then left.

Puerta del Sol
🚇 Gran Vía or Callao.
The epicentre of modern Madrid has a small monument displaying Madrid's coat of arms and an equestrian statue of Charles III. The clock on the former post office chimes midnight on New Year's Eve while locals eat a grape per second to bring luck the next year. Nearby, traditional shops with colourful wood fronts sell fans, mantillas and delicacies.

▶ Walk east through the Puerta del Sol square, then onto Alcalá.

Paseo del Prado

With the 18C drawing to a close, Charles III wanted to develop a public area worthy of Madrid's position as capital of Spain and Called upon the court's best architects for his project. In an area outside the city at the time Called Hermosilla, architects Ventura Rodríguez, Sabatini and Villanueva drained, embellished and built a curved avenue with two large fountains, Cybele and Neptune, at each end, and a third, Apollo, in the centre. To complete the project, the **Botanical Gardens**, **Natural History Museum** (now the Museo del Prado) and the **Observatory** were also built. The result combined the functional and the aesthetic, the sciences and the arts. Overnight the Paseo del Prado became a favourite place for Madrileños to meet and unwind. Today, the avenue retains its dignified air and a cluster of extraordinary museums that draw visitors from far and wide. A stroll along its tree-lined boulevard gives you a chance to appreciate the outsize vision and imagination of King Charles.

WALKING TOUR

2 BOURBON MADRID★★

See map of walking tour p132–133.

Charles III's Paseo del Prado remains a grand tree-shaded avenue lined by world-class museums, which lie within walking distance from Retiro Park.

Plaza de Cibeles★

Banco de España.

In the square is the 18C fountain of Cybele, goddess of fertility, emblematic of Madrid.

It's hard not to gasp at the sheer grandeur of this square and the impressive buildings that surround it such as the **Banco de España** (1891); 18C **Palacio de Buenavista** (Ministry of Defence); late-19C **Palacio de Linares**, now the home of the **Casa de América** (Po. de Recoletos 2; guided tours Sep-Jul Sat–Sun 11am, 12pm, 1pm; €8; ℘915 95 48 00; www.casa merica.es); and the **Palacio de Cibeles** (Post and Telegraph Office, 1919), where there is a cultural centre, **Centro Centro** (open Tue–Sun 10am–8pm, closed 1 and 6 Jan, 1 May, 24, 25 and 31 Dec; ℘91 480 00 08; www.centrocentro.org) with a viewing platform (open Tue–Sun 10.30am–1.30pm and 4–7pm) as well as a restaurant, café and bar.

Paseo del Prado★

This stately boulevard runs from Plaza de Cibeles to Plaza del Emperador Carlos V, past the Ministerio de la Marina and Museo Naval, the **Plaza de la Lealtad** (with an obelisk dedicated to the heroes of the Dos de Mayo Uprising), the Neoclassical **Bolsa** (Stock Exchange) and the emblematic **Hotel Ritz**, closed for renovations as of September 2019 (www.mandarinoriental.com).

Take the first left, Montalbán, after the Palacio de Cibeles.

Museo Nacional de Artes Decorativas

C. de Montalbán 12. Retiro. Open Tue–Sat 9.30am–3pm, Thu 5–8pm (Sep–Jun only), Sun & public hols 10am–3pm. Closed 1 and 6 Jan, 1 May, 24–25 & 31 Dec. €3; free Sun, Thu afternoon, Sat 2-3pm, 18 Apr, 18 May, 12 Oct, 6 Dec. ℘915 32 64 99. http://mnartesdecorativas.mcu.es.
This museum in a 19C mansion houses furniture and decorative objects as well as a complete tiled 18C kitchen.

Return to Paseo del Prado and continue south.

Museo Naval

Po. del Prado 3. Banco de España. Open year-round Tue–Sun 10am–7pm (Aug until 3pm). Closed public hols, 1 & 6 Jan, 24–25 Dec. €3 donation requested. ℘915 23 85 16. www.armada.mde.es/museonaval.
On display are ship **models**★, nautical instruments, weapons and paintings of naval battles. The **map of Juan de la Cosa**★★ (1500) is the first to show the American continent.

Continue on Paseo del Prado.

Plaza de Canóvas del Castillo

Banco de España.
This square, featuring the Fuente de Neptuno (Neptune Fountain), is overlooked by the Neoclassical **Palacio de Villahermosa** housing the **Museo Thyssen-Bornemisza**★★★ (see p141) and the iconic Westin Palace hotel.

Continue walking south, on the eastern side of the Paseo del Prado.

Museo del Prado★★★

See Museums.
The Neoclassical building housing one of the world's great art collections was built in the reign of Charles III, originally intended for the Institute of Natural Sciences. Behind it is Rafael Moneo's 2007 annexe, which incorporates the Jeronimos' monastery cloister and new iron doors

Palacio de Cristal, Parque del Buen Retiro

by Cristina Iglesias. Behind the Prado is the royal church, San Jerónimo el Real.

◯ Continue south to the Pl. de Murillo facing the Museum's southern facade.

Real Jardín Botánico

Pl. de Murillo, 2. Open Nov–Feb 10am–6pm; Mar and Oct until 7pm; Apr and Sept until 8pm; May–Aug until 9pm. €4. ℘914 20 30 17. www.rjb.csic.es.
The Botanical Garden, opened in 1781, was commissioned by Charles III and planned by Juan de Villanueva, who also built the Museo del Prado. Enter through the gate facing the Museum's southern facade. Apart from its meticulously tended beds, lawns and trees, the garden has a vine bower planted with grape varieties from around Spain and three greenhouses presenting ecosystems from desert to equatorial. The gift shop sells seeds and plants.

◯ Cross the Paseo to its western side.

Caixa Forum

Po. del Prado 36. Open daily 10am–8pm. Closed 25 Dec, 1 & 6 Jan. €5 exhibitions. ℘913 307 300. https://caixaforum.es/en/madrid
The latest major addition to the Paseo del Prado, Caixa Forum is worth a visit for its architecture alone: Jacques Herzog and Pierre de Meuron artfully converted a Modernist power station into this arts centre, whose vertical garden was designed by Patrick Blanc.

Inside, expect a mix of contemporary art exhibitions, concerts, talks and, on the top floor, a café-restaurant.

◯ Continue walking south, cross Calle Atocha and, 100m/110yd farther, turn right onto C. de Sta Isabel.

The former **Hospital de San Carlos**, an austere, imposing granite block with a towering extension and agora designed by architect **Jean Nouvel**, houses the **Museo Nacional Centro de Arte Reina Sofía★★** (♿see p143).

◯ Cross the Pl. del Emperador Carlos V to its southeastern side.

Estación de Atocha (Atocha Railway Station)

Pl. del Emperador Carlos V.
🚇 Atocha Renfe or Atocha.
Atocha station's vast 19C glass-and-wrought-iron **main hall** is a sight to behold. Enter to view the tropical patio garden, where turtles swim in pools (a highlight for kids), and to admire the soaring ceilings. The local train-station (Cercanías), nicknamed the 'pillbox', was designed by Rafael Moneo. There is a memorial to those who died in the 2004 bombing: A translucent cylinder, set partly beneath the ground and engraved with messages to the dead from loved ones (open daily 10am–8pm). Opposite, on the north side of Av Ciudad de Barcelona, stands the elaborate late-19C Ministry of Agriculture.

◯ Cross Av. Ciudad de Barcelona and turn right to the junction with C. de Alfonso XII.

Museo Nacional de Antropología

C. de Alfonso XII 68. Open Tue–Sat 9.30am–8pm, Sun & hols 10am–3pm. Closed 1 & 6 Jan, 1 May, 24, 25, 31 Dec. €3; free Sat after 2pm, Sun, 18 May, 12 Oct, 16 Nov, 6 Dec. ℘915 306 418. http://mnantropologia.mcu.es.
Housed in a Neoclassical building, this small museum, often overlooked, pre-

© Jon Arnold Images/hemis.fr

sents a fascinating ethnological collection of objects from around the world – particularly the Americas, Philippines and Africa – arranged thematically around ways of life.

▶ Follow Alfonso XII northeast, crossing to enter Retiro Park at the Puerta del Ángel Caído.

Parque del Buen Retiro★★ (Retiro Park)

Open daily Oct–Apr 6am–10pm; May–Sept 6am–midnight. ✆915 30 0041.
The Retiro is an emblem of noble Madrid and a favourite meeting place for Madrileños of all ages. Once the garden of a (long since destroyed) Hapsburg palace, , it takes in 130ha/321 acres of greenery with copses, a rose garden, fountains, temples, restaurants and terraces, a small zoo and statues.

Beside the central Lake (Estanque), where boats may be hired, is the imposing colonnade *Monumento a Alfonso XII*. Art exhibitions are held in the **Palacio de Velázquez**, built for the 1883 Exposición Nacional de la Minería, and in the fairy-tale **Palacio de Cristal★** (Glass Palace). (◉Ibiza; open Apr–Sep daily 10am–10pm; Oct 10am-9pm, Nov–Mar daily 10am–6pm; closed 1 & 6 Jan, 1 May, 24–25, 31 Dec and occasionally on rainy days; ✆91 774 1000, www.museoreinasofia.es).

▶ Stroll along Po. de México from the lake's northwestern corner to Pl. de la Independencia.

Puerta de Alcalá★ (Alcalá Gate)

Pl. de la Independencia. ◉ Retiro.
The arch at the centre of Plaza de la Independencia was built by Sabatini between 1769 and 1778 to celebrate the triumphant entry of Charles III into Madrid. During the Movida years, it became a symbol of democracy. The view from here down to Plaza de Cibeles is particularly grand at night.

🐾 WALKING TOUR

3 ROYAL MADRID★★

👣 See map of walking tour p132–133.

Madrid is home to the Royal Palace, the official (though not current) residence of the Spanish Royal family since 1764, and to convents and churches that sprang up around court life.

Plaza de la Armería

Along the vast arcaded square (south side) is the **Catedral de la Almudena** (◉Ópera; Cathedral open daily 9am–8.30pm (Jul–Aug until 9pm); museum and dome Mon–Sat 10am-2.30pm; €6; ✆915 42 22 00, https://museocatedral.archimadrid.es). The cathedral, begun in 1879, was finished in 1993. The neo-Baroque facade harmonises with the palace (but is arguably at odds with the rest of the structure). The view west extends over the Casa de Campo and the Campo del Moro gardens sloping down to the Manzanares river.

Palacio Real★★ (Royal Palace)

C. de Bailén. ◉Ópera. Open Oct–Mar daily 10am–6pm; Apr–Sep daily 10am–8pm; changing of the guard Wed 11am. For dates closed, see website or telephone. €12 palace, art gallery and armoury; guided tour of kitchen €6; audioguide €3. Free 18 May & 12 Oct. ✆914 54 87 00.
www.patrimonionacional.es.
Before going inside, get a postcard view of the palace from Paseo de Extremadura or the gardens of **Campo del Moro★** (open Oct–Mar daily 10am–6pm, Apr–Sep until 8pm). Europe's largest palace, built by the Bourbons following a fire at the Habsburg Alcázar, housed the royal family until 1931. It is still used for official ceremonies. Guadarrama granite and white stone were chosen for its construction, which reaches 140m/459ft and sits on a high bossaged base. The upper register, with alternating Ionic columns and Doric pilasters, is crowned by a limestone balustrade. The north face overlooks

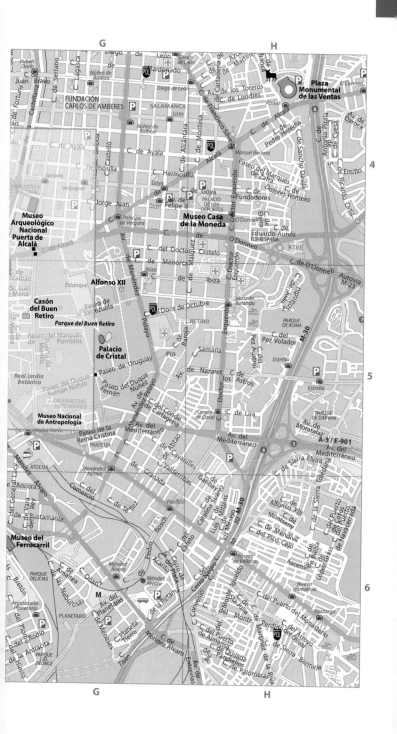

the manicured **Jardines de Sabatini**, where the stables once were. **Plaza de la Armería** is sandwiched between the west and east wings of the palace, while the east side faces **Plaza de Oriente**. The **Palacio (Palace)★★** itself welcomes you with a monumental staircase – presided over by a ceiling painted by Giaquinto – that leads to the Salón de Alabarderos (Halberdier Room), with a ceiling painted by Tiepolo.

This leads to the **Salón de Columnas** (Column Room) where royal celebrations and banquets are held. The **Salón del Trono** (Throne Room) retains decoration from the period of Charles III and is resplendent with crimson velvet hangings and a dynamic ceiling by Tiepolo (1764) titled *The Apotheosis of the Spanish Monarchy*. The consoles, mirrors and gilded bronze lions are of Italian design.

The following three rooms were the king's quarters, occupied by Charles III in 1764. The Saleta Gasparini, the king's dining room, retains a ceiling painted by Mengs.

The Gasparini antechamber also has a ceiling by Mengs and **Goya** portraits of Charles IV and María Luisa of Parma. The **Cámara Gasparini** is awash with dazzling Rococo decoration.

The Salón de Carlos III was the king's bedroom. The decor is from the period of Ferdinand VII. The **Sala de Porcelana** is, along with its namesake in Aranjuez Palace, the masterpiece of the Buen Retiro Porcelain Factory. Official banquets are held in the Alfonso XII **Comedor de Gala,** or Banqueting Hall, which seats 145 and is adorned with 16C tapestries. Two music rooms contain instruments including the only known **Stradivarius Quartet★**. In the chapel are frescoes by Giaquinto and paintings by Mengs *(Annunciation)* and Bayeu *(St Michael the Archangel)*.

The **Real Farmacia** (Royal Farmacy) holds ornate 18C-20C jars including a fine specimen from Talavera.

Museo de Colecciones Reales

Under construction as of September 2019, this museum off of the southwest corner of the palace has (inexplicably) taken 22 years to build at a cost of €160 million. It is due to open in 2020 and will display 1 000 objects from the royal collection on a rotational basis. The first floor will be dedicated to the House of Asturias, the second to the House of Bourbon and the top to temporary exhibitions.

▷ The palace faces Plaza de Oriente.

Plaza de Oriente

This stately arched square between the east facade of the Palacio Real and the Teatro Real is pleasant for a stroll. The rearing equestrian statue of Philip IV is the work of Pietro Tacca (17C), who consulted with Galileo on its construction.

Teatro Real

Pl. de Oriente. ⊚ Ópera. Guided tours (see website for details on special technical, artistic and nocturnal tours) daily on the half hour 10.00am– 1pm and audio guide tours 9.30am-3.30pm. Closed 1 Jan, 24–25, 31 Dec. Guided tour €8, audio guide €7. ☏915 16 06 00. www.teatroreal.es.

This hexagonal Neoclassical building was opened as an opera house in 1850 for Isabel II. It reopened in 1997 and is now one of the world's great opera houses and musical performance venues. The venue has a fine-dining restaurant, café and shop too.

▷ On the western side of Pl. de Oriente, Calle Pavia leads to Pl. de la Encarnación.

Real Monasterio de la Encarnación★ (Royal Convent of the Incarnation)

Pl. de la Encarnación 1. ⊚ Ópera. Guided tours (45min) Tue–Sat 10am–2pm, 4–6.30pm, Sun & hols 10am–3pm. See website for dates closed. €6; free Wed & Thu pm for EU citizens and 18 May. ✆914 54 87 00. www.patrimonionacional.es.

This convent, on a delightful square near the former Alcázar, was founded in 1611 by Margaret of Austria. The collection of paintings from the 17C Madrid School is particularly rich and includes the *Exchange of Princesses on Pheasant Island* (Van der Meulen, 1615). There is a polychrome sculpture of *Christ at the Column* by Gregorio Hernández on the first floor.

The **Relicario★**, whose ceiling was painted by Vicencio Carducci, holds 1 500 relics. The church with quasi-Herreran portals was reconstructed in the 18C after the Alcázar fire.

▶ Returning to the Teatro Real, turn left up Carlos III, then follow Arenal and turn left up San Martín.

Monasterio de las Descalzas Reales★★

Pl. de las Descalzas. 🚇Ópera. Guided tours (45min) Tue–Sat 10am–2pm, 4–6.30pm, Sun & hols 10am–3pm. See website for dates closed. €6; free Wed & Thu pm for EU citizens and 18 May. ✆914 54 87 00. www.patrimonionacional.es.

Joanna of Austria, Emperor Charles V's daughter, founded this convent of the Poor Clare order in the palace where she was born.

The magnificent grand **staircase★** is blanketed with frescoes. In a former dormitory is an extraordinary collection of **tapestries★★** depicting the Triumph of the Church, woven in Brussels in the 17C to cartoons by Rubens. The **33 small chapels** – particularly that of the Virgin of Guadalupe – are sumptuously decorated.

Convent treasures include portraits of the royal family by Rubens, Sánchez Coello and others.

▶ Take Postigo de San Martín to Pl. del Callao. Turn left on Gran Vía.

Plaza de España

🚇Plaza de España.

Gran Vía★, built by Alfonso XIII before his wedding, is the city's main artery and busiest shopping street. It leads west to the urban **Plaza de España**, closed until late 2020 for a €62 million refurbishment and pedestrianisation. From here, C. Princesa, lined with budget restaurants and shops, slopes northwest toward Moncloa and the **Ciudad Universitaria** (University City). From its southernmost corner, C. Bailén leads back to the Royal Palace via the formal, geometric **Jardines de Sabitini★** (🕐open daily May–Sep 9am–10pm; Oct–Apr 9pm).

👣 WALKING TOUR

4 LITERARY MADRID

🕐See map of walking tour p132–133.

This maze of cobblestoned streets east of **Plaza de Santa Ana** is known as Barrio de las Letras, as it was home to great writers and dramatists during Madrid's Golden Age. Cervantes, Quevedo and Lope de Vega, its most famous denizens, were buried in the Iglesia de San Sebastián. Here you will also find one of the country's finest theatres, **Teatro Español**, on Plaza Santa Ana, and the **Círculo de Bellas Artes** with its lively rooftop bar, on Marqués de Casa Riera. There are excellent antiquarian bookshops to explore by day, while after dark, visitors and locals flock to its swish tapas bars and nightclubs.

Around Plaza Santa Ana

Across from the Teatro Español, the **ME Madrid Reina Victoria** hotel (🕐see page 146), now a trendy hotspot, was once a meeting place for bullfighters. On the square's south side, **Cervecería Alemana**, a favourite haunt of Ernest Hemingway and Ava Gardner famous for its fried calamari, remains blissfully unchanged (and decidedly un-German, despite the name). The streets spoking out from the square teem with locals.

Catch a flamenco show at the floridly tiled **Villa Rosa** (www.tablaoflamencovillarosa.com), a legendary *tablao*, and have a nightcap at either **La Venencia** on C. Echegaray, a creaky-floored sherry bar, or across the street in the David Rockwell-designed lobby of the historic **Gran Hotel Inglés**, which reopened in 2018.

▶ Take C. del Prado, turn right down León and left down Cervantes.

Casa Museo de Lope de Vega★

C. de Cervantes 11. 🚇 Anton Martín. Guided tours (35min) Tue–Sun 10am–6pm. Closed national and local public hols. Booking required. ☎914 29 92 16. www.casamuseolopedevega.org. By the time Lope de Vega bought this house, he was Spain's most famous playwright. The top two floors and garden were recreated based on an inventory and his writings. Of special interest are the chapel and his study, where he wrote such works as *Fuentevejuna*.

▶ Turn left out of the house; take San Agustín (the first left) to Pl. de las Cortes.

When you emerge on the Plaza, you'll be facing the **Congreso de los Diputados**, Spain's parliament, held at gunpoint during the attempted military coup on 23 February 1981. Walking left up San Jeronimo, and then right down C. Sevilla to Alcalá, you'll pass embassies and old banks.

Real Academia de Bellas Artes de San Fernando★
(San Fernando Royal Fine Arts Academy)

C. de Alcalá 13. 🚇 Sevilla, Sol. Open Tue–Sun & public hols 10am–3pm. Closed 1 & 6 Jan, 1 & 30 May, Aug, 9 Nov, 24–25 & 31 Dec. €8; free 18 May, 12 Oct, 6 Dec and every Wed. ☎915 24 08 64. www.realacademiabellasartes sanfernando.com.

Among the Royal Academy's valuable collection of 16C–20C paintings are works by Ribera, **Zurbarán**, Murillo, Alonso Cano (*Christ Crucified*) and **Velázquez**, but street scenes and a self-portait by **Goya**, a member of the Academy, are the crown jewels.

SALAMANCA – LA CASTELLANA
Museo Arqueológico Nacional★★
(Archaeological Museum)

C. de Serrano 13. 🚇 Serrano. Open Tue–Sat 9.30am–8pm, Sun & public hols 9.30am–3pm. Closed 1 & 6 Jan, 1 May, 24–25 & 31 Dec. €3. Free Sat 2–8pm, Sun morning, 18 April, 18 May, 12 Oct, 6 Dec. ☎915 77 79 12. www.man.es. Remodelled in 2014, this Museum boasts artefacts dating from prehistory to the Middle Ages. Among early pieces are the bronze **Costix bulls★** (Talaiotic culture, Iron Age, Balearic Islands) and a faithful eproduction of the cave paintings at **Cuevas de Altamira★** . Iberian sculpture is exhibited at its peak of artistic expression: The **Dama de Elche★★★** (*Lady of Elche*) is a rivetingly expressive stone bust with a sumptuous headdress and corsage, while the **Dama de Baza★★** is a realistic goddess figure of the 4C BC. Medieval decorative arts include the **votive crowns of Guarrazar★★** (Visigothic period), made of embossed gold plaques that meld Germanic and Byzantine techniques. The Romanesque portals, engravings, grilles, tombs and capitals, along with the Gothic sculpture, convey a lingering Moorish influence.

The collection also includes a reconstruction of a Mudéjar interior complete with an intricate **artesonado★★** ceiling. North of the Museo Arqueológico is the Plaza de Colón (Columbus Square) with a statue of the navigator on a column. The Archaelogical Museum shares real estate with the **Biblioteca Nacional** (National Library; Po. de Recoletos 20–22; 🚇Serrano; exhibition galleries open Tue–Sat 10am–8pm, Sun & public hols 10am–2pm; closed 1 and 6 Jan, 1 May, 24–25 & 31 Dec; ☎915 80 78 00; www.bne.es), whose collection of manuscripts is one of the richest in Spain.

Museo Lázaro Galdiano★

C. de Serrano 122. ⓜ Núñez de
Balboa or Av. América. Open Tue–Sat
10am–4.30pm (Sun until 3pm). Closed
2–3 Apr, 15 May, 15 Aug, 12 Oct, 9 Nov,
24–25 & 31 Dec. €7; guided tours
5.30–7pm (reserve in advance) €10.
Free daily during last hour.
☏915 61 60 84. www.flg.es.

This mansion houses the collections of
editor and art connoisseur José Lázaro
Galdiano (1862–1947). On the **lower
level** are samples of outstanding paintings by the Master of Perea, Mengs, Zurbarán and Sánchez Coello.

The **main floor**, which retains ceilings
painted by Villaamil and period furniture – is devoted to 15C–19C Spanish
art and stands out foor its Gothic and
Renaissance panels. The **second floor**
centres on the **Flemish School** and the
third houses decorative arts (some 4
000 items): **ivories and enamel★★★**,
among other materials.

Museo Sorolla★★

Po. del General Martínez Campos, 37.
ⓜ Gregorio Marañón or Iglesia. Open
Tue–Sat 9.30am–8pm, Sun & public hols
10am–3pm. Closed 1 Jan, 6 Jan, 1 May,
24–25 & 31 Dec, and other local hols. €3.
Free Sat 2–8pm, Sun, 18 April, 18 May,
12 Oct, 6 Dec. ☏913 10 15 84. www.
museosorolla.es.

The Madrid abode of Joaquín Sorolla
(1863–1923) – the Valencian Surrealist
painter renowned for his evocative portraits and glowing Mediterranean beach
scenes – is meticulously preserved and
takes in the artist's studio and many of
his famous works (e.g., *The Horse's Bath*;
The Pink Robe). Round out your visit with
quiet time in the garden, a leafy oasis
with benches and burbling fountains.

♟ Museo de Cera

Po. de Recoletos, 41. ⓜ Colón. Open
Mon–Fri 10am–2.30pm, 4.30–8.30pm,
weekends and holidays 10am–8.30pm.
€21, under 12s and over 65s €14. ☏913
199 330. www.museoceramadrid.com.

Among the many **wax replicas** here
– which are convincing if haphazardly
laid out – are historical figures like

Cleopatra, actors like Penélope Cruz and
football giants like Cristiano Ronaldo.

Museo Casa de la Moneda (Royal Mint Museum)

C. del Doctor Esquerdo, 36. ⓜ
O'Donnell. Open Tue–Fri 10am–5.30pm,
weekends and holidays 10am–2pm.
Closed 1 & 6 Jan, 19 Mar, 1 May, 24–25 &
31 Dec. ☏915 66 65 44.
www.museocasadelamoneda.es.

One of the world's largest royal mint
collections, it covers not only coins,
stamps and medals but also lottery
tickets and gambling.

MONCLOA – CASA DE CAMPO DISTRICT
Museo Cerralbo★

C. de Ventura Rodríguez, 17. ⓜ Ventura
Rodríguez. Open Tue–Sat 9.30am–3pm
(Thu also 5–8pm), Sun & public hols
10am–3pm. Closed 1 & 6 Jan, 1 May,
24–25 & 31 Dec. €3. Free Sat 2–3pm,
Thu 5–8pm, Sun, 18 Apr, 18 May,
12 Oct, 6 Dec. ☏915 47 36 46.
http://museocerralbo.mcu.es.

Housed in a late-19C mansion and
recently restored, the Museo Cerralbo
displays the collection of the Marquis
of Cerralbo, a patron of the arts, including Spanish paintings, furniture, fans,
clocks, armour and weaponry, porcelain, and archaeological finds.

Parque del Oeste★ (Western Park)

This sprawling park on the Right Bank
of the Manzanares was designed at the
beginning of the 20C. In the southern
part stands the small 4C BC Egyptian
Temple of Debod (C. de Ferraz 1;
ⓜVentura Rodríguez; open 10am-7pm
year-round; closed 1 & 6 Jan, 1 May,
24–25 & 31 Dec; ☏913 66 74 15; www.
madrid.es/templodebod), rescued from
Nubia when the Aswan Dam was being
built. The abutting tree-lined **Paseo del
Pintor Rosales** has pavement cafés with
primo people- (and pup-) watching.

Fresco by Goya, Ermita de San Antonio de la Florida

Ermita de San Antonio de la Florida★

Glorieta de la Florida 5. On the edge of the Parque del Oeste. 🚇 Príncipe Pío. Open Tue–Sun & hols 9.30am–8pm. Closed 1 Jan, 1 May, 24, 25 and 31 Dec. 🖉915 42 07 22. www.madrid.es/ermita
Goya was buried (per his request) in this chapel, built in 1798 under Charles IV. The interior was frescoed by Goya with female angels around a central narrative scene on the cupola. One of the painter's first great realist works, these **frescoes★★** illustrate the miracle of St Anthony of Padua.

🚹🚺 Casa de Campo★

Clocking in at six times the size of New York's Central Park, Casa de Campo is popular among runners, walkers and cyclists.
Top spots include the lake, a public pool and the **Parque de Atracciones de Madrid★ 🚹🚺**, which has over 40 attractions ranging from kid-friendly rides to white-knuckle roller coasters; it's packed to the gills on summer evenings (Ctra. de Extremadura; 🚇Batán; see website for opening times and dates; €34 at the door, online from €21, see website for child price; 🖉912 00 07 95; www.parquedeatracciones. es). The **Teleférico★★** (cable car) connects the city (Rosales Station) to the Casa de Campo with views on the way (Po. del Pintor Rosales–Cerro Garabita; 🚇Argüelles; see website for opening

times and dates; €6 return; 🖉914 06 88 40; www.telefericodemadrid.es).
The **Zoo-Aquarium★★ 🚹🚺** houses one of the largest assortments of animals anywhere in Europe (Casa de Campo; 🚇Casa de Campo; see website for opening times and dates; €22.95 at the door, advance online tickets €17.90, see website for child price; 🖉902 34 50 14; www.zoomadrid.com).

Museo del Traje (Garment Museum)

Av. Juan Herrera 2. 🚇 Moncloa. Open Tue–Sat 9.30am–7pm (Thu Jul & Aug 10.30pm), Sun & public hols 10am–3pm. Closed 1 & 6 Jan, 1 May, 24–25, 31 Dec. €3; free Sat from 2.30pm, Sun, 18 April, 18 May, 12 Oct, 6 Dec. 🖉915 50 47 00. http://museodeltraje.mcu.es.
A showcase of fashion from the 18C to the 20C. Couturiers Mariano Fortuny and Balenciaga are featured among everyday designs. A tranquil white-tablecloth restaurant looks out onto the gardens.

Museo de América★ (Museum of the Americas)

Av. Reyes Católicos 6. 🚇 Moncloa. Open Tue–Sat 9.30am–3pm (Thu 7pm), Sun & public hols 10am–3pm. Closed 1 & 6 Jan, 1 May, 24–25, 31 Dec. €3; free Sun, 18 Apr, 18 May, 12 Oct, 6 Dec. 🖉915 49 26 41. www.mecd.gob.es/museodeamerica.
Over 2 500 objects, accompanied by maps, models, reconstructions of dwell-

ings, etc, focus on the ties between Europe and America.

Outstanding are the Stele of Madrid (Mayan), the **Treasure of Los Quimbayas★** (Colombian), the **Tudela Manuscript** (1553) and the prized **Maya Tro Cortesiano Manuscript ★★★**, one of only four remaining. The darkened map room memorably recreates early navigators' cartography.

Faro de Moncloa (Moncloa Beacon)

Av. de los Reyes Católicos. 🚇 Moncloa. Open Tue–Sun 9.30am–8pm. €3. 📞91 550 12 51. www.esmadrid.com/en/tourist-information/faro-de-moncloa.

From this 92m/301ft high, UFO-like **observatory★★**, built in 1992 and reopened in 2015, you'll spot key landmarks like the triumphal Arco de la Victoria, commissioned by Franco, and the foothills of the Sierra de Guadarrama.

MUSEUMS

MUSEO NACIONAL DEL PRADO★★★

Allow 3–4 hours. Po. del Prado (ticket office at northern entrance by Pl. Cánovas del Castillo), 🚇 Banco de España or Atocha. Open Mon–Sat 10am–8pm (Sun & public hols until 7pm; 6 Jan, 24 & 31 Dec until 2pm). Last entry 30 mins before closing. Closed 1 Jan, 1 May and 25 Dec. €15; free (permanent collection only) year-round Mon–Sat 6–8pm, Sun & hols 5–7pm. 📞913 30 28 00. www.museodelprado.es.

The Prado, which rang in its 200th anniversary in 2019, is the greatest gallery of Classical paintings in the world. The Neoclassical building was originally designed as a science museum by Juan de Villanueva under Charles III. After the Peninsular War, Ferdinand VII instead installed the Habsburg and Bourbon collections of Spanish painting, expanded over the years. In 2007, the Jerónimos building was inaugurated, incorporating a 16C monastery cloister.

Teleférico, Casa de Campo

© Sime/Photononstop

Spanish Painting★★★ (1100-1910) Rooms 50–52, 56, 60–67, 75,

Bartolomé Bermejo (Santo Domingo de Silos) and **Yáñez de la Almedina** cultivated an international style. Vicente Masip and his son **Juan de Juanes** *(The Last Supper)* are associated with Raphael. Morales' favourite subject, a *Virgin and Child*, is also outstanding. In the rooms devoted to the Golden Age, two painters stand out: **Sánchez Coello** and his pupil **Pantoja de la Cruz**, a portraitist at the court of Philip II. **El Greco** exists in a category of his own within the Spanish School. Works here date to his early Spanish period *(The Trinity)* to his maturity *(Adoration of the Shepherds)*. He was a great portraitist, as anyone who's seen *The Nobleman with his Hand on his Chest* will attest. **Ribalta** introduced Tenebrism (a dramatic illumination style of painting using pronounced chiaroscuro) to Spain. **José (Jusepe) de Ribera** *(Lo Spagnoletto)* is represented by *Jacob's Dream* in which the vigorous use of chiaroscuro reflects Caravaggio's influence. The portraits and still lifes of **Zurbarán** are peaceful compositions in which chiaroscuro and realism triumph. **Murillo** mainly painted the Virgin (*The Immaculate Conception*) but also plain folk (*The Holy Family with a Little Bird*). Works from Spanish historical painting include *The Last Will and Testament of Isabel the Catholic* by Rosales (Rm 61B), *Juana the Mad* by F Pradilla and *The Execution of Torrijos and his Colleagues on the Beach at Málaga* by A Gisbert.

Spanish Painting★★★
(1550-1850)
Rooms 7–18 & 32–38

The Prado contains not only the most iconic paintings of **Diego Velázquez** (1599-1660) but the world's largest collection of his work, displayed in rooms 10, 11, 12, 14 , 15, 15a & 27. He spent time in Italy (1629–31), where he painted *Vulcan's Forge* and began to use richer, more subtle colours and developed his figure compositions (*Christ on the Cross*). On his return he painted *The Surrender of Breda* in which his originality emerges. Pay special attention to the artist's masterful interpretation and expression of light. Velàzquez strove toward naturalism in his royal hunting portraits of *Philip IV* and *Prince Baltasar Carlos as a Hunter* (1635, a wonderful rendering of a child) and in his equestrian portraits of the royal family, in particular *Prince Baltasar Carlos on Horseback*, with the sierra in the background. In 1650 he returned to Italy where he painted landscapes (*The Medici Gardens in Rome*).

In his masterpiece, *Las Meninas* (c. 1656; Rm 12), the Infanta Margarita is portrayed in the artist's own studio from a thought-provoking perspective. In the later *The Spinners* (c. 1657), Velázquez explored labour and femininity in an allusion to the fable of Arachne.

The paintings of **Francisco Goya** (1746-1828) – encompassing portraits of the royal and famous, war scenes, depictions of everyday life, and the *Majas* – are in rooms 32–38 and 64–67 on the first floor and in 85 and 90–94 on the second floor. The museum contains 40 cartoons painted by Goya in oil between 1775 and 1791 for the Real Fábrica (Royal Tapestry Works). *Third of May 1808* (Rms 64-65) was inspired by the rebellion against the French occupation (see ARANJUEZ, p152). The artist's late works, the disturbing, macabre series of so-called Black Paintings he frescoed on the walls of his house, hang in Room 67.

Flemish Painting★★★
(1430–1700)
Rooms 16b, 28, 29, 55–58, 76, 76b

The exceptional collection of Flemish painting reflects Spain's royal ties with (and one-time dominance of) the Low Countries.

Among the Flemish Primitives are Robert Campen, the Mester of Flemalle (*St Barbara*). **Van der Weyden** added a richer colour palette and sense of composition (*Descent from the Cross*; Rm 58). Van der Weyden's drama was reimagined through melancholy by his successor, **Memling** (*Adoration of the Magi*; Rm 58A). There follow the bizarre, fantastical imaginings of **Hieronymus Bosch**, aka El Bosco (*The Garden of Earthly Delights*; Rm 56A), who in turn influenced Patinir (*Crossing the Stygian Lake*) and **Bruegel the Elder** (*Triumph of Death*; Rm 56A). **Rubens**, the most Baroque of all, brought motion and life to Flemish painting, as seen in *The Three Graces*. There is also a rich collection of his work completed by his disciples **Van Dyck** and **Jordaens**.

Dutch Painting (1700–1800)
Rooms B (Temporary), 41

Noteworthy works by **Rembrandt** include a *Self-Portrait* (Rm 41) and *Judith at the Banquet of Holofernes* (Rm B).

Italian Painting★★
(1450–1800) Rooms 4–7, 22–27, 40–44. (1300–1600) 49, 56b

The collection is especially rich in works by Venetian painters. The Italian Renaissance brought with it elegance and ideal beauty as in paintings by **Raphael** (*The Holy Family*, *The Cardinal*; Rm 49), Roman nobility and monumental bearing in the work of **Mantegna** (*The Death of the Virgin*; Rm 56B) and melancholic dreaminess in **Botticelli** (*Story of Nastagio degli Onesti*). The spirituality of the *Annunciation* by **Fra Angelico** belongs to the Gothic tradition.

Colour and sumptuousness define the Venetian school: **Titian** with his exceptional mythological scenes (*Danae and the Shower of Gold*; Rm 42, *Venus with* *the Organist*; Rm. 24) and portrait of *Charles V of Mühlberg*; **Veronese** with compositions set off by silver tones; **Tintoretto**'s gold-fleshed figures springing from shadow (*Christ Washing the Disciples' Feet*);and **Tiepolo**'s paintings intended for Charles III's royal palace.

French Painting (1600–1800)
Rooms 2, 3, 19, 39
The French are represented by **Poussin** (Rm 3) and **Lorrain**.

German Painting (1450–1800)
Room 55b
A selection includes **Dürer**'s figure and portrait paintings (*Self-Portrait, Adam and Eve*) and works by **Cranach**.

The **Cason del Buen Retiro**, a satellite of the Museo del Prado campus and the sole remnant of the Palacio del Buen Retiro, is a library today. It housed **Picasso**'s *Guernica* when it first returned to Spain (it's now at the Museo Nacional Centro de Arte Reina Sofía). Guided visits (Sun 12pm; arrive 30 minutes early to secure a spot) explore the Hall of the Ambassadors, crowned by the ceiling fresco The *Apotheosis of the Spanish Monarchy* (1697) by Luca Giordano.

MUSEO THYSSEN-BORNEMISZA★★★
Po. del Prado 8. 🚇 Banco de España, Atocha. Open Mon 12–4pm, Tue–Sun 10am–7pm; 24, 31 Dec until 3pm; last admission 1 hour before closing. Closed 1 Jan, 1 May, 25 Dec. €13 (temporary exhibitions additional charge). Free Mon 12–4pm (permanent collection only). 📞917 911 370. www.museothyssen.org. The Neoclassical Palacio de Villahermosa houses an outstanding private collection acquired by the Spanish State from **Baron Hans Heinrich Thyssen-Bornemisza**. The museum displays some 800 works from the late 13C to the present day, exhibited in chronological order on three floors. Temporary exhibitions are shown in a separate wing.

Second floor
The visit begins with the Italian Primitives (Gallery 1): **Duccio di Buoninsegna**'s *Christ and the Samaritan Woman*, with its concern for scenic realism.
Gallery 3 displays terrific examples of 15C Dutch religious painting such as **Jan van Eyck**'s *The Annunciation Diptych*. Next to it is the small *Our Lady of the Dry Tree* by **Petrus Christus**; Virgin and Child symbolise the flowering of the dry tree. The museum possesses a fantastic **portrait collection**. Gallery 5 contains examples from the Early Renaissance, which explore identity and autonomy; these come to the fore in the *Portrait of Giovanna Tornuaboni* by the Italian painter **Domenico Ghirlandaio**.
Raphael's *Portrait of an Adolescent* can be seen in the Villahermosa Gallery (Gallery 6), while Gallery 7 (16C) reveals **Vittore Carpaccio**'s *Young Knight in a Landscape,* in which the protagonist's elegance pops against a background heavy with symbolism.
The *Portrait of Doge Francesco Vernier* by **Titian** shows sober yet diverse tones. After admiring **Dürer**'s surprising *Jesus Among the Doctors* (1506, Gallery 8), move on to Gallery 9, with portraits from the 16C German School including *The Nymph from the Fountain*, one of several paintings by **Lucas Cranach the Elder**, and the *Portrait of a Woman* by **Hans Baldung Grien**. The 16C Dutch paintings in Gallery 10 include **Patinir**'s *Landscape with Rest on the Flight into Egypt*. Gallery 11 exhibits several works by **El Greco** as well as **Titian**'s *St Jerome in the Wilderness* (1575), with its characteristic use of flowing brushstrokes. One of the finest early works of **Caravaggio**, the creator of Tenebrism, *St Catherine of Alexandria*, hangs in Gallery 12. In the same gallery is a sculpture (*St Sebastian*) by Baroque master **Bernini**. Also here is the *Lamentation over the Body of Christ* (1633) by **Ribera**. The 18C Italian Painting section (Galleries 16–18) shows Venetian scenes by **Canaletto** and **Guardi**.
Also on this floor (Galleries 19–21) are 17C Dutch and Flemish works. Catch

Van Dyck's *Portrait of Jacques le Roy*, De Vos' *Antonia Canis* and two memorable Rubens, *The Toilet of Venus* and *Portrait of a Young Woman with a Rosary*, all in Gallery 19.

First floor

Galleries 22–26 represent 17C Dutch painting with landscapes and scenes of daily life. Note Frans Hals' *Family Group in a Landscape*, a fine collective portrait. Galleries 29 and 30 contain striking portraits from the 18C French and British schools as well as a handful of exceptional 19C North American paintings, which too often fly under the radar. These include works by Romantic landscape artists Cole, Church and Bierstadt and the Realist Homer. European Romanticism and Realism of the 19C are expressed in Constable's *The Lock*, Courbet's *The Water Stream* and Friedrich's *Easter Morning*, together with three works by Goya (Gallery 31).

Galleries 32 and 33 are dedicated to Impressionism and Post-Impressionism: Find works by Monet, Manet, Renoir, Sisley, Degas, Pissarro, Gauguin, Van Gogh, Toulouse-Lautrec and Cézanne here. *At the Milliner* by Degas is one of the artist's major canvases. Other easily recognisable works include Van Gogh's *'Les Vessenots' in Auvers*, which anticipates the explosion of brush-strokes in some of his later works; *Mata Mua* by Gauguin, from his Polynesian period; and Cézanne's *Portrait of a Farmer*, whose use of colour to build volumes is a forerunner of Cubism.

Expressionism is the focus of Galleries 35–40, just beyond a small display of Fauvist paintings in Gallery 34. The Expressionist movement, a highlight of this museum, supposes the supremacy of the artist's interior vision and colour over draughtsmanship. Two emblematic paintings by the German artist Grosz, *Metropolis* and *Street Scene*, hang in Gallery 40.

Ground floor

The first few galleries (41–44) contain eye-popping Experimental Avant-Garde works (1907–24) from European movements: Futurism, Orphism, Suprematism, Constructivism (note the female artists' work), Cubism and Dadaism. Room 41 displays Cubist works by Picasso (*Man with a Clarinet*), Braque (*Woman with a Mandolin*) and Juan Gris (*Woman Sitting*), while *Proun 1C* by Lissitzky and *New York City, New York* by Mondrian are in Room 43. Gallery 45 shows post-First World War European works by Picasso (*Harlequin with a Mirror*) and Joan Miró (*Catalan Peasant with a Guitar*), plus a 1914 abstract by Kandinsky (*Picture with Three Spots*). In the next gallery, mainly dedicated to North American painting, are *Brown and Silver I* by Jackson Pollock and *Green on Maroon* by Mark Rothko, fine examples of American Abstract Expressionism. The last two galleries (47 and 48) are given over to Surrealism, Figurative Tradition and Pop Art.

Carmen Thyssen-Bornemisza Collection

The 250-plus works on display build on those in the original collection. Notable are 17C Dutch painting, Impressionism and Post-Impressionism, North American painting and early Avant-Garde.

MUSEO NACIONAL CENTRO DE ARTE REINA SOFÍA★★ (QUEEN SOFÍA ART CENTRE)

C. de Santa Isabel 52. ⊙ Atocha. Open Mon & Wed–Sat 10am–9pm. Sun, Collection 1 10am–7pm, rest closes 2.15pm. Closed 1 & 6 Jan, 1 & 15 May, 9 Nov, 24–25, 31 Dec. €10; free Mon & Wed–Sat after 7pm, Sun 1.30– 7pm, 18 Apr, 18 May, 12 Oct, 6 Dec. ✆917 74 10 00. www.museoreinasofia.es.

The former Hospital de San Carlos was refurbished to house Spain's premier museum of contemporary art. A strikingly modern extension, designed by Jean Nouvel, holds large galleries designed for works of all sizes. The permanent collection, mostly contained within the original building, unfurls according to theme.

Permanent collection★
First floor.
Galleries around the patio garden show modern international work including **Juan Muñoz**'s *I Saw It in Bologna* (1991). The garden sculptures include pieces by Catalan artist **Joan Miró** and Basque sculptor **Eduardo Chillida**.

Second floor (galleries 201-210).
The museum's overview of Spanish art 1900–1945 (Collection 1) is structured around 'micronarratives' that give the wider context of Europe's avant-garde movements. However, the centrepiece of this floor – and of the larger museum – is undoubtedly **Picasso's Guernica★★★**, which hangs in gallery 206 (🚫 strictly no photography). Considered one of the great paintings of the 20C, it was commissioned for the Spanish Pavilion at the 1937 World Fair and inspired by the Fascist terror-bombing of Gernika. It is renowned for its Iberian symbolism, bone-chilling depictions of the atrocities of war and implied critique of Franco's dictatorship. Five other galleries give a narrative background to *Guernica*.

The Spanish masters **Miró** and **Dalí** are also found in this Collection; spot early works by Dalí and examples from his Surrealist period (*The Great Masturbator*). Gallery 208 is dedicated to the work of Madrid-born Cubist painter Juan Gris.

Fourth floor (Galleries 401-430).
Collection 2 galleries centre on art from 1945–1968 and features European works interwoven with pieces from North and Latin America. Some galleries highlight experimental Spanish pioneers such as Basque sculptor Oteiza. Photography and video are a strong suit throughout the collection, especially in this modern period. Trends from the late 1940s are also explained and well-represented; these include the avant-garde (in the early years of the dictatorship), abstract art in the 1950s, Neo-Realist photography and the realism of painters like Antonio López. Collection 3 spans 1962–1982 and contains more Experimental Art.

ADDITIONAL SIGHTS
Museo de Historia
C. de Fuencarral 78. 🚇 Moncloa. Open Tue–Sun & hols 10am–8pm. Closed 1 & 6 Jan, 1 May, 24–25 & 31 Dec. 🖉917 01 18 63. www.madrid.es/museosdehistoria. Housed in a former city hospice, this small museum, tracing the city's history, boasts a superb carved 18C decorative **portal★★** and, inside, among other artefacts, antique wells for storing ice hauled into town from the Sierra de Guadarrama.

Museo Nacional de Romanticismo
C. de San Mateo 13. 🚇 Tribunal. Open Tue–Sat 9.30am–8.30pm (Nov–Apr until 6.30pm), Sun & hols 10am–3pm. Closed 1 & 6 Jan, 1 May, 24–25 & 31 Dec. €3, free Sat from 2pm, Sun, 18 Apr, 18 May, 12 Oct, 6 Dec. 🖉914 481 045. http://museoromanticismo.mcu.es. Built in 1776 for the Marqués de Matallana, this Neoclassical palace houses a 19C decorative arts collection amassed by Benigno Valle-Inclán, the connoisseur who opened the museum in 1924. Two dozen rooms are beautifully appointed with period furniture. The ground-floor courtyard – access via the tea-room – is an oasis.

Plaza Monumental de las Ventas★ (Bullring)
C. de Alcalá 237. 🚇 Ventas. Guided tours daily 10am–5.30pm (with audioguide); on days of bullfight & during San Isidro, until 2pm. Closed 25 Dec, 1 & 6 Jan. 🖉687 73 90 32. €14.90. www.lasventastour.com. A few blocks east of Salamanca is Spain's largest bullring (built in 1931), a grand Neo-Mudéjar construction with a capacity of 22 300 spectators. There are bullfights every Sunday Mar–Oct and daily during the Feria de San Isidro in May. The **Museo Taurino** honours famed bullfighters.

👥 Museo del Ferrocarril (Railway Museum)
Po. de las Delicias 61. 🚇 Delicias. Open Oct–May Tue–Fri 9.30am–3pm, Sat–Sun 10am–7pm. Jun–Sep open 10am–7pm. Closed 25 Dec, 1 & 6 Jan €6

Matadero Madrid

© TRAVEL Collection/hemis.fr

(Sat & Sun €3). ☎902 22 88 22. www. museodelferrocarril.org.

The wrought-iron and glass Delicias railway station, where trains ran 1880–1969, has a collection of steam and diesel engines, clocks, models and a delightful restaurant car that youngsters love. The kid-friendly **Strawberry Train** (☞see page 152) leaves from here in the summer months.

👥 Museo Nacional de Ciencias Naturales

C. de José Gutiérrez Abascal 2. Ⓜ Gregorio Marañón. Open Tue–Fri, Sun & hols 10am–5pm, Sat 10am–8pm (Sat Jul–Aug closes 3pm). Closed 1 & 6 Jan, 1 May, 25 Dec. €7 ☎91 411 13 28. www.mncn.csic.es

Spain's premier natural science museum grew around an 18C royal collection, still on show as a cabinet of curiosities. But today's expansive collection of fossils and dinosaurs has been reoriented to delve into the world's past and exhibit its biodiversity.

Estadio Santiago Bernabéu

Av. de Concha Espina 1 (Tour tickets sold at Ticket Office 10 next to Gate 7, on Po. de la Castellana). ⓂSantiago Bernabéu. Open non match days Mon–Sat 9.30am–7pm, Sun & public hols 10.30am–6.30pm. Last tour 5 hours before kick off on match days. Closed 25 Dec, 1 Jan. €25, 14 and under €18. ☎913 98 43 70. www.realmadrid.com

Home to the mighty Real Madrid football (soccer) team, the tour takes you to the top of the stadium in a panoramic lift, into the Royal Box and changing rooms and onto the pitch through the tunnel from which teams emerge before an 80,000-strong crowd. The stadium will remain open through its four-year, €525 million renovation, which began in 2019.

Madrid Río (Madrid's Riverbanks)

River Manzanares. Ⓜ Príncipe Pío, Puerta del Ángel, Pirámides, Legazpi. www.esmadrid.com/en/tourist-information/madrid-rio.

A 32-km (20mi) riverside walkway has been opened up to pedestrians and cyclists. Four new bridges link the left and right banks' sports and leisure zones, which include 10 children's play areas along the Salón de Pinas. Parks and gardens are laid out around historic monuments, including the 18C Bridge of Toledo, Virgen del Puerto chapel (1718) and **Matadero Madrid**, a cutting-edge contemporary arts centre and leisure area (www.mataderomadrid. org) housed in a former slaughterhouse.

EXCURSIONS

👥 Parque Warner Madrid★

▶ San Martín de la Vega. 25km/15.5mi SE of Madrid. Open from 11am; see website for schedule. €41 at the door or from €30 online, see website for children's prices, parking €8 per day. ☎912 00 07 92. www.parquewarner.com.

This Warner Brothers theme park is a thrilling family-oriented getaway. Areas include Hollywood Boulevard, Movie World Studios, Super Heroes World, Old West Territory and Cartoon Village, each with rides and activities.

Movie WB World Studios will appeal to those who love special effects and car chases. In Super Heroes World you can experience spectacular combats between Batman and the forces of evil, or a 110m/360 ft freefall.

For the youngest visitors, Cartoon Village offers water games and recreates the magical world of old-fashioned heroes like Tom and Jerry. ☺ In summer, pack a hat: Shade is sparse.

👥 Faunia★

▶ Av. de las Comunidades 28, 5km/3mi E of Retiro Park. 🚇 Valdebernardo, Sierra de Guadalupe. Open from 10.30am, see website for schedule. €28 at the door, from €21 online, see website for children's prices; parking €5.50. 🖉911 54 74 82. www.faunia.es.

A zoo and nature park that recreates the planet's ecosystems, past and present, on a 140 000sq m/167 300sq yd site. It includes some 7 000 small- and medium-sized animals and birds, over 70 000 trees and plants and a several dinosaur models. One ecosystem is Europe's largest recreation of a polar ice cap. Popular with Madrileños and their children, Faunia may be visited time and again since the area is so large that it is difficult to explore it all in one visit.

Palacio Real Sitio de El Pardo★

▶ Manuel Alonso, El Pardo. 17km/ 10.5mi NW of Madrid. Open daily 10am–6pm (until 8pm Apr–Sep). See website for dates of closure. €9; free for EU citizens Wed & Thu Oct–Mar 3–6pm, Apr–Sep 5–8pm, all visitors 18 May and 12 Oct. 🖉913 76 15 00. www.patrimonionacional.es.

The palace was built by Philip III (1598–1621) on the site of Philip II's (1556–98) palace, destroyed in a fire in 1604. Franco lived here for 35 years and King Juan Carlos spent his teenage years here; today, it is used by heads of state on official visits. Decorations include more than 200 **tapestries★**; the

majority are 18C from the Real Fábrica de Tapices (Royal Tapestry Factory) in Madrid and based on cartoons by Goya, Bayeu, González Ruiz and Van Loo. The Casita del Príncipe – Prince's House – is a richly decorated pleasure pavilion. A short walk or drive away (1km/0.6m), at the Convento de Capuchines (Camino del Cristo de Pardo), is Gregorio Fernández's Cristo del Pardo (Christ Recumbent), a high point of **Spanish baroque sculpture** (open daily 9.30am–1pm, 4.30pm–8.30pm).

👥 Aquopolis

C. de la Mirasierra , Villanueva de la Cañada. Bus 627 every 10 minutes from Moncloa, or 25min drive via N6. Open mid-Jun–first week Sep from 12pm, see website for dates and times. €27 at door, from €17 online, see website for children's prices. 🖉912 00 07 91. www.villanueva.aquopolis.es.

Madrid's longest-established water park, with a wave pool, a dozen rides designed for all ages and tastes, a big swimming pool and bar-restaurants, is a blessing in the hot months.

Parque del Capricho

Av. de la Alameda de Osuna . 🚇 El Capricho. Open weekends and public hols 9am–9pm (Oct–Mar 6.30pm).

Here you'll find an 18C landscaped park with a boating lake, gazebos, a giant beekeeper's hive, a romantic cottage and classical colonnade. Paths connecting these run under century-old trees and between beautifully kept lawns.

Sierra de Guadarrama

Wrapping around the city's northern reaches, the Guadarrama range offers fantastic hiking and rural escapes. In 2013 it became Spain's fifteenth National Park (◐ See page 120). Starting points, at the foot of the slopes, may be reached by bus (Manzanares or Miraflores) or, in the case of Cercedilla, by train (from Atocha or Chamartín, about 1 hour's journey). A 20-minute walk above Cercedilla is the town's swimming pool, set among woods and filled by river water.

ADDRESSES

🛌 STAY

The Hat – C. Imperial 9 (Centro). 🚇 Sol. ☎917 72 85 72. www.thehatmadrid.com. 42 rooms. ☕€4. A far cry from the grubby hostels of yore, this ultramodern property steps from the Plaza Mayor has a rooftop bar (popular among locals) and private and multi-bunk rooms with white linens and blond wood furnishings.

Generator Madrid – C. de San Bernardo 2 (Centro). 🚇 Santo Domingo. ☎910 47 98 01. www.staygenerator.com. 129 rooms. ☕€7. Sleek, industrial interiors define this budget newcomer (opened 2018) with individual and group accommodations. Housed in a defunct petrol station, Generator stands out for its top-floor terrace and generous breakfasts.

Posada del León de Oro – C. Cava Baja 12 (Centro). 🚇 La Latina. ☎911 19 14 94. www.posadadelleondeoro.com. 27 rooms. ☕€12. Reminiscent of a small-town inn, this cosy, independently owned boutique hotel is located right on Cava Baja, for better (tapas heaven!) or for worse (can be noisy). The 300-bottle-deep wine list on the ground-floor restaurant is a boon to oenophiles. Rooms book far in advance; sister property Posada del Dragón, steps away, is a fine alternative.

Pestana Plaza Mayor – C. Imperial 8. 🚇 Sol (Centro). ☎910 05 28 22. www.pestanacollection.com. 87 rooms. ☕€24. Opened in May 2019, the newest Pestana outpost is Madrid's first Plaza Mayor hotel. It has a rooftop pool, spa, architectural elements from the original 17th-century building and – crucially –double-pained glass to keep out ambient noise.

Only YOU Atocha – Po. de La Infanta Isabel (Retiro). 🚇 Atocha. ☎914 09 78 76. www.onlyyouhotels.com. 205 rooms. ☕€19–27. The 2016 addition to the Only YOU family, towering above the Atocha railway station, wouldn't be out of place in Shoreditch or Kreuzberg with its subway-tiled bathrooms, high-design lobby and see-and-be-seen weekend brunches.

Room Mate Óscar Hotel – Pl. Vázquez de Mella, 12 (Chueca). 🚇 Banco de España or Chueca. ☎917 011 173. www.room-matehotels.com. 74 rooms. ☕€10. This sceney hotel in the heart of Madrid's 'gayborhood' is close to the museums yet removed from the tourist fray. There is contemporary art in the lobby, a minimalist pop café and glamourous rooftop terrace and pool.

Tótem Madrid – C. de Hermosilla 23 (Salamanca). 🚇 Serrano. ☎914 26 00 35. www.totem-madrid.com. 64 rooms. ☕€20. Hermosos y Malditos. A welcome dose of trendiness in an otherwise traditional barrio, Tótem is the ideal boutique hotel with its quiet side-street location, designer bedroom furnishings and slick cocktail bar and restaurant. Exterior-facing rooms with wrought-iron balconies are worth the extra coin.

ME Madrid Reina Victoria – Pl. Santa Ana 14. 🚇 Sol. ☎917 016 000. www.melia.com. 192 rooms. ☕€27. Restaurant Ana La Santa. One of the city's most iconic hotels, an old favourite of bullfighters, has been transformed into a stylish luxury accommodation complete with a rooftop bar and nightclub that's popular among local celebrities. The pleasant (if pricey) restaurant serves modern tapas created by the founder of Tragaluz (🕯️*See BARCELONA, p346*).

Villa Magna – Po. de la Castellana 22 (Salamanca). 🚇 Colón. ☎915 87 12 34. www.hotelvillamagna.es. 150 rooms. ☕€43. Tse Yang. Vying with the Ritz Madrid (closed for renovations at the time of writing) for the title of most luxurious hotel in Madrid, Villa Magna has elegance, tradition and every creature comfort you can imagine – with prices to match. The terrace-garden, where what's probably Madrid's best hotel breakfast is served, and Chinese fine-dining restaurant are major pluses, as is the Mytha Spa, revamped in 2019. Unwind in the new hammam, built with white marble imported from Turkey.

♥/EAT

Cerveriz – Pl. de San Miguel 2 (Centro). Sol. ✆915 59 67 67. Closed Sun. Improbably located across from the thronged Mercado de San Miguel in tourist central is this hidden gem that's literally a mom-and-pop restaurant (she tends bar; he cooks) known city wide for its Spanish omelette. The no-frills digs belie an eclectic wine list and soul-satisfying *abuela*-approved dishes including wine-braised whole squid, green beans with *jamón* and hand-carved lacón (Galician smoked ham) – all absurdly affordable.

Celso y Manolo – C. de la Libertad 1 (Chueca). Chueca or Banco de España. ✆915 31 80 79. www.celsoymanolo.es. In a district increasingly overrun with characterless chain restaurants, this just-trendy-enough neighbourhood *tasca* is a welcome surprise. Expect Spanish classics with a twist and locavore veg dishes.

Sylkar – C. de Espronceda 17 (Chamberí). Ríos Rosas or Gregorio Marañón. ✆915 54 57 03. Closed Sat eve and Sun. Genial service, comfort-food cooking, and throwback decor set this Chamberí stalwart apart from the hit-or-miss newfangled restaurants on neighboring Calle Ponzano. Dive your fork into the sinfully gooey Spanish omelette before moving on to dishes like griddled artichokes, burst-in-your-mouth croquettes and squid topped with ink sauce.

La Bola – C. de la Bola 5 (Centro). Santo Domingo. ✆915 47 69 30. www.labola.es. Closed Sun eve and 24 Dec. On a brisk day, try cocido madrileño, the local meat-and-chickpea stew served in multiple courses, at this this old-school tavern, which has been ladling it from earthenware pots cooked over a charcoal fire for over a century.

Sacha – C. de Juan Hurtado de Mendoza, 11 (Chamartín). Cuzco. ✆913 45 59 52. Closed Sun. Welcome to the dependably delicious bistro you wish your neighbourhood had. Presided over by a larger-than-life chef-owner, Sacha offers refined, seasonal dishes hinging on the freshest market ingredients. The intimate space, with candles, potted plants and soft lighting. will make you want to stay awhile. Regulars love the sea urchin 'lasagna', which never comes off the menu .

Sidrería Vasca Zerain – C. de Quevedo 3 (Las Letras). Antón Martín. ✆914 29 79 09. www.restaurante-vasco-zerain-sidreria.es. Closed Sun eve. A typical menu at this rustic Basque cider house near Plaza Santa Ana includes *tortilla de bacalao* (salt cod omelette) and *txuleton* (thick-cut grilled steak).

DiverXO – NH Eurobuilding, C. de Padre Damián 23 (Chamartín). Cuzco or Colombia. ✆915 70 07 66. www.diverxo.com. Closed Sun–Tue. David Muñoz's Spanish-Japanese fusion hotspot is Madrid's only three-Michelin-star restaurant. Expect billowing foams, mind-bending trompe-l'œil presentations and punk rock fine dining. Set tasting menus. Booking is essential.

Santceloni – Po. de la Castellana 57 (Chamberí). Gregorio Marañón. ✆912 10 88 40. www.restaurantesantceloni.com. Closed Sat lunch, Sun & public hols, Holy Week and Aug. Exquisite Michelin-starred Mediterranean cuisine has kept this well-oiled machine in business since 2001. The tasting menu and legendary cheese trolley change daily. 'Jacket and tie not compulsory but appreciated'. Booking is essential.

TAPAS

Casa González – C. del León 12 (Las Letras). Antón Martín or Sevilla. ✆914 29 56 18. www.casagonzalez.es. Open since 1931, this legendary purveyor of fine cheeses, meats and conservas has a dozen or so tables for sampling its wares; try to snag one in the picture window.

Docamar – C. de Alcalá 337 (Quintana). Quintana. ✆913 67 83 17. www.docamar.com. Closed Wed, Aug. The heavenly patatas bravas – perhaps the best in town – make Docamar well worth the (short) hike, out past Ventas.

Sala de Despiece – C. de Ponzano 11. Canal or Iglesia. ✆917 52 61 06, www.saladedespiece.com. Get your fix of cheffy ultramodern tapas at this Ponzano fixture modelled after a butcher shop. Top dishes include beef carpaccio slicked with truffle paste and a peeled whole tomato with basil .

Casa Labra – C. de Tetuán 12 (Centro). 🚇 Sol. 🖉 915 31 00 81. www.casalabra. es. This tavern dating to 1860 is an institution. Pablo Iglesias founded the Spanish Socialist Party (PSOE) here in 1879. House specialities are battered salt cod (*bacalao frito*) and salt cod croquettes; stand in the bar area or claim a marble table in the back.

Los Chuchis – C. de Puigcerdà (Salamanca). 🚇 Serrano. 🖉 915 75 41 25. Post up at the wrap-around steel bar and take your pick from the international tapas menu (think homemade pâte, baked feta or couscous) scrawled on the chalkboard overhead. Book ahead if you'd like to sit.

Cinco Jotas – C. de Puigcerdà (Salamanca). 🚇 Serrano. 🖉 915 75 41 25. Treat yourself to the best acorn-fed *jamón* money can buy at this posh outpost of the renowned '5J' brand.

La Venencia – C. de Echegaray 7 (Las Letras). 🚇 Sevilla. 🖉 914 297 313. This time-warpy sherry bar, frequented by Hemingway, serves *vinos generosos* straight from the cask alongside classic tapas like *mojama* (cured tuna) and fried almonds. (🚳 no photography).

CAFÉS

La Pecera del Círculo de Bellas Artes – C. de Alcalá 42. 🚇 Banco de España. 🖉 915 31 33 02. www. lapeceradelcirculo.com. Closed 24–25 Dec, 31 Dec–1 Jan. The 19C atmosphere of this café, with its soaring columns and windows, makes up for the unremarkable coffee and food. Ask to sit outside, weather permitting. The roof here boasts one of Madrid's best views.

Hola Coffee – C. del Dr. Fourquet 33. 🚇 Lavapiés. 🖉 910 56 82 63. www.hola. coffee. Let the baristas at this third-wave-coffee beacon pull you a perfect flat white, café con leche or americano using single-origin beans they roast themselves. Sister coffee shop Mision Café, near Pl. de España, has more space and a vegetarian-friendly food menu.

Chocolat – C. de Sta. María 30. 🚇 Antón Martín. 🖉 914 29 45 65. www. chocolatmadrid.com. Closed second half Aug. What most locals know and tourists don't is that the *chocolate con churros* here are far superior to those served at the better-known Chocolatería San Ginés.

Café de Oriente – Pl. de Oriente 2. 🚇 Ópera. 🖉 915 413 974. www. cafedeoriente.es. This upmarket institution opposite the Royal Palace is a delightful place for a drink, day or night.

NIGHTLIFE

Bendito Vinos y Vinilos – Mercado de San Fernando, stall #4. 🚇 Lavapiés. 🖉 661 750 061 www.benditovino.com. Closed Sun eve, public hols, 1 Jan, 7 Jan, 1 May, and 15 Aug. Natural wine unites Madrileños, expats and visiting oenophiles at this hole in the wall that's anything but pretentious.

Clamores – C. de Albuquerque 14. 🚇 Bilbao. 🖉 91 445 54 80 www.sala clamores.com. Drop by for a live jazz, Latin or flamenco show. The venue is a favourite with Spanish and international talent. Prices are reasonable.

Café Berlín – Costanilla de los Ángeles 20. 🖉 915 59 74 29. 🚇 Callao. www. berlincafe.es. Early evenings see live shows by a wide range of musicians (jazz, guitar, classical, flamenco and more); after midnight, disco-inflected DJ sets draw a young, trendy crowd.

Café Central – Pl. del Ángel 10. 🚇 Tirso de Molina. 🖉 913 69 41 43. www.cafe centralmadrid.com. The city's premier jazz venue since the 1980s, Café Central has nightly concerts 9–11pm.

Del Diego – C. de la Reina 12. 🚇 Gran Vía. 🖉 915 23 31 06. www.deldiego. com. Closed Aug, Sun, Holy Week. Open 7pm–3am. Perhaps Madrid's most iconic cocktail bar, Del Diego lures an over-40 crowd with classic drinks (think cosmos and white Russians) and *Wolf of Wall Street* vibes.

Macera – C. de San Mateo 21. 🚇 Tribunal or Alonso Martínez. 🖉 910 11 58 10. www.maceradrinks.com. Cocktails (€7 a pop) at this industrial-chic mixology hotspot centre on spirits macerated with local ingredients like rosemary, cucumber and almonds.

Pavoneo – C. de Belén 9. 🚇 Chueca. 🖉 646 79 64 85. Closed Sun–Tue.

This trendy new gay bar with low lights and bass-heavy tracks is the current place to be in Chueca. Expect a well-dressed thirtysomething crowd.

Ya'sta – C. de Valverde 10. 🚇 Gran Vía. ☎651 89 42 00. Open 11.45pm–6am. Closed Sun–Wed. Get a taste of Madrid's alternative scene at a techno, house, punk rock or reggaeton night at this long-established club.

FLAMENCO

Flamenco may not have been born in Madrid, but the city has long been a lively hub of flamenco culture. Performances unfold in every sort of venue, from auditoriums to outdoor festivals to restaurants and bars. Flamenco clubs, or tablaos, put on (often pricey and touristy) nightly shows; they vary in quality, so it's worth scoping out the artist du jour on Youtube before booking tickets.

Las Carboneras – Pl. del Conde de Miranda 1. ☎915 42 86 77. www. tablaolascarboneras.com. Open 7.30pm–12am. Closed Sun. Young, up-and-coming artists perform good modern flamenco in this sparsely decorated venue. The ticket comes with dinner or (the better option) a drink.

Corral de la Morería – C. de la Morería 17. 🚇 La Latina ☎913 658 446. www.corraldelamoreria.com. Open 6.30pm–12am. A midsize venue with top talent that puts on two shows a night, Corral de la Morería – in addition to its normal set menus – has a four-table Michelin-starred restaurant serving modern Andalucían fare.

Casa Patas – Cañizares 10. 🚇 Antón Martín. ☎913 69 04 96. www. casapatas.com. Open Mon–Fri 1–5pm, Mon-Thur 8-11pm, Fri-Sat 6.30pm-12am. Closed Sun. Enjoy tapas or supper in the tiled dining room before sitting down to an invigourating, foot-stomping flamenco show in the sardine-can performance area.

ENTERTAINMENT

Madrid's thriving film scene takes in dozens of cinemas showing un-dubbed and subtitled *versión original* (VO) films. The city also boasts 30 theatres (most plays in Spanish), numerous concert halls and a smattering of casinos. The

Auditorio Nacional (opened in 1988; www.auditorionacional.mcu.es) has a varied programme of classical music performed in two spaces; the **Teatro de la Zarzuela** (http://teatrodelazarzuela. mcu.es) hosts a wide range of dance, operettas (zarzuelas) and ballets; and the **Teatro Real** (www.teatro-real.com) offers mostly opera (most seats are sold as season tickets).

The **Teatro Español** (www.teatro espanol.es), a historic gem on Plaza Santa Ana, is a Spanish theatre buff's paradise, while productions at **El Matadero** (www.mataderomadrid.org) cultural centre are more eclectic and interpretative.

Veranos de la Villa (Jul–Aug; www. veranosdelavilla.com) is a varied music festival, and the **Festival de Otoño** (Nov–Dec; www.madrid.org/ fo) combines music, dance and opera. Both bring in international talent. **JAZZMADRID** (www.festivaldejazz madrid.com) is held in Nov.

SHOPPING

Cocol - Costanilla de S. Andrés 18. 🚇 La Latina. ☎919 19 67 70. www. cocolmadrid.es. Handmade Spanish artisan wares (such as ceramics, esparto baskets, textiles, leather items and glass) from this new independently run boutique make one-of-a-kind souvenirs.

Camper – Gran Vía 54 🚇 Gran Vía. ☎915 475 223 www.camper.com. The Mallorcan shoe firm combining high design and comfort is popular among visiting fashionistas, who take advantage of the lower home-turf prices.

Capas Seseña – C. de la Cruz 23. 🚇 Sevilla or Sol. ☎915 31 68 40. www. sesena.com. Closed Sun. Since 1901, this shop has made traditional and contemporary **capes**. Photos show such famed one-time clients as Picasso, Hemingway and Michael Jackson.

Antigua Casa Crespo – C. del Divino Pastor 29. 🚇 San Bernardo. ☎915 21 56 54. www.antiguacasacrespo.com. Closed Sun. Hand-woven **alpargatas** (espadrilles) in every colour and style – plus esparto grass baskets – can be found in this mid-19C shop. A basic pair will set you back just €20.

La Violeta – Pl. de Canalejas 6.
🚇 Sevilla. 🖉915 22 55 22. www.
lavioletaonline.es. Closed Aug, Sat in Jul,
Sun, public hols. This confectionery (est.
1915), renowned for its *marron glacé*
and violet products (glazed violets
and violet jam), was a favourite of King
Alfonso XIII and Valle Inclán. .

Art Galleries – Chueca, Salamanca
and Alonso Martínez have galleries
throughout. Purportedly Calle del Dr.
Fourquet, in Lavapiés, has the highest
concentration of galleries per square
metre in Spain. **ARCOmadrid** (www.
ifema.es/arcomadrid), held in February,
is the city's main contemporary art fair.

FIESTAS

15 May marks the the feast day of the
city patron, **San Isidro** (www.esmadrid.
com/sanisidro), rung in with outdoor
concerts and cultural events. Mid-
August sees the festivities of **La Paloma,
San Cayetano** and **San Lorenzo**, held
in La Latina, the Rastro Market area and
Lavapiés, respectively**.**

Alcalá de Henares★

**Alcalá has a historic centre★ of
16C–17C colleges and convents and
spacious squares. Medieval Calle
Mayor is adorned with impressive
gateways, and the university and
historic centre are a UNESCO
World Heritage site.**

A BIT OF HISTORY

Under the Romans the city was an
important centre known as **Complu-
tum**, now being excavated, but the history of Alcalá is mainly linked to that
of its university, founded by Cardinal
Cisneros in 1498. It became famous for
its language teaching and, in 1517, published Europe's first polyglot bible with
parallel texts in Latin, Greek, Hebrew
and Chaldean. The university was
moved to Madrid in 1836.
Alcalá's most famous denizen is **Miguel
de Cervantes**, Spain's greatest writer,
whose memory is honoured by a week
of celebrations every October. His
birthplace, the **Museo Casa Natal de
Cervantes**, recreated as a 16th-century
house with a collection of multilingual
editions of his novel *Don Quixote*, is
open to visitors (Mayor 48; open Tue–
Sun 10am–6pm; closed 1 & 6 Jan, 1
May, 24–25 & 31 Dec; 🖉918 89 96 54;
www.museocasanatalcervantes.org)

▶ **Population:** 193 751
⚲ **Michelin Map:** Michelin
maps 575 and 576
K 19 – Madrid.
ℹ **Info:** Plaza de Cervantes.
🖉918 80 33 00,
www.turismoalcala.es.
◗ **Location:** 33km/20mi
east of Madrid.
☺ **Don't Miss:** The
historic university.
🕐 **Timing:** Take a day trip
from Madrid.
👪 **Kids:** Tren de Cervantes.

GETTING THERE

The **cercanías** (commuter) train
takes 50 minutes and leaves from
Atocha.
Spanish-speaking kids love RENFE's
👪 **Tren de Cervantes**, which
runs every Sat from mid-May to
mid-Jul and mid-Sep to mid-Dec.
It departs Atocha at 10.45am and
returns from Alcalá at 6.35pm
(€22 adults, €16 children). Along
the way, actors perform scenes
from Cervantes' works. A guided
tour of Alcalá's sights is included
in the price. See the tourist office
website for details.

SIGHTS

Antigua Universidad & Colegio de San Ildefonso★

Pl. San Diego. Guided tours (40min) hourly Mon–Sat 10am–2pm, 4–8pm, Sun 10am-2pm. Closed 1 Jan, 25 Dec. From €6 (includes Capilla de San Ildefonso; other combinations available). ℘918 85 64 87. www.visitasalcala.es.

The original university, on Pl. de San Diego, has a **Plateresque facade★**(1543) by Rodrigo Gil de Hontañón crowned by a balustrade. The imperial escutcheon of Charles V decorates the pediment of the central section. The 17C **Patio Mayor** was designed by Juan Gómez de Mora, pupil of Herrera and architect of the Plaza Mayor and ayuntamiento (town hall) in Madrid; at the centre is a well-head with a swan motif, emblem of Cardinal Cisneros. Across the 16C Renaissance Patio de los Filósofos stands the delightful **Patio Trilingüe**,(1557) where Latin, Greek and Hebrew were taught. The **Paraninfoa** (1520), formerly used for examinations and degree ceremonies, now sees the solemn opening of the university year and the awarding of Spain's most important literary prize, the Cervantes. A gallery is in the Plateresque style, with **Mudéjar artesonado★★** work.

Capilla de San Ildefonso★

Next to the university.

This early-16C chapel is crowned with **Mudéjar artesonado** ceilings. The delicate **stucco** on the Epistle side of the church is Late Gothic, while the Evangelist side opposite is Plateresque. In the presbytery is the **Carrara marble mausoleum★★** of Cardinal Cisneros, by Domenico Fancelli and Bartolomé Ordóñez, one of the finest examples of 16C Spanish sculpture.

Catedral Magistral

Pl. de los Santos Niños. Open Mon–Sat 9am–1pm, 5–8.30pm, Sun & public hols 10am–1.30pm, 6–8.30pm. €3 for cathedral, museum and cloister, extra €2 for bell tower. ℘667 696 323. www.visitascatedraldealcala.org.

Built between 1497 and 1515, the cathedral has been remodelled several times. The central portal mixes Gothic, Plateresque and Mudéjar features.

Outside stork-nesting season (spring) you can visit the church tower. The cloisters (Calle Tercia) house a museum.

Palacio Arzobispal

In the 13C, the bishops of Toledo, lords of Alcalá, erected a palace-fortress on Pl. de Palacio. The Renaissance **facade**, by Alonso de Covarrubias, once fronted a courtyard; the Baroque coat of arms was added later. On adjoining Pl. de San Bernardo, the 17C church of the **Convento de San Bernardo** is crowned by an elliptical dome. The **Museo Arqueológico Regional de la Comunidad de Madrid** (archaeological museum), which has artefacts from the region – including the capital – dating from prehistoric times, is in the 17C former **Convento de la Madre de Dios** (open Tue–Sat 11am–7pm, until 3pm Sun & hols); ℘91 879 66 66).

El Corral de Comedias★★

Pl. de Cervantes 15. Guided tours (30 min) hourly Tue–Sun & hols 11.30am–1.30pm, 4.30, 5.30. €3. ℘91 877 1950. www.corraldealcala.com.

The oldest working theatre in Spain (if not in Europe) was a stage for Golden Age drama performed by and for university students. Glass sections in the floor allow visitors to view the original theatre floor.

ADDRESSES

🏨 STAY AND 🍴EAT

🍴🍴🍴 **Restaurante Miguel de Cervantes** –C. la Imagen 12. ℘918 83 12 77. www.hcervantes.es. Closed Sun eve and 24 Dec. This restaurant, behind Cervantes' birthplace in a restored town house, serves top-quality traditional cuisine in a Castilian setting. Set menus from €25; tapas also available. There are 13 basic rooms (🍴🍴) for those wishing to stay.

Aranjuez★★

Aranjuez, on the banks of the Tagus (Tajo), is an oasis in the Castilian plain, renowned for its green gardens and parkland, which are now a World Heritage landscape. The shaded walks, immortalised by composers (the most famous being Joaquín Rodrigo's haunting guitar piece 'Concierto de Aranjuez') and painted by artists, are popular at weekends and quiet during the week.

A BIT OF HISTORY

The Aranjuez Revolt (El Motín de Aranjuez) – In March 1808, Charles IV, his queen and the prime minister, Godoy, were at Aranjuez. They were preparing to flee (on 18 March) first to Andalucía, then to America, in the face of popular opposition to the right-of-passage privileges granted to Napoleon's armies. On the night of 17 March, Godoy's mansion was attacked by followers of the heir apparent, Prince Ferdinand; Charles IV then abdicated in favour of his son, but Napoleon soon forced both royals to abdicate in his own favour (5 May). These intrigues and the presence of a French garrison in Madrid stirred the revolt of May 1808, the beginning of the War of Independence.

SIGHTS
ROYAL PALACE AND GARDENS★★

The Catholic Monarchs enjoyed the original 14C palace, enlarged by Emperor Charles V. The present palace is mainly the result of an initiative by Philip II, who Called on the future architects of the Escorial to erect a new palace amid gardens. In the 18C, the town became a principal royal residence and was considerably embellished. It was ravaged by fire in 1727 and 1748, after which the present facade was built. Ferdinand VI built the town to a grid plan; Charles III added two palace wings, and Charles IV erected the delightful Labourer's Cottage.

▶ **Population:** 59 037
🕭 **Michelin Map:** 575 and 576 L 19 – Madrid.
🖸 **Info:** Plaza de San Antonio 9. ℘918 91 04 27. www.aranjuez.es.
◐ **Location:** Off the A4 linking Madrid with Andalucía, 47km/29.2mi from both the capital and Toledo. 🚃Aranjuez.
⊛ **Don't Miss:** The Palace and Prince's Garden.
🕔 **Timing:** Take a day trip from Madrid.
👪 **Kids:** El Tren de la Fresa is an 1851 steam train (℘902 228 822, www.esmadrid.com/en/strawberry-train; mid-May–late Sep, exc Jul–Aug; see website for schedule) that runs at weekends from Madrid's Museo del Ferrocarril to Aranjuez. Costumed staff serve strawberries (an Aranjuez speciality) along the way (from €30 for adults and €20 for children).

Palacio Real★

Pl. de Parejas. Open Tue–Sun 10am–8pm (Oct–Mar until 6pm). See website for dates closed. €9; free for EU citizens Wed & Thu 5–8pm summer, 3–6pm winter, free 18 May and 12 Oct. ℘91 45 87 00. www.patrimonionacional.es.
This Classical-style royal palace of brick and stone was built in the 16C and restored in the 18C. In spite of many modifications, it retains considerable unity of style. The entry and facades of the wings are marked by archways, and domed pavilions mark the angles. The apartments have been left as they were at the end of the 19C.
The **Salón del Trono** (Throne Room), with crimson velvet hangings and Rococo furnishings, has a ceiling painted with an allegory of monarchy.

Royal Palace

© JoseIgnacioSoto/iStockphoto.com

Ironically it was in this room that Charles IV abdicated in 1808.

The **Salón de Porcelana**★★ (Porcelain Room) is the palace's most notable room, covered in white garlanded porcelain tiles that illustrate, in relief, scenes of Chinese life, exotica and children's games. They were made in the Buen Retiro factory in Madrid in 1763.

In the king's apartments, a music room precedes the Smoking or Arabian Room – a reproduction of the Hall of the Two Sisters in the Alhambra. A Mengs *Crucifixion* hangs in the bedroom, and the walls of another room are decorated with 203 small pictures on rice paper with Asian motifs. A museum of palace life in the days of Alfonso XIII includes a gymnasium and a tricycle.

Parterre and Jardín de la Isla★ (Parterre and Island Garden)

Open Nov–Feb 8am–6.30pm, Mar 8am–7pm, Apr–15 Jun and 16 Aug–Sep 8am–8.30pm, 16 Jun–15 Aug 8am–9.30pm, Oct 8am–7.30pm.

The **Parterre** is a formal garden laid out before the palace's east front by the Frenchman Boutelou in 1746. The Fountain of Hercules brings a mythological touch to the balanced display. The **Jardín de la Isla** was laid out on an island in the Tajo river in the 16C.

Cross the canal to reach the park and its fountains hidden among chestnut, ash and poplar trees and boxwood hedges.

Jardín del Príncipe★★ (Prince's Garden)

Entrance on C. de la Reina.

This vast garden beside the Tajo (150 ha/371 acres) has four monumental gateways by Juan de Villanueva.

In 1763, Boutelou landscaped the park for the future Charles IV according to the romantic vision then in fashion. A farm, greenhouses with tropical plants and stables for exotic animals were added.

Casa del Labrador★★ (Labourer's Cottage) – €5. The 'cottage' at the eastern end of the Jardín del Príncipe, named after the humble cottages originally on the site, was built on the whim of Charles IV in Neoclassical style.

Casa de Marinos (Sailors' House)/ Museo de Falúas Reales– .

A curious museum beside the former landing stage exhibits **falúas reales**★★ (royal vessels) that ferried the royals and guests to the Labourer's Cottage. One, a gift to Philip V from a Venetian count, is remarkable for its ornate decoration in gilded, finely carved wood.

EXCURSION

Chinchón★

◗ 21km/13mi NE along the M 305.
Chinchón is famous for its namesake aniseed spirit and, more importantly, the Countess of Chinchón, wife of a 17C viceroy of Peru, to whom the West owes quinine, extracted from the bark of a Peruvian tree (dubbed chinchona in the countess's honour).

Plaza Mayor★★ – Chinchón is home to one of Spain's most postcard-perfect plazas, distinctive for its semicurcular layout. Presided over by a Covarrubias-designed church, it's lined with tapas bars and hemmed in by houses with wooden balconies. The tourist office is at no.6 (℘918 93 53 23; www.ciudad-chinchon.com). A passion play is held on Easter Saturday.

ADDRESSES

♀/EAT

⊜⊜ **Cuevas del Vino** – C. de Benito Hortelano 13, Chinchón. ℘918 94 02 06. Dine on Castilian home cooking in underground caves hung with goatskins, and wash things down with wine made on site. The *migas* (fried breadcrumbs with bacon), garlic shoots and grilled beef are excellent.

⊜⊜⊜⊜ **Casa Pablo** – C. del Almíbar 42, Aranjuez. ℘918 911 451. www.casapablo.net. Savour a hearty meal in the dining room, or post up at the wood-and-zinc bar strung with bullfighting paraphernalia to tuck into a variety of taPo.

Monasterio de
El Escorial★★★

This imposing building on the slopes of the Sierra de Guadarrama, commissioned by Philip II and designed by Juan de Herrera, heralded a style that combined regal grandeur with monastic austerity.

A BIT OF HISTORY

In memory of San Lorenzo – On 10 August 1557, St Lawrence's Day, Philip II defeated the French at St-Quentin. The king decided to dedicate a monastery to the saint, to serve as royal palace and pantheon. The outsize project – including 1 200 doors and 2 600 windows and involving 1 500 workmen – was completed in only 21 years (1563–84), which explains the exceptional unity of style. The general designs of Juan de Toledo were followed after his death in 1567 by **Juan de Herrera**.
In reaction to the excessive ornamentation of Charles V's reign, the architects produced a sober monument with clean, majestic lines.

⌚ **Michelin Map:** 575 or 576 K 17 – Madrid.

🛈 **Info:** Grimaldi 4, San Lorenzo de El Escorial. ℘918 90 53 13. ▭San Lorenzo de El Escorial. www.sanlorenzoturismo.es.

◗ **Location:** El Escorial is 56km/40mi NW of Madrid, at 1 065m/3 494ft.

◉ **Don't Miss:** The sumptuous royal apartments. The feast day of San Lorenzo (St Lawrence), the patron saint of the village and monastery, is celebrated on 10 August.

🕓 **Timing:** El Escorial makes an excellent day trip from Madrid, the full monastery visit taking an estimated 4 hours.

There is a good **view★** of the monastery and countryside from **Silla de Felipe II** (Philip II's Seat), from where the king oversaw construction (◗turn left after the monastery into the road marked Entrada Herrería-Golf).

© Turespaña

Real Monasterio de San Lorenzo de El Escorial

SIGHTS
Real Monasterio de San Lorenzo de El Escorial

Allow half a day. Av. de Juan de Borbón y Battemberg. Open Tue–Sun & public hols, Apr–Sep 10am–8pm (Oct–Mar until 6pm). Recommended last entry time 4 hours before closure. See website for dates closed. €12 (casitas extra). Free Wed & Thu 5–8pm summer, 3–6pm winter for EU citizens, free to all 18 May and 12 Oct. ℘914 54 87 00. www.patrimonionacional.es.

It is said that the monastery's gridiron plan recalls St Lawrence's martyrdom. Measuring 206m x 161m (676ft x 528ft), the austerity of its grey granite emphasises the severity of the architecture. When the king commanded an increase in height, Herrera positioned windows asymmetrically to lessen the monotony.

Palacios★★ (Royal Apartments)

While the Habsburgs remained on the Spanish throne, El Escorial was a place of splendour: The king resided in apartments encircling the church apse. The Bourbons preferred other palaces but, when in residence, occupied suites on the north side of the church. The palace took on renewed glory in the 18C in the reigns of Charles III and IV.

A staircase built in the time of Charles IV goes up (3rd floor) to the **Palacio de los Borbones** (Bourbon Apartments), with Pompeian ceilings and fine **tapestries★**, many of which were made in the Real Fábrica (Royal Tapestry Works) in Madrid based on cartoons by Spanish artists, notably Goya. Elsewhere are Flemish tapestries.

The large **Sala de las Batallas** (Battle Gallery) contains frescoes (1587): the Victory at Higueruela in the 15C against the Moors and, on the north wall, the Victory at St-Quentin.

The restraint of the **habitaciones de Felipe II** (Philip II's apartments, second floor) is striking in comparison with the Bourbon rooms. Those of the Infanta Isabel Clara Eugenia comprise a suite of small rooms with dados of Talavera ceramic tiles. The king's bedroom is off the church. When he was dying of gangrene in 1598, he could contemplate the high altar from his bed.

The paintings in the apartments include a *St Christopher* by Patinir and a portrait of the king in old age by Pantoja de la Cruz. Facing the gardens and the plain, the Salón del Trono (Throne Room) is hung with 16C Brussels tapestries. The Sala de los Retratos (Portrait Gallery), which follows, holds royal portraits.

Panteones★★ (Pantheons)

Access is through the Patio de los Evangelistas (Evangelists' Courtyard), with frescoes by Tibaldi and his followers.

A marble-and-jasper staircase leads down to the **Panteón de los Reyes★★★** (Royal Pantheon) and the remains of monarchs from the time of Charles V, with the exception of Philip V, Ferdinand VI and Amadeus of Savoy.

Biblioteca

The octagonal chapel was begun in 1617 under Philip III and completed in 1654. Facing the door is the jasper altar, flanked by 26 marble and bronze sarcophagi in wall niches (kings on the left, the queens whose sons succeeded to the throne on the right). The ornate chandelier is the work of an Italian artist. The 19C **Panteón de los Infantes★** (Infantes' Pantheon) includes princes and princesses and queens whose children did not rule. The sculptures are delicately carved. Overall, the room is phenomenally well-preserved.

Salas Capitulares★ (Chapter Houses)

Two fine rooms, with ceilings painted by Italian artists with grotesques and frescoes, form a museum of 16C–17C Spanish and Italian religious painting. The first room contains canvases by **El Greco** and **Ribera**, a *St Jerome* by Titian and *Joseph's Tunic* by Velázquez. The second room has works from the 16C Venetian school including paintings by Tintoretto, Veronese and Titian (*Ecce Homo*). A room at the back contains works by Bosch and his followers such as the imaginative *Haywain* and the satirical *Crown of Thorns (Los Improperios)*.

Basílica★★

Herrera based his final plan on Italian drawings. He introduced the flat vault, in the atrium. The interior owes much to St Peter's in Rome with a Greek Cross plan, a 92m/302ft high cupola above the transept crossing supported by four colossal pillars and transept barrel vaulting. The frescoes in the nave vaulting were painted by Luca Giordano

in Charles II's reign. Red marble steps lead to the sanctuary, which has paintings of the lives of Christ and the Virgin by Cambiasso. The massive **retable**, designed by Herrera, is 30m/98ft tall and is composed of four registers of jasper, onyx and red marble columns, between which stand 15 bronze sculptures by Leone and Pompeo Leoni.

The tabernacle is also by Herrera. On either side of the chancel are the royal mausoleums, with funerary figures at prayer by Pompeo Leoni. In the first chapel off the north aisle is the *Martyrdom of St Maurice* by Rómulo Cincinato, which Philip II preferred to that of El Greco (&See Nuevos Museos, below). In the adjoining chapel is a sculpture of Christ by Benvenuto Cellini.

Patio de los Reyes (Kings' Courtyard)

One of the three Classical gateways opens onto this courtyard, named for the statues of the Kings of Judea on the west front of the church.

Biblioteca★★ (Library)

2nd floor.

Easily one of the most memorable rooms in the complex, the library has shelving designed by Herrera, of exotic woods, and a ceiling painted by Tibaldi that represents the liberal arts, with Philosophy and Theology at each end. There are also portraits of Charles V, Philip II and Philip III by Pantoja de la Cruz and one of Charles II by Carreño. Philip II furnished the library with over 10 000 books, many of them lost in a 1671 fire. It is now a public library with over 400 00 books and historic manuscripts. The spines face inward for preservation purposes.

Nuevos Museos★★ (New Museums)

Paintings in the **Museo de Pintura** are on religious themes.

First room: 16C Venetian school canvases (Titian, Veronese and Tintoretto). **Second room:** two works by Van Dyck and a small painting by Rubens.

Third room: works by Miguel de Coxcie, Philip II's Court Painter.

Fourth room: Rogier Van der Weyden's sober and expressive *Calvary*, flanked by an *Annunciation* by Veronese and a *Nativity* by Tintoretto.

Fifth room: canvases by Ribera including *St Jerome Penitent*, the *Chrysippus* and *Aesop*, with vividly portrayed faces, and Zurbarán's *St Peter of Alcántara* and the *Presentation of the Virgin*.

Last room: paintings by Alonso Cano and Luca Giordano.

On the ground floor, paintings include El Greco's *Martyrdom of St Maurice and the Theban Legionary*★, commissioned by Philip II but later rejected by him. Ironically it is now considered one of El Greco's finest works.

OTHER ROYAL BUILDINGS
Casita del Príncipe★
(Prince's or Lower Pavilion)

Jardín de los Moes. SE along the station road. Same opening hours as Palacios, p153.
Charles III commissioned Juan de Villanueva to build a lodge for the future Charles IV. Its intricate decoration makes it a jewel of a palace in miniature. There are painted **Pompeian-style ceilings**★ by Maella and Vicente Gómez, silk hangings, canvases by Luca Giordano, chandeliers and a mahogany-and-marble dining room.

Casita del Infante
(Infante's or Upper Pavilion)

Ctra de Ávila. 3km/1.8mi SW beyond the golf course. Same opening hours as Palacio.
This 'hideaway' lodge was designed by Villanueva for the Infante Gabriel, Charles IV's younger brother. The interior is furnished in period style; the first floor was used by Prince Juan Carlos before his accession to the throne.

EXCURSION
Valle de los Caídos★

○ *16km/10mi NW on the M 600 and M 527. Open Tue–Sun & public hols Apr–Sep 10am–7pm (until 6pm Oct–Mar). Recommended last entry time 4 hours*
before closure. Closed 1 & 6 Jan, 1 May, 24–25, 31 Dec. €9 ticket includes basilica. Free Wed & Thu Oct–Mar 3–6pm and Apr–Sep 5–7pm for EU citizens, free to all 18 May. ℘918 90 54 11. www.valledeloscaidos.es.

The Valley of the Fallen is an ostentatious and hugely controversial monument to the dead of 'both sides' of the Spanish Civil War (1936–39), despite there being only two names on the tombs inside: those of Francisco Franco and the Falangist party founder, José Antonio Primo de Rivera. The complex, Western Europe's biggest and most recent example of Fascist architecture, was built by Franco's Republican prisoners. Today the palpably eerie site is a rallying point for neo-Nazis and Franco sympathisers.

Basílica★★

The Basilica, blessed by Pope Pius XII, is hollowed out of the rock face. Its west door is a bronze work crowned by a *Pietà* by Juan de Ávalos. At the entrance to the interior is a wrought-iron screen with 40 statues of saints and soldiers. The 262m/859.5ft nave is lined with chapels, between which hang copies of 16C Brussels tapestries of the Apocalypse. Above the chapel entrances are alabaster copies of famous Spanish statues of the Virgin Mary.

A **cupola**★, 42m/138ft in diametre, above the crossing, shows in mosaic the heroes, martyrs and saints of Spain approaching Christ and the Virgin Mary. On the altar stands a painted crucifix by Beovides. At the foot of the altar are the remains of José Antonio and Franco, though the current Socialist government is pushing for Franco's exhumation. Ossuaries hold remains of 40 000 soldiers and civilians. (Spain has the highest number of mass graves of any country on earth, barring Cambodia.)

La Cruz★

The cross is 125m/410ft high (150m/ 492ft including the base) and 46m/151ft wide. Statues of the Evangelists around the plinth and of the four cardinal virtues above are by Juan de Ávalos.

Castilla y León: Ávila, Salamanca & Zamora

The region of Castilla y León ('Castilla and León') sprawls across the northern part of Spain's *Meseta*, the dry central plain. Wide terraced valleys and moors are dotted with rock pinnacles, narrow defiles and gentle hills. Vast spaces open up with a grandeur one might associate with the American West: Some call it rustic and romantic, others harsh and monotonous. The region is crossed from east to west by one of the country's great rivers, the Duero. The area Castilla y León comprises today was a frontier territory in the Middle Ages, and many of its fortified towns remain; after all, Castilla was named for its castles. Its most famous one-time inhabitant is El Cid, the warrior who fought with and against the Moors.

Highlights

1 Walking the **city walls** by night in **Ávila** (p159)
2 Climbing the **Roman road** at the **Puerto del Pico** (p162)
3 People-watching in **Plaza Mayor, Salamanca** (p164)
4 Relaxing in the **quiet village** of **La Alberca** (p172)
5 Exploring the **Romanesque churches** of Toro (p174)

A bit of geography

The rocky Sierra de Gredos marks the southern border of Castilla y León, peaking at nearly 2 600m/8 530ft with glacial cirques and lakes. The towns at the foot of the southern slopes, which enjoy a benign climate, give access to gentle or adventur-ous walks up toward the peaks. Roads through the Sierra traverse historic passes that offer panoramic views to the south.

The towns of the north Meseta

Ávila, 107km/67mi northwest of Madrid, is a well-preserved medieval town whose 11C walls and romantic towers were never removed nor exceeded. For a period in the 16C, Ávila was the heart of Spanish religious life, thanks to its famous inhabitants, St Teresa of Ávila and St John of the Cross. The city is known for its brisk mountain air and austere, hardy Castilian character.

Salamanca, to the northwest, on the River Duero, is one of Spain's most impeccably preserved historic cities. The Universidad de Salamanca is as old as Oxford, and its students give the city a youthful verve. The double cathedral and the central plaza – grand architectural set-pieces – alone make the visit worthwhile. To the south and west of Salamanca, the Meseta's stark landscape softens into holm oak forests, where bulls and pigs graze lazily. Ciudad Rodrigo, 25km/15.5mi east of the Portuguese bor-der, set against that landscape, is another ly preserved town complete with nobles' mansions and palaces.

Close to Castilla y León's southern border with Extremadura, the plains turn into thickly wooded rolling hills that have kept a rural way of life and the popular stone architecture of past centuries. La Alberca, the best preserved of the towns and vil-lages, makes a good base for exploring Las-Batuecas National Park and Sierra de Francia.

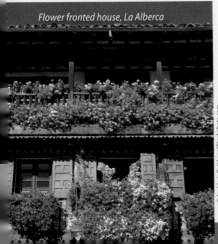

Flower fronted house, La Alberca

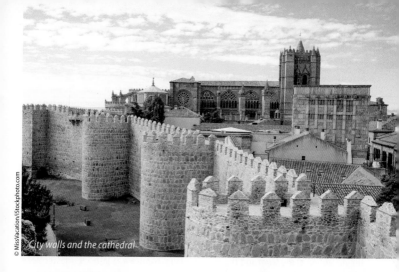
© MissVacation/iStockphoto.com
City walls and the cathedral

Ávila★★

Ávila is one of the best-preserved fortified cities in Europe; its numerous convents and churches peek above the crenellated 11C walls. The old town and churches outside the walls are a World Heritage site.

THE CITY TODAY

To tourists, Ávila is mostly a day-tripper's city, but a night here is worthwhile, preferably in the 16C Parador occupying a former palace (Calle Marqués Canales y Chozas 2; ☎920 54 79 79; www.parador.es). The town is hardly hopping, but there are enough tapas bars and drinking holes (particularly around the Plaza del Mercado Chico) to make a night of it. Wherever you go, you'll be reminded of the town's favourite daughter, Santa Teresa, since *yemas de Santa Teresa*, the egg-yolk-and-sugar confections produced by local nuns, are everywhere.

SIGHTS
Murallas★★
(City walls)

Entry at Pta. Alcázar, Carnicerías or Puente Adaja. Open Tue–Sun (daily 15 Jun–15 Oct) 31 Oct–31 Mar 10am–6pm, 1 Apr–30 Jun and 1 Sep–31 Oct 10am–8pm, Jul–Aug 10am–9pm. Last ticket 30min before closing. See website for days closed. €5. Free Tue

▶ **Population:** 59 008
♿ **Michelin Map:** 575 or 576 K 15 – Map 121 Alrededores de Madrid.
ℹ **Info:** Av. de Madrid 39. ☎920 350 000. www.avilaturismo.com.
◖ **Location:** Sitting at 1131m/ 3710ft, NW of Madrid, Ávila has a harsh and windy winter climate. 🚄Ávila (AVE).
☺ **Don't Miss:** The city walls.
◷ **Timing:** Start with the walls and Cathedral.

2–4pm exc hols. ☎920 35 00 00. www.muralladeavila.com.
Europe's most intact fortified medieval wall, with 90 bastions and towers and eight gateways, enclose an area 900m/ 2 953ft by 449m/1 476ft.
Most date to the 11C, and despite 14C modifications, maintain their unity. You can access the walls at various points to walk the sentry path along the top. The best **view** of the walls is from **Cuatro Postes**, on the Salamanca road.

Catedral★★

Pl. de la Catedral. See website for opening times. €6 (inc. museum). ☎608 48 68 08. www.catedralavila.es.
The fortified **east end** of the cathedral is set into the ramparts, crowned with

a double row of battlements. Granite and defensive design make it austere.

The 14C **north doorway** with French Gothic decoration, its stone eroded, was removed in the 15C from the **west front** during a renovation by Juan Guas. Its current placement, from the 18C, is more suited to a palace.

The surprisingly airy **interior** has a high Gothic nave, a chancel with sandstone patches of red and yellow and many **works of art★★**. The **trascoro** (1531) holds Plateresque statues (left to right): the *Presentation of Jesus in the Temple*, the *Adoration of the Magi* and the *Massacre of the Innocents*. The **choir stalls** are from the same period. There are two delicate wrought-iron **pulpits** – Renaissance and Gothic.

Construction spanned from 1135 to the 14C; windows in the apse are Romanesque. The large painted **altarpiece** (c. 1500) by Pedro Berruguete and Juan de Borgoña has a gilt wood surround with Isabelline features and Italian Renaissance pilasters.

Four carved panels on the high altar show the Evangelists and the four Holy Knights. The central panel is Vasco de la Zarza's masterpiece: the **alabaster tomb★★** of Don Alonso de Madrigal, Bishop of Ávila in the 15C, Called El Tostado (The Swarthy One). He is shown before a beautiful Epiphany.

Museo de la Catedral

The museum contains a notable 13C **sacristy★★** with an eight-ribbed vault, massive 16C altarpiece and sculptures of the Passion in imitation alabaster. Also on display are a head of Christ by Morales, painted on a tabernacle door; a portrait by **El Greco**; an Isabelline grille; late 15C antiphonaries; and a colossal 1571 monstrance (1.7m/5ft 8in) by Juan de Arfe. The Gothic **cloisters** are restored. In Pl. de la Catedral, the **Palacio de Valderrábanos**, now a hotel, has a fine 15C doorway with family crest.

Basílica de San Vicente★★

Pl. de San Vicente 1. Open May–Oct Mon–Sat 10am–6.30pm (Nov–Apr until 1.30pm then 4–6.30pm), Sun & hols 10am–2pm, 4–6pm. €2.50. ✆920 25 52 30. www.basilicasanvicente.es.

This vast 12C–14C Romanesque basilica, with ogive vaulting, is on the reputed site of the 4C martyrdom of St Vincent of Zaragoza and his sisters. The ensemble includes the 14C south gallery with slender columns, a cornice over the length of the nave, the tall west front porch and two incomplete towers.

The **west portal★★** is outstanding for the statue columns below the richly decorated cornice and lifelike covings. Beneath the 14C **lantern★** is the **martyrs' tomb★★**, a late 12C masterpiece under a rare 15C Gothic canopy with pagoda top. The martyrdom of St Vincent and his sisters is attributed to the unknown sculptor of the west portal. The scenes of their capture, flaying and torture are particularly powerful.

Monasterio de Santo Tomás★

Pl. de Granada 1. Open daily Sep–Jun 10.30am–2pm, 3.30–7.30pm and Jul–Aug 10.30am–9pm. Last ticket 1 hour before closing. €4 (church, Eastern art museum, cloisters and choir). ✆920 352 237. www.monasteriosantotomas.com.

This late-15C Dominican monastery, at times a summer residence of the Catholic Monarchs, was also the university. The **church** facade includes the common motifs of the monastery: Details are emphasised with long lines of dots, and the yoke and fasces (bound bundle of wooden rods) emblem of Ferdinand and Isabel. The church has a single aisle, its arches on clusters of slender columns. Two galleries were accessible only from the cloisters by the monks. The fine **mausoleum★** (1512) is of Prince Juan, the only son of the Catholic Monarchs. Its alabaster table with Renaissance sculpting is by Domenico Fancelli, who created the Catholic Monarchs' mausoleum in Granada. In a north chapel is the Renaissance tomb of Juan Dávila and his wife.

Claustro (Cloisters) – Beyond the plain 15C **Claustro de los Novicios** is the **Claustro del Silencio★**, intimate and generously carved on its upper gallery. The Catholic Monarchs' Cloister is larger and more solemn with curiously bare upper arching.

From the Claustro del Silencio, stairs lead to 15C Gothic **choir stalls** with pierced canopies and arabesques. In the high altar gallery is Berruguete's masterpiece, the **retable of St Thomas Aquinas★★** (c. 1495).

Iglesia de San Pedro

Pl. de Santa Teresa. Opening times vary; enquire at the tourist office. €1.50.
🖉920 229 328

This Romanesque church on the vast **plaza Santa Teresa** has Early Gothic pointed arches and a delicate rose window. Nearby are a number of urban palaces with facades to view from the street: the Gothic Reniassance **Mansión de los Verdugo** (C. Lopez Núñez, closed to the public), marked with a family crest, is flanked by two stout square towers; the **Mansión de los Polentinos** (C. Vallespín), now a barracks, has a Renaissance entrance and patio; the **Torreón de los Guzmanes** (Pl. Corral de las Campanas), also Called the Oñates Palace, has a massive square corner tower with battlements dating to the early 16C.

Near the Cathedral, the provincial Law Courts are housed in the **Palacio de Núñez Vela** (Pl. de la Catedral 10). This Renaissance palace of the Viceroy of Peru has windows framed by slender columns and coats of arms. The patio, accessible from the street, is a delight. Two 14C Gothic buildings with coats of arms give onto Plaza de Pedro Dávila and two others, belonging to the Episcopal Palace, face Plaza de Rastro.

Museo de Ávila

Pl. Nalvillos 3. Open Tue–Sun am & public hols 10am–2pm, 5–8pm (Oct–Jun 10am–2pm, 4–7pm). €1.20; free weekends & hols. 🖉920 354 000.
https://museoscastillayleon.jcyl.es
The 16C Dean's House contains Ávila Province's art collection including traditional objects, clothes and furniture; archaeological remains ranging from prehistoric to Visigothic times; and fine art. Among the paintings, in Room VII,

hangs an outstanding primitive triptych by Hans Memling.

Iglesia Santo Tomé el Viejo

Pl. de Italia. Visit included in Museum of Provincial Art ticket.

An annexe to the museum, this 13C Romanesque church displays pieces from the archaeological collection and a fine Roman mosaic.

🚗 DRIVING TOUR

SOUTH OF ÁVILA

120km/75mi. Allow half a day.

▷ Drive northeast to Burgos, then follow the N403 south for 40km/25mi toward San Martín de Valdeiglesias.

Embalse de Burguillo

This artificial lake on the River Alberche makes a   landscape set against the scrubby hills.

▷ Follow the N403 for another 10km/6mi before reaching San Martín de Valdeiglesias, then turn right at the signpost for Toros de Guisando.

Toros de Guisando

The granite Celtiberian Bulls of Guisando stand in a enclosure off the road. No one is certain of their meaning.

▷ Drive through San Martín de Valdeiglesias and take the N501 toward Madrid for 5km/3mi.

Pantano de San Juan

The winding road around the edge of the reservoir offers spectacular views down over the water, though often, in summer, its upper reaches are left bare by drought. Between the pine-covered slopes are areas for watersports and bathing, plus restaurants – busy in summer and tranquil the rest of the year.

Sierra de Gredos★★

The massif of the Sierra de Gredos includes Pico de Almanzor (2 592m/ 8 504ft), the highest peak in the Cordillera Central. The north face of the range is marked by glacial cirques and lakes and the south by a steep granite wall and gullies. Fertile valleys produce apples in the north and grapes, olives and tobacco on the sheltered south slope. Wildlife is protected in the Reserva Nacional de Gredos.

SIGHTS

San Martín de Valdeiglesias
This old market town with 14C castle walls was built by the Lord High Constable Álvaro de Luna. It's a starting point for explorations. **Comando G**, the buzzy bodega that put Sierra de Gredos on the winemaking map, is situated 12 minutes south, in Cadalso de Vidrios (www. comandog.es; reservation required).

Toros de Guisando
◉ 6km/3.7mi NW.
The **Bulls of Guisando** are four roughly carved granite figures in an open field. Similar ancient statues, possibly Celtiberian, are found elsewhere in Ávila province. They also resemble the stone **porcas** (sows) seen in the Trás-os-Montes region of Portugal.

Embalse de Burguillo★ (Burguillo Reservoir)
◉ 20km/12.4mi NW. ♿See p161.

Pantano de San Juan
◉ 8km/5mi E. ♿See p161.

◉ From San Martín de Valdeiglesias, take the N501 (which becomes the C501) toward Arenas de San Pedro.

- ◈ **Michelin Map:** 575 or 576 K 14, L 14.
- ▯ **Info:** Av. de Madrid 39, Ávila. ℘920 350 000. www.turismocastillayleon. com.
- ◉ **Location:** The sierra is almost due west of Madrid (M 501 via San Martín de Valdeiglesias) and south of Ávila (N 502 to Puerto del Pico).
- ◷ **Timing:** Start early and a day should allow you to fit most sights into a lesurely drive.
- 👪 **Kids:** Cuevas del Águila.

👪 Cuevas del Águila★ (Eagle's Caves)
◉ 9km/5.6mi S of Arenas de San Pedro. Take the C708 turn-off from the N502. Open 21 Sep–21 Mar 10.30am–1pm, 3–6pm; 22 Mar–20 Sep 10.30am–1pm, 3–7pm. €8. ℘920 37 71 07. www.cuevasdelaguila.com.
A single vast chamber is open to the public. Among the many concretions are lovely frozen streams of calcite, ochre crystals coloured by iron oxide and massive pillars still in the process of formation. ⊗ Pack a jumper.

Puerto del Pico road★
◉ 29km/18mi NE of Arenas de San Pedro.
The road through the sierra crosses the quaint town of **Mombeltrán** (15C castle) then winds upward, parallel to a Roman road. From the pass (1 352m/ 4 436ft) there are stunning **views**★ of mountains, the Tiétar Valley (south) and, the Tajo. The **Parador de Gredos**, the first in Spain (1928), stands in a **magnificent setting**★★ with far-reaching views.

Laguna Grande★
◉ 12km/7.4mi S of Hoyos del Espino.
⊗ Park at the end of the road.
🏃 A marked path leads to Laguna Grande (2hr), a glacial basin fed by mountain torrents. Halfway along is a **panorama**★ of the Gredos cirque.

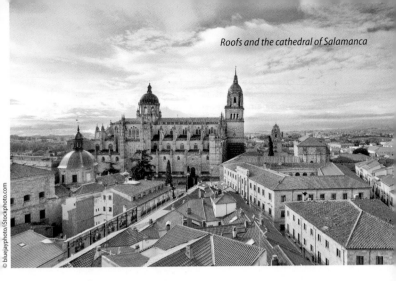

Roofs and the cathedral of Salamanca

© bluejayphoto/iStockphoto.com

Salamanca★★★

Salamanca wears its rich history on its sleeve with its medieval university, labyrinthine streets and buildings of golden stone. Blessed with what is widely regarded as the most picturesque main square in Spain, Salamanca has long been a favoured destination for foreign students and visitors alike. The old town is a World Heritage site.

THE CITY TODAY

The University of Salamanca may no longer be in the same league academically as the Oxfords and Harvards of the world, but its 30 000-or-so international and Spanish students bring a palpable *alegría* to the city. If you are young (or young at heart), want to study Spanish and experience a typical Spanish social life, this is your place.

A BIT OF HISTORY

A tumultuous past – Salamanca flourished under the Romans, who built the **Puente Romano** (Roman bridge). Alfonso VI took the city from the Moors in 1085. In 1520, Salamanca rose against the royal authority of Emperor Charles V (*See SEGOVIA, p174*) and around that time reached its artistic and intellectual zenith.

- ▶ **Population:** 144 692
- 🕭 **Michelin Map:** 575 and 576 J 12-13.
- 🄸 **Info:** Plaza Mayor 19. ☏ 902 30 20 02. www.salamanca.es.
- ▶ **Location:** Salamanca is in the western Castilla y León region, accessible from Ávila (98km/61mi SE on the N 501), Valladolid (115km/72mi NE on the A 62), and Zamora (62km/39mi N on the N 630). 🚃 Salamanca.
- ⊛ **Don't Miss:** The university and main square.
- 🕐 **Timing:** There's easily enough to fill two days.
- 🏃 **Kids:** A walk on the Ciudad Rodrigo ramparts.

Los Bandos – During the 15C, rivalry between noble factions *(bandos)* saw the city's streets bathed in blood.
The university was founded in 1218 by Alfonxo IX and grew under the patronage of kings of Castilla and high dignitaries.
Notable alumni include the Infante Don Juan; St John of the Cross and his teacher, the humanist **Fray Luis de León** (1527–91); and **Miguel de Unamuno** (1864–1936), rector, and philosopher, and professor of Greek.

Art in Salamanca – In the late 15C and early 16C, two major painters were working in Salamanca, **Fernando Gallego**, one of the best Hispano-Flemish artists, and **Juan of Flanders** (c. 1465–1519), whose work is outstanding for the subtle delicacy of its colours.

The 15C also saw the evolution of the original Salamanca patio arch, in which the line of the Mudéjar curve is broken by counter-curves and straight lines.

The 16C brought Salamancan **Plateresque** art to an ebullient climax.

WALKING TOUR

1 OLD CENTRE★★★

Allow one day.

Plaza Mayor★★★

The Plaza Mayor is the life and soul of Salamanca. All the city's major streets converge on the square, where locals and visitors rub shoulders. It was built by Philip V between 1729 and 1755 and is among the finest in Spain, designed principally by the Churriguera brothers.

Four ground-level arcades with rounded arches, decorated by a series of portrait medallions of Spanish kings and famous men such as Cervantes, El Cid and Columbus (and controversially, until 2017, Franco), support three storeys rising in perfect formation to an elegant balustrade.

On the north and east sides are pedimented fronts of the **ayuntamiento** (town hall) and the Pabellón Real (Royal Pavilion).

▶ Take Prior to Plaza de Monterrey, then Compañía.

Casa de las Muertes
(House of Death)

Closed to the public.

The Plateresque facade is attributed to Diego de Siloé; it stands out for the skulls carved on its upper part. The

edifice, built in 1500, is said to have received its macabre moniker following a quadruple homicide on the premises.

▶ Walk back on Calle de la Compañía.

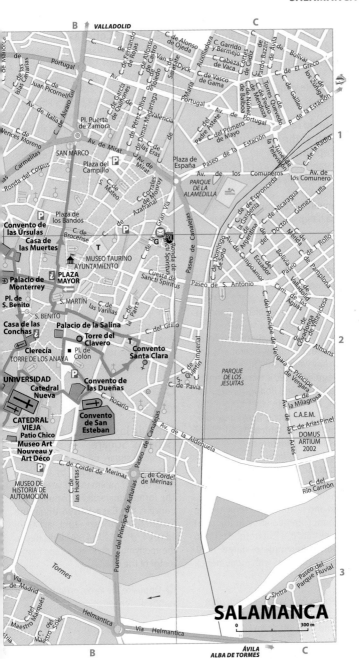

SALAMANCA

Palacio de Monterrey

Pl. de Monterrey 2. Open
10.30am–6.45pm (7.45pm in summer).
€5 guided tours every hour ex.
1.30–5pm:, tickets sold at Pl. Mayor

tourist office (not at palace). 📞923 21
83 42. www.fundacioncasadealba.com.
Advance booking required.
Built in 1539, this Plateresque palace
belonging to the House of Alba opened

to the public in 2018. On the 45-minute guided tour you'll see Ribera's two only known landscape paintings .

▶ Opposite stands the Iglesia de la Purísima.

Iglesia de la Purísima (Church of the Immaculate Conception)

Pl. de Monterrey. Open for Mass (the church may be viewed before or after). ☎923 21 27 38.
The **Immaculate Conception★** by **Ribera** hangs above the high altar.

▶ Take Ramón y Cajal to the end.

Colegio Arzobispo Fonseca★

C. de Fonseca 4. Chapel and cloisters open Mon-Fri 9am-2pm. ☎923 29 45 70.
Built in 1535 by Archbishop Fonseca, this is the last of the surviving four university colleges, almost perfectly preserved. Theology, liberal arts and canon law were taught here. Designed by **Diego de Siloé,** it was executed by Juan de Álava and Rodrigo Gil de Hontañón. The facade is strikingly simple. The main door is flanked by Ionic columns above which stand Saints Augustine and Ildefonso.
At the top a medallion frieze shows St James at the Battle of Clavijo. The portico to the patio is adorned with 128 medallions mixing Biblical, mythological and historical personalities. In the chapel, immediately to the right of the entrance, a Plateresque **retablo** by Alonso Berruguete, dated 1529, combines canvases with monumental statuary.

▶ Retrace your steps and turn right along Compañía to Rúa Antigua; turn right and then left down Libreros.

Plaza de San Benito

On this square are the **Iglesia de San Benito** and mansions of Salamanca's old noble rival families.

Casa de las Conchas★ (House of Shells)

C. de la Compañía 2. Patio: open Mon-Fri 9am-9pm, Sat-Sun & public hols 9am-3pm, 4-7pm. ☎923 26 93 17.
This late 15C house (now a library) is carved with 400 scallop shells in its golden stone wall. It has Isabelline windows and grand wrought-iron grilles. The **patio** has delicate mixtilinear arches and openwork balustrades (meant to evoke basketwork), carved lions' heads and coats of arms.

▶ Opposite stands the Jesuit College.

La Clerecía

C. de la Compañía 5. Open Mon-Fri 10am-12.45pm, 5-6.30pm, Sat, Sun & public hols 10.30am-1.30pm, 5-7.15pm. Guided tours €3.75. ☎923 27 71 00.
This Jesuit College was begun in 1617; its Baroque towers were finished by Andrés García de Quiñones in 1755. You can climb the towers for views over the city (€6 combined tickets available).

▶ Cross the Pl. de San Isidro and take Libreros.

Patio de las Escuelas★★★ (Schools' Square)

This small square off the historic Calle Libreros is surrounded by the best examples of Salamanca Plateresque. The former university principals' residence is the **Casa-Museo Unamuno** (open Mon-Fri 10am-2pm, last entry 1pm; €4; ☎923 29 44 00), dedicated to the eponymous philosopher and former rector of the university.

▶ Opposite the Patio, on Libreros, stands the University.

Universidad (University)

Patio de Escuelas. Open Mon-Sat 10am-6.30pm, Sun & public hols 10am-1.30pm. Limited access during academic events. €10 ticket includes entrance to the Escuelas Mayores; free Mon am, 18 May. ☎923 29 44 00. www.usal.es.

The University's 1534 **entrance★★★** is breathtakingly intricate. Above the twin doors, crowned with basket arches, carvings progress in ever greater relief, to compensate for increasing height. A central medallion in the first register shows the Catholic Monarchs, who presented the doorway; in the second are portrait heads in scallop-shell niches; in the third, flanking the pope supported by cardinals, are Venus and Hercules and the Virtues. The most famous motif – said to bring good luck if you can spot it – is the skull surmounted by a frog (spoiler: it's halfway up the right) symbolising the posthumous punishment of lust.

The lecture halls are around the **patio**: The **Paraninfo** (Great Hall) is hung with 17C Brussels tapestries and a portrait of Charles IV from Goya's studio. The hall where Fray Luis de León lectured in theology is as it was in the 16C.

The grand staircase rises beneath star vaulting, its banister carved with foliated scrollwork and, at the third flight, a mounted bullfight.

A gallery on the first floor has its original *artesonado* ceiling with stalactite ornaments and a low-relief frieze along the walls. A Gothic door with a fine 16C grille opens into the 18C library (sometimes closed) containing books, incunabula and manuscripts, some of which date to the 11C.

Escuelas Menores (Minor Schools)

Same opening hours as University.

Standing to the right of the hospital, and crowned by the same openwork Renaissance frieze, is the entrance to the Minor (preparatory) Schools – a Plateresque portal decorated with coats of arms, roundels and scrollwork.

The typical Salamanca **patio★★** (1428) has lovely lines. To the right of the entrance is a new exhibition room with a fine Mudéjar ceiling; the **University Museum** opposite exhibits what remains of the ceiling painted by Fernando Gallego for the former university library. This section of the **Cielo de Salamanca★** (Salamanca Sky) illustrates

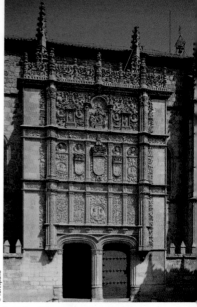
© Turespaña

Facade of the university entrance

constellations and signs of the zodiac. Several works by Juan of Flanders and Juan of Burgundy stand out.

▷ Exit the patio to the left.

Museo de Bellas Artes de Salamanca (Salamanca Fine Art Museum)

C. del Patio de Escuelas 2. Open Tue–Sun 10am–2pm, 5–8pm (Oct–Jun 4–7pm), Sun & public holis 10am–2pm. Closed Sun from 2pm, 1, 2 & 6 Jan, 24, 25 & 31 Dec. €1.20; free Sat, Sun and 18 May. www.museoscastillayleon.jcyl.es

The contents of Salamanca's fine arts museum, housed inside a small urban palace, cover 2 000 years of history. Many of its artistic treasures come from convents or monasteries; others are on loan from Madrid's Prado Museum. Outstanding is a 14C **sarcophogus** richly decorated with a narrative of the stigmatisation of St Francis, and a Mannerist *Llanto por Cristo* (*Mourning at the Tomb of Christ*). Its collection of modern paintings includes a portrait of *Don Miguel de Unamuno* by Basque painter Echevarria y Zunicalday and *Corrida en Azul★★*, a 1942 canvas by Luis de Horna, clearly influenced by Picasso's *Guernica*.

▷ Take Libreros toward the river and take the first left, Calderón de la Barca, to reach Pl. de Juan XXIII to enter the Cathedrals.

Catedral Nueva★★ (New Cathedral)

C. Benedicto XVI. Open Apr–Sep 10am–8pm (last entry 7.15pm), Oct–Mar until 6pm (last entry 5.15pm). €6. ℘923 21 74 76. www.catedralsalamanca.org.

Construction began in 1513, but additions continued to be made until the 18C – hence the variety of architectural styles.

The **west front★★★** is divided into four wide bays outlined by pierced stonework, carved as minutely as the keystones in the arches, the friezes and the pinnacled balustrades. The Gothic decoration of the central portal, which includes scenes such as a Crucifixion between St Peter and St Paul, overflows the covings and tympanum.

The **north doorway**, facing the **Colegio de Anaya**, bears a delicate low relief of Christ's entry into Jerusalem. The restored lower section of the last archivolt contains the anachronistic figure of an astronaut as well as a mythological animal eating ice cream.

The **interior** is notable for the pattern of the vaulting, the delicacy of the cornices and the sweep of the pillars. The eight windows in the lantern are given added effect by a drum with scenes from the Life of the Virgin painted in the 18C by the Churriguera brothers, who also designed the ornate Baroque stalls in the *coro*, the *trascoro* and the north organ loft.

Catedral Vieja★★★ (Old Cathedral)

Calle Benedicto XVI. Access via the Catedral Nueva. Same details as Catedral Nueva.

▷ Enter by the first bay off the south aisle in the New Cathedral.

The builders of the New Cathedral respected the fabric of the old, which is almost totally masked outside. It was built in the 12C and is a good example of the Romanesque, the pointed arching being a legitimate, if unusual, innovation; the *cimborrio* (lantern), or Torre del Gallo, with two tiers of windows and ribbing, is outstanding. Beneath the vaulting, capitals are carved with imaginary animals.

The **altarpiece★★** in the central apsidal chapel was painted by Nicholas of Florence in 1445; it comprises 53 compartments decorated in surprisingly fresh colours showing the architecture and garb of the era. *The Virgin of the Vega* is a 12C wooden statue plated in gilded and enamelled bronze.

Recesses in the south transept contain French-influenced 13C recumbent figures and frescoes.

Claustro – Capitals from earlier Romanesque galleries destroyed during the 1755 Lisbon earthquake remain in these cloisters. The adjoining **Capilla de Talavera** has a Mudéjar dome on carved ribs. A museum in three rooms and the Capilla de Santa Catalina contain works by Fernando Gallego and his brother Francisco in addition to others by Juan of Flanders (St Michael altarpiece).

The **Capilla Anaya** contains the outstanding 15C alabaster **tomb★★** of Diego de Anaya, archbishop of Salamanca and, subsequently, Sevilla. Surrounding it is a florid Plateresque grille. There is also a 15C **organ★** and 16C recumbent statues.

From the **Patio Chico** you can see the Old Cathedral apse and the scallop tiling on the **Torre del Gallo** (Cockerel Tower). From here, C. Arcediano leads to the romantic garden **Huerto de Calixto y Melibea**.

▷ From Pl. de Juan XXIII take Calle Tentenecio, then take the first left.

Museo de Art Nouveau y Art Déco (aka Casa Lis)★★

C. de Gibraltar 14. Open Tue–Fri 11am–8pm (Nov-Mar 11am–2pm, 4–7pm); Sat, Sun & hols 11am–8pm. Closed 1 & 6 Jan, 25 Dec. €4, free Thu 11am–2pm. ℘923 12 14 25. www.museocasalis.org.

This museum in the Modernist Casa Lis, dating to the beginning of the 20C, includes the house's own furnishings and bronzes, works by R Lalique, vases by E Gallé and sculptures by Hagenauer. Temporary shows focus on art of the period. There is a cafeteria and, in summer, live music events.

◗ From Calle Tentenecio take Po. de Rector Esperaba and C. Arroyo Sto Domingo

Convento de San Esteban★ (St Stephen's Monastery)

Pl. del Concilio de Trento. Open 10am–2pm, 4–6pm (Mar-Nov 4–8pm). €4. ℘923 21 50 00. www.conventosanesteban.es.

Gothic pinnacles adorn the side buttresses of this 16C–17C Dominican monastery; the sculpture of the facade★★ is quintessentially Plateresque. A low-relief *Martyrdom of St Stephen* is by Juan Antonio Ceroni (1610). In the 17C cloisters★★ , note the prophets' heads in medallions and grand staircase (1553). The large church has star vaulting in the gallery and a main altarpiece by José Churriguera. Crowning it is a painting of *The Martyrdom of St Stephen* by Coello.

◗ On the same square stands the Convento de las Dueñas.

Convento de las Dueñas

Pl. del Concilio de Trento. Open Mon–Sat 10.30am–12.45pm, 4.30–7.15pm; €2. ℘923 21 54 42.

The Renaissance cloisters★★ have profusely carved capitals that are extraordinarily forceful in spite of their small size.

◗ Take San Pablo toward the Plaza Mayor.

Palacio de la Salina★

C. de San Pablo 24. Open Tue–Sun 10.30am–1.30pm, 6-9pm. ℘923 29 32 33.

The city's salt was once kept in this palace, hence its name. The patio combines Salamanca mixtilinear arches at one end with a corbelled gallery – supported by distorted atlantes – on the right and an arcade on the left.

◗ Take San Pablo, then turn right on to San Justo and right again down Consuelo.

Torre del Clavero

C. Consuelo 34. Closed to the public. The octagonal keep is all that remains of a castle built in 1450. Mudéjar trellis-work decorates its turrets.

◗ Return to San Justo, follow it to the Pl. T. Bréton, then right to Santa Clara.

Convento de Santa Clara★

C. de Santa Clara 2. Open Mon–Fri 9.30am–12.45pm, 4.25–6.10pm. Sat, Sun & hols 9.30am–2.10pm. €3. ℘660 108 314.

This oft-overlooked convent was founded in the 13C, though the building dates to the 15C–18C . The church contains a retablo and, in the choir, frescoes uncovered in the 1970s. One wing of the convent is an ethnographic museum.

EXCURSIONS

Ciudad Rodrigo★

Ciudad Rodrigo appears high on a hilltop, guarded by the square tower of its 14C Alcázar (now a Parador) and medieval ramparts. A Roman bridge spans the Río Águeda from the Portuguese side. After the so-called Reconquista, in the 12C, the town was repopulated by Count Rodrigo González, for whom it is named; it subsequently became a border stronghold and played a role in all of the conflicts between the Kingdom of Castilla and Portugal.

Wellington's success against the French in 1812 won him the title of Duke of Ciudad Rodrigo and Grandee of Spain. The area is planted with ilex trees, under which pigs and bulls graze.

▶ WALKING TOUR

THE OLD TOWN
Start your visit on Plaza de
las Amayuelas.

Catedral de Santa María★★
Pl. San Salvador 1. Open Mon am only,
Tue–Sat 11am (from 12.45pm Sun)–2pm
and 4–7pm. €3 incl museum. Free Sun
after 4pm exc hols. ℘923 48 14 24.
www.catedralciudadrodrigo.com
The cathedral was built in two stages,
first from 1170 to 1230 and then in the
14C; in the 16C Rodrigo Gil de Hontañón added the central apse. Note
the delicate ornamentation of the blind
arcades. The 13C **Portada de la Virgen★**
(Doorway of the Virgin), masked outside by a Classical belfry, has a line of
Apostles carved between the columns
beneath the splayings and covings.
Inside, the Isabelline choir stalls in the
coro were carved by Rodrigo Alemán.
The fine Renaissance **altar★** in the north
aisle is adorned with an alabaster masterpiece by Lucas Mitata.
The **cloisters★** are made up of diverse
architectural styles. In the west gallery,
the oldest part, Romanesque capitals
illustrate man's original sin. Opening
off the east gallery is a Plateresque
door decorated with medallions. Three
flights and 140 steps lead to the bell
tower, where you can see a model of
the cathedral, an 8-min audiovisual, and
enjoy panoramic views.
The abutting **Museo Catedralicio** is
worth a visit. Note too the 16C **Palacio
de los Miranda** on Pl. de San Salvador.

▶ The arcaded Plaza del Buen
Alcalde is to the right.
Take the street to the left to reach
Plaza del Conde.

Palacio de los Castro★
(aka Palacio de los Condes
de Montarco)
Pl. Conde 3. Usually closed to the public.
This late-15C palace, on Plaza del Conde
(Count), has a long facade punctuated
by delicate windows.

The plateresque doorway is surrounded
by an *alfiz* (rectangular moulding) and
flanked by two twisted columns showing Portuguese influence. It is now a
wedding venue; the patio may be visited when not in use.

▶ Head to the Plaza Mayor, passing
the 16C Palacio de Moctezuma (right).

Plaza Mayor★
Two Renaissance palaces stand on
the lively main square: the first, now
the **ayuntamiento** (town hall), has
a facade with two storeys of basket
arcading forming a **gallery★** and a
loggia, while the second, the **Casa de
los Cueto**, has a decorative frieze.

▶ Continue onto Calle Juan Arias,
pausing to see the Casa del Príncipe
(aka Palacio de los Águila), a 16C
Plateresque building.

Murallas (Ramparts)
The walls, built on Roman foundations
in the 12C, were converted to a full
defensive system on the north and west
flanks in 1710. There are several stairways on the 2.25km/1.4mi sentry path.

▶ The imposing keep of Henry of
Trastámara's castle stands on the
SW corner of the walls alongside the
Roman bridge spanning the Águeda
river. The castle is the town's Parador.

Alba de Tormes
▶23km/14mi SE on the N 501 and C 510.
Only the massive keep remains of the
Castle of the Dukes of Alba (open
10am–2pm, 4–6.30pm; €3). This is also
where the tourist office is (℘923 30
00 24; www.villaalbadetormes.com)
The remains of St Teresa of Ávila are in
the Carmelite Convent. The Iglesia de
San Juan (open Mon–Fri 10am–2pm,
Sat–Sun & hols 10am–8pm; €2), featuring a Romanesque-Mudéjar east end,
contains an outstanding 11C **sculpture ensemble★** in the apse, showing
a noble Christ and the Disciples. Beyond
it is a small museum of local prehistoric
finds.

ADDRESSES

⌖ STAY

⊜ **Hostal Concejo** – Pl. de la Libertad 1. ℘923 21 47 37. www.hconcejo.com. Reservations recommended. 18 rooms. No breakfast. Cheap and cheerful, the centrally located Concejo is a cut above most *pensiones*. Rooms are simple, clean and comfortable.

⊜⊜ **Hostal Plaza Mayor** – Pl. del Corrillo 20. ℘923 26 20 20. www. hostalplazamayor.es. 19 rooms. No breakfast. You'd be hard-pressed to find a better location than this hostel behind Pl. Mayor opposite the Romanesque church of San Martín. Interiors are simple and old-fashioned. Garage parking available.

⊜⊜ **Hostería Casa Vallejo** – San Juan de la Cruz 3. ℘923 28 04 21. www. hosteriacasavallejo.com. 10 rooms. ⊑€5–14. Restaurant ⊜⊜⊜. Closed 2 weeks in Feb and Jul. This small hotel off Plaza Mayor. has refurbished interiors behind a 19C facade and includes a restaurant and down-home tapas bar.

⊜⊜⊜ **Hotel Rector** – Po. Rector Esperabé 10. ℘923 21 84 82. www. hotelrector.com. 13 rooms. ⊑€14. This high-end boutique hotel occupies part of a honey-coloured typical Salamanca stone town house that was formerly the mansion of a wealthy family. It enjoys spectacular views of the cathedral and elegant, well-appointed rooms presided over by professional staff.

⌖ EAT

⊜⊜⊜ **La Cocina de Toño** – Gran Vía 20. ℘923 26 39 77. www.lacocina detoño.es. La Cocina de Toño comprises an excellent pintxo bar and main dining area with rustic Castilian decor. The Basque-influenced menu encompasses dishes both classic and modern.

⊜⊜⊜ **Le Sablon** – C. Espoz y Mina 20, (Plaza de la Libertad). ℘923 26 29 52. www.restaurantlesablon.com. Closed Mon and Tue, Jul. Run by a husband and wife, Le Sablon has a meticulously furnished and classically elegant dining room. The cuisine is international with an emphasis on game dishes.

⊜⊜⊜⊜ **Víctor Gutiérrez** – C. Empedrada 4. ℘923 262 973. www. restaurantevictorguttierez.com. Closed Sun eve, Mon. Arguably the top table in town, this Michelin-starred institution is the brainchild of a Peruvian chef with boundless creativity. His fusion cuisine resists categorisation.

TAPAS

Tapas 2.0 – C. Felipe Espino 10. ℘923 21 64 48. Closed Tue–Wed. This locally famous *gastrotasca* has exquisite modern tapas like succulent lamb meatballs and 'Momofuku-style' crispy chicken. Expect high quality ingredients, down to the bread baked on the premises.

Mesón Cervantes – Pl. Mayor 15. ℘923 217 213. www.mesoncervantes.com. Take in fine views of the Plaza Mayor while nibbling Castilian tapas with a modern twist. Open until 2am, Cervantes fills up with a young crowd in late evenings. Try the house sangría.

Momo – San Pablo 13. ℘923 28 07 98. www.momosalamanca.com. Closed Sun, Jul & Aug. Attractively plated tapas and skewers come cold and hot; graze at the bar, or make a meal out of them in the the basement dining room.

CAFÉS AND BARS

Café Novelty – Pl. Mayor 2. ℘923 21 99 00. www.cafenovelty.com. The oldest café in town, opened in 1905, Novelty was a favourite haunt of Miguel de Unamuno. The wooden chairs, checkered black-and-white floor and marble tables conjure up a bygone era, and the terrace sprawls out onto the Plaza Mayor. The coffee may not be anything to write home about, but the ambiance is.

La Regenta Gin Club – C. Espoz y Mina 21. ℘923 12 32 30. A much-loved café with a 19C ambience, La Regenta – equally good for cocktails and coffee– is pricey by local standards but worth it.

The Doctor Cocktail - C. Dr. Piñuela 5. ℘923 26 31 51. Sip everything from martinis to *gin-tónics* to tiki drinks at this *coctelería* open daily until 1.30am.

La Alberca★★

La Alberca is a well-preserved village in the national park of Las Batuecas–Sierra de Francia. The sierra's rolling woodland is dotted by unspoilt villages with wooden-beamed architecture.

▶ **Population:** 1 107
ⓘ **Michelin Map:** 575 K 11.
ℹ **Info:** Plaza Mayor 11. ℘923 41 50 36. www.laalberca.com.
◗ **Location:** La Alberca is 42km/26mi E of Cuidad de Rodrigo and 77km/48mi S of Salamanca. 🚇Nearest station: Ciudad Rodrigo, 49km/30mi.

EXCURSIONS

Peña de Francia★★

◗ 15km/9.6mi W.

The Peña, a shale crag at 1 732m/5 682ft, is the peak of the Peña de Francia range. The approach affords stunning **panoramas★★** of the Hurdes mountains and the Sierra de Gredos. A 16C Dominican monastery with an excellent **hostelry** and restaurant is at the top (℘ 923 16 40 00; http://hospederiapeñadefrancia.com).

Avenida de Las Batuecas★

◗ To the S.

This road climbs to the Portillo Pass (1 240m/4 068ft) then plunges into a deep, green valley where the Batuecas Monastery is situated.

🚗 DRIVING TOUR

SIERRA DE BÉJAR AND SIERRA DE CANDELARIO

76km/47mi to the SE. Allow one day. Meander through the gorges of the Alagón and Cuerpo de Hombre rivers amid walnut and oak forests.

◗ Head east. After 2km/1.2mi, turn to Cepeda, then Sotoserrano. Head toward Lagunilla to reach the N 630 at Puerto de Béjar. **Baños de Montemayor**, a pleasant spa, and **Hervás**, with its old *Judería* (Jewish Quarter) are in this area. Return to Puerto de Béjar. One road heads toward Candelario.

Candelario★★

This picturesque village on the sierra's flanks retains traditional stone homes with elegant balconies.

Béjar

4km/2.5mi NW.

Béjar, known for its textiles, stretches along a narrow rock platform at the foot of the Sierra de Béjar.

◗ Leave Béjar along the SA 515.

Miranda del Castañar

34km/21mi W.

Pass the 15C **castle** and penetrate the old quarter through the Puerta de San Ginés; **Mogarraz** (10km/6.2mi W) and **San Martín del Castañar** (10km/6.2mi N) are charming villages worth a visit.

◗ Take the SA 202 back to La Alberca.

ADDRESSES

🏨 STAY AND 🍴 EAT

▱⊜⊜ **Hotel Antiguas Eras** – Av Batuecas 29, La Alberca. ℘923 415 113. www.antiguaseras.com. 34 rooms. Restaurant ⊜⊜⊜. This charming country hotel in the heart of La Alberca occupies wooden-beamed homes and affords sierra views.

Zamora★

Zamora rises above a plain on the banks of the River Duero. The 12C and 13C saw the construction of its cathedral and numerous Romanesque churches, which stand in the well-preserved old town.

A BIT OF HISTORY

Traces remain of the walls that made Zamora the western bastion along the Duero during the so-called Reconquista. The city figured in repeated struggles for the throne of Castilla.

SIGHTS

Catedral de Zamora★

Pl. de la Catedral. Open daily Apr 10am–2pm, 5–8pm; May–Sep 10am–8pm; Oct–Mar 10am–2pm, 4.30–7pm. Closed 1 & 6 Jan, 24 Dec pm, 25 Dec, 31 Dec pm. €5 (cathedral and museum), free Mon pm. ✆980 53 06 44.
The Cathedral was built between 1151 and 1174 and subsequently altered. The north front is Neoclassical in keeping with the square in front; it contrasts with the Romanesque bell tower and graceful cupola covered in scallop tiling. The south front, the only original part, has blind arcades and a Romanesque portal with unusual covings featuring openwork festoons.
The aisles are transitional Romanesque-Gothic, the vaulting ranging from broken barrel to pointed ogive.
Slender painted ribs support the luminous **dome★** above the transept. Late Gothic master woodcarvers worked here. Note the fine **grilles** enclosing the presbytery, *coro*, two 15C Mudéjar pulpits, certain chapels and **choir stalls★★** with biblical, allegorical and burlesque scenes.
The museum, off the cloisters, displays 15C Flemish and 17C **tapestries★★**. Note the 16C Renaissance monstrance and a Virgin and Child and Little St John sculpted by Bartolomé Ordóñez. The **Jardín del Castillo** (Castle Garden) to the rear commands fine views.

▶ **Population:** 63 831
⚙ **Michelin Map:** 575 H 12.
❚ **Info:** Avenida Príncipe de Asturias 1. ✆980 53 36 94. www.zamora-turismo.es.
◖ **Location:** Zamora is NW of Madrid, 65km/40mi N of Salamanca. ▭Zamora.
❚❚ **Kids:** The Museo Etnografico's costumes and shepherds' art will amuse children.
◷ **Timing:** Allow a long morning to visit the old town, then in the afternoon take one of the excursions below.

Baltasar Lobo Centro de Arte★

Pl. de la Catedral. Open Tue–Sun 10 –2pm, 6–9pm (Oct–Apr 10am–2pm, 5–8pm). ✆616 92 95 77. www.fundacionbaltasarlobo.com
This arts centre is dedicated to the work of sculptor Baltasar Lobo, whose marble and bronze works are kept here. Born in Zamora province, he lived and worked in Paris, where his work evolved toward abstraction under the influence of Jean Arp and Henry Moore.

Romanesque churches★

Open generally Tue–Sun 2 Mar–Sept 10am–1pm, 5–8pm; Oct–6 Jan 10am–2pm, 4.30–6.30pm.
Zamora and its environs boast a treasure trove of Romanesque churches. Built around the 12C, these have portals without tympana surrounded by multifoil arches and often possess heavily carved archivolts.
Larger churches had domes on squinches over the transept crossing. The best examples in Zamora, open to the public with coordinated times, are the **Magdalena** (C. Rúa de los Francos), **Santa María la Nueva** (Pl. de Santa María la Nueva), **San Juan de Puerta Nueva** (Pl. Mayor), **Santa María de la Horta** (Barrio de la Horta), **Santo Tomé** (Pl de . Santo Tomé) and **Santiago del Burgo** (Santa Clara).

Zamora with the cathedral and the Duero

© José Antonio Moreno/age fotostock

👥 Museo Etnográfico de Castilla y Léon★

C. Sacramento, Pl. Viriato.
Open Tue–Sun 10am–2pm, 5–8pm. €3,
free Sun pm and Tue–Thu 7–8pm, 6 Dec
23 Apr, 18 May, 12 Oct. ☏980 531 708.
www.museo-etnografico.com.
An wide-reaching collection of popular
and folk art from across the region with
videos and written explanations.

Seigniorial Mansions/ Museo de Zamora

Palacio del Cordón, Pl. de Santa Lucía
2. Open Tue–Sat 10am–2pm, 5–8pm
(Oct–Jun 4–7pm), Sun & public hols
10am–2pm. €1, free Sat, Sun.
☏980 51 61 50.
The museum features archaeology
and fine art; the **Palacio de los Momos**
(*San Torcuato 7*) has elegant Isabelline
windows.

EXCURSIONS

San Pedro de la Nave★

▶ 19km/11.8mi NW. Leave Zamora
on the N 122–E 82. Follow the N 122
for 12km/7.4mi, then turn right onto
Campillo.
The Visigothic church here (open Mar–
Sep Tue–Sun 10.30am–1.30pm, 5–8pm;
Oct–6 Feb Fri–Sat 10am–1.30pm, 4.30–
6.30pm, Sun 10am–1.30pm. ☏980 553
078) dates to the late 7C. Endangered

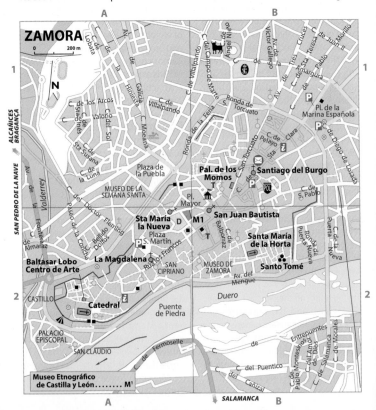

by the damming of the Esla, it was rebuilt with millimetric precision at El Campillo. It is remarkable for the Biblical carving on the transept **capitals**. The frieze, halfway up, presents Christian symbols including grapes and doves.

Arcenillas

❍ 7km/4.3mi SE on the C 605.

In the village church (Nuestra Señora de la Asunción; try your luck asking for the key at Bar Las Tablas, across the way), 15 **panels★** depicting the life, death and resurrection of Christ have been reassembled from the late 15C Gothic altarpiece designed for Zamora Cathedral by **Fernando Gallego**, one of the great Castilian painters of the age.

Benavente

❍ 66km/41mi N along the N 630.

The Renaissance **Castillo de los Condes de Pimentel** (✆980 51 44 98; www.parador.es), now a Parador, retains its 16C Torre del Caracol, with a carved artesonado ceiling and valley **views**. The **Hospital de la Piedad**, once a pilgrims' hospital (C. de Santa Cruz 5), keeps a magnificent cloister (access 9am–8pm). The transitional **Iglesia de Santa María del Azogue** (Pl. de Santa María; ✆980 66 42 58) has five apses and two Romanesque portals. A beautiful 13C **Annunciation** stands at the crossing. The **Iglesia de San Juan del Mercado** (Pl. de San Juan 4; ✆980 63 00 80) has a 12C carving on the south portal illustrating the journey of the Magi.

Toro

❍ 33km/21mi E along the N 122–E 82.

Toro, a wine town on the River Duero, has preserved an exceptional cluster of Romanesque churches, most notably **San Salvador de los Caballeros**: The brick Mudéjar Romanesque church was originally Templar, built on circular floorplans with elongated blind arcades on the curving facades; it holds Mudéjar frescoes and a surprisingly admirable selection of art (open Tue–Sun, hours as for the Colegiata). In the **Monasterio del Sancti Spiritus** (Tue–Sun, 1 hour guided tours 10.30, 11.30, 12.30, 4.30 and 5.30; €4.50) is an impressive collection of local Romanesque and other art. A number of the town's other recently restored monuments include the **Iglesia de San Lorenzo** and the bullring, one of the oldest in Spain. Wineries are open certain days of the week, and Toro's gutsy, high-octane reds – the best of which are made from gnarled centennial vines – feature in its handful of tapas bars.

Colegiata de Santa María La Mayor★

Pl. de la Colegiata. Open Tue–Sun Mar–Sep 10.30am–2pm, 5–7.30pm; Oct–Feb 10am–2pm, 4.30–6.30pm. €4. ✆980 69 47 47. www.romanicozamora.es.

Construction began in 1160 with the elegant transept lantern and ended in 1240 with the west portal. The Romanesque **north portal** illustrates the Old Men of the Apocalypse and angels linked by a rope. Note the Gothic **west portal★★**, repainted in the 18C.

Statues on the pier and tympanum jambs have youthful faces. Start beneath the **cupola★**, one of the first of its kind in Spain with two tiers of windows in the drum. Polychrome wood statues stand against the pillars at the end of the nave on consoles, one carved with an amusing version of the Birth of Eve (below the angel).

In the sacristy is the *Virgin and the Fly★*, a magnificent Flemish painting by either Gérard David or Hans Memling.

ADDRESSES

🏠 STAY AND ♈EAT

⊜⊜⊜⊜ **Parador de Zamora (Condes de Alba de Aliste)** – Plaza Viriato 5, Zamora. ✆902 54 79 79. www.Paradores.es. 52 rooms. ⊑€17. Sleep in an immaculately preserved 15C Renaissance palace replete with armour, tapestries, canopied beds and other baronial decor. There is a swimming pool. The restaurant serves elevated traditional fare.

Castilla y León:
Segovia, Valladolid & Soria

The central provinces of Spain's northern tableland offer landscapes of unexpected splendour. Segovia's mountains, the wheat plains of Valladolid and Soria's river valleys and gorges make for scenic drives and hikes. Segovia and Valladolid, court cities long before Madrid, have preserved contrasting architectural and artistic legacies. Soria is more understated but doesn't disappoint with its medieval spiritual retreats and military monuments that speak to its history as a frontier between Christian and Islamic Spain.

Highlights

1 Gazing in awe at the **Roman Aqueduct** of Segovia (p177)
2 Strolling in the gardens of **La Granja's** royal palace (p183)
3 Admiring richly coloured Baroque sculpture in **Valladolid's** museum (p185)
4 Roaming the cloisters of Santa María de Huerta, **Soria** (p190)
5 Visiting the Moorish ruins of **Gormaz castle**, the largest in Europe (p191)

Segovia

The Sierra de Guadarrama's hill towns provide cool refuge from the summer heat: Medieval Pedraza de la Sierra, for example, is a popular weekend bolt hole. At the foot of the sierra stands the Palacio de la Granja de San Ildefonso, whose lush, manicured gardens run up into woodland. To the north, Segovia is famous for its Roman aqueduct – a triumph of art and engineering – and Romanesque churches. Its fairytale castle (Alcázar) is actually a fanciful mid-19C recreation of the medieval original. Explore the winding streets of the *Judería* (Jewish Quarter) before indulging in Segovia's star dish, *cochinillo asado* (roast suckling pig).

Valladolid

By comparison Valladolid, once capital of Castille, is prosaic, although its Isabelline architecture and National Museum of Sculpture are outstanding. In Holy Week, church sculptures are processed through the streets in great solemnity. Elsewhere in the province is Tordesillas, where the famous treaty dividing the New World was signed. The castles of Medina del Campo, Montealegre Peñafiel and Simancas, rising up above the wide-horizoned vineyards and fields, are a reminder of battles fought here long ago.

Soria

Soria is one of Spain's least populated provinces, and that's precisely its allure. Its rugged expanses are dotted with medieval monasteries such as San Juan de Duero, a picturesque riverside ruin. Castles built on an epic scale to defend a warring medieval frontier, such as Gormaz, loom above dramatic, bare red rock.

A trio of small towns – Burgo de Osma, Peñaranda and Berlanga – hold unexpected artistic wealth. Excursions to see them may be combined with scenic day hikes.

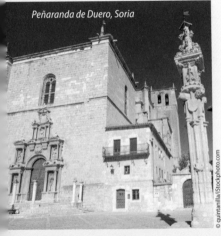

Peñaranda de Duero, Soria

© quintanilla/iStockphoto.com

Segovia★★★

This austere, imposing city, at 1 000m/3 280ft, rises on a triangular rock like an island in the Castilian plain. Its sturdy walls enclose a maze of narrow streets dotted with churches, mansions and Roman monuments. The old town and aqueduct are a UNESCO World Heritage site.

A BIT OF HISTORY

Noble Segovia, residence of King Alfonso X, the Wise, and King Henry IV, played a decisive role in the history of Castilla. It reached its zenith in the 15C, when its population numbered 60 000.

Isabel the Catholic, Queen of Castilla

On the death of Henry IV in 1474, many grandees refused to recognise the legitimacy of his daughter, Doña Juana, known as **La Beltraneja**. In Segovia, the grandees proclaimed Henry's half-sister, Isabel, Queen of Castilla – thus paving the way for Spain's unification (Isabel would marry Ferdinand, heir apparent of Aragón). La Beltraneja, aided by her husband, Alfonso V of Portugal, pressed her claim but renounced it in 1479 after defeats at Toro and Albuera.

The 'Comuneros'

In 1519, three years after Charles I (Carlos I) landed in Asturias to take possession of his Spanish dominions, he left the country to be proclaimed Holy Roman Emperor (as Charles V).
His absence, perceived allegiance to Flanders and push for higher taxes led to the peasant Revolt of the Comuneros, which sought to quash the aristocratic, Dutch dominance imposed by Charles I. The movement swept Castilla and culminated in a blockade of Segovia. Yet despite the Comuneros' efforts and widespread support across the Peninsula, they were ultimately crushed at Villalar in 1521.

▶ **Population:** 55 220
⚲ **Michelin Map:** 575 or 576 J 17 – map 121 Alrededores de Madrid.
▯ **Information:** Azoguejo 1. ☏921 466 720. www. turismodesegovia.com.
◖ **Location:** Segovia is 92km/57mi NW of Madrid. The AVE high-speed train service calls at Segovia-Guiomar, 6km/3.5mi from the town centre. ▭Segovia (AVE).
◉ **Don't Miss:** The Alcázar, Roman aqueduct and streets lined with palaces.
◕ **Timing:** Allow a full day in town, plus time for excursions.

👣 WALKING TOUR

CIUDAD VIEJA★★ (OLD TOWN)

4hr. ⚲See town plan.

Acueducto★★★

Pl. del Azogüejo.
This soaring structure with two tiers of arches was built during the reign of Trajan in the 1C to bring water from the River Acebeda to the upper part of town. It remains one of the finest examples of Roman engineering still standing, its boulders held together without a lick of mortar. It stretches 728m/2 388ft long and rises to 28m/92ft in Plaza del Azoguejo.

◖ Take Calle Cervantes.

Casa de los Picos

C. de Juan Bravo 33. Open year-round (patio and exhibitions only) daily 12–2pm, 7–9pm (Oct–Mar 6–8pm). ☏921 46 26 74.
www.turismodesegovia.com.
The 'house of spikes', faced entirely with granite blocks carved into pyramid-

Casa Solier.. R
Casa de los Lozoya.............................. V
Museo Esteban Vicente...................... M
Palacio de los Condes de Cheste........ F
Palacio de los Marqueses de Moya.... B
Palacio del Marqués de Lozoya.......... E
Palacio del Marqués de Quintanar..... K

shaped reliefs, is the most original of Segovia's 15C mansions. It is now home to an art school.

▶ Take Juan Bravo and turn onto Pl. de Platero Oquendo.

Casa del Conde de Alpuente

Pl. Conde Alpuente. Closed to the public. The elegant facade of this 15C Gothic house, now a government building, is adorned with *esgrafiado*.

▶ Continue down Platero Oqueno.

La Alhóndiga

C. de Alhóndiga 10.
This 15C granary is now an exhibition hall & public event space. Peek your head in to see what's on.

▶ Return to Juan Bravo.

Plaza de San Martín★

This square in the heart of the old aristocratic quarter epitomises Segovia's medieval splendour. Around the square stand the **Casa del Siglo XV** (15C House), aka Juan Bravo's house, with a gallery beneath the eaves; the 16C tower of the **Casa de los Lozoya**; the Plateresque facade of the **Casa Solier** (aka Casa de Correas); and ornate entrances to other large houses.

In the middle is the 12C **Iglesia de San Martín★**, a church framed on three sides by a covered gallery on pillars with carved strapwork and animal figures on the capitals.

▶ The Pl. de las Bellas Artes opens off Pl. San Martín.

Roman aqueduct

© René Mattes/hemis.fr

Museo de Arte Contemporáneo Esteban Vicente

Plazuela de las Bellas Artes. Open Thu–Fri 11am–2pm, 4–7pm; Sat 11am–8pm, Sun & public hols 11am–3pm. €3; free Thu. ℘921 46 20 10. www.museoestebanvicente.es.

This museum is set in the palace of Henry IV in the Hospital de Viejos (Old People's Hospital). The only trace of the original building is the fine chapel with a Mudéjar ceiling, now an auditorium. The museum exhibits the work of artist Esteban Vicente (1904–2001) and is also used for concerts.

▷ Follow Juan Bravo past the town's old prison.

Iglesia del Corpus Christi/ Antigua Sinagoga Mayor

Po. del Salón. Opening times vary; check with the tourist office. €1.

The convent, largely reconstructed following a fire, was formerly the Antigua Sinagoga Mayor, the city's largest synagogue. Close by is the **Centro Didáctico de la Judería,** or Centre for Interpretation of the Jewish Quarter (C. Judería Vieja 12; open Mon–Tue 10am–2pm, Wed–Fri 10am–2pm, 3pm-6pm, Thu-Sat 10am-1pm, 3–6pm, Sun 10am–1pm. ℘921 46 23 96, www. juderia.turismodesegovia.com).

▷ Take Isabel la Católica.

Plaza Mayor

Dominated by the impressive Cathedral, the arcaded square with its terrace cafés remains the centre of town life. Also on the square are the **ayuntamiento** (town hall) and Teatro Juan Bravo.

Catedral★★

C. Marqués del Arco 1. Open Mon–Sat 9.30am–6.30pm (Oct–Mar until 5.30pm), Sun 1.15–5.30pm. Closed 25 Dec, 1 & 6 Jan. €3; free Sun 9.30am–1.30pm. ℘921 46 22 05. www.catedraldesegovia.es

The domed behemoth you see today was built during the reign of Emperor Charles V over the ashes of another during the Comuneros' Revolt in 1521. It's a testament to the survival of the Gothic style in the 16C, when Renaissance architecture was at its height. The golden stone, soaring bell tower (which you can climb at 10.30am, 12.30pm or 4pm) and stepped east face with pinnacles and delicate balustrades bring grace to the imposing building. The width of the aisles combines with the decorative lines of the pillars and ribs in the vaulting to make the interior feel improbably airy and elegant. The chapels are closed by fine wrought-iron screens. The first off the south aisle contains as its altarpiece an *Entombment* by Juan de Juni. The *coro* stalls, in late-15C Flamboyant Gothic style, are relics from the earlier Cathedral.

Claustro★ – The 15C cloisters from the former Cathedral, near the Alcázar, were rebuilt on the new site. In the Sala

Capitular (chapter house), 17C Brussels **tapestries★** illustrate the story of Queen Zenobia.

◐ Follow Mqués del Arco and Daioz to Pl. de la Reina Victoria Eugenia.

Alcázar★★★

Pl. de la Reina Victoria Eugenia.
Open daily Apr–Oct 10am–8pm;
Nov–Mar 10am–6pm. Closed 24 Dec and 1& 6 Jan. €8; tower only, €2.50; free Tue (except holidays) 2–4pm for EU citizens.
✆921 46 07 59.
www.alcazardesegovia.com.
The Alcázar, jutting out on a cliff overlooking the valley, was built above a former (possibly Roman) fortress in the 13C and modified in the 15C and 16C by Henry IV and Philip II. In 1764, Charles III converted the building into the **Real Colegio de Artillería** (Royal Artillery School), but in 1862 it suffered a devastating fire. Reconstruction was completed at the end of the 19C, hence its neo-Gothic look.
The furniture and richly decorated Mudéjar artesonado work, mostly from the 15C, are original and were brought from various Castilian towns. Its keep is flanked by corbelled turrets.
The main rooms of note are the Royal Chamber (Cámara Real) and Sala de los Reyes (Monarchs' Room). The Sala del Cordón and terrace command a fine panorama of the fertile Eresma Valley, 15C Monasterio de El Parral and 13C Iglesia de la Vera Cruz, built by the Knights of Templar.
The artillery school pays tribute to the 18C chemistry lab once here, where French chemist Louis Proust formulated his law of definite proportion.
The views from the keep (152 steps) stretch across the city to the Sierra de Guadarrama.

◐ Take Velarde to Pl. de San Esteban, passing through the medieval Porte de la Claustra.

Iglesia de San Esteban (St Stephen's Church)

Pl. de San Esteban. Closed to the public.
One of the latest (13C) and most beautiful of Segovia's Romanesque churches has porticoes running along two of its sides with finely carved capitals. The five-storey **tower★** has elegant bays and slender columns on the corners.

◐ Take Valdeláguila to Pl. de la Trinidad.

Iglesia de la Santísima Trinidad (Holy Trinity Church)

Pl. de la Trinidad 6. Open during Mass.
This austere Romanesque church has a decorated apse with blind arcading and capitals carved with imaginary beasts and plant motifs.

◐ Take Trinidad and San Agustín and turn left down Zuloaga to Pl. de Colmenares.

Iglesia de San Juan de los Caballeros

Pl. de Colmenares. Open Wed 9am–4pm.
€1. ✆921 46 06 13.
www.turismodesegovia.com.
This is Segovia's oldest Romanesque church (11C). Its portico (taken from the church of San Nicolás) has carvings of portrait heads, plant motifs and animals. The church, which was almost in ruins at the turn of the 20C, was bought in 1905 by Daniel Zuloaga, who converted it into his home and workshop. Today it houses the **Museo Zuloaga**, exhibiting ceramics by the artist and his nephew Ignacio Zuloaga.

Plaza del Conde de Cheste

On the square stand the palaces of the Marqués de Moya, the Marqués de Lozoya, the Condes de Cheste and the Marqués de Quintanar.

OUTSIDE THE WALLS
Museo de Segovia★

Casa del Sol – C. del Socorro 11.
Open Tue–Sat 10am–2pm, 4–7pm (Jul–Sep 5–8pm), Sun & public hols

10am–2pm. €1; free weekends, hols. ℘921 460 613.
www.turismodesegovia.com.

Segovia's archaeological, ethnological and fine arts museum collection ranges from exhibits on early hydraulic systems and present-day drovers' roads to exceptional pieces of classical art. Galleries show prints by Rembrandt and Dürer and sculpture and altarpieces from local monasteries and churches. Glass works made at La Granja's Royal Factory are a highlight.

Iglesia de San Millán★

Av. Fernández Ladreda.
Open during Mass.

The early-12C church stands in the middle of a large square, which allows a full view of its pure, primitive Romanesque lines and two porticoes with finely carved modillions and capitals. The three aisles have alternating pillars and columns as in Jaca's cathedral. The apse has blind arcading and a decorative frieze. The transept has Moorish ribbed vaulting.

Monasterio de El Parral★

Alameda del Eresma. Open Wed–Sun 11am–5pm. Donations. ℘921 43 12 98.
www.monjesjeronimos.es.

The monastery was founded by Henry IV in 1445 and later entrusted to the Hieronymites. The **church**, behind its unfinished facade, has a Gothic nave with beautifully carved doors, a 16C altarpiece by Juan Rodríguez and, on either side of the chancel, the Plateresque tombs of the Marquis and Marchioness of Villena.

Iglesia de la Vera-Cruz★

Camino de Zamarramala. Open Tue–Sun 10.30am–1.30pm, 4–7pm (Oct–Mar until 6pm). Closed Tue am. €2, free Tue pm. ℘921 43 14 75.
www.turismodesegovia.com.

The unusual polygonal chapel was erected in the 13C, probably by the Templars; it now belongs to the Order of Malta. A circular corridor surrounds two small chambers, one above the other, where secret ceremonies were conducted. The Capilla del Lignum Crucis holds an ornate Flamboyant Gothic altar. There is a good view of Segovia.

EXCURSIONS

Palacio Real de Riofrío★

❯ Bosque de Riofrío, Navás de Riofrío. 11km/6.8mi S of Segovia on the N 603. Open year round Tue–Sun & public hols 10am–8pm (Oct–Mar until 6pm). See website for dates closed. €4; free Wed–Thu 5–8pm summer, 3–6pm winter for EU citizens, for all 18 May & 12 Oct. ℘914 54 87 00.
www.patrimonionacional.es.

The palace at Riofrío was planned by Isabel Farnese as the equal of La Granja, which she had to vacate on the death of her husband, Philip V. Construction began in 1752, but at 84m x 84m (276ft x 276ft) it was never more than a hunting lodge. It's built around a grand Classical-style courtyard. The green-and-pink facade reflects Isabel's Italian origins.

Castillo de Coca★★

❯ Camino Antigua Cauca Romana, Coca. 52km/32mi NW of Segovia along the C 605 and SG 341. Guided tours Mon–Fri 10.30am–1pm, 4.30–6pm, Sat–Sun & hols 11am–1pm, 4–6pm. Closed 1st Tue of month, Jan and 25 Dec. €2.70. ℘617 57 35 54. www.castillodecoca.com.

This pink-tinged picturebook fortress is the most outstanding example of Mudéjar military architecture in Spain. It was built in the late 15C by Moorish craftsmen for the archbishop of Sevilla, Fonseca, and consists of three concentric perimetres flanked by polygonal corner towers and turrets. A massive keep sits at its heart. The **Torre del Homenaje** (keep) and **capilla** (chapel), which contains Romanesque wood carvings, are open to the public.

Arévalo

❯ 60km/37mi NW along the C 605.
Isabel the Catholic spent her childhood in the 14C **castle**, whose massive crenellated keep dominates this town with Romanesque-Mudéjar brick churches and several old mansions.

Plaza de la Villa★ is one of the best-preserved town squares in Castilla with its half-timbered brick houses resting on pillared porticoes.

Pedraza★★

◖ 40km/25mi NE of Segovia on N 110.
🅘 Real 40. ✆921 50 86 66.
www.pedraza.info.

Pedraza is a popular weekend retreat from Madrid, bounded by medieval walls and veined with winding streets. The **Puerta de la Villa** gateway opens into a maze of country-style houses. The first medieval building of interest is the **Cárcel de la Villa** (open daily 11.30am–2pm, 3.30–7.30pm, until 3.45pm weekdays; €3; ✆921 50 99 55), the former jail. The ancient **Plaza Mayor** is surrounded by ancient porticoes topped by balconies and the slender Romanesque bell tower of San Juan. The medieval **castle** (open Wed–Sun, summer 11am–2pm, 5–8pm, winter 4–6pm; guided tours every 30 mins; €6; ✆921 50 98 25; www.museoignaciozuloaga.com) houses works by artist **Ignacio Zuloaga** (◖see p178).

From Pedraza you can continue on the N110, once a Roman road, to Riaza and Ayllón, quaint, non-touristy Castilian towns. Ayllón gives access to **Tiermes archaeological sight★★** (via Montejo and the SO-P-4120; open Tue–Sat 10am–2pm and 4–7pm, 5–8pm Jul–Sept, morning only public hols; €5; ✆975 35 20 52; www.museodetiermes.es), a Celtiberian town hewn into a sandstone cliff. Its amphitheatre is stunning.

Sepúlveda

◖ 25km/15.5mi N of Segovia. 🅘Santos Justo y Pastor 8. ✆921 54 04 25. www.sepulveda.es.

As you approach this attractive village, you'll get a good view of its terraced **position★** on the slopes of a deep gorge. Park at the town hall square, overlooked by castle ruins, then walk up to the **Iglesia de San Salvador** (Subida al Salvador 10; open Sat-Sun 11am-6pm; free guided tours available in summer; ✆921 54 04 25) for a fine view. The church is typical Segovia Romanesque

with one of the oldest side doors in Spain, dating to 1093.

On Calle Conde de Sepúlveda, the **Casa del Parque Hoces del Río Duratón (Duratón Gorges)** (open Jul–Aug Mon–Thu and Sun 10am–3pm, Fri–Sat & hols until 6pm, check website for further opening hours; €1; ✆921 54 03 22, www.patrimonionatural.org) provides information about hiking routes and local canoeing. The park runs along the middle stretch of the river, hemmed in by spectacular 70m/230ft walls and sheltering the Romanesque hermitage of San Frutos.

🚗 DRIVING TOUR

From Segovia to Madrid via La Granja and El Paular
159km/99mi.
Allow one day for visits to the palace and monastery or two days to walk in the mountains.

The bare peaks of the **Sierra de Guadarrama★**, visible from Segovia, rise above steep granite and gneiss slopes blanketed in oak and pine. Mountain-born streams feed the province's reservoirs. At the foot of the sierra's slopes on the western side stands La Granja's royal summer palace. On the eastern side, you can visit the restored medieval monastery of El Paular.

◖ Take the CL 601 from Segovia to La Granja.

Palacio Real de La Granja de San Ildefonso★★
Pl. de España 17. Open year round Tue–Sun 10am–8pm (Oct–Mar until 6pm). from €9 incl gardens; fountains only, €4. Free Wed–Thu 5–8pm summer, 3–6pm winter for EU citizens and for all 18 May and 12 Oct. ✆914 54 87 00. www.patrimonionacional.es.

La Granja is a little Versailles at 1 192m/3 911ft, built in 1731 by Philip V in pure nostalgia for the palace of his childhood. Philip V and his second wife, Isabel Farnese, are buried in the collegiate church.

Palace

Galleries and chambers, faced with marble or hung with velvet, are lit by chandeliers. The **Museo de Tapices★★** (Tapestry Museum) contains principally 16C Flemish hangings, notably (**3rd gallery**) nine of the *Honours and Virtues* series and the 15C Gothic *St Jerome*, modelled after a cartoon by Raphael.

Gardens★★

Open Oct and Mar 10am–6.30pm, Apr until 8pm, Nov–Feb until 6pm, May–15 Jun and Sep until 8pm, 16 Jun–Aug until 9pm. Fountains on for Holy Week, 30 May, 25 Jul, 25 Aug and (water levels allowing) 5.30pm Sat–Sun & public hols.

The ground was levelled with explosives before the French landscape gardeners (Carlier, Boutelou) and sculptors (Dumandré, Thierry) descended. They stand in contrast to the more organic woodland vistas. The chestnut trees, brought from France at great expense, are majestic. The **fountains★★** begin at the Neptune Basin, go on to the New Cascade (Nueva Cascada), a multicoloured marble staircase in front of the palace, and end at the Fuente de la Fama (Fame Fountain), which jets up a full 40m/131ft.

▶ Head south on the CL-601.

♟♟ Real Fábrica de Cristales de La Granja (Royal Glass Factory)

Museum: Open Apr–Sep Tue–Sat 10am–6pm, Sun until 3pm; Oct–Mar Tue–Fri and Sun 10am–3pm, Sat until 6pm. Glass blowing: Open Tue–Fri and Sun 10am–2.45pm, Sat 11am–1.45pm, 4–5.45pm. Guided tours available. Closed 1 & 6 Jan, 25 Dec. €6, free Wed Apr–Sep 3–6pm. ℘921 01 07 00. www.fcnv.es.

The present building, erected in 1770 under Charles III, contains magnificent exhibits of contemporary glass and offers glass-blowing demonstrations, equally fascinating to kids and adults.

▶ Leave La Granja on the CL 601; it soon starts to climb steeply, with hairpin bends.

Puerto de Navacerrada★

1 860m/6 102ft.

The pass, a ski resort on the borders of the two Castillas, commands a beautiful **view★** of the Segovian plateau.

▶ Take the M 604 at the junction on the pass.

Puerto de los Cotos

1 830m/6 004ft.

The pass is a base for ski lifts. 🏃 From the upper terminus at Zabala, hike in summer to the Laguna de Peñalara (15min), a former glacial cirque, the Picos de Dos Hermanas (Summit of the Two Sisters, 30min) and Peñalara (2 429m/7 967ft), the highest point in the sierra (45min). Trails for longer walks are also marked; enquire at the information centre at Zabala.

▶ Continue on the M 604 (the descent is gentler than the ascent).

Monasterio de Santa María de El Paular★

2km/1.2mi from Rascafría.
Guided tours of Monastery available daily (see website for current schedule); full-sung Mass at 12pm Sun & hols. ℘918 69 19 58.
www.monasteriopaular.com.

Castilla's earliest Carthusian monastery (1390) stands in the cool Lozoya Valley. The reconstructed complex includes a hotel in a former palace. The **church** has a Flamboyant doorway by Juan Guas. There is a 15C alabaster **altarpiece★★** illustrating the Lives of the Virgin and Christ. More than 50 canvases portraying Carthusian history, painted by Vicenzo Carduccio, have been rehung in the cloister, for which they were specially painted in 1635. Close to the monastery stands the old stone Puente de Perdón (Absolution Bridge), named for those who walked across it to the gallows. It gives access to a recreational area with summer river pools and walking paths to the sierra's foothills.

Rascafría

2km/1.2mi from El Paular.

This lively and oft-overlooked small town, a green oasis most of the year, is the capital of the Upper Lozoya valley. Its main buildings cluster around an old bridge over the river. Restaurants, bars and rural charm abound.

▶ From Rascafría you can continue on the M 604 along the Lozoya valley, (32 km/20 mi) through small villages to join the A1 to Madrid, or take minor roads to Puerto de la Morcuera and Manzanares el Real.

Puerto de la Morcuera

As you reach the pass (1 796m/5 892ft), an extensive view opens toward El Vellón reservoir. A descent through moorland brings you to the wooded Lozoya depression. Río Lozoya is a well-known trout stream.

Manzanares El Real

The pride of this village is its **Castillo Viejo★** (open Mon–Fri 10am–4pm, Sat–Sun 10am–6pm; €5; ℘91 853 00 08; www.manzanareselreal.org), built in the 15C and one of the best-preserved medieval fortresses in Spain.

▶ The M 608 and M 607 lead to Madrid.

ADDRESSES

🛏 STAY

Hostal Don Jaime – C. Ochoa Ondategui, 8. Segovia. ℘921 444 790. www.hostaldonjaime.com. 6 rooms. €4. A plain and comfortable Castilian house close to the aqueduct.

Hotel Las Sirenas – C. Juan Bravo 30, Segovia. ℘921 46 26 63. http://hotelsirenas.webs3.mirai.es. 39 rooms. €10. A traditional hotel in the old quarter with an elegant stone facade, ornate staircase and and kitsch decor.

Hotel Spa La Casa Mudéjar – C. Isabel la Católica 8, Segovia. ℘921 46 62 50. www.lacasamudejar.com. 40 rooms. €14. Beautifully renovated hotel with modern spa facilities and delightful decoration including a coffered mudéjar-style ceiling. Enjoy Castilian and Sephardic cuisine on the patio.

La Posada de Don Mariano – Mayor, 14, Pedraza. ℘921 509 886. www.hoteldonmariano.com. 18 rooms. €9.50. Pretty bedrooms, helpful service and a terrace restaurant opening onto the Plaza Mayor.

Parador de la Granja – Los Infantes 3, Palacio de la Granja de San Idelfonso. ℘902 54 79 79. www.parador.es. 127 rooms. €19. Built in the 18C, the princes' pavilion, once part of the royal palace, is now a luxury hotel with a spa and landscaped swimming pool.

🍽/EAT

El Sitio – C. Infanta Isabel 9, Segovia. ℘921 46 09 96. A meeting place for locals, this easygoing tapas bar serves suckling pig at a bargain price.

Taberna López – C. San Cristobal 3, Segovia. ℘921 43 36 18. Meat lovers shouldn't miss this tavern serving hefty portions of grilled and roasted delicacies.

Narizotas – Pl. Medina del Campo 2, Segovia. ℘921 46 26 79. www.narizotas.net. This traditional restaurant is renowned for its roast suckling pig and a tasting menus; there's often music on the terrace.

Casa Felipe – Ctra. de Soria Plasencia, Torrecaballeros. ℘921 40 11 71. www.casafelipe.net. Delicious grilled meats cooked over an open fire and a pleasant terrace make this under-the-radar roadside *asador* a local favourite.

Mesón de Cándido – Pl. del Azoguejo 5, Segovia. ℘921 42 59 11. www.mesondecandido.es. Fittingly, Segovia's most iconic restaurant is set in a 15C house beneath the aqueduct. Feast here on Castilian classics served with panache.

FESTIVALS

The Hay Festival (www.hayfestival.com), which celebrates English and Spanish literature, visits Segovia each September.

Valladolid★

The former capital of Castilla and of a great empire, now a bustling modern city, stands amid vineyards and cereal fields.

A BIT OF HISTORY

From the 12C, Castilla's kings frequently resided at Valladolid. Peter the Cruel married there, as did Ferdinand and Isabel; it was the birthplace of Philip IV and his sister Anne of Austria, mother of Louis XIV.

THE CENTRE

The historic centre of Valladolid is a blend of carefully tended plazas and lively pedestrian ways that empty onto the Campo Grande park. The 16C Plaza Mayor, with more international chains than one might hope, remains the centre of activity.

SIGHTS

Colegio de San Gregorio

Cadenas de San Gregorio 1–2.
This is Valladolid's most impressive Isabelline building. On the sumptuous entrance★★★, attributed to Gil de Siloé and Simon of Cologne, fantasies from savages to interwoven thorn branches create a firm hierarchical composition rising from the doorway. The college is the seat of the **Museo Nacional de Escultura★★★** (👁see below).

Museo Nacional de Escultura★★★ (National Museum of Sculpture)

Cadenas de San Gregorio 1–2. Open Tue–Sat 10am–2pm, 4–7.30pm, Sun & public hols 10am–2pm. Closed 1, 6 Jan, 1 May, 8 Sept, 24–25, 31 Dec. €3; free Sat pm, Sun am, 18 April, 18 May, 12 Oct, 6 Dec. ℘983 25 03 75.
www.mecd.gob.es/mnescultura
From the 16C to the 17C, Valladolid was a major centre for sculpture, reflected in this museum's unparalleled collection of religious statues and processional figures in polychrome wood, a material well-suited to the expression of the dramatic.

▶ **Population:** 300 795
👁 **Michelin Map:** 575 H 15 (town plan).
🚇 **Info:** Acera de Recoletos (Pabellón de Cristal). ℘983 21 93 10. www.info.valladolid.es.
◐ **Location:** The city is at the centre of the northern section of the Spanish Meseta with an AVE high-speed train service from Madrid to Valladolid-Campo Grande.
🚆Valladolid (AVE).
👪 **Kids:** The interactive Museo de la Ciencia.

On the ground floor of the Palacio de Villena, aside from paintings (including an attractive *Pietà* by Pedro Berruguete) are sculptures of two 16C Mannerist masters: **Alonso Berruguete** (a remarkable altarpiece designed for the San Benito church) and **Juan de Juni** (*The Crucifixion* and portentous ensemble *Burial of Christ*). Works by **Gregorio Fernández**, a leading 16C exponent of Castilian Baroque, include *Passage to the Sixth Agony* and *Christ Recumbent*. There are also works of the Andalucían School (Martínez Montañés, Pedro de Mena, Alonso Cano).
On the second floor are works from the Renaissance by **Diego de Siloé** (*The Holy Family*) and **Felipe Vigarny** (*Virgin and Child*, a model of grace and elegance). There is also a fine **Rubens** (*Democritus and Heraclitus*).
On the third floor are Late Baroque (18C) works such as *St Francis of Assisi* by Salzillo and *Head of St Paul* by Juan Alonso de Villabrille y Ron. On the way down, admire a magnificent *Neapolitan nativity* of more than 180 figures.

Capilla del Colegio de San Gregorio★

Located within the Colegio.
Designed by Juan Guas, this Gothic chapel with an elevated *coro* contains an altarpiece by Berruguete, a tomb by Felipe Vigarny and carved choir stalls.

Holy Week procession in front of the entrance of Colegio de San Gregorio

© JoseIgnacioSoto/iStockphoto.com

Iglesia de San Pablo (St Paul's Church)

Pl. de San Pablo 4. Open before and after Mass. ✆983 35 17 48.

The **facade★★★** is outstanding. The lower section, by Simon of Cologne, consists of a portal with an ogee arch framed in a segmental arch; above, you'll see a large rose window and two coats of arms supported by angels.

Catedral★

C. Arribas 1 (entry from Pl. de la Universidad). Open Tue–Fri 10am–1.30pm, 4.30–7pm, Sat–Sun & public hols until 2pm. €4. ✆983 30 43 62.

The cathedral, commissioned ca. 1580 by Philip II, was distorted by the architect's 17C and 19C successors – in the octagonal tower, and the Baroque upper facade by Alberto Churriguera. Never completed, the **interior** remains one of Herrera's triumphs, though some critique the building's overall harmony. The altarpiece (1551) in the central apsidal chapel is by Juan de Juni.

Museo Diocesano y Catedralicio★

In the funerary chapels of the former Gothic Cathedral. Same entrance hours and as the cathedral; extra €4.

Note the Mudéjar cupolas in the Capilla de San Llorente. There is a **collection★** of sculptures, paintings and ornaments. Also on display are busts by Pedro de Mena (*Ecce Homo* and *Dolorosa*), 13C tombs, 13C Christs (one Protogothic with four nails), a dramatic *Ecce Homo* by Gregorio Fernández, the sculpture group *Lament for Christ* (c. 1500) and a 16C silver monstrance by Juan de Arfe. Outside, on the Baroque University facade, see sculptured and heraldic decoration by Narciso and Antonio Tomé.

Colegio Mayor de Santa Cruz

Cardenal Mendoza 1. Closed to the public.

This late-15C college is one of the first Renaissance buildings in Spain; the carved decoration at the entrance is Plateresque, but the rusticated stonework is Classical. The Neoclassic balconies and windows are 18C additions.

Iglesia de Nuestra Señora de las Angustias

C. de las Angustías 6.

The church, built by one of Herrera's disciples, contains Juan de Juni's masterpiece, the **Virgen de los Siete Cuchillos★** (*Virgin of the Seven Knives*).

Palacio Pimentel★

Pl. San Pablo ; enter via Agustinas .

Once a royal residence, where Charles V stayed, the building's facade has Plateresque details. Today it houses government offices. Meeting rooms Salón de Plenos and Sala de Comisiones have Mudéjar ceilings, which can be viewed 9am–3pm. The entrance hall, with a tiled frieze depicting key moments in Spanish history, is also open in the afternoons.

Museo Patio Herreriano de Arte Contemporáneo Español (Modern Spanish Art Museum)

Jorge Guillén 6. Open Tue–Fri 11am–2pm, 5–8pm, Sat 11am–8pm,

Sun 11am–3pm. Closed 25 Dec, 1 Jan. ℘983 36 29 08. www.museoph.org.
The **Herreran patio★** of the ex-monastery of San Benito houses this collection of Spanish art dating from 1918 with works by Dalí, Chillida, Miró and others.

Casa-Museo de Cervantes

Rastro 2. Open Tue–Sat 9.30am–3pm, Sun 10am–3pm. Closed 1 & 6 Jan, 1 May, 24–25 and 31 Dec. €3; free Sun, 18 Apri, May, 12 Oct, 6 Dec. ℘983 30 88 10. http://museocasacervantes.mcu.es.
The author of **Don Quixote** lived in this house from 1603 to 1606; some of his simple furnishings remain.

BEYOND THE CENTRE
👥 Museo de la Ciencia (Science Museum)

Av. Salamanca 59. Open Tue–Fri 10am–6pm, Sat & hols 10am–7pm, Sun 10am–3pm. From €4. Closed 1 & 6 Jan; 24, 25, 31 Dec. ℘983 14 43 00. www.museocienciavalladolid.es.
Valladolid's science museum includes a planetarium (see website for schedule) and thrilling temporary exhibitions.

EXCURSIONS
Castillo de Simancas

◐ 11km/6.8mi SW. Only the archive is open to public; www.mecd.gob.es.
This picturesque fortress was first used by Charles V as a state archives repository; it still fulfils that function.

Peñafiel★

◐ 55km/34mi E along the N 122.
Peñafiel was a stronghold on the Duero during the so-called Reconquista, and its massive 14C **Castillo★** (open Oct–Mar Tue–Sun 10.30am–2pm, 4–6pm; Apr–Sep Tue–Sun 10.30am–2pm, 4–8pm; closed 1 & 6 Jan, 24–25, 31 Dec; €6.60 castle and museum; guided wine tasting €9.20; ℘983 88 11 99; www. turismopenafiel.com) is positioned at the meeting point of three valleys. Its keep, reinforced by machicolated turrets, houses the **Museo Provincial del Vino**, which hosts tastings.

Also notable in Peñafiel is the Convento de San Pablo (ask at the tourist office about opening times; guided tours available; ℘983 881 526, www.turis-mopenafiel.com). Its church (1324) has a Mudéjar east end with Renaissance vaulting in the 16C Capilla del Infante.

Tordesillas

◐ 30km/19mi SW along the A 62.
The kings of Spain and Portugal signed the famous **Treaty of Tordesillas** here in 1494, dividing up the New World.

Real Monasterio de Santa Clara★

◐ C. de Alonso del Castillo Solorzano. Open Tue–Sat 10am–2pm, 4–6.30pm, Sun & public hols 10.30am–3pm. €6 incl Arabic baths; free Wed pm & Thu pm for EU citizens and for all 18 May. ℘914 54 87 00. www.patrimonionacional.es.
The palace built by Alfonso XI in 1350 was converted into a convent by Peter the Cruel. He installed María de Padilla here, to whom he might have been married. For María, homesick for Sevilla, he commissioned Mudéjar decoration. The **patio★** has multifoil and horseshoe arches, strapwork decoration and multicoloured tiles. In the **Capilla Dorada** (Gilded Chapel) are mementos and works of art. The choir has a particularly intricate **artesonado ceiling★★**.

Medina del Campo

◐ 54km/34mi SW along the A 62 and the A 6; 24km/15mi from Tordesillas.
🚌 Av. de la Estación 27.
In the Middle Ages, Medina was famous for its fairs, and a bustling market is still held in Medina del Campo on Sundays. Isabel the Catholic died here in 1504.

Castillo de la Mota★

Av. del Castillo. Open Apr–Sep Mon–Sat Visitor Centre 11am–2pm, 3–7pm (Oct–Mar 6pm). Sun & public hols 11am–2.30pm. Closed 2 Sept, 1 & 6 Jan, 24–31 Dec. €4. Guided visits available (book in advance). ℘983 81 00 63. www.castillodelamota.es.
Juana the Mad often stayed in this classic medieval castle. Cesare Borgia, the

Italian nobleman said to have inspired Machiavelli's *The Prince*, was locked up in the keep for two years.

Villa de Almenara-Puras: Museo de las Villas Romanas (Museum of Roman Villas)

◗ 51km/31.8mi S by the N 601. Turn at Almenara and continue 3km/1.9mi S. Open Tue–Sun 10.30am–2pm, 4.30–8pm; (Oct–Mar 4–6pm). Closed Jan, 24–25 and 31 Dec. €3. ✆983 62 60 36.
This museum features the remains of a sumptuous Roman villa of the 4C and its underlying 3C mosaics.

Castillo de Montealegre

◗ 35km/22mi NW from Valladolid along the VA 900 and the VA 912. Visitor centre open Apr–Sep Fri 5.30–7pm, weekends & hols 11.30am–1pm, 5–7pm. Castle open daily 7–9pm. ✆680 857 148. www.provinciadevalladolid.com.
The castle of Montealegre looms above low-lying wheat fields. Twice besieged, by Peter the Cruel and Charles V, its stalwart walls, 4m/13ft thick and 24m/79ft high, keep original Arab-medieval structures. In modern times it became a grain silo before restoration. Today it is home to the Centro de Interpretación del Medievo (Medieval Culture Centre).

Medina de Rioseco

◗ 40km/25mi NW along the N 601.
The picturesque narrow main street, or **Rúa**, of this agricultural centre is lined by porticoes on wooden pillars.
The 16C Iglesia de Santa María (Pl. de Santa María; open Tue–Sun 11am–2pm, 4–7pm; guided tours available; closed 1, 5 & 6 Jan, 24–25 & 31 Dec; €3; ✆983 72 50 26) features a central altarpiece carved by Esteban Jordán. Other churches house Holy Week processional sculptures and religious art, and the **Capilla de los Benavente★** (Benavente Chapel, 16C) contains a 16C retable by Juan de Juni.

ADDRESSES

🛏 STAY

🍴🛏 **Hotel El Nogal** – C. Conde Ansurez 10, Valladolid. ✆983 34 03 33. www.hotelelnogal.com. 24 rooms. ⬜€4.50. This hotel lies at the heart of the old town. Rooms are bright, airy and well-equipped. The restaurant offers a bargain €15 prix-fixe lunch Mon–Sat.

🍴🛏 **Hotel Zenit Imperial** – C. Peso 4. ✆983 33 03 00. http://imperial.zenit hoteles.com. 63 rooms. ⬜€9. Restaurant 🍴🛏🛏. A Valladolid institution, with good online deals, set in an impeccably maintained redbrick 16C Gallo mansion.

🍴🛏🛏🛏 **Abadía Retuerta LeDomaine** – Ruetuerta, Valladolid. ✆983 68 03 14. www.abadia-retuerta. com. 30 rooms. No 'best hotels in Spain' list is complete without Abadía Retuerta, the ultra-luxurious retreat and winery surrounded by vineyards outside Valladolid. It takes in a 12C abbey and Michelin-starred restaurant (🍴🛏🛏🛏).

🍴 EAT

🍴 **Pita.gr** – C. Bajada de la Libertad 3, Valladolid. ✆983 45 47 21. Closed Tue. Fresh mezes, gyros and flavourful stews lure locals to this laid-back (and family-friendly) Greek restaurant.

🍴🛏🛏 **Molino de Palacios** – Av. de la Constitucion 16, Peñafiel. ✆646 20 37 70. Closed dinner daily, Mon, 1st fortnight in Jul. Roast milk-fed lamb is this riverside *asador's* speciality; adventurous eaters shouldn't miss the locally made blood sausage (*morcilla*).

🍴🛏🛏 **El Figón de Recoletos** – C. Acera de Recoletos 3. ✆983 39 60 43. www.elfigonderecoletos.es. Closed Sun eve & 20 Jul–12 Aug. Popular for business lunches and family meals, this standby offers terrific vegetable dishes and *lechazo*, roast lamb.

SHOPPING

Mercado del Val - C. Sandoval . ✆983 71 30 79. www.mercadodelval.com. Closed Sun from 4pm. Stock up on Ibérico ham and other Spanish delicacies at this 19C traditional market with multiple tapas bars within.

Soria★

This tranquil provincial capital stands on the banks of the Duero. The scenery and medieval atmosphere were lyricised by poets like Gustavo Adolfo Bécquer and Antonio Machado.

▶ **Population:** 39 987
⚙ **Michelin Map:** 575 G 22.
🚩 **Info:** Pl. Mariano Granados 4.
  ℘975 21 20 52.
  www.turismosoria.es.
◑ **Location:** Soria, in NE Spain, sits at an altitude of 1 050m/3 445ft on a plateau buffeted by the winds of the Meseta. 🚆 Soria.

SIGHTS

Iglesia de Santo Domingo★

Pl. de los Condes de Lérida 3. Open 7am–9pm.

The west front of this church has two tiers of blind arcades and a richly carved **portal★★**. The church's founders were Alfonso VIII and his queen, Eleanor Plantagenet (they appear on either side of the portal), hence the French appearance. Scenes include the early chapters of Genesis (on the capitals of the jamb shafts), the 24 Elders of the Apocalypse playing stringed instruments, the Massacre of the Innocents and Christ's childhood, Passion and Death.

Palacio de los Condes de Gómara (Palace of the Counts of Gómara)

Pl. de Aguirre 3.

The long facade – part Renaissance, part Classical – the bold tower and double patio exemplify late 16C opulence. Today the palace houses the city's law courts.

Iglesia de San Juan de Rabanera

Caballeros. Open for Mass. Ask at the tourist office about opening times.

The Romanesque portal taken from a ruined church dedicated to St Nicolas recalls the saint's life in the capitals on the slender columns on the right, and on the tympanum. The decoration at the east end shows Byzantine and Gothic influences. Crucifixes inside are Romanesque over the altar and Baroque in the north transept.

Museo Numantino (Numancia Museum)

Po. del Espolón 8. Open Tue–Sat 10am–2pm, 5-8pm (Oct–Jun 4–7pm), Sun & public hols 10am–2pm. Closed 1 Jan, 24–25 and 31 Dec. €1.20; free Sat–Sun. ℘975 22 13 97.

The collections in this recently restored museum include an outstanding range of artefacts from Celtiberian necropolises and coloured pottery from Numancia (7 km north of Soria).

Concatedral de San Pedro

Pl. de San Pedro. Open Sat 11am–2pm, 4–7pm, Sun 11am–2pm.

This 16C Gothic Cathedral is light and spacious; the **cloisters★** are even older, with three Romanesque galleries. The capitals have been delicately re-sculpted in Romanesque style.

Monasterio de San Juan de Duero★★

C. San Agustín 16. Open Tue–Sat 10am–2pm, 4–7pm, Sun & public hols 10am–2pm. €1; free Sat–Sun & hols. ℘975 22 13 97.

This monastery founded by the Hospitallers of St John of Jerusalem enjoys a rustic setting along the Duero. Only the graceful gallery arcading, with four different orders, remains of the 12C–13C **cloisters★**. The intersecting, overlapping arches owe much to Moorish art. The church contains a small lapidary museum. Two small chambers with beautiful historiated capitals stand at the entrance to the apse; the ciborium effect is unusual, as one might find in an Orthodox church. The site was the inspiration for Bécquer's *El Monte de las Ánimas* (*The Mountain of Souls*).

Parque Natural Laguna Negra y Circos glaciares de Urbión

Ermita de San Saturio

Camino de San Saturio. 1.3km/0.8mi S of N 122. Open Tue–Sat 10.30am–2pm, 4.30–7.30pm (6.30pm Nov–Mar, 8.30pm Jul–Aug), Sun 10.30am–2pm. ℘975 18 07 03.

A shaded path beside the Duero leads to the site where a hermit once sat in meditation. Today, in its place, there's an 18C octagonal chapel, with frescoes, hewn into the rock.

EXCURSIONS

Monasterio de Santa María de Huerta★★

◐ The monastery is just off the A 2 highway linking Madrid and Zaragoza (131km/82mi NE). It is 85km/53mi SE of Soria via the SC 20 A 15 and CL 116. Allow 1 hr for the visit. Open Mon–Sat 10am–1pm, Sun 10am–11.15am, daily 4–6pm. €3. ℘975 32 70 02. www.monasteriohuerta.org.

In 1144, a Cistercian community came to this border region between Castilla and Aragón. Monks settled in Huerta in 1162. The monastery is entered through a 16C triumphal arch.

Claustro Herreriano (Herreran Cloisters)

The 16C-17C buildings around the cloisters are the monks' living quarters.

Claustro de los Caballeros★ (Knights' Cloisters)

These 13–16C cloisters owe their name to the knights buried there. The arches at ground level are elegant, pointed and purely Gothic; above, the 16C gallery has all the exuberance and imagina-tion of the Plateresque. The decorative medallions are of prophets, apostles and Spanish kings.

Sala de los Conversos (Converts' Hall)

The 12C room is divided by stout pillars crowned with stylised capitals. The **kitchen** is famed for its monumental central chimney. The **Refectorio★★** (refectory), a masterpiece of 13C Gothic, rises 15m/49ft above the 35m/114.8ft long hall and has a rose window. An elegant staircase, its arches on slender columns, leads to the **lectern**.

Iglesia

The church has been restored to its original state, although the royal chapel has kept sumptuous Churrigueresque decoration. Between the narthex and the aisles is an intricate 18C wrought-iron screen. The **coro alto** (choir) is beautifully decorated with Renaissance panelling and woodwork. The Talavera *azulejos* on the floor are also worthy of note.

El Burgo de Osma★

◐ 56km/35mi SW of Soria and 139km/87mi SE of Burgos. ▣ Plaza Mayor 9. ℘975 340 107. www.burgodeosma.com. This town with porticoed streets and squares has long been a bishop's seat. Its notable buildings include the San Agustín hospital and imposing **Cathedral★** (Pl. de la Catedral; open Tue–Sun 10.30am-1.30pm, 4–7.30pm, Oct-Jun Tue-Sat 10.30am-1pm, 4-6pm (Sat 7pm); €2.50; ℘975 34 03 19).

The east end, transept and chapter house were built in the 13C; the Late Gothic cloisters and chancel received Renaissance embellishments. The sacristy, royal chapel and 72m/236ft belfry are from the 18C.

There is Gothic decoration on the late 13C **south portal**. The interior is remarkable for the elevation of the nave, the delicate wrought-iron screens (16C) by Juan de Francés, the **high altar retable** by Juan de Juni and the 16C white-marble **pulpit** and **trascoro altarpiece**. The 13C polychrome limestone **tomb of San Pedro de Osma★** is in the west transept. In the **museum** you'll find a richly illustrated 1086 **Beatus** and a 12C manuscript with the signs of the zodiac. Returning to Soria (25km/15.5mi NE on the N 122), **Calatañazor** sits just off the main road. Time has stood still in its steep, stone-paved streets and castle ruins, from where you can view the plains.

Peñaranda de Duero★

❍ 47km/29mi W of El Burgo de Osma along the N 122 and BU 924.
The Castilian village (pop. 583), one of the province's most scenic, has castle ruins and medieval buildings. Around the 15C pillory in the **Plaza Mayor★** are half-timbered houses on stone piers. To one side is the **Palacio de los Condes de Miranda (Avellaneda)★** (open Tue–Sat 10am–2pm, 3–7pm, Oct–Mar 3–6pm, Sun 10am–2pm; last entry 1 hour before closing; ℘947 55 20 13, www.peñarandadeduero.es), a palace with a Renaissance facade. The patio with a two-tier gallery,the grand staircase and chambers with **artesonado ceilings★** make this one of the finest Renaissance residences in Spain. An 18C pharmacy, **Botica de Ximeno**, with books and instruments, may also be visited by arrangement with the tourist office.

Cañón del Río Lobos

❍ 15km/10mi N on the SO 920 (best access from the south). Centro de Interpretación del Parque Natural. ℘975 36 35 64.
The landscape along this 25km/15.5mi stretch of the Río Lobos is riddled with caves, depressions and chasms.

Castillo de Gormaz

These 10C Moorish castle ruins, overlooking the Duero, are the largest in Europe (446m/1 463ft in length) and boast 26 towers.

Berlanga del Duero

❍ 28km/17.4mi SE on C 116 and SO 104.
Berlanga, below its massive 15C castle, was a strongpoint on the Duero frontier. Some 8km/5mi southeast in **Casillas de Berlanga** is the **Iglesia de San**

Baudelio de Berlanga (open Wed–Sat 10am–2pm, 4–8pm, Oct–Mar until 6pm; ℘975 22 13 97), an unusual 11C Mozarabic chapel whose roof is supported by a massive pillar. Its 12C frescoes were removed in the 20C, though hunting scenes and geometric patterns can still be made out.

🚗 DRIVING TOUR

SIERRA DE URBIÓN★★

Roads may be blocked by snow Nov–May.

This hilly green part of the Sistema Ibérico mountain range rises to 2 228m/ 7 310ft. Streams rush through pinewoods and meadows; one is the source of the Duero, one of Spain's longest rivers (910km/565mi).

Laguna Negra de Urbión★★

53km/33mi NW of Soria via the N 234. Allow 1hr.

❍ At Cidones, bear right toward Vinuesa; after 18km/11mi, head for Montenegro de Cameros. After 8km/5mi, bear left onto the Laguna road (9km/5.6mi).

The **road★★**, after skirting the Cuerdo del Pozo reservoir (embalse), continues through pines to **Laguna Negra** (alt 1 700m/5 600ft), a small glacial lake at the foot of a semicircular cliff over which cascade two waterfalls.

Laguna Negra de Neila★★

86km/53mi NW of Soria via the N 234.

❍ At Abejar, turn right toward Molinos de Duero; continue to Quintana de la Sierra, then turn right for Neila (12km/7mi) and left for Huerta de Arriba; 2km/1mi on the left is the road to Laguna Negra.

The **road★★** through picturesque countryside affords changing views of the valley and Sierra de la Demanda. The lake lies at 2 000m/6 561ft.

Castilla–La Mancha

The southern *meseta*, which stretches south from Madrid to the Andalucían border through Castilla–La Mancha's, is a vast tableland slightly tilted toward the west and watered by two large rivers – the **Tajo** (Tagus), which cuts a deep gorge through the limestone Alcarria region, and the trickling **Guadiana**. The word La Mancha comes from the Arab *manxa*, meaning dry land, which is abundant, particularly in summer. Yet there is considerable cultivation, with wind-ruffled cereal fields, stretches of saffron turned purple in the flowering season (September), and serried ranks of olives and vines. Most of Spain's table wine comes from here, and the area is also renowned for its manchego cheese. **La Mancha**'s most famous personality is **Don Quixote**, created by **Cervantes** some four centuries ago. A Quixote trail leads in his (fictional) footsteps and includes (real) windmills and old towns. The region doesn't see nearly as many tourists as its southern neighbour, which makes it ideal for quiet getaways.

Highlights

1 Gazing upon **Toledo** from the other side of the Tajo (p193)

2 The iconic 'Don Quixote windmills' at **Consuegra** (p204)

3 The Museum of Abstract Art, set in a **casa colgada** in **Cuenca** (p211)

4 The spectacular natural formations of the **Serranía de Cuenca** (p212)

5 The sculptures and museum in the cathedral at **Sigüenza** (p215)

Toledo and West

Toledo is the jewel of Castilla-La Mancha. It is surrounded, moat-like, on three sides by the Tajo, with parts of its city wall and gateways still intact, little changed in appearance over the centuries. Until 1560, when the capital moved to Madrid (70km/43.5mi north), the city was the nerve centre of not only the Peninsula but of a burgeoning empire. In the following years it declined rapidly and slid into political irrelevance. The silver lining for today's visitors? 'Progress' bypassed the city, and its old town remained largely untouched. It is UNESCO World Heritage-listed with copious reminders of its multi-faith past. Some 80km west of Toledo, Talavera de la Reina is famous for the ceramic work that decorates its palaces, mansions and chapels, and nearby Oropesa is a charming village home to a fine Parador.

The South

The flat landscapes of the south conjure up the archetypal Don Quixote images of La Mancha. But there are surprises here too such as Belmonte, with a 15C fortress, and Almagro, once the headquarters of the Military Order of the Knights of Calatrava.

Cuenca city and province

Cuenca's 'hanging' houses, old town and Museum of Abstract Art put the small city high on most visitors' itineraries. Around the town a limestone plateau, pitted with swallow-holes *(torcas)* and cut by gorges, *(hoces)* makes for a curious and highly explorable landscape.

Northeast

La Mancha extends north to hug Madrid Province's eastern edge; here, you'll find a cooler, less arid landscape than in the southern part of the region. With fewer than 6 000 inhabitants, Sigüenza is remarkable for two outsize buildings dwarfing its medieval streets: the cathedral, which features outstanding sculpture and would be more at home in a major metropolis, and the fortress which was a Moorish alcázar and subsequently a Christian stronghold. (Today it is a Parador that caters to travellers who like getting off the beaten track). Workaday Guadalajara is worth a visit for the late-15C Palace of the Duke of Infantado.

Toledo★★★

As if pulled from *Game of Thrones*, Toledo rises dramatically on a granite eminence encircled by a steep ravine of the Tajo (Tagus). It is as spectacular in setting as it is rich in history, buildings and art. The city stands as a relic of a golden age in which Eastern and Western societies and Christian, Jewish and Islamic cultures not only intertwined but flourished.

THE CITY TODAY

On busy days (weekends in spring and autumn) Toledo is like a medieval theme park with hordes of visitors, bused in from Madrid, clogging its narrow streets. Shop windows here flaunt fearsome displays of Toledan steel, once the deadliest weaponry in the world, wielded by Spanish heroes from El Cid to the Conquistadores. Nowadays such steel is marketed as the 'official' weaponry of Hollywood films such as **Lord of the Rings**. Whenever you visit, try to stay the night and do the bulk of your exploration early (before the groups arrive) and late (after they've gone). Don't expect much nightlife as Toledo after dark is a fairly staid place.

A BIT OF HISTORY

Roman town to Holy Roman city – The Romans fortified the strategic settlement into a town they named Toletum. It passed into the hands of the barbarians and in the 6C to the Visigoths, who made it a royal seat until they were defeated by the Berbers at Guadalete in 711.

After the revolt of the taifas in 1012, Toledo was capital of an independent kingdom. In 1085 it was conquered by Alfonso VI, who soon moved his capital from León. Alfonso VII was crowned emperor in Toledo, hence the title of imperial city. The city, by this time filled with Moors, Jews and Christians, began to prosper.

The Catholic Monarchs gave it the Monastery of St John but lost interest after

- ▶ **Population:** 83 226
- ⚇ **Michelin Map:** 576 M 17 (town plan) – map 121 Alrededores de Madrid – Castilla–La Mancha (Toledo) .
- 🛈 **Info:** Plaza del Consistorio. ☎925 25 40 30. www.toledo-turismo.com.
- ◗ **Location:** Toledo is 71km/44mi SW of Madrid. 🚆Toledo (AVE).
- 🅿 **Parking:** Try to park below the centre of the city, and walk or take a taxi up.
- ✆ **Don't Miss:** El Greco's masterpiece, *The Burial of the Count of Orgaz.*
- 🕐 **Timing:** Monumental Toledo is compact. Walk around for an overview, then return for a visit to the sites of most interest.

they reconquered Granada in 1492. Emperor Charles V had the Alcázar rebuilt. In his reign the city took part in the Comuneros' Revolt, led by **Juan de Padilla**, a Toledan. This was one reason why, in 1561, Philip II named Madrid as Spain's capital, relegating Toledo to the role of spiritual centre.

Toledo and the Jews – In the 12C the Jewish community numbered 12 000. **Saint Ferdinand III** (1217–1252) encouraged diversity, which brought about a cultural flowering, and the city developed into a great intellectual forum. **Alfonso X the Wise** (1252–1284) gathered a court of learned Jews and established the **School of Translation**. In 1355 a pogrom was instigated by supporters of Henry IV of Trastamara. After repeated attacks, the Jews were expelled in 1492.

Mudéjar art in Toledo – The Mudéjar style established itself in Toledo after the so-called Reconquista in palaces (Taller del Moro), synagogues (El Tránsito, Santa María la Blanca) and churches. Brick was widely used.

Moorish stuccowork, *artesonado* and *azulejos* became commonplace. In the 13C and 14C, most Toledan churches were given Romanesque semicircular east ends. Blind arcades took on variations unknown elsewhere, and **belfries** were built square and decorated to resemble minarets. Edifices here often have a nave and two aisles – a Visigothic influence – Roman tripartite apses and Moorish wood vaulting.

CATHEDRAL★★★

Pl. del Ayuntamiento. Open Mon–Sat 10am–6pm (last admission), Sun & public hols 2–6pm. See website for free days. Closed 1 Jan, 25 Dec. €12.50. ✆925 22 22 41. www.catedralprimada.es.

The cathedral dominates the **Plaza del Ayuntamiento**. Construction began under Ferdinand III (St Ferdinand) in 1227. Unusually, the design was French Gothic, but as building continued until the end of the 15C, its architecture came to reflect Spanish Gothic. Despite later additions, the cathedral remains notable for its decoration and works of art.

Exterior

The **Puerta del Reloj** (Clock Doorway), in the north wall, from the 13C, was modified in the 19C. The **main facade** is pierced by three tall 15C portals; the upper registers were completed in the 16C and 17C. The central **Puerta del Perdón** (Pardon Doorway) is crowded with statues and crowned with a tympanum illustrating the Virgin presenting the 7C bishop of Toledo with a chasuble. The harmonious tower is 15C; the dome was designed by El Greco's son in the 17C. In the south wall is the 15C **Puerta de los Leones** (Lion Doorway) designed by Master Hanequin of Brussels and decorated by Juan Alemán. The Neoclassical portal is from 1800.

▶ Enter through the Puerta del Mollete, left of the west front, which leads you into the cloister.

Interior

The size and sturdy character of the cathedral are striking. Twinkling stained glass (1418–1561) and elaborate wrought-iron grilles enclose the chancel, **coro** and chapels.

Capilla Mayor

The chancel, the most sumptuous section, was enlarged in the 16C. The immense **polychrome retable★★**, intricately carved Flamboyant style with the Life of Christ, is awe-inspiring. The silver statue of the Virgin at the predella dates to 1418. The Plateresque marble tomb of Cardinal Mendoza on the left is by Covarrubias.

Coro

14C high reliefs and wrought-iron-enclosed chapels form the perimetre of the choir, itself closed by an elegant iron screen (1547). The lower parts of the 15C and 16C **choir stalls★★★** were carved by Rodrigo Alemán to recall the conquest of Granada; the alabaster 16C upper parts, by Berruguete *(left)* and Felipe Vigarny *(right)* portray Old Testament figures. The central low relief, the Transfiguration, is also by Berruguete. His style creates the impression of movement. Two organs and a Gothic eagle lectern complete the set. The 14C marble **White Virgin** is French.

Girola

The double ambulatory, surmounted by an elegant triforium with multifoil arches, is bordered by seven apsidal chapels separated by small square chapels. The vaulting is a geometrical wonder.

There is little room to step back for a good look at the **Transparente★**, the contentious but famous work by Narciso Tomé that forms a Baroque island in the Gothic church.

Illuminated through an opening in the ambulatory roof (made to allow light to fall on the tabernacle), the **Transparente** appears as an ornamental framework of angels and swirling clouds and rays surrounding the Virgin and the Last Supper. Elsewhere, in the **Capilla de San**

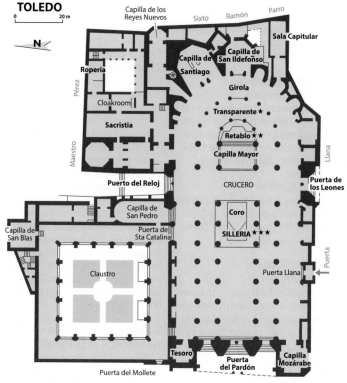

Plaza del Ayuntamiento

Ildefonso (Chapel of San Ildefonso), the central tomb of Cardinal Gil de Albornoz (14C) is the most notable.

Sala Capitular (Chapter House)

The antechamber has an impressive Mudéjar ceiling and two Plateresque carved walnut wardrobes. Remarkable Mudéjar stucco doorways and carved Plateresque panels precede the chapter house with its multicoloured **Mudéjar ceiling★**. Below frescoes by Juan de Borgoña are portraits of former archbishops including two by **Goya**.

Sacristía (Sacristy)

The first gallery, its vaulted ceiling painted by Lucas Jordán, includes **paintings by El Greco★** of which **El Expolio** (*The Disrobing of Christ*, c. 1577) is striking, with Christ front and centre dressed in a sheeny crimson robe.

Other works include a remarkable portrait of *Pope Paul III* by Titian, a *Holy Family* by Van Dyck, a *Mater Dolorosa* by Morales and the *Taking of Christ* by Goya, a triumph in composition, light and portraiture. Pedro de Mena's (17C) famous sculpture *St Francis of Assisi* is in a glass case. In the vestry are portraits by **Velázquez** (*Cardinal Borja*), Van Dyck (*Pope Innocent XI*) and **Ribera**.

The old laundry (*ropería*) contains liturgical objects dating to the 15C. T**he Nuevas Salas del Museo Catedralicio** (Cathedral Museum's New Galleries; C. de Cardenal Cisneros; open same hours as cathedral but closed Corpus Christi & 15 Aug) displays works by Caravaggio, El Greco, Bellini and Morales.

Tesoro (Treasury)

A Plateresque doorway by Covarrubias opens into the chapel under the tower. Beneath a Mudéjar ceiling, note the 16C silver-gilt **monstrance★★** by Enrique de

Arfe, weighing 180kg/392lb and measuring 3m/10ft high, paraded at Corpus Christi. The pyx at its centre is fashioned from gold plundered by Columbus.

Capilla Mozárabe
(Mozarabic Chapel)

The chapel beneath the dome was built by Cardinal Cisneros (16C) to celebrate Mass according to the Visigothic or Mozarabic ritual, which had been threatened with abolition in the 11C.

Claustro (Cloisters)

The simplicity of the 14C lower gallery contrasts with the bold murals by Bayeu of the Lives of Toledan Saints (Santa Eugenia and San Ildefonso).

Campana Gorda
(Bell Tower)

Ascend the 90m/295ft high north tower (built 1380-1440), from which there are panoramic views of Toledo. It takes its moniker, 'Fat Bell', from its 17-ton bell cast in 1753.

👣 WALKING TOUR

CENTRE OF OLD TOLEDO★★★

Allow 1 day. See town plan.
Surrounding the square before the Cathedral are the 18C **Palacio Arzobispal** (Archbishop's Palace); the 17C **ayuntamiento** (Town Hall), with a classical facade; and the 14C **Audiencia** (Law Courts).

Iglesia de Santo Tomé

Pl. del Conde. Open daily 10am–6.45pm (5.45pm mid-Oct–Feb). Last ticket 30min before close. €3. Closed 1 Jan, 25 Dec. 📞925 25 60 98. www.santotome.org.
The church, like that of San Román, has a distinctive 14C Mudéjar tower, but its raison d'être is **El Greco**'s most famous painting, **The Burial of the Count of Orgaz★★★** (c. 1586), housed here. The interment is transformed by the miraculous appearance of St Augustine and St Stephen. Figures in the lower register are portraits of personalities of the day; the sixth from the left is said to be El

Greco. Above, Christ prepares to receive the soul of the count.

Casa-Museo de El Greco★
(El Greco Museum)

Samuel Leví. Tue–Sat 9.30am–7.30pm (Nov–Feb until 6pm), Sun & hols 10am–3pm. €3, free Sat from 2pm, Sun, 18 Apr, 18 May, 12 Oct, 6 Dec. 📞925 99 09 82. http://museodelgreco.mcu.es.
In 1585, El Greco moved into a house similar to this one. In what would have been the artist's workroom is a signed *St Francis and Brother León*.
On the first floor are an interesting *View and Plan of Toledo* and the complete series of individual portraits of the Apostles and Christ (later and more mature than those in the cathedral). The **capilla** on the ground floor, with a multicoloured Mudéjar ceiling, has a picture in the altarpiece of *St Bernardino of Siena* by **El Greco**.

Sinagoga del Tránsito★★★
(Synagogue of El Transito)

C. Samuel Leví. Opening hours same as Casa-Museo de El Greco. Closed 1 & 6 Jan, 1 May, 24–25, 31 Dec. €3. 📞925 22 36 65. http://museosefardi.mcu.es.
Of the ten synagogues that once stood in the Jewish quarter (Judería), only this and Santa María la Blanca remain. It was financed in the 14C by Samuel Ha-Levi, treasurer to Peter the Cruel and, in 1492, converted into a church. El Tránsito is the best-preserved medieval synagogue in Spain.
Unassuming from the outside, it is covered inside with ornate **Mudéjar decoration★★**. Above the rectangular hall is an *artesonado* ceiling of cedarwood; just below are 54 multifoil arches, some blind, others pierced with delicate stone tracery. Below again runs a frieze, decorated at the east end with *mocárabes* and on the walls with inscriptions in Hebrew to the glory of Peter the Cruel, Samuel Ha-Levi and the God of Israel. In the east wall, inscriptions describe the synagogue's foundation. The women's balcony opens from the south wall.
The adjoining rooms, once a monastery, hold the **Museo Sefardí** (Sephardic

Sinagoga del Tránsito

Museum; hours and admission as above), with tombs, books and other artefacts, of which several are gifts from descendants of Jews expelled in 1492.

Casa Museo Victorio Macho★

Pl. de Victor Macho. Open Mon–Sat 10am–7pm, Sun 10am–3pm. Closed 1 Jan, 25 Dec. €3. ✆925 284 225. www.realfundaciontoledo.es

This exhibition space with dramatic views of the Tagus and San Martín bridge, occupies the home of avant-garde sculptor Victorio Macho, who fled to Peru on the outbreak of the Spanish Civil War. Alongside works on temporary show are many pieces by Macho including a portrait of his brother.

Sinagoga de Santa María La Blanca★★

C. de los Reyes Católicos 4. Open daily 10am–6.45pm last admission (5.45pm Oct–Feb). €3. ✆925 22 72 57.

Step into the principal synagogue of Toledo in the late 12C. In 1405 it was given to the Knights of Calatrava as a church, hence its incongruous name. Surprisingly, subsequent modifications left the Almohad-style nave untouched, with five tiered aisles separated by octagonal pillars supporting horseshoe-shaped arches. The white-washed pillars set off intricately carved capitals★. The wood altarpiece is 16C.

Monasterio de San Juan de los Reyes★ (St John of the Kings Monastery)

C. de los Reyes Católicos 17. Open daily Apr–Oct 10am–6.45pm (Oct-Feb 10am-5.45pm). €2.80. ✆925 22 38 02. www.sanjuandelosreyes.org.

This Franciscan monastery commemorates the victory over the Portuguese at Toro in 1476. The overall style is Isabelline: Covarrubias designed the north portal, including in the decoration the figure of John the Baptist. The fetters depicted are said to have been taken from Christians jailed by the Moors.

Claustro (Cloisters)

The cloisters boast Flamboyant bays and Plateresque upper galleries (1504) crowned with a pinnacled balustrade and Mudéjar *artesonado* vaulting.

Iglesia

The church, burned by the French in 1808, has an Isabelline single wide aisle; at the crossing are a dome and a lantern. The sculptured decoration★ by Flemish architect Juan Guas provides a delicate stone tracery (*crestería*) that, at the transept, forms twin tribunes for Ferdinand and Isabel. The transept walls are faced with a frieze of royal escutcheons, supported by an eagle, symbol of St John. Close by are a Visigothic palace and the *Puerta del Cambrón*, once part of the town perimetre, rebuilt in the 16C.

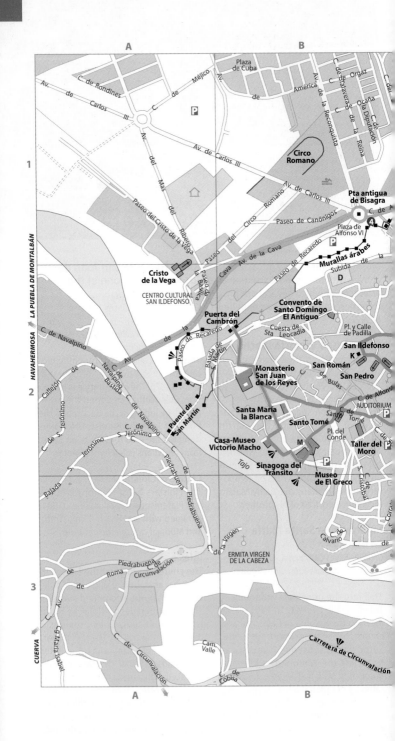

A · B

1

2

3

CUERVA

HAVAHERMOSA

LA PUEBLA DE MONTALBÁN

Plaza de Cuba

C. de Rondines

Av. de Carlos III

C. de Méjico

C. de

Av. de la Reconquista

Av. de Talavera de la Reina

C. de Orgaz

C. de la Diputación

Av. de Carlos III

Circo Romano

Av. de Carlos III

Paseo del Cristo de la Vega

Paseo del Circo Romano

Paseo de Canónigos

Pta antigua de Bisagra

C. de A

Plaza de Alfonso VI

4

Paseo del

Av. de la Cava

Paseo de Recaredo

Murallas árabes

Subida de la

Cristo de la Vega

CENTRO CULTURAL SAN ILDEFONSO

Puerta del Cambrón

Convento de Santo Domingo El Antiguo

D

Cuesta de Sta. Leocadia

Pl. y Calle de Padilla

Paseo de Recaredo

C. de Navalpino

San Ildefonso

K

San Román

San Pedro

C. de Navalpino

C. de Navalpino

C. de la Bastida

Callejón de S. Jerónimo

S. Jerónimo

C. de S. Jerónimo

Monasterio San Juan de los Reyes

Bajada de S. Martín

Puente de San Martín

Santa María la Blanca

Santo Tomé

C. de Alfons

AUDITORIUM

P

C. de

Santo Tomé

C. de Bulas

Pl. del Conde

Taller del Moro

P

Casa-Museo Victorio Macho

M

C. de Piedrabuena

S. Jerónimo

C. de Piedrabuena

Tajo

Sinagoga del Tránsito

P

Museo de El Greco

C. de S. Cristóbal

Bajada de S. Jerónimo

C. de la Virgen

C. de Piedrabuena

ERMITA VIRGEN DE LA CABEZA

C. de Calvario

C. de

Piedrabuena

C. de Roma

Circunvalación

C. de Circunvalación

Av. María Isabel

Cam. Valle

C. de Cobisa

Carretera de Circunvalación

A · B

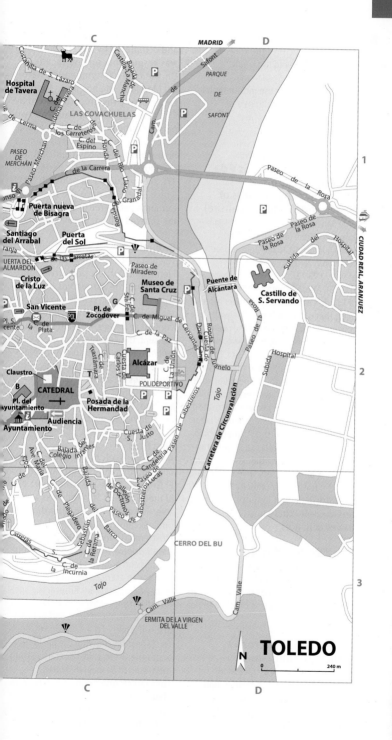

MADRID

PARQUE DE SAFONT

Hospital de Tavera

LAS COVACHUELAS

PASEO DE MERCHÁN

Paseo de la Rosa

Puerta nueva de Bisagra

Santiago del Arrabal

Puerta del Sol

CIUDAD REAL ARANJUEZ

HUERTA DEL ALMARDÓN

Paseo de Miradero

Cristo de la Luz

Museo de Santa Cruz

Puente de Alcántara

Castillo de S. Servando

San Vicente

Pl. de Zocodover

Hospital

Claustro

Alcázar

CATEDRAL

POLIDEPORTIVO

Pl. del Ayuntamiento

Ayuntamiento

Audiencia

Posada de la Hermandad

Carretera de Circunvalación

Tajo

CERRO DEL BU

Tajo

Cam. Valle

ERMITA DE LA VIRGEN DEL VALLE

TOLEDO

N

0   240 m

Return to San Juan and take Calle Ángel to Santo Tomé, then take the picturesque Travesía de Campana alley to the small Pl. del Padre Juan de Mariana. Cross the plaza past the monumental Baroque facade of the Iglesia de San Ildefonso and that of the Iglesia de San Pedro.

Iglesia de San Román: Museo de los Concilios y de la Cultura Visigoda★ (Museum of the Councils of Toledo and Visigothic Culture)

C. de San Román. Open Tue–Sat 10am–2pm, 4–6.30pm (4–7pm summer), Sun & public hols 10am–2pm. Closed 1 Jan, 1 May, 24–25 and 31 Dec. ✆925 22 78 72.

This 13C Mudéjar church, at the summit of Toledo's old town, has a tower resembling that of Santo Tomé. The walls are covered in 13C frescoes of the raising of the dead, the Evangelists and, on the far wall, one of the Councils of Toledo. The apse was modified in the 16C with a cupola by Covarrubias. The collections include fine bronze jewellery and copies of Visigothic votive crowns decorated with cabochon stones from Guarrazar (originals in the Museo Arqueológico, Madrid). On the walls are steles, fragments from capitals, balustrades from the choir and pilasters. In Plaza de San Vicente, note the Mudéjar east end of the **Iglesia de San Vicente**. Continue up Calle de la Plata, with its houses with carved entrances.

Plaza de Zocodover

The triangular Zocodover is the heart of Toledo. It was rebuilt after the Civil War, as was the Arco de la Sangre (Arch of Blood), which opens onto Calle de Cervantes.

Museo de Santa Cruz★★ (Santa Cruz Museum)

Miguel de Cervantes 3. Open Mon and Sat 10am–7pm, Sun & public hols 10am–2.30pm. Closed 1, 6 & 23 Jan; 1 May; 24–25, 31 Dec. €5, free 18 & 31 May. ✆925 22 14 02.

These Plateresque hospital buildings were begun by Enrique Egas and completed by Covarrubias, who was responsible for the **facade★★**. On the gateway tympanum, Cardinal Mendoza, the hospital's sponsor, kneels before the Cross supported by St Helena, St Peter, St Paul and two pages; on the arches are the cardinal virtues. Above, two windows frame a high relief of St Joachim and St Anne. The museum is known for its **16C and 17C art★** including 18 paintings by **El Greco**. The large nave and transept – forming a two-tiered Greek cross – and the coffered ceilings are outstanding.

Ground floor

The first part of the nave contains 16C Flemish tapestries, **primitive paintings★** and the *Astrolabios* or *Zodiac* tapestry, woven in Flanders in the mid-15C for Toledo cathedral, still strikingly original in design. Note, in the south transept, the *Ascension* and the *Presentation of Mary in the Temple* by the Maestro de Sijena. In the second part of the nave hangs the immense pennant flown by Don Juan of Austria at the Battle of Lepanto. The north transept contains a *Christ at the Column* by Morales.

First floor

A staircase leads to the upper gallery of the north transept with paintings by **El Greco★**. There are gentle portraits of the Virgin and St Veronica as well as a version of the *Expolio*, later than the original, hung in the cathedral.

Most famous is the late **Altarpiece of the Assumption★**, from 1613, with Baroque stylings and notably elongated figures. The south transept contains a *Holy Family at Nazareth* by **Ribera**, the specialist in tenebrism who here shows himself a master of light and delicacy. In the first part of the nave are 16C Brussels tapestries showing the life of Alexander the Great; and 17C statues from the studio of Pascual de Mena.

The **Plateresque patio★** has bays with elegant lines complemented by the openwork balustrade and enhanced by Mudéjar vaulting and by the magnificent **staircase**★ (Covarrubias). Adjoining rooms house a museum of archaeology and decorative arts.

WITHIN THE CITY WALLS
Alcázar (Museo del Ejército)
Cuesta de Carlos V 2. Open Thu–Tue 10am–5pm. Closed 1 & 6 Jan; 1 May; 24–25, 31 Dec. €5; free Sun, 29 Mar, 18 Apr, 12 Oct, 6 Dec. ℘925 238 800. www.museo.ejercito.es

The Alcázar, destroyed and rebuilt multiple times, is now home to the National Army Museum. Emperor Charles V converted the 13C fortress, of which El Cid had been the first governor, into an imperial residence. The work was entrusted to Covarrubias (1538–1551) and then to Herrera, who designed the austere south front. An eight-week Republican seige in 1936 left the fortress in ruins. The Falangist commander defending it allowed his son to be shot rather than surrender. Franco later enshrined the site as a monument to Nationalist power.

The Alcázar would be restored to its former glory in 2010 after a long renovation. In the museum, 6 500 items tell the story of Spain's complex military past.

Posada de la Hermandad (House of the Brotherhood)
C. Hermandad 6.
This 15C building, once a prison, has an exhibit worthwhile for those interested in seige warfare.

Puerta del Sol
Callejón San José 2.
The Sun Gate in the second perimetre, rebuilt in the 14C, is a fine Mudéjar construction with two circumscribing horseshoe arches. At the centre a later low relief shows the Virgin presenting San Ildefonso with a chasuble. At the top, the brick decoration of blind arcading incorporates an unusual sculpture of two girls bearing the head of the chief *alguacil* (officer of justice), allegedly a rapist, on a salver.

Mezquita del Cristo de la Luz (Christ of the Light Mosque)
Cta. de Carmelitas Descalzas. Open Mar–Oct 10am–6.45pm, Nov–Feb 10am–5.45pm. €2.80. ℘925 25 41 91.
Summing up Toledo's multifaceted past, this 12C Mudéjar church succeeded a mosque, which in turn replaced a Visigothic church. It's named for the miraculous appearance of a lamp illuminating a crucifix in the mosque when Alfonso VI first entered Toledo. Arches of different periods, intersecting blind arcades, and a line of horizontal brickwork surmounted by Cufic characters make up the facade. Inside, Visigothic pillars support superimposed arches like those in Córdoba's mosque.
Nine domes, each different, rise from square bays.The gardens lead to the Puerta del Sol. Enjoy the panorama from the top.

Iglesia de Santiago del Arrabal (St James on the Outskirts)
Pl. Santiago del Arrabal 4. Closed to the public, though discreet visits may be possible before/after evening Mass. ℘925 22 06 36.
San Vicente Ferrer is said to have preached from the Gothic Mudéjar pulpit of this restored church whose 12C tower is the oldest in the region.

Puerta Nueva de Bisagra (New Bisagra Gate)
Puerta de Bisagra.
The gate was rebuilt by Covarrubias in 1550 and enlarged under Philip II. Massive round crenellated towers, facing the Madrid road, flank a giant imperial crest.

Puerta Antigua de Bisagra (Old Bisagra Gate)
Po. Recaredo.
Alfonso VI entered Toledo in triumph through this Moorish gate in 1085.

ADDITIONAL SIGHTS
Hospital de Tavera★
Cardenal de Tavera 2. Open 10am–2.30pm, 3–6.30pm, Sun am only. Guided tours every 45min. €6. ℘925 22

04 51. www.fundacionmedinaceli.org/
monumentos/hospital.

The Hospital de San Juan Bautista (better known as the Hopital de Tavera) was begun in 1541 and completed in the 17C. After the Civil War, the Duchess of Lerma rearranged her **apartments**★ in 17C style; these hold an outstanding collection of paintings. In the vast library, the hospital archives contain volumes bound in leather by Moorish craftsmen. El Greco's *Holy Family* is arresting, the portrait of the Virgin perhaps the most beautiful by the artist. Note also the *Birth of the Messiah* by Tintoretto, the *Philosopher* by **Ribera** and, in an adjoining room, his strange portrait of the *Bearded Woman*.

On the first floor, in the reception hall, is El Greco's sombre portrait of *Cardinal Tavera*, painted from a death mask. Beside it are *Samson and Delilah* (Caravaggio) and two portraits of the *Duke and Duchess of Navas* (Antonio Moro). A gallery leads to the **church** from the twin patio.

The retable at the high altar was designed by El Greco, whose last work, a **Baptism of Christ**★, is displayed. The artist's use of brilliant colours and elongated figures is awe-inspiring.

The hospital pharmacy, facing the patio, has been restored.

Talavera Ceramics

Since the 15C, the name Talavera has been associated with high-quality **ceramic tiles** used to decorate the palaces, mansions and chapels. Visit the town's Basilica and **Museo de Cerámica Ruiz de Luna** (Pl. de San Agustín; ℘925 80 01 49) to see ceramics dating to the 15C to modern times. Talavera now manufactures decorative crockery, and green-coloured items are made in **El Puente del Arzobispo**, a village (34km/21mi SW) specialising in pottery drinking jars.

Puente de Alcántara

At the ends of the 13C bridge are a Mudéjar tower and a Baroque arch. Across the Tajo, behind ramparts, is the restored 14C **Castillo de San Servando** (now a youth hostel; ℘925 22 45 54). A plaque on the town wall by the bridge recalls how *St John of the Cross* (1542–1591) escaped through a window from his monastery prison nearby.

Puente de San Martín

The medieval bridge, rebuilt in the 14C, is marked at its south end by an octagonal tower; the north end is 16C.

Iglesia de Cristo de la Vega

Travesía Cristo de la Vega.

The Church of Christ of the Vega, formerly St Leocadia, stands on the site of a 7C Visigothic temple.

VIEWPOINTS

The city's incomparable **geographic position**★★★ is best appreciated from the **Carretera de Circunvalación** (ringroad) that parallels the loop of the Tajo from the Puente de Alcántara (Alcántara Bridge) to the Puente de San Martín. Drive or take a leisurely uphill walk to its **viewpoints** among olive groves. The terrace of the Parador (&see Addresses), above the **carretera de circunvalación**, is a superb vantage point.

EXCURSIONS

Talavera de la Reina

◗ 80km/50mi W of Toledo. ⌂ Ronda del Cañillo 22. ℘925 82 63 22. www.turismotalavera.com.

On the bank of the Tajo, spanned by a 15C bridge, Talavera retains part of its medieval walls and Mudéjar churches. Its name is synonymous with the *azulejos* (ceramic tiles) that brought it fame from the 15C, when they were used to decorate chapels and noble homes.

Basílica de Nuestra Señora del Prado

Jardines del Prado 6. Open daily 7am–2pm, 5–10pm (4–9pm during summer). ✆925 80 14 45.
www.basilicavirgendelprado.es.

The church, virtually an *azulejo* museum, shows the evolution of the local style. The earliest tiles, geometrically patterned and yellow in colour, are in the sacristy.

In the basilica, later tiles (16C–18C) are distinguished by blue narrative scenes. Nearby, the Museo Ruiz de la Luna (♿see p202) displays more tiles.

Oropesa

➲ 32km/20mi W.

Visitors to this hilltop village are greeted by its castle★, rebuilt in 1402. A portion is open to visitors (Pl. del Palacio 1; open Tue–Sat 10am–2pm, 4–6pm, Sun & public hols 10am–2pm; €3; ✆925 26 76 66; www.parador.es/en); the remainder is a Parador with far-reaching views across the Sierra de Gredos.

Montes de Toledo

Within the low wooded mountains lying southwest of Toledo, a central area of 1 000sq km /385sq m is protected as the Parque Nacional de Cabañeros, home to rare wildlife and an ancient shepherds' culture.

ADDRESSES

🛌 STAY

⊜🍽 **Hostal Santo Tomé** – C. Santo Tomé, 13. ✆925 221 712. www.hostalsantotome.com 10 rooms. No breakfast. In the heart of the old town, with balconies in upgraded rooms and fine views from the top floor, this family-run hotel offers bright, spacious rooms.

⊜⊜ **Hotel La Almazara** – 3.5km/2mi SW. ✆925 45 48 04. www.almazara devaldeverdeja.com. 28 rooms. Closed early Dec–Mar, Aug. Follow a lane shaded with olive trees to this former olive press. Spacious bedrooms afford views of Toledo. Loaner bikes are a plus.

⊜🍽🍽 **Hacienda del Cardenal** – Po. Recaredo 24. ✆925 22 49 00. www.hostaldelcardenal.com. 27 rooms. 🍴€9. This charming hotel, formerly a cardinal's residence, stands at the foot of the city walls. Behind the stone facade, there's an indoor pool and rooms decorated with wood furnishings and antiques. The refined restaurant is popular among locals (⊜🍽🍽🍽).

⊜🍽🍽 **Antídoto Rooms** – C. Recoletos 2. ✆689 76 66 05. www.antidotorooms.com. 10 rooms. 🍴€9. Finally, a hotel in Toledo with some modern design sense: Antídoto seamlessly melds the new (polished concrete floors) with the old (beamed ceilings).

⊜🍽🍽🍽 **Parador de Toledo** – Cerro del Emperador via Ctra de Circunvalación. ✆902 54 79 79. www.parador.es. 79 rooms. 🍴€17. The modern building was recently given a facelift; rooms are comfortable, and there is a swimming pool. Its terraced dining room has a magnificent city view

🍴 EAT

⊜ **Bar Ludeña** – Pl. de la Magdalena 10. ✆925 223 384. The Toledan speciality of *carcamusas* – stewed pork with garlic and paprika – is the must-try tapa here.

⊜🍽 **Colección Catedral** – C. Nuncio Viejo 1. ✆925 224 244. www.grupoadolfo.com. Visit this modern bar and restaurant, in a 1920s building near the cathedral, for prix-fixe tapas menus, a great value.

⊜🍽🍽 **Cervecería El Trébol** – C. de Santa Fe 1 ✆925 281 297. www.cerveceriatrebol.com. Come for the locally brewed craft beer; stay for comfort-food dishes like *bombas,* ultra-crisp orbs of mashed potato packed around a molten core of spiced meat.

SHOPPING

Keep an eye out for **damascene ware,** black steel inlaid with metal thread, and **marzipan**, often sold at convents.

FESTIVALS

The **Corpus Christi** procession is one of the largest of its kind in Spain (late May/early Jun, www.spain.info).

Ruta de Don Quijote ★

The Quixote route, created to celebrate the 400th anniversary of the publication of Cervantes' great novel *Don Quixote* (1605), was the EU's first approved cultural route dedicated to a literary figure. Even if you don't know the first thing about Spanish literature, it's a useful guideline for exploring La Mancha's most pleasing and historically significant places.

🚗 DRIVING TOUR

Consuegra
90km/56mi NE of Belmonte along the N 420.

A row of 12 **molinos de viento** (windmills) stands alongside the 13C castle on a hill overlooking the town, making up what's perhaps the most iconic image of Castilla–La Mancha.
The **Castillo de Consuegra** (open Mon–Fri 10am-2pm and 3.30-6pm, Sat, Sun & hols 10am-6pm; Closed 1 and 6 Jan, 25 Dec. €7, incl windmills; ☎925 47 57 31, www.consuegra.es) once belonged to the Knights of St John . Some of the rooms have been interpreted according to this period. In late October, when the saffron croci are in bloom, the town hosts a **Saffron Festival** complete with rides, local dance and a farmers market.

Puerto Lápice
23km/14mi SE of Consuegra along the E 5/A 4.
Puerto Lápice has retained the rambling 17C inn, **Venta del Quijote**, said to have inspired the one that Don Quixote mistook for a castle and its innkeeper a lord. The patron, taking pity on the old man, 'knighted' him. The inn holds a marvellous collection of Don Quixote memorabilia ranging from tasteful to kitsch. You can enjoy local food here as well.

▶ **Population:** 1 938 (Belmonte)
🚗 **Michelin Map:** 576 N 21 – Castilla–La Mancha (Cuenca).
ℹ **Info:** Av. Luis Pinedo Alarcón. ☎967 17 00 08. www.belmonte.es.
▶ **Location:** Belmonte is 157km/98mi NW of Madrid and on the 250km/155mi Ruta de Don Quijote.
👥 **Kids:** Consuegra's windmill-dotted hillsides are straight out of a fairytale.
🕐 **Timing:** You can easily spend two or three days exploring the region.

▶ Take the N420 toward Cuenca for 32km/20mi.

Campo de Criptana
Windmills open 10am–2pm, 5–7.45pm. ☎926 562 231. www.tierradegigantes.es
Three of the ten windmills on the hill above this blue-and-white town date to the times of Don Quixote, and one, which stands next to the windmill housing the tourist office, retains its original working mechanism. The walk up to the windmills gives good views over the heart of La Mancha. Below the mill, a 16C miller's house, Cerro de la Paz (opening times same as windmills; €1) may be visited. Alongside the highest windmill is a local collector's mass of wire models, as surreal as Don Quixote's universe.

▶ Take N420 for 2km /0.8mi toward Cuenca. Turn left onto CM3162 for 18km/11mi (Quintanar de la Orden).

El Toboso
www.eltoboso.es
Dulcinea, Don Quixote's tragicomically distant love – they met only a handful of times – came from this tiny village. A wealthy woman of the time, Doña Morales, who may have inspired the character of Dulcinea, lived here in a 16C farmstead, which is well-preserved

(Museo Casa de Dulcinea; open mid-Jun–mid-Sep Tue–Sat 9.45am–1.45pm, 4–7.30pm; Sun 10am–2pm; €3, free Sun; ☏925 197 288). Nearby, the Convento de Trinitarias has a small museum of religious art. True Cervantes devotees shouldn't miss the **Centro Cervantino** (open Tue–Sun 10am–2pm, 4–7pm; €2; ☏925 568 226) housing a polyglot collection of 198 editions of *Don Quixote* from around the world.

▶ CM 3162, then N301 for Cuenca.

Belmonte★

Belmonte's whitewashed houses are clustered around its church and castle.

Iglesia Colegial de San Bartolomé★

Open Tue–Sun 11am–2pm, 4.30–7.30pm (6.30pm Oct–Mar). Sun pm only. €2. ☏699 840 947.

This 15C collegiate church holds 15C–17C altarpieces. **Choir stalls★** from the cathedral in Cuenca starkly illustrate scenes from Genesis and the Passion.

Castillo de Belmonte★

Open Tue–Sun 10am–2pm. Also May–mid-Sep 4.30–8.30pm, Mar–Apr 4–7pm, mid-Sep–Feb 3.30–6.30pm. Closed 1 Jan and 25 Dec. €9 (€10 Aug & public hols). ☏678 64 64 86.
www.castillodebelmonte.com.
Open after years of restoration, this 15C fortress with six circular towers was built by the Marqués de Villena but lay long abandoned.
The rooms are now interpreted with period furnishings and feature original **Mudéjar artesonado★** ceilings – that of the audience chamber is jaw-dropping – and delicately carved stone window surrounds. Follow the curtain walls to the stepped merlons for views over the terracotta roofs and countryside.

▶ 6km/3.7mi NE along the N 420.

Villaescusa de Haro

The 1507 **Capilla de la Asunción★** (Chapel of the Assumption) of the parish church boasts a Gothic-Renaissance altarpiece and a wrought-iron screen with florid Gothic arches (Open for Mass only).

▶ Take the N420 and CM 3103 S.

Argamasilla de Alba

Cervantes is said to have conjured up Don Quixote here while he languished in prison for fraud during his stint as a tax collector. At the time, Don Rodrigo de Pacheco, a fantasist like Cervantes's fictional character, lived here, perhaps inspiring Cervantes. You can visit the basement prison under the tourist office (C. de Cervantes 7; open Tue–Sat 10am–2pm, 5–8 pm/4–7pm Oct–Mar; ☏926 52 32 34; www.argamasilladealba.es), and in the Iglesia de San Juan Bautista you can see Don Rodrigo's portrait, in the chapel of the Virgen de la Caridad. The church, begun in 1542, was never finished.

▶ Take the CM3109 toward La Solana, then the CM 3127 to Villanueva.

Villanueva de los Infantes

Perhaps the most charming town on the Quixote route, Villanueva claims to be the 'certain village in La Mancha, which I do not wish to name' of the famous opening sentence of Cervantes' novel. Here, it is said, the knight lived before setting out on his adventures, and where he returned to die.
The great Spanish poet **Francisco de Quevedo** (1580–1645) is buried in the **Convento de Santo Domingo**, founded in 1526. You can see the cell inside the convent, now a hotel. The spacious Plaza Mayor sits to one side of the old town, a maze of small streets with stone houses decorated by over 200 carved shields. The **alhóndiga**, or granary, and late Renaissance Iglesia de San Andrés are worth peeking into if open.

Almagro★

Almagro's facades with time-worn coats of arms hark back to a bygone era. The 16C Convento de San Francisco is now a Parador. From here, day-trip to La Mancha Húmeda, the 'wet' area dotted with lagoons and marshland.

A BIT OF HISTORY

The impressive architecture of this charming town, the birthplace of the explorer Diego de Almagro (1475–1538), is rooted in its noble history.

From the 13C–15C, Almagro was the stronghold of the Order of the Knights of Calatrava and the base from which they administered their possessions. Between 1750 and 1761, the town the province's capital thanks to the favours of the Count of Valparaíso, then-minister of finance under Ferdinand VI. From 16C–19C, religious orders established convents and monasteries here.

SIGHTS

Quiet streets lead past treeless, whitewashed neighbourhoods to historic convents and monasteries.

Plaza Mayor★★

This square is one of the most picturesque in Spain. Stone columns demarcate its base, above which rest 16C houses with cheery green trim. Tapas bars serve the town's namesake garlicky pickled **berenjenas** (eggplant).

Corral de Comedias★

Pl. Mayor 18. Open daily, see website for times; €4 self-guided tours, from €7 theatrical tours; ℘926 86 15 39. www.corraldecomedias.com.

Thisis the only intact original 17C theatre in Europe. Wooden porticoes, oil lamps, a stone well and open ceiling combine to form an incomparable example of popular architecture. It's at its liveliest at the annual International Festival of Classical Drama (www.festivaldealmagro.com).

- ▶ **Population:** 8 922
- ⌖ **Michelin Map:** 576 P 18 – Castilla–La Mancha (Ciudad Real).
- **Info:** Plaza Mayor 1. ℘926 86 07 17. www.ciudad-almagro.com.
- ◖ **Location:** Almagro is on the plain south of Madrid. ▭Almagro.
- ⊛ **Don't Miss:** A walk through streets frozen in time.

🥾 WALKING TOUR

HISTORICAL ALMAGRO★

Allow 2–3 hours.

From the statue of Diego de Almagro in the **Plaza Mayor**, take Nuestra Señora de las Nieves (note its fine doorways) to the left, to the triangular Plaza Santo Domingo, surrounded by mansions. Turn left onto Bernardas to face the Baroque door of the **Palacio de los Condes de Valparaíso**. Follow Don Federico Relimpio, then go left on Don Diego de Almagro, dominated by the 16C **Convento de la Asunción de Calatrava** (open daily, see website for opening hours, Sun 11am–2pm year round; €2; ℘926 69 33 32, www.ciudad-almagro.com), with its fine Renaissance staircase. Loop back to the Pl. Mayor and turn right at the end onto Gran Maestre, where you'll find the **Museo Nacional del Teatro** (open Tue–Sun; check website for opening times; closed public hols; €3, free Sat pm, Sun am, 27 Mar, 18 Apr, 18 May, 12 Oct, 12 Nov, 6 Dec; ℘926 26 10 14; http://museoteatro.mcu.es) showing old scripts, costumes and models of theatre sets.

EXCURSIONS

Parque Nacional de las Tablas de Daimiel

◖ 31km/19mi N by the CM 4107 and N 420. From Daimiel, take a tarmac road to the right (7km/4.5mi).

Centro de Información, 9am–9pm (8.30am–6.30pm in winter). ☎926 850 371. www.lastablasdedaimiel.com.

These wetlands are the smallest of Spain's national parks with an area of 1 928ha/4 764 acres. The flooding of the Cigüela and Guadiana rivers creates floodplains colonised by various species of birds including migratory herons, egrets, red-crested pollards and wintering pintails and shovelers. The park almost disappeared due to agricultural mismanagement, but after a slap on the wrist by the European Commission and concerted efforts by environmentalists, the aquifers have bounced back some 20m/66ft since their nadir in 2009; lost bird populations have also returned.

Parque Natural Lagunas de Ruidera

◗ 67km/42mi NE. Centro de Información, Av Castilla La Mancha . www.lagunasderuidera.es.

Drive along the country road across these 3 772ha/9 320 acres with 15 Caribbean-blue lagoons conneted by streams, gullies and waterfalls. Avoid Jul–Sep (dry season).

San Carlos del Valle★

◗ 46km/29mi E.

The 18C Plaza Mayor★is charming with its Baroque church. The former hospice at no. 5 retains a typical patio.

Valdepeñas

◗ 34km/21mi SE along the CM 412. ▰Paseo de la Estación.

La Mancha produces more wine – most of it table wine – than any other viticulturalregion on earth, and Valdepeñas is its nerve centre. Blue and white houses rise above shady porticoes on the spacious Plaza de España.

Visit the Museo del Vino (C. Princesa 39; open Tue–Sat 10am–2pm, 5–8pm, Sun year-round 11am–2pm; €3; ☎926 32 11 11, www.museodelvinovaldepenas.es), installed in one of the town's oldest bodegas, to get a taste of the local stuff.

Sacro Castillo y Convento de Calatrava la Nueva★

◗ 32km/19.8mi SW. 7km/4.3mi SW of Calzada de Calatrava, turn right onto a paved road (2.5km/1.5mi). Open Oct–Mar Fri-Sun 10.30am-2pm, 2-6pm. Apr-May Thur-Sun 10am-2pm, 4-8pm, Jun-Aug Tue-Sun 10am-2pm, 5-7.30pm (am only Tue-Thur), Sep Thu-Sun 10.30am-2pm, 4-8pm. €4. ☎ 926 69 31 19. www.castillodecalatrava.com.

This semi-ruined citadel occupies a magnificent hilltop site visible on the route to Andalucía.

The gateway leads into vaulted stables. The second perimetre, built into rock, houses religious buildings including the impressive church, lit by a rose window, and brick swallow's nest vaulting, probably the work of Moorish prisoners. The towers look onto the ruined Castillo de Salvatierra. Cracks caused by the 1755 Lisbon earthquake are clearly visible.

Viso del Marqués★★

◗ El Viso de Marqués.

The Renaissance Palacio de Álvaro de Bazán (open Tue-Sun 9am-1pm, 4-6pm, until 2pm Jul–Aug; €3; ☎926 33 75 18) towers over the village. It was the home of the Marqués de Santa Cruz, admiral to Philip II.

Note the damage left by the Lisbon earthquake, which destroyed the corner towers. The austere facade belies delicate frescoes (patio) and an ornate double staircase. In the upstairs living quarters there's a collection of model boats (Museo de la Marina). A crocodile marks the entrance to the chapel where the Marqués was buried in 1588, weeks before he was to command the 'Invincible' Armada.

Beside tourist office, the Museo de Ciencias Naturales (Natural Science-Museum; open Tue–Fri 10am–2pm, 5–7pm/4–6pm winter, Sat pm 1hr later, Sun am only; ☎926 33 68 15, www.museocienciasnaturalesavan.es) houses a surprisingly varied collection of butterflies.

Albacete

Albacete (from *Al-Basit*, 'plain' in Arabic), capital of the province of the same name, stands on a dry plateau that juts into the fertile east. Heritage structures are grouped with modern buildings and residential districts.

SIGHTS

Museo de Albacete

Parque Abelardo Sánchez. Open Tue–Sat 10am–2pm, 4.30–7pm, (Jul Tue–Sat 10am–2pm), Sun & public hols 9.30am–2pm. Closed 1 Jan, Maundy Thu, Good Fri, 25 Dec. €3; free Wed pm, Sat pm, Sun am, 18 & 31 May. ℘967 22 83 07. www.albacete.es.

This modern building has two main sections. The principal one is the archaeology museum, displaying artefacts from the province: Iberian sculptures – including the *Sphinx of Haches*, the *Hind of Caudete*, the lion from Bienservida – and **Roman dolls with movable joints★** There is a small Fine Arts section.

Catedral de San Juan Bautista

Pl. de la Virgen de los Llanos. Open 10.45am–12.45pm, 5.45–8.45pm. ℘967 63 00 04.

Construction began in the late 16C. The facade and side doorway are additions. Three naves are separated by large Ionic columns. Mannerist paintings decorate the sacristy. The Capilla de la Virgen de los Llanos is a fine chapel dedicated to the Virgin of the Plains, the city's patron. The Renaissance altarpiece is by the Maestro de Albacete. Recent restoration has returned the original colours to the 19C ceiling frescoes.

Pasaje de Lodares

This narrow conservatory passageway, lined by shops and homes, links Calle Mayor with Calle del Tinte. Its Modernist architecture, dating from 1925, is emblematic of Albacete and was inspired by Milanese decoration. Allegorical figures proliferate.

▶ **Population:** 173 050
◐ **Michelin Map:** 576 O-P 24 Castilla–La Mancha (Albacete).
▤ **Info:** Plaza del Altozano. ℘967 630 004. www.albacete.es
◑ **Location:** The A 35 and A 30 lead to Valencia (NE) and Murcia (SE); the A 32 runs SW to Andalucía. AVE high-speed trains use the central station. ▰▰Albacete (AVE).
◈ **Don't Miss:** Pasaje de Lodares to experience old Albacete.
◔ **Timing:** A morning in town, then drive out to visit caves and castles.

EXCURSIONS

Alarcón★

◑ 103km/65mi NW.

◑ Take the A 31 to Honrubia, then turn right onto the A 3.

Alarcón, named for Alaric, its Visigothic founder, rises above a loop of the Júcar river. The 13C–14C castle is a Parador. The **location★★★** made the fortress practically impregnable; it follows a triangular plan, with a double protective enclosure.

Don Juan Manuel (1282–1348) wrote many of his cautionary tales while living there. Amid the whitewashed facades of Albacete, note the **Iglesia de Santa María** (Dr Agustín Tortosa), a Renaissance church with an elegant Plateresque doorway and a fine sculpted 16C altarpiece. On **Plaza de Don Juan Manuel** are the **ayuntamiento** (town hall), with its porticoed facade; the Iglesia de San Juan Bautista, a Herreran church; and the Casa-Palacio, adorned with elaborate grilles.

Alcalá del Júcar★

▶ 60km/37.3mi NE along the CM 3218.
The road winds through steep **gorges**.
The Júcar river encircles the magnificent **site★** of the village between its castle and church overlooking a fertile plain on the bottom of the gorge, unusual for arid La Mancha. A walk through Alcalá's maze of steep alleyways reveals hidden nooks and lookout-points. Dwellings hollowed out of rock have long corridors leading to cliffside balconies; some can be visited.

Cueva de la Vieja

▶ 70km/43.5mi E along the A 35, via Alpera. By phone appt only. ✆ 967 330 001 (town hall).
Some of the over 100 discernible cave paintings here – of human figures, phalluses, tribal customs, hunting stags with bows and arrows and more – date back 5 000 years.

Almansa

▶ 74km/46mi E along the A 35.
🚌 Plaza 1º de Mayo.
Almansa's labyrinthe of streets and lanes spreads across a limestone crag crowned by a picturebook castle.

Iglesia de la Asunción – Below the castle. The church owes its mix of styles to a remodelling. The Renaissance portal is attributed to Vandelvira.

Palacio de los Condes de Cirat (Pl. de Santa María) – The fine Manneriststyle doorway of this mansion, the **Casa Grande**, bears an escutcheon flanked by crude figures.

Castillo de Almansa – Restored 15C ramparts, perched along the rock ridge, command a view of the plain. Keystones in the keep *(torre de homenaje)* bear the coat of arms of the Marqués de Villena, the one-time feudal lord of the town. (Closed for construction as of Sep 2019; ✆ 967 344 771.)

Alcaraz

▶ 79km/49mi SW along the A 32.
Alcaraz, the historic capital of the sierra of the same name, stands isolated on a red clay rise. The town grew rich manufacturing carpets and retains its Renaissance character in buildings influenced by the great architect **Andrés de Vandelvira**, born here in 1509.

Plaza Mayor – On the main square are: the 15C Pósito, once a granary; 16C **ayuntamiento** (town hall) with an emblazoned facade; 17C **Lonja** del Corregidor, standing against the **Torre del Tardón** (clock tower); and 15C **Iglesia de la Santísima Trinidad**. Old houses front the **Calle Mayor**. Note a facade with the two warriors and the Plateresque **Puerta de la Aduana** (Customs Doorway) of the Casa Consistorial. Stepped alleys head from the right-hand side of the square. Guided visits to the old town, including the town's revived artisan carpet workshops, must be reserved in advance (Cherry Tours, 90 mins; from €5; ✆ 647 809 255). The path to the cemetrey passes under two arches, leading to fine views over rooftops and countryside.
From Alcaraz you can make a picturesque **excursion** 46km/28.5mi south to the **source of the River Mundo** where there are wooded valleys, springs, caves and falls.

Source of the Río Mundo

▶ 62 km/38.5mi S of Alcaraz on the CM 412.
Where the Río Mundo, a tributary of the Segura, emerges above ground, a spectacular waterfall tumbles from a sheer wall of rock into pools below at the foot of the Sierra del Calar. The source's flow varies greatly from spring (strong) to high summer (weak). It is best visited early in the day before coaches arrive.
🚶 From the car park, waymarked footpaths lead into the surrounding countryside.

Cuenca★★

Cuenca's spectacular setting★★ is a rocky, gravity-defying platform hemmed in by the Júcar and Huécar ravines *(hoces)*. The phenomenally preserved old city is on the UNESCO World Heritage List. Its beauty drew artists here in the 1960s; many left works for public enjoyment.

▶ **Population:** 56 703

Michelin Map: 576 L 23 – Castilla–La Mancha (Cuenca)

Info: Alfonso VIII 2. ℘969 24 10 51; Avenida Cruz Roja 1. ℘969 24 10 51. www.turismo.cuenca.es.

Location: Cuenca lies 164km/102mi E of Madrid in the Montes Universales, on the edge of the central Meseta. AVE high-speed train services from Madrid and Valencia call at Cuenca Fernando Zóbel station on the edge of town. Cuenca (AVE).

Parking: Follow signs for the *Casco Antiguo*. Cross Plaza Mayor and leave your car in the free car park.

Don't Miss: The 'hanging houses' and the vertiginous views.

WALKING TOUR

CIUDAD ANTIGUA★★ (OLD TOWN)
Allow 2hr 30min.

▶ From the car park, pass through the 16C Renaissance-style Arco del Bezudo, follow San Pedro to the San Pedro church, then turn left onto Ronda de Julián Romero.

Ronda Julián Romero
This stepped alley runs above the Huécar gorge to the cathedral.

Convento de las Carmelitas
Find contemporary art on display at the **Fundación Antonio Pérez** (see Sights), housed in an ex-Carmelite convent.

Catedral de Santa María La Mayor★
Pl. Mayor. Open Sun-Fri 10am-5pm, Sat & hols 10am-7pm. Closed 1 Jan, 25 Dec. From €4.80. ℘969 22 46 26. www.catedralcuenca.es
The cathedral was started in the 13C in Norman-Gothic style. One of two towers collapsed after an early 20C fire. The interior, a mix of Gothic and Renaissance decoration, has wrought-iron **chapel grilles★**, a twin ambulatory, a triforium and a **Plateresque door★** into the chapter house with carved walnut panels by Alonso Berruguete.

▶ Walk along the right-hand side of the Cathedral and take Canónigos.

This street is lined by the Bishops Palace, housing the **Museo Tesoro de la Catedral★** (same opening times as cathedral; €3.50, sold separately; www.catedralcuenca.es) and the **Museo de Cuenca** (see Sights).

Casas Colgadas★★ (Hanging Houses)
These restored 14C houses clinging to a windswept clifftop contain the **Museo de Arte Abstracto** (see Sights) and a restaurant. The best **view★** of the buildings is from across the **Puente de San Pablo**, an iron bridge that leads to the city's Parador. The panorama is particularly enchanting when illuminated.

▶ Return to the cathedral and head along José T Mena.

Iglesia de San Miguel
Bajada de San Miguel. Open for events and performances only (summer).
This Gothic-style former church is one of the main venues for Cuenca's **Religious Music Week** (www.smrcuenca.es).

▶ Return to the Plaza Mayor. Follow Severo Catalina and Pilares.

Plaza de las Angustias★

An 18C Franciscan monastery and a Baroque hermitage, the Virgin in Anguish, stand in this quiet square between the town and the ravine.

▶ Return to San Pedro and continue to the San Pedro church. For a good view, bear left into an alley that ends at the edge of the Júcar ravine.

SIGHTS

Museo de Arte Abstracto Español★★★

Casas Colgadas, C. de los Canónigos. Open Tue–Fri & public hols 11am–2pm, 4–6pm (until 8pm Sat), Sun 11am–2.30pm. See website for dates closed. ℘969 21 29 83. www.march.es/arte/cuenca.

The views from the Museum of Abstract Spanish Art are as thrilling as the collection, hung in plain galleries within stripped-back traditional houses, some overhanging the gorge. Works of unparalleled value by Chillida, Tàpies, Saura, Zóbel, Cuixart, Sempere, Rivera and others were amassed by painter Fernando Zóbel to make this museum the best of its kind in Spain.

The project grew around the friendships of the Cuenca Group of abstract artists formed in the 1960s, of whom Gustavo Torner was born in Cuenca.

Museo Provincial de Cuenca★

Obispo Valero 6. Open Tue–Sat 10am–2pm, 5–7pm (mid-Jul–mid-Sep 5–7pm), Sun & public hols 10am–2pm. ℘969 21 30 69. www.patrimoniohistoricoclm.es.

Prehistoric objects, sculpture, coins and ceramics found in Roman excavations. Note the top of a **Roman altar★** found at Ercávica illustrating ritual items.

Fundación Antonio Peréz★

Rda Julián Romero 20. Open Tue–Sun 11am–2pm, 5–8pm. Closed 18–21 Sep. €2. Free Wed pm. ℘969 23 06 19. www.fundacionantonioperez.com

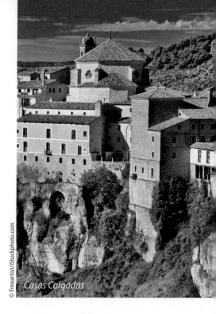

© Freeartist/iStockphoto.com

Casas Colgadas

Within a 17C Carmelite friary, works of modern Spanish art donated by the late local collector hang against a plain backdrop. Canvases by Millares and Saura, among others, sit alongside small installations.

Fundación Antonio Saura – Casa-Museo Zavala

Pl. de San Nicolás 4. Open 11am–2pm, 4–7pm (5-8pm in summer). Closed Mon & Tue in summer. ℘969 23 60 54.

Of the city's quartet of contemporary art spaces, this one, in a 17C palace with views over the Júcar gorge, is known for temporary shows. The first floor holds works by artist Antonio Saura (1930–1998), who lived in the town.

▲▲ Museo de las Ciencias de Castilla–La Mancha

Pl. Merced 1. Open Tue–Sat 10am–2pm, 4–7pm, Sun 10am–2pm. Closed 1 Jan, Maundy Thu, Good Fri, 18-21 Sep, 24, 25, 31 Dec. €5; free 18 & 31 May. ℘969 24 03 20. http://pagina.jccm.es/museociencias. This modern science museum has a planetarium.

EXCURSIONS

Las Hoces (Ravines)

▶ Round tour of 15km/9.6mi.

The roads that trace the river circling Cuenca afford views of the hanging houses. The **Hoz del Júcar** is the shorter, more enclosed ravine.

The **Hoz del Huécar** course swings from side to side between gentler slopes given over to family farms.

◐ Turn left at the end of the ravine for Buenache de la Sierra and left again for the Convento de San Jerónimo.

In a right bend, there's a **view★** of grey rock columns and, in the distance, Cuenca. Enter through the gateway.

Las Torcas★

◐ Take the N 420, then bear left after 11km/6.5mi.

The road crosses a conifer wood punctuated by *torcas*, odd and occasionally dramatic depressions.

🚗 DRIVING TOUR

SERRANÍA DE CUENCA★
270km/168mi. Allow 1 day.

Wind and water formed these whimsical landscapes in limestone amid pines and numerous streams. Heading north you reach a Roman settlement and Renaissance monastery, both of which have been on the main route from Madrid to the Mediterranean since Classical times.

Ventano del Diablo

◐ 25.5km/15.8mi from Cuenca along the CM 2105.

The Devil's Window, an opening in rock, overlooks the depths of the **Garganta del Júcar** (Júcar Gorges).

Ciudad Encantada★

◐ Follow the road signposted to the right of the CM 2105.

🔼 A circuit directs visitors through the Enchanted Forest to the Tobogán (Toboggan Slope) and Mar de Piedras (Sea of Stones).

◐ To reach the Mirador de Uña (2km/1mi) viewpoint, take the road from the car park.

Enjoy the **view** of the Júcar Valley and Uña's green lake flanked by towering cliffs.

👥 Los Callejones de las Majadas
3km/1.8mi from Las Majadas.
🚻 Leave your car on the esplanade.
'The Alleways' are a secluded, otherworldly maze of paths among enormous eroded boulders.

Nacimiento del Río Cuervo★ (Source of the Cuervo)
30km/18.6mi N of Las Majadas toward **Alto de la Vega.** 🚻 Leave your car after the bridge and walk up 500m/547yd.
A footpath leads to **waterfalls★** and mossy grottoes.

Hoz de Beteta★ (Beteta Ravine)
30km/18.6mi NW along the CM 2106 and CM 2201 toward Beteta.
This impressive ravine was cut by the River Guadiela. From Vadillos, a road to the left leads to the spa of Solán de Cabras. The road (CM 210) continues through the **River Escabas valley.** Before reaching Priego (3km/1.8mi), a branch to the right leads to the **Convento de San Miguel de las Victorias**, in an impressive **setting★**.

◐ Take the N320 E, then turn S along the CM 2006 and CM200 to the A40, which leads you to the A3. From there follow signs to Uclés.

Uclés
The monastery here was the seat of the Order of Santiago from 1174 to 1499.

Castillo Monasterio d'Uclés

Open Jun–Aug 10am–8pm, Mar–May and Sep–Oct until 7pm, Nov–Feb until 6pm. Guided tours (extra €2) Sat–Sun 11am, 12.30pm. Closed 1 & 6 Jan, 25 Dec. €5. ℰ969 13 50 58. www.monasteriuocles.com.

This massive, castle-like monastery was begun in 1529 in Plateresque style. Most of the work was undertaken by Herrera's disciple, **Francisco de Mora** (1553–1610), hence his nickname, the Little Escorial. The entrance is via a beautiful **Baroque portal★★**. Note too the Baroque well and the **artesonado★** ceiling in the refectory. The ramparts command a fine view.

Parque Arqueológico de Segóbriga

In Saelices, 14km/8.7mi S of Uclés.

▶ Leave the A 3 at exit 103/104 and follow signs toward Casas de Luján.

Begin your visit at the **Centro de Interpretación** (Ctra. Carrascosa de Campo a Villamayor de Santiago; open Apr–Sep Tue–Sun 10am–3pm, 4–7.30pm; Oct–Mar Tue–Sun 10am–6pm; €6; ⊙allow 2–4 hours for a visit; ℰ629 75 22 57) for an overview of this 5C BC Celtiberian site that became an important Roman waypoint. By 1C AD, it had a theatre and an imposing **amphitheatre★**, with a capacity for 5 000 spectators. Parts of its baths and ramparts also remain.

ADDRESSES

🛏 STAY

⊖⊜ **Posada Huécar** – Po. del Huécar 3, Cuenca. ℰ969 21 42 01. www.posadahuecar.com. 20 rooms. Find excellent value in the old part of Cuenca at this inn with a garden and simply furnished rooms, all with TV. Free coffee and pastries for breakfast.

⊖⊜ **Posada San José** – Ronda Julián Romero 4, Cuenca. ℰ969 21 13 00. www.posadasanjose.com. 22 rooms.

⊒€9. This welcoming hotel occupies an old-fashioned beamed hanging house. The large, comfortable rooms with tile floors have a country feel. The public areas – sitting room and cafeteria for breakfast and dinner – hang over the gorge.

⊖⊜⊜⊜ **Parador de Cuenca** – Subida a San Pablo, Cuenca. ℰ902 54 79 79. www.parador.es. ⊒ €20. Sitting on the far bank of the River Huécar, the Parador can been seen from afar. Built within a 16C convent, it offers a view over the old town and its hanging houses. The tasteful decoration includes old tiles in the dining room.

🍴 EAT

⊖⊜ **Mesón Mangana** – Pl. Mayor 3. ℰ969 22 94 51. Closed 15 Oct–15 Nov, Thu. The perfect spot for a meal when visiting the old quarter, Mangana serves good, rustic home cooking like blistered sausages, aged manchego and grilled meats. The set menus are a good value.

⊖⊜⊜ **Figón del Huécar** – Ronda Julián Romero 6. ℰ969 24 00 62. www.figondelhuecar.es. Closed Sun eve, Mon. Cuenca's most legendary restaurant is this gastro-tavern with modern Manchegan fare occupying a medieval home. The dining room looks out over the old town.

⊖⊜⊜⊜ **Trivio** – C. Colón 25. ℰ969 03 05 93. www.restaurantetrivio.com. Closed Sun eve, Mon. It's not all meat and potatoes in Cuenca anymore, thanks to this experimental Michelin-starred hotspot serving tweezed, foamed and torched dishes using local ingredients.

FESTIVALS

The Holy Week processions unfurl throught the steep, narrow streets of the old town. Don't miss the Procesión de las Turbas (Procession of the Crowd), which sets out around dawn (5.30–6.00am) to the sound of drumbeats through silent streets, terminating at the Calvary. Around this time of year there is also a festival of holy music.

Facade of Palacio del Infantado

© Javier Larrea/age fotostock

Guadalajara

In the 14C, Guadalajara ('valley of stones' in Arabic) became the fief of the Mendozas. This illustrious Spanish family includes the poet Íñigo López de Mendoza, the first Marquis of Santillana (1398–1458); his son, Cardinal Pedro González de Mendoza (1428–95); and the second Duke of Infantado, who built the palace at the north entrance in the 15C.

▶ **Population:** 255 336

🜚 **Michelin Map:** 576 K 20 – map 121 Alrededores de Madrid – Castilla–La Mancha (Guadalajara).

🄸 **Info:** Glorieta de la Aviación Militar Española. 𝒫949 88 70 99. www. turismoenguadalajara.es.

◗ **Location:** Guadalajara is NE of Madrid along the A 2 motorway. High-speed AVE trains link to Madrid and Barcelona (station 9km/5.5mi from town centre). 🚄 Guadalajara (AVE station 9km/5.5mi from town centre).

😊 **Don't Miss:** The Palacio del Infantado.

SIGHTS
Palacio del Infantado★
(Palace of the Duke of Infantado)
Pl. de los Caídos. Open: Patio Tue–Sun 9am–2pm, 4–8pm. Museo: Tue–Sat 10am–2pm, 4–7pm (mid-Jun–mid-Sep closed pm), Sun & public hols 10am–2pm. Closed 1 & 6 Jan, Good Fri, 1 May, 8 & 11 Sep, 24 & 25 Dec. €3 (museum), patio free. 𝒫949 21 33 01.
This late 15C palace, by Juan Guas, is a masterpiece of Isabelline civil architecture fusing Gothic and Mudéjar styles. The **facade★** is adorned with diamond-studded stonework and the Mendoza coat of arms. The upper gallery is a series of paired ogee windows interposed between corbelled loggias. The effect is impressive in spite of windows added in the 17C. The two-storey **patio★** is just as remarkable with multifoil arches on turned columns and extremely delicate Mudéjar ornamentation.

The once-sumptuous interior was damaged during the Spanish Civil War. The palace houses the **Museo Provincial de Guadalajara** with ethnographical, archeological and arts collections.

EXCURSIONS
Pastrana
◗ 42km/26mi SE on the N 320.
The picturesque town of Pastrana was the seat of the **Princess of Eboli**, involved in intrigues in the time of Philip II. She was imprisoned by her husband for the last five years of her life in the palace on the Plaza de la Hora, so called because she was allowed to show herself at the window for an hour a day. The 16C **Iglesia Colegiata** (Melchor Cano 1; open daily 11.30am–2pm, 4.30–7pm, Jun–Aug 5–8pm, Sun & public hols 1–2pm, 4.30–7pm; free for church; €5 for entry to crypt, church and museum; 𝒫949 37 00 27, www. pastrana.org/turismo), a collegiate church, contains four **Gothic tapestries★** woven in Tournai after cartoons by Nuno Gonçalves. These illustrate the capture of Arzila and Tangier by Alfonso V of Portugal in 1471 and reveal a mastery of composition, an eye for detail

(armour and costume) and talent for portraiture.

Sigüenza★

⬤ 75km/46mi NE on the E 90 N 2 then the CM-1101. 🚊Sigüenza. 🅱 Serrano Sanz 9. ☏949 34 70 07. www.siguenza.es. Sigüenza descends in pink and ochre tiers below a cathedral fortress and castle. The old quarter is a maze of narrow streets lined by Romanesque mansions.

Catedral★★

Pl. del Obispo Don Bernardo 6. Open 9.30am–2pm, 4.30–8pm. ☏949 23 13 70. www.catedralsiguenza.es. €6.

The nave, begun in the 12C, was completed in 1495. In the **north aisle**, the **doorway★** into the Capilla de la Anunciación is decorated with Renaissance pilasters, Mudéjar arabesques and Gothic cusping. In the north transept is a fine **sculptured unit★★**: a 16C porphyry doorway opens onto cloisters of marble. The **sacristy ceiling★** by Covarrubias is a profusion of heads and roses between which peer thousands of cherubim.

The chancel (presbiterio) has a 17C wrought-iron grille framed by alabaster **pulpits★**. The **Doncel tomb★★**, (open only by guided tour weekends 11am–2pm) in the south transept features a realistic figure of a youth, a major work of sepulchral art.

The holdings of the **Museo Diocesano** (Pl. Obispo Don Bernardo; open Wed, Thu, Sun 11am–2pm, 4–7pm, Fri & Sat until 8pm; €3; ☏949 391 023), on the cathedral's west facade, were largely sourced from small churches in the surrounding countryside and include a 14C alabaster Virgin, a Pietà attributed to Morales and a Salzillo statue of the prophet Eli.

Valverde de los Arroyos★

⬤ 68km/45mi N via CM 1003 & 1006. Around Ocejón (2 048m/6 700ft) are the so-called **pueblos negros** or black slate villages. Among these, Valverde is especially attractive, its houses adorned with wooden balconies and its plaza retaining its original fountain. A footpath

leads to the **Despeñal Agua** waterfall that tumbles 100m/110ft down.

ADDRESSES

🛏 STAY

🍽 **Tryp Guadalajara Hotel**– Av. Eduardo Guitián 7, Guadalajara. ☏949 209 300. www.melia.com. 159 rooms. 🍽 €11. Sitting on the edge of the town, the Tryp hotel, Melià's budget subsidiary, is tall modern building with good views, simple decoration and dependable brand-name service.

🍽🍽 **Parador de Sigüenza** – Pl. del Castillo. ☏902 54 79 79. www.parador.es. 79 rooms. 🍽 €11. This 12C castle has been putting up kings and queens for centuries – including Ferdinand and Isabella and the current king, Felipe VI – and you'll feel like one while staying here, thanks to the sumptuous antique furnishings, soaring halls and refined restaurant. The inner patio, with a garden where you can relax with a drink, is very atmospheric. Secure parking.

🍴 EAT

🍽 **El Mesón** – C. Seminario 14, Sigüenza. Closed Mon. ☏949 39 06 49, www.hostalelmeson.com. Regional specialities, many using tender local lamb, are served in an rustic, beamed dining room that fills up on weekends. Save room for the homemade desserts.

🍽 **Bar Alameda** – Po. de la Alameda 4, Sigüenza. ☏949 39 05 53. Closed Thu. Locals pile into this raucous bar to eat their weight in regional tapas like sliced blood sausage and stuffed mushroom caps.

🍽🍽 **Casa Palomo** – Cuesta San Miguel 5, Guadalajara. Closed Jul. ☏949 23 06 32. www.casapalomo.es. Locally sourced ingredients are a mainstay of this cosy restaurant. If wild mushrooms are on the menu, spring for them.

🍽🍽 **Calle Mayor** – C. Mayor 21, Sigüenza. ☏949 39 17 48. www.restaurantelacasa.com. Traditional and creative dishes intermingle on the menu of this elegant restaurant in a historic building in the centre of old Sigüenza.

Extremadura

Much of the boundary between Spain and Portugal is formed by Extremadura, which means 'beyond the River Duero'. In Roman times it was at one with present-day Portugal, when the larger territory was known as Lusitania. This was the heyday of the region, when Mérida, the home of Emperor Augustus, was its capital. Some 1 500 years later Charles V also chose to retire here, far from the cares of the world. Like La Mancha, Extremadura has been shaped by the harsh, unforgiving climate of La Meseta. Add to this its isolation from the rest of Spain (as of 2019, there's still no decent train servicing the region) and centuries of absentee landlord farming, and it is no wonder that the region has seen generations of brain drain to Madrid. Extremadura's most famous denizens were its Conquistadores: Cortés, conqueror of Mexico; Pizarro, conqueror of Peru; Hernando de Soto, first European discoverer of the Mississippi; and many more. This is one of Spain's least densely populated regions; in many areas sheep outnumber humans while storks wheel majestically overhead and nest on tall buildings and towers. Extremaduran summers are punishingly hot, but its spring and autumn might be Spain's best-kept secrets.

Highlights

1 Wandering the time-capsule streets of old **Cáceres** (p219)

2 Crossing the Puente Romano bridge near **Monfragüe's** natural parkland (p221)

3 Taking a coffee in the Plaza Mayor in charming **Trujillo** (p222)

4 Paying homage to the Virgin in the Monasterio de **Guadalupe** (p223)

5 Sitting in **Mérida's** Teatro Romano, imagining the past (p226)

Medieval Majesty

Upper Extremadura has the most fertile land in the region, especially in the verdant Valle de la Vera, where crops include cotton and around 80% of Spain's tobacco. The hilltop town of Plasencia, with its market, is a highlight. Built mostly between the 12C and 14C, its old mansions and churches retain their atmosphere, and the cathedral is one of Extremadura's finest. Close by is the monastery of Yuste, the retirement home of Charles V, a haven of tranquility at the foot of the mountains. In the centre of the region, the ancient walled city of Cáceres, designated a World Heritage site, offers a feast of medieval architecture, including one of Spain's finest assemblies of Gothic and Renaissance mansions.

Conquistador Towns

Guadalupe is famous for its Mudéjar monastery, the second most important Marian shrine in the country, home to the effigy of the Virgin of Guadalupe.

The cult of the Virgin and the village's name were exported by the Conquistadores and remain widespread throughout Latin America. Trujillo is a beguiling small town, plush with Conquistador wealth with mansions built from the riches plundered by Pizarro (and his four half brothers, also from Trujillo), de Orellana and other adventurers. Small cities and towns in the south have kept extraordinary architecture and art. Mérida was the headquarters of Western Roman Iberia and retains many important monuments including the Roman Theatre, where plays are staged each summer. Olivenza, close to the Portuguese border, is awash with Manueline architecture; its 15C castle is now a Parador. Stay the night, and you'll be following in the footsteps of Hernán Cortés, who posted up here before striking out for the so-called New World. In fact, some of Spain's most coveted Paradors are in Extremadura in Plasencia, Trujillo, Guadalupe, Cáceres and beyond, where you can literally sleep on the region's rich history.

Plasencia★

In this tranquil, oft-overlooked provincial town are stunning Renaissance buildings such as the New Cathedral. Between February and July, migrating storks nest on rooftops and towers.

BARRIO VIEJO (OLD QUARTER)
Houses with wrought-iron balconies define the neighbourhood.

Catedrales★
Pl. de la Catedral. Open Apr–Sep Tue–Sun 11am–2pm, 5–8pm (Oct–Mar 4–7pm). €4 (Old Cathedral). ℘927 42 44 06. www.catedralesdeplasencia.org
Enter by the north door, edged with Plateresque decoration. A door left of the coro opens into the 13-14C Old Cathedral (parish church of Santa María). The cloisters have pointed arches and Romanesque capitals, while the chapter house is covered by a fine dome. In the shortened nave is a museum of religious art.
Inside the 15C Catedral Nueva (New Cathedral), the tall pillars and slender ribs illustrate the mastery of architects Juan de Java, Diego de Siloé and Alonso de Covarrubias. The altarpiece★ is decorated with statues by the 17C sculptor Gregorio Fernández; the choir stalls★ were carved in 1520 by Rodrigo Alemán.

Start from Plaza de la Catedral and – leaving on your right the Casa del Deán (Deanery), with its unusual corner window, and the Casa del Dr Trujillo, now the Law Courts (Palacio de Justicia) – head toward the Gothic Iglesia de San Nicolás, which faces the facade of the Casa de las Dos Torres (House with Two Towers).

Continue to the Palacio Mirabel (open by appt only; ℘927 410 701). Flanked by a massive tower, it contains a two-tiered patio and the Museo Cinegético (Hunting Museum). A passage beneath the palace (door on right) leads to Calle

▶ **Population:** 40 141
♧ **Michelin Map:** 576 L 11 – Extremadura (Cáceres).
Info: Calle Santa Clara. ℘927 423 843. www.plasencia.es.
Location: Plasencia stands where the Sierra de Gredos meets the Extremadura plain. Plasencia.

Sancho Polo and an area with stepped alleys (near the ramparts) and white-walled houses with washing drying overhead. Turn right onto the Plaza Mayor, bounded by porticoes and full of busy cafés.

EXCURSIONS
Monasterio de Yuste★
▶ 1.8km/1mi from Cuacos de Yuste. Open Tue–Sun 10am–8pm (until 6pm Oct–Mar). €7. Free for EU citzens Wed–Thu last 3 hrs, for all 18 May & 2 Oct. ℘927 17 28 58.
www.patrimonionacional.es.
In 1556, a weary Emperor Charles V retired to this modest Hieronymite monastery in a serene mountain setting. The structure, devastated during the War of Independence, is partially restored. Of Charles V's small palace, the dining hall, royal bedroom adjoining the chapel, Gothic church and two fine cloisters – one Gothic, the other Plateresque – remain. Leave time to wander down to Cuacos de Yuste (pop. 846), the tiny village below the monastery where Charles V's illegitimate son, Don Juan of Austria, grew up.

Coria★
▶ 42km/26mi W.

▶ Take the N 630 S. After 7km/4.3mi turn right onto the EX 108.

This atmospheric town, overlooking the Alagón Valley, retains Roman walls and gateways, rebuilt in the Middle Ages.

*River Tajo running through the
Parque Nacional de Monfragüe*

© Juan Carlos Cantero/age fotostock

Walk through its old streets to reach
the cathedral.

Catedral de la Asunción de Nuestra Señora★

Pl. de la Catedral. Closed for construction
as of Sep 2019. ℘927 50 39 60.
The Gothic cathedral, embellished
with Plateresque motifs in the 16C, is
crowned with a Baroque tower and has
a sculptured frieze.
The tall single aisle has vaulting
adorned with lierne and tierceron ribs
typical of the region. Note the 18C altarpiece and, in the *coro*, the wrought-iron
grilles and Gothic choir stalls. Within the
cathedral is a museum of religious art,
most of which was culled from nearby
churches.

Parque Nacional de Monfragüe

The National Park of Monfragüe, lying
southeast of Plasencia, protects 500sq
km/19 sq mi of rolling hill country
around the dammed valleys of the River
Tagus and Tiétar.
The Mediterranean scrub and woodland here, unbroken by large towns
or farmland, has become a refuge for
wildlife: Rare birds can be seen, albeit
at a distance, from the road or lookout
points, with remarkable ease. The entry
point to the park is **Villarreal de San
Carlos**, where there are two information
centres: one explains the park's ecosystems and the other its fauna (Centro

de Información, Villareal de San
Carlos, off the EX208 from Plasencia;
open 9.30am (from 9am Sat & Sun)
–7.30pm, 6pm Sep-Mar; ℘927 19 91 34;
www.magrama.gob.es/es/red-parques-
nacionales). The little town offers simple
pensiones and taverns and is the starting point of hiking and driving routes.
One road (12km/7.5mi) leads to the lake
formed by the dam, which overlooks
farmland outside the park; here fighting bulls and black pigs graze under
holm oaks. A second (8km/5mi) winds
through the hills, past a lookout point
to the Salto del Gitano (Gypsy's Leap),
a peak where imperial eagles, black
storks and kites breed (the park is home
to some 20 birds of prey). Just beyond,
you can park and climb to Monfragüe
fortress, which gives a 360° view from
the top. Some of the other wildlife in
the park, such as the Iberian lynx and
genets, are difficult to see, but slow
driving often perks up red deer and
wild boar.

ADDRESSES

🏠 STAY

🍽 **Casa Rural Al-Mofrag** – Villareal de
San Carlos 19. ℘927 199 205. www.casa
ruralalmofrag.com. 6 rooms. Expect
simple but comfortable rural
accommodation. Rooms with kitchens
and jacuzzis available.

🍽🏠🏠🏠 **Parador de Jarandilla de la
Vera** – Av. de García Prieto 1, Jarandilla
de la Vera, Cáceres. ℘902 54 79 79.
www.parador.es. 52 rooms. ⚏ €15. This
rural stunner is housed in a modest
15C castle, entered through a long
courtyard. It offers tranquil gardens and
nearby mountain walks and is an ideal
base for exploring the Plasencia area.

🍽/EAT

🍽 **La Pitarra del Gordo** – Pl Mayor 8.
Plasencia ℘927 41 45 05. A handy
refueling station for tapas or lunch, this
lively traditional city-centre bar serves
fine Extremaduran ham. The rough red
pitarra wine is made from local grapes.

Cáceres★★★

The Almohad walls of this World Heritage site, a provincial capital, enclose a rare ensemble of superbly preserved Gothic and Renaissance noble houses.

THE CITY TODAY

Cáceres was a thriving commercial hub as far back as 35 BC under Roman rule, when it was Called Norba Caesarina. It retains a heady mix of Roman, Moorish, Sephardic and Renaissance architecture within its medieval walls.

 WALKING TOUR

CIUDAD MONUMENTAL★★★ (OLD CÁCERES)

1hr30min.

Moorish walls hem in a number of Gothic and Renaissance mansions beyond compare in Spain. The shields on the unadorned, ochre facades of the 15C and 16C reflect their owners, the Ulloas, the Ovandos and the Saave-dras, who in battles won prestige, not wealth. Infuriatingly, the fortified tow-ers of Cáceres were demolished on the command of Queen Isabel in 1477. Pass beneath the **Arco de la Estrella** (Star Arch; Pl. Mayor), which was built into the wall by Manuel Churriguera in the 18C.

Plaza de Santa María★

You're surrounded by ochre facades. The front of the **Palacio Mayoralgo** (Mayoralgo Palace; closed to the pub-lic) has elegant paired windows, while the **Palacio Episcopal** (Bishop's Palace; free access to the patio portico) has a 16C bossed doorway flanked with medallions of the Old and New Worlds.

Concatedral de Santa María

Pl. Santa María. Open daily; see website for times. €4. ℰ927 21 53 13. www.concatedralcaceres.com.
This 16C church has three Gothic aisles of almost equal height, with

- ▶ **Population:** 95 617
- ◔ **Michelin Map:** 576 N 10 (town plan) – Extremadura (Cáceres).
- ▤ **Info:** Plaza de Santa Clara. ℰ927 111 222. www.turismocaceres.org.
- ▶ **Location:** Cáceres is strategically situated at the heart of Extremadura in west-central Spain. ▬Cáceres (AVE planned 2014).
- ⊛ **Don't Miss:** The city walls and mansions, especially at night.
- ◷ **Timing:** Allow a half-day in Cáceres, then explore the region.

lierne and tierceron vaulting from which ribs descend into slender columns engaged in the main pillars. The sumptuously carved retable (16C), unpainted according to local custom, is difficult to see. Rub the feet of the statue of San Pedro de Alcántara in the corner for good luck.

▶ Continue to the top of Calle de las Tiendas.

Palacio de Carvajal

C. Amargura 1 . Open Mon–Fri 8am–8.45pm, Sat 10am–1.45pm, 5–7.45pm, Sun & public hols 10am–1.45pm ℰ927 25 55 97.
Built between the 15C and 16C, blend-ing Gothic and Renaissance styles, this palace – the only one open to the public, barring the one occupied by the Museo de Cáceres – is flanked by a medieval tower. It's filled with period furniture and art and has an information centre on Cáceres province. Of special interest is the architectural model of Cáceres old town.

▶ Take the narrow alley opposite, Adarve Obispo Álvarez de Castro.

a vaulted arcade. Inside are a Baroque altarpiece and side chapels with tombs with decorative heraldic motifs.

On Calle Orellana, the 15C **Torre de la Plata** (Silver Tower) and **Casa del Sol** (Sun House, for the Solís family crest over the arch) have unusual parapets.

▷ Walk back to Plaza San.

Palacio de las Cigüeñas

Plaza de San Mateo. Open Sat–Sun & hols 11am–1pm.
The House of the Storks retains the town's only 15C battlemented tower.

▷ Turn left toward Plaza de las Veletas.

Casa de las Veletas

Pl. de las Veletas. Open Tue–Fri 9am–2.30pm, 4–8pm; Sat 10am–2.30pm, 4–8pm; Sun & hols 10am–3pm. Closed 1 & 6 Jan, 23 Apr, 31 May, 24, 25 & 31 Dec. €1.20; free for EU citizens. ℰ927 01 08 77. www.museodecaceres.juntaex.es
The **Museo de Cáceres** occupies this 12C Moorish mansion. Collections include Bronze Age steles, Celtiberian statues of wild boar (*verracos*) and local dress and crafts. Its original 11C *aljibe* (cistern) is still fed from the roof and sloping square.

▷ Take Calle Ancha opposite Iglesia San Mateo.

Casa del Comendador de Alcuéscar

Ancha 6.
This palace, also Called the **Palacio de Torreorgaz**, houses the city's Parador. It has a Gothic tower, delicate window surrounds and an unusual corner balcony. Down the alley within the ramparts is the **Palacio de los Golfines de Arriba** (Ⓒsee above). Further on, on C. Santa Ana, the **Palacio de Adanero★** is now home to the law school.

▷ Go through the ramparts opposite.

Palacio Toledo Moctezuma

The 14–16C palace is now the city's history archive. Its curious name derives from the marriage of conquistador Juan Cano de Saavedra to the daughter of Aztec king Moctezuma II.

▷ Return to Plaza Sta María.

Palacio de los Golfines de Abajo★ (Lower Golfines Palace)

Pl. de Santa María. Closed to the public.
This late-15C Gothic-Plateresque mansion has a paired window, a style that derives from the Moorish *ajimez*.
A Plateresque frieze with winged griffons was added in the 16C.

▷ Plaza San Jorge is adjacent to Plaza Sta María.

Plaza San Jorge

Note the austere 18C facade of the Jesuit church of **San Francisco Javier**.

▷ Take Cuesta de la Compañía to Pl. San Mateo.

Iglesia de San Mateo

Pl. de San Mateo. Open for Mass.
The church's High Gothic nave, begun in the 14C, abuts a 16C *coro alto* set on

The steps to Plaza Mayor del General Mola afford a fine view of the walls.

ADDITIONAL SIGHTS

Iglesia de Santiago
(St James' Church)

Pl. de Santiago

The Romanesque church outside the city walls is the birthplace of the Military Order of the Knights of Cáceres, precursor to Order of the Knights of St James. Its altarpiece, by Berruguete (1557), bears scenes from the Life of Christ. The church was renovated in the 16C by Valladolid-born architect Hontañón. The **Palacio de Godoy** opposite has an impressive coat of arms on the corner and a fine inner patio.

EXCURSIONS

Santuario de la Virgen de la Montaña

◯ Sierra de la Mosca. 3km/1.8mi E. Open daily 8.30am–2pm, 4–8pm (9pm in summer). Closed 22 Apr–1st Sun in May. ℘927 22 00 49.

In this 17C Baroque shrine, set among olive trees, is a statuette of the Virgin (a *romería*, or pilgrimage, is held the first Sunday in May). The esplanade offers a **view★** of the plateau.

Museo Vostell-Malpartida

◯ 18km/11mi E. Follow the N 521 to Malpartida de Cáceres, then signposts. Open Tue–Sun, see website for times; closed 1 & 6 Jan, 28 Feb, 24 & 25 Dec. €2.50, free Wed. ℘927 01 08 12. www.museovostell.org.

Set in an 18C wool-washing plant, this quirky museum was created by Hispano-German artist Wolf Vostell, co-founder of the 1960s Fluxus movement, whos wife was Extremaduran. It includes late 20C works by Canogar, the Crónica team, Saura and Brecht and the fruits of Vostell's zany imagination including a Cadillac encompassed by dinner plates. The surroundings are a work of art in themselves: You're in the heart of Los Barruecos nature reserve, known for its bizarre rock formations.

Arroyo de la Luz

◯ 20km/12.4mi W along the N 521 and C 523.

The 16C altarpiece of the **Iglesia de la Asunción** has 16 **painted tablets★** and four medallions by **Morales the Divine**, a rare, stunning assemblage. The tourist office (Plaza de la Constitución 21, open Wed–Sat 9.30am–2pm, 4.30–8pm; Sun 10am–2pm; ℘927 270 437), directly opposite, opens the church for visitors.

Alcántara

◯ 65km/40mi NW via the N 521and C 523.

Alcántara is famed for its Roman bridge from which it took its ancient name (*Al Kantara* in Arabic).

Puente Romano★

◯ 2km/1.2mi NW on the road to Portugal. This bridge (106 AD) of unmortared granite blocks has withstood formidable floodwaters. Note the small temple at one end.

Convento de San Benito

Regimiento de Argel. Free guided tours. Call for times. ℘927 39 00 81.

The old headquarters of the Military Order of Alcántara stands high above the Tajo. The 16C monastery has a Plateresque church with star vaulting, a Gothic patio and a well-restored refectory. The graceful Renaissance amphitheatre is used as the backdrop for plays.

ADDRESSES

🍴 STAY AND 🍽️ EAT

🍲🍲🍲🍲 **Atrio** – Av de España 30 (pasaje) ℘927 24 29 28. www. restauranteatrio.com. Closed last 2 weeks of Jul, Sun pm, Mon. Chef Toño Pérez's passion project has single-handedly put Cáceres on the gourmet map with his two-Michelin-star tasting menus blending local and far-flung flavours. Many ingredients are grown on the premises. Ask to see the Château d'Yquem cave in the basement cellar. There are ultra-luxurious rooms with collectible art in the Mansilla + Tuñón-designed boutique hotel above.

Trujillo★★

Trujillo is an idyllic medieval gem of a town that most Spaniards would just as soon not tell you about. It was fortified by the Moors in the 13C and later embellished with mansions built by those who had made their fortunes in the Americas.

A BIT OF HISTORY

Cradle of the Conquistadores – **Francisco de Orellana** left here in 1542 to explore the country of the Amazons. Native son **Francisco Pizarro** (c. 1475–1541) plundered the riches of the Inca Emperor Atahualpa and was murdered amid untold riches in his own palace.

SIGHTS

OLD QUARTER

Trujillo's mansions, built in the late 16C and 17C, are decorated with arcades, loggias and corner windows. Its **Plaza Mayor★★** – one of the most beautiful in Spain – is oblong and lined with mansions. At night it's like a *Game of Thrones* set – but with tapas instead of horse jerky and stallion hearts (a number of scenes from the famous show were filmed here).

The 16C **Iglesia de San Martín** (open daily 10am–2pm, 4–6.30pm; €1.50) encloses a nave chequered with funerary paving stones. The 17C **Palacio de los Duques de San Carlos★** (Palace of the Dukes of Saint Charles) is now a convent. The granite facade, decorated in Classical Baroque style, has a corner window topped by a crest with a double-headed eagle. Calle Sillería leads away from the southeastern corner of the square. A Renaissance loggia, the **Palacio de los Marqueses de Piedras Albas** (Palace of the Marquises of Piedras Albas) has been accommodated into the original Gothic wall. On the other side of the square stands the **Palacio de los Marqueses de la Conquista** (Palace of the Marquises of the Conquest), in reality the palace of Hernando Pizarro, the conquistador's brother. To the left of a

- ▶ **Population:** 9 193
- ⊛ **Michelin Map:** 576 N 12 – Extremadura (Cáceres).
- ⒤ **Info:** Plaza Mayor. 𝒫927 32 26 77. www.turismotrujillo.es.
- ◖ **Location:** Trujillo is situated on the A 5 linking Madrid and Badajoz. 🚃Nearest station: Cáceres (46km).
- ⊚ **Don't Miss:** The Plaza Mayor and Old Town alleyways.

Plateresque corner **window★**, added in the 17C, are busts of Francisco Pizarro and his wife; on the right are Hernando and his niece, whom he married. Other buildings on the plaza include the old town hall, now law courts, fronted by Renaissance arcades and the Casa de las Cadenas (House of Chains), where Christians freed from the Moors are said to have shed their fetters. Its Mudéjar belfry is a favourite nesting spot for storks. The **Iglesia de Santiago** (open daily 9am–2pm, 5–8pm) hosted council meetings in the Middle Ages. It's 13C Romanesque belfry and the tower of the Palacio de los Chaves frame the Arco de Santiago (St James Arch), one of Trujillo's seven gates.

Trujillo's pantheon is the 13C **Iglesia de Santa María la Mayor★** (Pl. de Santa María; open daily 10am–2pm, 5–8pm, Nov–Mar 4.30–7.30pm; €2; 𝒫927 32 26 77). The panels of the **Gothic retable★** are by Fernando Gallego. Climb to the top of the belfry, and you'll be rewarded with a terrific **view** over the terracotta roofs, the Plaza Mayor arcades and the castle. The **Castillo de Trujillo** (Cerro Cabeza de Zorro; open daily 10am–2pm, 5–8pm, Oct–May 4–7pm; €1.50; 𝒫927 322 677) is perched on a granite ledge, its massive crenellated wall reinforced by heavy towers. Above the keep is the patron of Trujillo, Our Lady of Victory. There are fine views from the walls.

Guadalupe★★

Guadalupe's monastery bristles with battlements and turrets above a picturesque village with brown tile roofs. Richly endowed by rulers and deeply venerated by the people, the 'miraculous' Virgin of Guadalupe, in the monastery's church, made this an important place of pilgrimage in the 16C and 17C. Ferdinand and Isabelle received Christopher Columbus here, and Native Americans were summoned to its church to be forcibly baptised. Today the Virgin remains a symbol of *Hispanidad*, across Spanish-speaking cultures. The road above the old village★ commands a fine view★.

▶ **Population:** 1 887
⊙ **Michelin Map:** 576 N 14 – Extremadura (Cáceres).
🅱 **Info:** Plaza Santa María de Guadalupe. ☎675 28 69 87. www.turismoextremadura. com.
◖ **Location:** Guadalupe is SW of Madrid, on the slopes of the Guadalupe range. 🚉Nearest station: Mérida (127km).
⊗ **Don't Miss:** The monastery, and processions celebrating Día de Hispanidad (2 Oct).

SIGHTS

MONASTERIO★★

Guided tours (1hr) daily 9.30am–1pm 3.20–6pm. €5. Entrance includes museums. ☎927 36 70 00. www.monasterioguadalupe.com.

It's hard to overstate the jaw-dropping grandeur of this monastery complex, which dates to the late 14C–early 15C and eclipses the tiny town that surrounds it. It contains many artistic treasures, several of which reflect the Hieronymite monks' craftsmanship tradition in embroidery, gold, silversmithing and illumination.

Facade

Golden in hue and exuberant in its Flamboyant Gothic decoration, the facade overlooks a medieval square. Moorish influence is apparent in the sinuous decoration. Bronze reliefs on the 15C doors illustrate the Lives of the Virgin and Christ.

Iglesia (Church)

One of the first buildings to be constructed, the 14C church received 18C additions. A 16C grille by Valladolid ironsmiths closes the sanctuary, which has a Classically ordered 17C retable by Giraldo de Merlo and Jorge Manuel Theotocopuli, son of El Greco. The Virgin of Guadalupe in the altarpiece (1) can be seen more clearly from the **camarín★**.

Camarín★

This 18C chapel-like room is where the Virgin of Guadalupe rests. Riches of every description abound: jasper, gilded stucco, marble, precious wood

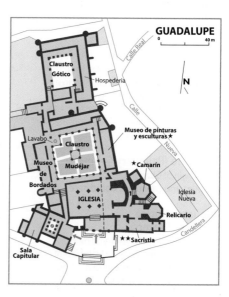

Camarín, Monasterio de Guadalupe

– you name it. There are nine canvases by Luca Giordano. The Virgin sits on an enamelwork throne (1953), a small 12C figure carved in darkened oak, obscured beneath embroidered veil and mantle.

Sala Capitular (Chapter House)

The chapter house contains a collection of 87 antiphonaries and books of hours with **miniatures★** by the monks.

Claustro Mudéjar

The 14C–15C cloisters are remarkable for their size and the two storeys of horseshoe arches. Note a small Mudéjar Gothic temple and, in a corner, a lavabo faced with multicoloured tiles.

Sacristía★★ (Sacristy)

Canvases by Carreño de Miranda hang in the antechamber. The 17C sacristy combines Classical architecture and ornate Baroque decoration. The unexpected harmony and rich colouring set off **paintings by Zurbarán★★** to perfection. The 11 canvases, painted in a serene yet forceful style between 1638 and 1647, depict Hieronymite monks and scenes from the Life of St Jerome such as *The Temptation*.

Relicario (Reliquary Cabinet)

The Virgin of Guadalupe's processional mantles and crown are stored here.

Claustro Gótico
(Gothic Cloisters)

In the *hospedería* (hostelry). The cloisters were built in the 16C in Flamboyant Gothic style to serve as a dispensary for the monastery's four hospitals.

Museo de Bordados
(Embroidery Museum)

The museum, in the former refectory, displays copes and **altarfronts★★** embroidered in minute detail by the monks between the 15C and 19C.

Museo de Pinturas y Esculturas★
(Painting and Sculpture Museum)

Works include a 16C triptych of the *Adoration of the Magi* by Isembrandt, an ivory Christ attributed to Michelangelo, an *Ecce Homo* by Pedro de Mena, eight superb small canvases of the monks by **Zurbarán** and **Goya**'s *Prison Confession*.

EXCURSION

Puerto de San Vicente
(San Vicente Pass)

▷ 40km/25mi E on the C 401.
The **road★** to the pass crosses the Las Villuercas range. The climb (8km/5mi) beyond the Guadarranque Valley affords **views★** of jagged green peaks above the wild moorland.

ADDRESSES

🍽 STAY

🛏🍴🟦 **Hospedería del Real Monasterio** – Pl. Juan Carlos I. ☎927 36 70 00. www.hospederiaguadalupe.com. 47 rooms. ☄ €8. Restaurant🛏🍴. Closed 15 Jan–15 Feb. The hotel's unbeatable setting, around the monastery's Gothic cloisters, and its comfortable, quiet rooms with old-fashioned decor, ensure a memorable stay. It's a great value to boot.

🛏🍴🟦🟦 **Parador de Guadalupe** – Marqués de la Romana 12. ☎902 54 79 79. www.parador.es. 41 rooms. ☄ €17. Guadalupe's Parador occupies the old monastery hospital, once famed as a school of humanities and medicine. The cloister is planted with lemon trees, and there's a delightful garden and swimming pool. Bedrooms evoke the buildings' ancient atmosphere with antique carved-wood furnishings. The restaurant serves Extremaduran cuisine with modern twists

Badajoz

Once an Arab fortress, Badajoz crowns a hill along the Guadiana river and is a border town with Portugal. Much of the old city was destroyed during the Spanish Civil War, but original walls, a fortress and ramparts, the 16C Puente Royal bridge and Mudéjar houses are reminders of the past.

- ▶ **Population:** 150 530
- ⏾ **Michelin Map:** 576 P 9 (town plan) – Extremadura (Badajoz).
- ℹ **Info:** Paseo de San Juan. ℘924 22 49 81. www.turismobadajoz.es.
- ▶ **Location:** The A 5 links with Mérida (62km/39mi W), the EX 100 connects the town with Cáceres (91km/57mi NE). 🚆Badajoz (AVE planned 2014).

A BIT OF HISTORY

In the 11C Badajoz became the capital of a Moorish kingdom. Because of its frontier location, it was besieged and pillaged in the Wars of the 16C.

SIGHTS

The 13C Gothic **Catedral de San Bautista** was considerably remodelled during the Renaissance (Pl. de España; museum open Tue–Sat 11am–1pm, 6–8pm, Sep-Jun 5–7pm; €1 museum; ℘924 22 49 81, www.aytobadajoz.es). Its tower boasts delicate Plateresque friezes and window surrounds. The impressive *coro* has 16C stalls and the sacristy holds fine 17C Flemish tapestries. The cathedral museum has canvases by Luis de Morales.

The **Museo Arqueológico Provincial** is a modern museum in the 16C **Palacio de la Roca** in the **alcazaba** (Pl. de José Álvarez y Sáenz de Buruaga; open Tue–Sun 9am–3pm; closed 1 & 6 Jan, 24 & 31 Dec; ℘924 00 19 08; museoarqueo-logicobadajoz.juntaex.es). It displays prehistoric and protohistoric steles and figurines; Roman mosaics and bronze tools; Visigothic pilasters carved with plant and geometric motifs; medieval artefacts; and Islamic pieces. Unique are the finds from Cancho Ruano, the only excavated Tartessan site in Spain. The **Museo de Bellas Artes,** in two elegant 19C mansions, holds 19C and 20C paintings, sculpture and sketches (Duque de San Germán 13; open Tue–Sun 10am–2pm, Tue–Fri 5-7pm, 6–8pm Jun–Aug; closed public hols; ℘924 21 24 69; muba.badajoz.es). The contem-porary art **Museo Extremeño e Iberoamericano de Arte Contemporáneo**, set inside the town's old prison, has experimental exhibits (open Tue–Sat 9.30am–1.30pm, 4–8pm, Sun 9.30am–1.30pm; closed hols; ℘924 01 30 60; www.meiac.es).

EXCURSIONS

Olivenza

▶ 25km/15.5mi SW.

Olivenza's Portuguese influence shows in its graceful white-walled town centre surrounded by olive groves. The town is administered by Extremadura but is in a disputed border territory. The Manueline **Iglesia de Santa María Magdalena**★★ is worth peeking your head into.

Albuquerque★

▶ 49km/30mi N of Badajoz on EX110.

Albuquerque, close to the Portuguese frontier, is presided over by the **Castillo de Albuquerque** (not to be confused with the Castillo de los Duques de Alburquerque in Segovia province). Dating to at least the 12C, it switched hands a several times between the Moors and the Christians. Note the curious pentagonal tower crowned with battlements. There's also a small 13C church on the grounds dedicated to Santa María del Castillo. .

Mérida★

Mérida was the capital of
Roman Lusitania and retains an
extraordinary series of classical
monuments that have earned it
World Heritage status – even if the
modern city is rather unmemorable
by comparison. Today it is
Extremadura's regional capital.

ROMAN MÉRIDA★★

In 25 BC, the Romans founded **Emerita
Augusta** on the River Guadiana and at
the junction of major Roman roads.
They lavished upon it temples, a theatre, an amphitheatre and even a circus.

Museo Nacional de Arte Romano★★ (National Museum of Roman Art)

José Ramón Mélida. Open Tue–Sat
9.30am–8pm (Oct–Mar 6.30pm); Sun
& hols 10am–3pm. Closed 1 Jan, 1 May,
24–25 & 31 Dec. €3. Free Sat pm,
Sun am, 18 Apr, 18 May, 12 Oct, 6 Dec.
℘924 31 16 90.
http://museoarteromano.mcu.es.
An imposing brick **building★** by Rafael
Moneo Vallés, reminiscent of a Roman
amphitheatre, displays Mérida's rich
archaeological collections. Sculptures
include the head of Augustus (at the
end of the second bay). In the last bay
are statues, caryatids and giant medallions (Medusa and Jupiter) which made
up the frieze of Mérida's forum. **Mosa-
ics★** may be viewed up close. In the
basement are remains of Roman villas
and tombs. The room of Visigothic art
is temporarily closed as of September
2019.

Teatro Romano★★ (Roman Theatre)

Av. de los Estudiantes. Open daily Apr–
Sep 9am–9pm. Oct–Mar 9am–6.30pm.
€15 (combi-ticket). ℘924 31 25 30.
www.turismomerida.org.
The theatre, built by Agrippa in 24 BC,
seated 6 000. A high stage wall was
decorated in Hadrian's reign (2C) with
a colonnade and statues. Enormous

- ▶ **Population:** 57 797
- ⌖ **Michelin Map:** 576 P 10 –
  Extremadura (Badajoz).
- 🛈 **Info:** Paseo José Álvarez Saénz
  de Buruaga. ℘924 33 07 22.
  www.turismomerida.org.
  A combined entrance ticket
  (€15), on sale at all the
  city's major monuments,
  allows entry to the theatre,
  amphitheatre, Roman
  houses, Alcazaba etc.
- ◖ **Location:** Mérida is close to
  the A 5 highway to Portugal.
  🚃Mérida (AVE planned 2014).
- 😊 **Don't Miss:** The main
  Roman sites and museum.

granite blocks over the passages are
skilfully secured without mortar.

Anfiteatro★★★ (Amphitheatre)

Pl. José Álvarez Saenz de Buruega. Open
same hours/ticket as Roman Theatre.
This 1C BC arena once held 14 000 spectators. It staged chariot races and was
flooded for mock sea battles. Original
steps remain and a few tiers are reconstructed. A wall crowned by a cornice
protected the noble spectators from
wild beasts during gladiatorial combats.

Casa Romana del Anfiteatro (Roman Villa)

Adjacent to Amphitheatre. Closed for
renovations. ℘924 31 20 24.
Water channels, pavement foundations
and mosaics remain in this large villa,
which, by 2020, will finally open to the
public after years of bureaucratic dis-
putes and drawn-out restorations.

Casa del Mitreo

Oviedo. Open 9.30am–2pm, 4–6.30pm
(Apr–Sep 9am-9pm); same ticket as
Roman Theatre.
The patios of this 1C villa served to
distribute light and collect rainwater.
Visible remains include the **Cosmologi-
cal Mosaic★**.

Templo de Diana

C. Santa Catalina 7.

Soaring Corinthian columns and make this Roman temple stand out. Its stones would be in the 16C to build the palace of the Count of Corbos. Two Roman **bridges** still span the Albarregas and Guadiana.

Alcazaba

Graciano. Open same hours/ticket as Roman Theatre. ℘924 00 49 09.

The Moors built this fortress in the 9C to defend the 792m/866yd **Puente Romano**★ (Roman Bridge) across the Guadiana. It has a cistern.

Zona Arqueológica de Morería★

Po. de Roma. Open 9am–3pm; check website for pm hours. €6. ℘924 00 49 08. www.turismoextremadura.com.

The active riverside Morería archaeological site displays artefacts from Roman to medieval times, ranging from sections of Roman wall to 15C–17C craftsmen's workshops.

Cripta de la Basílica de Santa Eulalia★

Av. de Extremadura 15. Open same hours/ticket as Zona Arqueológica.

The structure was first a palaeo-Christian necropolis, then a 5C basilica and now a 13C Romanesque church. (The central basilica is open during hours of worship only).

EXCURSIONS

Zafra

◗ SW of Madrid 27m/4.3mi W of the N 630.

A 15C **Alcázar** (now a Parador) guards this white-walled town, one of the oldest in Extremadura. The fortress, with nine round towers, was built by the Dukes of Feria. The 18C **Plaza Grande**★ and adjoining smaller 16C **Plaza Chica**★ are lined with arcaded houses. The 16C transitional Gothic-Renaissance **Iglesia de la Candelaria** (Rotonda de la Candelaria) holds an altarpiece by Zurbarán painted in 1644.

Zafra is the birthplace of **Fray Ruy López**, who penned one of the first European works on chess.

Llerena

◗ 42km/26mi from Zafra SE along the N 432.

The **Plaza Mayor** here is pleasingly harmonious. Its **Iglesia de Nuestra Señora de la Granada** (Church of Our Lady of Granada; Pl. San Juan) has a facade with superimposed arcades that contrast with the mass of a great Baroque belfry.

Jerez de los Caballeros

◗ 42km/26mi SW along the EX 101 and EX 112.

This is the birthplace of **Vasco Núñez de Balboa** (1475–1519), who crossed Panama and in 1513 'discovered' the Pacific Ocean. The town's name stems from the Knights Templar – Caballeros del Temple – to whom the town was given in 1230 by Alfonso IX on its recapture from the Moors. Iit has lanes lined with Andalucían-esque white-walled houses that wouldn't be out of place in the other Jerez (de la Frontera).

Today it's a centre of ham-making and hosts an annual congress. The aroma of ham fills the streets and surrounding hillsides, where black-footed pigs snuffle.

ADDRESSES

⌂ STAY

⌷⌷⌷⌷ **Parador de Zafra** – Pl Corazón de María, 7, Zafra ℘902 54 79 79. www.parador.es. 51 rooms. ⌸ €16. Housed in the Alcázar, this 15C castle Parador offers the chance to stay where conquistador Hernán Cortés passed time before sailing to conquer Mexico.

FESTIVALS

From late July to late August, the Roman theatre reverts to its original function to host the prestigious Merida Classical Theatre Festival, which has been running since 1953. www.festivaldemerida.es.

Atlantic Spain

Las Médulas, El Camino de Santiago
© photohampster/iStockphoto.com

Atlantic Spain

0   100 km

OCÉ

Rías Altas

Costa Verde

Costa da Muerte

A Coruña

Mondoñedo

Gijón   Villa

Betanzos

AG 55

A 8

R. Navia

Oviedo

Costa Verde

AP 9

A 6

Valles del Oeste

A 64

SANTIAGO DE
COMPOSTELA

N 547

Lugo †

ASTURIAS

Río Miño

DESFILADERO
DE LOS BAYOS

Rías Baixas

AP 9

AP 53

Pontevedra

CAMINO

Villafranca
del Bierzo

Sil

AP 66

León

Ría de Vigo

Vigo

Ribadavia

† Ourense

Río Miño

DE

AP 71

Baiona

Tui

A 52

Allariz

GALICIA

Astorga

A 6

A 66

S

A 52

A 52

R. Esla

A 52

N 123

N 630

A 6

N 601

Támega

Río

IP 4

R.

PORTO

A 4

DOURO

Río Duero

Río Tormes

A 66

A 11

A 1

RÍO

A 24 - IP 3

Embalse de
Almendra

A 62

A 50

A 25 - IP 5

IP 2

PORTUGAL

A 62

A 66

A 5

A 23

Río

Zêzere

Río

Alagón

EX A1

A 23 - IP 6

EXTREMADURA

N

PICOS DE EUROPA	★★★	Worth a special journey
Burgos	★★	Worth a detour
Lugo	★	Interesting
Reinosa		Other sight described in this guide
	– – – – –	Camino de Santiago (Chemins de St-Jacques)

OCÉANO   ATLÁNTICO

BORDEAUX

FRANC

Villaviciosa

Costa de Cantabria

FITO

Santillana del Mar

Santander

Costa de Bizkaia

Costa de Gipuzkoa

Donostia/ San Sebastián

Hondarribia

PICOS DE EUROPA

ERO YOS

LIESBA

Reinosa

CANTABRIA

Bilbao

Gernika

S. Ignacio de Loiola

LA RHUNE

PICO DE TRES MARES

Aguilar de Campoo

P. N. de Valderejo

NERVIÓN

Tolosa

Oñati

Vitoria-Gasteiz

Orreaga/ Roncesvalles

Pamplona

NAVARRA

Leyre

CASTILLA Y LÉON

Labastida

Laguardia

Estella/ Lizarra

SANTIAGO

Burgos

Haro

Viana

Puente-la-Reina

Sangüesa

Sto Domingo de la Calzada

Nájera

Logroño

Olite

Palencia

Covarrubias

La Rioja

Tudela

Sto Domingo de Silos

RÍO   DUERO

ZARAGO

CASTILLA Y LEÓN

CASTILLA LA MANCHA

ARAGO

Río Tajo

Embalse de Entrepeñas

R. Guade

MADRID

Navarra

The most geographically varied region of the north, Navarra (Navarre) sweeps from the lush, mountainous belt facing France to a semi-arid desert in the south. Both Basque (Euskera) and Castilian are spoken, hence the co-official names of its towns and cities. In the Middle Ages Navarra found fame and wealth as a staging point on the Camino de Santiago, which left a legacy of churches, monasteries and pilgrims' hospices. Navarran gastronomy is one of Spain's finest: Cheese is made with milk from its endemic *latxa* sheep, and though its wines are less prestigious than those of neighbouring La Rioja, they sing alongside regional dishes like fried trout and stuffed piquillo peppers.

Highlights

1. Visiting the new Museo Universidad de Navarra in **Pamplona** (p233)
2. Spooky witches' caves near **Zugarramurdi** (p236)
3. Hiking between villages on the **Camino de Santiago** (p240)
4. Discovering the rich royal and pilgrimage legacies of **Estella-Lizarra** (p245)
5. Staying at the Parador **Palacio Real de Olite**, Olite/Erriberri (p246)

Pamplona/Iruña

Synonymous with the hair-raising 'running of the bulls' festival of San Fermín (first week of July), Pamplona is a sleepy old city every other time of year. It has been the capital of Navarra for more than a thousand years. The characterful medieval old town, crumbling citadel and fine cathedral make it a good base from which to explore the rest of this largely undiscovered and often-surprising region.

East of Pamplona

Estella-Lizarra was not only a medieval royal capital but also one of the main stops on the Camino de Santiago – it still is today – and it retains a rich medieval legacy. Like Estella, Sangüesa was once an important pilgrim's pit stop and has all the historic religious trimmings to prove it including some remarkable church stone carvings. Outside the town stands the impressive Castillo de Javier, and it's worth journeying beyond to the Monasterio de Leyre, which not only occupies a privileged position but also contains an atmospheric church and crypt.

South of Pamplona

Olite and Tudela are two more charming medieval towns. Olite castle, today a Parador, was once the fortress of the kings of Navarra. Continue to Tudela to see its cathedral and to sample its vegetable-centric cuisine, and journey on to the Bardenas Reales, a desert landscape with wind-battered rock formations that wouldn't be out of place in the American West.

North of Pamplona

Welcome to the lush pre-Pyrenees, a popular day-trip destination for **Pampilonenses** fleeing the heat for hikes around the Valle de Bidosa's 'five villages'. One of the finest garden estates in Spain, the Jardín de Señorío de Bertiz, is nearby at the threshold to the national park of the same name, where, if you're lucky, you might spot a Pyrenean salamander.

Los Sanfermines de Pamplona

© Eduardo Blanco/age fotostock

Pamplona/ Iruña★

The old quarter of Pamplona is veined with narrow medieval streets that empty onto arcaded squares. Around the Plaza del Castillo, streets are named after old trades: Zapatería (shoemaker) and Tejería (tilemaker), for instance. If you visit during San Fermín, expect crowds and round-the-clock revelling; outside the July festivities, the city is rather sedate.

▶ **Population:** 199 066
⌖ **Michelin Map:** 573 D 25 (town plan).
🛈 **Info:** Plaza Consistorial ℘948 42 01 00. www.pamplona.es.
◗ **Location:** Modern Pamplona extends south from the riverside old town. Roads lead to Roncesvalles in the Pyrenees and to Hendaye, France. 🚊Pamplona.
🅿 **Parking:** Don't try to park in the old city.

A BIT OF HISTORY

Pamplona was founded by the Roman leader Pompey, who gave his name to the town. The Moors briefly took over in the 8C but were repelled by Charlemagne, who demolished the walls. The townspeople in turn massacred Charlemagne's rearguard. In the 10C Pamplona became the capital of Navarra, though it was torn for a time between Castilla and France.

SIGHTS

Catedral★★

Pl. de la Catedral. Mon–Sat 10.30am–7pm (until 5pm Oct–Mar). €5 for Museo Catedralicio. ℘948 21 25 94. www.catedraldepamplona.com.
The Gothic cathedral was built in the 14–15C. At the end of the 18C, Ventura Rodríguez rebuilt the west front.
Interior★– The nave has wide arches and windows and great bare walls, typical of Navarra Gothic. In front of the finely wrought grille closing the sanctuary stands the alabaster **tomb★★**, commissioned in 1416 by Charles III, the Noble. The reclining figures and **mourners** were carved by Janin Lomme. Note the late-15C Hispano-Flemish altarpiece (south ambulatory chapel).
Claustro★– The 14C–15C cloisters appear delicate, with Gothic arches surmounted by gables. Sculptured tombs and doors add interest. Off the east gallery is the Capilla Barbazán with 14C star vaulting. On the south side, the doorway of the Sala Preciosa is a masterwork of the period, its tympanum carved with scenes from the Life of the Virgin and two statues forming an Annunciation. In the southeast corner, a lavabo is turned into a shrine commemorating the Battle of Las Navas de Tolosa.

Epic Poems

According to legend, Roncesvalles was the site where the Basques of Navarra massacred the rearguard of Charlemagne's army in 778 as Roland was retreating through the Pyrenees to France. The early-13C poem of **Bernardo del Carpio** describes Bernardo as a national hero who fought alongside his Basque, Navarran and Asturian companions in arms to avenge the Frankish invasion of Spain; the 12C **Song of Roland**, the first French epic poem, on the other hand, glorifies the heroic but ultimately vain resistance of a handful of valiant Christian knights against hordes of Saracen fanatics.

Museo Catedralicio★

Dormitalería 3–5.

The Diocesan Museum is in the old refectory and kitchen, which date to 1330. The former, a lofty hall with six pointed arches, contains a rostrum decorated with an enchanting scene of a unicorn hunt. The latter has a central lantern rising to 24m/79ft. Displays include a 13C *Reliquary of the Holy Sepulchre* donated by St Louis (Louis IX of France) and polychrome wood statues of the Virgin and Christ.

Follow the narrow, picturesque Calle del Redín to the ramparts.

Murallas (Ramparts)

La Cuenca de Pamplona zone.

A bastion, now a garden, looks out over the Puerta de Zumalacárregui (a gate below and to the left), a stretch of the old walls and a bend in the rivers Arga and Monte Cristóbal. Learn about the walls at the **Centro de Interpretación** (Fortín de San Bartolomé; Tue–Sun 11am–2pm and mid-Mar–Oct 4–7pm, Nov–mid-Mar 3–6pm; ✆948 211 554; www.murallasdepamplona.com).

Museo Universidad de Navarra★★

Campus Universitario. Open Tue–Sat 10am–8pm. Sun & hols 12pm–2pm. Free guided tours (reserve in advance) Tue–Fri 6pm, Sat, Sun 12pm. Closed 1 & 6 Jan, Good Fri, 7-14 Jul, 24–25 & 31 Dec. €4.50. ✆948 42 57 00.

http://museo.unav.edu/visita.

This museum, which was designed by Rafael Moneo and opened in 2015, contains the Colección de Maria Josefa Huarte with works by Picasso, Kandinsky and Rothko, and also the university's photography collection, which has images from the art's origins up to the present day, including works by photojournalists such as Robert Capa and Henri Cartier-Bresson. It houses a theatre, a cafe and a gourmet restaurant too.

Museo de Navarra★

C. Santo Domingo 47. Open Tue–Sat 9.30am–2pm, 5–7pm. Sun & hols 11am–2pm. Closed 1 Jan, 6-7 Jul, 25 Dec. €2; free Sat pm, Sun, 18 May, 27 Sep, 12 Oct, 3 & 6 Dec. ✆848 426 492. www.cfnavarra.es/cultura/museo.

This museum is on the site of the 16C Hospital de Nuestra Señora de la Misericordia. Only a Renaissance gateway and the chapel remain. The Roman period (basement and first floor) is represented by funerary steles, inscriptions and **mosaic★** pavements from 2C and 4C villas. The main exhibit in the Hispano-Moorish section (Room 1.8) is an 11C ivory **casket★** from San Salvador de Leyre sculpted in Córdoba. Romanesque **capitals★** are from the former 12C cathedral of Pamplona, brilliantly carved with the Passion, the Resurrection and the Story of Job.

The museum also contains **Gothic wall paintings★** from Artaíz (13C), Artajona (14C), Pamplona (14C) and elsewhere in the province. They share an unobtrusive emphasis on faces and features reminiscent of French miniaturists. The reconstruction of the interior of the **Palacio de Oriz** is decorated with 16C monochrome panels depicting Adam and Eve and the wars of Charles V.

On the third floor are 17C–18C paintings by Luis Paret and Francisco de Goya (*portrait of the Marqués de San Adrián*).

Iglesia de San Cernín/San Saturnino★

C. de San Saturnino. Open Mon–Sat 9.15am–12pm, 6–7.30pm. Sun & public hols 10am–1.30pm, 6–7.30pm. ✆948 22 11 94.

Set in a tangle of narrow streets in the old quarter, this church mingles Romanesque brick towers, and 13C Gothic **portals★** and vaulting.

Casa Consistorial (Town Hall)

Pl. Consistorial. Closed to the public.

San Fermín is rung in at 12pm on 6 July from the balcony to great fanfare. The building has a reconstructed **Baroque facade★** (originally late 17C) with statues, balustrades and pediments.

EXCURSIONS

Museo Oteiza

▶ Cuesta 7, Alzuza. 7 km/4.3mi E. Take the NA 150, then immediately turn left. Open Sep–Jun Thu–Fri 10am–3pm, Sat 11am–7pm, Sun 11am–3pm. Guided visits at 11am and 1pm Tue (book in advance). Jul–Aug Tue–Sat 11am–7pm, Sun 11am–3pm. €4. Free Fri (exc hols). ℘948 33 20 74. www.museooteiza.org.
Jorge Oteiza (1908–2003) was a key figure of modern Spanish abstract sculpture. The museum is beside his house.

Santuario de San Miguel de Aralar★

▶ 45km/28mi NW. Follow the A 15. Shortly before Lecumberri, turn onto the NA 751, which crosses the Sierra de Aralar through beech woods to this sanctuary. Open 10am–2pm, see website for afternoon opening times. ℘948 37 30 13. www.sanmigueldearalar.info.
The sanctuary consists of an 8C Romanesque **church** which encloses a free-standing chapel. The gilt and enamel **altar front★★** is one of the major works of European Romanesque gold- and silverwork, attributed by some to a late 12C Limoges workshop. It consists of gilded bronze plaques adorned with enamel and mounted precious stones, arranged as an altarpiece. The multicoloured honeycomb enamelwork is decorated with arabesques and plant motifs.

Roncesvalles/Orreaga★

▶ 47km/29mi NE along the N 135.
🏠 Antiguo Molino ℘948 76 03 01. www.roncesvalles.es.
This 12C ensemble of buildings served as an important hostelry for pilgrims to Santiago de Compostela. Its funerary chapel is now the Capilla del Sancti Spiritus (Chapel of the Holy Spirit); its collegiate church is rich in relics.

Iglesia de la Real Colegiata

Única. Open daily 8am–9pm. Closed 6 Jan–6 Feb, 8 Sep, 25 Dec, 1 & 6 Jan. €5.20. ℘948 79 04 80. www.roncesvallesorreaga.blogspot.com.
This Gothic collegiate church, inspired by those of the Paris region, was con-

'Sanfermines'

The **feria** of San Fermín runs from 6–14 July. Visitors pour in from around the globe, tripling the town's population, to enjoy the carnival atmosphere (described by Hemmingway in *The Sun Also Rises*) and, to an increasingly lesser extent, to watch bullfights. The festival's centrepiece is the **encierro** (around 8am), when the bulls run through the streets to the bullring. Many foolhardy festival-goers join the stampede; there are grave injuries each year. 🚫 It is illegal to run while intoxicated. The festival has come under scrutiny recently as more and more women report being groped or attacked. Avoid walking alone at night.

secrated in 1219. Beneath the high altar canopy is the silver-plated statue of **Nuestra Señora de Roncesvalles**, created in France in the late 13C.

Sala Capitular (Chapter House)

The Gothic chamber contains the tombs of the founder, Sancho VII (1154–1234), the King of Navarra and his queen.

Museo★

Única. Same opening hours as Iglesia de la Real Colegiata. €3. ℘948 79 04 80.
The museum contains fine pieces of ancient plate: a Mudéjar casket; a Romanesque book of the Gospel; a 14C enamelled reliquary known as 'Charlemagne's chessboard'; a 16C Flemish triptych; an emerald, said to have been worn by Sultan Miramamolín el Verde in his turban on the day of the Battle of Las Navas de Tolosa in 1212; and a *Holy Family* by Morales.

🚗 DRIVING TOUR

VALLE DEL BIDASOA★

134km/83mi. Allow one day.

The Bidasoa Valley cuts through the lower foothills of the western Pyrenees, where villages of typical Basque houses lie amid lush meadows. The Bidasoa river is renowned for its salmon and trout.

▶ Exit Pamplona from the PA-30 ring road toward Ezcaba. Then take the the N 121A. Near the exit to Oricaín, take the N 121B and exit at Oronoz, then follow the signs to the Parque Natural de Señorío Bértiz.

Señorío Bértiz Natural Park

Access beside the petrol station, on the edge of town. ℰ948 592 421. www.parquedebertiz.es.

A natural park since 1984, this area covers 2040 ha/5 000 acres, about half of which is forest (mainly oak and beech). Its woods and meadows are home to diverse wildlife, from salamanders to Pyrenean desman (a type of mole). Pedro Ciga was its last lord, custodian of the land gifted by King Charles III in the 14C. He planted exotics in the garden (situated at the entrance to the park and now open to the public) and built a new palace in the Art Nouveau style, while restoring the old. In 1949 he bequeathed the lands to the Navarran government, under the proviso that everything be maintained as it was given. The palace overlooks the Aizkolegi peak, the park and the surrounding valleys.

Several marked trails leave from the park entrance (ask for a map at the gate). The shortest (700m/765yd) and easiest bears left to follow the River Bidasoa. Others snake into the forest along the path marked Aizkolegi (the only one on which you can cycle – follow the green signage).

▶ From the centre of Oronoz, take the N 121B, toward Elizondo.

Elizondo, the capital and gateway of the **Valle del Baztán**, has numerous traditional Basque houses decorated with armorial bearings known as *caseríos*. It's a pleasant place to wander and soak up the atmosphere, pausing to sample the village's sweet speciality, hazelnut chocolate.

▶ From Elizondo, head to Elbete and take the N 121B (from here, the road has hairpin bends). At Otxondo take the NA 4402 to Leoriaz and then the NA 4401 to Zugarramurdi.

The quiet enclave of **Zugarramurdi** 🏃🏃 is home to one of the most extraordinary sites in the region, the Cuevas de las Brujas, or witches' caves. Over 120m/130yd long and set over various levels deep in the woods, they are an eerie sight, made even more evocative by the fact that they were an alleged meeting place for medieval witches. One of the caves, Cueva de Zugarramurdi, has been turned into a visitor attraction along with a Museo de las Brujas (museum and caves open Tue– Sun year round and Mon 15 July–15 Sep; check website for opening times; €4.50 cave, €4.50 museum; ℰ948 59 90 04; www.turismozugarramurdi.com). Many were tortured and executed here by an Inquisition that targeted women and children on the fringes of society.

▶ Take the N 4401 to Urdax, then follow the signs to N 121B. Close to Oronoz, follow the signs to N121A toward Bera/Vera de Bidasoa.

The **houses in Bera** (Vera) de Bidasoa are adorned with coats of arms, particularly along the main street. The typically Basque facades have deep eaves over balconies with delicate balustrades.

ADDRESSES

🏠 STAY

▪️ **Hotel Yoldi** – Av. de San Ignacio, 11. ℰ948 22 48 00. www.hotelyoldi.com. 50 rooms. ⊆ €11.10. This central, modern hotel has a tapas bar. Rooms are small but nicely decorated.

▪️ **Palacio Guendulain** – C. de la Zapatería 53. ℰ948 22 55 22. www. palacioguendulain.com. 25 rooms. ⊆ €20. There's a refined Basque restaurant with wide terrace in this old-world hotel housed in an 18th-century palace.

¶/EAT

Churrería La Mañueta – C. Mañueta 8. Open Sat 8–11.30am in Jun; 6–11am daily for San Fermín; Sun 7.45–11am in Oct. ℘948 22 76 27. Churros are fried in Navarran olive oil over beechwood flame at this churrería, the oldest in Spain, going on its 148th year.

Baserriberri – C. San Nicolás 32. ℘948 22 20 21. www.baserriberri.com.

Get the solomillo (beef fillet) al roquefort at this packed tapas spot.

Rodero – C. Emilio Arrieta 3. ℘948 22 80 35. www.restaurante rodero.com. Closed Sun & Holy Week. This family-run Michelin-starred restaurant behind the bullring serves refined Navarran cuisine accompanied by wine pairings.

Monasterio de San Salvador de Leyre★

At the end of a winding road, a splendid **panorama★★** opens up: Limestone crests tower above appear the ochre walls of the monastery.

A BIT OF HISTORY

By the early 11C, the Abbey of San Salvador de Leyre was the spiritual centre of Navarra and the final resting place of kings. In the 12C, after union with Aragón, Leyre was neglected, and by the 19C, abandoned. But in 1954 a Benedictine community from Silos moved in and restored the 17C and 18C conventual buildings, today a hostelery (⬮⬮⬮).

IGLESIA★★

Open 10am–7pm, Nov–Mar until 6pm. Closed 24 & 25 Dec, 1 & 6 Jan. €3.20, guided visit €3.70.

East End – Three apses, the nave, turret and a square tower, all 11C, make a delightful group.

Crypt★★ – The robust 11C crypt, built to support the Romanesque church above, looks even older. The vaulting is relatively high but divided by arches with enormous voussoirs.

Interior★ – In the 13C the Cistercians rebuilt the central aisle with a bold Gothic vault while retaining earlier Romanesque bays with barrel vaulting, engaged pillars and perfectly hewn stone. In the north bay a wooden chest contains the remains of the first kings of Navarra.

Michelin Map: 573 E26.

Info: ℘948 88 41 50. www.monasteriodeleyre.com.

Location: Near the Yesa reservoir; 50km/31mi SE of Pamplona and 16km/10mi NE of Sangüesa. Nearest station: Pamplona (50km).

Timing: Hear the monks' Gregorian chants inside the church daily at 7pm.

West Portal★ – The 12C portal is Called the Porta Speciosa for its decorative richness. Carvings cover every available space. On the tympanum are archaic statues – Christ (centre), the Virgin Mary and St Peter (left) and St John (right); the covings teem with monsters and fantastic beasts.

EXCURSIONS

Hoz de Lumbier★

14km/8.7mi W.

The Irati gorge between Lumbier and Liédana is barely 5km/3mi long and so narrow that it appears at either end as a crack in the cliff face. There is a good **view** of the gorge from a lookout point on the road (N 240).

Hoz de Arbayún★

31km/19.2mi N along the N 240 and NA 211.

The River Salazar is steeply enclosed within limestone walls. From a point north of Iso, there a splendid **view★★** to the end of the canyon, where the cliff walls are clad in lush vegetation.

Detail of the south portal, Iglesia de Santa María la Real

Sangüesa/ Zangoza★

On the Río Aragón, Sangüesa still stands guard over the bridge that, in the Middle Ages, brought the region and city so much prosperity. Its monumental and artistic heritage stems from its location on the Camino de Santiago.

▶ **Population:** 4 960

⊙ **Michelin Map:** 573 E 26.

🛈 **Info:** C. Mayor 2. ℘948 87 14 11. www.sanguesa.es.

▶ **Location:** Sangüesa is 5km/3mi from the N 240, linking Jaca with Pamplona, 36km/22mi away.
🚃Nearest station: Pamplona (48km).

⊙ **Timing:** Allow a couple of hours in town.

SIGHT
Iglesia de Santa María la Real★

C. Mayor. Only by guided tour; prior booking required. €2.30. ℘620 110 581. The glory of the church is its late-12C–13C **Portada Sur★★** (South Portal), crowded with sculptures executed by the Master of San Juan de la Peña. The Gothic **statue columns** derive from those at Chartres and Autun. On the **tympanum**, God the Father, at the centre of a group of angel musicians, receives Jesus with his right arm and with left reproves sinners. The **covings** swarm with motifs; the second innermost shows the humbler trades: clogmaker, lute-maker and butcher.
The older upper arches, marked by an Aragonese severity of style, show God surrounded by the symbols of the Evangelists, two angels and the disciples.

EXCURSIONS
Castillo de Javier★

▶ Javier. 7km/4.3mi NE on the NA 541. Open Mar–Nov 10am–6.30pm, Dec–Feb until 4pm. Call ahead. Closed 1 Jan, 24–25, 31 Dec. €3. ℘948 88 40 24. www.santuariojaviersj.org
St Francis Xavier, the patron saint of Navarra, was born in this picturesque fortress in 1506. He founded the Society of Jesus (with Ignatius Loyola), died in 1552 and was canonised in 1622. The castle was in part destroyed by Cardinal Cisneros in 1516. Its **oratorio★** (oratory) contains a 13C Christ in walnut and an unusual 15C fresco of the Dance of Death.

Sos del Rey Católico★

▶ 13km/8mi SE along the A 127.
🏛 Palacio de Sada. ℘948 88 85 24.
www.sosdelreycatolico.com.

It was in the historic town of Sos del Rey, in the **Palacio de Sada**, that Ferdinand the Catholic was born in 1452. The town still has a medieval air. On the **Plaza Mayor** stand the imposing 16C ayuntamiento (town hall), with large carved-wood overhangs, and the Lonja (Exchange), with wide arches.

Iglesia de San Esteban★

Pl. de la Iglesia. Guided tours by appt with tourist office. ℘948 88 82 03.

The Church of St Stephen is reached through a vaulted passageway. The 11C **crypt★** is dedicated to Our Lady of Forgiveness (Virgen del Perdón). Two of the three apses are decorated with fine 14C **frescoes**. The central apse contains outstanding capitals carved with women and birds. The statue columns at the **main door** have the stiff and noble bearing of those at Sangüesa. The church, in transitional style, has a beautiful Renaissance **gallery★**. A chapel contains a 12C wide-eyed Romanesque Christ.

Uncastillo

▶ 34km/21mi SE; 21km/13mi from Sos del Rey Católico.

The Romanesque Iglesia de Santa María (Pl. de la Villa) in this village has an unusual 14C tower adorned with machicolations and pinnacle turrets. The delicate carving on the **south portal★** makes it one of the most beautiful doorways of the late Romanesque period. The church gallery with Renaissance **stalls★** and the **cloisters★** are 16C Plateresque.

Cáseda

▶ 12km/7.5mi SW. Head from Sangüesa toward Sos del Rey Católico, and turn right after 1km/.06mi onto NA 5341.

Perched on a hillside and hemmed in by fields and the Aragon River, this picturesque village has a Gothic church and medieval stone bridge. Upstream, 10km/6mi W via the NA5321, **Gallipienzo**/Galipentzu's hilltop church peeks above the remains of fortified walls, from where you can enjoy a **view★** of the surrounding landscape.

ADDRESSES

🏨 STAY

🛏🛏 **Hostal Rural JP** – Av. Padre Raimundo Lumbier 3, Sangüesa.
℘948 87 16 93. 7 rooms. 🍽 €4.50.
This friendly, bare-bones hostal with views of the River Aragón has simply-decorated rooms and a café-bar.
♿ Steep stairs may pose a problem for guests with mobility issues.

Sangüesa and the Camino de Santiago

Fear of the Moors compelled Christian Sangüesans to live on the Rocaforte hillside until the 10C, but by the 11C the citizens had moved down to defend the bridge and clear a safe passage for pilgrims. Sangüesa reached its zenith at the end of the Middle Ages, when prosperous citizens began to build elegant residential mansions. These contrasted with the austere Palacio del Príncipe de Viana (Palace of the Prince of Viana), residence of the kings of Navarra, now the ayuntamiento (town hall), with its facade (seen through the gateway) flanked by two battlemented towers. The main street, the Calle Mayor which was once part of the pilgrim road, is lined with quaint brick houses, with Classical carved-wood eaves and windows with Gothic or Plateresque surrounds. On the second street on the right (coming from the bridge) you'll find the Baroque front of the Palacio de Vallesantoro, a palace protected by monumental overhangs carved with imaginary animals.

Camino de Santiago★★★

Way of St James

The discovery of the tomb of the Apostle James in the 9C transformed Santiago de Compostela, Galicia, into the most important medieval pilgrimage destination in Europe. In the 11C, the veneration of his saintly remains gave rise to the Camino de Santiago (Way of St James), still trekked by thousands of pilgrims – and interested tourists of all faiths – today. The Camino Francés, the French Way, also crosses Navarra. The route and its many monuments hold UNESCO World Heritage status.

- **Michelin Map:** 573.
- **Info:** Rúa do Vilar, 63. ☎ 981 555 129. ww.santiagoturismo.com. Confraternity of St James. www.csj.org.uk.
- **Location:** El Camino de Santiago runs from the Pyrenees to Santiago (☝️ see map opposite).
- **Timing:** If you're fit and healthy, you can cover about 25km/15mi a day, and therefore walk between Roncesvalles and Santiago de Compostela in about a month.

A BIT OF HISTORY

The discovery St James's remains created a furore among European Christians, and by the 11C, Santiago was as popular a pilgrimage site as Rome or Jerusalem.

St James had a particular appeal for the French, who at the time were united with the Spanish against the Moors, but others came from even farther, along routes blazed by the Benedictines, Cistercians and Knights Templar. Purpose-built hospitals and hospices received the sick and weary. Most travellers donned the same uniform: a heavy cape, long staff with a hollowed-out gourd attached (to carry water), sturdy sandals and a broad-brimmed felt hat marked with scallop shells.

A *Pilgrim Guide* of 1130, said to be the first tourism guide ever written, describes the inhabitants, climate, customs and sights on the way. Churches and towns along the route prospered, receiving between 500 000 and two million pilgrims a year.

Those from England who 'took the cockleshell' often sailed from Parson's Quay in the Plymouth estuary to Soulac and followed the French Atlantic coast – or docked in A Coruña or in Portugal.

Routes through France from Chartres, St-Denis and Paris joined at Tours. Villages along the main route grew into towns, and some were settled by foreigners, often from France.

With time, the faith that impelled the pilgrims began to diminish; crime, particularly from bandits, increased; and infighting among Christians reduced the faithful. In 1589, Drake attacked A Coruña and the bishop of Santiago removed the relics from the cathedral. They were lost, and for 300 years the pilgrimage was virtually abandoned. In 1879 they were recovered, recognised by the Pope, and the pilgrimage was reborn. In Holy Years, on 25 July, when the feast day of St James falls on a Sunday, elaborate religious and cultural celebrations in the major stops of St James Way attract even more pilgrims.

THE WAY IN SPAIN

The Camino Francés (French Way) is the most popular of the handful of *caminos* to Santiago. Routes from France converge at either Roncesvalles or Somport and cross the Pyrenees. The easier southerly route (from Somport) goes via Jaca, Santa Cruz de la Serós, San Juan de la Peña, the Monasterio de Leyre and Sangüesa and features churches and monasteries influenced by French architecture. Both routes converge at Puente la Reina.

Puente la Reina★

The town's 11C arched bridge was built for the pilgrims; a bronze pilgrim statue marks where routes converged.

The wide N 111 circles the old town, outside whose walls stands the Iglesia del Crucifijo (Church of the Crucifix; open daily 9am–6pm, until 8pm Apr-Oct). A second nave was added to the 12C main aisle in the 14C and contains a Y-shaped crucifix with an Expressionist **Christ★** fashioned out of wood, said to have been brought from Germany in the 14C.

◐ Walk along the narrow, elegant main street, Calle Mayor, fronted by houses of golden brick with carved-wood eaves, to the bridge. You'll see the **Iglesia de Santiago** (Church of St James; open Mon–Sat 10.30am–8pm, Sun & hols 9.39am–7.30pm), its **doorway★** crowded with carvings now almost effaced. Note two statues facing the entrance: St James the Pilgrim, in gilded wood, and St Bartholomew.

Iglesia de Santa María de Eunate★

◐ Muruzábal. 5km/3mi E of Puente la Reina. Open daily (check website for hours). €1.50, guided €2 (appt only) ℘948 741 273.
www.santamariadeeunate.es.

Human bones indicate that this octagonal Romanesque sanctuary, with enigmatic origins, might have been a funerary chapel like that of Torres del Río (℅see below).

Cirauqui★

Steep, winding alleyways are lined with houses with rounded doorways, their upper fronts adorned with iron balconies, coats of arms and carved cornices. At the top of the village (difficult climb) stands the Iglesia de San Román with a multifoil 13C **portal★**.

Estella★ and Monasterio de Irache★

℅ See Estella-Lizarra, p244.

Los Arcos

The **Iglesia de Santa María de los Arcos** (Church of St Mary of the Arches; Pl. de Santa María; opens 30 mins before Mass. ℘649 909 514),has a high tower and Spanish Baroque interiors, with overpowering stucco, sculpture and painting covering every available space. Above the high altar rises the 13C polychrome wood statue of the Black Virgin of Santa María de los Arcos. The cloisters are 15C Gothic.

Torres del Río

The **Iglesia del Santo Sepulcro★** (Church of the Holy Sepulchre; Mayor; ℘666 988 255) is a tall octagonal Romanesque building that might have been a funerary chapel, dating to ca.1200. The Mudéjar-inspired star-shaped **cupola** is geometrically perfect. Note also the fine 13C crucifix.

Nájera and Santo Domingo de la Calzada★

℅ See LA RIOJA, p265.

Burgos★★★

See BURGOS, p308.

Iglesia de Frómista★★

See PALENCIA, p315.

Villalcázar de Sirga

The vast Gothic **Iglesia de Santa María la Blanca** (open Sat–Sun & hols 10am–2pm, 4–6pm; €2.50; 979 88 80 76) has a fine carved **portal★** and two outstanding Gothic **tombs★**. The recumbent statues of the brother of Alfonso X (who had the king murdered in 1271) and his wife Eleanor are carved in great detail.

Carrión de los Condes

The 11C **Monasterio de San Zoilo**, rebuilt during the Renaissance, and now housing a well-reviewed upscale hotel and restaurant (www.sanzoilo.com), has **cloisters★** (Obispo Souto Vizoso; open Apr–15 Oct Tue–Sun 10.30am–2pm, 4.30–8pm, 16 Oct–Mar Tue–Fri 10.30am–2pm, Sat–Sun & hols 10.30am–2pm, 4–7pm; closed Jan–Feb; €2; 979 88 00 50; www.sanzoilo.com) designed by Juan de Badajoz with distinctive vaulting. The keystones and bosses are adorned with figurines and medallions. The Iglesia de Santiago (C. Adolfo Suárez 2; open Tue–Sun 12–2pm, 5–7pm; €1; 979 88 00 72) has 12C carvings on the facade.

León★★

See LEÓN

Astorga

Astorga.

Astorga is known for its *mantecados*, phenomenally flaky biscuits made with lard and lemon rind.

Catedral de Santa María★

Pl. de la Catedral. Open 10.30am–8.30pm (until 6pm Nov–Mar). €5; free Sun 10am–12pm. 987 61 58 20. www.catedralastorga.com.

Construction began in the late 15C, and was not completed until the 18C, which explains the Renaissance and Baroque facade and towers. The front **porch★** low reliefs illustrate the Expulsion of the Moneylenders and the Pardoning of the Adulterous Woman. Above the door is a beautiful Deposition.

The interior is surprisingly large, with an upsweeping effect created by innumerable slender columns. Behind the high altar is a 16C **retable★**. Gaspar de Hoyos and Gaspar de Palencia are behind the painted, gilt decoration.

The **Museo Catedralicio** contains a 13C gold filigree Holy Cross reliquary and a 10C reliquary of Alfonso III, the Great (same hours as cathedral).

Palacio Episcopal de Gaudí

Pl. de Eduardo de Castro.

Open Oct–Apr Tue–Sat 11am–2pm, 4–6pm, Sun 11am–2pm; May–Sept Tue–Sat 10am–2pm, 4–8pm, Sun 10am–2pm. €5. 987 61 68 82. www.palaciodegaudi.es.

This fantastic pastiche of a medieval palace was created by a fledgling **Gaudí** in 1889 for a rich cleric. The original interior decoration, especially in the neo-Gothic chapel on the first floor, is a profusion of mosaics, stained glass and intersecting ribbed vaults, but it pales in comparison to the storybook exterior. The palace is home to the **Museo de los Caminos,** where medieval art reflects the theme of pilgrimage.

Ponferrada

Ponferrada.

The centre of a mining area, Ponferrada owes its name to an 11C iron bridge built across the River Sil for pilgrims. Above the town are the ruins of the **Castillo de los Templarios** (Templars' Castle; open Jun–15 Oct 9am–9pm, 16 Oct–May 9am–7pm; €6, free Wed, 23 Apr, 12 Oct, 6 Dec; 987 40 22 44; www.castillodelostemplarios.com).

Peñalba de Santiago★

21km/13mi SE.

Peñalba stands in the heart of the Valle del Silencio. Its houses are schist-walled with wooden balconies and slate roofs. The Mozarabic **Iglesia de Santiago** (open 10am–2pm, 4–8pm and 5–9pm

May–Sep, Sun 10am–2pm), is all that remains of a 10C monastery.

Las Médulas★

◐ 22km/14mi SW.

A Roman gold mine transformed the slopes of the Aquilianos mountains into a magical landscape of rocky crags and strange-shaped hillocks of pink and ochre, covered by gnarled chestnut trees. It is a World Heritage site. The information centre, offering maps and guided tours (€3, appt only) is in the village of Carucedo (open 11am–2pm; ℘619 25 83 55; www.espaciolasmedulas.es). There's also a small **Archaeology Museum** (open Mon–Fri 10am–2pm, Sat & Sun 10am–1.30pm, 4–6pm; €2). Snap a postcard-perfect picture from the **Orellán viewpoint**.

Cebreiro

Near the Puerto de Piedrafita (Piedrafita Pass, 1 109m/3 638ft), Cebreiro is a reminder of the hardship of the pilgrims' journey. Drystone and thatched houses (pallozas) are little more than ancient Celtic huts; in one is an **Ethnographic Museum** (Museo Etnográfico; open Tue–Sat 16 Sep–14 Jun 11am–6pm, 15 Jun–15 Sept 8.30am–2.30pm). A pilgrim inn remains beside the small 9C mountain church where pilgrims venerated the relics of the miracle of the Holy Eucharist Relics, in silver caskets presented by Isabel.

Portomarín

Before this ancient village was drowned by a dam, its fortified **church★** of the Knights of St John of Jerusalem (open Tue–Sun 10.30am–1pm, 4.30–7pm) was moved stone by stone. It features massive arches and Romanesque doors with delicately carved covings. The west door depicts Christ in Majesty with the 24 Elders of the Apocalypse.

Vilar de Donas

◐ 6.5km/4mi E of Palas de Rei.

Enter the village **church** (open Tue–Sun 11am–2pm, 3–6pm) via its Romanesque doorway. Lining the walls are tombs of the Knights of the Order of St James, slain in battle. 15C **frescoes★** decorate the apse, illustrating Christ in Majesty with St Paul and St Luke on his left and St Peter and St Mark on his right. On the chancel walls are the faces of the elegant young women (donas in Galician) who give the church its name.

Santiago de Compostela★★★

♨See SANTIAGO DE COMPOSTELA

ADDRESSES

🛏 STAY

⊜⊜ **Hotel El Castillo–** Av. el Castillo 115, Ponferrada. ℘987 45 62 27. 48 rooms. Simple and centrally located near its namesake castle, El Castillo is a fine resting place for Camino walkers and overnighters.

⊜⊜ **Hotel Rural Bidean** – C. Mayor 20, Puente la Reina. ℘948 34 11 56. www.bidean.com. 20 rooms. It's rare to find a hotel at this price with such character and rustic, antique charm. Pilgrims get a special rate. A restaurant (⊜) serves home-cooked dishes.

⊜⊜⊜ **Hotel Real Monasterio San Zoilo** – Obispo Souto, Carrión de los Condes. ℘979 88 00 49. www.sanzoilo.com. 49 rooms. ⊠ €10.75. Restaurant ⊜⊜⊜. This former Benedictine monastery is now a delightful, welcoming hotel with elegant architecture. Rates are a great value.

♚/EAT

⊜⊜⊜ **La Peseta** – Pl. San Bartolomé 3, Astorga. ℘987 61 72 75. www.restaurantelapeseta.com. This popular family-run restaurant serves heaped portions of cocido maragato, the local boiled dinner with chickpeas and pork (perfect for refueling after a long day of hiking), and homemade desserts.

Estella-Lizarra★★

Estella was the 12C capital of the Kingdom of Navarra and the 19C base of the Carlists. It is an important stage on the Camino de Santiago.

▸ **Population:** 13 673
🖰 **Michelin Map:** 573D 23.
🗊 **Info:** San Nicolás 1.
 ✆948 55 63 01. www.
 estellaturismo.com.
◖ **Location:** Estella is in NE Spain near the Pyrenees on the slopes of the Sierra de Andía, along the N 111 linking Pamplona and Logroño (48km/30mi SW). 🚆Nearest station: Pamplona (43km).
◕ **Timing:** Allow a few hours for leisurely wandering in the Old Town.

SIGHTS

Plaza de San Martín

The once-bustling small square was originally the heart of the freemen's parish. On one side is the former **ayuntamiento** (town hall) dating to the 16C. On the other side of the Río Ega, on Calle de la Rúa (Pilgrim Road), stands the **Casa de Cultura Fray Diego de Estella** (✆948 55 17 47), built in 1565, at no. 7, with an emblazoned Plateresque facade. Newly renovated but still rather empty, it hosts occasional art exhibitions.

Palacio de los Reyes de Navarra★ (Palace of the Kings of Navarre)

San Nicolás 1. Open Tue–Fri 9.30am–1.30pm. Sat Sun & pub hols 11am–2pm. Closed 1 Jan, 25 Dec. ✆948 54 61 61. www.museogustavodemaeztu.com.

This rare 12C Romanesque civil building is punctuated by arcades and twin bays with remarkable capitals. It houses the contemporary art museum **Museo Gustavo de Maeztu y Whitney**, featuring the works of Gustavo de Maeztu y Whitney (1887–1947).

Son of a Cuban father and French mother, he grew up in Bilbao and then moved to Paris, but travelled extensively through Spain. In 1936 he settled in Estella until his death. His œuvre, which focusses on landcapes and portraits, is marked by colour and attention to detail. The first floor of the museum holds portraits of women, and the second, drawings, sketches and rural scenes.

Iglesia de San Pedro de la Rúa★

C. San Nicolás 2. Mon– Sat 10am–1.30pm, 6–7pm (pm only Nov–Mar), Sun & hols 10am–12.30pm

The church stands facing the royal palace, on a cliff spur formerly crowned by the city castle. It retains outstanding 12C and 13C features.

The unusual **doorway★** at the top of a steep stairway in the north wall has an equilateral scalloped arch of Caliphate influence. Similar portals can be seen in Navarra and in the Saintonge and Poitou regions of France. Inside, note the transitional Romanesque Virgin and Child, a Gothic Christ and an unusual column of intertwined serpents in the central apse. A Romanesque Crucified Christ is in the apse on the left.

The Romanesque **cloisters** lost two galleries when the nearby castle was blown up in the 16C. The skill and invention of the masons are evident in the remaining **capitals★★**; the north gallery series illustrates scenes from the lives of Christ, St Lawrence, St Andrew and St Peter, while plant and animal themes enliven the west gallery.

Iglesia de San Miguel

C. Mayor 46. Open 30 mins before Mass ✆948 55 00 70.

The church juts above a quarter that retains narrow streets and a medieval atmosphere. On the tympanum of the north **portal★** is a figure of Christ surrounded by the Evangelists and mysterious personages. The covings are full

Cloisters, Iglesia de San Pedro de la Rúa

© Susanne Kremer/Sime/Photononstop

of sculptures. The capitals illustrate the childhood of Christ.

On the upper register of the walls are eight Statue columns of the Apostles; on the lower register, two **high reliefs★★**, accomplished and expressive, show St Michael slaying the dragon (left) and the three Marys coming from the Sepulchre. The noble bearing, the elegant drapery and the facial expressions make the carving a Romanesque masterpiece.

EXCURSION

Monasterio de Irache★

◐ Irache. 3km/1.8mi SW of Estella. Open Wed–Sun 10am–1.30pm, 4–6pm. Closed for renovation until Jun 2020. ☎948 550 070.

A Benedictine abbey occupied the site in the 10C. Later, it was a major pilgrimage stop and a Cistercian community before becoming a university under the Benedictines, in the 16C.

Iglesia★ – The 12C–13C church's apse is purely Romanesque with a rib-vaulted nave. The dome on squinches and the *coro alto* are Renaissance; the facade and most of the structures were rebuilt in the 17C. Brackets and capitals illustrate the lives of Christ and St Benedict in the **claustro**.

🚗 DRIVING TOUR

SIERRA DE ANDÍA AND SIERRA DE URBASA★
94km/58mi. About 3hr.

◖ Leave Estella on NA 120 north toward the Puerto (pass) de Lizarraga. The road crosses beechwoods and rises to a pass that affords extensive views.

Monasterio de Iranzu
9km/5.6mi N of Estella. Signposted from NA 120. Open 10am–2pm, 4–8pm (Oct–Apr 4–6pm). €3. ☎948 52 00 12.

This 12C Cistercian monastery is now home to a college. Isolated in a wild **gorge★**, it is a fine example of the Cistercian transitional style from Romanesque to Gothic, combining robustness and elegance. The cloister bays have Romanesque blind arcades, oculi and wide relieving arches. The church, with primitive vaulting, has a flat east end decorated with three windows, symbolising the Trinity, a signature Cistercian feature.

Puerto de Lizarraga Road★★
Once out of the tunnel (alt 1 090m/ 3 576ft), pause at the **viewpoint★** over the Ergoyena Valley before the descent through woods and pastures.

◖ Continue to Etxarri-Aranatz; take N 240 W to Olatzi; turn left to Estella.

Puerto de Urbasa road★★
The road climbs steeply between great boulders and dense copses. Beyond the pass (alt 927m/3 041ft) tall limestone cliffs add character to the landscape before the road enters the gorges of the sparkling river Urenderra.

Palacio Real de Olite

Olite/Erriberri ★

Olite was the favourite residence of the kings of Navarra in the 15C and retains the seat of power, a now-restored fairytale palace the size of a small village. Olite's idyllic setting and handful of museums and nearby wineries attract plenty of summer visitors.

SIGHTS

▲▲ Palacio Real de Olite ★

Pl. de los Teobaldos, between the Parador and Iglesia de Santa María. Open daily; see website for hours. Closed 1, 6 Jan, 25 Dec. €3.50, guided tours €4.90. ℘948 74 00 35.
www.guiartenavarra.com/palacio.
The Royal Palace of Olite is divided into the Palacio Viejo (Old Palace), now a Parador, and the Palacio Nuevo (New Palace), open to visitors.
The latter was built by Charles III (the Noble) in 1406. His French origins – as Count of Evreux and native of Mantes – explain the fortifications, a transition between the massive stone constructions of the 13C and the royal Gothic residences of the late 15C with galleries and courtyards. During the Peninsular War, a fire almost destroyed the building. Behind the 15 or so towers marking the perimetre were hanging gardens,

▶ **Population:** 3 931
⏚ **Michelin Map:** 573 E 25.
🛈 **Info:** Pl. de los Teobaldos 10. ℘948 74 17 03. www.olite.es.
◖ **Location:** Olite stands at the heart of the Navarran plain, 4km/2.5mi from the A 15 motorway linking Zaragoza and Pamplona/Iruña (43km/26mi S). 🚃Nearest station: Pamplona (45km).
▲▲ **Kids:** Palacio Real de Olite.
🕙 **Timing:** The last week of August, Olite celebrates a theatre festival.

along with inner halls and chambers decorated with *azulejos*, painted stuccowork and coloured marquetry ceilings.
The most impressive rooms are the Guardarropa (Wardrobe), the Sala de la Reina (Queen's Room) and the Galería del Rey (King's Gallery).

Iglesia de Santa María la Real ★

Pl. de los Teobaldos. Open 30min before Mass, Sun 11am and 6.30pm. €1.50.
The church is the former royal chapel. An atrium of slender multifoil arches predates the 14C **facade★**, a fine exam-

ple of Navarra Gothic sculpture. The only figurative carving illustrates the lives of the Virgin and Christ. A painted 16C retable frames a Gothic statue of Our Lady.

Museo del Vino de Navarra★

Pl. de los Teobaldos 4. Open Holy Week–mid-Oct Mon–Sat 10am–2pm, 4pm–7pm, Sun 10am–2pm; rest of the year Mon–Fri 10am–5pm, Sat & Sun 10am–2pm. Closed 1 & 6 Jan, 25 Dec. €4. ℘948 741 273.

www.museodelvinodenavarra.com.

This museum abutting the tourism office explains the basics of Navarran wine through objects and informative placards. Each floor introduces a different theme such as the history of wine, vineyard management, bottling or aging. Perhaps most memorable is the nosing and tasting room with various scents and flavoured bonbons to help you improve your palate. Some displays have fallen into disrepair. No wheelchair access.

EXCURSIONS

Ujué★

⬤ 19km/11.8mi NE of Olite, along NA 5 300 (Ctra de San Martin de Unx) to San Martín de Unx, then follow the NA 5310. www.ujue.info

Medieval Ujué, clustered on a hilltop overlooking the Ribera region, has narrow streets, nearby wineries and a historic windmill.

Iglesia de Santa María

Open 10am–6.30pm (5.30 in winter). Guided tours of church and fortress by appointment. ℘618 820 414.

A Romanesque church was built at the end of the 11C. In the 14C, Charles II, the Bad, began a Gothic church, but the Romanesque chancel happily remains. The central chapel contains the venerated Santa María la Blanca, a plated Romanesque statue honoured with a *romería* (pilgrimage) the Sunday after St Mark's Day (25 April).

Fortaleza
(Fortress)

The church towers command a view out to Olite, Mt Montejurra and the Pyrenees. Of the medieval palace there remain lofty walls and a covered watch path circling the church.

Monasterio de La Oliva★

⬤ Ctra de Lerida, Carcastillo, 27km/ 16.7mi S of Ujué. Open Mon–Sat 9.30am–12pm, 3.30–6pm, Sun & public hols 9.30am–11.30am, 4–6pm. €2.50. ℘948 72 50 06.

www.monasteriodelaoliva.org.

La Oliva was one of the first Cistercian monasteries built outside France. The buildings, stripped of treasure and trappings, retain a pure Cistercian beauty.

Iglesia★★ – The facade of this late 12C church is mostly unadorned, a perfect setting for the interplay of lines of the portal and two rose windows. The interior is surprisingly deep with pillars and pointed arches lined with thick polygonal ribs in austere Cistercian style.

Claustro★ – The bays in the late-15C cloisters appear exceptionally light. Ogival vaults rise from Romanesque capitals at the entry to the 13C **Sala Capitular** (chapter house). The monastery makes its own wine, available for purchase from €5 a bottle.

Laguna de Pitillas★

⬤ 13km/8.7mi SW of Olite on the N-121 to Pitillas. Observation area open Sat, Sun & hols, times vary with the seasons. Guided tours available. www.lagunadepitillas.org.

This marshy area covers 87ha/216 acres with an average water depth of 3m/9.8ft; a dyke regulates the level. The site was declared a nature reserve in 1987 because of its ecological importance. It also lies on the migratory routes of many species of birds that use the marshes as a breeding ground. The best time for birdwatching is winter. A free bird observation area (*Observatorio de Aves*) provides telescopes.

Tudela/Tutera★

Tudela was once part of the Córdoba Caliphate, evident from its large Moorish quarter, the Morería. Following the so-called Reconquista, an abundance of churches were built. Another legacy of Tudela's Moorish past is its sophisticated irrigation system that waters the surrounding Ribera farmland.

▶ **Population:** 35 593
◈ **Michelin Map:** 573 F 25.
🖪 **Info:** Pl. de los Fueros
  ℘948 84 80 58.
  www.tudela.es/turismo.
◐ **Location:** Tudela is on the right bank of the River Ebro in NE Spain, 50km/31mi S of Olite via N 121 and N 134.
  ▤▤Tudela/Tutera.
◔ **Timing:** During the Festival de Santa Ana, at the end of July, is a great time to visit.

SIGHTS

Catedral★

Pl. Vieja. Open Tue–Sat 11.30am–1.30pm, 4–7pm; Sun 11.30am–1.30pm. €4 incl museum and cloisters. ℘948 40 21 61. www.catedraldetudela.com.

The 12C–13C cathedral exemplifies the transitional Romanesque-Gothic style. The **Last Judgement Doorway★** (Portada del Juicio Final), though difficult to see, is carved with 120 groups of figures. Gothic works include early 16C choir stalls, the high altar retable and the Byzantine-looking 13C stone reliquary statue of the White Virgin. In the **Capilla de Nuestra Señora de la Esperanza★** (Chapel of our Lady of Hope), 15C masterpieces include the tomb of a chancellor of Navarra and the main altarpiece. The 12C–13C **cloisters★★** (claustro) are beautifully harmonious. Romanesque arches rest alternately on columns with historiated capitals with scenes from the New Testament and the lives of the saints in a style inspired by the carvings of Aragón. A door of an earlier mosque remains.

St Anne's Feast Day

26 July – Like a (much) smaller San Fermín, this fiesta involves several days of street fairs, concerts and cultural events. During Holy Week, an event known as the Descent of the Angel takes place on the picturesque **Plaza de los Fueros**, which served as a bullring in the 18C.

Palacio Decanal y Museo de Tudela

Pl. Vieja 2. Mon–Fri 10am–1.30pm, 4–7pm. Sat & hols 10am–1.30pm. Jul & Aug guided tours of cathedral, Mon–Fri 12pm & 4pm, Sat & hols 10am. €4, free Wed 5–7pm. ℘948 40 21 61. www.palaciodecanaldetudela.com.

The former bishop's palace, built in the 16C, houses the Museum of Tudela with its collection of sacred art. Before entering the museum, which also includes a visit to the cloisters, take time to admire its magnificent Plateresque portico.

Plaza de la Judería

Until the Jews were expelled from Navarra in1498, Tudela was home to a large and learned Jewish population that lived within the castle walls. On one side of this square, in the former Jewish Quarter (Judería), is the 16C Renaissance Palacio del Marqués de San Adrián. Note the Aragonese style arches and eaves, carved by Esteban de Obray in 1519. The interior houses a fine courtyard.

Museo Muñoz Sola de Arte Moderno (Modern Art Museum)

Pl. Vieja 2. Open Wed–Sun, see website for seasonal opening hours. €1. ℘948 402 640. www.castelruiz.es.

A native of Tudela, the painter César **Muñoz Sola** (1921–2000) amassed an extensive collection of 19C French

Bardena Blanca, Bardenas Reales

paintings, on display here. Girodet Roucy, Hugard Tower, Julien Tavernier Foubert and – of course – Muñoz Sola are represented.

EXCURSIONS
Bardenas Reales★★

◯ Visitor Centre: Ctra. del Polígono de Tiro, km. 6, on the NA134 15km/9mi north of Tudela, just before Arguedas. Park: open 8am–1 hr before sunset. Visitor Centre: Apr–Aug 9am–2pm, 4–7pm, Sep–Mar 9am–2pm, 3–5pm. ℘948 83 03 08.
www.bardenasreales.es. ⊛ Take water and food as there are few facilities.

This semi-desert resembling parts of the American West spans 42 500ha/105 000 acres and takes in stunning gypsum, clay and sandstone formations. The park is divided into several areas according to vegetation: The northern swath and southern *Bardena Negra* are characterized by pines and oaks, while the central *Bardena Blanca* has the most spectacular landscape.

The diversity of terrain and flora in the park attracts many species of birds. By ancient decree, sheep are allowed to graze here during the cooler months, their arrival celebrated September 18.

Entering via the road from Arguedas, you'll pass a military base before the surreal beauty of the Bardenas begins. From here, you can loop around the **Bardena Blanca**, where centuries of erosion created an eye-popping moonlike landscape.

Enter by Nuestra Señora del Yugo, a shrine housing a 15C Madonna, to access the Bardena Blanca, the main attraction, renowned for colourful sites like Pisquerra, Sanchicorrota and the Ralla Rallón.

ADDRESSES

🍽 STAY

⊜⊜⊜⊜ **Aire de Bardenas** – Ctra. de Ejea, km 1. ℘948 11 66 66. 22 rooms. ⊑€15.40. The Navarran hotel gracing magazine covers the world over is this futuristic luxury retreat composed of 'bubble' rooms strewn across the arid basin. It doesn't get much more remote than this: Aside from hotel staff and guests, there's no one around.

Basque Country and La Rioja

The Basque Country (*País Vasco* in Castilian, *Euskadi* in Basque), which sits in the crook of the Bay of Biscay on the French border, is as picturesque as it is enigmatic: No one knows when or how the Basques arrived in this rocky corner of Spain, nor the origins of their language, Euskera, puzzlingly non-Indo-European. Today the autonomous region – in particular San Sebastián and Bilbao – is Spain's gastronomic nerve centre with a vibrant *pintxos* (Basque tapas) scene and more Michelin-starred restaurants per capita than anywhere else on earth (barring Kyoto). Its tiny fishing villages and timber farmhouses (*caseríos* or *basseriak*) are exceptionally charming. La Rioja, the renowned wine region, lies to the south. In the Middle Ages, Basque and Riojan towns expanded as staging points on the Camino de Santiago, which left a legacy of religious buildings.

Highlights

Costa Vasca

The Basque coastal region is known as Bizkaia (Biscay) and is famous for its capital, Bilbao (Bilbo in Euskera). Just as the 1992 Olympics led to the reinvention of Barcelona, the 1997 inauguration of Frank Gehry's stunning Guggenheim Museum launched what was a fading industrial city onto the global cultural map. Of course, the city's splendid fine arts museum and characterful old quarter were here long before then. The crown jewel of the Costa Vasca is San Sebastián (Donostia in Euskera): It boasts one of Europe's finest urban beaches, La Concha, on a sandy bay, and draws Spanish holidaymakers, a fashionable international set and food connoisseurs. The atmospheric Parte Vieja (old town) is chock-a-block with pintxo bars serving refined small bites.

Basque Country interior

The inland Basque regions of Gipuzkoa and Álava (Araba in Euskera) are too often eclipsed by the hedonistic delights of the coast, but those who make the effort to visit cities like Vitoria-Gasteiz, the sophisticated Basque capital with fine museums and galleries, and old towns like Oñate (Oñati in Euskera) and Santuario de Arantzazu are duly rewarded.

La Rioja

Irrigated by the Ebro river, much of Rioja's 5 034sq km/1 944sq mi is blanketed with vines of tempranillo, graciano, viura and more to make world-class *crianzas* and *reservas*, young and reserve wine, respectively. Haro is the epicentre of the region's wine scene with historic bodegas lined up one next to the other. Logroño, the scruffy industrial capital has a few characterful corners and some the best tapas bars in the region, on Calle Laurel.

La Concha, Donostia-San Sebastián

© Javier Larrea/age fotostock

Donostia-San Sebastián★★

San Sebastián wraps around a scallop-shaped bay framed by three hills. Just off shore lies the storybook Isle of Santa Clara, visible from the expansive beaches of La Concha and Ondarreta. Gardens, promenades and statuary new and old decorate the town, most notable of which is *El Peine del Viento XV* (Windcomb 15), by abstract sculptor Eduardo Chillida.

A BIT OF HISTORY

Unhumble beginnings – Queen María Cristina of Habsburg chose San Sebastián, then fishing village, as her summer residence in the 19C, establishing it as an aristocratic resort; the *Belle Époque* feel hasn't waned since.

A culinary revolution – Txokos, local (traditionally male-only) gastronomic clubs, paved the way for San Sebastián's 20C *nueva cocina* movement, spearheaded by Pedro Subijana, Juan Mari Arzak and Martín Berasategui.

SIGHTS

Parte Vieja★★

The narrow streets of the old town (rebuilt after a fire in 1813) contrast with the wide avenues of modern Donostia. The area comes alive at the apéritif hour, when locals and (ever more) tourists pack the bars lining Portu, Muñoa, 31 de Agosto and Fermín Calbetón streets on protracted pintxo crawls.

Basílica de Santa María

C. Mayor. Open Jun–Sep 8am–2pm, 4–8pm; Oct–May 8.30am–2pm, 5–8pm. €3. ℘943 42 31 24.

The church has an exuberant late-18C portal, Baroque altars and modern art by Chillida and Maximilian Peizmann.

Museo de San Telmo

Pl. Zuloaga 1. Open Tue–Sun & hols 10am–8pm. Closed 1 & 20 Jan, 25 Dec. €6. Free Tue. ℘943 48 15 81. www.santelmomuseoa.eus.

▶ **Population:** 186 095
◔ **Michelin Map:** 573 (town plan or 574 C 23-24.
🛈 **Info:** Alameda Boulevard 8. ℘943 48 11 66. www.san sebastianturismo.com.
◑ **Location:** Donostia-San Sebastián is on the Gulf of Vizcaya, 25km/15.5mi W of the French border, 102km/63.3mi E of Bilbao. 🚊Donostia-San Sebastián (only train to Bilbao airport is a local one, takes 2.5hrs).
🅿 **Parking:** Space is limited in the old quarter; walking is preferable.
🚫 **Don't Miss:** A walk in the old quarter, and a fine seafood repast.
🕓 **Timing:** Allow a day in town and a days for excursions.
👥 **Kids:** The Aquarium, Eureka Science Museum.

The entrance leads to the Renaissance cloisters of this former monastery, where Basque stone funerary crosses from the 15C–17C are on display. Interior quarters are lined with paintings by Ribera, El Greco and 19C artists. The chapel was decorated by **José María Sert** with scenes from the city's history. Temporary exhibitions are often thought-provoking.

Paseo Nuevo★ (Pasealekua Berria)

This oceanside promenade with excellent **views** traces the base of Monte Urgull.

👥 Aquarium San Sebastián★

Pl. Carlos Biasca de Imaz 1. Open Jul–Aug 10am–9pm; Holy Week–Jun and Sep Mon–Fri until 8pm, Sat–Sun until 9pm; Oct–Holy Week Mon–Fri until 7pm, Sat–Sun until 8pm. Closed 1 & 20 Jan, 25 Dec. €13; child €6.50. ℘943 44 00 99. www.aquariumss.com.

After marveling at rare, colourful aquatic life in tanks and learning about whaling history, traverse the **Oceanarium★**, an underwater glass tunnel.

Mercado de la Bretxa

Blvd Zumardia 3. Open: Market Mon–Sat 8am–9pm. www.cclabretxa.com.
You might bump into a star chef at this traditional market (est. 1870) selling top-quality Basque ingredients like Getaria anchovies, pickled chillies (*piparrak*) and Espelette pepper.

Kursaal

Zurriola 1. Only open for events. ℘943 00 30 00. www.kursaal.com.es.
Spanish architect Rafael Moneo's glowing cube-shaped hall is a modernist triumph. It hosts the **International Film Festival** and International Jazz Festival.

EXCURSIONS

Monte Ulía★

◗ 7km/4.3mi E. Follow the N 1 toward Irún and take a right before the summit. The twisting drive up affords excellent **views** of San Sebastián and the coast.

Astigarraga

◗ N 10km/6mi S toward Hernani.

Basque Cider House Museum (Sagardoetxea)

Nagusia Kalea 48. Open Tue–Sat (Jul–Aug daily) 11am–1.30pm, 4pm–7.30pm, Sun & hols 11am–1.30pm; €4. ℘943 550 575. www.sagardoarenlurraldea.eus.
The Basques have been making cider for centuries if not milennia. Learn how it's made, and stroll orchards of endemic apple trees, at this museum that caps off visits with a tasting.

♟♟ Eureka! Zientzia Museoa (Science Museum)

Mikeletegi Pasealekua 43. Open Mon 10am–4pm, Tue–Fri 10am–7pm, Sat–Sun 11am–8pm. Extended hrs Jul–Aug & hols. €10; add €4 planetarium. ℘943 012 478. www.eurekamuseoa.eus.
Each room of this state-of-the-art museum focusses on a different scientific principle (light, energy, the senses etc.). brought to life by interactive, hands-on displays. There is a planetarium (open Tue–Sun; sessions in Spanish and Basque; see website for times) and several motion simulators (extra charge).

♟♟ Parque de Aiete

It's a long, uphill walk from town; buses 19 & 31 offer service.
Escape the tourist hubbub in this quiet neighbourhood park shaded by Atlas cedars, ginko biloba and plane trees. It surrounds a **Neoclassical palace** built in 1878 for the Duke and Duchess of Bailen and, later, used by Franco as a summer residence; today it's a cultural centre. There are playgrounds, benches and wide lawns great for picnicking.

Tolosa

◗ 26kms/16mi south on the N1.
Tolosa's historic centre, with colourful houses, quaint squares and a recently restored windmill, hugs the River Oria. A bustling **farmers market★** takes place on Saturdays in Pl. Euskal Herria.
Tolosa's most notable church is the Baroque Santa María, situated on the square of the same name. From here, wander along the typically Basque Kale Nagusia, stopping at the Palacio Atodo No. 33 to admire the handsome coat of arms and eaves in the vernacular Basque style, before heading to the 15C Torre Andia. Tolosa is famous for its beans (*alubias*), colloquially Called 'black pearls' for their sheen and price, which you can try in down-home restaurants.

ADDRESSES

🏨 STAY

🌐🌐🌐 **One Shot Tabakalera House** – Po. Duque de Mandas 52, San Sebastián. ℘943 930 038. www.hoteloneshottabakalerahouse.com. ⊑€14. Opened in 2015 in the shiny new Tabakalera cultural centre, this four-star by the train station has highly Instagrammable designer furnishings.

⊖⊖⊖⊖ **Hotel Akelarre** – Padre Orkolaga Ibilbidea 56, San Sebastián. ✆943 31 12 08. www.akelarre.net. 22 rooms. It doesn't get more sybaritic than having dinner at Pedro Subijana's three-Michelin-star restaurant (⊖⊖⊖⊖) and then swanning straight up to a luxurious pad overlooking the Bay of Biscay. Suites add in-room whirlpools.

⍩ EAT

⊖ **Txepetxa** – Arrandegi Kalea 5, San Sebastián. ✆943 42 22 27. Closed Mon–Tue. One (or four) of Txepetxa's anchovy canapés is the optimal first bite on a *txikiteo* (pintxo crawl). Wash it down with txakoli, the fizzy local white.

⊖⊖ **La Cuchara de San Telmo** – C. 31 de Agosto 28, San Sebastián. Closed Tue lunch, Mon. ✆943 44 16 55. Getting an order in at this perennially jammed pintxo bar can feel downright Darwinian, but the chaos is instantly worth it when you taste killer pintxos like braised beef cheeks or 'orzotto' enriched with Idiazabal cheese.

⊖⊖⊖ **Casa Julián** – Sta. Klara Kalea 6, Tolosa. ✆943 67 14 17. www.casajulianmg.com. Closed Mon. If the Basques are religious about their beef, then Casa Julián – the most famous *asador* (grill) in Spain – is their temple. Expect thick-cut steaks flame-licked to juicy perfection every time.

⊖⊖⊖⊖ **Martín Berasategui** – Loidi Kalea 4, Lasarte-Oria. ✆943 36 64 71. Closed Mon–Tue, Sun pm. A quick jaunt south of San Sebastián, and you're at the namesake restaurant of Martín Berasategui, who holds 10 Michelin stars. Weather permitting, sit on the terrace, and enjoy haute-cuisine dishes like eel-and-foie-gras millefeuille.

Costa de Gipuzkoa★★

The Basque Coast (Costa Vasca) stretches from the Bay of Biscay to the headland of the Cabo de Machichaco. The steep, impenetrable shoreline, serrated with cliffs, belies coves with peaceful fishing villages.

🚗 DRIVING TOUR

HONDARRIBIA TO BILBAO
70km/43mi. Allow one day.

Hondarribia★

🚈 Nearest train station: Irún (4km). Today Hondarribia is largely a resort, but it retains its old fishermen's quarter, **La Marina,** with white timbered houses edged with colourful trim. Overlooking the River Bidasoa, the steep **Old Town** retains its 15C walls, penetrable via the Puerta de Santa María, a gateway with twin angels venerating the Virgen de Guadalupe. The corner placement of

- 🕭 **Michelin Map:** 574 B-C 21 to 24 – Basque Country (Gipuzkoa, Vizcaya).
- 🗊 **Info:** www.bizkaiacosta vasca.com.
- ◖ **Location:** The Basque Coast runs from the French border to Bilbao.
- 👫 **Kids:** Museo del Ferrocarril Vasco.
- 🕓 **Timing:** The Basque Coast can be very wet at any time of year.

escutcheons on noble houses here is a local architectural oddity.

The Iglesia de Santa María on Calle Mayor is Gothic with massive buttresses. It was remodelled in the 17C and given a Baroque tower.

The Castillo de Carlos V (Pl. de Armas 14), a fortress towering over the harbour, was constructed in the 10C by Sancho Abarca, King of Navarra, and restored by Charles V in the 16C; today it's a well-reviewed Parador.

From the harbour you can take a ferry (⚓ 10min) across the French border to **Hendaye★**, with fine beaches for surfing and plentiful shops.

◗ Leave Hondarribia on the harbour road.

Cabo Higuer★
4km/2.5mi N.
Turn left; as the road climbs, catch a fantastic **view★** of the beach, the town and the quayside and, from the end of the headland, the French coast.

◗ Take the Behobia road, then the first right after the Palmera factory. Bear left at the first crossroads.

Ermita de San Marcial
9km/5.6mi SE.
A narrow road leads to the wooded hilltop (225m/738ft). The **panorama★★** from the hermitage includes Hondarribia, Irún and Isla de los Faisanes (Pheasant Island) in the mouth of the River Bidasoa on the border. In the distance are San Sebastián and Hendaye.

Jaizkibel Road★★
Aim to **drive★★** this seaside road (GI 3440) at sunset for stunning views. After 5km/3mi you reach the Capilla de Nuestra Señora de Guadalupe (Chapel of our Lady of Guadalupe) where there is a lovely **view★** of the French coast. Past pines and gorse is the Hotel Jaizkibel (www.hoteljaizkibel.com), at the foot of a 584m/1 916ft peak, and a lookout with another great **view★★**. The road down affords tantalising **glimpses★** of the indented coast, the Cordillera Cantábrica range and the mountains above San Sebastián.

◗ Travel 17km/10.5mi W along the Jaizkibel road.

Pasaia/Pasajes
Pasaia comprises three villages around a sheltered bay. Pasai Antxo is a trading port; **Pasai Donibane★** and Pasai San Pedro are deep-sea fishing ports, processing cod. To get to Pasai Donibane,

park at the village entrance or take a motorboat from San Pedro. The view from the water is gorgeous – picture slender houses with brightly painted balconies jutting above a classic harbour scene. A path runs to the lighthouse (🚶 45min).

Donostia-San Sebastián★★
See DONOSTIA-SAN SEBASTIÁN

◗ Take the N 1; 7km/4.3mi S of San Sebastián, then the N 634 toward Bilbao.

Zarautz
Surfers and Spanish families flock to this beach resort that was Queen Isabel II's summer residence in the 19C. The old quarter isn't as impressive as the beach, but it does have two palaces: the Renaissance **Palacio Narros** (Elizaurre Kalea 2; by guided tour only; ℘943 833 641) and 15C **Luzea tower** (open only during exhibitions; ℘943 83 09 90) on the Plaza Mayor, with mullioned windows and a machicolated balcony. The modern **Photomuseum** (San Ignacio 11; Tue–Sun 10am–2pm, 5–8pm; ℘943 130 906; €6; www.photomuseum.es) traces photography from its beginnings to the digital age. Beyond Zarautz, the road rises to a picturesque **corniche★★**.

Getaria★
Getaria is known for its top-quality anchovies (antxoak). It's distinguished by a rocky peak colloquially called el ratón (the mouse) for its shape. Native son **Juan Sebastián Elcano** set out from here with Magellan and in 1522 became one of the first sailors to circumnavigate the globe. A narrow street, lined with picturesque houses, leads to the 13–15C Iglesia de San Salvador (C. Mayor 39; open 9.30am–afternoon Mass; ℘943 14 07 51), whose chancel rests on an arch above an alleyway. The gallery is Flamboyant Gothic.
The **Cristóbal Balenciaga Museoa★** (Aldamar Parkea 6; open Tue–Sun Nov–Feb 10am–3pm, Mar–Oct 10am–7pm, Jul–Aug 10am–8pm; €10; ℘943

00 88 40; www.cristobalbalenciaga-museoa.com) showcases some 1 200 key designs from the Getaria-born couturier's career in the house – now with a massive, geometric modern addition – he was born in.

Zumaia

Zumaia has two fine beaches: Itzurun, set between cliffs, and Santiago. Near the latter is the **Espacio Cultural Ignacio Zuloaga** (open a few days each month; check website for full schedule; *℘* 677 078 445, www.espaciozuloaga. com), devoted to the artist who lived here 1870–1945. His paintings – showing realistic and popular scenes with vivid colours and strong lines – are in the company of works by Goya, El Greco, Rodin, Toulouse-Lautrec and Manet. Note the remains of a Romanesque chapel.

In town, the 15C **Iglesia de San Pedro** contains a 16C altarpiece by Juan de Anchieta.

▶ Past Zumaia, go left onto the GI 631.

Santuario de San Ignacio de Loyola

Zumaia. Open Jun–Sep 10am–1.30pm, 3.30–7.30pm (until 7pm Oct–May). Santa Casa €3; other buildings free. *℘* 943 02 50 00. www.loyola.global.

This sanctuary was built by the Jesuits to plans by Italian architect Carlo Fontana around the Loyola family manor near Azpeitia at the end of the 17C. It is an important place of pilgrimage, especially on St Ignatius' day (31 Jul). The basement casemates of the 15C tower are vestiges of the original Loyola manor house, the **Santa Casa**.

The rooms in which Ignatius was born have been transformed into profusely decorated chapels. The Baroque basilica is more Italian than Spanish in style, circular with a cupola (65m/213ft high).

▲▲ Museo Vasco del Ferrocarril

(Azpeitia Railway Museum)
Julián Elortza Hiribidea 8, Azpeitia. Open Tue–Fri 10am–1.30pm, 3pm–6.30pm, Sat 10.30am–2pm, 4-7.30pm, Sun &

hols 10.30am–2pm. Steam train rides throughout the year. Museum €3, train rides €3. *℘* 943 150 677. www.museoa. euskotren.eus.

A disused railway station is the perfect setting for a railway museum, its platforms and warehouses used for exhibits of clunky machinery and old locomotives. Train rides go to neighbouring Lasao.

▶ Return to the coast. The journey by road to Deba is one of the region's most scenic.

Deba

The **Iglesia de Santa María la Real** (Pl. Zaharra 7; open 9am–1pm, Tue until 12pm; *℘* 943 12 24 52; www.deba.eus) in this fishing port conceals a superb Gothic portal decorated with lifelike statues. The cloister galleries have intricate tracery. There is a splendid **view★** of the coast from the **cliff road★** between Deba and Lekeitio, another delightful fishing village. At **Mutriku** is the tree-backed beach of **Saturraran**.

ADDRESSES

🏠 STAY

🛏🛏🛏 **Hotel Obispo** – Pl. del Obispo, Hondarribia. *℘* 943 64 54 00. www. hotelobispo.com. 16 rooms. ⚏ €12. Quiet comfort sans pretension defines this hotel in a 14C–15C palace on the upper ridge of the old quarter.

🍽 EAT

🍽🍽🍽 **Iribar** – Kale Nagusia Kalea 34, Getaria. *℘* 943 14 04 06. Closed Thu, 2 wks Apr & Oct. Drop in for a straightforward, seafood-centric meal at this village restaurant with affordable grilled dishes.

🍽🍽🍽 **Elkano** – C. Herrerieta 2, Getaria. *℘* 943 140 024. Closed Mon & Tue. Anthony Bourdain put this fine-dining seafood restaurant on the fast track to international fame when he raved about its grilled turbot on *Parts Unknown*. The whole, wild-caught flat fish is carved tableside with panache.

Bilbao★

Bilbao has far more to offer than its flashy Frank Gehry-designed Guggenheim Museum: a romantic riverside esplanade, a palpable artsy pulse, charming old buildings and – take note, San Sebastián – sensibly priced pintxos, for starters. The modern, well-run metro system, with entrances by Norman Foster, makes it easy to get around.

A BIT OF HISTORY

The city – Founded in the early 14C, old Bilbao lies on the right bank of the Nervión, under the Santuario de Begoña (Begoña Sanctuary). It was originally named **Las Siete Calles** (the Seven Streets) for its layout. The modern **El Ensanche** ('enlargement') business district, across the river, developed in the 19C. A wealthy residential quarter spreads around Doña Casilda Iturriza park and Gran Vía de Don Diego López de Haro.

Industry – Industry developed in the middle of the 19C when iron mined nearby was shipped to England. Iron and steelworks were subsequently established. Unthinkably, many of these were built in the centre of town, causing most Spaniards to lose hope that it could regain its erstwhile splendour. **Greater Bilbao and the Ría** – Since 1945 Greater Bilbao has included the towns spanning from Bilbao itself to Getxo, on the sea. Industry is concentrated along the left bank in the districts of Baracaldo, Sestao, **Portugalete** – popular among tourists for its **transporter bridge** built in 1893 – and Somorrostro, where there is an oil refinery.

Santurtzi is known for its sardines. **Algorta**, a residential town on the right bank, is a contrast to heavy industry; **Deusto** is famous for its university.

MUSEO GUGGENHEIM★★★

Av. Abandoibarra 2. Open Tue-Sat 10am-8pm. Closed 1 Jan, 25 Dec. €17. ℘944 35 90 00.
www.guggenheim-bilbao.eus.

▸ **Population:** 345 821
‍ **Michelin Map:** 573 C 21 (town plan) – Basque Country (Bizkaia)

 Info: Plaza Circular 1. ℘944 79 57 60. www.bilbaoturismo.net.

 Location: Bilbao is in northeastern Spain's Basque Country. Vitoria-Gasteiz is 69km/43mi to the S, Donostia-San Sebastián 102km/63mi to the E and Santander 103km/64mi to the W. Estación de Abando is the major train station. Trains do not run to the city centre from Bilbao airport.

 Don't Miss: The Guggenheim is a must-see for Spain, not just Bilbao, but art lovers shouldn't miss the oft-overlooked Museum of Fine Arts.

 Timing: Spend a few hours in and around the Guggenheim, then stroll along the esplanade to the old town.

 Kids: Museo Marítimo Ría del Bilbao.

This is the European showcase for the collection founded in New York by art patron Solomon R. Guggenheim (1861–1949) and the youngest of the museums managed by the Guggenheim Foundation. With this eye-popping museum complex, inaugurated in 1997, acclaimed architect **Frank Gehry** created one of the great buildings of the late 20C, a counterpart to Frank Lloyd Wright's famous 1950 spiral housing the Guggenheim's Fifth Avenue museum.

Emblem of the City

The museum rises from the banks of the Nervión like a ship from the future with billowing sails. Formal geometry and symmetry are abandoned to free forms, creating harmony and lines

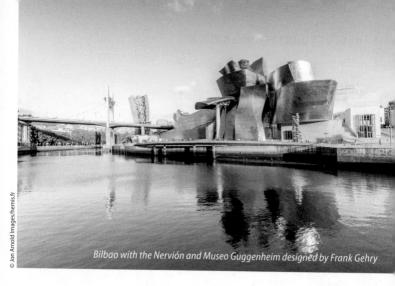

Bilbao with the Nervión and Museo Guggenheim designed by Frank Gehry

flowing both gracefully and chaotically. The composition, shimmering in titanium, must be seen from all angles to appreciate how it plays with light and space. The south entrance, of golden limestone, opens to a soaring **central atrium** (50m/164ft high) echoing Wright's great spiral, a whirl of smoothly moulded shapes and natural light on the ground floor.

Access to the galleries is by glass-fronted lifts or vertiginous suspended walkways and staircases, the largest measuring 130m/426.5ft by 25m/82ft.

Collections

Drawing on the vast Guggenheim collections (more than 6 000 paintings, sculptures and works on paper), the Bilbao collection focusses on the 1950s to the present. Well represented are Modern masters (Picasso, Mondrian, Kandinsky) and major movements such as Abstract Expressionism (Rothko, De Kooning, Pollock), Pop art (Oldenburg, Rosenquist, Warhol), and Conceptual and Minimalist art (Carl André, Donald Judd). Contemporary artists likely to be on view include Anselm Kiefer, Francesco Clemente and Damien Hirst.

The museum's own acquisitions include a vast mural by Sol LeWitt and Richard Serra's Snake, three gigantic sheets of undulating steel. Notable Spanish works are by **Antoni Tàpies, Eduardo Chillida, Francesc Torres, Cristina Iglesias** and **Susana Solano**.

SIGHTS

Museo de Bellas Artes★

Pl. del Museo 2. Open Wed–Mon 10am –8pm (2pm Dec 24 & 31 unless Tue). Closed 1 & 6 Jan, 25 Dec. €10. ℘944 39 60 60. www.museobilbao.com.

The city's fine arts museum is in two buildings in Doña Casilda Iturriza park. The **ancient art section★★** (old building, ground floor) exhibits 12–17C Spanish paintings. Romanesque works include a 12C Crucifixion from the Catalan School. The 16–17C Spanish Classical section has works by **Morales, El Greco**, Valdés Leal, **Zurbarán, Ribera** and **Goya**. Dutch and Flemish canvases (15C–17C) include The Usurers by Quentin Metsys, a Pietà by Benson and Holy Family by Gossaert.

The Basque art section (first floor) holds works by the great Basque painters: Regoyos, Zuloaga, Iturrino et al. The contemporary art section (new building) displays works by artists both Spanish – Solana, Vázquez Díaz, Gargallo, Blanchard, Luis Fernández Otieza, Chillida and Tàpies – and foreign – Delaunay, Léger, Kokoschka and Bacon.

Euskal Museoa Bilbao (Basque Museum)

Pl. Miguel de Unamuno 4. Open Mon–Fri 10am–7pm (exc Tue), Sat 10am–1.30pm, 4–7pm, Sun 10am–2pm. Closed Tue, public hols. €3; free Thu. ℘944 15 54 23. www.euskal-museoa.eus.

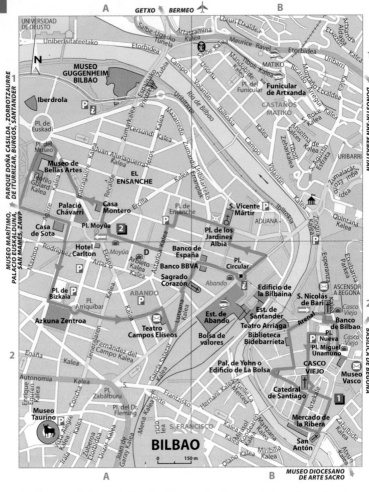

Set in the ex-**Colegio de San Andrés** in the Old Town, this collection sheds light on traditional Basque culture and activities (weaving, arts and crafts, fishing). The El Mikeldi stone animal figure, which may be more than 4 000 years old, is a feather in the museum's cap.

Alhóndiga Bilbao★

Arriquibar 4. Open Mon–Thu 7am–11pm, Fri until midnight, Sat 8.30am–midnight, Sun until 11pm. 944 01 40 14. www.azkunazentroa.com.

This Modernist wine warehouse was restored to designs by Philippe Starck, transforming the complex into a giant cultural venue encompassing the performing arts, a huge leisure complex, plus library, shops, cafes and restaurants.

Itsasmuseum★★

Muelle Ramón de la Sota. Open Jun–Oct Tue–Sun 10am–8pm, Nov–May Tue–Fri 10am–6pm, Sat, Sun 10am–8pm. €6; €3 per person for families; free Tue. 946 08 55 00. www.itsasmuseum.eus.

This interactive family-friendly museum explains Bilbao's important maritime history and culture. The ground floor occupies the outbuildings of the city's old shipyards (*astilleros*) and illustrates the changes to the city's estuary over the centuries; there's a room devoted to **Evaristo de Churruca** (1841–1917), the engineer who constructed the city's first port. The second level focusses on Bilbao's commercial and industrial maritime prominence and the industrialisation of the city through historic maps, documents and models.

Outside in the dry docks, the tour ends with a display that includes a life boat, old wooden fishing boats and a tug from 1928, which visitors can board.

🚗 DRIVING TOUR

Costa de Bizkaia

The beaches and coves that dot the coast of Gipuzkoa province are backed by rolling green hills and make for an ideal retreat from busy Bilbao – particularly the area around the Urdaibai Biosphere Reserve. Touring the coastline, you'll discover towns and villages brimming with Basque history and charm. For outdoor enthusiasts there are ample opportunities for sports and hiking.

▷ Exit Bilbao W along the A-8 in the direction of Vitoria-Gasteiz. At exit 14, take the N-624 toward San Sebastián, then the GI-638 toward Mutriku. Once there, take the Bi-633.

Ondarroa
10km/6.2mi W of Deba along GI 638.
The 15C church, winding river and slender Basque houses with washing at the windows make up a postcard-perfect ensemble★. Canning and fish-salting are the main industries.
Continue around the point for a fine view★ of the next settlement, Lekeitio, its beach and the island of San Nicolás-joined to the mainland at low tide.

▷ Leave W along BI 3438.

Lekeitio
12km/7.4mi W.
A deeply indented bay at the foot of Monte Calvario, divided by an island, makes up Lekeitio's fishing harbour. The 15C Iglesia (Independentzia Enparantza; open 8am–12pm, 5–7.30pm; ☏ 946 84 09 54) by the har-

bour has three tiers of flying buttresses and a tall Baroque belfry.
Nearby are good beaches.

Ispaster
This sleepy town has a pretty 15C church and Renaissance and Baroque mansions including the Palacio Arana (1700). To get to the coast, take the road on your right just before the cemetrey on the outskirts of the village. It runs though the forest before reaching Ogeyi Beach.

▷ Continue NW BI 3438.

Ea
11km/6.8mi NW of Lekeitio
This miniature harbour stands between two hills at the end of a quiet creek.
Old houses follow the banks of the river, which is spanned by stone bridges and makes for a pleasant, shaded walk.
To the left of the church of Nuestra Señora de Jesús, at the entrance to the village, follow the yellow-and-white markings. The walk continues through woods and meadows. Once you reach two houses overlooking the main road, take the path at the side of the second. Back on the road, follow it left to the houses where you return to the main path. It leads to the coast and the hermitage of Talako Ama, revealing a beautiful sea view★ (🚶 90min).

▷ Continue NE along BI 3438.

Elantxobe★
7km/4.3mi NW of Ea.
Fishermen have long used the bay as a natural harbour and built their houses overlooking the water, against steep-sided Cabo Ogoño (300m/1 000ft).
Beyond Playa de Laga, a rose-coloured beach circling Cabo Ogoño, you can see the estuary of Gernika Ría★, Izaro island, the white outline of the town of Sukarrieta on the far bank and Chacharramendi island. The resort of Playa de Laida, on the ría, is popular with Gernika residents.

▷ Go SW and bear left at Kortezubi.

Cuevas de Santimamiñe

Barrio Basondo, Kortezubi. Access by guided tour only (1hr 30mins), phone reservation required. Most tours start at 10am. 5€. ☏944 65 16 57. www.santimamiñe.com.

Wall paintings and engravings from the Magdalenian period (around 17 000 to 11 000 years ago) were discovered in these caves in 1917.

◉ Return to the main road and bear south.

Gernika

14km/8.7mi S of Elantxobe.

The town is of course famous for Picasso's painting, *Guernica* (◉ see MADRID, p143), depicting the Spanish Civil War atrocity here on 26 April 1937, when Nazi planes destroyed the town, with Franco's blessing, killing over 1 000 in the world's first mass bombing of a civilian population.

The topic is explored in the moving **Fundación Museo de la Paz** (Pl. de Foru; open Mar–Sept Tue–Sat 10am–7pm, Sun 10am–2pm; Oct–Feb Tue–Sat 10am–2pm, 4–6pm, Sun 10am–2pm; €5; ☏946 27 02 13, www.museodelapaz.org). The museum is divided into three sections: The first attempts to define the concept of peace through quotes from famous historical figures such as Martin Luther King, Jr, and Gandhi, while the second discusses Gernika's tragic history. The third addresses the concept of peace today, focussing on the Basque conflict, political prisoners and torture.

◉ Head south on the BI 2224 and BI 3231 for 18km/11mi.

The **Balcón de Vizcaya★★** (Balcony of Biscay) viewpoint overlooks a lovely perspective over meadows and forests.

◉ Return to Gernika.

Two viewpoints before Mundaka enable you to take a last look back the ocean. As the road drops downhill, you get a stellar **view★** of Bermeo.

Bermeo

15km/9mi NW Gernika on BI 2235.

The fishermen's quarter, still crowded onto the Atalaya promontory overlooking the old harbour, was once protected by ramparts (traces remain), and the grim granite Torre de Ercilla, now the **Museo del Pescador/Arrantzaleen Museoa** (pl. Torrontero; open Tue–Sat 10am–2pm, 4–7pm, Sun 10am–2pm; €3.50; ☏946 88 11 71), is dedicated to local fishermen.

A reconstruction of a 17C whaling boat anchored in the port, near the tourist office, is another of Bermeo's golden age of fishing and is part of **The Whaling Interpretation Centre, Aita Guria** (C. Lamera; closed Mon; €2; ☏946 17 91 21; www.aitaguria.bermeo.org). An audioguide introduces the captain's cabin, galleys and the hold and explains the living conditions onboard. Call before visiting; access depends on the tides.

◉ Turn left toward Mungia.

Alto del Sollube★
(Sollube Pass)

The road up to the low pass (340m/ 1 115ft) affords a good view of Bermeo.

◉ Return to Bermeo, follow the coast road left for 3km/1.8mi, then turn right.

Faro (Lighthouse) de Machichaco

From just left of here there is a good view west. The road winds to a **viewpoint★** over the storybook **San Juan de Gaztelugache** headland and its windswept hermitage (access via a pathway), a *Game of Thrones* filming location and the site of a *romería* (pilgrimage) each Midsummer's Day (23 Jun). There are extensive views from the **corniche road★** between Bakio and Arminza, and a belvedere also commands a fine **view★** of the coast, Bakio, valley farms and wooded hinterland.

Arminza

Arminza is the only harbour along this section of wild, largely uninhabited coast.

▶ Continue SW.

Gorliz

7km/4.3mi SW of Arminza.

Gorliz is an attractive beach resort at the mouth of the River Butrón. **Plent-zia** nearby (2km/1.2mi) is a resort and oyster-farming centre.

Castillo de Butrón

Closed to the public.

This folly, built on the remains of a 14C–15C construction and inspired by Bavarian castles, was commissioned buy a fanciful marquis to be looked at, not lived in.

Getxo

13km/8mi SW of Gorliz.

The **paseo marítimo** (sea promenade) overlooks the coast. From the road up to Getxo's well-known golf course there is a view of the Bilbao inlet and, on the far bank, Santurtzi and Portugalete.

Bilbao★

See BILBAO.

ADDRESSES

STAY

⊖ **Optimi Rooms** – Areiltza Doktorearen Zumarkalea 58, Bilbao. ☎627 11 38 59. www.optimirooms.com. 50 pods. Spain's first capsule hotel, opened in 2019, has futuristic pods decked out with smart TVs, USB sockets and wake-up-light alarm clocks.

⊖⊜⊜ **NH Collection Villa de Bilbao** – Gran Vía 87, Bilbao. ☎944 416 000. www.nh-hotels.com. 142 rooms. ☐€13–32. This renovated four-star in the centre offers comfortable, minimalist rooms – some with balconies and jacuzzis – as well as a restaurant serving contemporary Basque cuisine (⊖⊜⊜).

⊖⊜⊜⊜ **Castillo de Arteaga** – Gaztelubide Street 7, Gautegiz de Arteaga (40km/25mi NW of Bilbao). ☎946 240 012. www.castillodearteaga. com. 13 rooms. Nestled in the Urdaibai nature reserve, this mid-19C castle

hotel has turret rooms with sumptuous furnishings and a white-tablecloth restaurant (⊖⊜⊜⊜).

⏧EAT

⊖⊜ **Gatz** – C. Sta. Maria 10, Bilbao. ☎944 15 48 61. www.bargatz.com. Closed Sun eve. Try the salt cod cloaked in *pil-pil* (garlic-oil) sauce at this no-frills bar with prize-winning pintxos.

⊖⊜ **Rio-Oja** – Txakur Kalea 4, Bilbao. ☎944 15 08 71. Closed Mon. In the old town, this popular restaurant and bar serves affordable tapas like *croquetas* and *gambas al ajillo* (garlic prawns) as well as mains like roast monkfish with potatoes.

⊖⊜ **Mercado de la Ribera** – C. de la Ribera 20, Bilbao. ☎944 79 06 95. Closed Sun. Bilbao's traditional market doubles as a raucous food court with ground-floor tapas stalls serving delectable bites ranging from freshly shucked oysters to sliced jamón to generously stacked *gildas* (anchovy-olive skewers).

⊖⊜⊜⊜ **Mina** – Muelle Marzana, Bilbao. ☎944 795 938. www. restaurantemina.es. Closed Mon & Tue. Located in the south of the city next to the river, this Michelin-star restaurant decorated in earth tones hinges on the finest market-fresh ingredients. Tasting menus from €90.

SHOPPING

La Bendita - C. Bidebarrieta 16, Bilbao. ☎946 523 623. www.labenditabilbao. com. Stock up on the finest ingredients – biscuits, digestifs, txakoli, anchovies and more – at this tiny shop wedged beneat the cathedral.

Vitoria-Gasteiz★

Vitoria-Gasteiz is the capital of the largest Basque province and the seat of the regional government, sited in a cereal-covered plateau. It was founded in the 12C and was surrounded by walls. The old quarter is in the upper section.

CIUDAD VIEJA★★

Concentric streets – each named after a trade – ring the cathedral in the old town. The liveliest spots are to the left of the Plaza de la Virgen Blanca. Nearby is the **Iglesia de San Pedro** (Fundadora de las Siervas de Jesús 2), with a Gothic facade.

Plaza de la Virgen Blanca

The square, dominated by the Iglesia (church) de San Miguel, is surrounded by house fronts with glassed-in balconies, or *miradores*. The massive monument at the square's centre commemorates Wellington's victory on 21 June 1813 that put to flight King Joseph Bonaparte and his army. It connects to the nobly ordered 18C **Plaza de España** (aka Plaza Nueva).

Iglesia de San Miguel

Escaleras de San Miguel 1.
Guided tours available Jul–Sep, organised by the tourist office.
In a jasper niche in the church porch is a polychrome Late Gothic statue of the Virgen Blanca, the city's patron. In the late 14C portal, the tympanum shows the Life of St Michael. In the chancel are an altarpiece by Gregorio Fernández and a Plateresque sepulchral arch.

Plaza del Machete★★

This small, long square lies behind the **Arquillos**, an arcade which links the upper and lower towns. A niche in the east end of San Miguel church contains the '*machete*' (actually a cutlass), on which the procurator general had to swear to uphold the town's laws (*fueros*).

▶ **Population:** 249 176
◔ **Michelin Map:** 573 D 21-22 (town plan) – Basque Country (Álava).
🗊 **Info:** España Plaza 1. ℘945 16 15 98. www.vitoria-gasteiz.org.
▶ **Location:** Vitoria-Gasteiz is 62km/38mi south of Bilbao. ▭Vitoria-Gasteiz.
🕔 **Timing:** Allow a day to explore the city. Vitoria hosts a jazz festival (www.jazzvitoria.com) each July attracting international talent.

The 16C **Palacio de Villa Suso**, on the right side, is now a municipal building with occasional exhibitions (open Mon–Fri during exhibitions 8.30am–1.30pm, until 9pm in summer; guided tours available by reservation via tourist office).

▶ Climb the steps adjoining the palace.

A stroll along **Calle Fray Zacarías Martínez**, with wood-framed houses and palaces, is pleasant. The Renaissance north doorway of the Palacio de los Escoriaza-Esquivel, built on the old town walls, is worth a look; if it is open, go inside to see its lovely covered courtyard.

Catedral de Santa María★★

C. Cuchillería 95–97. Open 10am–2pm, 4–8pm. Closed 1 Jan, 25 Dec. Guided hard-hat tours (60min) with prior online booking. From €8.50. ℘945 25 51 35. www.catedralvitoria.com.
The construction of this Gothic church-fortress, part of the city's first defensive ring, began at the end of the 13C, but the diocese has stuggled for centuries to keep the cathedral from crumbling. A programme to realign its walls has been running for several years, and the visitor centre has turned lemons into

lemonade by launching one-of-a-kind hard-hat tours of the premises.

Still on Calle Cuchillería, old meets new in the exciting BIBAT complex (& see below) that juxtaposes cutting-edge 21C architecture with the Renaissance **Palacio de Bendaña**. The latter is notable for its corner turret and doorway with *alfiz* surround; part of its delightful **patio** has also been preserved.

Museo BIBAT★ (Playing Cards Museum and Archaeological Museum)

C. Cuchillería 54. Open Tue–Fri 10am–2pm, 4–6.30pm, Sat 10am–2pm, Sun & public hols 11am–2pm. &945 20 37 00.

Occupying the older building is the Naipes (playing cards) museum, founded in 1868 by Heraclio Fournier, a descendant of a Parisian family famous for printing playing cards. The collection has 20 000 sets of cards from around the world dating to the 14C to the present. The museum also covers topics including print media, paper-making and textiles.

The Archeological Museum (architect Patxi Mangado) occupies the striking modern annex and displays finds from excavations in Álava province. Note the dolmen collections and Roman monuments. At Cuchillería 24, the 16C **Casa del Cordón** is sometimes open for exhibitions.

CIUDAD NUEVA

As Vitoria-Gasteiz grew in the 18C, Neo-classical constructions began to appear such as the **Arquillos** arcade in what is referred to as the modern town.

In the 19C, the town expanded south and added the **Parque de la Florida** (Florida Park), **Catedral Nueva** (New Cathedral, 1907) and two wide avenues: Paseo de la Senda and Paseo de Fray Francisco. The latter has mansions like the Palacio de Ajuria Enea, seat of the Lehendakari (Basque government), and two museums, the Museo de Armería and Museo de Bellas Artes.

Near España Plaza is the modern Plaza de los Fueros, the work of architect José Luis Peña Ganchegui and sculptor Eduardo Chillida.

Museo Artium★

Francia Kalea 24. Open Tue–Fri 11am–2pm, 5pm–8pm; Sat–Sun 11am–8pm. €5, by donation Wed. &945 20 90 00. www.artium.org.

This contemporary art museum and cultural centre focusses on the foundations of modern art. A significant selection from its **collection★** – 1 800 works of Spanish artists, from the Avant Garde of the twenties and thirties (forming the majority of the collection) almost to the present – is shown on a rotating basis. Featured artists include Miró, Gargallo, Tàpies, Oteiza and Chillida.

Museo de Armería★ (Museum of Arms and Armour)

Po. de Fray Francisco 3. Open Tue–Fri 10am–2pm, 4–6.30pm, Sat 10am–2pm, Sun & public hols 11am–2pm. Closed 1 Jan & Good Fri. &945 18 19 25.

Military history buffs will appreciate this well-presented collection of weaponry in the Basque Country from prehistoric axes to early-20C pistols. Note the **armour** including 17C **Japanese** examples.

Museo Diocesano de Arte Sacro (Diocesan Sacred Art Museum)

C. Cadena y Eleta. Open Tue–Fri 11am–2pm, 4–6.30pm Sat–Sun & public hols, 11am–2pm. €3, free first Sat of the month. &945 15 06 31. www.museoartesacro.org.

Set in the ambulatory of the **Catedral Nueva, the Diocesan Museum** exhibits Gothic images, Flemish works (*Descent from the Cross* by Van der Goes, *The Crucifixion* by Ambrosius Benson), 16C–18C canvases (*St Francis* by El Greco, several Riberas, *The Immaculate Conception* by Alonso Cano) and various silverware.

Street art

Anorbin and Carnicerías streets & surrounds.

In the last decade, Vitoria has become an improbable hotbed for graffiti artists, whose **ephemeral paintings** and murals (state-sanctioned and otherwise) around the modern city are often politically charged and show exceptional skill.

Museo de Bellas Artes (Fine Arts Museum)

Po. de Fray Francisco de Vitoria 8. Open Tue–Sat 10am–2pm, 4–6.30pm, Sun 11am–2pm. Closed 1 Jan & Good Fri. *945 18 19 18.*

This collection, housed in the early-20C Historicist **Palacio de Agustí**, displays Spanish art of the 18C and 19C and a selection of Basque *costumbrista* painting by such artists as Iturrino, Regoyos and Zuloaga. Highlights include *La Cuidad con Sol* by Fernando de América.

EXCURSIONS

Santuario de Estíbaliz

◖ 10km/6.2mi E. Leave Vitoria-Gasteiz via Av. de Bruselas, take the A 132 toward Argadoña. Bear left after 4km/2.5mi. Open Sat 5–7pm, Sun 11.30am–1.30pm. €2 (75min guided tours Sat 5.30pm, €4). *660 766 383.*

This Late Romanesque pilgrim shrine has an attractive wall belfry on the south front and a 12C Romanesque statue of the Virgin.

EAST OF VITORIA-GASTEIZ: MEDIEVAL PAINTINGS

◖ 25km/15.5mi along the E5-N1 motorway as far as junction 375.

Gazeo/Gaceo

Vivid 14C **Gothic frescoes**★★, discovered in 1967, decorate the chancel of the Iglesia de San Martín de Tours (guided tours by phone appt; €2; *945 30 29 31*). The south wall shows hell as a whale's gullet, the north, the Life of the Virgin. On the roof are scenes from the Life of Christ.

Alaiza

◖ Follow the A 4111 for 3km/1.8mi, turn right, then left after a few metres.

The **paintings**★ on the walls and roof of the Iglesia de la Asunción apse (guided tours, hours and fees as Gazeo) probably date to the late 14C. Strange red outlines represent castles, churches and soldiers.

Oñati/Oñate

◖ At the foot of Monte Alona, (1 321m/4 333ft), 45km/28mi NE of Vitoria-Gasteiz and 74km/46mi SW of San Sebastián

Secluded in the Udana Valley, Oñati, with its seigniorial residences, monastery and old university, figured prominently in the First Carlist War.

The **Edificio de la Antigua Universidad (Old University Building)**★ (Universitate Etorbidea 8, open only by prebooked guided tour; *943 78 34 53*), now the administrative headquarters of Gipuzkoa province, was founded in 1542 and functioned as a university until the early 20C. The gateway, by Pierre Picart, is surmounted by pinnacles and crowded with statues.

The **ayuntamineto**★ is housed in a fine 18C Baroque building designed by Martín de Carrera.

The Gothic church, **Iglesia de San Miguel**, facing the university, was modified in the Baroque period. In the Renaissance chapel, off the north aisle, closed by beautiful iron grilles, note the gilded wood altarpiece. The golden stone cloister exterior is in **Isabelline Plateresque** style (guided tours by prior appt with tourst office; *943 78 34 53*).

Santuario de Arantzazu★

◖ 9km/5.5mi S of Oñati along the GI 3591. €2.50, by prebooked guided tour only. *943 71 89 11.*
www.arantzazu.org.

The **scenic cliff road**★ follows the River Arantzazu through a narrow gorge. The **shrine** at 800m/2 625ft in a mountain **setting**★ faces the highest peak in the province, Mount Aitzgorri (1 549m/5 082ft). A startlingly modern bell tower, 40m/131ft high, is studded with diamond-faceted stones symbolising the hawthorn bush (*arantzazu* in Basque) in which the Virgin is said to have appeared to a local shepherd in 1469.

ADDRESSES

🛏 STAY

🛏 **Hotel Dato** – Eduardo Dato Kalea 28. ℘945 14 72 30. www.hoteldato. com. 14 rooms. Centrally located, this cheerful hotel offers traditional decor with Belle Époque flourishes.

🛏 **Hotel Palacio de Elorriaga** – Elorriaga 15, 1.5km/1mi E along Av. de Santiago and the N 104. ℘945 26 36 16. www.hotelpalacioelorriaga.com. 21 rooms. ☕€6. Restaurant 🍽. This quiet 16C–17C mansion with sober brick and stone walls is filled with antique furniture. Rooms are cosy and have en-suite bathrooms.

🛏 **Parador de Argómaniz** – C. del Parador 14, Argómaniz, 14km/9mi NE of Vitoria. ℘915 293 200. www. parador.es. 53 rooms. ☕€16. A restored 17C palace houses this retreat outside Vitoria overlooking rolling farmland. Be sure to dine at the upscale Basque restaurant (🍽🍽🍽), popular among locals and hotel guests alike.

🍽 EAT

🍽 **El Rincón de Luis Mari** – Rioja Kalea 14. ℘945 25 01 27. Closed Tue. Step into this tile-floored bar near the old quarter for affordable tapas like marinated white anchovies, seared blood sausage and mini baguette sandwiches.

🍽 **Gurea** – Pl. de la Constitución 10. ℘945 24 59 33. www.gurearestaurante. com. Closed Sun–Wed pm, Tue, 2nd fortnight Aug. Updated Basque home cooking is this smart-casual white-tablecloth restaurant's speciality.

🍽 **El Portalón** – Correría Kalea 151. ℘945 14 27 55. www. restauranteelportaloncom. Rustic stone walls, beamed ceilings and antique furnishings welcome you to this ultra-traditional Basque tavern housed in a 15C timbered inn.

La Rioja★★

The Ebro Valley in La Rioja is carpeted with vineyards and vegetable fields in the shadow of the Sierras de Cantabria and de la Demanda. The region, which takes its name from the Río Oja, a tributary of the Ebro, flourished first on the pilgrim route to Santiago de Compostela and only later became famous for its wine.

A BIT OF GEOGRAPHY

Confusingly, La Rioja takes in not just the eponymous autonomous community but also portions of Navarra and the Basque Country (**Rioja Alavesa**). **Rioja Alta** (Upper Rioja), to the west around Haro, is the main hub for quality winemaking, while **Rioja Baja** (Lower Rioja) is more rural, given over to vegetable cultivation. The main towns are **Logroño**, **Haro** and Calahorra.

▶ **Population:** 150 927 (Logroño)

🚗 **Michelin Map:** 573 E 20-23, F 20-24 – La Rioja, Navarra, Basque Country (Álava).

ℹ **Info:** Logroño: Portales 50. ℘941 29 12 60; Nájera: Plaza San Miguel 10. ℘941 36 00 41; San Millán de la Cogolla: Monasterio de Yuso. ℘941 37 32 59; Santo Domingo de la Calzada: Mayor 70 ℘941 34 12 38. www.lariojaturismo. com, www.turismo. euskadi.eus. 🚉Logroño.

▶ **Location:** La Rioja covers approximately 5 000sq km/ 1 930sq mi in the regions of La Rioja, Navarra and Basque Country.

🕐 **Timing:** 2–4 days to tour the vineyards.

TAPAS

Calle del Laurel in Logroño is one of Spain's great tapas streets with a huge choice of bars serving delicious local specialities (sweet peppers, mushrooms etc.) and, of course, local wines.

SIGHTS

Logroño

The urban capital of the autonomous community hugs the the Ebro. Pilgrims to Santiago de Compostela would have entered through the stone gateway overlooking the cathedral.

Concatedral de Santa María la Redonda

C. Portales 14. Open Mon–Sat 8am–1pm, 6.30–8.45pm, Sun 9am–2pm, 6.30–8.45pm. ℘941 25 76 11. www.laredonda.org.
Dating to 1435, the cathedral has two Baroque towers, three naves, three polygonal apses and chapels in its side aisles.

Museo de la Rioja

Pl. de San Agustín. Open Tue–Sat 10am–2pm, 4–9pm, Sun & public hols 11.30am–2pm ℘941 29 12 59. www.museodelarioja.es.
Rioja's regional museum, with art and artefacts from prehistory to the 20C, is set in an 18C Baroque palace.

Laguardia/Guardia★

Hillside Laguardia is the most attractive town in Rioja Alavesa; many top bodegas are located nearby. The two imposing towers visible as you approach are San Juan, to the south, and the 12C tower of the abbey, to the north.

Iglesia de Santa María de los Reyes

C. Mayor. Guided prebooked tour only. €2. ℘945 60 08 45.
The late-14C **portal★★** with 17C polychrome decoration is the only of its kind in Spain. The tympanum is divided into three scenes relating the Life of the Virgin. Note the figure of Christ holding a small child in his hands, representing the soul of the Virgin.

Labastida

▶ 20km/12mi W of Laguardia via A 124.
The capital of Rioja Alavesa, this frontier town is perched on a rocky outcrop. Its pretty old town, **La Mota★**, has narrow streets lined with stone houses with studded doors.

Bodegas Ysios★

▶ N of Laguardia on Camino de la Hoya. Guided tours (approx 2 hrs) with tasting. Prior booking required. €16. ℘945 60 06 40. www.ysios.com.
Designed by renowned Valencian architect Santiago Calatrava, and nestled at the base of the Sierra de Cantabria Mountains, the outline of this stunning *bodega* (winery) evokes both the shape of wine barrels and the mountains' curves in its undulating form. Inside, vats and bottles are stored in soaring wall-less, arc-like spaces that allow air to circulate.
The upstairs tasting room is characterised by a high ceiling and a fabulous view onto the vineyards.

Herederos de Marqués de Riscal

▶ 5km/3.1mi S of Laguardia on the A2310. C. Torrea 1, Elciego. Guided tours (1hr 30min) and tasting with prior booking. €16. ℘945 60 60 00. www.marquesderiscal.com.
In the tiny village of **El Ciego**, Frank Gehry, of Guggenheim fame, designed the eye-popping luxury hotel and spa of traditional winemaker Marqués de Riscal. Tthe cellars are also open to the public; the visit ends at 'La Catedral', where a bottle of wine from each year of the company's long history is kept.

Centro Temático del vino Villa Lucía (Villa Lucía Wine Centre)

Ctra Logroño. Call to reserve a tour. €11 (inc tasting with tapas). ℘945 60 00 32. www.villa-lucia.com.

Wines of La Rioja

In 1902, Rioja was the first Spanish appellation to be stamped with the Denominación de Origen Calificada (DOC) imprimatur, and today over 500 *bodegas* (wineries) dot the region. The wine, mostly mass produced in enormous wineries, is the result of more than seven centuries of tradition and a superb position in the Ebro Valley between the Sierra de la Demanda and the Sierra de Cantabria. The wine region contains three sub-zones: Rioja Alavesa, Rioja Baja and Rioja Alta.

Rioja Alavesa vineyards, Laguardia

© F. J. Fdez. Bordonada/age fotostock

Although 16 grape varieties are permitted, Tempranillo and Garnacha are the most widely planted. Red wine accounts for 75% of production, and the most prestigious bottles are aged in (traditionally American) oak barrels for extended periods. They are classified according time spent in both barrel and bottle: Crianza (at least one year in the barrel, one year in the bottle), Reserva (one year, two years) and Gran Reserva (two years, three years in the bottle). Crianzas are fruity and fresh, while Reservas and Gran Reservas have earthier, more leathery notes. Rustic rosé table wine (*clarete*), served in stemless glasses, is a mainstay of traditional *tabernas* and seldom makes it outside the region.

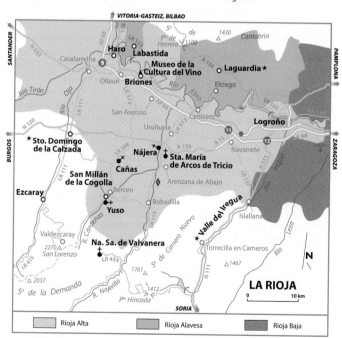

The museum on this lovely estate traces the history and viticulture of wines and within its tours includes a '4-D' presentation. The **panorama** from the **Balcón de Rioja**★★ or Rioja Balcony 12km/7.4mi northwest of Laguardia near the Puerto de Herrera (Herrera Pass, 1 100m/3 609ft), is extensive.

Haro

This small town is famous for its wines. Elegant 16C and 18C facades recall a prestigious past. In **Plaza de la Paz** note the Neoclassical town hall (ayuntamiento), built by Juan de Villanueva in 1769, and the Baroque tower of the **Iglesia de Santo Tomás**.

Vivanco★

◯ 5km/3mi from Haro, in **Briones** (442km/275mi on the N 232).

Museo de la Cultura del Vino

See website for opening times. €15 for museum, €18 guided tour, €12 guided tours (reserve in advance), €30 winery and museum. ℘902 32 20 13. www.vivancoculturadevino.es.
Vivanco winery houses what's perhaps Spain's top wine museum, with interactive exhibitions and an unparalleled, quirky collection of wine openers from every era.

Santo Domingo de la Calzada★

This staging post town on the Camino de Santiago was founded in the 11C and owes its name to a hermit, Dominic, who built a bridge for pilgrims. Parts of the 14C ramparts can still be seen. The **old town**★ huddles around the **Plaza del Santo**, dominated by the cathedral and ex-hospital, now a Parador. The streets around the square, particularly Calle Mayor, retain 16C and 17C stone houses with fine doorways. The 18C ayuntamiento (town hall), in nearby Plaza de España, is crowned by a formidable escutcheon.

Catedral★

Entrance via the 14C cloisters, housing the cathedral museum. Pl. del Santo. Open Mon–Sat 9–10.30am, 11.45am–7pm, Sun 9am–12pm, 2–7pm. €7 (€8 prebooked guided tour). ℘941 34 00 33. www.catedralsantodomingo.com
The church is Gothic, apart from the ambulatory and apsidal chapel, which are Romanesque (second half of the 12C). The saint's tomb (13C), beneath a 1513 canopy, is in the south transept, and opposite is a sumptuous Gothic cage containing a live white rooster and hen, which pay homage to a miracle attributed to the saint.
The **retable**★★ at the high altar (1538) is an unfinished work by Damián Forment. The Cathedral also contains the **Capilla de la Magdalena**★ (Evangelist's nave) with Plateresque decoration. Visitors may also ascend the cathedral's freestanding tower for a view.

Abadía de Cañas/El Monasterio de la Luz

C. Real, Cañas. ◯ 13km/8mi SE of Santo Domingo de la Calzada. Open Tue–Sat 10.30am–1.30pm, 4–6pm, Sun 11am–1.30pm, 4–6pm (Apr–Oct opens 10am, Tue–Sat closes 7pm). €4. ℘941 37 90 83. www.monasteriodecañas.es.
This monastery has been inhabited by Cistercian monks since 1170. The 16C church and chapter house exemplify the purity and simplicity of Cistercian art. A small shop sells delicious sweets made by the Carmelite nuns who live here.

Ezcaray

This delightful village is a summer resort and ski area. It features houses with stone-and-wood porticoes, noble mansions and the **Iglesia Santa María la Mayor** (guided tours available through tourist office; ℘941 35 46 79) as well as a former tapestry factory founded by Charles III in 1752.

Nájera★

Navarra's capital until 1076, this small town is home to **Monasterio de Santa María la Real**★ (Pl. de Santa María; open daily; see website for seasonal hours; €4; ℘941 36 10 83; www.santamaria lareal.net) was founded by Don García III, King of Navarra, in 1032, when a statue of the Virgin was found here. The bays in the lower galleries of the **cloisters**★ are filled with Plateresque stone tracery. Beneath the gallery of the **church**★ is the **Panteón Real**★ of 11C and 12C princes of Navarra, León and Castilla.

Basílica de Santa María de Arcos de Tricio

◑ 3km/2mi SW of Nájera in Triciclo. Open Sat 10.30am–1.30pm, 4.30–7.30pm, Sun 10.30am–1.30pm. €2. Call prior to visit. ℘620 92 36 44.
This ancient church, originally a 3C Roman mausoleum, was transformed into a Christian basilica in the 5C.

San Millán de la Cogolla★

Turn-off from the LR 113 at Bobadilla. Home to two World Heritage sites (Yuso and Suso monasteries) this village became famous in the 5C when San Millán and his followers settled here as hermits. In the 13C, Gonzalo de Berceo wrote the first-known Castilian Spanish manuscripts here. The town's warm, honey-coloured stone buildings nestled in rolling green valleys make it a pleasant place to explore.

Monasterio de Yuso★

San Millán de Cogolla. Open only by guided tour (50min) Holy Week–Sept Tue–Sun (Mon in Aug) 10am–1.30pm, 4–6.30pm. Oct– Holy Week Tue–Sun 10am–1pm, 3.30–5.30pm (closed Sun pm). €7, by guided tour only. ℘941 37 30 49. www.monasteriodeyuso.org.
Housed in a Mozarabic building partly hollowed out of the rock, this monastery overlooks the Cárdenas Valley. Its proudest posessions are **ivories**★★, from two 11C reliquaries.

Monasterio de Nuestra Señora de Valvanera

Anguiano. Via the LR 113. Open daily 9am–7pm. ℘941 37 70 44. www.monasteriodevalvanera.es.
Secluded in a wooded mountain **setting**★★, The church houses a 12C statue of the Virgen of Valvanera, patron of La Rioja. There is also a simple hotel.

Valle del Iregua★

◑ 50km/31mi S of Logroño on N 111.
Near Isallana appear the **rock faces**★ of the Sierra de Cameros, overlooking the Iregua Valley at 500m/1 640ft. In the **Villanueva de Cameros**, half-timbered houses are roofed with circular tiles.

ADDRESSES

⌂ STAY

🍽🍽🍽 **Echaurren** – Padre José García 19, Ezcaray. ℘941 35 40 47. www. echaurren.com. 27 rooms. ⊐ €20. Gastronomes will love staying at this food-obsessed family-run hotel with two buzzy restaurants (🍽🍽🍽).

🍽🍽🍽 **Parador de Santo Domingo de la Calzada** – Pl. del Santo 3, Santo Domingo de la Calzada. ℘902 54 79 79. www.parador.es. 61 rooms. ⊐ €18. Restaurant 🍽🍽🍽. Unwind in this former pilgrims' hospital on the Camino de Santiago with Gothic features including a spectacular hallway.

⑂/EAT

🍽 **Restuarante Ariño Jatetxea** – C. Frontin 28, Labastida. ℘945 33 10 24. Expect textbook Basque country fare and a mix of locals and visitors. Set menus are a steal.

🍽🍽 **La Taberna de Baco** – C. San Agustín 10, Logroño. ℘941 213 544. www.latabernadebaco.com. This wine bar with genial staff is famous for its griddled pig's ear smothered in spicy *brava* sauce.

🍽🍽🍽 **Terete** – C. Lucrecia Arana 17. ℘941 310 023. www.terete.es. Closed Mon. A 19C wood-burning oven turns out shatteringly crisp roast lamb in this one-time stagecoach inn.

Cantabria and Asturias

In the centre of Spain's northern Atlantic coast lie Asturias, to the east, and Cantabria, to the west. This verdant swath is blessed – or cursed, depending on your perspective – with more rain than any other area of Spain. Its shamrock-green foothills and misty villages liken it to Switzerland or Ireland – a far cry from the Spain of Don Quixote. Roads wind along valley floors hemmed in by lush meadows, cider-apple orchards and woodland. Cows outnumber humans in many parts, and butter is the cooking fat of choice (translation: sinfully good comfort food and desserts). Maize remains an important crop as evidenced by the *hórreos* (stilted granaries) that dot Asturian villages. The coast has deep inlets and dramatic cliffs with idyllic beaches scattered throughout.

Highlights

1 Marvelling at the prehistoric paintings at **Cueva de Altamira** (p271)
2 Relaxing on the broad golden sands at **El Sardinero** (p273)
3 Exploring the old town of **Santillana del Mar** (p276)
4 The Mirador del Cable view point at **Fuente Dé** (p278)
5 The technicolour fishing village of **Cudillero** (p288)

Asturias

Asturias is said to be the only part of Spain never conquered by the Moors. This had its pros and cons: The region preserved its ancient customs and Romance language but was also isolated from the rich cultural exchanges happening farther south. Its relative isolation spurred the development of a unique art and architectural style known as Asturian Pre-Romanesque, which can still be seen in 14 buildings, mostly churches, built between the 8C and 10C. They symbolise the birth and development of the both the Asturian Monarchy and the first Christian kingdom on the Peninsula.

Other idiosyncratic Asturian features include bagpipes – keep an ear open for students practising in city squares – harking back to the region's Gallic origins, and cider (*sidra*), favoured over wine. *Sidrerías* (cider houses) are a mainstay; protocol states that the tipple be theatrically poured from a height of some 30cm/1ft, in order to aerate it. Slug it down in one fell swoop, or risk getting the side-eye from the bartender. Asturias is also renowned for its cheeses, particularly the blue-veined *Cabrales*, matured in dank mountain caves, and stews, especially *fabada*, made with smoked sausages and local white beans. With such enviable ingredients available year round – seafood from the ocean and beef and produce from the hills – it's no wonder Asturias has turned out acclaimed chefs like José Andrés.

Cantabria

Cantabria is sandwiched between the Bay of Biscay and the mountains of the Cantabrian Cordillera; in fact, mountains are so prevalent here that Cantabria is known colloquially as 'La Montaña'. Its Picos de Europa national park has ski slopes and a far-reaching network of hiking trails. The region is too cool and wet for most northern European vacationers' taste – their loss: Cantabria has oodles of unspoilt medieval villages, unparalleled landmarks and wonderfully scenic beaches.

Santillana del Mar, deemed 'the prettiest village in Spain' by Jean-Paul Sartre, is the jewel of the Cantabrian coast. Its time-warpy centre is a preserved historical monument showcasing architectural styles from the 14C to the 18C. Nearby is the world-famous Altamira Cave, 'the Sistine Chapel of Prehistoric Art', with ancient drawings of animals and human forms.

Santander, the regional capital, is arched around a sandy bay and is the region's main cultural hub. It's been on the up-and-up since the Centro Botín contemporary art centre opened on the *bahía* in 2017.

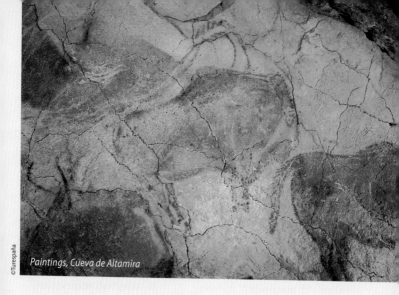

Paintings, Cueva de Altamira

The Altamira Caves

▶ 2km/1.2mi SW of Santillana del Mar. 🚃 Narrow-gauge train service from Santander (35 min). Neocueva Museum open May–Oct Tue–Sat 9.30am–8pm, Nov–Apr Tue–Sat 9.30am–6pm. Sun and pub hols 9.30am–3pm. Closed 1 & 6 Jan, 1 May, 24– 25, 31 Dec. €3; free Sat pm, Sun, 18 Apr, 18 May, 12 Oct, 6 Dec. ☎942 81 80 05. www.museodealtamira.mcu.es. 🅿 Every Fri at 10.40am, five lucky visitors are allowed inside the caves (35min tour) on a first-come-first-served basis; arrive no later than 8.30 if you want any shot at getting in.

Cantabria has the world's richest heritage of Palaeolithic cave art. Across the region, underground caverns hold treasure troves of paintings rendered by the ancients, often dazzling in detail, colour and vivacity.

The most famous of these sites is Cueva de Altamira. The complex consists of a series of galleries with wall paintings and engravings thought to date to the Solutrean Age, 20 500 years ago. The most impressive paintings are in the **Sala de los Polícromos** (Polychrome Chamber), whose ceiling, painted mainly in the Magdalenian period (15 000–12 000 BC), shows colourful bison – asleep, crouched and galloping – with extraordinary realism.

The forms were discovered in 1880 by a local amateur archaeologist, Marcelino Sanz de Sautuola, who was led to the entrance of the caves by his young daughter. Due to the paintings' sophistication, their authenticity was immediately challenged. Sanz de Sautuola was even charged with forgery. The paintings forever changed our perception on the 'primitiveness' of our ancient ancestors.

The caves were open to the public in the 1960s and 70s, but studies showed that human breath damaged their delicate state, leading them to be closed to mainstream tourism. A fantastic replica (the **Neocueva**) near the site has since been installed. An adjacent museum covers human evolution and daily life in the Upper Palaeolithic period.

Santillana del Mar

Santander★

Santander enjoys a postcard-worthy location★★, on a bay bathed by the azure waters of the Cantabrian Sea. It is easily explored on foot, its long maritime *paseo* – one of the finest in Spain – lined by gardens and outdoor restaurants. Beaches here draw (mostly Spanish) summer visitors.

THE CITY TODAY

The constant trickle of passengers to and from the boat terminal in summer combined with the crowds of students who pack the plazas and bars the rest of the year, keeps the city continually abuzz. The much-ballyhooed 2017 opening of **Centro Botín**, Spain's newest major modern art space, has breathed new life into the local culture scene.

SIGHTS

On a stroll down the **Paseo de Pereda★**, along the seafront, you'll spot the Neoclassical Banco de Santander building and the Palacete del Embarcadero exhibition centre.

The stilted building on the *bahía* that looks like a moored UFO is the new **Centro Botín** arts and culture complex.

Museo de Prehistoria y Arqueología de Cantabria★

Open Oct-Apr Tue-Sun 10am-2pm, 5-7.30pm, May-Sep 10am-2pm, 5-8pm, Sat, Sun & hols 10am-2pm, 5-8pm. €5. *&*942 20 99 22. www.museosdecantabria.es/prehistoria.

Finds from prehistoric caves in Cantabria and remains of extinct animals from the Quaternary era round out the Prehistory and Archaeology Museum's collection. The best-represented period is the Upper Palaeolithic, from which there are engraved bones and **batons★** made of horn. Three large circular steles, used for funerary purposes, are representative of the apogee of ancient Cantabrian culture (Bronze Age). Roman finds

▶ **Population:** 172 044
🚗 **Michelin Map:** 572 B 18.
🅘 **Info:** Jardines de Pereda *&*942 20 30 00. www.turismo.santander.es.
◐ **Location:** Santander sprawls to the west of the bay. The A 8 motorway runs SE to Bilbao (116km/72mi). 🚉 Santander.
👪 **Kids:** Museo Marítimo del Cantábrico. El Sardinero zoo, Parque de la Naturaleza de Cabárceno.
🕐 **Timing:** The International Music and Dance Festival (www.festivalsantander.com) is in August.

are mostly from Julióbriga and Castro Urdiales and include coins, bronzes and pottery figurines.

Catedral de Nuestra Señora de la Asunción

Pl. del Obispo José E Eguino. Cathedral: Mon–Sat 10am–1pm, 4–7.30pm (Sat until 8pm), Sun 8am–2pm, 5–8pm. Guided tours Jul–Aug every 30 min. Tower: Tue–Sat scheduled entries at 10.30am, 11.45am, 4.45pm, 6pm, Sun 10.30am & 11.45am. *&*942 20 30 99.

This fortress-like cathedral was damaged in a 1941 fire but rebuilt in its original Gothic style.

A Baroque altarpiece dominates the presbytery; the font to the right of the ambulatory was brought from Sevilla by soldiers of the so-called Reconquista. **Iglesia del Cristo★** – Access to the 13C crypt is through the south portal. Excavations in the Evangelist nave have brought to light the remains of a Roman house with the relics of St Emetreio and St Celedonio, patron saints of the city.

Centro Botín★★

Muelle de Albareda, Po. de Pereda. *&*942 04 71 47. www.centrobotin.org.

2017 saw a new artistic awakening in Santander with the opening of Centro

Botín, a contemporary art centre on the banks of the bay. Spain's first building by renowned Italian architect Renzo Piano, it hosts cutting-edge exhibitions spotlighting local and international artists; a recent success was 'Calder Stories' with 80 works culled from the Calder Foundation's holdings.

Biblioteca de Menéndez Pelayo

C. Rubio 6. Open Mon–Sat 10.30am–1pm, 5.30-8pm, Sat 10.30am–1pm only, also Tue & Thu 4.30–9pm during school term. Closed hols. ℘942 23 45 34. www.bibliotecademenendezpelayo.org. **Marcelino Menéndez y Pelayo** (1856–1912), one of Spain's greatest historians, founded this Hogwarts-like library of nearly 43 000 books and manuscripts.

👥 Museo Marítimo del Cantábrico

San Martín de Bajamar. Open Tue–Sun 10am–7.30pm (Oct–Apr 6pm). Closed 1 & 6 Jan; 24–25, 31 Dec. €8. ℘942 27 49 62. www.museosdecantabria.es/maritimo. This thoroughly modern museum on the seafront covers all aspects of the region's maritime past and present.

Península de la Magdalena★★

With its privileged position and sublime views, this peninsula is one of Santander's major sights. The small **zoo** 👥 (free) on the El Sardinero side, and the replicas of the galleons in which Francisco de Orellana explored the Amazon, are popular with children. The **Palacio de la Magdalena** was a summer residence for Alfonso XIII; today it's occupied by the Menéndez Pelayo International University.

Walk to Cabo Mayor★

🚶 2hr; 4.5km/3mi round trip from the junction of C. García Lago and C. Gregorio Marañón, at the far end of El Sardinero. By car, 7km/4.3mi N. This attractive walk, adjoining the Mataleñas golf course, runs along the coast, offering magnificent views all the way.

Santander disasters

The old port and centre of Santander have been ravaged twice over the last century or so. In 1893 the *Cabo Machichaco* cargo boat blew up, killing more than 500 people and destroying much of the port area. On 15 February 1941, as the city was still in shambles following the Civil War, a tornado struck: The sea swept over the quays and a fire broke out, almost completely destroying the centre. Reconstruction was undertaken to a street plan of blocks no higher than five storeys, and space was allocated to gardens beside the sea, such as those on Paseo de Pereda, and to squares, such as Plaza Porticada.

EXCURSIONS

El Sardinero★★

With its three magnificent **beaches**, the residential and resort area of El Sardinero is one of Santander's main attractions.

👥 Parque de la Naturaleza de Cabárceno★

Obregón.15km/9.3mi S. Open daily; check website for seasonal hours. €30. ℘902 210 112. www.parquedecabarceno.com. An old iron mine in the Sierra de Cabarga is part of an environmental rehabilitation project that includes this superb **wildlife park** with jaguars, tigers, rhinos, gorillas and other animals. Don't miss the raptor displays.

Castañeda

🔾 24km/15mi SW via N 623 and N 634. The late-12C **Colegiata** (open for guided tours and 12pm Sun Mass), a former collegiate church, stands in a pretty valley.

Cueva de El Castillo★

🔾 Puente Viesgo, 26km/16mi SW along the N 623. Guided tours (45min) mid-Jun–mid-Sept Tue–Sun 9.30am–2.30pm,

3.30–7.30pm. Rest of year reduced hours /days, see website. €3. ℰ942 59 84 25. http://cuevas.culturadecantabria.com. Cave dwellers began engraving and painting the walls of these caves toward the end of the Palaeolithic.

🚗 DRIVING TOUR

COSTA CANTÁBRICA★

The Cantabrian coast is a succession of gulfs, capes, peninsulas, *rías*, bays (most notably at Santander and Santoña), beach resorts and fishing villages. The area is also rich in caves bearing traces of human life since the Palaeolithic.

Castro Urdiales

The medieval heart of this attractive holiday resort is set above a vast bay. It clusters around the Gothic **Iglesia de Santa María de la Asunción** (open Mon–Fri 10am–12pm, 4–6pm; ℰ942 86 15 86). A ruined castle and lighthouse add charm. Beaches lie east and west.

Laredo

25km/15.5mi W of Castro Urdiales off N 634.
The **old town** adjoins a long beach lined by modern buildings.

Limpias

8km/5mi S of Laredo.
The fishing village on the banks of the Ría Asón is known for its top-quality elvers (*angulas*), which you can try in local restaurants for a pretty penny.

Santuario de Nuestra Señora de la Bien Aparecida

12km/7.4mi SW of Limpias.
A road winds up to the Baroque shrine offering a splendid **panorama★**.

Santoña

17km/10.5mi NW of Laredo.
This fishing port facing Laredo was a French headquarters in the Peninsular War. **Iglesia de Nuestra Señora del Puerto** (Alfonso XII 11; open daily 10am–1pm, 4–8pm; ℰ942 66 01 55), remodelled in the 18C, has Romanesque carved capitals and a font.

Bareyo

14km/9mi W of Santoña off CA 141.
The diminutive **Iglesia de Santa María** overlooks the Ría de Ajo. It retains Romanesque moulded arches and historiated capitals. The **font** is probably Visigothic.

Peña Cabarga

35km/22mi SW of Bareyo off E 70.
A steep road rises to the summit (568m/1 863ft) and a monument to the Conquistadores and the Seamen Adventurers of Castilla. From the top there is a **panorama★★**.

▷ Return to the E 70 and follow signs to **Santander★** (🕮 see p274). Leave the town centre heading W on the A 67 to **Santillana del Mar★★** (🕮 see p276), where you can visit the **Museo de Altamira★★** (🕮 see p271).

Comillas★

54km/33.5mi W of Santander off E 70.
Comillas is a seaside resort with a lovely plaza, beach and easy access to the vast sands at Oyambre (5km/ 3mi W). In the late 19C it received royal patronage. In its large park is the neo-Gothic **Palacio de Sobrellano and Capilla Panteón (chapel mausoleum) de los Marqueses de Comillas** (call for opening times; €3; ℰ942 72 03 39). The chapel features fittings by Gaudi; also in the park is Gaudí's fairytale-like **El Capricho★**, a summer house built in 1883 for a relative of the Marquis of Comillas, newly reopened (open Nov–Feb 10.30am–5.30pm, Mar–June & Oct 10.30am–8pm, Jul–Sep 10.30am–9pm; €5, guided tours available. ℰ942 720 36. www.elcaprichodegaudi.com).

San Vicente de la Barquera★

11km/6.8mi W of Comillas on N 634.
Tourists flock to the **beach★**, across the inlet. The hilltop **Iglesia de Nuestra Señora de los Ángeles** has two Roman-

esque portals, Gothic aisles and tombs from the 15C and 16C. On the Unquera road is a fine **view**★ of San Vicente.

Cueva el Soplao★

Near Rábago, 20km/12.4mi S of San Vicente de la Barquera. See website for opening times. Reservations advised. €12.50, Adventure price €32. ℘902 82 02 82. www.elsoplao.es.

You can visit these impressive caves , once lead and zinc mines, as a regular tourist (aboard an open mine-train carriage) or in 'Adventure' mode (exploring remote parts with boots and a helmet).

ADDRESSES

STAY

⊜⊜ **Las Brisas** – La Braña 14, El Sardinero. ℘942 27 50 11. www.las-brisas-es.book. direct. 13 rooms. ⊊ €8. This terrific family-run hotel is housed in a flossy 1905 mansion; its comfortable little rooms have a classic yet comfy style, thanks to eye-catching antiques.

⊜⊜ **Hotel Escuela Las Carolinas** – Po. General Dávila. ℘942 03 34 02. www.hotelescuelalascarolina.13 rooms. ⊊ €7.50. This hospitality school–hotel hybrid is set in a 19C mansion on a hill, with fantastic views of Santander. The city centre is a 10-minute walk away.

⊜⊜⊜ **Hotel Gerra Mayor** – Los Llaos, Gerra. 5km/3mi NE of San Vicente de la Barquera. ℘942 71 14 01. www. hgerramayor.com. 22 rooms. ⊊ €5. Closed Dec 15–Mar 1. This rural hotel, formerly a farmhouse, has sea and mountain views. It is a peaceful base from which to explore the coastline.

⊜⊜⊜⊜ **Hotel Palacio de la Peña** – Barrio la Peña 26, Ajo. 37km/22mi E of Santander. ℘942 67 05 67. www. hotelpalacio.es. 8 rooms. Just because this tastefully decorated boutique luxury hotel is housed in a 16C palace doesn't mean you have to forego modern amenities like whirlpool tubs, laundry service and a spa.

EAT

⊖ **Mesón Rampalay** – Daoíz y Velarde 9, Santander. ℘942 31 33 67. www. meson-rampalay-santander.com. Closed Tue. Sidle up to the long bar for local specialities such as red peppers with tuna and mushrooms with cod.

⊖⊖ **El Bodegón** – Av. Los Soportales, San Vicente de la Barquera. ℘942 71 00 43. Closed Tue. www.elbodegonsvb. com. Generous portions of ocean-fresh seafood – squid, razor clams and sundry fish – are this restaurant's claim to fame.

⊖⊖⊖⊖ **El Serbal** – Andrés del Rio 7, Santander. ℘942 22 25 15. www. elserbal.com. Closed Sun eve, Mon. Expect refined (but not frilly) modern Cantabrian fare at this Michelin-starred restaurant with good-value tasting menus starting at €48.

⊖⊖⊖⊖ **Mesón Marinero** – La Correría 23, Castro Urdiales. ℘942 86 00 05. www.mesonmarinero.com. This famous name in Cantabrian gastronomy specialises in seafood. The fried *calamares* are killer.

SHOPPING

You can find terrific culinary souvenirs (anchovies, sweets, jams etc.) in Santander's old-school **Mercado de la Esperanza** (Pl. de la Esperanza; closed Sat pm, Sun) and at in **Mantequerías Cántabras** (Mercado del Este, Hernán Cortés 4; closed Sun), whose buttery *sobaos pasiego* cakes have been making Santanderinos chubbier since 1860.

FESTIVALS

Santander rings in the fiesta of St James (Santiago) in July with a range of popular concerts, dance performances and other cultural events.

In late July, **Loredo** hosts a horse race ('derby') on its wide, sandy beach.

BOAT TRIPS

Throughout the year, vessels known as reginas provide a shuttle service between Santander and Somo and Pedreña (two districts on the other side of the bay). In summer, excursions around the bay and along the Cubas river are also available for visitors, with departures from the **Embarcadero del Palacete** dock on Po. de Pereda (℘942 216 753; www.losreginas.com).

Santillana del Mar★★

Depsite its name, Santillana del Mar is located a few kilometres inland. The town retains its medieval appearance, with mansions embellished by family coats of arms.

A BIT OF HISTORY

Santillana developed around a monastery that sheltered the relics of St Juliana, who was martyred in Asia Minor – the name Santillana is a contraction of Santa Juliana. Throughout the Middle Ages, the monastery was famous as a place of pilgrimage and was particularly favoured by the Grandees of Castilla. In the 11C it became powerful as a collegiate church; in the 15C, the town was named the seat of a marquisate and enriched with aristocratic mansions that still stand today.

👣 WALKING TOUR

The town★★ has two main streets, both leading to the collegiate church. Start on **Calle de Santo Domingo**, with the 17C Casa del Marqués de Benemejís to the left and the Casa de los Villa, with its semicircular balconies, to the right. Turn left onto Juan Infante. Along the vast triangular square of **Plaza de Ramón Pelayo** are the Parador Gil Blas and the 14C Torre de Merino (Merino Tower, right); the Torre de Don Borja, with its pointed doorway; and (left) the 18C ayuntamiento (town hall), Casa del Águila and Casa de la Parra. Calle de las Lindas (end of the square on the right) runs between massive houses with austere facades to Calle del Cantón and Calle del Río, which lead to the collegiate church.
As you approach the church, you will see several noble residences on the right. On the left, the house of the Archduchess of Austria is decorated with coats of arms. The **Colegiata★** (collegiate church; Pl. del Abad Francisco

- ▶ **Population:** 4 172
- ⏱ **Michelin Map:** 572 B17.
- ℹ **Info:** Calle Jesús Otero. 𝄞942 81 82 51. www.santillanadel marturismo.com.
- ◐ **Location:** Santillana is surrounded by verdant hills, between Santander and Comillas (16km/10mi W). 🚃Santillana del Mar; narrow gauge station Puente San Miguel (4 km); nearest RENFE station Torrelavega (10 km).

Navarro; open Tue–Sun 10am–1.30pm, 4–7.30pm; €3, incl cloister); 𝄞942 81 88 12) dates to the 12–13C. The design of the 12C **cloister★** and the east end is Romanesque.

◐ Return to Calle de Santo Domingo.

The restored 16C Convento de Clarisas (Convent of the Poor Clares) houses the **Museo Diocesano** (open Tue–Sun 10am–1.30pm, 4–7.30pm/6.30pm Oct–May; €2; 𝄞942 84 03 17; www.santillana museodiocesano.es), featuring paintings, sculptures, metalwork, ivory and Baroque carvings.

ADDITIONAL SIGHTS
Museo de la Tortura El Solar
Escultor Jesús Otero, 1. Open Mon–Fri 10am–8.30pm, Sat–Sun until 9pm. Closed 1 Jan, 25 Dec. €4. 𝄞942 840 273. The range of punishments used by the Inquisition, and others, from the Middle Ages onwards, is catalogued in this grim, graphic collection of 70 instruments of torture. 🚫 Not suitable for children.

Museo y Fundación Jesús Otero
Plaza del Abad Francisco Navarro. Open Tue–Sat 10am–1.30pm, 4–8pm (Tue opens 11.30am). 𝄞942 84 01 98. This collection is devoted to the town's favourite sculptor, born here in 1908.

Picos de Europa★★★

The Picos de Europa is the highest range in the Cordillera Cantábrica yet a mere 30km/18.6mi from the sea. Its vertiginous gorges are veined with gushing mountain rivers, and its snow-capped peaks are jagged and severe.

The south face is less steep than the north, where the higher climes are concentrated, and looks out over a rugged terrain of outstanding natural beauty. The Parque Nacional de los Picos de Europa, covering 64 660ha/159 775 acres, protects the region's flora and fauna.

🚗 DRIVING TOURS

1 DESFILADERO DE LA HERMIDA (LA HERMIDA DEFILE) ★★

From Panes to Potes
27km/16.7mi. Allow about 1hr.

A defile (**ravine**)★★, 20km/12.4mi long, extends to either side of a basin containing the hamlet of La Hermida. The narrow gorge is bare and shadowed.

Iglesia de Nuestra Señora de Lebeña★
Lebeña. Open summer Tue–Sun 10am–1.30pm, 4.30–7.30pm. Winter by appointment, €2. ☎942 840 317.
The small 10C Mozarabic church stands amid poplars at the foot of cliffs. The belfry and porch are later additions. Note the 15C sculpture of the Virgin Mary.

Tama
This charming mountain village is situated in a lush basin and surrounded by the sharp peaks of the Central Range. There are many operators offering adventure activities here plus the excellent Sotama **visitor centre** (open daily Apr–Oct 9am–8pm, Nov–Mar until 6pm; ☎942 738 109).

- 🛈 **Michelin Map:** 572 C 14-15-16.
- 🛈 **Info:** Cangas de Onís: Avenida de Covadonga. ☎985 84 80 05; Covadonga: El Repelao. ☎985 84 61 35. www.turismoasturias.es.
- ▶ **Location:** The Picos de Europa rise along the northern coast, between Gijón and Santander. 🚂Picos De Europa. Narrow-gauge trains run from Santander to Arriondas (7km north of Cangas de Onís) and Unquera (40km north of Potes).
- 🕐 **Timing:** Roads are busy Jul–Aug. Skiing is best Dec–Mar.

Potes
9km/5.6mi S of Lebeña along N 621.
Potes is a delightful stone village in a fertile basin set against jagged crests. Two rivers run through it. From the bridge, admire the old stone houses and the 15C **Torre del Infantado**, now the town hall.

2 THE CLIMB TO FUENTE DÉ★★
30km/19mi on the N 621.
Allow about 3hr.

Monasterio de Santo Toribio de Liébana★
Bear left on the signposted road (CA 885) off CA 185. 🅿 If approaching from the W, do not turn right on Barrio Congarna (dangerous road); instead, continue on CA 185 toward Potes and loop back on CA 885. Open daily 10am–1pm, 4–7pm (until 6pm in winter) ☎942 73 05 50. www.santotoribiodeliebana.org.
The monastery was founded in the 7C and grew to considerable importance when a fragment of the 'True Cross' was placed in its safekeeping. A chapel set above and behind the altar contains the largest-known chunk of it, contained in a silver gilt wooden *lignum crucis* Crucifix reliquary.

The monastery was the house of **Beatus**, the 8C monk famous for his *Commentary on the Apocalypse*, copied in the form of illuminated manuscripts. There is a fine **view★** of Potes and the central mountain range from the lookout point at the end of the road.

Fuente Dé★★

21km/13mi W of Liébana.
A Parador stands at 1 000m/3 300ft. Nearby, a cable car (**teleférico**) rises 800m/2 625ft to the top of the sheer rock face (open weather permitting Oct–Jun 10am–6pm; Jul–Sep 9am–8pm; €17 return; ℘942 73 66 10, www. cantur.com). On the **ascent,** keep your eyes peeled for chamois. The **Mirador del Cable★★** commands a splendid panorama of the upper valley of the Deva and Potes. A path leads to the Aliva refuge. Erosion of the karst limestone produces stony plateaus and sinkholes (**hoyos**).

3 PUERTO DE SAN GLORIO (SAN GLORIO PASS)★

From Potes to Oseja de Sajambre
83km/52mi. Allow about 3hr.
The road crosses the Quiviesa Valley, then climbs through pastures.

Puerto de San Glorio★

Alt 1 609m/5 279ft.
A track leads north from the pass (1hr there and back) to near the Peña de Llesba and the **Mirador de Llesba**, a magnificent **viewpoint★★**.
To the right is the east range and to the left, the steep south face of the central massif. In the left foreground is Coriscao peak (2 234m/7 330ft).

▶ At Portilla de la Reina, bear right onto LE 243.

Puerto de Pandetrave★★

19km/12mi NW of Puerto de San Glorio.
This pass (1 562m/5 125ft) affords a **panorama** of the three ranges: in the right foreground, the Cabén de Remoña and Torre de Salinas, both in the central

massif. In the distance, in a hollow, is the village of Santa Marina de Valdeón. The Santa Marina de Valdeón/Posada de Valdeón road is narrow but passable.

Puerto de Panderruedas★

21km/13 mi NW.
The road climbs to pastures at 1 450m/4 757ft. Walk up the path to the left (15min there and back) to the **Mirador de Piedrahitas★★** (viewing table) for an impressive view of the immense cirque that closes the Valdeón Valley.

RIBADESELLA

Arriondas **San Pedro de Villanueva**
N 625
N 634
OVIEDO
Cueva del Bux
Cangas de Onís
P
AS 262
Covadonga CO 4
★★La Reina
R. Dobra
R. Sella
R. Ponga **PARQU**
R. Ponga **★★★DESFILADERO DE LOS BEYOS**
N 625
★★Oseja de Sajambre
Niaja
1732 △
OVIEDO **Oseja de Sajambre**
1290
★Puerto del Ponton
1490 C 635 N 625
Puerto de Tarna
E. de Riaño Riaño
LÉON

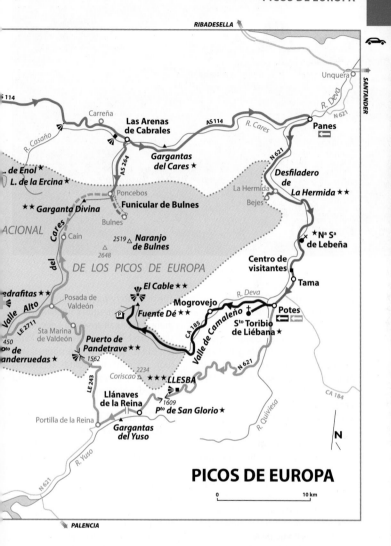

PICOS DE EUROPA

0   10 km

To the northeast is the Torre Cerredo peak (2 648m/8 688ft), the highest in the range.

Puerto del Pontón★

8km/5mi SW of Puerto de Panderruedas. Alt 1 280m/4 200ft. The pass offers a **view★★** of the Sajambre Valley. The descent to Oseja de Sajambre begins with hairpin bends below the western range and continues as a tunnel through the mountain.

④ DESFILADERO DE LOS BEYOS★★★ (LOS BEYOS DEFILE)

From Oseja de Sajambre to Cangas de Onís

8km/23.6mi. About 1hr along N 625.

Mirador de Oseja de Sajambre★★

There is an awe-inspiring **view★★** of the Oseja de Sajambre Basin: The sharp Niaja peak at its centre rises to 1 732m/5 682ft, and the Los Beyos defile opens between walls of rock strata.

Picos de Europa

© Slawek Staszczuk/age fotostock

Desfiladero de Los Beyos★★★
4km/2.5mi NW of the Mirador de
Oseja de Sajambre.
This is one of the most beautiful gorges
in Europe, 10km/6.2mi long, carved by
the River Sella. The limestone is thick,
marked by the occasional clinging tree.

Cangas de Onís
26km/16mi N of the Desfiladero
de Los Beyos.
A humpbacked **Roman bridge** *(Puente
Romano)* crosses the Sella to the west.
The Capilla de Santa Cruz (open daily
11am-2pm, 4.30-7.30pm, €2), also west,
in Contranquil, commemorates the
victory of Covadonga and houses the
region's only dolmen (megalithic tomb).
The Aula del Reino de Asturias (Iglesia
Santa María Evaristo Sanchez; open Jul–
Sept Mon–Sat 11am–2pm, 4–8pm, Sun
12pm–2pm, 5–8pm; ℘985 84 80 05) is
a small museum that traces the modern
history of the town.
On the outskirts, toward Arriondas, is
the **Monastery of San Pedro de Villanueva**, a former 17C Benedictine
monastery with a Romanesque church.

Villanueva
4km/2.5mi N of Cangas de Onís.
The 17C Benedictine **Monasterio de
San Pedro** stands in a picturesque site,
by the river at the end of the village.

The monastery was built around a pre-
existing Romanesque church of which
there remains an apse and a decorated
side portal. The complex is now a Parador but is open to non-residents; two
rooms display archaeological remains
(especially ceramics) found during
refurbishment work.

⑤ THE ROAD TO COVADONGA AND THE LAKES★★

From Cangas de Onís to Covadonga
35km/22mi. About 3hr.

Cueva del Buxu
By guided tour only (30min) Wed–Sun
10.15am, 11.15am, 12.15pm, 1.15pm.
Reservation recommended; max 6
persons per tour. €3, free Wed. ℘608 17
54 67. No children under 8.
The cave in the cliff face contains charcoal drawings and rock engravings from
around 14 000 years ago including a
stag, horse and bison, brought to life
by Marta, the expert guide.

Covadonga
16km/10mi SE of La Cueva del Buxu.
This famous shrine is nestled in a dramatic **setting★★★** at the bottom of a
narrow valley surrounded by soaring
forested peaks. It commemorates the
(somewhat disputed) victory of Don

Pelayo over the Moors at Covadonga in 722 that traditional historians say marked the beginning of the Reconquista.

Santuario de Covadonga

Open 9am–6.30pm. ✆ 985 84 60 35. www.santuariodecovadonga.com.
A statue of Don Pelayo stands before this neo-Romanesque Basilica, built 1886–1901. Its museum (open daily 10.30am–2pm, 4–7.30pm; €2.50; ✆ 985 84 60 96) contains gifts to the Virgin.

La Santa Cueva

Open 8.30am–8pm. ✆ 985 84 60 35.
This holy cave, dedicated to the Virgin of the Battlefield, holds the coveted 18C wooden statue of the Virgin, *La Santina*, patron of Asturias. The remains of Don Pelayo are also buried here.

Lago de Enol★ and Lago de la Ercina★ (Lake Enol and Lake Ercina)

Lakes Enol and Ercina (alt. 1 232m/ 4 042ft), are two of the most popularplaces in the *sierra,* served by parking facilities, paved roads, walking trails, a restaurant and a museum.

🚶 There is a walking trail around both (3km/1.86mi, 1h), or you can follow a longer circuit (8km/5mi) for a less crowded experience. From mid-July to early September, vehicular access to the lakes is restricted between 8.30am and 8.30pm. Shuttle buses depart regularly from Cangas de Onís.
The Pedro Pidal Visitor Centre, (Buferrera services; open mid-Jun–mid-Oct 10am–6pm) has thematic exhibitions on the Picos de Europa explaining their ecosystems and a reproduction of a shepherd's hut.

▶ Continue to the lakes along the steep C0 4; stop and look back occasionally to enjoy the extensive panoramas.

After 8km/5mi, arrive at **Mirador de la Reina★★** with a view of the rocky peaks that make up the Sierra de Covalierda. Beyond the pass, two rock cirques are the settings for lakes Enol and Ercina.

6 GARGANTAS DEL CARES (CARES GORGES)★★

From Covadonga to Panes

90km/56mi. Allow one day.

Beyond Portillo la Estazadas village there is a **panorama★★** of the rock wall, which closes off the Río Casaño Valley. From a viewpoint on the right, shortly after Carreña de Cabrales, catch a glimpse of the fang-like crest of **Naranjo de Bulnes** (2 519m/8 264ft).

Las Arenas de Cabrales

10km/6.2mi E of Las Estazadas, along the AS 114.
This is the main production centre for Cabrales, Asturias's devilishly pungent blue cheese made from ewes' milk.
Beyond Arenas, the **gorges★** are mossy with the occasional tree. Arched stone bridges span the emerald waters.

▶ Bear right onto AS 264, which runs through the Upper Cares Valley.

Upper Cares Valley

The Poncebos road leads south, through a **ravine★**. After the *embalse* (reservoir) at Poncebos, a track (🚶 3hr return) leads up to Bulnes hamlet. A quicker and, frankly, extortionate, ascent can be made on the **Bulnes Funicular** (access at Poncebos at the intersection of the Sotres road; open Jun–Sep & hols 10am–8pm, rest of year 10am–12.30pm, 2–6pm; €17 one way, €22 return, ✆ 985 84 68 00; www.alsa.es) which connects to the Bulnes ski station (alt. 400m/1 312ft) in 7 minutes. On a clear day, there are great views of the summit.
🚶 From Poncebos to Caín (3hr30min one way) a path follows the Cares into the **gorge★★** to the foot of the central massif (from here, hire a taxi back to Poncebos).

▶ Return to Arenas de Cabrales.

Oviedo★★

The capital of Asturias has a long and eventful history. Its old quarter is sprinkled with enchanting plazas and streets lined with sculptures. Strolling about this World Heritage site is a delight.

THE CITY TODAY

Oviedo is excellent for shopping and is particularly well-known for its leather goods. A 21 000-student-strong university keeps the city vibrant with a buzzy nightlife. Enjoy Oviedo's boisterous *sidrería* (cider house) culture on Calle Gascona before satisfying your sweet tooth at any of the city's formidable bakeries.

A BIT OF HISTORY

The capital of the Kingdom of Asturias (9C–10C) – Alfonso II, the Chaste (791–842), moved his court to Oviedo and rebuilt the former Muslim town. The heir to the throne of Spain is still Called the Prince of Asturias.

The Two Battles of Oviedo – In 1934, Oviedo was heavily damaged in fighting between miners and right-wing government forces. In 1936, it was the scene of a three-month siege when the garrison rose in revolt against the Republican government during the Civil War.

The Prince of Asturias Awards have been presented in Oviedo since 1981 for achievements in sciences, humanities and public affairs.

OUTSIDE THE OLD QUARTER

Antiguo Hospital del Principado

Leave Oviedo on Conde de Toreno (marked on the plan).
The facade of the 18C former principality hospital, now the Hotel Reconquista, bears a fine Baroque **coat of arms★**.

▶ **Population:** 220 020
⚙ **Michelin Map:** 572 B 12
🛈 **Info:** Calle Marqués de Santa Cruz 1. ✆985 22 75 86. www.turismoviedo.es
◖ **Location:** The A 66 links Oviedo to the north coast at Gijón (29km/18mi) and to León (121km/75mi S). 🚂Oviedo.
🅿 **Parking:** Avoid the old town.
🕐 **Timing:** Stroll the old town first, so you won't be rushed later.

Iglesia de San Julián de los Prados★

C. Selgas 2. Open May–Jun Mon 10am –12.30pm; Tue–Sat 10am–12.30pm, 4–6pm. Jul–Sep Mon 10am–1pm, Tue–Fri 9.30am–1pm, 4–6pm, Sat 9.30am–12.30pm, 4–6pm. Oct–Apr Mon–Sat 10am–12pm. €2.
✆687 052 826.
This early-9C work has a characteristic porch, twin aisles, wide transept and, at the east end, three chapels with barrel vaults. The walls are covered in **frescoes★** of Roman influence. A fine transitional Romanesque **Christ in Glory★** is in the central apse.

Centro de Recepción e Interpretación del Prerrománico Asturiano

C. Antiguas Escuelas del Naranco. Open Jul–Aug 10am–2pm, 3.30–7.30pm. Rest of year: Wed–Fri 10am–1.30pm, 3.30–6pm; Sat–Sun & hols 10am–2pm, 3.30–6.30pm. ✆902 306 600. www.prerromanicoasturiano.es. Palacards (Spanish only) explain ancient Asturian art; a video is in English.

Iglesia de Santa María del Naranco★★

Monte del Naranco. 4km/2.5mi along Av. de los Monumentos to the NW. Open Apr–Sep Tue–Sat 9.30am–1pm, 3.30–7pm, Sun–Mon 9.30am–1pm;

Oct–Mar Tue–Sat 10am–2.30pm, Sun & Mon 10am–12.30pm. €3, mandatory guided; free Mon, self-guided. ☏638 260 163. www.santamariadelnaranco.es

This harmonious church incorporates part of the 9C summer palace of Ramiro I. It is supported by grooved buttresses and lit by vast bays. The lower floor is a vaulted crypt. On the upper floor (a former reception hall), two loggias open off the great chamber. Its decoration is delicate and unified. From outside, there is a fine **view** of Mount Aramo, with Oviedo in the foreground.

Iglesia de San Miguel de Lillo★

Monte del Naranco. 15min on foot.
Hours as Iglesia de Santa María. €3; free Mon. ☏902 306 600.

What remains is perhaps only a third of the original church, which likely collapsed in the 13C.

The aisles are narrow. Several claustral-type windows remain. The delicate carving is a delight: On the door, **jambs★★** are identical scenes in relief of arena contests. An Asturian cord motif is repeated on the capitals and on vaulting in the nave and gallery.

WALKING TOUR

OLD TOWN

Allow 1hr30min.

▶ Enter by Calle San Francisco and hug the right side of the street.

Antigua Universidad

The austere 17C stone-fronted university was restored after the Civil War. Opposite the facade is *Mujer Sentada (Seated Woman)* by Manolo Hugué.

Plaza de Porlier

View the cathedral in the next plaza. The **Palace of the Count of Toreno** (right) dates to 1673; the **Camposagrado** (opposite), an 18C edifice, houses the Law Courts (note spread eaves).

▶ Continue along C. San Francisco.

Plaza de de Alfonso II el Casto (Plaza de la Catedral)

Note the coat of arms on the facade of the 17C **Palacio de Valdecarzana**. The majestic Cathedral rises at the far end of the square. The **Palacio de la Rúa** was built at the end of the 15C.

▶ The cathedral is on the eastern side of the square.

Catedral de Oviedo★

Pl. de la Catedral. Open Mon–Fri 10am–1pm, 4–5pm exc Mar-May, Oct (4-6pm), Jun (4-7pm), Sat 10am–1pm, 4pm–5pm exc Jul-Sep, 10am-5pm. €7. ☏985 22 10 33. www.catedraldeoviedo.com.

The main work was carried out between 1412 and 1565 in Flamboyant Gothic style. The south tower tapers into a delicate openwork spire. Three 17C Gothic portals pierce the asymmetrical facade; figures of the Transfiguration are above the central portal. On the walnut-panelled doors (also 17C) are figures of Christ and St Eulalia.

Interior – The Cathedral has three aisles, the triforium surmounted by tall stained-glass windows, and an ambulatory. A 16C polychrome **high altarpiece★★** shows scenes from the Life of Christ. On either end of the transepts are 18C Baroque panels, and in the south transept, next to the main chapel, the 17C polychromed stone image of The Saviour.

The **Capilla de Alfonso II 'El Casto'** (The Chaste), on the site of the original church, is the pantheon of the Asturian kings. The decoration inside the gate (end of north transept) is Late Gothic. In the embrasures are figures of the Pilgrim St James, St Peter, St Paul and St Andrew, and on a mullion, a Virgin of Milk. Renaissance and Baroque elements intermingle.

The **tesoro★★** (treasury) in the apse includes outstanding ancient gold and silver plate: the *Cruz de los Ángeles* (Cross of the Angels), a gift from Alfonso II in 808, studded with gems; Roman cabochons and cameos; and the *Cruz de Victoria* (908), faced with chased gold, gems and enamel, supposedly carried by Pelayo at Covadonga.

The reliquary chapel of Cámara Santa (see below) is preceded by an antechapel, enlarged in the 12C. Its 12 **statue columns**★★, representing the Apostles, are among the most masterly sculptures of this period in Spain and obviously influenced by the *Pórtico de la Gloria* (Doorway of Glory) in Santiago Cathedral. Capitals illustrate the marriage of Joseph and Mary, the Holy Women at the Tomb and lion and wild boar hunts.

Cámara Santa

Access by steps from the south transept. Open daily, same access as cathedral.

The Cámara Santa was built by Alfonso II early in the 9C to hold holy relics and was reconstructed in the Romanesque period. The Arca Santa (Holy Chest) is a precious reliquary brought to Asturias after Toledo fell to the Moors.

Claustro

Same hours as Cathedral.

The Gothic **cloisters** (14C–15C) have intersecting pointed arches and delicate tracery in the bays. The **Capilla de Santa Leocadia** (to the left on entering) contains an altar, tombs from the time of Alfonso II and an unusually small stone altar. The **sala capitular** (chapter house) contains fine 15C stalls.

▶ Return to Pl. de Alfonso II El Casto.

To the right of the Cathedral (leaving), low reliefs and busts compose a homage to the Kings of Asturias. To the left, at Calle Santa Ana, note the unexpected Moorish *alfiz* window enclosure in the east wall of the 9C **Iglesia de San Tirso**.

▶ Turn left onto Tránsito de la Virgen, alongside the Cathedral.

Beyond the arch that connects the cathedral to the Palacio Arzobispal (archbishop's palace, left) is the Romanesque former cathedral. Ahead in Plaza de la Corrada del Obispo is the busy facade of the Palacio Arzobispal (late

16C) and the imposing 18C Puerta de la Limosna (alms gate).

▶ Continue along San Vicente.

Museo Arqueológico

C. San Vicente 5. Open Wed–Fri 9.30am–8pm, Sat 9.30am–2pm, 5–8pm, Sun & public hols 9.30am–3pm. ℘985 20 89 77. www.museoarqueologicodeasturias.com.

This archaeological museum is set in the former Convento de San Vicente (16C–18C). Two galleries off the 15C Plateresque cloisters display pre-Romanesque art. Fragments and reproductions evidence the sophistication of Asturian art. Among exhibits (placards in Spanish only) are the Naranco altar, low reliefs showing Byzantine influence and column bases from San Miguel de Lillo. Upon exiting, go under the arch and cross the **Plaza de Feijóo**, past the Iglesia de Santa María la Real de la Corte and the palace-like facade of the 18C Monasterio de San Pelayo.

▶ Turn right onto Jovellanos and look back at the city wall. Return to Santa Ana.

Museo de Bellas Artes de Asturias (Fine Arts Museum)

Santa Ana 1–3. Open Sep–Jun Tue–Fri 10.30am–2pm, 4.30–8.30pm, Sat 11.30am–2pm, 5–8pm, Sun & public hols 11.30am–2.30pm; Jul–Aug Tue–Sat 10.30am–2pm, 4–8pm, Sun & public hols 10.30am–2.30pm. ℘985 21 30 61. www.museobbaa.com.

The museum is in three buildings. The core collection of Spanish painting is enriched by Italian and Flemish works. There is also a sculpture collection. Among the works in the 18C Palacio de Velarde are a complete *Apostolado* by **El Greco** (ground floor); the Gothic panels of the *Santa Marina Retable* (on the stairway); a *Burial of Christ* and magnificent *Apostle* by **Ribera**; a *Crucifixion* by **Zurbarán**; a *San Pedro* by Murillo; and two portraits by **Goya** (*Jovellanos* and *Charles IV*) on the first floor. The second floor is devoted to Asturian and Spanish art of the 19C and early 20C.

A passageway leads to the second floor of the 17C Casa Oviedo-Portal, which houses a gallery dedicated to J Sorolla plus paintings by **Picasso**, Gutiérrez-Solana, Regoyos and Nonell.

As you leave, take in the Plaza de Trascorrales, with its brightly coloured houses and its sculpture of *The Milkmaid*.

▶ Take Cimadevilla to reach Plaza de la Constitución.

Along **Plaza de la Constitución** are the **ayuntamiento** (City Hall), with 17C and 18C porticoes, and the Iglesia de San Isidoro, from the same era.

▶ Take Fierro, where there is a covered market, to Fontán.

Fontán is a picturesque area. Porticoed houses have enchanting courtyards, reached by multiple archways.

▶ Leave by the archway that faces Plaza de Daoíz y Velarde.

The sculpture in the tree-lined **Plaza de Daoíz y Velarde** is *Las Vendedoras del Fontán*, honouring Oviedo's female street vendors over the centuries.

EXCURSIONS
Iglesia de Santa Cristina de Lena★

▶ 34km/21mi S on the A 66 (junction 92) At Pola de Lena, head for Vega del Rey, then take the signposted road. Park before the rail viaduct (road becomes impassable) and walk up the steep path (15min) to **Iglesia de Santa Cristina de Lena** (open Tue–Sun Apr–Oct 11am–1pm, 4.30–6.30pm/ Dec-Mar 11am-1pm, 4-6pm, closed Nov; €1.50; free Tue. ℘984 49 35 63). This small but well-proportioned pre-Romanesque 9C golden stone church stands on a rocky crag and enjoys a **panorama★** of the Caudal Valley.
The building has a Greek cross plan, unusual in Asturias. It features traditional stone vaulting, with blind arcades, and columns with pyramid-shaped capitals emphasised by a cord motif. The nave is separated from the raised choir by an iconostasis in which the superimposed arches increase the impression of balance. The low reliefs in the chancel are Visigothic sculptures with geometric figures and plant motifs.

Teverga

▶ 43km/27mi SW on the N 634 and AS 228. The road follows the River Trubia, which, after Proaza, enters a narrow gorge. Glance back for a **view★** of the Peñas Juntas cliff face. Beyond the Teverga fork the road penetrates the **desfiladero de Teverga★** (Teverga Ravine). Beyond La Plaza village is the **Colegiata de San Pedro de Teverga** (guided tours Sat–Sun 12pm and 4.30pm; call ahead to check times; €1.50; ℘696 816 915). This late 12C collegiate church was built in a continuation of pre-Romanesque Asturian style and includes a narthex, a slender nave and a flat east end. The narthex capitals are carved with stylised animal and plant motifs.

ADDRESSES

🏠 STAY

⊖⊖⊖ **Eurostars Hotel de la Reconquista** – C. Gil de Jaz 16, Oviedo. ℘913 342 196. www.hoteldelareconquista.com. 142 rooms. ⌑ €20. What was a hospice in the 18C is now Oviedo's most respected hotel. It has spacious rooms, charming courtyards and an old-world feel.

🍽/EAT

⊖⊖ **Sidrería Tierra Astur Gascona** – C. Gascona 1. ℘985 202 502. www.tierra-astur.com. Closed Tue. Calle Gascona is lined with teeming cider bars, and this is the most consistent of the bunch. At lunch, spring for a prix-fixe menu that might include *fabada* or octopus stewed with white. beans. Cider is a must, of course.

Costa Verde ★★

The Costa Verde (Green Coast) is so named for its lush pine and eucalyptus forests that fringe the shores. Inland, cows graze lazily on mountainsides. The most scenic towns are hidden in secluded coves. On a clear day the Picos de Europa and Cordillera Cantábrica are a stunning backdrop.

🚗 DRIVING TOURS

Along the rocky coast, low cliffs are interrupted by sandy inlets; the estuaries are narrow and deep. West of Cudillero, the coastal plain ends in sheer cliffs overlooking small beaches.

1 LLANES TO GIJÓN
145km/90mi.

Llanes

The clifftop promenade gives a good view of the once-fortified port, the rampart ruins and castle and the squat Iglesia de Santa María. In mid-August the **Fiestas de San Roque** (www.san-roque.com) take place here with dancers in brilliant local costume parading through the streets.

▶ Take the E70 20km/12.5mi to Colombres.

Fundación Archivo de Indianos - Museo de la Emigración

San Vicente de la Barquera. Open Jun–Sep daily 10am–2pm, 4–8pm; rest of the year Tue–Sat 10am–2pm, 4–7pm. Closed 1 & 6 Jan, 24–25 & 31 Dec. €6. ☎985 412 005. www.archivodeindianos.es.
Housed in the sumptuous Quinta Guadalupe palace, this museum tells the story of hundreds of thousands of Asturians who emigrated to Latin America in the 19C, an event that shaped the region and its culture.

▶ Take the E70 W back to Llanes, where it turns in to the Autovía del Cantábrico. Continue to Ribadesella.

🚲 **Michelin Map:** 571 and 572 (town plan of Gijón) B8-15.

🛈 **Info:** Gijón: C. Rodriguez Sampedro. ☎985 34 17 71; Llanes: C. Posada Herrera, 15 (La Torre building). ☎985 40 01 64; Valdés (Luarca): Plaza Alfonso X El Sabio. ☎985 64 00 83. www.turismoasturias.es.

◗ **Location:** The N 634 runs along the northern coast of Asturias and affords sea and mountain views.

👪 **Kids:** The Centro de Arte Rupestre Tito Bustillo and MUJA, the Jurassic Museum, are unmissable.

Ribadesella

The town and port of Ribadesella are on the right side of the estuary opposite the holiday resort.

👪 Centro de Arte Rupestre Tito Bustillo ★

Av. de Tito Bustillo. Cave open by guided tour only (1hr), Apr–Oct Wed–Sun 10.15am–5pm (last tour). Reservation recommended for cave tour. Cave Art Centre open Jul–Aug Wed–Sun 10am–7pm; Sep–Dec & Feb–Jun Wed–Fri 10am–2.30pm, 3.30–6pm, Sat–Sun & hols 10–2.30pm, 4–7pm. Closed 8 & 9 Aug, 24–25 & 31 Dec. €9.59 cave & art centre; free 18 May, Wed. ☎902 306 600. www.centrotitobustillo.com.
These caves are well-known for their Palaeolithic **paintings** ★ (ca. 20 000 BC) of horses, stags and a doe.

◗ 26km/16mi W of Ribadesella on the A-8. Squat drying sheds, or *hórreos*, typical of Asturias, stand beside the houses in the small, attractive village of **La Isla**.

👪 MUJA (Museo del Jurásico de Asturias – Jurassic Museum)

Rasa de San Telmo, Colunga. Open Jul–Aug 10.30am–8pm. Feb–Jun & Sep–Dec Wed–Fri 10am–2.30pm, 3.30–6pm,

Sat–Sun & hols 10.30am–2.30pm, 4–7pm .Closed Jan, 24–25 & 31 Dec. €7.21; free Wed. ℘902 30 66 00. www.museojurasicoasturias.com Between Colunga and Lastres, this museum is dedicated to the dinosaurs that once roamed this area.

◗ 12km SE of La Isla on AS 260.

Mirador del Fito★★★

This dramatic and oft-Instagrammed high-diving-board-style viewpoint gives a fabulous panorama of the Picos de Europa and the coast.

◗ 17km/10.5mi W of Fito.

Priesca

The capitals in the chancel in the **Iglesia de San Salvador** (℘985 97 67 12) resemble those at Valdediós (👓 see entry below).

◗ 11km/6.8mi W of Priesca via N 632.

Villaviciosa

Emperor Charles V arrived here in 1517 to take possession of Spain. The **Iglesia de Santa María** (open Tue–Sun 11am–1pm, 5–7pm) is decorated with a Gothic rose window.

◗ 3km/1.8mi S of Villaviciosa.

Amandi

The bell tower of **Iglesia de San Juan** (open Tue–Sat 11.30am–1.30pm, Jul–Sep also 5.30-7.30pm; ℘985 891 759) stands on high ground. The remodelled church retains a 13C portal with sophisticated **decoration★**. Inside the **apse★**, the frieze from the facade reappears to form a winding ribbon that follows the curves of the intercolumniation.

◗ 7km/4.3mi S of Villaviciosa.

Valdediós★

The **Iglesia de San Salvador** was consecrated in 893 and is known as *El Conventín*. The adjacent **Monasterio de Santa María** consists of a 13C Cistercian church and cloisters dating to the 15C,

17C and 18C (open Tue–Sun Apr–Sep 11am–2pm, 4.30–7.30pm, Oct–Mar 11am–1.30pm; €4 both sites; ℘670 242 372; www.monasteriovaldedios.com).

◗ Take the AS 112, A 66 and Autoveia Minera N to Gijón.

Gijón

36km/22mi NW of Valdediós.

🚄Gijón (high speed line under construction).

Gijón is a lively urban city with a population of 271 843. On Plaza del Marqués is the crenellated late-17C **Palacio de Revillagigedo** (open depending on exhibition, generally Tue–Sat 11.30am–1.30pm, 5–8pm, Sun & hols 12pm–2.30pm; ℘985 34 69 21), now a cultural centre.

Nearby is the fishermen's quarter, Cimadevilla. Vestiges of Gijon's Roman past include the **Termas Romanas del Campo Valdés** (Roman baths) in the old quarter (Campo Valdés; open Tue–Fri 9.30am–2pm, 5–7.30pm; Sat–Sun 10am–2pm, 5–7.30pm; closed 1, 6 Jan, 15 Aug, 24, 25, 31 Dec; €2.50, free Sun; ℘985 18 51 51, http://museos.gijon.es). Nearby, the **Torre del Reloj** (Recoletas 5; open Mon–Fri 9am–2pm; ℘985 181 120) has history displays and views over the city.

② FROM GIJÓN TO CASTROPOL
179km/118mi.

Luanco

The charming port village of Luanco mixes a workaday fishing port with tourist development, as seen in the new buildings multiplying on the watefront. Calle La Riva is the main street, with three notable Baroque monuments: the Torre del Reloj (clock tower), the Palacio de los Menéndez Pola and, overlooking the beach, Santa Maria church. Afterward, stroll the Paseo del Muelle, where restaurants overlook the charming bay.

Avilés

With 81 659 inhabitants, Avilés is the third-largest city in Asturias. Industrial and set back from the coast, it is worth a visit for its old neighbourhood, concentrated around the town hall, and new cultural centre, designed by Brazilian architect Oscar Niemeyer.

Plaza de España is the heart of the old city, dominated by the City Hall, a former palace built in 17C and modelled on that of Oviedo. Opposite is the Baroque **Palacio Ferrera**. On the adjacent Calle San Francisco, the 17C **Fuente de los Canos de San Francisco** was once the city's main water source.

The striking **Centro Niemeyer** (open 9am–midnight; guided visits available; ℘984 835 031; www.niemeyercentre. org) is situated 500m/550yd from the Plaza de España, over the river via a footbridge. A curious avant-garde landmark given the location, Oscar Niemeyer's clean, white rationalist forms spread out over a giant swath of reclaimed industrial land.

Avilés's nearest beach, **Salinas**, is a rapidly expanding resort. The rock islet of La Peñona affords a **view** of the beach, one of the longest on the Costa Verde.

Ermita del Espíritu Santo

Muros de Nalón. 19km/11.8mi W of Salinas. The hermitage commands an extensive **view**★ west along the coastal cliffs.

Cudillero★★

9km/6mi W of la Ermita.

This fishing village, with its **pastel-painted houses**★ perched on a series of cliffs around a bay, calls to mind Italy's Cinque Terre or the Amalfi Coast. Beneath them is a boat launch and quaint harbourside restaurants. Continue west for some of the area's best beaches: Playa Concha de Artedo (4km/2.5mi), Playa de San Pedro (10km/6.2mi) and, the most secluded and stunning of alll, Playa del Silencio (15km/9.3mi).

Cabo Vidio★★

14km/8.7mi NW of Cudillero.

Catch the coastal **views**★★ from near the lighthouse on this headland with 100m/328ft-tall near-sheer cliffs.

Excursion to the Narcea River

91km/57mi to Cangas del Narcea along the N 634 and AS 216, branching S at the Cabo Busto.

Tineo

50km/31mi SW of Cabo Vidio.

An aerie 673m/2 208ft up the mountainside, the town of Tineo commands an immense mountain **panorama**★★.

Monasterio de Corias

28km/17mi SW of Tineo. Open to prebooked groups. ℘983 48 40 02. www.bodegamonasterio.com.

This 11C monastery, rebuilt after a 19C fire, was occupied for 800 years by Benedictines. It is now a wine producer.

▶ Return to the coast road (N 632).

Luarca★

Luarca is in a remarkable **site**★ at the mouth of the winding Río Negro, spanned by seven bridges. A lighthouse, church and cemetrey stand on the headland once occupied by a fort.

Excursion along the Navia Valley

82km/51mi along the AS 12 (2hr30min each way).

The River Navia flows along a wild valley below several peaks. After Coaña, turn right at the sign 'Castro'. Circular foundations and paving remain from a **Celtic village**. For a striking **panorama**★★ of the **Arbón dam**, pause at the viewpoint. Past Vivedro, there is another **panorama**★★, and as the road climbs, the **confluence**★★ of the Navia and the Frío is impressive from a giddy height. Beyond Boal, the valley is blocked by the high **Doiras Dam**.

The **Museo Etnográfico** at Granda de Salime (Av. del Ferreriro; open Tue–Sun; €1.50, free Tue; ℘985 627 243; www. museodegrandas.com) traces Asturian life through period rooms and artefacts.

▶ Return to Navia, then continue W along the N 634. From Figueras on the Ría Ribadeo you can view **Castropol**, which resembles an Austrian village.

Galicia

This remote region, around the size of Belgium or Maryland, spans the northwest corner of the Iberian Peninsula, above Portugal. In appearance and culture it is akin to the Celtic regions of Ireland, Wales and Brittany, far removed from the archetypal images of southern Spain. Geologically Galicia is an ancient eroded granite massif, and the overall impression is that of a hilly and mountainous region. The climate is influenced by the ocean: Temperatures are mild and rainfall is abundant – hence the northern coast's nickname, 'Green Spain'. The largely untouristed interior is agricultural: maize, potatoes, grapes and rye, and cattle in Ourense province. Galicia is Spain's chief fishing region, renowned for its seafood both fresh and canned (*conservas*). Spaniards view *Gallegos* as a hardy and serious yet friendly people. Like Asturians, they have their own heritage, folklore and language, which sounds like a singsong mix of Castilian and Portuguese.

A Coruña and the Rías Baixas

The former capital of Galicia, A Coruña (La Coruña in Castilian) is a bustling port city with a stately cobbled old town of narrow alleyways and pretty plazas. The Rías Altas, deep inlets backed by pine and eucalyptus, stretching eastwards from A Coruña, shelter some fine beaches and low-key resorts. By contrast, many a ship has been dashed against the rocks at the wind-whipped Costa de la Muerte, but is worth a visit for its drama and (occasionally) calm beauty. The Rías Baixas – its inlets, creeks and coastline more scenic than those farther north – is Galicia's major holiday area and Spain's premier white wine region, producing internationally adored Albariño. There are several good resorts, chief among them A Toxa (La Toja in Castilian). The most idyllic beaches are on the Islas Cíes, a nature reserve reached by boat from Vigo, Spain's leading fishing port. The area's other urban centre, Pontevedra, has a charming historic old quarter.

Camino de Santiago

Ther's no official starting point for the Camino de Santiago (Way of St James), though the Spanish leg (750km/465mi) begins at the French border, runs across the Pyrenees, then west through Navarra, Rioja, Castilla and Galicia, waymarked by the pilgrim's symbol of a scallop shell. Numerous, often rudimentary, inns providing victuals and shelter line the route, which ends at Santiago de Compostela, whose narrow granite-paved streets and towering cathedral rank among Spain's highlights.

Highlights

1 Standing in front of the Cathedral at **Santiago de Compostela** (p290)

2 Relaxing in a wonderful setting on the beach at **A Toxa** (p296)

3 Touring the **Ría de Vigo** and taking in the wonderful views (p297)

4 Strolling the delightful Old Quarter at **Pontevedra** (p299)

5 Walking atop the Roman city walls at **Lugo** (p302)

Beach of Islas Cíes, Rías Baixas

Catedral de Santiago de Compostela

© AdamGregor/iStockphoto.com

Santiago de Compostela★★★

In the Middle Ages Santiago de Compostela attracted pilgrims from all of Europe in search of eternal salvation. Today around 200 000 pilgrims make a similar trek to the city, declared a UNESCO World Heritage Site, each year. Whatever the spiritual benefits gained en route, its highlight is – literally – the final step of the journey, onto the Praza do Obradoiro beneath the wondrous Cathedral. The continual influx of walkers lends the city a jovial and cosmopolitan feel. 🕐 Pilgrims get discounts at many tourist sights.

▶ **Population:** 95 612
🖾 **Michelin Map:** 571 D 4 (town plan).
🖪 **Info:** Rúa do Vilar 63. 𝄞981 55 51 29. www.santiagoturismo.com.
▶ **Location:** This pilgrimage city in NW Spain is connected by the AP 9 to Vigo (84km/52mi S) and A Coruña (72km/45mi N) and by the N 547 with Lugo (107km/67mi E). The AP 53 runs SE to Ourense/Ourense (111km/69mi). 🚆Santiago de Compostela (AVE).
🕐 **Don't Miss:** The Cathedral.

THE CITY TODAY

Despite its large number of visitors, Santiago de Compostela is one of Spain's most enchanting cities with its old quarter and maze of narrow streets lined with bars and restaurants. The city's 30 000 or so university students mix with the hundreds of thousands of annual visitors from across the globe to keep this ancient city feeling young.

A BIT OF HISTORY

History, tradition and legends – The Apostle **James the Greater** crossed the seas to convert Spain to Christianity. He returned to Judaea where he fell victim to Herod Agrippa. His disciples fled to Spain with his body. A star is said to have pointed out of his grave to shepherds early in the 9C.

In 844, during an attack against the Moors at **Clavijo**, a knight on a charger bearing a white standard with a red cross appeared on the battlefield and brought victory. The Christians recognised St James, naming him *Matamoros* or Moorslayer. The Reconquista, and ultimately Spain, had found a patron saint.

In the 11C devotion spread until a journey to St James' shrine ranked with one to Rome or Jerusalem.

SIGHTS

Praza do Obradoiro/Plaza del Obradoiro

The vastness of this square makes it a fitting setting for the Cathedral.

Catedral★★★

Praza do Obradoiro. Closed for renovations until late 2020. Pórtico de la Gloria (advance booking required) & museum open 10am–8pm, from 9am Apr–Oct; closed 1 & 6 Jan, 25 July, 24 Dec pm, 25 Dec, 31 Dec. ☎981 58 35 48. €12 museum & Pórtico combined. www.catedraldesantiago.es.

The cathedral, most of whose interior is closed (Mass included) for renovations in preparation for the 2021 Año Jacobeo (jubilee), dates mostly from the 11–13C. Its Baroque **Fachada do Obradoiro★★★** (Obradoiro facade), a masterpiece by **Fernando Casas y Novoa** completed in 1750, was newly unveiled after a five-year restoration in 2018. The cen-

tral area, given true Baroque movement by the interplay of straight and curved lines, rises to what appears to be a long tongue of flame.

Pórtico de la Gloria★★★ (Doorway of Glory) – Behind the facade stands the narthex and Pórtico de la Gloria, a late 12C wonder by **Maestro Mateo**. The statues of the triple doorway are exceptional both as a composition and in detail. Entry is limited to fewer than 100 visitors a day; advance booking (via the website) is required.

The doorway is slightly more recent than the rest of the cathedral and shows Gothic features. Mateo, who also built bridges, had the crypt reinforced to bear the weight of the portico. The central portal is dedicated to the Christian Church, the left to the Jews and the right to the Gentiles. The central portal tympanum shows Christ surrounded by the Evangelists, while on the archivolt are the 24 Elders of the Apocalypse.

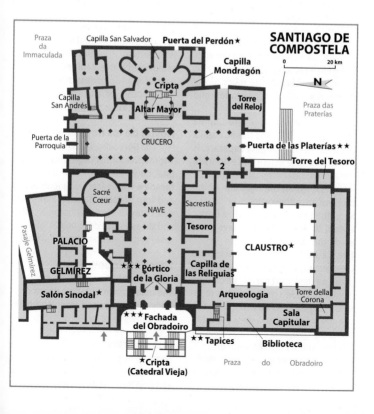

The engaged pillars are covered in statues of Apostles and Prophets. Note the figure of Daniel with the hint of a smile, a precursor to the famous Smiling Angel in Reims Cathedral in France. The pillar beneath the seated St James bears finger marks; traditionally, on entering the Cathedral, exhausted pilgrims placed their hands here in token of safe arrival. On the other side of the pillar, the statue of Santos Croques is known colloquially as the Saint of Bumps as it supposedly imparts memory and wisdom upon touching one's brow against it.

Interior – The immense Romanesque cathedral displays all the characteristics of medieval pilgrim churches: a Latin Cross plan, vast proportions, an ambulatory and a triforium. The side aisles are covered with 13C groin vaults. At major festivals (none celebrated until renovations are complete, in late 2020) a huge thurible, the **botafumeiro** (displayed in the library), is swung, fuming, from the transept dome keystone.

The **altar mayor,** or high altar, surmounted by a sumptuously dressed 13C statue of St James, is covered by a gigantic baldaquin. Beneath the altar is the **cripta★**, (crypt) built into the 9C church. It enshrines the relics of the saint and his disciples, St Theodore and St Athanasius.

The Gothic vaulting of the Capilla Mondragón (1521), and the 9C Capilla de la Corticela, formerly separate, is impressive. The Renaissance doors to the **sacristía** (sacristy) (**1**) and *claustro* (cloisters) (**2**) on the right arm of the transept are noteworthy.

Enter the **tesoro** (treasury), in a Gothic chapel to the right of the nave, from inside the cathedral.

The Cathedral Museum (incl Palcio Gelmírez temporary exhibitions) is located in the westernmost part of the cloister; exhibits include a gold and silver monstrance by Antonio de Arfe (1539–66). Use the side entry to access the **biblioteca** (library); **sala capitular** (chapter house), with its granite vault and 16C Flemish tapestries; and adjoining rooms with **tapestries★★** by Goya, Bayeu, Rubens and Teniers.

Claustro – Access via the museum. This Renaissance cloister was designed by Juan de Álava, who combined a Gothic structure with Plateresque decoration. **Puerta de las Platerías★★ (Silversmiths' Doorway)** – This is the only intact 12C Romanesque doorway. Not all of the entrance is original. The most impressive figure is David playing the viola on the left door. Adam and Eve can be seen being driven out of the Garden of Eden; the Pardoning of the Adulterous Woman is on the right corner of the left tympanum.

The **Torre del Reloj** (Clock Tower) was added at the end of the 17C. To the left stands the **Torre del Tesoro** (Treasury Tower). The 18C Baroque facade of the **Casa del Cabildo** is opposite the *fuente de los caballos,* or horse trough.

Palacio Gelmírez and Las Cubiertas (Cathedral rooftop tours)★

Praza do Obradoiro. Palacio Gelmírez. Closed until 2021. ℘902 55 78 12.

This was formerly the bishops' palace; the **Salón Sinodal★** (Synod Hall) is more than 30m/98ft long and has sculptured ogive vaulting. A guided tour of the roof offers a topsy-turvy perspective of the Cathedral and unforgettable views of the city.

Hostal de los Reyes Católicos★

Praza do Obradoiro. www.parador.es.
The massive former pilgrim inn and hospital, now a parador, has an impressive **facade★** with a Plateresque doorway and four elegant patios. Even if you don't stay the (pricey) hotel, a coffee and slice of *tarta de Santiago* (almond cake) in its restaurant are a fine treat.

Casco Antiguo★★ (Old Town)

The many-streeted tangle opens onto lively squares centred around burbling fountains.

Rúa do Franco

Gaze up at old colleges, such as the Renaissance-style Colegio de Fonseca, and pop into the shops and bars. The

Porta de la Faxeiras leads to Paseo de la Herradura, a setting for fairs. The excellent **view★** includes the cathedral and rooftops of Santiago.

Fundación Eugenio Granell

Pl. del Toral. Open Oct–May Tue–Fri 11am–2pm, 4–8pm, Sat 12pm–2pm and 5–8pm. Extended hours in summer. €2. ℘981 57 63 94.
www.fundacion-granell.org.
Inside the Pazo de Bendaña, an 18C noble building, the foundation displays rotating art exhibitions with an emphasis on Surrealism.

Rúa do Vilar

Stroll past arcaded ancient houses here and on the parallel **Rúa Nova**.

Plaza de la Quintana★★

This square at the east end of the Cathedral teems with student life. Here are the **Casa de la Canónica** (former Canon's Residence) and 17C Monasterio de San Peiayo de Antealtares. The latter is home to the **Museo de Arte Sacra** (Sacred Art Museum; open Apr–Dec Mon–Sat 10.30am–1.30pm & 4–7pm, Sun 4–7pm. €1.50. ℘981 56 06 23, www.santiagoturismo.com/museos/museo-de-arte-sacra). Opposite, the doorway in the Cathedral's east end, known as the **Puerta del Perdón★** (Door of Pardon), designed by Fernández Lechuga, is opened only in Holy Years (when the feast day of St James, 25 July, falls on a Sunday, next occurring in 2021). It incorporates statues of the Prophets and Patriarchs carved by Maestro Mateo for the original Romanesque *coro*.

Monasterio de San Martín Pinario★

Pl. de la Inmaculada 5. Open 11am–7pm. Church €4, monastery €6.
℘981 58 30 08.
The monastery church has an ornate Plateresque front. The interior, with coffered barrel vaulting, is lit by a Byzantine-style lantern without a drum. The Churrigueresque high altar **retable★** is by the great architect Casa y Novoa

(1730). A grand staircase beneath a cupola leads to 16C–18C cloisters. The facade overlooking Plaza de la Inmaculada is colossal with Doric columns. Plaza de la Azabachería, opposite, is named for the jet ornament craftsmen *(azabacheros)* who once toiled in this square.

Museo do Pobo Galego (Museum of the Galician People)

Open Tue–Sat 10.30am–2pm, 4–7.30pm, Sun & public hols 11am–2pm. Closed 1 Jan, 25 Dec.€3; free Sun. ℘981 58 36 20. www.museodopobo.gal.
This regional museum, housed in the former Convento de Santo Domingo de Bonaval (17C–18C), provides an introduction to Galician culture. Rooms are devoted to the sea, crafts, painting and sculpture. The building has an impressive triple **spiral staircase★**.
Opposite stands the **Centro Galego de Arte Contemporáneo** (open summer Tue–Sun 11am–8pm; ℘981 54 66 19; www.cgac.org).

Museo de las Peregrinaciones (Pilgrimage Museum)

C. San Miguel 4. Open Tue–Fri 9.30am–8.30pm, Sat 11am–7.30pm, Sun & public hols 10.15am–2.45pm. Closed 1, 6 Jan; 1 May; 24–25, 31 Dec. €2.40, Free Sat pm and Sun. ℘981 58 15 58.
http://museoperegrinacions.xunta.gal.
The history of pilgrimages to Santiago is explored with multimedia displays.

Colegiata de Santa María la Real del Sar★

Pl. de la Colegiata de Sar.
Open 11am–2pm, 4.30-7.30pm. Museum closed for renovation. ℘981 56 28 91.
This 12C collegiate church is the city's second-most important Romanesque structure after the cathedral. A glance inside at the astonishing slant of the pillars explains the 18C buttresses. Only a single elegant cloister gallery remains, its paired **arches★** decorated with floral and leaf motifs. A museum (closed for renovation as of Sep 2019) displays gold and silverwork.

EXCURSIONS

Pazo de Oca★

◗ 25km/15.5mi S on N 525. Gardens: open 9am–6.30pm (Apr–Oct until 8.30pm). €6. ℰ986 58 74 35. www.fundacionmedinaceli.org.

This austere Galician **manor**, or *pazo*, with a crenellated tower, lines two sides of a vast square.

The romantic **park★★** is a gorgeous surprise (&see INTRODUCTION – Spanish Gardens, p100) and has been dubbed the 'Generalife of the North'. There are shady arbours, terraces covered with rust-coloured lichen, pools and a lake with a stone boat.

Monasterio de Santa María de Sobrado

◗ Pl. Portal. 56km/35mi W. Open 10am–1pm, 4.30–7.30pm. €1. ℰ981 78 75 09. www.monasteriodesobrado.org.

Sobrado is a vast weatherworn **monastery** built between the Renaissance and Baroque periods.

Despite the severe church facade, the interior displays a fertile imagination in the design of the **cupolas** in the transept, the sacristy and the Rosary Chapel. Medieval parts of the monastery include the kitchen, chapter house and Mary Magdalene Chapel.

ADDRESSES

🏠 STAY

⊖⊜ **Hostal Mapoula** – Entremurallas 10, 3rd floor. ℰ981 58 01 24. www.mapoula. com. 11 rooms. The recently renovated family-run hotel in the old quarter has simple rooms with en-suite bathrooms.

⊖⊜ **Hotel San Clemente** – Rúa San Clemente 28. ℰ981 56 93 50. www. pousadasdecompostela.com. 10 rooms. ⌦ €6.50. A couple of minutes' walk from Praza do Obradoiro, this hotel has plain, cosy rooms decorated in wood.

⊖⊜⊜ **Casa Grande de Cornide** – C. Cornide 82, Teo. 11.5km/7mi SW of Santiago. ℰ981 89 30 44. www.casa grandedecornide.es. 11 rooms. ⌦€7.50. This traditional Galician manor is a peaceful refuge. The decor, a mix of

the old and new, create a comfortable environment. There's an outdoor swimming pool.

⊖⊜⊜⊜ **Parador de Santiago de Compostela** – Pl. del Obradoiro 1. ℰ981 58 22 00. www.parador.es. 137 rooms. ⌦€22. Two restaurants ⊖⊜⊜⊜. The former Royal Hospital founded by the Catholic Monarchs in 1499 is now a parador. Of note are its inner patios, which trace the typology of such hospitals in the 16C. Some rooms have four-poster beds.

🍽 EAT

⊖⊜⊜ **O Dezaseis** – R. de San Pedro 16. ℰ981 57 76. www.dezaseis.com. Reservations recommended. Closed Sun. Perennially packed for a reason, O Dezaseis serves local comfort food like gratinéed scallops and grilled octopus in a stone dining room or on the grapevine-shaded terrace.

⊖⊜⊜ **Don Quijote** – Rúa das Galeras 20. ℰ981 58 68 59. www. quijoterestaurante.com. The seafood rice is particularly standout at this old-school stalwart.

⊖⊜⊜⊜ **Casa Marcelo Santiago** – Rúa das Hortas 1. ℰ981 55 85 80. www. casamarcelo.net. Closed Sun eve, Mon. Savour creative Galician haute cuisine at this Michelin-starred favourite.

TAPAS

Bierzo Enxebre – Rúa da Troia 10. ℰ981 58 19 09. www.bierzoenxebre.es. Get the griddled *solomillo* (filet) or the blistered padrón peppers here.

Abastos 2.0 – Praza de Abastos, Rúa das Ameas 13. ℰ981 57 61 45. Bona fide market-based tapas are the draw at this trendy *nueva cocina* spot across from the eponymous market that sources the bulk of its ingredients from there.

La Bodeguilla de San Roque – Rúa de San Roque 13. ℰ981 56 43 79. www. labodeguilla.gal. This bodega has a good reputation for its revueltos (scrambled-egg dishes), chorizo and wines. There's a pleasant restaurant on the first floor.

A Gamela – Rúa da Oliveira 5. ℰ981 58 70 25. Tuck into the best fried *calamares* in town as well as delectable mushroom dishes

Rías Baixas★★

This is Galicia's most attractive region for beach holidays and typical Spanish resorts such as A Toxa. The coastline is famed for its deep, fjord-like flooded inlets (*rías*), which afford safe harbour.

🚗 DRIVING TOURS

1 RÍA DE MUROS Y NOIA★★

From Muros to Ribeira
71km/44mi. About 1hr15min.

This *ría* is delightfully wild, its low coastline strewn with rocks. The northern bank is wooded. **Muros** is a seaside town with local-style houses. **Noia** is notable for its square looking out to sea, upon which stands the Gothic **Iglesia de San Martín★** (Pl. Suárez Oviedo; ✆981 82 01 31) with a carved portal and rose window.

2 RÍA DE AROUSA

From Ribeira to A Toxa
115km/71mi. About 3hr

Ría de Arousa, at the mouth of the Ulla, is the largest and most indented inlet. **Ribeira** is a large fishing port with vast warehouses. **Mirador de la Curota★★** is 9km/5.6mi northeast of Ribeira.

🔵 Take the LC 302 W toward Oleiros, and after about 4km/2.5mi, turn right onto a narrow road up to the viewpoint.

From a height of 498m/1 634ft there is a **panorama★★** of the four inlets of the Rías Baixas.

Padrón
41km/25.5mi NE of Ribeira.
According to legend, St James landed by boat at this village. Its mooring stone (*pedrón*) can be seen beneath the altar in the parish church. The town, renowned for its namesake green peppers, which

---

🖋 **Michelin Map:** 571 D-E-F 2-3-4.

🈺 **Info:** Baiona: Paseo da Ribeira. ✆986 68 70 67; Vigo: Canovas del Castillo 3. ✆986 22 47 57; Tui: Colón 2. ✆986 60 17 89. www.turismoriasbaixas.com.

🔵 **Location:** The Rías Baixas are four inlets: the Ría de Muros y Noia; the Ría de Arousa; the Ría de Pontevedra; and the Ría de Vigo, all along the northern coast.

👥 **Kids:** The Acuario de O Grove and Museo do Mar (Vigo) offer hands-on fishy fun.

---

in recent years have become a trendy menu item the world over, was home to poet **Rosalía de Castro** (1837–85). Her house is a **museum** (Jul–Sep Tue–Sun 10am–2pm, 4–8pm, Oct–Jun 10am–1.30pm, 4–7pm; €2; ✆981 81 12 04; www.rosalia.gal).

Vilagarcía de Arousa
32km/19.8mi SW of Padrón off AP 9.
A garden-bordered promenade overlooks the sea. The **Convento de Vista Alegre**, founded in 1648, on the outskirts, is an old *pazo* (manor house) with square towers, coats of arms and pointed merlons.

Mirador de Lobeira★
4km/2.5mi S. Take a signposted forest track at Cornazo.
The view from the lookout takes in the whole *ría* and the hills inland.

Cambados★
12km/7.4mi SW of Vilagarcía de Arousa along PO 549.
The alleys of the old quarter are bordered by beautiful houses. At the northern entrance is the **Plaza de Fefiñanes★**, bounded on two sides by the emblazoned Fefiñanes *pazo* and on the third by a 7C church. On the other

ered in scallop shells. The seaside resort and fishing harbour of **O Grove,** on the other side of the causeway, is renowned for its seafood.

🏊 Acuario do Grove

Punta Moreiras, Reboredo. From O Grove, head toward San Vicente and turn off at Reboredo. Open Holy Week and mid-Jun–mid-Oct 10.30am–8.30pm; rest of year Wed–Fri 10am–6pm, Sat & Sun 10.30am–7.30pm. €15. ☎986 73 23 27. www.acuariodogrove.es. The only aquarium in Galicia, it has over 150 species, local and exotic, on display in 18 tanks. The **road★** from A Toxa to Canelas affords views of sand dunes and rock-enclosed beaches such as **La Lanzada.**

3 RÍA DE PONTEVEDRA★

From A Toxa to Hío

62km/39mi. About 3hr.
Sanxenxo is a lively summer resort with one of the best climates in Galicia. Further east at Samieira, a small road leads to the Monasterio de Santa María de Armenteira (open daily 9am–sunset; ☎986 71 83 00), a Cistercian monastery, where a 12C church and 17C Classical-style cloister can be visited. Some 12km/7.4mi east of Sanxenxo along PO 308 is **Combarro★**, a fishing village with winding alleyways that has a good many Calvaries and is famed for its **hórreos★** (drying sheds). Beyond Combarro is **Pontevedra★** (♥ see PONTEVEDRA, p299).
8km/5mi southwest of Pontevedra along PO 11 is **Marín**, headquarters of the Escuela Naval Militar (naval academy). A further 19km/11.8mi southwest along AP 9 is Hío, a village at the tip of the Morrazo headland that has a famous intricately carved **Calvary★**.

side of the village are the romantic ruins of **Santa Mariña de Dozo,** a 12C parish church. On the northern fringes of town, **Bodegas del Palacio de Fefiñanes** (Pl. de Fefiñanes; open Mon-Sat 10am–2pm, 4–8pm; reservation required; prices vary; ☎986 54 22 04; www.fefinanes. com) offers terrific Albariño tastings.

Illa da Toxa/Isla de La Toja★

20km SW of Cambados off PO550.
According to local lore, a sick donkey abandoned on the island was the first creature to discover the health-giving properties of its spring. It has since run dry, but this pine-covered island, in a wonderful **setting★★**, remains the most elegant resort on the Galician coast, adorned with luxury villas and an early-20C palace. Its small church is cov-

4 RÍA DE VIGO★★

From Hío to Baiona
70km/43mi. About 3hr.

The deep Ría de Vigo is sheltered inland by hills and out to sea by the Islas Cíes. The scenery at Domaio, where the wooded banks draw together and the narrow channel is covered in mussel beds, is particularly beautiful.
From Cangas and Moaña you can see the white town of Vigo covering the hillside across the inlet.

Vigo
38km/23.6mi SE of Hío. www.turismodevigo.org. 🚃 Vigo-Ursáiz (AVE).
Vigo is Spain's principal transatlantic and fishing port. Its **setting★** is outstanding, in an amphitheatre on the south bank of the Ría de Vigo surrounded by parks and pinewoods. There are magnificent **views★★** from El Castro hill. Berbés is the picturesque fishermen and sailors' quarter. Adjacent is the A Pedra market, where fishwives sell oysters; try them in the local bars.
MARCO (Museo de Arte Contemporáneo) (Príncipe 54; open Tue–Sat 11am–2.30pm, 5–9pm, Sun 11am–2.30pm; 🕿986 11 39 00; www.marcovigo.com) displays the works of avant-garde artists, sculptors and architects.
At Punta de Muíño are far-reaching **views** of the *ría*. The **Museo do Mar** 👥 (Av. Atlántida 160; open mid-Jun–mid-Sep Tue–Sun 11am–2pm, 5–8pm; mid-Sep–mid Jun Tue–Sun 10am–2pm, 5–7pm; €3; 🕿986 24 77 50; www.museodomar.com) explores the history of Vigo and the sea and includes an aquarium.

Islas Cíes★
🚢By boat from Baiona, Vigo or Cangas; operates Holy Week to Oct; €18.50 return). 🕿986 22 52 72.
www.mardeons.com.
This stunning archipelago surrounded by crystalline water with powdery white-sand beaches guards the entrance to the Ría de Vigo. Its three islands and Playa de Rodas beach are part of the **Parque Nacional de las**

Islas Atlánticas de Galicia. A ⚠camping permit is required for overnights (apply at www.autorizacionillasatlanticas.xunta.gal).

Mirador la Madroa★★
6km/3.7mi. Leave Vigo along the airport road. After 3.5km/2mi turn left, following signposts to the Parque Zoológico.
The corniche commands a fine **view★★** of Vigo and the *ría*. The beaches of Alcabre, Samil and Canido stretch along the coast south of Vigo.

Panxón
14km/9mi SW along the C 550.
This seaside resort lies at the foot of Monte Ferro.

Playa América
2km/1.2mi S of Panxón.
A popular, elegant resort in the curve of a bay.

Baiona/Bayona★
5km/3mi SW of Playa América.
www.baiona.org
It was here, on 10 March 1493, that Christopher Columbus's caravel *Pinta*, captained by **Martín Alonso Pinzón**, gave the first reports of the so-called New World.
Today Baiona is a summer resort with a harbour fronted by a promenade of terrace cafés. In the old quarter, houses have coats of arms and glassed-in balconies.
The former collegiate church (Pl. de Santa Liberata 1; open 11am–12.30pm, 4.30–6.30pm; 🕿986 68 70 67) at the top of the town was built in a transitional Romanesque-Gothic style.

Monterreal
Open daily 10am–10pm. €1; €5 vehicles. 🕿986 35 50 00.
The Catholic Monarchs had a wall built around Monterreal promontory at the beginning of the 16C. The fort within is now the Parador de Baiona, surrounded by pinewood.
A walk round the battlements★ (🚶 30min), rising above the rocks, gives

views★★ of the bay, Monte Ferro, Estela islands and the coast to the Cabo Silleiro headland.

5 BAIONA TO TUI★

58km/36mi.

The coast between Baiona and La Guarda is flat and semi-deserted.

Virgen de la Roca

Open Tue-Sun 11am-2pm, 4pm-7pm, €1.50.

This towering granite statue (15m/50ft high) of the Virgin holding a boat in her right hand was built by architect Antonio Palacios in 1930. It can be climbed, Statue of Liberty-style, via a spiral staircase. The view over the bay and the ocean from the top is impressive.

Oia

This fishing village clusters around the recently restored Cistercian abbey of **the Real Monasterio** (by prebooked tour only; see website for times; €5; www.monasteriodeoia.com).

A Guarda

13km/8mi S of Oia along PO 552.

From this fishing village at the southern end of the Galician coastline, you can see **Monte Santa Tecla★** (341m/1 119ft) rising above the mouth of the Miño, a fine **view★★**.

▶ Take Citania de Santa Trega signs.

On the slopes are the extensive remains of a **Celtic city**, inhabited from the Bronze Age to the 3C.

▶ From La Guarda, the PO 552 heads inland parallel to the Miño river.

Tui★

27km/17mi NE of La Guarda along PO 552. Ancient Tui stands across the border from Portugal in a striking **setting★**. Its old quarter, with its emblazoned houses and narrow stepped alleys, climb the rocky hillside to the Romanesque-Gothic **catedral★** (open 10.45am–1pm, 4–7pm, May–Sep until 8pm; €4; ℘986 60 05 11; www.catedraldetui.com), consecrated in 1232. The **Parque de Santo Domingo**, including a Gothic church of the same name, commands a good view of Tui and the Portuguese coast.

ADDRESSES

🏨 STAY

🛏 **Canaima** – Av. de García Barbón 42, Vigo. ℘986 43 09 34. www.hotelcanaima vigo.es. 50 rooms. This no-frills hotel may be a bit frayed around the edges, but its rock-bottom prices and terrific location make up for its minor shortfalls (e.g., paper-thin walls).

🛏🛏🛏🛏 **Parador de Baiona** – Av. Arquitecto Jesús Valverde, Baiona. ℘986 355 000. 🍴 €20. www.parador.es. 122 rooms. Housed in a stone castle, Baiona's Parador has well-kept old-fashioned rooms with ocean views and four-poster beds .

🍴 EAT

🍴🍴🍴 **Bitadorna** – Ecuador 56, Vigo. ℘986 13 69 51. www.bitadorna.com. Closed Sun eve. When you've had your fill of the stick-to-your-ribs classics, make a beeline for this modern restaurant serving a lighter, fresher take on Galician cuisine.

🍴🍴🍴 **O Fogón da Ría** – Fontecarmoa 3, Vilagarcia De Arousa. ℘986 50 79 62. www.ofogondaria.com. Closed Sun & Mon eve, Tue. This lovely old establishment has two dining rooms with rustic decor with a varied menu and good wine list.

🍴🍴🍴 **Posta do Sol** – Ribeira de Fefiñáns 22, Cambados. ℘986 54 22 85. The speciality is seafood; try the empanadas (savoury pies) and homemade desserts. The lunch *menú del día* is a great value.

Pontevedra★

Pontevedra has a pleasant mix of attractive buildings, plain arcades, cobbled streets and leafy parks. Colourful flowers tumble down its wrought-iron balconies. Terrace cafés teem in summer, while wood-panelled bars are a cosy retreat in winter.

▶ **Population:** 82 400
⏱ **Michelin Map:** 571 E 4.
ℹ **Info:** Casa da Luz, Praza da Verdura. ☏986 09 08 90. www.visit-pontevedra.com, www.turismoriasbaixas.com.
▶ **Location:** Pontevedra, near the northern coast, is linked by motorway with Vigo (27km/17mi S) and Santiago de Compostela (57km/35mi N).
🚆 Pontevedra.

CASCO ANTIGUO★

The **Old Quarter** is between Calle Michelena, Calle del Arzobispo Malvar, Calle Cobián and the river. Glass-covered passages and picturesque squares (**Plaza da la Leña; del Teucro, de la Pedreira**) are enchanting. There are endless places to stop for a drink plus busy shopping streets such as **Sarmiento**.

The **Plaza de la Leña★** has beautiful facades; two 18C mansions have been converted into the **Museo de Pontevedra** (Pasantería 2–12; open Tue–Sat 10am–9pm, Sun & public hols 11am–2pm; closed 1 Jan, 25 Dec; ☏986 80 41 00; www.museo.depo.es). The ground floor holds Bronze Age **Celtic treasures★** and pre-1900 silverware. One storey up you'll find paintings including several 15C Aragonese Primitives.

The second mansion includes a reconstruction of a stateroom from a 19C Spanish frigate, the *Numancia*. On the upper floor are an antique kitchen and 19C Sargadelos ceramics. The museum also encompasses the ruins of the Iglesia Santo Domingo and the ex-collegiate Iglesia de la Compañía de Jesús, beside the Iglesia de San Bartolomé.

Alleyways and gardens surround the 15C–16C Plateresque **Basílica de Santa María la Mayor★** (Av. de Santa María 24; museum and tower open 10am-12pm, 5-9pm; €1 tower; ☏986 09 08 90). The **west front★** is carved like an altarpiece, divided into separate superimposed registers on which are reliefs of the Assumption of the Virgin and the Trinity.

At the summit is the Crucifixion at the centre of an openwork coping, finely carved with oarsmen and fishermen. The **interior** mingles Gothic (notched arches), Isabelline (slender cabled columns) and Renaissance (ribbed vaulting) styles.

San Bartolomé is an 18C Baroque church with fine sculptures including some by Pedro de Mena (Sarmiento 51; open Tue–Sun 9am-1pm, 6-10pm; ☏986 85 13 75).

Overlooking the gardens of Plaza da Ferrería is the simple Gothic facade of **San Francisco** church (Jardines de Castro San Pedro; open daily 7.30am-12.45pm, 4.30-6.45pm; ☏986 09 08 90). The interior features timber vaulting.

A small 18C **Pilgrim's Chapel** (Capilla de la Peregrina; Pl. de la Peregrina; open daily 9am–9pm; ☏886 15 15 55), with scallop-shaped floor plan and convex facade, contains a venerated statue of the patron saint of Pontevedra.

The **Ruínas de San Domingos** (Po. de Montero Ríos; closed for renovation as of Sep 2019; ☏986 80 41 00) are a study in medieval romanticism: The Gothic east end is overgrown with ivy. Inside are Roman steles, Galician coats of arms and tombs of nobles and craftsmen (beside the tools the latter used).

Ourense

Ourense (Orense in Castilian) has been famous for its hot springs since Antiquity. Its Roman bridge was and still is a crossing for pilgrims to Santiago de Compostela. The pedestrianised old town is packed with cafés and restaurants, whose terraces spill out on to the streets, shaded by the numerous churches and the town's solid Baroque *casonas* (houses).

▶ **Population:** 105 505

Michelin Map: 571 E 6, F 6 (town plan) – Galicia (Ourense).

Info: Isabel La Católica 2. ℘988 36 60 64. www.turismo deourense.gal.

Location: Ourense is 101km/ 62.7mi E of Vigo along the A 52 motorway; 100km/62mi SE of Pontevedra via the N 541; 105km/65mi SE of Santiago de Compostela on the N 525 and the AP 53. ▬Ourense (AVE).

SIGHTS

Catedral★

Pl. del Trigo 1. Open Mon–Sat 11am–2.30pm, 4-7pm, Sun 1–3pm, 4-7pm (Oct–Feb Mon–Thu and Sun until 6pm) €5. ℘988 22 09 92. www.catedralourense.com.

The 12–13C cathedral has been repeatedly modified. The **Portada Sur** (South Door), in the Compostelan style, is profusely decorated with carvings. The **Portada Norte** (North Door) has two statue columns and, beneath, a great ornamental arch, a 15C Deposition framed by a *Flight into Egypt* and statues of the Holy Women.

The interior is noteworthy for its pure lines. At the end of the 15C, a Gothic-Renaissance transitional-style **lantern★** was built above the transept. The ornate Gothic high altar retable is by Cornelius de Holanda. The 16C and 17C **Capilla del Santísimo Cristo** (Chapel of the Holy Sacrament), off the north transept, is decorated with exuberant sculpture in the Galician Baroque style.

The triple-arched **Pórtico del Paraíso★★** (Paradise Door), at the west end, has carvings and bright medieval colouring. The central arch shows the 24 Old Men of the Apocalypse; to the right is the Last Judgement. The pierced tympanum above, like the narthex vaulting, is 16C. A door in the south aisle opens onto the 13C chapter house, housing the **Museo Catedralicio** with a church plate, statues, chasubles and a 12C travelling altar.

♁ Termas (Hot Springs)★★

On the banks of the Río Minho.

A dozen or so hot spring facilities line the Río Minho; some are public and geared toward family (though splashing is forbidden); others are private and serene. **Termas Chavasqueira** (Mercado da Feira; Closed Mon; ℘988 214 821; www.termaschavasqueira.com) is the most popular with public (free) and private pools of varying temperatures.

Museo Arqueológico y de Bellas Artes

Pl. Mayor. Buildings have separate hours; see website for details. ℘988 22 38 84. www.musarqourense.xunta.es

Collections in the former bishop's palace on the Plaza Mayor include prehistoric specimens, cultural objects (mainly statues of warriors) and an early 18C woodcarving of the **Camino del Calvario★** (Stations of the Cross).

EXCURSIONS

Monasterio de Oseira★

▶ 34km/21mi NW. Leave Ourense on the N 525. After 23km/14mi turn right toward Cotelas. Visit only by guided tour Mon–Sat 10am, 11am, 12pm, 3.30pm, 4.30pm, 5.30pm, 6.30pm; Sun 12.45pm only. €3. ℘988 28 20 04. www.mosteirodeoseira.org.

This grand 12C Cistercian monastery, known as the 'Escorial of Galicia', was founded by Alfonso VII. It stands isolated in the Arenteiro Valley, a region that once abounded in bears, as the name suggests. The **facade** (1708) is in three sections. In a niche below the statue of Hope, which crowns the doorway, is the figure of a Nursing Madonna with St Bernard at her feet. Of note are the **escalera de honor** (grand staircase) and the **Claustro de los Medallones** (Medallion Cloisters), decorated with 40 busts of historic figures. The **church** (12C–13C), hidden behind a Baroque facade restrained in its Cistercian simplicity, saw the late-17C addition of frescoes. The **chapter house★** dates to the turn of the 16C and has outstanding rib vaulting.

Verín

❯ 69km/43mi SE along the A 52.

Verín is a lively, picturesque town with narrow paved streets, houses with glassed-in balconies, arcades and carved coats of arms. It is best known for its thermal springs, which were already famous during the Middle Ages and reputed for their treatment of rheumatic and kidney disorders.

Castillo de Monterrei

❯ 6km/3.7mi W. Open Wed–Sun 10.30am–1pm, 4–7pm. ℘988 41 80 02.

This formidable fortress compound was a frontier post throughout the Portuguese-Spanish wars. The complex included a monastery, hospital and houses, abandoned in the 19C.

The approach is up an avenue lined with lime trees that commands a **panorama★** of the valley below. Entering the castle youl pass through three walls, the outermost dating from the 17C. At the centre stands the square 15C Torre del Homenaje (Keep) and 14C Torre de las Damas (Lady's Tower). The courtyard is bounded by a three-storey arcade and is less austere than the rest of the building. The 13C church has a **portal★** delicately carved with a notched design and a tympanum showing Christ in Majesty between the symbols of the Evangelists. Opposite is the Parador de Verín.

Celanova

❯ 26km/16mi S on the N 540.

Celanova is famous for its **Monasterio de San Rosendo** (guided tours Mon-Sat 11am-12.30pm, 4.30-6pm, Sun 12.30pm; €2; ℘988 43 14 87), founded in 936 by San Rosendo, Bishop of San Martín de Mondoñedo. The **church** is a monumental late-17C edifice built in Baroque style. The coffered vaulting is decorated with geometrical designs, the cupola with volutes. An immense altarpiece (1697) occupies the back of the apse.

The **cloisters★★**, among the most beautiful in the region, took from 1550 until the 18C to complete.

Behind the church, the **Capilla de San Miguel** (opening hours as above; €1), is one of the monastery's earliest buildings (937) and a rare Mozarabic monument still in good condition.

Santa Comba de Bande

❯ 52km/32.5mi S along the N 540 (26km/16mi S of Celanova). 10km/6.2mi beyond Bande, head along a road to the right for 400m/440yd.

The small 7C Visigothic **church★** (call to arrange a visit; ℘988 44 31 40) overlooks the lake. The plan is that of a Greek cross, lit by a lantern turret. The apse is square and is preceded by a horseshoe-shaped triumphal arch resting on four pillars with Corinthian capitals.

Río Sil★

❯ 65km/40.3mi E. Follow the C 536; after 6km/3.7mi, turn left toward Luintra; continue 18km/11mi.

The ex-Benedictine monastery is now occupied by the **Parador de Santo Estevo** in a lush mountain **setting★**. The former church's Romanesque east end and cloisters were built to grandiose proportions, largely in the 16C.

Return downhill on the road to the left, toward the River Sil. Two dams control the river, which flows through **deep gorges★**; their sides are dotted with vineyards.

Lugo★

Lugo was capital of Roman Gallaecia, the legacy of which includes the town walls, old bridge and thermal baths. The old quarter huddles around the cathedral.

OLD TOWN
Murallas★★

Ronda de la Muralla.
The 2km/1.5mi-long Roman walls were built in the 3C, although they have been significantly modified. A UNESCO World Heritage site, they are made of schist slabs levelled at a uniform 10m/32.8ft in a continuous 2km/1.2mi perimetre with 10 gateways.

Catedral de Lugo★

Pl. Santa María. Open 8am–8.30pm; museum 11am–1pm. €5. ℘982 23 10 38.
The original Romanesque church (1129) saw Gothic and Baroque additions. The Chapel of the Wide-Eyed Virgin at the east end, by Fernando Casas y Novoa (who built the Obradoiro facade of the cathedral in Santiago de Compostela) has a Baroque rotunda and stone balustrade. The north doorway has a Romanesque **Christ in Majesty★**. The figure is above a capital curiously suspended, carved with the Last Supper.The nave has barrel vaulting and galleries, a feature common in pilgrimage churches. There are two immense wooden Renaissance altarpieces at the ends of the transept; the south one is signed by Cornelis de Holanda (1531). A door in the west wall of the south transept leads to the small but elegant **cloisters**.

City squares

The 18C **Palacio Episcopal**, facing the north door of the cathedral on **Plaza de Santa María**, is a typical *pazo*, one storey high with smooth stone walls, advanced square wings framing the central facade and decoration confined to the Gil Taboada coat of arms on the main doorway.

▶ **Population:** 98 007
Michelin Map: 571 C 7 (town plan) – Galicia (Lugo).
Info: Rúa Miño 10–12. ℘982 231 361. www.lugo.gal.
▶ **Location:** Lugo is 96km/ 59.6mi SE of A Coruña along the A6, 94km/58.4mi NE of Ourense on the N 540 and 135km/83.8mi SW Santiago de Compostela on the A 6 and A P9. ▰Lugo.
Don't Miss: The sundials of the Museo Provincial.
Timing: See the Cathedral and walls first, then explore the surrounding area.

Plaza del Campo, behind the palace, is lined by old houses. Calle de la Cruz, with its bars and restaurants, and **Praza Maior**, dominated by the 18C **town hall**, with its gardens and esplanade, are popular meeting places. The **Alejo Madarro** sweet shop (Reina 13; ℘982 22 97 14; www.madarro.net), famed for its tea cake (*pastas de té*), opened in 1891.

Museo Provincial de Lugo

Open Mon–Fri 9am–9pm, Sat 10.30am–2pm, 4.30–8pm. Sun & public hols 11am–2pm. Closed 1, 6 Jan; 22 May; 24, 25, 31 Dec. ℘982 24 21 12. www.museolugo.org.
This museum of regional art is housed in the former Monasterio de San Francisco. A room is devoted to ceramics from Sargadelos, and there are sundry artefacts from the Roman period. The former cloister of San Francisco contains a curious collection of sundials as well as several altars and sarcophagi.

A Coruña★

This aristocratic Galician city is set on a rocky islet linked to the mainland by a strip of sand. The charming old Ciudad quarter, at the northern end of the harbour with small squares and Romanesque churches, contrasts with to the wide streets of the business centre on the isthmus.

The warehouses and industry of the Ensanche district are a reminder that A Coruña is Spain's sixth-largest port and the main economic engine of the region.

▶ **Population:** 1.1 million
Michelin Map: 571 B 4 (town plan) – Galicia (A Coruña).
Info: Pl. María Pita 6. ℘981 92 30 93. www.turismocoruna.com.
Location: A Coruña, on the north coast, links to Santiago de Compostela by the AP 9 motorway. The A 6 heads SE past Lugo (97km/60mi SE) and on to Madrid. 🚆La Coruña/A Coruña (AVE).
Kids: Aquarium Finisterrae.

A BIT OF HISTORY

Spanish Armada – Philip II's ill-fated 'Invincible Armada' set out for England from A Coruña in 1588. A year later, Elizabeth I sent Drake to burn the city; fortunately it was saved by local heroine **María Pita**, who gave the alarm. **Fraught 19C politics** – During the Peninsular War, Marshal Soult of France clashed with the English in the Battle of Elviña/A Coruña in 1809. In the late 19C, A Coruña was a hotbed of liberal insurgents and suffered severe authoritarian reprisals.

SIGHTS

Colegiata de Santa María del Campo

Pl. Santa María 1. Open before and after Mass. ℘981 22 03 86.

This Romanesque church has a triple barrel-vaulted nave strengthened by arches with plaster borders. Note the fine 13C–14C portal, Gothic rose window and tower. A **Museum of Sacred Art** (*Arte Sacro*) is on one side of the church. In the square stands a 15C Calvary.

Iglesia de Santiago

Parrote 1. Open Mon–Fri 11am-1.30pm, 6.30-7.30pm. ℘981 20 56 96.

The building is Romanesque-Gothic and features a carved stone pulpit.

EL CENTRO (CENTRAL DISTRICT)
Avenida de la Marina★

The avenue facing the harbour has an arched, unbroken line of houses with glassed-in balconies, one of Galicia's most pleasing architectural sights. Along one side is the Paseo de la Dársena, and on the other, the **Jardines de Méndez Núñez**, gardens with a variety of flowering trees. Beneath it are two well-kept **urban beaches**, Orzán (popular for surfing) and Riazor.

Plaza de María Pita

The vast, café-lined square honours the city's heroine. This is a terrific place to begin an evening of tapas-crawling.

Museo Arqueolóxico e Histórico Castelo de Santo Antón

Pas. del Parrote. Open Jul–Aug Tue–Sat 10am–9pm, Sun & public hols 10am–3pm; Sep–Jun Tue–Sat 10am–7.30pm, Sun & public hols 10am–2.30pm. €2. ℘981 18 98 50. http://museos.xunta.gal/en/arqueoloxico-coruna.

This fortress dates to the period of Philip II and houses an archaeological museum with exhibits of prehistoric gold and silver.

Museo de Bellas Artes

Avda. Zalaeta. Open Tue–Fri 10am–8pm, Sat 10am–2pm, 4.30–8pm, Sun 10am–2pm. Closed hols. €2.40; Free Sat pm, Sun am, 18 May. ✆881 88 17 00. http://museobelasartescoruna.xunta.gal. Light and spacious exhibition rooms are dedicated to art from the 16–20C including sketches by **Goya**.

▲▲ Domus

Santa Teresa 1. Open Jan–Apr Mon–Fri 10am–6pm, Sat, Sun & public hols 11am–7pm; May, June, Sept–Dec Mon–Fri 10am–7pm, Sat, Sun & public hols 10am–7pm; July, Aug 10am–8pm. €2; Cinema free. ✆981 18 98 40. www.mc2coruna.org/domus.

This landmark modern **building★** by **Arata Isozaki** – a double curve evoking a sail that's covered in slate – is houses the city's museum of mankind. Its boasts 150 interactive stations and a 3D cinema.

▲▲ Aquarium Finisterrae

Po. Marítimo. Open Jan–Apr Mon–Fri 10am–6pm, Sat, Sun & public hols 11am–8pm; May, Jun, Sep–Dec Mon–Fri 10am–7pm, Sat, Sun & public hols 11am–8pm; Jul, Aug 10am–9pm. €10. ✆981 18 98 42.

The local aquarium with 338 species highlights local marine ecosystems.

La Casa de las Ciencias

Parque de Santa Margarita. Open, same hours as Domus (✆see above). €2. ✆981 18 98 40.

This hands-on museum features a planetarium and three floors of interactive exhibits. A Foucault pendulum oscillates in the central stairwell.

Torre de Hércules★

Av. de Navarra. Open Oct–May 10am–6pm, Jun–Sep 10am–9pm. €3; free Mon. ✆981 22 37 30. www.torredeherculesacoruna.com.

This is the oldest functioning lighthouse in the world, a UNESCO World Heritage site, dating to the 2C. The original outer ramp was enclosed in 1790. From the top (104m/341ft), there is a good **view** of the town and the coast.

EXCURSIONS

Costa de la Muerte (Coast of Death)

The coast between A Coruña and Cabo Finisterre is wild, harsh and majestic; whipped by storms, it's the graveyard of many a ship.

Tucked in its more sheltered coves are fishing villages like **Malpica de Bergantiños**, protected by the Cabo de San Adrián (opposite the Islas Sisargas, with a bird sanctuary) and **Camariñas**, a lively port town famous for its bobbin lace, which can be bought in various shops around the harbour.

Cabo Finisterre or Fisterra★ (Cape Finisterre)

Legend has it that the Romans arrived here and christened it Finis Terrae ('the end of the earth'). The lighthouse on the headland commands a fine **panorama★** of the Atlantic and the bay.

The coast **road★** to the cape looks down over the Bahía de Cabo Finisterre, a bay enclosed by three successive mountain chains. **Corcubión★**, west of Cabo Finisterre, is an old harbour town of emblazoned houses with glassed-in balconies. South of here the coast is a succession of coves, harbours and beaches against a backdrop of hills dotted with windmills. At **Ezaro** you can make a detour on the Rio Xallas, turning left onto the CA 2308, then right toward the **Noveira** waterfall. You will find several small waterfalls and natural pools up toward the Fervenza reservoirs.

Other nearby highlights include the long beaches 8km south of Ezaro at **Caldebarcos**; one is 6km long and 1km deep – to access it, go down the small road that runs past the church and continue straight to the car park.

Carnota

7km/4mi south of Caldebarcos, the village of Carnota is home to the longest **hórreo★** (granary on stone pillars) in Galicia. Built in 1760, it is 35m/115ft long, a triumph in popular architecture.

Rías Altas★

The Rías Altas are characterised by deep inlets that are backed by thick forests of pine and eucalyptus, thriving despite the low altitude of Galicia's northern coast.
The weather is grey and gusty in the winter, but the summer welcomes holidaymakers with plenty of sunny days. The *rías* described below are ordered from east to west.

- **Michelin Map:** 571 A 5-7, B4-8, C 2-5, D 2 – Galicia (Lugo, A Coruña).
- **Info:** Ferrol: Praza Camilo José Cela. ℘981 33 71 31; Foz: Edificio Cenima, Av. de Ribeira. ℘982 13 24 26; Viveiró: Av. de Ramón Canosa. ℘982 56 08 79. www.turismo.gal.
- **Location:** In the far NW corner of the Iberian Peninsula. 🚋 Nearest station La Coruña/A Coruña

SIGHTS

Ría de Ribadeo
See also COSTA VERDE.
The Ría de Ribadeo is the estuary of the Eo, which slackens its pace to wind gently between wide banks. There is a **view★** up the estuary from the bridge across the mouth of the river.
The old port of **Ribadeo** is an important regional centre and summer resort.

Praia das Catedrais★
The 'Beach of the Cathedrals' is so called for the curious shape of its cliffs, carved by the sea to resemble buttresses. Pass under the arches and you'll also find caves to explore, but beware high tides .

Ría de Foz
Foz, at the mouth of its namesake *ría*, is a small port with a fishing fleet. Its two beaches are popular in summer.

Iglesia de San Martín de Mondoñedo★
Barrio Caritel, Foz. 5km/3mi S of Foz. Take the Mondoñedo road, then immediately turn right. Open Jun-Sep Tue-Sat 11am-2pm, 4pm-8pm, Sun 11am-3pm, Oct-May Wed-Fri am only, Sat-Sun 11am-2pm, 4.30-7pm .
℘982 13 26 07.
On a summit, this ancient church was once part of a monastery and an episcopal seat until 1112. Unusually for the region, it shows no sign of Compostelan influence. The east end, with Lombard bands, is supported by massive buttresses; the transept **capitals★** are naively carved and rich in anecdotal detail: One shows a table overflowing with food while a dog licks the feet of a suffering Lazarus.

Mondoñedo
23km/14mi SW along the N 634.
The small town of Mondoñedo rises out of the hollow of a lush valley. Streets are lined with balconied white houses bearing coats of arms. The cathedral square is quaint with its arcades and *solanas* (glassed-in galleries).
The immense facade of the **Cathedral★** (Pl. Catedral; open 10am–2pm, 4–8pm; €2 museum; ℘982 50 7 77) combines the Gothic grace of the three large portal arches and the rose window, all dating to the 13C, with the grandiose Baroque style of towers added five centuries later.
Late 14C frescoes decorate the interior, one above the other (below the extraordinary 1710 organ) illustrating the Massacre of the Innocents and the Life of St Peter. There is a Rococo retable at the high altar and a polychrome wood statue of the Virgin in the south ambulatory; it is known as the English Virgin as the statue was brought from St Paul's, London, in the 16C. The classical **cloisters** were added in the 17C.

Ría de Viveiro

All **Viveiro** retains of its town walls is the Puerta de Carlos V (Charles V Gate), emblazoned with the emperor's arms. In summer, the port becomes a holiday resort, and on the fourth Sunday in August, visitors from all over Galicia flock to the Romeria do Naseiro festival. Holy Week processions are particularly dramatic here with participants walking on their knees.

Ría de Santa María de Ortigueira

The *ría* is deep and surrounded by green hills. **Ortigueira** has quays bordered by well-kept gardens. In mid-July it hosts Spain's largest **Celtic music festival★** (www.festivaldeortigueira.com).

Santuario de San Andrés de Teixido★

Open June–Sep 9am–10pm; Oct–May 9am–6pm. ℘981 48 24 96.
This stone hermitage has long been a site of pilgrimage and is worth a visit for the views alone.

Ría de Cedeira

Here lies a small, deeply enclosed *ría* with beautiful beaches. The road gives good **views** of **Cedeira** (summer resort).

Ría de Ferrol

The *ría* forms a wide harbour entered by a channel guarded by two forts. In the 18C, **Ferrol** (🚌Avenida de Compostela) became (and remains) a naval base. The symmetry of the old quarter dates to the same period.

Betanzos★

Betanzos, a medieval port that has long since silted up, stands on a hill at the end of a *ría*. Its old quarter retains three richly ornamented Gothic churches and white houses with glassed-in balconies, and its taverns serve the local speciality, *tortilla de Betanzos*, an ultra-runny rendition of the classic Spanish omelette.

Iglesia de Santa María del Azogue★

Pl. de Fernán Pérez de Andrade. Open Jun-Sep 10am-1.30pm, 4.30-7pm, Sep-May 10am-1.30pm, 4.30-6pm. ℘981 77 04 62.
Visit this 14–15C church at dusk, when its curiously asymmetrical facade glows pink. Niches flanking the door hold statues of the Virgin and the Archangel Gabriel.

Iglesia de San Francisco★

Pl. de Fernán Pérez Andrade. Open same hours as preceding church. Guided tours available. ℘981 770 110.
This Franciscan monastery church in the shape of a Latin Cross was built in 1387 by the Count Fernán Pérez de Andrade. It is remarkable for the many tombs along its walls, including Pérez de Andrade's own, supported by a wild boar and a bear, his heraldic beasts. Scenes of the hunt adorn the sides of the tomb.

Iglesia de Santiago

Pl. de Lanzós. Open same hours as preceding churches. Guided tours available. ℘981 77 66 66.
The local tailors' guild erected this church was built in the 15C. Above the main door is a carving of St James Matamoros (Moorslayer) on horseback. Alongside is the arcaded 16C **ayuntamiento** (town hall).

Museo das Mariñas

Emilio Romay 1. Open Mon–Fri 10am–1pm, 4–8pm; Sat 10.30–1pm. €1.20. ℘981 77 19 46.
Despite its nautical name, this is a local history and ethnography museum. Housed in a former convent, it features displays of Roman archaeology, traditional dress and Galician art.

Ría de A Coruña

♿See A CORUÑA

Castilla y León: Burgos, León and Palencia

These three provinces of Castilla y León occupy the northern part of Spain's semi-arid *meseta*. Fortified towns such as Léon and Palencia rise above vast plains of cereal crops and remind today's visitors of this area's importance in the establishment of the Kingdom of Castille and its power during the so-called Reconquista. Most of the region's population is concentrated in the thriving university towns of Burgos and León, but there are dozens of isolated, sparsely populated villages where life continues largely as it did in centuries past. Adapted to the hardy climate, the cuisine here is largely stick-to-your-ribs fare – think bean stews, lentils, pork sausages and – a León delicacy – *cecina*, air-dried cured beef, all washed down with black-horse wines like Mencía (red) or Albarín (white).

Reclics of a glorious past

León was once the capital of a kingdom that covered nearly a quarter of present-day Iberia, and its old centre retains splendid monuments from this period. In the 15C, to restore royal authority and promote Catholicism in the region, Ferdinand and Isabella became patrons of the arts; León's Cathedral, with the richest stained glass in Spain, and its Pantéon Real, are emblematic of the era. The old town's buzzing bars entertain a sizeable student population out for tapas and *cortitos* (local jargon for quarter-pints of beer). **Burgos** was the ancient capital of Castilla and is known the world over for its Gothic cathedral, one of the most awe-inspiring in Europe. It houses the remains of El Cid.

The city benefited from a restoration programme that widened and pedestrianised the old town's riverfront. Summer festivals, like those of San Pedro y San Pablo, and the Día de las Peñas, are celebrated with processions, bullfights and street food including the city's nationally famous *morcilla de Burgos*, black pudding made with rice. **Aguilar de Campoo** marks the northeast border of the region, and from the nearby Pico de Tres Mares, there is a gorgeous panorama across to the Picos de Europa in Cantabria.

Highlights

1 Gasp-worthy **Burgos cathedral**, a triumph in Gothic architecture (p308)

2 Panorama from the **Pico de Tres Mares** (p314)

3 The 900-year-old church **San Martín de Frómista** (p315)

4 Ancient and modern artwork at **León's Museo and MUSAC** (p318)

5 Rock formations at the **Cuevas de Valporquero** (p319)

Burgos cathedral

Burgos★

Burgos sits on the banks of the River Arlanzón on a windswept plateau at the heart of the Meseta. Its raison d'être is its colossal cathedral, whose lofty Gothic spires soar above the city's skyline.

A BIT OF HISTORY

Founded in 884, Burgos was capital of Castilla (and from 1230, of Castilla y León) until the fall of Granada in 1492. Commerce and the arts flourished afterward: The town became a wool centre for the sheep farmers of the Mesta association (see SORIA, p189), and architects and sculptors from northern Europe arrived and transformed monuments.

Burgos would become Spain's capital of Gothic architecture with outstanding works built including the cathedral, Monasterio de las Huelgas Reales (Royal Convent of Las Huelgas) and Cartuja de Miraflores Carthusian monastery. The end of the 16C saw the decline of the Mesta and with it the town's prosperity.

Land of El Cid (c. 1040–99) – The exploits of Rodrigo Díaz of Vivar light up the late-11C history of Castilla. This brilliant captain, better known as El Cid, supported the ambitious King of Castilla, Sancho II, then Alfonso VI, who succeeded his brother in dubious circumstances. Alfonso, jealous of El Cid's exploits against the Moors, banished the hero. As a result, Díaz joined forces with the Moorish King of Zaragoza and subsequently fought Christian and Muslim armies with equal fervour. Most famously, he captured Valencia at the head of 7 000 men, chiefly Muslims, after a nine-month siege in 1094. He was finally defeated in 1099 by the Moors at Cuenca and died soon after. His widow held Valencia against the Muslims until 1102, when she set the city ablaze and fled to Castilla with El Cid's body. The couple were buried in San Pedro de Cardeña (10km/6.2mi SE

of Burgos), their ashes moved to Burgos Cathedral in 1921.

Legend – and a dose of nationalist propaganda – transformed the stalwart but ruthless warrior, also known as the Campeador (Champion) of Castilla, into a national hero. The epic poem *El Cantar del Mío Cid* first appeared in 1180 and was followed by ballads. In 1618, Guillén de Castro wrote a romanticised version, *Las Mocedades del Cid* (Youthful Adventures of El Cid), upon which Corneille, in 1636, based his drama *Le Cid*. In 1961, Charlton Heston immortalised El Cid in the eponymous Hollywood epic.

It's no coincidence that Franco, who fancied himself a knight protecting some mythical Spanish past, ruled from Burgos from 1936 to 1938.

SIGHTS

Cathedral★★★

Pl. Santa María. Open third wk Mar–Oct 9.30am–7.30pm; rest of year 10am–7pm. Closed 25 Dec & 1 Jan. €7. 947 204 712. www.catedraldeburgos.es.

The third-largest Cathedral in Spain (after Sevilla and Toledo), Burgos illustrates the transformation of French and German Flamboyant Gothic into an exuberant Spanish style. Ferdinand

---

▶ **Population:** 176 115

Michelin Map: 575 E 18 –19 (town plan).

Info: Nuño Rasura, 7 947 288 874 . www.turismoburgos.org.

Location: Burgos is in the north of Spain, 88km/54.6m from Palencia, 117km/73mi from Vitoria-Gasteiz and 120km/74.5mi from Valladolid; at 856m/2 808ft, it is exposed to bitter winds in winter. Burgos.

Don't Miss: The cathedral, monasteries and circular main square.

Timing: A full day or slightly less.

III laid the first stone in 1221. Maurice the Englishman, then-Bishop of Burgos, had collected drawings on a journey through France (at that time influenced by the Gothic style) that inspired the design of the nave, aisles and portals, built by local architects. The 15C saw the construction of the west front spires and the Capilla del Condestable (Constable's Chapel). Foreign architects and sculptors were brought in by another Burgos prelate, Alonso de Cartagena, on his return from the Council of Basel; they found inspiration in Mudéjar arabesques and other Hispano-Moorish elements. The most talented of the lot, Burgundian **Felipe Vigarny**, Fleming **Gil de Siloé** and Rhinelander **Johan of Cologne**, assimilated fast and, with their progeny, created what was essentially a Burgos school of sculpture. The cloisters were added in the 14C, while the magnificent lantern over the transept crossing – the original of which collapsed after some overly ambitious design work by Simon of Cologne – was rebuilt by Juan de Vallejo in the mid-16C.

Exterior – A walk round the cathedral reveals how the architects took ingenious advantage of the sloping ground (the upper gallery of the cloisters is level with the Cathedral pavement) to introduce small precincts and closes.

West front – The ornate upper area, with its frieze of Spanish kings and two openwork spires, is the masterwork of Johan of Cologne.

Interior – The design of the interior is French-inspired, while the finishings bear a clearly Spanish stamp.

Portada de la Coronería – The statues at the jambs have the grace of their French Flamboyant Gothic originals, though their robes show more movement. The Plateresque **Portada de la Pellejería** (Skinner's Doorway) in the transept was designed by Francis of Cologne early in the 16C.

Near the east end, the Constable's Chapel, with its Isabelline decoration and lantern with pinnacles, sticks out as a late additions.

Portada del Sarmental – The covings are filled with figures from the Celestial Court. The tympanum is a remarkable showing of each Evangelist in a different position as he writes.

Crucero, Coro and Capilla Mayor★★ – The splendid star-ribbed lantern of the transept crossing rises on four massive pillars to 54m/177ft above the funerary stones of El Cid and Ximena, inlaid in the crossing pavement. The imposing unit of 103 walnut choir stalls, carved by Felipe Vigarny between 1507 and 1512, illustrates biblical stories on the upper, back rows and mythological and burlesque scenes at the front. The handsome recumbent statue of wood (13C), plated with enamelled copper, on the tomb at the centre is of Bishop Maurice. The high altar retable is a 16C Renaissance work in high relief against a Neoclassical background of niches and pediments.

Claustro – The 14C Gothic cloisters are a panorama of Burgos sculpture in stone, terracotta and polychrome wood.

The **Capilla de Santiago** (St James' Chapel) contains the Cathedral treasure of plate and liturgical objects.

In the **Capilla de Santa Catalina** (St Catherine's Chapel) are manuscripts and documents including the marriage contract of El Cid. On the carved and painted consoles (15C), Moorish kings pay homage to the King of Castilla.

The **sacristía** (sacristy) houses the *Christ at the Column* by Diego de Siloé, a supreme example of Spanish Expressionism in post-16C Iberian sculpture. The **sala capitular** (chapter house) displays, in addition to 15C and 16C Brussels tapestries symbolising the theological and cardinal virtues, a Hispano-Flemish diptych, a *Virgin and Child* by Memling and, above, a painted wood Mudéjar *artesonado* ceiling (16C).

Capilla del Condestable★★ – An elaborate grille closes off the area. The Isabelline chapel, founded by Hernández de Velasco, Constable of Castilla, in 1482 and designed by Simon of Cologne, is lit by a lantern surmounted by a cupola with star-shaped vaulting.

All the great early Renaissance sculptors of Burgos cooperated in the decoration of the walls and altarpiece; the heraldic displays in the chapel are striking.

On either side of the altar, the Constable's escutcheon, held by male figures, seems to hover over the balustrades of the tribune.

Statues of the Constable and his wife lie on their tomb, carved in Carrara marble; beside them is an immense garnet-coloured marble funerary stone for their descendants. To the right, a Plateresque door leads to the sacristy (1512), where there is a *Mary Magdalene* painted by Pietro Ricci.

Girola★ – The *trasaltar* (at the back of the high altar), carved partly by **Felipe Vigarny**, shows the Ascent to Calvary.

Escalera Dorada aka Escalera de la Coronería – The harmoniously proportioned golden, or coronation, staircase was designed in pure Renaissance style by Diego de Siloé in the early 16C. Twin flights are outlined by a gilded banister by the French master ironsmith Hilaire. Each of the side chapels is a museum of Gothic and Plateresque art: **Gil de Siloé** and Diego de la Cruz collaborated on the huge Gothic altarpiece in the **Capilla de Santa Ana★**, which illustrates the saint's life. In the centre is a Tree of Jesse with, at its heart, the first meeting of Anne and Joachim, and at the top, the Virgin and Child.

At the beginning of the Cathedral nave, near the roof, is the Papamoscas, or **Flycatcher Clock**, with a jack that opens its mouth on the striking of the hours.

In the **Capilla del Santo Cristo** (Chapel of Holy Christ) is a Crucifixion complete with hair and covered with buffalo hide to resemble human flesh.

The **Capilla de la Presentación** (Chapel of the Presentation) contains the tomb of the Bishop of Lerma, carved by Felipe Vigarny, and the **Capilla de la Visitación** (Chapel of the Visitation), the tomb of Alonso de Cartagena by Gil de Siloé.

Museo de Burgos★

C. Miranda 13. Open Jul–Sep Tue–Sat 10am–2pm, 5–8pm, Sun & hols 10am–2pm; Oct–Jun Tue–Sat 10am–2pm, 4–7pm, Sun & public hols 10am–2pm. €1.20; Free Sat–Sun, 23 Apr, 18 May, 12 Oct, 6 Dec. ✆947 26 58 75. www.museodeburgos.com.

Learn about the region's ethnography at this excellent museum.

Prehistoric and Archaeological Department – This section, in a Renaissance mansion, holds objects from the Prehistoric to Visigothic periods. Of particular interest are the rooms devoted to Iron Age sites, the Roman settlement of Clunia and funerary steles.

Fine Arts Department – The Casa de Ángulo houses 9C-20C Castilian art. There are several precious items from the Santo Domingo Monastery at Silas: an 11C **Hispano-Moorish casket★**, carved in ivory and highlighted with enamel plaques; the 12C **Frontal** or **Urn of Santo Domingo★**, in enamelled copper; and a 10C **marble diptych**. On the **tomb★** of Juan de Padilla, Gil de Siloé beautifully rendered the face and robes of the deceased. The collection of 15C paintings includes a *Christ Weeping* by Jan Mostaert.

👤👤 Museo de la Evolución Humana★

Paseo Sierra de Atapuerca. Open Tue –Fri 10am–2.30pm, 4.30–8pm; Sat, Sun and Jul–Aug 10am–8pm. Closed 1 & 6 Jan, 16 & 29 Jun, 25 Dec. €6. Free Wed pm, Tue & Thu after 7pm. ✆902 024 246. www.museoevolucionhumana.com

This sprawling, ultramodern museum, opened in 2010, chronicles human evolution from its beginnings to the present with exhibition themes including the archaeological site of Atapuerca, Darwin's theories, hunter-gatherer societies and more. Life-size models and hands-on stations bring the material to life.

Arco de Santa María★

Po. del Espolón. Interior open Tue–Sat 11am–2pm, 5–9pm, Sun 11am–2pm. Closed public hols. ✆947 28 88 68.

The 14C gateway in the city walls was modified to form a triumphal arch for Emperor Charles V and embellished with statues of the famous including (top right) El Cid with Charles V. Inside are the **Sala de Poridad**, with magnificent Mudéjar cupola, and the pharmacy of the ex-Hospital de San Juan.

Iglesia de San Esteban: Museo del Retablo

C. San Esteban 1. Open Tue–Sun 11am–2pm, 5–8pm. €2. ℘947 27 37 52. www.museodelretablo.com.
Within this 14C Gothic church★ are 18 retables, exhibited in three naves according to their religious significance. The *coro alto* contains a small collection of gold and silverwork.

Iglesia de San Gil Abad

C. San Gil 12. Open mid-Jul–mid-Sep Mon–Sat 10am–2pm, 4–7pm; Oct–Jun before or after Mass only.
℘947 26 11 49. www.sangil.org
A sober facade belies a splendid Late Gothic interior. Noteworthy are the Nativity and Buena Mañana chapels, the latter containing a retable by Gil de Siloé.

Casa del Cordón

Pl. de la Libertad. Patio open Mon–Fri 12pm–2pm, 7–9pm. ℘947 251 791.
The 15C palace of the Constables of Castilla (now a cultural centre) displays a thick Franciscan cord motif, hence its moniker. Columbus was received by the Catholic Monarchs here on his return from his second voyage to America.

Museo Marceliano Santa María

Pl. de San Juan. Open Tue–Sat 11am–2pm, 5–9pm, Sun 11am–2pm. Closed public hols. ℘947 20 56 87.
Impressionist canvases by Marceliano Santa María (1866–1952) are shown in the ruins of the former Benedictine monastery of San Juan.

Hospital del Rey

Founded by Alfonso VIII as a hospital for pilgrims, the hospital retains its entrance, the Patio de Romeros, with its fine 16C Plateresque facade. Today, it is the seat of the University of Burgos.

Castillo de Burgos

Open Jun–Sept 10am–8:30pm, Apr–Jun 11am–6.30pm, Oct–Mar 11am–2.30pm. ℘947 20 38 57.
This largely ruined (yet recently restored) hilltop fortress once protected the city from invaders. Built around 9C, it was destroyed by Napoleon's troops. Views from here are terrific.

EXCURSIONS

Monasterio Santa María Real de las Huelgas★★ (Royal Convent of las Huelgas)

Compases. ◑ 1.5km/1mi W of Burgos; take Av. del Monasterio de las Huelgas. Open Tue–Sat 10am–2pm, 4–6.30pm, Sun 10.30am–3pm. €6, free for EU citizens Wed & Thu pm and for all 18 May. ℘947 20 16 30.
www.monasteriodelashuelgas.org, www.patrimonionacional.es.
Las Huelgas Reales, the summer palace of the kings of Castilla, was converted in 1180 into a convent by Alfonso VIII and his wife Eleanor, daughter of Henry II of England. The nuns were Cistercians of high lineage, the abbess all-powerful; by the 13C the convent's influence, both spiritual and temporal, extended to more than 50 towns, and it had become a place of retreat for members of the house of Castilla and the royal pantheon.
Rearrangement over the centuries has resulted in a somewhat divided building, featuring the Cistercian style of the 12C and 13C alongside Romanesque and Mudéjar features (13C–15C) as well as Plateresque furnishings.
The clean lines of the church are textbook Cistercian. The interior is divided by a screen: from the transept, open to all, you can see the revolving pulpit (1560), in gilded ironwork, which enabled the preacher to be heard on either side. Royal and princely tombs, originally coloured, rich in heraldic devices and historical legend, line the aisles, while in the middle of the nave (the nuns' *coro*) is the tomb of Alfonso VIII and Eleanor of England. The rood screen retable, carved and coloured in

the Renaissance style, is surmounted by a fine 13C Deposition. The altar is flanked on each side by two handsome 13C and 14C tombs.

Enough fragments of Mudéjar vaulting stucco remain in the 13–15C **Gothic cloisters** to suggest the delicacy of the strapwork inspired by Persian ivories and fabrics.

The **chapter house** holds the **pendón★**, a trophy from the Battle of Las Navas de Tolosa, adorned with silk *appliqué*.

The **Romanesque cloisters** (late 12C) has elegant slender paired columns topped by stylised capitals. Several rooms in this part of Alfonso VIII's former palace were decorated by Moors.

The **Capilla de Santiago** (Chapel of St James) retains an *artesonado* ceiling with original colour and stucco frieze. According to legend, the statue of the saint with articulated arms conferred knighthoods on princes of royal blood. The fabrics, court dress and finery displayed in the **Museo de Telas Medievales★** provide a vivid view of royal wear in 13C Castilla. Some of these exhibits were found in the royal tombs; the most valuable came from the tomb of the Infante Fernando de la Cerda (who died in 1275), son of Alfonso X, the Wise: Fortunately escaping the French desecration of 1809, the tomb yielded a long tunic, *pellote* (voluminous trousers with braces) and large mantle, all of the same material embroidered with silk and silver thread. Note too the *birrete*, a silk crown adorned with pearls and precious stones.

A diminutive but worthwhile textile museum rounds out the visit.

Cartuja de Miraflores (Miraflores Carthusian Monastery)

Ctra. de la Cartuja. ❯ 4km/2.5mi E. Open Mon–Sat 10.15am–3pm, 4–6pm, Sun & public hols 11am–3pm, 4–6pm. ℘947 25 25 86. www.cartuja.org.
This former royal foundation, entrusted to the Carthusians in 1442, was chosen by Juan II as a pantheon for himself and his second wife, Isabel of Portugal. The church was completed in Isabelline Gothic style in 1498.

Iglesia★ – The sobriety of the facade, relieved only by the buttress finials and the founders' escutcheons belies elegant interior vaulting and gilded keystones.

Sculpture ensemble in the Capilla Mayor★★★ – Designed by the Fleming Gil de Siloé at the end of the 15C, this ensemble comprises the high altarpiece, the royal mausoleum and a funerary recess. The polychrome **altarpiece**, by Siloé and Diego de la Cruz, is striking: The usual rectangular compartments are replaced by circles crowded with biblical figures. The white marble **mausoleo real** (royal mausoleum) is in the form of an eight-pointed star in which you can make out recumbent statues of Juan II and Queen Isabel, parents of Isabel the Catholic. Dominating the exuberant Flamboyant Gothic decoration of scrolls, canopies, pinnacles, cherubim and armorial bearings, executed with rare virtuosity, are the four Evangelists. In an ornate **recess** in the north wall is the tomb of the Infante Alfonso, whose premature death gave the throne to his sister Isabel the Catholic. The statue of the prince at prayer is technically brilliant if informal (compared to that of Juan de Padilla in the Museo de Burgos (❍see Sights, p308).

Also in the church are a 15C Hispano-Flemish triptych (to the right of the altar) and Gothic **choir stalls** carved with an infinite variety of arabesques.

Sierra de Atapuerca

❯ Take the N 120 toward Logroño. In Ibeas de Juarros (13km/8mi), head to the Emiliano Aguirre hall (beside the main road). See website for times. €6 for the archaeological site and €5 for the Experimental Archaeology Centre. ℘947 42 1000. www.atapuerca.org.
These scrubby hills are the site of one of the world's most important palaeontological sites. Excavations at **La Dolina** uncovered remains of hominids who lived around 800 000 years ago. The fossil register at the **Sima de los Huesos** (Chasm of Bones) is the largest in Europe, dating to 400 000 –200 000 years ago. Visitors can walk along the

trench and visit a small archaeological museum.

Covarrubias★

The quintessentially Castilian village of half-timbered houses and a Renaissance palace is partly surrounded by medieval ramparts. Covarrubias is the burial place of Fernán González, one of Castilla's great historic figures and the catalyst for the kingdom's independence.

The Gothic collegiate church, the **Colegiata★**, contains 20 medieval tombs, including those of Fernán González and the Norwegian Princess Cristina who married the Infante Philip of Castilla in 1258 (Pl. Rey Chidasvinto 3; prebooked guided visits from 10.30am Wed–Mon; ℘947 40 63 11).

Note the paintings by Pedro Berruguete and Van Eyck in the **Museo Paroquial** (Pl. Rey Chindasvinto 3; open Wed–Mon 10.30am–2pm, 4–7pm; €2). A 15C Flemish **triptych★**, with central relief of the Adoration of the Magi, is said to be by Gil de Siloé.

Monasterio de Santo Domingo de Silos★★

Valle de Tabladillo. ❷ 18km/11mi SE. Phone for monastery opening times. Cloisters open Tue–Sun 10am–1pm, 4.30–6pm. Closed 1 & 6 Jan, 19 Mar, 15 Aug, 12 Oct, 1 Nov; 8, 20 & 25 Dec. €3.50 ℘947 39 00 68. www.abadiadesilos.es. This site, originally Visigothic, was occupied by Benedictine monks from France in 1880. The monastery is renowned for its concerts of Gregorian chants. The **cloisters★★★** are among the most beautiful in Spain.

Garganta de la Yecla

❷ 3km/1.8mi SW of Santo Domingo de Silos via the BU 910 – 🚶 20min. A footpath follows a narrow gorge.

Lerma

❷ 23km/14.3mi W along the C 110. Lerma owes its splendour and Classical town plan to the extravagance and corruption of the **Duke of Lerma**, Philip III's early-17C favourite.

Cloisters, Monasterio de Santo Domingo de Silos

© Mike Randolph/age fotostock

The quarter built by the duke retains steep cobbled streets and houses with wood or stone porticoes, charming despite – to the chagrin of visitors – somehow resisting pedestrianisation. The ducal palace, with its austere facade, stands on the spacious **Plaza Mayor★**. The **Colegiata** church (guided tours organised by tourist office; ℘947 17 70 02; www.citlerma.com) has a 17C gilded bronze statue by Juan de Arfe of the duke's nephew, Archbishop Cristóbal de Rojas.

Quintanilla de las Viñas

❷ 24km/15mi N. Take the C 110, the N 234 toward Burgos, then bear right onto a signposted road.

The road follows the Arlanza Valley. Below and to the right are the ruins of the **Monasterio de San Pedro de Arlanza**. Though only the apse and transept of the **Iglesia de Quintanilla de las Viñas★** remain, it is of great archaeological importance (phone for opening hours; ℘947 28 15 00).

ADDRESSES

🛏 STAY

🛏 **Hotel Mesón del Cid** – Pl. Sta. María 8. ℘947 20 87 15. www.mesondelcid.es. 55 rooms. This family-run hotel in a 15C printing press exists at the intersection of comfort and affordability. Request a cathedral-facing room.

🍴 EAT

🍽🍽🍽 **Casa Ojeda** – Calle Vitoria 5. ℘947 20 90 52. www.restauranteojeda. com. Closed Sun eve. A 19C wood-burning oven still churns out sigh-worthy roast meats, like suckling pig and milk-fed lamb, at this Burgos stalwart in business since 1912.

Aguilar de Campoo

The Castillo de Aguilar stands on a desolate outcrop typical of this part of the Meseta. Below the castle stretches the medieval old town, with its handsome main square, gateways, walls, and mansions adorned with coats of arms.

- ▶ **Population:** 6 842
- ⚲ **Michelin Map:** 575 D 17.
- **Info:** Paseo Cascajera 10. ☎979 12 36 41. www.aguilardecampoo.com.
- **Location:** Aguilar is 115km/71mi NE of Burgos. 🚂Aguila de Campoo.
- **Don't Miss:** A drive to the Pico de Tres Mares.
- ⏱ **Timing:** Allow half a day.

SIGHTS

Colegiata de San Miguel

Closed for renovation as of Sep 2019. ☎979 12 36 41.

This Gothic church has Romanesque elements and two fine 16C tombs bearing statues of the Marquesses of Aguilar at prayer. Look for the lifelike sculpted tomb of archpriest García González.

Monasterio de Santa María la Real

Ctra. de Cervera. On the edge of town toward Cervera de Pisuerga. Open Sep-Jun Mon-Sat 10am-1pm, 4-6pm; Jul-Aug 10am-2pm, 5-8pm. Guided visits €5. ☎979 12 30 53. www.santamarialareal.org.

This thoroughly restored transitional (12C–13C) monastery houses a Romanesque interpretation centre. There is also a hotel and restaurant.

🚗 DRIVING TOUR

Pico de Tres Mares via Reinosa

66km/41mi N.

Cross the vast plain and ascend the south face of the Cordillera Cantábrica.

▷ Follow the A 67.

Cervatos

The **antigua colegiata**★ (open 10am–2pm), a Romanesque former collegiate church, bears imaginative carved **decoration**★. The portal tympanum bears a meticulous openwork design. There is a frieze of lions , while varied figures decorate the modillions.

The carving on the capitals and consoles supporting the arch ribs is dense and sophisticated, and the 14C nave has intersecting rib vaulting.

▷ Continue 5km/3mi, then turn right.

Retortillo

Only an oven-vaulted apse and arch with capitals illustrating warriors remain of a small Romanesque **church**. Adjacent are the ruins of a villa of the Roman city of **Julióbriga.**

▷ Return to the A 67.

Reinosa

The nearby Embalse del Ebro (a reservoir) and Alto Campoo ski resort (☎942 77 92 22; www.altocampoo.com) make this a growing tourist centre.

▷ From Reinosa, take the CA 183 to the Pico de Tres Mares (27km/17mi).

Pico de Tres Mares★★★

On the way, paths from Fontibre lead to a greenish pool, the **source of the Ebro** (Fuente del Ebro), Spain's largest river, at an altitude of 881m/2 890ft. ⛷To the Pico de Tres Mares by chairlift (Dec–Apr). Rivers flow from the peak (2 175m/7 136ft) to three seas. At the crest is a splendid **panorama**★★★.

Palencia

Palencia is a tranquil provincial capital situated in the fertile Tierra de Campos region. Alfonso VIII created the first Spanish university here in 1208. Irrigation of the region has opened up an important horticultural industry.

CATHEDRAL★★

Pl. de la Inmaculada. Open May–Oct Mon–Fri 10am–1.30pm, 4–6pm, 6.35 –7.30; Sat 10am–2pm, 4–5.30pm, 6.45 –7.30pm; Sun 4.30–8pm (Nov-Apr Sun 4-7pm). €5. Guided tours available. ℘979 70 13 47. www.catedraldepalencia.org.

Palencia's oft-overlooked cathedral is a 14C–16C Gothic edifice with Renaissance features. The original 7C Visigothic chapel lay forgotten during the Moorish occupation until Sancho III de Navarra came upon it while hunting.

Interior★★

The cathedral contains an impressive concentration of art in all the styles of the early 16C: Flamboyant Gothic, Isabelline, Plateresque and Renaissance. The monumental high altar **retable** (early 16C) was carved by Felipe Vigarny and painted by Juan of Flanders and is surmounted by a Crucifix by Juan de Valmaseda.

The 16C tapestries on the sides were commissioned by Bishop Fonseca. The *coro* grille, with a delicately wrought upper section, is by Gaspar Rodríguez (1563). The choir stalls are Gothic; the organ gallery, above, is dated 1716.

The **Capilla del Sagrario** (Chapel of the Holy Sacrament) is exuberantly Gothic with a rich altarpiece by Valmaseda (1529), and the central **triptych★** is a masterpiece, painted in Flanders by Jan Joest de Calcar in 1505 – the donor, Bishop Fonseca, is shown at its centre. The collection of the **Museo Catedralicio★** includes a *St Sebastian* by El Greco and four 15C Flemish **tapestries★** of the Adoration, the Ascension, Original Sin and the Resurrection of Lazarus.

▶ **Population:** 81 552
⚙ **Michelin Map:** 575 F 16.
🖹 **Info:** Mayor Principal 31. ℘979 70 65 23. www.palenciaturismo.es.
◉ **Location:** Palencia is close to the A 62 heading NW to Burgos (88km/55mi) and SE to Valladolid (50km/ 31mi) and Salamanca (166km/104mi). 🚇Palencia.
◈ **Don't Miss:** The cathedral.

EXCURSIONS

Iglesia de San Martín de Frómista★★

◉29km/18mi NE along the N 611. Open Apr–Sep 9.30am–2pm, 4.30–8pm; Oct–Mar 10am–2pm, 3.30–6pm. €1.50. ℘979 81 01 28.

Pilgrims on the way to Santiago de Compostela used to stop here; however, the only vestige of the once-famous Benedictine **Monasterio de San Martín** is a church, built in 1066, with beautifully matched stone blocks of considerable size. The structure was a model for many others in the region.

Baños de Cerrato

◉14km/8.7mi SE.

◉ Cross the railway at Venta de Baños; turn right toward Cevico de la Torre. Bear left at the first crossroads.

Iglesia de San Juan Bautista★

Open Tue–Sun Apr–Sep 10.30am– 2pm, 5–8pm; Oct–Mar 11am–2pm, 4–6pm. €2; Free Wed, 18 May, 24 Jun, 23 Aug. ℘979 77 03 38.

This is the oldest church in Spain, built by the Visigothic king, Recceswinth, while he was taking the waters in Baños de Cerrato, in 661.

León★★

León, once the capital of a kingdom, was an important pilgrim stop on the Camino de Santiago and retains many superb Romanesque and Gothic monuments. Buoyed by the arrival of the AVE high-speed train, today it is a university town with an electric tapas scene that's on the up-and-up.

- ▶ **Population:** 125 754
- ⏱ **Michelin Map:** 575 E 13.
- 🚩 **Info:** Plaza de San Marcelo 3. ☏987 87 83 27. www. turismoleon.org.
- ▶ **Location:** León is on the northern edge of the Meseta. The AP 66 motorway runs north to Oviedo (121km/75mi). Palencia (128km/79.5mi) and Valladolid (139km/86.3mi) are to the southeast. 🚍León (AVE).
- 👁 **Don't Miss:** The cathedral.

THE CITY TODAY

León is a lively city, thanks in no small part to its 14 000-strong student population, with lots of good places to eat and drink and party. The centre of activity at night is the Plaza de San Martin in Barrio Húmedo on the edge of the historic centre; an older, more sedate crowd hangs around the Plaza Mayor. León also has good shopping with many clothing boutiques and gourmet shops.

A BIT OF HISTORY

The medieval town – In the 10C, the kings of Asturias moved the capital from Oviedo to León, and fortified it. By the 11C and 12C León had become virtually the centre of Christian Spain.
Ramparts and peeling stucco over old brick in the east of the city recall the early medieval period.
The most characterful quarter, the Barrio Húmedo (the 'wet quarter', named for its proliferation of small bars), lies between the **Plaza Mayor** and the **Plaza de Santa María del Camino**, an attractive square with wooden porticoes.
The modern city – León could rest on its medieval laurels – the cathedral alone lures tourists by the thousands – but the city has a modern, forward-looking attitude, epitomised by the eclectic MUSAC contemporary art centre, and a pulse all its own.

PUERTA DEL CASTILLO

A good starting point for exploring León is the Puerta del Castillo, the only remaining entrance arch along the ancient city walls.

Built between 1–3C and rebuilt in the 12–15C, the arch's walls originally formed a quadrangle punctuated by 72 semicircular towers (plus the eight towers that flanked the entrances). There are now 36, from the Torre de los Ponces behind the Plaza Mayor to the tower of San Isidoro.

CATHEDRAL★★★

Pl. Regla. Open May–Sep Mon–Fri 9.30am–1.30pm, 4–8pm; Sat 9.30am–12pm, 2–6pm; Sun 9.30–11am, 2–8pm (May 9.30am–2pm). See website for remaining opening times. Closed public hols. €6. ☏987 87 57 70. www.catedraldeleon.org.
Built mainly between the mid-13C and late 14C, the cathedral is Gothic through and through, down to the soaring, French-inspired nave with its vast stained-glass windows, some of the most impressive in Europe.
The **facade** is pierced by three deeply recessed and richly carved portals. The gently smiling Santa María Blanca (a copy; original sculpture in the apsidal chapel) stands at the pier of the central doorway; on the lintel is a Last Judgement. The left portal tympanum illustrates scenes from the Life of Christ; the right portal includes the Dormition and the Coronation of the Virgin.

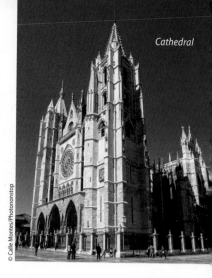

Cathedral

© Calle Montes/Photononstop

The statues decorating the jambs of the central doorway on the south facade are extremely fine. Inside, the cathedral's outstanding **stained-glass ★★★** – 125 windows and 57 oculi with an area of 1 200sq m/12 917sq ft– is the finest in Spain; the structure is so suffused with it that it weakens the walls (hence the frequent restoration work).

The west front rose and the three central apsidal chapels contain 13C–15C glass; the Capilla de Santiago (St James Chapel) shows Renaissance influence. The Renaissance **trascoro★**, by Juan de Badajoz, includes four alabaster high reliefs framing Esteban Jordán's triumphal arch.

The high altar **retable**, painted by Nicolás Francés, is a good example of the 15C international style. To the left is a remarkable **Entombment★**, showing Flemish influence, attributed to the Master of Palanquinos.

A silver reliquary contains the remains of San Froilán, the city patron. Several Gothic tombs can be seen in the ambulatory and transept, in particular that of Bishop Don Rodrigo – in the Virgen del Carmen Chapel to the right of the high altar – which is surmounted by a multifoil arch.

The galleries of the **claustro★** are contemporary with the 13C–14C nave, but the vaulting, with ornate keystones, was added at the beginning of the 16C. The galleries are interesting for the frescoes by Nicolás Francés and for the Romanesque and Gothic tombs.

Museo Catedralicio

Open Jun–Sep daily 9.30am–1.30pm, 4–8pm. Oct–May Mon–Sat 9.30am–1.30pm, 4–7pm; Sun 10am–2pm. Same ticket as cathedral (incl cloisters).
Among items in the museum are a French-inspired 15C statue of St Catherine, a Christ carved by Juan de Juni in 1576 (meant to be viewed from below) and a Mozarabic Bible.

SIGHTS

Real Colegiata de San Isidoro de León★★

Pl. de San Isidoro 4. Open Jul–Sep Mon–Sat 9am–9pm, Sun & public hols 9am–3pm. May & Jun Mon–Thu 10am–2pm & 4–7pm, Fri–Sat 10am–2pm & 4–8pm, Sun & public hols 10am–3pm. Rest of year Mon–Sat 10am–2pm & 4–7pm, Sun 10am–2pm. Closed 1, 6 Jan, 25 Dec. €5, Thu after 4pm. €5. ℘987 87 61 61. www.museosanisidorodeleon.com.
The **basilica**, built into the Roman ramparts, was dedicated in 1063 to Isidore, Archbishop of Sevilla, whose ashes had been brought north for burial in Christian territory. Of the 11C church only the pantheon remains. The apse and transept of the present basilica are Gothic; the balustrade and the pediment on the south front were added during the Renaissance.

Panteón Real★★★

Colegiata Real de San Isidoro de León. This Royal Pantheon is one of the earliest examples of Romanesque architecture in Castilla. The **capitals★** on the short, thick columns bear traces of the Visigothic tradition yet exhibit notable advances in sculpture, showing scenes for the first time. The 12C **frescoes★★★** are outstanding, illustrating not only New Testament themes but also country life. The pantheon is the resting place of 23 kings and queens.

Real Colegiata de San Isidoro de León

© KarSol/iStockphoto.com

Tesoro★★

Colegiata Real de San Isidoro de León.
The 11C reliquary containing the remains of San Isidoro is made of wood, faced with embossed silver and covered in a Mozarabic embroidery. The famous **Cáliz de Doña Urraca★** (Doña Urraca chalice) comprises two Roman agate cups mounted in the 11C in a gold setting inlaid with precious stones. The plaques of the 11C **Arqueta de los Marfiles★** (Ivory Reliquary) each represent an Apostle. The library contains over 300 incunabula and a 10C Mozarabic Bible.

Convento de San Marcos★ (Monastery of St Mark)

Pl. de San Marcos 7. ℘902 54 79 79. www.parador.es.
This former monastery, connected with the Knights of the Order of Santiago (St James) since the 12C, is now a Parador. The 100m/328ft long **facade★★** has a remarkable unity of style in spite of the addition of an 18C Baroque pediment. It has two storeys of windows, niches friezes and cornices, engaged columns, pilasters and medallions in high relief illustrating biblical and Spanish personages. The **church** front (on the extreme right), emblazoned with scallop shells, symbols of the pilgrimage to Santiago de Compostela, remains incomplete.

MUSAC (Museo de Arte Contemporáneo de Castilla y León)

Av. de los Reyes Leoneses 24. Open Tue–Fri 11am–2pm, 5–8pm; Sat, Sun 11am–3pm, 5–9pm. Closed 1 Jan, 25 Dec. €3, Free Sun pm, 18 May, 12 Oct, 6 Dec. ℘987 09 00 00. www.musac.es.
This striking crayon-box-like building by cutting-edge architects Mansilla + Muñón is covered in coloured crystals – echoing the stained glass of the cathedral – and focusses on living artists.

Museo de León★

Pl. de Santo Domingo 8. Open Oct–Jun Tue–Sat 10am–2pm, 4–7pm; Jul–Sep Tue–Sat 10am–2pm, 5–8pm, Sun & public hols 10am–2pm. €1; free Sat, Sun, 23 Apr, 9 & 18 May, 12 Oct, 6 Dec. ℘987 23 64 05. www.museodeleon.com.
This history museum includes the 10C Votive Cross of Santiago de Peñalba and the **Cristo de Carrizo★★★**, an 11C Byzantine-influenced ivory crucifix. The **cloister** galleries, built between 16C–18C, serve as a lapidary museum. The northeast corner contains a low relief of the Nativity with an interesting architectonic perspective by Juan de Juni. The **sacristy★** is a sumptuous creation by Juan de Badajoz (1549) with decorated ribbed vaulting.

Casa de Botines★

Pl. de San Marcelo 5. Open 11am–2pm, 4–8pm exc Wed am and Sun pm. €8; guided tours available. ℘987 35 32 47. www.casabotines.es.

The neo-Gothic Casa de los Botines, one of Gaudí's few buildings outside Catalonia, since 2017 houses a museum containing some 5 000 works with eight centuries' worth of paintings by such renowned artists as Solana, Sorolla, Madrazo and Gutiérrez.

The building was commissioned by wealthy textile firm Fernández y Andrés (its official name is Casa Fernández-Andrés), and construction began in 1891. Impressively, it was completed the following year.

Unlike most of Gaudí's fantastical buildings, it is a heavy, squared-off affair. Note the statu above the entrance of Saint George slaying the dragon by Antonio Cantó and Vicenç Matamala. In front of the building is a bronze statue of Gaudí sitting on a bench.

Palacio de los Guzmanes★

Pl. de San Marcelo 6. Open Jul–Sep, 10am–2pm, 4–8pm; Oct–Jun, Mon–Fri; Oct–Jun, 9am–2.30pm, 4.30–6.30pm. ℘987 29 21 00.

Built in the late 16C by the influential Guzmán family, this Renaissance palace is the work of two great architects, Rodrigo Gil de Hontañón (famous for the university buildings in Alcalá de Henares, among others) and Juan del Ribero. Flanked by two towers and built on three levels, the palace bears heraldic decoration, such as the Guzmáns' shield, a cauldron with snakes crawling out of it. There is also a relief of St Agustín washing Christ's feet.

EXCURSIONS

Monasterio de San Miguel de Escalada★

❱ 28km/17.4mi W. Leave León via N 601 to Gradefes. Open Tue–Sun May–Oct 10.30am–2.30pm, 4.30–7.30pm; Nov–Apr 10am–2pm. Guided tours available. Closed 1 & 6 Jan; 2 May; 24, 25, 31 Dec. €3. ℘618 866 790

In the 11C, Alfonso III bequeathed this abandoned **monastery** to refugee monks from Córdoba. Today the surviving church is the best-preserved Mozarabic building in Spain.

The **outside gallery★**, built in 1050, has horseshoe arches resting on carved capitals at the top of smoothly polished columns. An earlier church (**iglesia★**) from 913 has wooden vaulting, and a balustrade of panels carved with Visigothic (birds, grapes) and Moorish (stylised foliage) motifs.

Cuevas de Valporquero★★

❱ 47km/29mi N on the LE 311. Guided tours (1hr 15min) daily mid-May–Sept 10am–6pm, rest of year 10am–5pm. €8.50. ℘987 57 64 08. www.cuevadevalporquero.es.

Well-placed lighting sets off the countless bizarre forms in these vast caves – there is even a stalactite 'star' hanging from the roof of the largest chamber. Other features include petrified 'waterfalls', 'church organ pipes ' and a green lake. Choose between the 1.6km/1mi and 2.5km/ 1.5mi routes.

Puebla de Sanabria

Puebla de Sanabria is an attractive mountain village along the A 52 motorway, close to the Embalse de Cernadilla (reservoir), near the Portuguese border. The 15C castle of the Count of Benavente overlooks its white houses and late -12C church.

Valle de Sanabria

❱ 19km/11.8mi NW. Follow the lake road; turn right after 14km/8.7mi; after a further 6km/3.7mi, turn left.

This valley, a nature reserve, its at the foot of the Sierras de Cabrera Baja and Segundera. Hiking, hunting and fishing are popular activities.

Lago de Sanabria is the largest glacial lake in Spain, at 1 028m/3 373ft. It is used for water sports and for salmon-trout fishing.

There are **views★** of the rushing Tera and the mountain-encircled lake out to the Galician-looking village of **San Martín de Casteñada**, with its 11C Romanesque **church**.

Mediterranean Spain

Sagrada Família, Barcelona
© José Fuste Raga/age fotostock

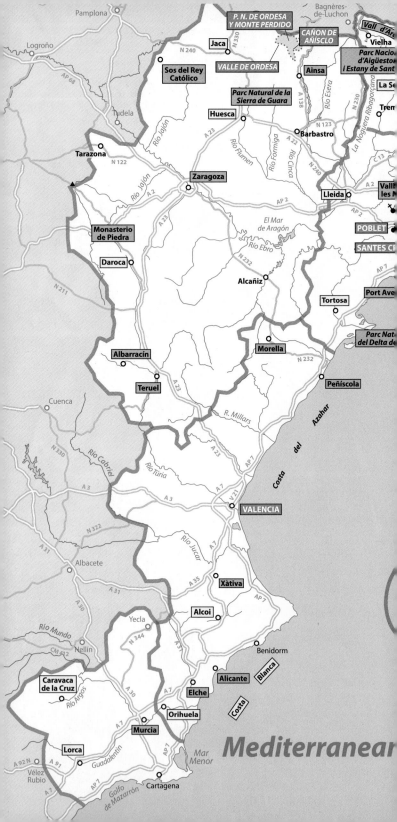

FRANCE

PERPIGNAN

Argelès
Colliore

Céret

SANT PERE
DE RODES

N

Principat
d'Andorra

N 116

'Aran
tha
cional
stortes
ant Maurici

a Seu d'Urgell

N 260

El Segre

Camprodon

Figueres

Cadaqués

remp

Ripoll

Empúries

C 14

Solsona

El Ter

Vic

C 16

C 25

Girona

COSTA BRAVA

allbona de
es Monges

C 25

Manresa

C 17

Terrassa

AP 7

C 32

Serra de
Montserrat

Costa de Barcelona-Maresme

AP 7

Montblanc

C 32

CREUS

BARCELONA

Sitges

TARRAGONA

aventura

Costa Daurada

Natural
a de l'Ebre

MAR

MEDITERRANEO

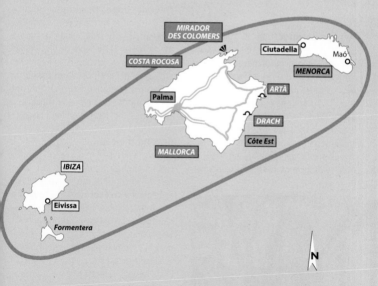

MIRADOR
DES COLOMERS

COSTA ROCOSA

Ciutadella

Maó

MENORCA

ARTÀ

Palma

DRACH

Côte Est

MALLORCA

IBIZA

Eivissa

Formentera

N

| | 0 | 20 km |

BARCELONA	★★★	Worth a special journey
Teruel	★★	Worth a detour
Alcoi	★	Interesting
Cartagena		Other sight described in this guide

n   Spain

Barcelona and around

Barcelona is the capital of Catalunya and the favourite Spanish city of many foreign visitors –and who can blame them? Not only does it have a fascinating history, unparalleled Gothic quarter and enviable architectural legacy; it's bathed in sunlight and surrounded by palm-fringed beaches to boot. The city has become so popular, in fact – to the tune of nearly 16 million international visitors a year (2019) – that local lawmakers are toying with hitting incoming holidaymakers with a tourist 'tax'.

Highlights

Art and architecture

The best way to see Barcelona is on foot, to take in its manifold architectural assets. The city has long been renowned for its architecture and has used the medium to make civic improvements in times of prosperity. When feisty Catalans were a force to be reckoned with on the Mediterranean trade routes, the Barri Gòtic was born; today it is an atmospheric, moody ensemble of Medieval buildings that is a joy to wander.

Similarly, the **Modernisme** period, with its keynote buildings by Antoni Gaudí, was ushered in when Catalans started a brisk trade with the newly discovered Americas. Barcelona's museums are world-class. The one-time resident Pablo Picasso bequeathed an extensive collection of his early work, while Joan Miró's purpose-built museum illustrates the genius of this ground-breaking abstract surrealist. A millennium's-worth of Catalan art, from ancient Romanesque frescoes to modernista decorative pieces can be seen at the MNAC. Spaces showcasing some of the world's best contemporary art include the Caixaforum and MACBA, a gleaming white edifice whose opening kick-started the makeover of the Raval district. Yet for most, Barcelona's charms lie in its smaller pleasures: delightful squares linked by networks of winding streets, colourful neighbourhood markets and the palpable exuberance that locals have for their city.

Beyond the capital

Cataluyna has garnered a reputation for cutting-edge gastronomy, thank in large part to Ferran Adrià, the self-taught chef and figurehead of **cocina de vanguardia** (avant-garde cuisine). His Costa Brava restaurant El Bulli may have closed just as Adrià was reaching his creative and professional peak, but his influence lingers in high-end restaurants across the region. One of Barcelona's greatest assets is its ease of escape. An efficient regional transport network can have you scaling the peaks of Montserrat or soaking up the sun on the beach in fashionable, LGBT-friendly Sitges in under an hour. Farther afield lies the quintessentially Catalan city of Terrassa, well off the tourist trail.

© Xavier Forés & Joana Roncero/age fotostock

Left:
Plaça de Sant Felip Neri, Barri Gòtic

Barcelona★★★

Combining urban sophistication with Mediterranean *alegria*, Barcelona is elegant and welcoming, traditional and avant-garde. .

THE CITY TODAY

Far from just a vacation spot, Barcelona is a *city* city –an industrial centre and major port, a university town and seat of the regional government. It also has a thriving artistic, cultural and music scene.

The 1992 Olympic Games brought large-scale planning projects and were the catalyst of the tourism boom. Catalunya has long had a separatist streak, and tensions reached a fever pitch 1 October 2017, when the regional government held a referendum on Catalan independence in defiance of the Spanish constitution; police descended violently on voting stations and broke up protests in Barcelona. Catalan separatism remains the most hot-button issue in Spanish politics today.

A BIT OF HISTORY

Founding and expansion – Settled by the Phocaeans, the city grew as Roman **Barcino**, within a 3C fortified wall. In the 12C, Barcelona was already the capital of Catalunya and seat of the expanding kingdom of Aragón-Catalunya. Catalan Gothic architecture blossomed.

Catalunya sided with the Archduke of Austria in the War of the Spanish Succession (1701–14) and in defeat lost its autonomy. Montjuïc hill was fortified, and construction was prohibited except in the old city. Building outside the walls began again in the mid-19C. Industrialisation followed, along with International Exhibitions in 1888 and 1929. Modernista architecture flowered, with Antoni Gaudí its figurehead.

Art & identity – The Catalan language, which was banned under Franco, is many locals' mother tongue, though everyone speaks Spanish. Artists like **Picasso**, **Miró** and **Dalí** all lived here.

▶ **Population:** 1.6 million

◔ **Michelin Map:** 574 H 36 (town plan) – map 122 Costa Brava. Michelin City Plans Barcelona 40, 41 and 2040 – Catalunya (Barcelona).

🛈 **Info:** Main office Pl. de Catalunya 17 ℘932 853 834. Other offices (no℘): Pl. de Sant Jaume, Estació de Sants Cabina Rambla, Catedral, Aeroport (1 & 2), Terminals de Creuers, Triangle, Mirador de Colom plus other tourist 'cabines' in various locations. www.barcelonaturisme.com.

◔ **Location:** Barcelona is the hub of northeastern Spain. The AP 7 motorway runs from Murcia to Girona and France; the C32 heads to the resorts to the north and south to Tarragona; the C 16 veers inland to Manresa (59km/37mi NE) and the C 17 to Vic. 🚃Plaça Canonge Rodó (Clot Aragó); Av. Marquès de l'Argentera (Estació de França); Po. de Gràcia; Pl. de Catalunya Estació; Pl. Estació (Sant Andreu Comptal); Pl. dels Països Catalans (Sants).

🅿 **Parking:** Don't even think about driving in Barcelona. Use the excellent Bus Turístic to see the sights (www.barcelonabusturistic.cat).

☺ **Don't Miss:** Sagrada Família church and the Modernist masterpieces of architecture in the Eixample district.

◔ **Timing:** See the Gothic Quarter and continue to the Ramblas, Passeig de Gràcia and Sagrada Família before all else.

👪 **Kids:** El Poble Espanyol; Parc Güell; Aquarium; Chocolate Museum; Museu Blau; beach.

GETTING FROM A TO B

Airport – ☎902 40 47 04. www.
aena.es. 18km/11mi from the city
centre. Can be reached by local train
from Terminal 2 (Línea 2, Cercanías;
☎900 202 220) every 30min from
5.42am to 11.38pm, or by the regular
no.46 TMB bus service from the Plaça
de Catalunya and Plaça d'Espanya,
departing every 15min from 5.30am to
12.15am (€2.20 single; ☎902 07 50 27).
The Aerobus (every 10 mins) makes
fewer stops and takes approx 35 mins
(€5.90 single). A taxi to or from the city
centre will run you €25–35.

Taxis – The city's hailable black-and-
yellow taxis are convenient yet pricey.
Radio Taxi Barcelona: ☎932 25 00 00,
or via the Amb Taxi Barcelona app.

Ride-Hailing Apps – Massive protests
by official taxi drivers drove Uber out
of town (again) in early 2019; Cabify,
however, is back after a brief hiatus.

Metro – Metro stations are shown on
the maps in this guide as 🚇. (☎932
987 000; www.tmb.cat.) Info on
access for disabled travellers can be
obtained on the website. The network
is open Mon–Thu and Sun 5–12am,
Fri 5am–2am, Sat and days preceding
public holidays 24 hours.
Metro **tickets and cards** can be used
on buses, the 'Tramvía Blau' (a tourist
tram in the Diagonal section of the
city) and train services operated by
FGC (Ferrocarriles de la Generalitat
de Catalunya). In addition to single
tickets, multi-journey cards include
the T-1 (valid for ten trips), T-DIA
(unlimited travel for one day), T50/30
(50 trips in 30 days) and the T-MES
(unlimited travel for one month).

Tram/Streetcars – There are six
lines (T1, T2, T3, T4, T5 and T6).

Regional railway network –
Main station: Barcelona Sants (AVE).
Airport to Sants: 20 mins. €4.20 single.
Ferrocarriles Catalanes train stations
are shown on the maps in this guide
(☎900 90 15 15; www.fgc.cat). Free
connections to the metro system may
be made at these stations: Avinguda
Carrilet /L'Hospitalet, Espanya,
Catalunya and Diagonal/Provença.

Bus Turístic – The service offers visitors three itineraries. Daily departures
from Plaça de Catalunya starting at
9am (€30 day; €40 2 days; www.barce-
lonabusturistic.cat).

Boat trips – Las Golondrinas organises
trips around the port (approx 35min;
from €7.70). Departures from Portal
de la Pau, opposite the Columbus
monument. ☎934 42 31 06. www.
lasgolondrinas.com.

CULTURAL EVENTS

Publications – The **Guía del Ocio**
(www.enbarcelona.com) is a weekly
online and print guide to cultural
events. Tourist offices also provide
visitors with free booklets and leaflets
produced by the Generalitat de
Catalunya's Department of Industry,
Commerce and Tourism.

DISCOUNTS

🎟 Most of the main sights offer
reduced-price tickets online.

Barcelona Card – The official three-in-
one transport, museum and discount
card (3, 4 or 5 days; €46/€56/€61).

Articket – Visit CCCB, Fundació Antoni
Tàpies, La Pedrera, Fundació Joan
Miró, MNAC, MACBA and Museu
Picasso for €35 (www.articketbcn.org).

Arqueoticket – For entry to Museu
d'Arqueologia de Catalunya, Museu
Egipci de Barcelona, Museu Marítim
de Barcelona and Museu d'Història
de la Ciutat de Barcelona (€14.50;
valid one year; http://bcnshop.
barcelonaturisme.com).

The above cards and passes are sold
online and at local **tourist offices**. For
further information: ☎932 853 832;
www.barcelonaturisme.com.

Ruta del Modernisme – A guidebook
and discount booklet with discounts
of up to 50% on admission to the

main Modernist buildings by Gaudí, Domènech i Montaner and Puig i Cadafalch. Available from the tourist office in Plaça Catalunya (€12). ℘932 853 834. www.rutadelmodernisme.com)

DISTRICTS

Barri Gòtic – Following an intense restoration programme undertaken during the 1920s, the area containing the city's major historical buildings was renamed the Gothic Quarter.

Ciutat Vella – The old city includes districts as diverse as Santa Anna, La Mercè, Sant Pere and El Raval. The last, which used to be known as the Barri Xino (Chinatown), contains Barcelona's leading cultural centres and is a fine example of urban renovation.

Eixample – The Eixample ('extension') developed following the destruction of the city's medieval walls. The district personifies the bourgeois, elegant Barcelona of the end of the 19C with its prestigious boutiques, smart avenues and some of the best examples of Modernist architecture. It is also where many of the main hotels are concentrated.

Gràcia – This *barrio*, situated at the end of the Passeig de Gràcia, is one of the city's most characterful – if quickly gentrifying – areas. Once an agrarian area on the fringes of town, it grew as a result of the influx of shopkeepers, artisans and factory workers. It hosts a number of popular fiestas.

Ribera – With its narrow alleyways and Gothic architecture, this former mercantile quarter still retains an old-world charm, particularly in the EL Born district near the port. Its main attractions are the Carrer Montcada (where the Picasso Museum is located) and the Església de Santa Maria del Mar.

Barceloneta – Seaside Barceloneta is famous for its outdoor stalls, fish restaurants and nautical atmosphere as well as its eponymous beach, the most easily accessed from the city centre.

Vila Olímpica – The Olympic Village was built to accommodate athletes participating in the 1992 games. Nowadays, it is a modern district with wide avenues, landscaped areas and direct access to some of Barcelona's restored beaches.

Les Corts – This district is located at the upper end of Diagonal and includes the **Ciudad Universitaria** and **Camp Nou**, the home of Barcelona Football Club and its much-visited **Museu FC Barcelona**.

Sarrià – Sarrià hugs the foot of the Serra de Collserola and has managed to retain its traditional, tranquil character. The neighbouring districts of **Pedralbes** and **Sant Gervasi de Cassoles**, at the base of Tibidabo, are a favourite hangout of the city's upper-crust denizens.

Sants – A true-blue working-class district surrounds the railway station of the same name.

Horta-Guinardó – This *barrio* at the foot of Collserola was first populated by peasants and then by factory workers. It is home to the **Laberinto de Horta** (to the north), an 18C property with attractive gardens, and the **Velódromo**, a venue for sporting events and major music events.

Poble Sec – Nestled at the foot of Montjuïc – the city's garden and museum belt – Poble Sec is a cozy neighbourhood of pretty 19C apartment buildings and outdoor cafés.

Street Signs: Castilian vs Catalan

Castilian	Catalan
Ayuntamiento	Ajuntament
Avenida	Avinguda
Calle	Carrer
Capilla	Capella
Iglesia	Església
Paseo	Passeig
Plaza	Plaça

Castell on the Plaça Sant Jaume, Festival of Our Lady of Mercy on 24 September

© Anna Serrano/hemis.fr

WALKING TOUR

BARRI GÒTIC★★

The Gothic quarter, named for the many buildings constructed between the 13C and 15C, holds traces of Roman settlement and massive 4C walls.

Plaça Nova

This is the heart of the quarter, where the Romans built an enclosure with walls 9m/29.5ft high. Two watchtowers that flanked the West Gate (converted to a house in the Middle Ages) remain. Opposite the cathedral, the **Collegi d'Arquitectes** (College of Architects; Pl. Nova amb carrer del Bisbe) is a contemporary building with a facade bearing an etched mural designed by Picasso.

Catedral Santa Eulàlia (La Seu)★

Pl. de la Seu. Open Mon–Fri 8am–12.45pm, 1pm–5.30pm, 5.45–7.30pm. Sat 8am–12.45pm, 1–5pm, 5.15–8pm. Sun & hols 8am–1.45pm, 2–5pm, 5.15–8pm. €3 ea choir & roof, or €7 donation; free before 12.45pm (1.45pm Sun) & after 5.45pm.
🖋 933 42 82 62. www.catedralbcn.org.
The cathedral was built on the site of a Romanesque church. The facade and spire are 19C, based on old French designs.
The Catalan Gothic **interior**★ has an outstanding elevation with slender pillars. The nave is lit by a fine lantern-tower; the perspective is broken by the **coro**★★, with double rows of beautifully carved **stalls**. Note the humorous scenes adorning the misericords. In the early 16C, the backs were painted with the coats of arms of knights of the Order of the Golden Fleece by Juan de Borgoña, in one of the most impressive achievements of European heraldry.

The side chapels hold exquisite retables and marble tombs. The white marble **choir screen**★ was sculpted in the 16C after drawings by Bartolomé Ordóñez. Statues illustrate the martyrdom of St Eulàlia, patron of Barcelona; her relics lie in the **crypt**★ in a 14C Pisan-style alabaster sarcophagus. The **Capella del Santísimo** (right of the entry) contains the 15C *Christ of Lepanto*, said to have been on the prow of the galley of Don Juan de Austria in the Battle of Lepanto (1571). In the next chapel is a Gothic retable by Bernat Martorell, also the artist of the **retable of the Transfiguration**★ in the ambulatory.

Cathedral roof visit – by lift from an ambulatory chapel. Metal walkways under the imposing silhouettes of the cathedral towers and cupola afford exceptional **views**★★ of the city.

The **cloisters**★ are home to a flock of 13 geese, one for each year of co-patron saint Eulalia's life before her martyrdom.

In the chapter house, a museum houses a *Pietà* by Bermejo (1490), altarpiece panels by the 15C artist Jaime Huguet and the missal of St Eulàlia, enhanced by delicate miniatures.

Around the corner from the cathedral is the **Museu Diocesà de Barcelona** (Av. de la Catedral 4; open Nov–Feb 10am–6pm, Mar–Oct until 8pm; closed 1 Jan, 25–26 Dec; €15, free 18 May; ℘932 687 582).

○ Facing the facade of the Cathedral, turn right on Carrer Sant Llúcia.

Casa de l'Ardiaca★

Santa Llúcia 1. Open Mon–Fri 9am–8.45pm (exc Jul–Aug, 9am–7pm), Sat 9am–1pm. ℘933 181 195.
Constructed in the 12C and altered in the 15C, the Archdeacon's House (now housing Arxiu Històric de la Ciutat or Historical City Archives) combines Gothic and Renaissance elements.

○ Left on Carrer del Bisbe and take the first right.

Plaça de Sant Felip Neri

The Renaissance houses on this square were moved here when Via Laietana was built.

○ Return to Carrer del Bisbe.

Carrer del Bisbe

To the left is the side wall of the Palau de la Generalitat (Provincial Council). Above a door is an early-15C medallion of St George by Pere Johan. On the right side is the **Casa dels Canonges** (Canons' Residence), residence of the President of the Generalitat.
A neo-Gothic covered gallery (1929), over a star-vaulted arch, links the two.

○ Continue along Carrer del Bisbe.

Plaça Sant Jaume

This handsome square, once the main crossroads of the old Roman city, is the hub of Catalan political life; major celebrations (and protests) take place here.

Palau de la Generalitat

Pl. de Sant Jaume 4. Open to the public 23 Apr, 11 & 24 Sep. Guided tours (50min); online booking required. http://catalangovernment.exili.eu.
This vast 15C–17C edifice is the seat of the Autonomous Government of Catalunya. It has a Renaissance-style facade on Plaça de Sant Jaume (c. 1600).

Casa de la Ciutat
(Town Hall)

Pl. de Sant Jaume 1. Open Sun 10am–2pm; 11 Feb, 23 Apr, 15 Jun 10am–8pm. ℘934 02 70 00.
The town hall facade on Plaça Sant Jaume is Neoclassical; that on Carrer de la Ciutat is an outstanding 14C Gothic construction.

○ Cross Plaça St. Jaume, turn left.

Carrer del Paradis

At no. 10 stand four Roman **columns★**, remains of the Temple of Augustus (same ticket as MUHBA, see below). Carrer Paradis leads to Carrer de la Pietat, bordered on the left by the Gothic facade of the Casa dels Canonges. The cathedral cloister doorway opposite is adorned with a wooden 16C *Pietà*.

○ Right on Baixada de Sant Clara.

Plaça del Rei★★

On this splendid square stand the Palau Reial Major (at the back), the **Capella de Santa Àgata** (right) and the **Palau del Lloctinent**. In the right corner, the Casa Clariana-Padellàs, housing the **Museu d'Història de Barcelona (MUHBA)★★**, is a 15C Gothic mansion moved stone by stone in 1931.

Museu d'Història de Barcelona (MUHBA)★★

Pl. del Rei. Multiple sites, Tue-Sat 10am-7pm, Sun 10am-8pm. €7. ℘932 56 21 22. http://ajuntament.barcelona.cat.
The ticket covers 12 various locations including the the Temple of Augustus, Roman City, and Palau Reial Major.

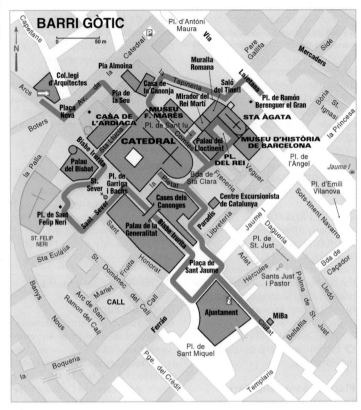

The Roman city★★★

Under the museum and Plaça del Rei are Roman foundations. In adjoining vaulted rooms are 1–4C sculptures (busts of Agrippina, Faustina and Antoninus Pius). Gothic frescoes were uncovered in the Sala Jaime I in 1998.

Palau Reial Major

Built in the 11C and 12C, the palace acquired its present appearance in the 14C. It was the seat of the counts of Barcelona and the kings of Aragón. Arches link huge buttresses in the facade, with rose windows. The lofty 14C **Saló del Tinell**, 17m/56ft high, is topped with a double-sloped ceiling set on six monumental arches. It is said that the Catholic Monarchs welcomed Columbus here after his first voyage.

Capella Reial de Santa Àgata★★

This 14C palatine chapel is covered by intricate polychrome woodwork panelling. The **Altarpiece of the Constable★★** by Jaime Huguet (1465) depicts the life of Jesus and the Virgin. In the centre, the *Adoration of the Three Wise Men* is a Catalan masterpiece. A staircase leads to the **Torre del Rei Martí**, a five-storey tower, which is closed to the public but can be seen on a visit to the MUHBA.

▶ Return to Baixada de Sant Clara and turn right onto Carrer Comtes.

Palau del Lloctinent

The 16C late-Gothic palace was the residence of the viceroys of Catalunya.

▶ Continue on Carrer Comtes.

Museu Frederic Marès★

Pl. de Sant Lu 5–6. Open Tue–Sat 10am
–7pm, Sun & hols 11am–8pm. Closed
1 Jan, 1 May, 24 Jun, 25 Dec. €4.50;
free first Sun & every Sun from 3pm.
☏923 56 35 00.
www.museumares.bcn.cat.
The threshold to this eccentric
museum is on the tiny **Plaça de Sant
Lu**, which is always full of mime artists and street musicians. The collections were left to the city by
sculptor Frederic Marès (1893–1991).
Sculpture Section – The works on
two floors and in the crypt are in
chronological order from the Iberian
period to the 19C. Note the **Christs and
Calvaries★** in polychrome wood (12C–
14C), Romanesque and Gothic **Virgins
with Child★**; a 16C **Holy Entombment★**
and **The Vocation of St Peter★**, an
expressive 12C relief by Cabestany.
Gabinete del Coleccionista – Everyday objects, mainly 19C, include items
from recreational rooms, the smoking
parlour and the women's boudoir (spectacles, fans, clothes etc.).

▶ Return to Plaça de la Seu; right on
Carrer Tapinera; follow it to the end.

Plaça de Ramon Berenguer el Gran

From the Plaça, Roman walls are visible,
incorporated into the Palau Reial.

 WALKING TOUR

LA RAMBLA★★

The most famous promenade in
Barcelona, La Rambla's five sections
follow an old riverbed bordering the
Gothic quarter. La Rambla separates the
Eixample district from the old quarter
and is alive at all hours with locals, out-
of-towners and vendors. This is tourist
central: Forego dining here. The upper
section, by Plaça de Catalunya, is Rambla de Canaletes, followed by Rambla
dels Estudis or Rambla dels Ocells (Avenue of the Birds). Watch your wallet.

▶ Walk S (towards the port) and stop
at the corner of Carrer Portaferrisa.

Palau Moja

The former home of poet Jacinto Verda-
guer (1845–1902) is a Baroque late-18C
palace. It houses a bookshop specialising in Catalan history and culture.

▶ Continue south.

Església de Betlem

La Rambla 107. Free.
This Baroque church, whose interior was
razed in the Civil War, has retained its
imposing facade, facing Carrer Carme.

▶ Walk in the same direction to the
corner of Carrer Carme and turn right.

Antic Hospital de la Santa Creu

Hospital 56.
The Gothic, Baroque and Neoclassical
buildings are a haven from the hubbub.
An ex-hospital is the Library of Catalunya. A charming planted **Gothic patio★**
(Jardines de Rubio y Lluch) is situated
through a hall decorated with *azulejos*.

▶ Return to La Rambla.

Rambla de les Flors

This stretch of La Ramblas is named for
the abundance of flower stalls, a scene
immortalised by many a local painter.

Palau de la Virreina★

La Rambla 99. Open Tue–Sun & hols
12pm–8pm. Free. ☏933 16 10 00.
www.ajuntament.barcelona.cat.
The elegant 1778 palace of the Vicereine
of Peru, with Baroque and Rococo
decorations, hosts exhibitions on
the theme of image. Alongside is the
traditional Mercat (market) de Sant
Josep (La Boqueria).
Down La Rambla on the right side
stands the city's opera house, the **Gran
Teatre del Liceu★** (La Rambla 51–59;
☏934 85 99 00; www.liceubarcelona.
cat), rebuilt after a 1994 fire. Opposite is
Plaça de la Boqueria, a charming esplanade whose pavement was decorated
by **Joan Miró**.

Plaça Reial

© Xavier Forés & Joana Roncero/age fotostock

Mercat de la Boqueria★★★

La Rambla 91. Mon–Sat 8am–8.30pm.
www.boqueria.barcelona.
One of the world's great food markets,
La Boqueria is a gastronomic Disney-
land welcoming some 45 000 people
per day. Join the hordes wandering its
stalls, with pristine local produce, and
stop at whichever tapas counter takes
your fancy.

◗ Turn left into Carrer Cardenal
Casañas.

Església/Basílica de Santa Maria del Pi★

Pl. del Pi 7. Open daily 10am–6pm.
€4.50. Guided tours available. ℘933
18 47 43. www.basilicadelpi.cat.
This lovely 14C Catalan Gothic church
is striking for its simplicity and the size
of its single nave. The plaza is noted for
its tapas bars.

Palau Güell★★

Nou de la Rambla 3. Open Tue–Sun
10am–8pm (5.30pm Nov–Mar). Closed
Dec 25 & 26, Jan 1, 6. €12; free summer
Sun (limited tickets) & first Sun in winter
(similar restrictions). Guided tours Tue
2pm (no additional charge). ℘934 725
775. www.palauguell.cat.
Gaudí designed the Güell residence
(1886–90). Note the parabolic entry
arches and the extravagant bars typical of the Modernist movement. The
most striking interior features are the
grand hall and the treatment of light
as a design element.
La Rambla meets the sea at **La Rambla de Santa Mònica**. The former
Convent de Santa Mònica (no. 7;
open Tue–Fri 2–9pm, Sun 11am–7pm;
free; ℘935 67 11 10; www.artssanta
monica.cat) is a modern art centre with
rotating exhibitions.
The ♨♨ Wax Museum **(Museu de Cera)**
is also here (Pas. de la Banca 7; open
Mon–Fri 10am–1.30pm, 4–7.30pm, Sat–
Sun & hols 11am–2pm, 4.30–8.30pm;
summer 10am–10pm; €15; ℘933 17 26
49; www.museocerabcn.com).

Plaça Reial★★

This lively pedestrianised square
shaded by palms and lined with cafés
is surrounded by Neoclassical buildings.
Gaudí designed the lampposts by the
fountain. A stamp and coin market is
held on Sunday mornings.

Mirador de Colom

Pl. Portal de la Pau. Open
8.30am–8.30pm (until 7.30pm Oct–Feb).
Closed 1 Jan, 25 Dec. €6. ℘932 853 854.
This famous 1886 landmark monument
commemorates Christopher Columbus.
A lift to the top gives a view over the sea
and Ramblas; it can be uncomfortably
crowded in the small viewing space.

ADDITIONAL SIGHTS

Museu d'Art Contemporàni de Barcelona (MACBA)★★

Pl. dels Àngels 1. Open Mon, Wed–Fri 11am–7.30pm, Sat 10am–8pm, Sun & public hols 10am–3pm; third week Jun– third week Sep extended hours Mon– Sat. Closed 1 Jan, 25 Dec. €11; free Sat 4–8pm. ✆934 12 08 10. www.macba.es.

The landmark **building**★★, designed by American architect Richard Meyer, fuses the rationalist Mediterranean tradition with contemporary architecture. Two significant works sit outside: *La Ola* by Jorge Oteiza and Eduardo Chillida's mural *Barcelona*.

The **permanent collections**★, set in dazzling white halls, cover major artistic movements of the past 50 years. Exhibits include works influenced by Constructivism and Abstract art (Klee, Oteiza, Miró, Calder, Fontana), as well as creations by experimental artists (Kiefer, Boltanski, Solano) and names of the 1980s (Hernández, Pijuán, Barceló, Tàpies, Ràfols Casamada, Sicilia). There is also an excellent Modernista collection. Views from the roof terrace are spectacular.

Centre de Cultura Contemporània de Barcelona (CCCB)

Montalegre 5. Open (usually) Tue–Sun 11am–8pm. Closed 1 Jan, 25 Dec. from €6; free Sun 3–8pm. ✆93 306 41 00. www.cccb.org.

This is another important cultural and creative arts centre. Its **patio**★ combines original mosaics and silk-screen floral motifs with modern elements including a wall of mirrored glass.

 WALKING TOUR★★

L'EIXAMPLE & MODERNIST ARCHITECTURE

Barcelona's Eixample (or enlargement) grew in the 19C. Ildefons Cerdà's 1859 grid plan circumscribe blocks of houses (*mançanes* in Catalan or *manzanas* in Castilian), octagonal in shape with trimmed corners.

The busy thoroughfares of avinguda Diagonal and La Meridiana cross to meet on Plaça de les Glòries Catalanes. In this ordered new section, architects transformed L'Eixample into the centre of Modernism in Barcelona.

Plaça de Catalunya

This vast square is considered the centre of the city and acts as a link between the old town and Eixample. Always buzzing, it is also Barcelona's principal transport hub and is lined with well-known department stores, the city's main tourist office and the long-established Café Zurich, a popular people-watching spot.

▶ N along the Passeig de Gràcia, then left on Carrer de la Diputació, then second right on Carrer de Balmes.

Museu del Modernisme★

Carrer de Balmes 48. Tue–Sat 10.30am–7pm, Sun & hols until 2pm. Closed 1 & 6 Jan, 1 May, 25 & 26 Dec. €10. ✆932 722 896. www.mmbcn.cat.

Housed in a Modernista textile warehouse dating to1902 and designed by Enric Sagnier, this museum, opened in 2010, is the only in Europe dedicated to this style of architecture. The exhibits, from a private collection, include furniture, sculpture and decorative arts by all the main players.

▶ Continue up Carrer de Balmes and take the second right on Carrer d'Aragó.

Fundació Antoni Tàpies★★

Aragó 255.Open Tue–Sun 10am–7pm. Closed 1, 6 Jan, 25, 26 Dec. €8. ✆934 87 03 15. www.fundaciotapies.org.

Tàpies established his foundation in an ex-publishing house designed by Domènech i Montaner. The brick building is crowned by a sculpture by the artist, *Núvol i Cadira* (cloud and chair), the emblem of the museum. The renovated interior, where white walls are contrasted with original wooden detailing, is lit by skylights (a cupola and a pyramid). Paintings and

Gaudí (1852–1926)

Antoni Gaudí, born in Reus, studied architecture in Barcelona. His style was influenced first by Catalan Gothic architecture, with its emphasis on volume (e.g., wide naves and soaring ceilings), and subsequently by the Islamic and Mudéjar styles. He also studied nature, observing plants and animals, which inspired his shapes, colours and textures. He gave full rein to these images – liana-like curves, the rising and breaking of waves, rugged rocks and the serrations on leaves and flowers – when designing his buildings. Part of his originality lay in his use of parabolic arches and spirals (as can be seen in the chimneys of Casa Milà). Deeply Christian, Gaudí also drew upon religious symbols in the adornment of his buildings, especially the Sagrada Família (Church of the Holy Family), on which he worked for over 40 years. He spent his last years hidden away in a small room in the middle of the site, until he was tragically killed by a tram. Gaudí worked a great deal for the banker **Eusebi Güell**, his patron and admirer, who asked him to design his private houses. Gaudí's main works in Barcelona are the Sagrada Família, Casa Batlló, La Pedrera, Casa Vicens, Palau Güell, Pavellons Güell and the Parc Güell.

sculptures trace the development of Tàpies' work since 1948.

▶ Continue N along Passeig de Gràcia to Carrer Valencia and turn left.

Museu Egipci de Barcelona – Fundació Arqueològica Clos

Valencia 284. Open Mon–Sat 10am–8pm (early Jan–third wk Jun & mid-Sep–Nov closed 2–4pm, exc Easter & hols); Sun & hols 10am–2pm. Closed 1, 6 Jan, 25-26 Dec. €12. ☎934 88 01 88. www.museuegipci.com.
This fascinating private museum has about 600 exhibits representing various periods of Egyptian civilization in addition to pieces from the Roman period.

▶ Return to Passeig de Gràcia.

Passeig de Gràcia★★

Along this boulevard, with elegant wrought-iron **street lamps**★ by Pere Falqués (1900), is some of Barcelona's finest Modernist architecture – on the **Illa de la Discordia**★★ (Block of Discord): no. 35 **Casa Lleó Morera**★ (1905) by Domènech i Montaner, no. 41 **Casa Amatller**★ (1900) by Puig i Cadafalch (guided 1hr tours at 11am in English and 1pm in Spanish; €23.50; ☎934 617 460; www.amatller.org), and no.

43 **Casa Batlló**★★ (1904–06) by Gaudí, with its extraordinary mosaic facade and fairy-tale dragon-like roof (open 9am–9pm; €25; ☎932 16 03 06; www.casabatllo.es).

▶ Continue in the same direction until you reach the corner of Carrer Provença.

La Pedrera (Casa Milà)★★★

Provença 261–265. Open Mon–Sun 9am-6.30pm, 7-9pm. Closed 1, 6 Jan, 25–26 Dec. From €25. ☎902 202 138. www.lapedrera.com.
With its unmistakable shapes and undulating lines, this magnificent Gaudí building is an icon of the city. Visit the **roof and attic**★ and a **residential floor**★. The **Espai Gaudí** exhibits drawings and models by the artist. The roof, with its forest of chimneys resembling medieval knights, provides fine **views**★. **El Piso**★ is a re-created apartment of an early-20C upper-class family. There is a smart café-restaurant (open 8.30am-midnight; www.lapedrera.com) on the ground floor and a noteworthy gift shop selling wares made by local artisans.

▶ Continue along Passeig de Gràcia to the busy Avinguda Diagonal, and turn right.

© Anna Serrano/hemis.fr

La Pedrera (Casa Mila)

Avinguda Diagonal

Palau Baró de Quadras, a Modernista building on the right (no. 373), was designed by **Puig i Cadafalch** and houses the Institut Ramón Llull (Mon–Fri 9am–5.30pm), which promotes Catalan language and culture abroad.

Along on the left (no. 416), his **Casa de les Punxes (Casa Terrades★)** bears the stamp of Flemish influence.

◗ Continue along the Diagonal to the intersection of Carrer Mallorca. Continue along Carrer Mallorca in the same direction.

La Sagrada Família★★★ (Church of the Holy Family)

Mallorca 401. Open Apr–Sep 9am–8pm (Mar & Oct until 7pm; Nov–Feb until 6pm); 25–26 Dec, 1 & 6 Jan 9am–2pm. €17–32 depending on experience. ℘932 08 04 14. www.sagradafamilia.org.

Slated for completion in 2026, the Sagrada Familia was begun in 1882 and taken over by Gaudí in 1883. It will be the tallest religious structure in Europe when finished. Gaudí planned a Latin Cross church with five aisles and a transept with three aisles. Three facades were each to be dominated by four spires representing the Apostles with a central spire to represent Christ and the Evangelists. The nave was to be a forest of columns. In his lifetime, only the crypt, the apsidal walls, one of the towers and the **Nativity facade★★** were completed. The Nativity facade comprises three doorways, Faith, Hope and Charity. Work resumed in 1940. The Passion facade was completed in 1981. The top of the east spire affords a wonderful **view★★** of the work on the church, and of Barcelona.

Domènech i Montaner's **Hospital Sant Pau★** (Sant Antoni Maria Claret 167; guided tours daily in English at noon and 1pm; €15; ℘93 553 78 01, www.santpaubarcelona.org), with its remarkable glazed roof tiles, may be seen at the end of Avinguda de Gaudí.

ADDITIONAL SIGHTS
Casa Vicens★★

Carrer de les Carolines 20. Open Mon–Sun 10am–8pm (last visit 7pm). Closed 1 & 6 Jan, 25 Dec. €16. ℘93 547 59 80. www.casavicens.org

A long-unvisitable Gaudí masterpiece, Casa Vicens was the first private house the architect, designed in 1883, and his first important commission. The result was this candy-striped tiled fantasy of a dwelling. Wander through the original rooms and the charming garden, then visit the permanent exhibition on the second floor.

Teatre Nacional de Catalunya

Plaça de les Arts 1. ℘933 06 57 00. www.tnc.cat.

Built by local architect Ricardo Bofill, Catalunya's National Theatre is a synthesis of modern and classical architecture. Shows are performed exclusively in Catalan.

Torre Agbar

Plaça de les Glòries Catalans .
Designed in 2005 by French architect
Jean Nouvel, the Torre Agbar is a new
city landmark. A LED system lights up
the building's cigar-shaped form in hues
of red, blue and green.

🏛 Parc Güell★★

Olot 1–13. Open Apr, Sept, Oct & Apr
8am–8.30pm, May–Aug 8am–9.30pm,
Jan-Feb 8.30am-6.30pm, Mar
8.30am-7pm. Free to enter Park;
Monumental Zone (limited numbers)
€10. 📞902 200 302.
www.parkguell.barcelona.
Gaudí's imagination shines with his
mushroom-shaped pavilions; a mosaic
dragon; the **Chamber of the Columns**, whose undulating mosaic roof
covers a forest of sloping columns;
and a remarkable **rolling bench★★**.
The aforementioned are all in the '
Monumental Zone'.
Not included in the zone is the **Casa-
Museu Gaudí** (Ctra del Carmel entrance;
open daily Oct–Mar 10am–6pm; Apr–
Sep 9am–8pm; closed during the
afternoon of 1 & 6 Jan and 25 & 26 Dec;
€5.50; 📞932 19 38 11; www.casamuseu-
gaudi.org), which offers the chance to
see how much of his work the architect
actually took home with him.

👣 WALKING TOUR★

LA RIBERA

Mercat de Santa Caterina

Av. Fransesc Cámbo 16. Closed Sun.
Originally opened in 1848, this is
Barcelona's oldest market and has
all the charm of La Boqueria without
the bulldozing crowds. In 2004 it was
crowned with an undulating roof scattered with colourful mosaic patterns
of fruit and vegetables. Inside, the
Espai Santa Caterina (open Jul–Sep
Mon– Sat 10am–2pm, rest of the year
until 3pm, and 8pm Thur–Fri) highlights
the remains of the former Dominican
Convent of Santa Catarina that stood
on this site.

▷ Facing the market's entrance,
take the street on the right (Carrer
Giralt el Pellisser) and follow it to
the end.

Carrer de Montcada★★

During the 13C and 14C, the Catalan fleet exercised unquestionable
supremacy over the western basin
of the Mediterranean. Important
merchant families acquired considerable social status and the Carrer de
Montcada became a showcase for
their wealth. The street, named after an
influential family of noble descent, is a
unique ensemble of merchants' palaces
and aristocratic mansions, most dating
back to the late Middle Ages; many are
occupied by museums and galleries.
Behind the austere facades are beautiful
patios with galleries and porches typical
of Catalan Gothic architecture.

Palau Berenguer d'Aiguilar★

This magnificent residence (Montcada
15, part of the Picasso Museum) which
was modified in the 15C and again in
the 18C has retained many architectural
elements typical of the noble houses of
medieval Barcelona. The sober facade
features decorative windows on the
lower floor, while a central patio (now
the entrance to the museum) is enliv-
ened by arches and mouldings.

Museu Picasso

Montcada 15–23. Open Tue–Sun &
public hols 9am–7pm (Thu until 9.30pm).
Closed 1 Jan, 1 May, 24 Jun, 25 Dec. €12;
exhibitions €6.50; joint ticket €14; free
Thu from 6pm. 📞932 56 30 00.
www.museupicasso.bcn.cat/en.
The Gothic palaces of Berenguer de
Aguilar and Baron de Castellet and the
Baroque Palau Meca are the setting for
the museum. Works here are dedicated,
in most cases, to Picasso's friend Sabar-
tès, shown in several portraits.
Picasso's early genius is evident in his
(conventional) portraits of his family,
First Communion and *Science and Charity*
(1896). Examples of his early Paris work
are *La Nana* and *La Espera; Los Desem-
parados* (1903) is from his Blue Period,

Modernista Architecture

Catalan Modernism developed between 1890 and 1920 alongside similar movements in other parts of Europe, such as Art Nouveau in France and Great Britain and Jugendstil in Germany. Modernista architecture sprang from artistic exploration that combined new industrial materials with modern techniques, using decorative motifs like curve and counter-curve and asymmetrical shapes in stained glass, ceramics and metal. The Catalan cultural movement of Modernisme was an expression of the region's striving for autonomy at a time when large fortunes were being made as a result of industrialisation: Designs frequently contained symbols of Catalan identity. The most representative architects of the style were Antoni Gaudí, Domènech i Montaner, Puig i Cadafalch and Jujol. A parallel movement in Catalan literature known as Renaixença (Renaissance) also flourished during the period. The mixture of regional and foreign architectural tradition in the work of **Josep Puig i Cadafalch** (1867–1956) reflects the Plateresque and Flemish styles. His main works are the Casa de les Punxes, the Casa Macaya (1901) and the Palau Baró de Quadras (1904). **Lluís Domènech i Montaner** (1850–1923) expressed his decorative style through extensive use of mosaics, stained glass and broken glazed tiles (*trencadís*). His main works include the Palau de la Música Catalana and Castell dels Tres Dragons.

Casa Vicens by Antoni Gaudí

© Lucas Vallecillos/age fotostock

Señora Casals from his Rose Period. His **Las Meninas series★** consists of variations on the masterwork by Velázquez. Picasso's skill as an engraver is seen in his outstanding etchings of bullfighting, and his talent as a ceramicist shines through in his vases, dishes and plates from the 1950s.

◉ Continue to the end of Carrer de Montcada.

Església/Basílica de Santa Maria del Mar★★

Pl. de Santa Maria 1. Open Mon–Sat 9am –1pm, 5–8.30pm; Sun 10am–2pm, 5–8pm. Guided visits available. ☏933 10 23 90. www.santamariadelmarbarcelona.org.

This is one of the most beautiful churches in the Catalan Gothic style, built in the 14C by ordinary sailors to compete with the cathedrals of the wealthy. The result is a graceful church of outstanding simplicity.

The west front is adorned only by a portal gable and the buttresses flanking the superb Flamboyant **rose window★**. The **interior★★★** gives the impression of spaciousness due to the elevation of the nave and the slenderness of the pillars.

Fossar de les Morenes (Mulberry Graveyard)

Opposite the Santa Maria del Mar, this little square is surrounded by pink-hued apartment buildings. An 'eternal flame' has been burning here since 1999 in memory of the victims of the 1714 siege on the city.

◉ From the rear entrance of the Santa Maria del Mar, stroll along the Passeig del Born to the end.

Mercat del Born

This steel structure, by Josep Fontseré (1874), was once the city's principal wholesale market. One of the first examples of Spanish industrial architecture, it is being converted into a museum of the La Ribera neighborhood and a library. The first part of the conversion, the **El Born Centre Cultural** (open Mar–Sept Tue–Sun 10am–8pm; until 7pm Oct–Feb Tue–Sat; €3; http://elbornculturaimemoria.barcelona.cat) opened in 2013. One of its main objectives is to illustrate iife in the city before and after the siege of 1713–14. The conversion was complicated by the fact that substantial remains of the medieval city were found when work started; these are also on display. A food court (open until 12am) was recently added.

▷ Take the Carrer del Comerç.

▲▲ Museu del Xocolata (Chocolate Museum)

Comerç 36. Open Mon–Sat 10am–7pm, Sun & hols 10am–3pm. Closed 1 & 6 Jan, 1 May, 25 & 26 Dec. €6. ℘932 68 78 78. www.museuxocolata.cat.

This lively 'museum' traces the history of commercial worldwide chocolate making with special emphasis on local specialities such as *monas,* elaborate chocolate sculptures that are a Catalan Easter tradition.

▷ Turn left out of the museum onto Passeig Picasso.

Parc de la Ciutadella★

Open daily 10am–dusk.

A citadel was built here by Philip V to control the rebellious city inhabitants but was demolished in 1868 and replaced by gardens. Gaudí collaborated on the design of the park waterfall while still a student. In 1888 the World Fair was held here, and the **Castell dels Tres Dragons★★** is a surviving pavilion, built in neo-Gothic style using unadorned brick and iron by Domènech i Montaner. It houses the Laboratori de Natura zoology centre (closed for renovations).

▲▲ **Zoo Barcelona** (check website for seasonal opening hours; ticket office closes 1hr before zoo; closed afternoon 25 Dec; €21.40; ℘902 45 75 45; www.zoobarcelona.cat) covers much of the park. Animals from all over the world are kept in settings ranging from 'natural' habitats to unsettlingly small cages. There's a vibrant primate community. A dolphin show is held in its Aquarama.

ADDITIONAL SIGHT

Palau de la Música Catalana★★

Palau de la Música 4–6. Guided tours every 30 mins (55 mins) Aug 9am–6pm, Easter & Jul 10am–6pm, rest of the year

Mercat del Born

Palau de la Música Catalana

10am–3.30pm. €20; advance purchase recommended. ☎93 295 72 00. www.palaumusica.cat.

This concert hall (1905–08) is Domènech i Montaner's most famous work. The **exterior★** displays lavish mosaics. Inside, an **inverted cupola★★** of polychrome glass is decorated with sculpted groups and mosaic figurines. A concert in this remarkable venue is a memorable occasion.

👣 WALKING TOUR

SEAFRONT★

Allow half a day. Bus 157, 57 follows the seafront to Vila Olímpica.

The seafront, from Montjuïc to the Besòs river, was completely redesigned for the 1992 Olympic Games, turning Barcelona once again toward the sea. The wide promenade is a great place to people-watch and escape the bustle of the city.

Drassanes (Shipyards)★★ and Museu Marítim★★

Av. de les Drassanes. Open daily 10am–8pm. €10; free from 3pm Sun. ☎93 342 99 20. www.mmb.cat.

The **old shipyards** that are home to the museum are among the best examples of civil Gothic architecture in Catalunya. Ten sections remain, under a timber roof supported by sturdy stone arches. The museum is currently in the final phases of a major restoration and not all areas may be open to visitors; see the website for details.

Among its many impressive models is a lifesize replica of the **Royal Galley of Don Juan of Austria★★**, Christian flagship at the Battle of Lepanto (1571). Also of note is The **Portulan of Gabriel de Vallseca** (1439), a nautical map that belonged to Amerigo Vespucci.

On the waterfront in Portal de la Pau is the restored 1918 schooner **Santa Eulàlia★** (Apr–Oct Tue–Fri & Sun 10am–8.30pm, Sat 2–8.30pm; Nov–Mar Tue–Fri & Sun 10am–5.30pm, Sat 2–5.30pm; €3), named after the city's patron saint. Pleasure boats depart from here too. The area around the port includes the palm-lined promenade known as the Moll de Bosch i Alsina (**Moll de la Fusta**), where there is a sculptre by American Pop Artist Roy Lichtenstein.

Monument a Colom

♿See La Rambla.

Port Vell★

The old harbour is a lively leisure area featuring bars, the **Maremàgnum** shopping and leisure centre (www.maremagnum.es) and an **aquarium**.

▶ From the Passeig Isabel II, cross the 'Rambla del Mar' footbridge in front of the Columbus Monument.

👥 Aquàrium★

Moll d'Espanya del Port Vell. Open Jan-Mar and Nov-Dec Mon-Fri 10am-7.30pm, Jun and Sep 10am-9pm, Jul-Aug 10am-9.30pm, Apr-May and Oct 10am-8pm; last admission one hour before closing. €21.

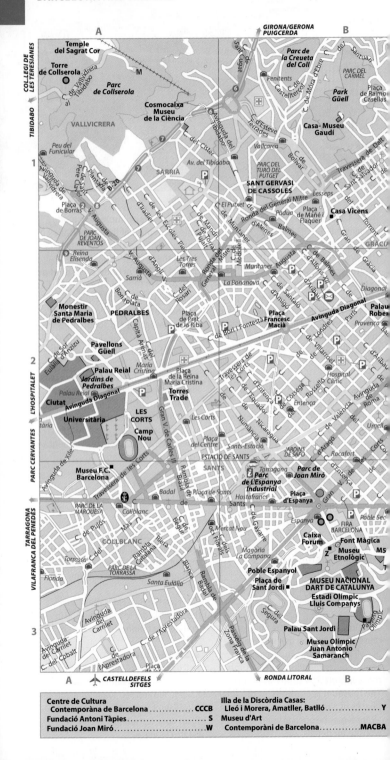

Centre de Cultura Contemporàna de Barcelona	CCCB
Fundació Antoni Tàpies	S
Fundació Joan Miró	W
Illa de la Discòrdia Casas: Lleó i Morera, Amatller, Batlló	Y
Museu d'Art Contemporàni de Barcelona	MACBA

Barceloneta beach

© rastika2000/iStockphoto.com

932 21 74 74. www.aquariumbcn.com. One of Europe's most impressive aquariums, the highlight is a spectacular viewing tunnel, 80m/262ft long.

▶ Return to Passeig del Colom and turn right, following the water's edge to the intersection of Via Laitana.

La Llotja★

Pas. Isabel II 1. 935 478 849. www.casallotja.com.
The building housing the Chamber of Commerce and Industry was completely rebuilt in the 18C. The **Gothic hall★★**, a lofty chamber with three naves, remains from the medieval building.

Porxos d'en Xifré

After the 'discovery' of America, many Catalans went there to seek their fortune. When they returned, these so-called *Indianos* built garish mansions to flaunt their wealth. Josep Xifré Cases (1777–1856) amassed such a large fortune in Cuba that he became the richest man in Barcelona. This block of Neoclassical buildings – all with arcades – now (rather ironically) houses cheap electrical goods stores.

▶ Head S to the marina.

👥 Museu d'Història de Catalunya★

Palau de Mar, Pl. de Pau Vila 3. Open Tue, Thu–Sat 10am–7pm, Wed 10am–8pm, Sun & public hols 10am–2.30pm. €4.50; free 12 Feb, 23 Apr, 18 May, 11 & 24 Sep, last Tue Oct–Jun.

932 25 47 00. www.mhcat.net.
This museum, set in an ex-warehouse, details Catalunya from prehistory to now. Kid-friendly sections include pulling water from a reproduction of a 12C well. Many descriptions are in Catalan only.

▶ Continue walking S along Passeig Joan de Borbó, either following the marina or venturing into the maze of streets just inland.

La Barceloneta★

The 'Iberian Naples' has quaint narrow streets plus restaurants and stalls offering seafood dishes.

▶ At the end of Passeig Joan de Borbó, you will hit the beach. Take the boardwalk in the opposite direction.

Vila Olímpica★

Built for the 1992 Olympics, this is one of Barcelona's most modern areas. Gardens and avenues of the Olympic Village are dotted with sculptures.
The **marina★★**, designed by JR de Clascà, has bars, restaurants and pavement cafés. The **view★★★** takes stretches to Mallorca on a clear day.

ADDITIONAL SIGHTS
Basílica de la Mercè★

Pl. de la Mercè 1. Open 10am–1pm, 6–8pm. 933 15 27 56.
www.basilicadelamerce.com.
This 1760 church has an unusual curved Baroque facade. The facade on Carrer

Ample is Renaissance and was moved from elsewhere. A Gothic statue in the interior, the **Mare de Déu de la Mercè★**, is by Pere Moragues (1361).

👥 Museu Blau

Parque del Forum, Plaza Leonardo da Vinci. Mar–Sep Tue–Sat 10am–7pm, Sun until 8pm. Oct–Feb Tue–Fri 10am–6pm, Sat until 7pm, Sun until 8pm. Closed 1 Jan, 1 May, 25 Dec. €6, €5 exhibitions; free Sun from 3pm, first Sun of the month, 12 Feb, 18 May, 24 Sep. ℘932 566 002. http://museuciencies.cat.

Continue east along the seafront and you'll come to the Natural Science Museum's journey through life on earth, from its origins to the present day and beyond. The multi-media exhibiton has plenty to interest all the famiy, though some say the new CosmoCaixa (👉see ADDITIONAL SIGHTS) is more interesting and up-to-date.

👣 WALKING TOUR

MONTJUÏC★

Alllow 1 day, including museum visits.
The **Castell** (castle) built on this 173m/568ft hill during the 1640 rebellion is visitable after a multi-year renovation (open Mar–Oct 10am–8pm, rest of year 10am–6pm; €5; guided tours available, €9, 11am English; ℘932 56 44 40; http://ajuntament.barcelona.cat/castelldemontjuic); it offers 360-degree city and harbour **views★**.

The **Plaça d'Espanya** remains from the 1929 exhibition, along with the illuminated **fountain** (Font Magica) by Carles Buïgas, the reconstructed **reception pavilion★★** by Mies van der Rohe (an icon of Modern architecture), and the Spanish Village (Poble Espanyol, or Pueblo Español in Castilian).

👥 Poble Espanyol★ (Spanish Village)

▶ Av. Francesc Ferrer i Guàrdia 13. Open Mon 9am–8pm, Tue–Thu & Sun 9am–12am. Fri 9am–3am, Sat 9am–4am. Shops close 6–8pm. From €6.30. ℘935 08 63 00. www.poble-espanyol.com.

This Disneyesque Spanish folk village-cum-architectural museum reflects life in the various parts of Spain and was built for the 1929 exhibition. Its re-creations are convincing and contain many original artefacts; in minutes, you can wander from a small Castilian square to a street in an Andalucían village with white houses and geraniums, and so on. The scene is lively: There are craftsmen making traditional Spanish wares plus shops, restaurants, bars and even two nightclubs.

▶ Walk down Av. Francesc Ferrer i Guàrdia.

CaixaForum

Av. Francesc Ferrer i Guàrdia 6–8. Open 10am–8pm (Wed Jul & Aug 11pm). Closed 1, 6 Jan, 25 Dec. Permanent exhibitions free, temporary exhibitions from €4. ℘934 76 86 00. www.caixaforum.es/barcelona.

This early-20C textile factory, a magnificent Modernist landmark, was built by **Puig i Cadafalch**. It now houses a social and cultural centre with exhibits from a modern art collection of more than 800 works alongside experimental modern art exhibitions.

▶ Climb the stairs to the MNAC.

Museu Nacional d'Art de Catalunya (MNAC)★★★

Palau Nacional, Parc de Montjuïc. Open Tue–Sat 10am–8pm (Oct–Apr 6pm); Sun & public hols year-round 10am–3pm. €12 (two days), roof €2; free 12 Feb, 18 May, 11 & 24 Sep, Sat from 3pm and first Sun. ℘936 22 03 60. www.museunacional.cat.

The Palau Nacional was built for the 1929 fair; its museum of Catalan art includes remarkable **Romanesque and Gothic collections★★★**.

Romanesque art – The display evokes contemporary churches. Note 12C frescoes by Sant Joan de Boí (Room 2); the late-11C lateral apses by Sant Quirze de Pedret (Room 3); the Santa Maria de Taüll ensemble (12C), dominated by a fine *Epiphany;* and Sant Climent de Taüll

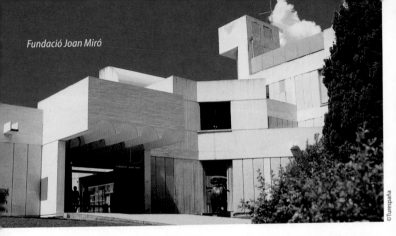

Fundació Joan Miró

©Turespaña

(Room 5) with the remarkable *Christ in Majesty*: The apse is a Renaissance masterpiece. Note the anti-naturalism and geometry.

Altar frontals are painted on a panel or carved. In the magnificent sculpture galleries is the polychrome *Majestad de Batlló* (13C). The museum also presents **capitals★** (Room 6), silverware and enamels. Paintings from **Sigena** (1200) evidence a great stylistic shift.

Gothic art – Exhibits of 13C–14C Catalan Gothic art include stone retables attributed to **Jaime Cascalls** (Rooms 15 and 16); the collection of Catalan Gothic art (Room 30), with works by **Guerau Gener, Juan Mates, Ramon de Mur, Juan Antigó, Bernardo Despuig** and **Jaime Cirera**; and a room dedicated to **Bernardo Martorell** (no. 32), for whom detail and shading were paramount; works by the **Master of La Seu d´Urgell** (Room 34); and 14C–15C funerary sculpture (Room 50).

Other Collections – The **Cambó Collection** includes painters of the rank of **Zurbarán**, Tintoretto, **El Greco**, Rubens, Cranach the Elder and **Goya**. The **Thyssen-Bornemisza Collection**, selected from the Museu Thyssen, comprises works from the Middle Ages to the 18C, notably paintings of the Virgin and Child. Portraits represent several schools of the 15C–18C.

In the **Renaissance and Baroque** section are Flemish and Italian masters along with works of Ayne Bru, Pere Nunyes and Pedro Berruguete. Other **19C–20C** artworks include Fortuny paintings, Modernista furniture and playful posters by **Gaudí, Domènech i Montaner**, Casas, Rusiñol et al.

◉ Go to the rear of the MNAC and take the escalator to Av. l' Estadi.

Anella Olímpica★

High on the mountainside is the 'Olympic Ring' complex. The **Olympic Stadium★**, with its 1929 facade, now hosts athletics chamionships and major concerts. The nearby **Palau Sant Jordi★★**, designed by Arata Isozak, was one of the main venues of the 1992 Summer Olympics. It also hosts major sporting events, concerts and shows. The **telecommunications tower** is the work of Santiago Calatrava.

◉ Continue on Av. l' Estadi, following the signs to the Fundació Joan Miró.

Fundació Joan Miró★★★

Parc de Montjuïc. Open Tue–Fri & Sat 10am–6pm (8pm Jul–Sep), Thu 10am–9pm, Sun & public hols 10am–3pm. €13. ℘934 43 94 70. www.fmirobcn.org.

The works of Avant-Garde artist **Joan Miró** (1893–1983) are ubiquitous in Barcelona: a mural at the airport, pavement mosaics on La Rambla, the logo of La Caixa bank and on and on. Born in Barcelona, Miró spent 1921 and 1922 in Paris; his painting *La Masía* signalled his departure from figurative art. Between 1939 and 1941 he executed *Constellations*, 23 panels expressing the horrors of World War II.

Miró's Foundation is housed in a modern building of harmonious proportions designed by Josep Lluís Sert, a close friend.

The 10 000 items were largely executed in the last 20 years of his life. A small exhibition of contemporary art includes Alexander Calder's *Fountain of Mercury*.

ADDITIONAL SIGHTS

Museu d'Arqueologia de Catalunya (MAC)★

Pg. de Santa Madrona 39–41. Open Tue–Sat 9.30am–7pm, Sun & public hols 10am–2.30pm. €5.50; free last Tue Oct–Jun, 12 Feb, 23 Apr, 18 May, 11 & 24 Sep. ℘934 23 21 49. www.mac.cat.

Household effects, ceramics and votive figures trace the history of Catalunya from Palaeolithic times through to the Visigothic. The collection is housed in the former Palace of Graphic Arts on Montjuïc, which was built for the 1929 International Exhibition.

Monestir de Santa Maria de Pedralbes★★

Bajada Monestir 9. Open Oct–Mar Tue–Fri & hols 10am–2pm, Sat–Sun 10am–5pm. €5; free Sun from 3pm and first Sun. ℘932 56 34 34. http://monestirpedralbes.bcn.cat.

Founded in the 14C by King James II of Aragón and his fourth wife, the monastery has a fine Catalan Gothic **church★** with the tomb of the foundress.

The three-storey **cloisters★** surrounded by cells and oratories are sober and elegant. The Sant Miquel Chapel is adorned with beautiful **frescoes★★★** by Ferrer Bassá (1346), whose works combine the style of the Siena School with a Tuscan sense of volume and perspective. Restoration works are in process; certain areas may be cordoned off.

Disseny Hub Barcelona

Plaça de les Glòries, Av. Diagonal 686. Open Tue–Sun 10am–8pm. Closed 1 Jan, 1 May, 24 Jun, 25 Dec. €6; free Sun 3–8pm, first Sun, 8 & 12 Feb, 24 Sep ℘932 56 68 00. www.museudeldisseny.cat.

This futuristic stunner, opened in 2014, houses three major art collections:

The **Museu de les Arts Decoratives** (Decorative Arts) is a rich collection that spans domestic objects from the medieval to the *Modernista* and contemporary industrial – movements Catalans have excelled at. Exhibits ranging from chests and desks, lamps, chairs and even bottles illustrate the changing face of design vis-à-vis technological breakthroughs and mass production.

The **Museu Tèxtil i d'Indumentaria** (Textile & Clothing) takes you on a journey from 16C fashion to today with the work of Spanish designers (such as Balenciaga and Paco Rabanne), Dior and Karl Lagerfeld. Also noteworthy is the jewellery collection, comprising some 500 pieces produced in Spain.

The **Museu de Ceràmica** (Ceramics) has a rotating collection of Catalan and Valencian pieces, focussing on 18C and 19C – in particular Alcora, a Valencian town that excels in the medium. Don't miss the works of Catalan ceramicist **Josep Llorens Artigas**, alongside those of **Picasso** and **Miró**.

Camp Nou

Av. Aristides Maillol. Open daily, see website for times. From €31.50. ℘934 963 600. www.fcbarcelona.com/camp-nou.

FC Barcelona stadium seats some 100 000, and its extensive facilities include the **Museu FC Barcelona**, where fans can ogle the many trophies won by their beloved Barça team. Stadium tours go through the same tunnel the players emerge from during home matches.

👥 CosmoCaixa★

Isaac Newton . Open 10am–8pm. Closed 25 Dec & 6 Jan. €5. ℘932 12 60 50. www.cosmocaixa.es.

The city's newer Science Museum combines facts and fun in exhibits such as a Foucault pendulum, a giant soaring geological wall and an 'Amazon' rainforest complete with 82 aimal and 52 plant species and – yes – rain. You'll also find a 3-D Planetarium and dozens of hands-on stations including the Toca-Toca

(Touch-Touch) animal area. The gift shop is great for buying gifts for kids.

ADDRESSES

🏨 STAY

The Barri Gòtic has the highest concentration of cheap accommodation. Crossing La Rambla, the Raval district should be approached with caution by night. For the most chic, and generally safest, accommodation, the Eixample has a wide range of luxury and design hotels.

🛏🍴🛎 **Hotel Condal** – Bouería 23 (Barri Gòtic). 🚇 Liceu. 𝄢933 18 18 82. www.hotelcondal.es. 52 rooms, 🚮 €6. Situated between La Rambla and the Barri Gótic, this smart, bright hotel is a fine base. Request a quieter rear room.

🛏🍴🛎 **Hotel Gaudí** – Nou de la Rambla 12 (Ciutat Vella). 🚇 Liceu. 𝄢933 17 90 32. www.hotelgaudibarcelona. com. 73 rooms, 🚮 €12. The location opposite the Palau Güell and Modernist décor evoke the namesake artist. Upper-floor rooms and those withbalconies enjoy superb views of the city and Palau Güell.

🛏🍴🛎 **Hotel Hesperia Barri Gòtic** – Ample 31 (Barri Gòtic). 🚇 Jaume I. 𝄢933 10 51 00. www.hesperia.com. 71 rooms, 🚮 €18.90. This hotel close to the waterfront is on a narrow street in the old quarter, between the post office and the Basílica de La Mercè. The lobby in a covered patio is a highlight. Room service available.

🛏🍴🛎🛎 **Hotel Granvía** – Gran Via de les Corts Catalanes 642 (Eixample). 🚇Cataluyna. 𝄢933 18 19 00. www. hotelgranvia.com. 53 rooms, 🚮 €14. This impressive banker's residence from the late 19C was converted into a hotel in 1936 and has minimalist rooms with clean lines and earth tones.

🛏🍴🛎🛎🛎 **Sir Victor** – Carrer del Rosselló 265 (Eixample). 🚇Girona. 𝄢932 71 12 44. www.sirhotels.com. 91 rooms, 🚮 €29. Welcome to the city's buzziest new hotel. Opened in June 2019, it embodies the form-over-formality philosophy of Barcelona's newest crop of designer properties, featuring some 330 original works by Catalan artists. An oasis in the heart of the tourist fray, it also has a spa and rooftop pool and bar.

🍽EAT

🍴🍴 **Senyor Parellada** – L'Argentaria 37 (Ribera). 🚇 Jaume I. 𝄢933 10 50 94. www.senyorparellada.com. Tuck into Catalan comfort food like fish soup and goat chops at this restaurant adorned with chandeliers. Request a ground-floor table in the covered patio. Skip the paella – it's not their strongest suit.

🍴🍴🍴 **Los Caracoles** – Escudellers 14 (Ciutat Vella). 🚇 Liceu. 𝄢933 01 20 41. www.loscaracoles.es. Founded in 1835, this legendary restaurant specialises in escargot (as its name suggests), though many come here for the rice and meat dishes – all served in a tiled dining room amid wine barrels, murals and photos.

🍴🍴🍴 **L'Olivé** – Balmes 47 (Eixample). 🚇 Passeig de Gràcia. 𝄢934 52 19 90. www.restaurantlolive.com. Closed Sun eve. An old stone house is the setting for this romantic restaurant with terrific seafood dishes. Start with the cod fritters.

🍴🍴🍴🍴 **Tragaluz** – Pas. de la Concepció 5 (Eixample). 🚇 Diagonal. 𝄢934 87 06 21. www.grupotragaluz.com. One of Barcelona's most hopping modern restaurants, known for Mediterranean-fusion cuisine, takes up three storeys and has a sliding greenhouse roof.

🍴🍴🍴🍴 **Casa Leopoldo** – Sant Rafael 24 (Ciutat Vella). 🚇 Liceu. 𝄢934 41 30 14. www.casaleopoldo.es. Closed Sun eve (all day in Jul) and Mon. When the El Raval stalwart came under new ownership in 2017, locals shuddered: *another old-school classic bites the dust.* But their fears were allayed, since the menu and decor have hardly changed a lick; in fact, some say the food is better than ever. As you devour dishes like saucy seafood meatballs and fried calamari, take in the gorgeous tiles and bullfighting memorabilia. .

🍴🍴🍴🍴 **Casa Calvet** – Casp 48 (Eixample). 🚇 Urquinaona. 𝄢934 12 40 12. www.casacalvet.es. Closed Sun & public hols. It's not every day that you get to sit down to a refined (and well-priced) Catalan feast in a dining room designed by Gaudí – so soak it up.

🍽🍽🍽🍽 **Enigma** – Carrer de Sepúlveda 38-40 (Sant Antoni). 🚇 Poble Sec. 📞616 69 63 22. www.elbarri. com. Closed Sun–Mon. Albert Adrià, of El Bulli fame, is back with a vengeance at this mind-bending restaurant from the future that'll set you back around €350 a head. Multi-hour tasting menus, which resist categorisation, unfold with gustatory surprises and plenty of pyrotechnics.

TAPAS

Euskal Etxea – Placeta Montcada 1–3 (Ribera). 🚇 Jaume I. 📞933 10 21 85. www.euskaletxeataberna.com. Closed half of Aug. By the church of Santa Maria del Mar, this Basque-inflected pintxo bar has delectable pork chops and fried fish. Wash things down with txakoli, the Basque Country's effervescent white.

Tickets – Paral·lel 164 (Poble Sec). 🚇 Poble Sec. 📞606 225 545. Reserve in advance online at www.elbarri.com, or call to see if there are any cancellations. Closed Sun and Mon. The Adrià brothers serve ultra-experimental tapas at this gastronomic playground. Dishes like asparagus with green-almond ice cream and the legendary spherified olive make Tickets one of the most sought-after tables in town

El Xampanyet – Montcada 22 (Ribera). 🚇 Jaume I. 📞933 19 70 03. Closed Sun, Holy Week and Aug. In an alleyway close to the Picasso Museum, this riotous bar is famous for its anchovies and cava (sparkling wine).

BARS / CAFÉS

Nomad Coffee La & Shop – Passatge Sert 12 (Ciutat Vella). 🚇 Urquinaona. 📞628 56 62 35. www.nomadcoffee.es. The third-wave coffee shop behind Barcelona's coffee renaissance, Nomad roasts its own beans locally for its expertly pulled flat whites, pour-overs, coldbrew and more.

Café de la Opera – Rambla dels Caputxins 74 (Ciutat Vella). 🚇 Liceu. 📞933 17 75 85. www.cafeoperabcn.com. A colourful history, Modernist facade and 19C atmosphere keeps this café (est. 1929) perennially packed.

Jamboree – Pl. Reial 17 (Ciutat Vella). 🚇 Liceu. 📞933 017 564. www.jamboree jazz.com. Top jazz musicians perform here night in, night out.

Luz de Gas – Muntaner 246 (Eixample). 🚇 Barceloneta. 📞932 09 77 11. www. luzdegas.com. This upscale nightclub picks up after 1am with DJ sets; security guards can be grouchy about letting in all-male groups.

Els 4Gats – Montsió 3 bis (Ciutat Vella). 🚇 Catalunya. 📞933 02 41 40. www.4gats.com. A byword for Modernist Bohemian Barcelona, this landmark café was a meeting place for artists such as Picasso, Casas and Utrillo. Disclaimer: It's more about the ambiance than the food.

SHOPPING
ANTIQUES

Bulevard dels Antiquaris – Pas. de Gràcia 55 (Eixample). 🚇 Diagonal. 📞932 15 44 99. www.bulevarddelsantiquaris. com. Explore a 'shopping mall' of 73 shops selling fine artwork and antiques.

Plaça de la Catedra – Ciutat Vella. 🚇 Jaume I. A small market with stalls selling antiques is held here on holidays.

Plaça Sant Josep Oriol – Ciutat Vella. 🚇 Liceu. Shop mirrors, furniture and art at this popular weekend market.

La Palla and Banys Nous – Ciutat Vella. 🚇 Liceu. These two streets are lined with reputable antique shops.

FASHION

Mango – Passeig de Gràcia 65 (Eixample). 📞932 15 75 30. www.mango.com. Browse the flagship of the international fashion chain that started in Barcelona.

La Manual Alpargatera – Carrer Avinyó 7 (Barri Gòtic). 📞933 01 01 72. www. lamanualalpargatera.es. Walk out wearing a new pair of hand-sewn espadrilles.

ART GALLERIES

Barcelona's most prestigious galleries are centred around Carrer Consell de Cent, along the Rambla de Catalunya and the Carrer Montcada in La Ribera.

Terrassa

Terrassa (Tarrasa in Castilian) is synonymous with textiles, the industry that made it prosperous. It's surrounded by the mountains of the Sant Llorenç del Munt i l'Obac natural park. Along its streets, industrial and Modernista architecture meld to reflect the city's early-20C economic growth.

▶ **Population:** 218 535
♿ **Michelin Map:** 576 H 36.
🛈 **Info:** Plaça Freixa i Argemí 11. ℰ937 39 70 19. www.visitaterrassa.cat.
◖ **Location:** 31km/19mi NW of Barcelona along the C 58. 🚇Metro link with Barcelona
👫 **Kids:** Museu de la Ciència y la Tècnica de Catalunya.
🕐 **Timing:** Terrassa makes a good day trip from Barcelona.

SIGHTS

Conjunto Monumental de Esglésias de Sant Pere★

Open Tue–Sat 10am–1.30pm, 4–7pm, Sun & hols 11am–2pm. Closed 1 Jan, 1 May, 25, 26 Dec. €5.50. ℰ937 83 37 02.
The **Antiguo baptisterio de Sant Miquel★** was built in the 9C using late Roman remains. The dome rests on eight pillars; four have Roman capitals, four are Visigothic. Alabaster windows in the apse filter light onto 9C–10C pre-Romanesque wall paintings. The crypt's three apses have horseshoe arches.
The Romanesque Lombard church of **Santa Maria★** has an octagonal cupola and a *cimborrio* (lantern); a 5C mosaic survives in front. A 13C wall fresco in the south transept, of the martyrdom of Thomas Becket, retains bright colours. Note the 15C north transept altarpiece by Jaime Huguet of **St Abdon and St Sennen★★**.
Sant Pere (6C) follows a trapezoid plan with a Romanesque transept crossing. In the apse is a **stone altarpiece★**.

Castell Cartoixa de Vallparadís

Salmerón. Open Wed–Sat 10am–1.30pm, 4–7pm; Sun 11am–2pm. €3; free first Sun. ℰ937 85 71 44.
Built in the 12th century, this castle and former monastery houses the local history museum.

👫 Museu de la Ciència y la Tècnica de Catalunya★

Rambla d'Ègara 270. Open Sep–Jun Tue–Fri 10am–6pm, Sat–Sun 10am–2.30pm, 4.30-8.30; Sun & hols 10am-2.30pm. Jul–Aug Tue–Sun 10am–2.30pm. Closed 1, 6 Jan, 25–26 Dec. €4.50; free first Sun. ℰ937 36 89 66. www.mnactec.cat.
Catalunya's shiny Museum of Science and Technology is housed in an Art Nouveau woollen mill.

Museu Textil

Salmerón 25. Open Fri-Sun 10am-2pm, Tue & Thu 10am-2pm, 4-7pm. ℰ937 31 52 02. www.cdmt.es.
This museum of textile and fashion presents a comprehensive overview of the local industry. Vividly coloured silks are a highlight of the collection.

Masía Freixa★

Parc de San Jordi.
The 1907 modernist building houses the tourist office. Note the pleasing repetition of parabolic arches.

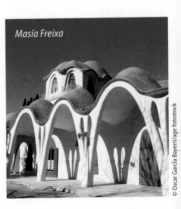

Masía Freixa

© Oscar García Bayerri/age fotostock

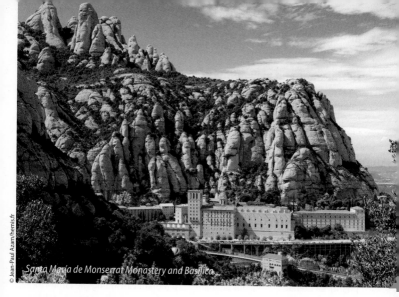
Santa María de Monserrat Monastery and Basilica

© Jean-Paul Azam/hemis.fr

Serra de Montserrat★★

The grand site★★★ of the Macizo de Montserrat (Montserrat Massif) was the setting for Wagner's *Parsifal*. Here, hard Eocene conglomerates rise above eroded formations. It is the main place of devotion to the Virgin in Catalunya. Views★★ from the road are impressive. The Montserrat cable car runs from near Monistrol de Montserrat.

- **Michelin Map:** 574 H 35.
- **Info:** Pl. de la Creu, opposite the funicular 1. ℰ938 77 77 01. www.montserratvisita.com
- **Location:** 49km/31mi NW of Barcelona along the C 58, 19km/12mi E of Terrassa. Metro link with Barcelona, Plaça Espanya station.

A BIT OF GEOGRAPHY

Montserrat (the serrated mountain) is a mountain range of impressive beauty. Long a source of inspiration for musicians, poets, geographers and travellers, it is considered Catalunya's spiritual heart and remains an important place of devotion.

VISIT

Santa María de Monserrat Monastery and Basilica

Open Mon–Fri 10am–5.45, Sat & Sun until 6:45pm. €7 ℰ938 77 77 66. www.abadiamontserrat.net.

The most-visited site in Barcelona's environs is indubitably this sprawling cliffside monastery. The Benedictines arrived in the 9C, and every century since has seen additions to the structure. In 1812, it was ransacked by the French. The present buildings are 19C and 20C. Inside the dark, ornate **basilica** (15C) is **La Moreneta ★★**, the shrine of the Black Madonna. According to legend, this 12C polychrome statue of the Black Madonna, now above the high altar, was discovered in a cave by shepherds.

Learn more about the history of the monastery in its musuem.

The Basilica is famous for its **Gregorian chant**, usually sung at Mass at 11am and Vespers at 6.45pm. The **Escolanía**, one of the world's oldest boys' choirs, is another transcendent aural experience (Mon–Thu 1pm and 6.45pm, Fri 1pm, Sun & festivals 12pm and 6.45pm; ℰ938 77 77 67; www.escolania.cat).

Hermitages and viewpoints

Access via the mountain trails, cable cars or funiculars - all run regularly, but note the closing times, particularly out of season. 📞 93 204 10 41 www.cremallerademontserrat.com.

The 13 hermitages, abandoned since the arrival of Napoleon's troops, offer historical interest and fine views. To make the most of the surrounding scenery without tiring yourself out, take the cable car or funicular up, then walk back down.

Ermita de la Trinitat (🚶45min on foot), secluded in a bucolic plain, sits beneath three mountains: El Elefante (The Elephant), La Preñada (Pregnant Woman) and La Momia (The Mummy). On a clear day, **Sant Jeroni★** (🚶 1hr30min on foot, or go by car), at 1 238m/4 062ft, offers a **panorama** from the Pyrenees to the Balearic Islands. **Ermita de Santa Cecilia** features an attractive 11C **Romanesque church★** that hosts temporary art exhibitions (prices vary). Its east end is encircled by Lombard bands. The statue of the Virgin was found in **Santa Cova** (holy cave, 🚶 1hr walk), which has views of the Llobregat Valley. **Sant Miquel★** (🚶 30min from the monastery; 1hr from the upper terminal of the Sant Miquel funicular) has a general view of the monastery. **Sant Joan** (🚶 30min from upper terminal of the Sant Joan funicular) offers a fantastic panorama including the Ermita de San Onofre, which clings to the rock face.

Sitges★★

Sitges is a beach town famous for its crystalline waters, exemplary Modernist architecture and riotous Carnival, well-loved (and attended) by LGBT+ folk from across Spain and Europe. In fact, Sitges is perhaps Spain's most popular LGBT+ resort, though it's frequented by holidaymakers of every orientation. The seafront promenade, Passeig Marítim, is dotted with hotels and luxury residences.

▶ **Population:** 28 969.
⚭ **Michelin Map:** 574 I 35 – Catalunya (Barcelona)
ℹ **Info:** Plaza Eduard Maristany, 2. 📞 938 94 42 51. www.visitsitges.com.
◖ **Location:** Between Barcelona and Tarragona. 🚆 Sitges.
👥 **Kids:** The Museu del Ferrocarril is the place to admire steam engines.
🕐 **Timing:** While away a few days at the beach.

OLD TOWN★★

1hr 30min.

The parish church dominates the breakwater of La Punta. Balconies of white houses erupt with flowers. Museums in neo-Gothic mansions display canvases from the late 19C, when Rusiñol and Miguel Utrillo (father of the French painter) painted here.

Museu Cau Ferrat★★

Fonollar. Open Tue–Sat Jul–Sep 10am–8pm, Mar–Jun & Oct until 7pm, Nov–Feb until 5pm. €10, combined with Museu Maricel. 📞 93 894 03 64. www.museusdesitges.cat.

Santiago Rusiñol (1861–1931) added Gothic features to two 16C fishermen's houses, which he left to the town along with ceramics, paintings and sculptures. Among the **paintings**, note two remarkable works by **El Greco**: *Penitent Mary Magdalene* and *The Repentance of St Peter*. The gallery also contains canvases by Picasso, Casas and Rusiñol himself *(Poetry, Music and Painting)*. The museum takes its name from its **wrought-iron** collection *(cau ferrat)*.

Sitges

Museu Maricel★

Fonollar . Same hours and price as Museu Cau Ferrat. www.museusdesitges.cat. Next door to Museu Cau Ferrat, this museum in a 14C hospital takes visitors on a tour of the different periods of art from the 10th to early 20th centuries. Modernisme features prominently.

Fundació Stämpfli - Art Contemporani★

Plaça de l'Ajuntament. Open Jul–Sep Wed–Sun, Oct–Jun Fri–Sun; see website for seasonal hours. €5. ☎93 894 03 64. www.fundacio-stampfli.org.
This former fish market houses one of the the region's finest contemporary art collections. There are 60 works by 90 artists from around the world.

Casa Bacardí★

Plaça Ajuntament. Wed-Sat 12-2pm, 4-8pm, Sun 12-2pm, 4-7pm. €15. ☎938 94 81 51 . www.casabacardi.es.
The founder of the Bacardí brand, Facundo Bacardí Massó (1814-1886), was raised in Sitges before emigrating to Cuba. The 'museum' tells the company's story and ends with a rum tasting.

Museu Romàntic★

Sant Gaudenci 1. Closed for renovation. www.museusdesitges.cat.
This late-18C house gives a good idea of bourgeois life during the Romantic period with its frescoed walls, English furniture, mechanical devices and musical boxes.

Festivals in Sitges

Sitges is known for its Corpus Christi flowers, Fantasy & Horror Film Festival (early October; http://sitgesfilmfestival.com), vintage car rally (Mar) and international theatre festival (Jun). Its major fiesta Sant Bartomeu (24 Aug), celebrated with fireworks and a traditional parade of giant figures. The town is also renowned for its exuberant Carnival. For many LGBT+ vacationers, every night is a festival here: There are tons of gay bars, nightclubs and ticketed events.

Sitges Carnival

The **Lola Anglada collection** is an outstanding display of 17–19C dolls from all over Europe.

EXCURSIONS

Vilanova i la Geltrú★

⏵7km/4.3mi SW. 🚆Vilanova i la Geltrú. Set in a small bay, this is an important fishing harbour and a holiday resort.

Museu Romàntic Can Papiol★

Major 32. Open Fri-Sat 11am–2pm, 4–6pm (Jun–Sep 6–8pm), Sun 10am–2pm. Guided visits only, on the hour. €4. ☏938 93 03 82. www.museucanpapiol.cat.
The Papiol family mansion, built 1780–1801, evokes the life of the devout, well-to-do industrial middle class. Austerity reigns in the library with its 5 000 volumes, in the chapel with its strange relic of St Constance and in the reception rooms with their biblical scenes in grey monochrome. However, there's an opulent streak in the furnishings and in the ballroom.

Biblioteca-Museu Balaguer★

Av. Víctor Balaguer. Open Mon-Fri 9.30am-2pm, Weds 9.30am-7pm. €4. ☏938 15 42 02. www.victorbalaguer.cat.
This library-museum in a curious Egyptian-Greek building was an initiative of poet-historian-politician **Víctor Balaguer** (1824–1901). The **contemporary art collection** includes Catalan works from the 1950s and 1960s (*Legado 56*). There are also **16C and 17C paintings** (El Greco, Murillo, Carducho, Maino, Carreño etc.) and Egyptian and Asian art.

👥 Museu del Ferrocarril★

Pl. d'Eduard Maristany. Open mid-Jul–Aug 10.30am–2.30pm, 5–8pm; Sep–mid-Jul Tue–Sun 10.30am–2.30pm (Sat 4–6.30pm). €6. ☏938 15 84 91. www.museudelferrocarril.org.
This is one of the most impressive collections of railway engines in Spain.

Vilafranca del Penedès★

⏵29km/18mi NW by the C 158 and C 15. 🚆Vilafranca del Penedès.

Situated in the centre of the Penedés wine-growing region, Vilafranca proudly wears the badge of 'Catalunya's Wine Capital'. The Penedés is synonymous with **cava**, Spain's famed bubbly, and you can visit all the big names here such as Cordoníu, whose cellars are a glorious Modernista affair (www.codorniu.com/es/cavas), and Freixenet (www.freixenet.es). There are some 60 more smaller bodegas within the area, including the more highly esteemed Recaredo and Raventós i Blanc, and many can be visited (www.enoturismepenedes.cat).

Vinseum – Museu de les Cultures del Vi de Catalunya ★★

Pl. Jaume I5. Open Tue–Sat May–Sep 10am–7pm, Oct–Apr Tue–Sat 10am–2pm, 4–7pm; Sun 10am–2pm. Closed Mon, 1 May, 25–26 December, 1 & 6 Jan. €7, free first Sun & 18 May. ☏938 900 582. www.vinseum.cat.
This delightful centre celebrates the culture of wine, the evolution of the region through wine production and and even how local music and folklore have been inspired by wine.

ADDRESSES

🛏 STAY

🍴🍴 **Hotel Medium Romàntic** – Sant Isidre 33. Sitges. ☏938 94 83 75. www.mediumhoteles.com. 69 rooms. This establishment takes up two 19C buildings, each with period decor and a certain decadent charm.

🍴🍴🍴 **ME Sitges Terramar** – Passeig Marítim 80, Sitges. ☏938 94 00 50. www.melia.com. ⊞ €20. 213 rooms. Opened in 2018, the ME (a Meliá subsidiary) has a rooftop pool fringed with Balinese beds, a bar right on the beach and bright, understated rooms.

🍴/EAT

🍴 **La Oca** – Parellades 41, Sitges. ☏938 94 79 36. www.laocadesitges.com. Closed mid-Oct–mid-Dec and 25 & 31 Dec. This inexpensive, modern restaurant in the centre of Sitges is known for its grilled meats.

Northern Catalunya and Principat d'Andorra

Geographically, Catalunya is a triangle of varied landscapes, from snow-topped peaks to sun-kissed beaches, set between the French border, Aragón and the Mediterranean. Culturally, however, it's more or less a nation unto itself: It has its own language, cuisine, customs and proud history. Barcelona has long been the face of Catalunya on the international stage, but as early as the 1950s, Northern Europeans were flocking to the blue water and pine-fringed coves of the Costa Brava. The Pyrenees and the Principality of Andorra, on the other hand, welcome mostly domestic and cross-border visitors, skiers and walkers.

The mountains

The Pyrenees, between Andorra and the Cap de Creus headland, is a green wooded area with peaks over 3 100m/ 10 170ft. It's phenomenal walking country, dotted with quaint villages and a smattering of ski resorts and veined with waymarked trails. Andorra, a tax haven, is famous for its shopping but has great mountain fun as well: The Port d'Envalira pass, the highest in the range, is particularly majestic. The Pyrenees also contain one of Spain's richest cultural legacies. During the 10C and 12C, Romanesque art and architecture became prolific here as Catalunya emerged as a force to be reckoned with. In the Vall de Boí, a UNESCO World Heritage site, stout, slate-roof Romanesque churches are an ancient part of the bucolic landscape. Art of the period is distinguished by highly expressive religious frescoes featuring vivid colour and elongated, doe-eyed creatures. Most of the originals have been moved to Barcelona's MNAC, but sensitive reproductions evoke a sense of time and place.

Highlights

1. **Girona** in early May during the flower festival (p351)
2. The romantic, art-filled village of **Cadaqués** (p356)
3. The coastal scenery of the **Cap de Begur** on the Costa Brava (p360)
4. The surreal Teatre-Museu Dalí in **Figueres** (p365)
5. Romanesque art and architecture in the **Vall de Boí** (p376)

former Jewish quarters in Europe. Nearby, the villages of Besalú and Figueres, the latter being the spiritual home of Salvador Dalí, will dazzle even the most doubtful art sceptic (or jaded connoisseur).

Costa Brava and inland

The Costa Brava was 'discovered' and made fashionable by artists such as Dalí, Picasso and Marc Chagall and was clobbered by the first wave of Spain's mass tourism boom. Fortunately, with a few unsightly exceptions (we're looking at you, Lloret de Mar), it has largely remained true to its name, meaning 'wild' or 'rugged' coast. Beaches range from rocky coves to long, talc-fine golden stretches. The international gateway to the coast is landlocked Girona, a well-preserved city with a distinctive character and history – plus one of the most stunning

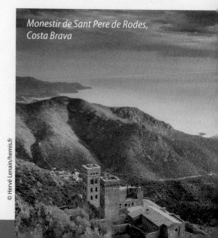

Monestir de Sant Pere de Rodes, Costa Brava

© Hervé Lenain/hemis.fr

Vic★★

This important commercial centre and thriving industrial town (leather goods, food processing and textiles) is in the foothills of the Pyrenees. Monumental buildings testify to its history as a Roman centre. Vic makes a good base for exploring the mountains while also being within striking distance of Barcelona.

▶ **Population:** 42 498

◔ **Michelin Map:** 574 G 36 – Catalunya (Barcelona).

▤ **Info:** Pl. del Pes. ℘938 86 20 91. www.victurisme.cat.

◔ **Location:** Vic is in NE Spain, 70km/43mi N of Barcelona. ▭Vic.

◉ **Don't Miss:** Museu Episcopal.

◔ **Timing:** A famous farmer's market is held in Vic's main square (Plaça Major) every Saturday.

THE CITY TODAY

Vic sees few overnighting Northern European visitors, but those in the know return time and again for the soul-satisfying Catalan cuisine served in its restaurants.

SIGHTS

Old Quarter★

Wide avenues *(ramblas)* follow the old walls, of which a few remnants remain.

Museu Episcopal★★★

Pl. Bisbe Oliba 3. Open Apr–Sep Tue–Sat 10am–7pm, Sun & public hols 10am–2pm; Oct–Mar Tue–Fri 10am–1pm, 3–6pm, Sat 10am–7pm, Sun & public hols 10am–2pm. Closed 1, 6 Jan, Easter Sunday, 25–26 Dec. €8. ℘938 86 93 60. www.museuepiscopalvic.com.

This magnificent museum displays Romanesque and Gothic works, along with fabrics and costumes, jewellery, ceramics and other arts.

Sala del Románico★★★ (Romanesque Gallery) – On exhibit are the *Descent of Erill la Vall*, a sculptural ensemble; the painting *Canopy of Ribes de Freser;* and outstanding **altar fronts**. The *Lluça Altar* marks the transition to the Gothic style.

Salas del Gótico★★★ (Gothic Galleries) – Among items from the early Gothic period (after 1275) are a marble altarpiece by **Bernat Saulet**, a *Virgin of Boixadors*, the altar front of Bellver de Cerdanya and parts of an altarpiece by **Pere Serra**. The collection of international Gothic altarpieces (15C) includes the **Santa Clara** and *Sant Antoni i Santa Margarida* altars, both by Borrasà; the *de Guimerà* altar, the work of Ramon de Mur; and the *Verdú* altarpiece of Jaume Ferrer II.

Paintings by Jaume Huguet mark the transition to the Renaissance.

Tejido e Indumentari★★★ (Textiles and Costumes) – Feast your eyes on flamboyant liturgical wear and 13C–18C textiles.

Catedral★

Pl. de la Catedral. Open 10am–1pm, 4–7pm. ℘938 86 44 49.

An elegant 11C Romanesque belfry and crypt remain from earlier churches. The Neoclassical Cathedral was built between 1781 and 1803. In 1930, Catalan artist **Josep Maria Sert** decorated the **interior★** with wall paintings. These were burned during the Civil War and repainted by Sert before his death in 1945.

The **paintings★★** have a power reminiscent of Michelangelo. They evoke the mystery of the Redemption (chancel) from the time of Adam's original sin (transept) to the Passion (apse), the Evangelists and the Martyrs (nave). Scenes on the back of the west door illustrate the triumph of human injustice in the Life of Christ: Jesus chasing the moneylenders (right), Jesus condemned (centre) and the road to Calvary (left). The monochrome golds and browns in the murals lend the effect of a relief.

The former high altar **retable★★** (end of the ambulatory) is a 15C alabaster work in 12 panels. Tracery-filled 14C arches surround the small **clasustro★**. In a cloister gallery is the tomb of the painter, surmounted by his unfinished *Crucifixion*.

Palau Episcopal

Santa Maria. ✆938 86 15 55.
The 12C episcopal palace has been modified significantly. The **Sala dels Sínodes**, decorated in 1845, and the patio are the main features.

Plaça Major★

Note the facades with Modernist, Gothic and Baroque details on this busy arcaded square. A popular market is held on Saturday.

EXCURSIONS

Monestir de Sant Pere de Casserres★

➲17km/11.6mi NE of Vic. Take the C 153 NE from Vic, then turn right toward Tavernoles and the Parador. At the Parador take a paved lane to the left (3.5km/2.2mi). Open Tue–Sun: Oct–May 10am–5.30pm, Jun–Sep until 7.30pm. Closed 1 & 6–31 Jan, 24–25 Dec. €3. ✆937 44 71 18.
www.santperedecasserres.com.
Stop just before the Parador for a fine **view★★**. The small Romanesque monastery enjoys a picturesque **location★★** at the end of a long, narrow peninsula in the marsh. For centuries, Sant Pere de Casserres was the only working Benedictine Monastery in the Osona region. Monastic life ended at the hands of King Carlos III in 1797, but the complex's medieval structures have been well preserved for posterity.

Monestir de Santa Maria de L'Estany★

➲ 24km/15mi SW of Vic. Leave Vic on the C 25 toward Manresa. Go right at exit 164, follow the BP 4313 to L'Estany. Open 20 Jan–20 Dec Tue–Sun & pub hols 10am–2pm. €3.50. ✆938 30 30 40. www.monestirestany.cat.
The village of **L'Estany★** grew up around this medieval Augustinian monastery. The bell tower of the 12C Romanesque church was rebuilt in the 15C. The arcades of the **cloisters★** are supported by matching columns and decorated with 72 **capitals ★★**.

The north gallery is Romanesque and narrative; the west, decorative with palm fronds and gaunt griffons; the south, geometrical and interlaced; and the east, awash with popular scenes of weddings and musicians.

🚗 DRIVING TOURS

Serra de Montseny★

The Serra de Montseny, an extension of the Pyrenees, is a granite massif covered in beeches and cork oaks. To the southeast, the **Parque Natural de Montseny** covers 17 372ha/42 925 acres; its highest peaks are Matagalls (1 695m/5 560ft) and **Turó de l'Home** (1 707m/5 601ft).

Vic to Sant Celoni via the Northern Road

60km/37.3mi. Leave Vic to the S; turn left after 6km/3.7mi.
The road goes through pine and beechwoods past delightful **Viladrau**. After **Arbúcies**, it runs beside the river then turns for **Breda**, with the Romanesque tower of the **Monestir de Sant Salvador★**, and Sant Celoni (🚌Plaça de l'Estació).

Beyond Campins, the road rises with **views** to the lake *(embalse)* of Santa Fè (1 130m/3 707ft). The **Ermita de Sant Marçal★★** hermitage is 7km/4.3mi ahead on Matagalls ridge. There are good **views** of the serra from the road between Sant Celoni and Tona via **Montseny★**. Beyond Montseny, the road rises to a wild area, then descends to Tona past the Romanesque church in **El Brull** and the tower of **Santa Maria de Seva**.

Girona★★

Girona (Gerona in Castilian) stands on a strategic site that has made it the target of repeated sieges. Its ramparts were built and rebuilt by Iberians, Romans and Catalans. The city has always been scrappy: In 1809, it resisted Napoleon's troops for more than seven months.

- **Population:** 96 722
- **Michelin Map:** 574 G 38 (town plan) – map 122 Costa Brava – Catalunya (Girona).
- **Info:** Rambla de la Llibertat 1 ✆972 22 65 75. www.girona.cat/turisme.
- **Location:** Girona connects with Barcelona (97km/60.2mi SW) and France via the N II and AP 7. The C 255 leads to Palafrugell (39km/24mi SW) and the C 250 to Sant Feliu de Guíxols (36km/22mi SW), both on the coast. Gerona (no train transfer from Barcelona airport).
- **Parking:** Park along one of the wider streets and walk into the old city.
- **Don't Miss:** A jaunt through the old Jewish quarter is essential.
- **Timing:** Allot extra time to wander aimlessly among the orange-and-ochre heritage buildings.

THE CITY TODAY

Once seen as merely the waypoint for adventures farther afield, today Girona is a destination in itself, a place where curious visitors who have 'done' Barcelona can find culture and history without the crowds. A mix of atmospheric streets and ancient sights reflecting a rich multicultural heritage is found in the compact centre, which straddles the confluence of four rivers.

WALKING TOUR

BARRI VELL (OLD TOWN)

Allow 3hr

Narrow alleys lead up to the Cathedral, with its monumental stairway, the **Escaleras de la Pera**. The 14C **Pia Almoina** building (right) is a fine example of Gothic architecture.

For a view of the old town, ascend to the **Paseo de la Muralla** (Wall Walk) where you can stroll along the path tracing the millennium-old walls. There are various entrances and exits.

Antic Hospital Santa Caterina

Plaça de l'Hospital. Pharmacy: Sat–Sun & hols 11am–1pm. ✆972 20 38 34.

Facing the Plaça Pompeu Fabra, this baroque building was modernised with a glass annex when it became the home of the Generalitat (local government) in 2010. But you can still admire its elegant Neoclassical facade and austere lines. The building also houses a large Catalan library and an auditorium, the latter in the old chapel. Its pharmacy, with a collection of 300 apothecary jars from the 18C, opened to the public in 2015.

After Plaça Pompeu Fabra, cross Plaça de Catalunya, over the river.

Rambla de Llibertat

Following the Onyar River and lined with cafés and shops, the lively Rambla de la Llibertat is the main route of entry into the old town. Beyond the stone bridge, medieval arcades once housed a large market. La Rambla flows onto the Carrer Argenteria, which is much narrower but just as colourful, and then leads to the bridge of Sant Agustí.

At the bridge, turn right into Plaça Lucerne, then right again on Carrer Bonaventura Carreras Peralta.

Girona by the Onyar

Fontana d'Or

Known by this name since the 18C, this Romanesque building has had various functions over the centuries. It now hosts art exhibitions.

▷ Return to Plaça Lucerne.

El Call

Parallel to the Carrer Bonaventura Carreras Peralta, the Carrer de la Força winds through the 'Call', the former Jewish quarter of Girona. This ensemble of tall buildings is crisscrossed with alleyways and steep staircases winding around the site of an ancient synagogue.

This road leads directly to the cathedral, but rather than heading straight on, meander around the looped side streets. Although the current layout no longer corresponds entirely to that of medieval times, and buildings have undergone various transformations, it is still a very atmospheric quarter.

Museu d'Història dels Jueus (Museum of Jewish History)

Carrer Força 8. Open Sep–Jun Tue–Sat 10am–6pm, Sun, Mon & hols 10am–2pm; Jul–Aug: Mon–Sat 10am–8pm, Sun & hols 10am–2pm. Closed Jan 1 and 6, 25–26 Dec. €4; free first Sun.
☏ 972 216 761. www.girona.cat/call/cat.
This museum reveals a moving and ultimately tragic history and tells the daily life of the Jewish community of 10C Girona through documents, text panels and engravings. They narrate the Jews' trajectory, from when they were protected by the Church and by the Catalan-Aragonese state, to their devastating banishment.

Along the same street, the **Centre Ca Porta Bonastruc** is located at the site of the ancient synagogue; it houses the Nahmanides Institute of Jewish Studies, named after the physician, philosopher and Rabbi Moshe ben Nahman (1194–1270), a leading member of Girona's Jewish community.

Girona and Judaism

Girona's Jewish community, which settled on both sides of **Carrer de la Força** in the city's old quarter, was the second-largest in Catalunya after Barcelona's and became famous in the Middle Ages for its prestigious Kabbalistic School, which operated for over 600 years, from the 9C until the expulsions of 1492. This contemplative past can be felt in atmospheric narrow alleyways such as Carrer Cúndaro and Carrer Sant Llorenç, the latter home to the **Centro Bonastruc ça Porta**, dedicated to the town's Jewish history.

Museu d'Història de Girona

Força 27. Open Tue–Sat May–Sep 10.30am–6.30pm, Oct–Apr until 5.30pm; Sun & hols until 1.30pm. Closed 1 & 6 Jan, 25–26 Dec. €4, free first Sun. ☏972 222 229. www.girona.cat/museuhistoria.

This fascinating museum housed in a former monastery gives an overview of the city, from its Roman origins (check out the Roman wall in the basement) until the end of Franco's reign. The 14 exhibition rooms include info about the town's industrial heritage, the local *sardana* dance and the Civil War.

▶ Continue along Carrer de la Força.

Catedral★

Pl. de la Catedral. Open Apr–Oct 10am–7.30pm; Nov–Mar 10am–6.30pm. €7 (including nave, cloisters and museum); free Sun (10am–2pm cloister and treasury). ☏972 21 58 14. www.catedraldegirona.cat.

The Baroque facade of the Cathedal resembles an altarpiece with a huge single oculus. Barring the 11C Torre de Carlomagno (Charlemagne Tower) – from an earlier Romanesque cathedral – the structure is Gothic, and its single nave★★ is, remarkably, the largest Gothic nave in the world. It remains largely unadorned. The chancel (1312) is surrounded by chapels. A silver-gilt embossed 14C altarpiece★ traces the Life of Christ. In the Sant Honorat chapel is the impressive tomb, set in a Gothic niche, of Bishop Bernard de Pau.

Museu-Tresor de la Catedral★★

The treasury houses one of the most beautiful copies of the Beatus★★, or *St John's Commentary on the Apocalypse* (8C), in existence In the 10C embossed silver Hixem Casket is a fine example of Caliphate art, and there is Gothic silver and plate of the 14C and 15C. The end room contains the Tapís de la Creació★★★ (Tapestry of Creation), dating from about 1100, showing Christ in Majesty surrounded by creation. The 12–13C cloisters★ remain (like the 11C tower) from the Romanesque cathedral.

Museu d'Art de Girona★★

Pujada de la Catedral 12. Open May–Sep Tue–Sat 10am–6.30pm, Sun 10am–1.30pm; Oct–Apr Tue–Sat 10am–5.30pm, Sun 10am–1.30pm. Closed 1, 6 Jan, 25–26 Dec. €6. ☏972 20 38 34. www.museuart.com.

Set in the Palau Episcopal, the city 's principal art collection dates to the Romanesque to the present. Holdings include a 10C portable altar from Sant Pere de Rodes of embossed silver, a 12C–13C beam from the village of Cruïlles★ and apse paintings from Pyrenean churches.

Among altarpieces in the Throne Room is one from Sant Miquel de Cruïlles★★ by Luis Borrassá (15C), Catalunya's greatest Gothic artist. Note the Púbol altarpiece★, by Bernat Martorell (1437), and the Sant Feliu altarpiece, by Juan de Borgoña.

▶ Return to Carrer de la Força and take the first stairs on the left.

Basilica de Sant Feliu★

Pujada Sant Feliu 29. Open Mon–Sat 10am–5.30pm, Sun 1–5.30pm. €7. ☏972 20 14 07. www.catedraldegirona.cat.

This church outside the walls must have originally been a martyry over the tombs of St Narcissus, Bishop of Girona, and St Felix. The later Gothic church holds eight early-Christian sarcophagi★, two with carvings including a spirited lion hunt★.

▶ Return to Carrer de la Força, cross it and veer left.

Banys àrabs★ (Arab Baths)

Ferran el Católic. Open Apr–Sep Mon–Sat 10am–7pm, Sun & public hols 10am–2pm; Oct–Mar 10am–2pm. Closed 1, 6 Jan, 25–26 Dec. €2. ☏972 19 09 69. www.banysarabs.org.

These picturesque late-12C baths were built in Muslim tradition. Steps opposite lead to the Passeig Arqueològic, with its view of the Ter Valley.

Monestir de Sant Pere de Galligants/Museu d'Arqueologia★

Santa Lucía 8. Open Tue–Sat Jun–Sep 10am–7pm, Oct–May until 6pm; Sun & public hols 10am–2pm. Closed 1 & 6 Jan, 24–26 Dec. €6; free last Tue Oct–Jun. &972 20 26 32. www.macgirona.cat

The fortified Romanesque church of Sant Pere, set into the town walls, houses the **Museu Arqueològic.** Highlights include its medieval memorial plaques and the 4C Roman **tomb of Las Estaciones★**.

ADDITIONAL SIGHTS
Casa Masó

Ballesteries 29. Prebooked tours only. €6. &972 413 989. www.rafaelmaso.org.

Before heading into the Jewish quarter, consider exploring the home of architect Rafael Masó (1880-1935). It overlooks the river and is is in the *noucentisme (1900s)* style, which continued on from *modernisme*. The sumptuous interior is filled with antiques dating from the 18C.

Museu del Cinema

Sèquia 1. Open Oct–Apr Tue–Fri 10am–6pm, Sat 10am–8pm, Sun & hols 11am–3pm. May–Jun and Sep Tue–Sat 10am–8pm, Sun & hols 11am–3pm. Jul–Aug 10am–8pm. Closed Jan 1 & 6, 25–26 Dec. €6; free first Sun. &972 412 777. www.museudelcinema.cat.

This quirky collection brings to life the early days of cinema through screenings and varied exhibits. From silhouette montages to delightful magic lanterns, you'll time-travel to an age lacking modern technology but beholden to an exuberant imagination.

Plaça de la Independencia

Designed by architect Martí Sureda Deulovol in 1855 (yet completed in 1993, according to his design), this pretty square is surrounded by Neoclassical buildings and affords glimpses of the colourful facades along the Onya River.

Parc de la Devesa★

This park contains the largest grove of plane trees in Catalunya.

EXCURSION
Casa-Museu Castell Gala Dalí★

▶ In Púbol. 16km/10mi E along the C 66 towards La Bisbal d'Empordà. Open mid-Mar–6 Jan, Tue–Sun (& Mon Jun–Sep) from 10am; see website for seasonal closing times. Closed 7 Jan. €8. &972 48 86 55. www.salvador-dali.org.

In 1970 Salvador Dalí gifted this 14C castle to his wife Gala. It now displays her effects in a Surrealist setting.

🚗 DRIVING TOUR

GIRONA TO SANTA PAU

64.5km/40mi. Allow one day.

▶ Head N from Girona along the C 66.

Banyoles

20km/12.4mi NW of Girona.

This small town enjoys a beautiful lakeside setting. The **Museu Arqueològic Comarcal★** (Placeta de la Font 11; open Tue–Sat 10.30am–1.30pm, 4–6.30pm/7.30pm summer, Sun 10.30am–2pm; €3; &972 57 23 61, www.museusdebanyoles.cat) is set in a Gothic building; the star exhibit is its Palaeolithic Jaw of Banyoles.

An 8km/5mi road around the lake passes the 13C **Església de Santa Maria de Porqueres★**; its columns are sculpted with odd figures (Ctra Circumval·lació de l'Estany; open by arrangement; enquire at the Museu Arqueològic Comarcal).

Estany de Banyoles★

Lake Banyoles, over 2km long and 235m wide (1.2mi by 770ft), is flanked to the west by the Serra de Rocacorba and overlooks planes of oak trees alternating with green fields. Besides the beauty of its landscape, it is of great ecological importance because of the protected marine species that dwell here such as sunfish, black bass and

Medieval bridge, Besalù

© Lucas Vallecillos/age fotostock

tench. Rowing is popular, and the lake was a gorgeous setting for the 1992 Olympic regatta events.

▶ Take the C-66 7kms/4.3mi N.

Serinya

The church in this little village, devoted to Sant Andreu, is a remarkable example of 13C Romanesque architecture, with a gate adorned with archivolts.
Archaeological finds in the area include some splendid Middle and Upper Paleolithic remains in two caves: the Cova dels Encantats and Cova del Mollet (enquire about visiting at the Museu Arqueològic Comarcal).

▶ Continue Non the C-66 for 7kms/4.3mi.

Besalú★★

The first view of Besalú, across the river with its Roman **fortified bridge★**, rebuilt in the medieval period, is memorable. This small, **ancient city★★** retains ramparts and many medieval buildings including the Romanesque **Església de Sant Pere★** with an unusual lion-flanked window.
In the former Jewish quarter are 12C **ritual baths** (church and baths may be visited on guided tours arranged through the Tourist Office, C. del Pont 1, ℘972 59 12 40, www.besalu.cat/turisme).

▶ Head 14km/8.7mi W along the N 260.

Castellfollit de la Roca★

This village set in the **Parc Natural de la Garrotxa★** has a medieval centre around the church of Sant Salvador.

▶ Continue 8km/5mi on the N 260.

Olot★

The 18C Neoclassical and Baroque **Església de Sant Estève★** houses an evocative painting by El Greco, *Christ Bearing the Cross★*.
The **Museu Comarcal de la Garrotxa★** displays a **collection of paintings and drawings★★** by 19C and 20C Catalan artists (Hospici 8; open Tue–Fri 10am–1pm, 3–6pm; Sat 11am–2pm, 4–7pm; Sun & public hols 11am–2pm; €3; free first Sun; ℘972 27 11 66; https://museus.olot.cat/museu-garrotxa).
Note also the splendid **Modernist facade★** of the **Casa Solà-Morales★** by Domènech i Montaner.

▶ Take the GI 524 E 9.5km/6mi.

Zona Volcánica de la Garrotxa

Casal dels Volcans, Av. Sta Coloma de Farners. ℘972 266 012.
www.gencat.cat/parcs/garrotxa.
Declared a national park in 1982, the Zona Volcanica de la Garrotxa covers 11 300ha (27 923 acres) through the upper Fluvià valley. Thirty Strombolian-type volcanic cones, craters and more than 20 basaltic lava flows have created a striking, moonlike landscape. (Volcanic activity is extinct.) In the valleys it's not uncommon to see

wild cats and boars. The park has also become a sanctuary for birds: nearly 150 species have found refuge here. On the road from Olot to Santa Pau, the Fageda d'en Jordà is an ancient beech forest standing on hardened lava. From here there are easy ⓧwalks to El Croscat (the youngest volcano in the park) and to the Santa Margarida volcano, the largest in Garrotxa, measuring 110m/360ft high and 1 200 m/3 930 ft wide and covered in vegetation. Four waymarked routes start from the information point of Can Serra (open 10am–3pm; parking €5 all day).

Santa Pau★

The Castillo de Santa Pau and the 15C–16C parish church stand on the arcaded square of this village.

ADDRESSES

🏠 STAY

⊝⊜ **Pensió Bellmirall** – Bellmirall 3, Girona. ℘972 204 009. www.bellmirall.eu. 7 rooms. In the heart of the old town, this B&B is in an attractive three-storey house furnished with antiques. Free public parking nearby.

⊝⊜⊜⊜ **Llegendes de Girona Catedral** – Portal de la Barca 4, Girona. ℘972 22 09 05. www.llegendeshotel.com. 15 rooms, ⊑€12. Next to Sant Feliu church, this four-star offers contemporary, gentlemanly rooms in an atmospheric old building. There is a cocktail bar on the ground floor.

Ⓨ/EAT

⊝⊜⊜ **Café Le Bistrot** – Pujade de Sant Domènec 4, Girona. ℘972 21 88 03. www.lebistrot.cat. Always dependable, this Parisian-style restaurant serves fresh, pan-European cusisine served in a Parisian-style cuisine. There's a pleasant outdoor terrace.

⊝⊜⊜⊜ **Divinum** – Albereda 7, Girona. ℘972 872 08 02 18. www.dvnum.com. Closed Sun. Tweezed and foamed Catalan cuisine makes this Michelin-starred restaurant perfect for special occasions. There are lunchtime set menus and a superb wine list.

⊝⊜⊜⊜ **Celler de Can Roca**– Carrer de Can Sunyer 48, Girona. ℘972 872 08 02 18. www.cellercanroca.com.Closed Sun & Mon. Consistently named one of the world's best restaurants, this culinary mecca presided over by the Roca brothers lives up to its hype with tasting menus that are equal parts clever and delicious. Book months (or years) ahead.

Cadaqués★★

It doesn't get much more charming than this idyllic fishing village in Catalunya. Located on the southern coast of Cape Creus, a peninsula that marks the meeting point between the Pyrenees and the Mediterranean, its picturesque streets and bohemian atmosphere fascinated many famous artists in the first half of the 20C: Picasso, Man Ray, Buñuel, Lorca and Thomas Mann, to name a few. Salvador Dalí spent much of his life in nearby Port Ligat. Cap de Creus became a recurring theme in his work.

▸ **Population:** 2 752
◔ **Michelin Map:** 574 F 39.
🛈 **Info:** Cotxe 1. ℘972 258 315. www.visitcadaques.org.
◗ **Location:** 36km/21mi S of the French border and 39km/24mi E of Figueres. �Nearest train station: Figueres (34km).
◔ **Timing:** July/August can be very crowded.

Parque Natural de Cap de Creus

© Gonzalo Azumendi/agefotostock

THE TOWN TODAY

In high summer, Cadaqués remains a fashionable retreat for Catalans and a large number of French visitors, so at times it can feel more like a resort on the French Riviera than a remote village in northern Spain – shoulder season is a better bet. Chic galleries and cafés line the waterfront, and the local fleet of fishing boats is joined by pleasure yachts. Such is the town's cachet that a seaside development in China, Kadakaisi, was built in 2017 to emulate its whitewashed, bougainvillea-covered houses.

The town hosts an international music festival (late Jul–early Aug; www.festivalcadaques.com).

SIGHTS

Museu de Cadaqués

Narcís Monturiol 15. See website for opening times and prices. ℰ972 25 88 77. www.visitcadaques.org.
The town's museum holds temporary exhibitons by local artists and by those associated with Cadaqués. There are also permanent displays on Dalí.

Església de Santa Maria

Pl. Dr Callis 15. Open Mass only: Sat 7pm, Sun 11am (altarpiece can be viewed from the exterior via window).
Overlooking the **casco antiguo** and the focal point of the village, the Església de Santa Maria has a sober facade that belies a sumptuous interior: Note the **Baroque altarpiece★★** in gilded wood by Joan Torres.

EXCURSIONS

Port Lligat★

Less than a mile northeast of Cadaqués, this eensy village is set in a small bay on the Cap de Creus peninsula. Blending into a charming cluster of whitewashed fishermen's houses is the **Casa-Museu Salvador Dalí★**, where the artist lived and worked from 1930–82. Works inspired by the local scenery include *The Sacrament of the Last Supper*, and *The Madonna of Port Lligat*. Dalí's workshop, library, rooms and garden are open. (Open mid-Jun–mid- Sep 9.30am–9pm; rest of year Tue–Sun 10.30am–6pm; reservation required; closed 25 Dec, 1-2 Jan, 9 Jan–second week Feb, 29 May, 2 Oct; €12; ℰ972 25 10 15; www.salvador-dali.org.)

Parque Natural de Cap de Creus★★

Steep roads and paths wind between cliffs and hidden bays to Cap de Creus, Spain's most eastern point. Many come to enjoy the spectacular **view at sunset ★★★** from the terrace of the Restaurant Cap de Creus (ℰ972 19 90 05), by the lighthouse.

Costa Brava★★★

Spain's Costa Brava (literally 'Wild Coast') is the twisted, rocky shoreline where the Catalan mountains meet the sea. Fairytale inlets, Caribbean-blue waters, quiet harbours and leisure and sporting activities are its main draws. Inland there are unspoilt medieval towns and villages.

- **Michelin Map:** 574 E 39, F 39, G 38-39 – Catalunya (Girona).
- **Info:** Girona: Rambla de la Llibertat 1. ℘972 22 65 75; Blanes: Pg. Catalunya 2. ℘972 33 03 48; Cadaqués: Cotxe 1. ℘972 25 83 15. en.costabrava.org.
- **Location:** The Costa Brava is the coastline from Blanes up to Portbou on the border with France. Lloret de Mar, Tossa de Mar and Platja d'Aro are major tourist centres; towns to the north are more low-key.
- **Kids:** Beaches are the main attractions.

🚗 DRIVING TOURS

1 BLANES TO PALAMÓS

51km/31mi. Allow one day.

The circuit through two narrow coastal roads (GI 682 from Blanes to Sant Feliu and C 253 from Sant Feliu to Palamós) affords sweeping views of the coast.

Blanes★

🚉 Blanes

The **Passeig Marítim★** offers a lovely panorama of Blanes and its beach. The remains of the Castillo de Sant Joan are to the east, above the 14C Gothic Església de Santa Maria.

To the southeast is the **Jardí Botànic de Marimurtra★** (Pg. Karl Faust; open daily; Apr–Oct 9am–6pm/Jun–Sept 8pm; Nov–Mar 10am–5pm; €7; ℘972 33 08 26, www.marimurtra.cat), a botanical park with 5 000 plant species including many exotic varieties. At each bend the twisting paths reveal **views★** of the bay of Cala Forcadera and the coastline.

Created in 1945, the **Jardí Botànic Pinya de Rosa★** (Platja Santa Cristina, above the Marimurtra Jardí Botánic; open 9am–6pm; closed 1 Dec-30 Jan; €4; ℘972 350 689, www.pinya-de-rosa.es) is the largest cactus garden in the world, with over 7 000 varieties. Its founder, engineer Fernando Riviere de Caralt, spent decades on its development. Trails through the garden meander over the side of a steep cove, leading to a small pool surrounded by palm trees.

The foothills of the Serra de l'Albera form huge enclosed bays, like those of Portbou and El Port de la Selva. The clifftop **road section★★** from Portbou to Colera offers views of one of the most craggy strips of coastline in Catalunya.

▶ Take the G1 682 NE for 7km/4.3mi.

Lloret de Mar

Lloret de Mar has become the epitome of bucket-and-spade tourism on the Costa Brava, replacing its hushed maritime charm with the din of highrise hotels, outdoor discos, water parks and overcrowded beaches.

Jardins de Santa Clothilde★★

Leave Lloret de Mar in the direction of Blanes. Open 10am–5pm (Apr–Oct until 8pm). Closed 25 Dec & 1, 6 Jan. €5. ℘972 370 471. www.lloretdemar.org. This oasis in Lloret de Mar was created in 1919 by architect and landscape designer Nicolau Maria Rubió i Tuduri (1891–1981). Jazz concerts are held here in summer. It draws inspiration from the Italian Renaissance, its terraced gardens crossed by paths and ivy-cloaked stairs. Pines and cypresses bristle skyward.

▶ Take the G1 682 NE for 11km/6.8mi.

Tossa de Mar★

🚌 Tossa de Mar

Painter Marc Chagall, who spent some 40 summers here, called Tossa 'blue paradise'. Its long sandy beach with large rock formations curves toward Punta del Faro, the promontory on which stand the lighthouse and the 13C walls of the **Vila Vella★** (old town).

The **Museu Municipal★** (Pl. Pintor Roig i Soler; open Jun–Sep 10am–8pm; Oct–May Tue–Fri 10am–1.30pm, 3–5pm; Sat 10am–2pm, 4–6pm; Sun 10am–2pm; €3; ☎972 34 07 09; www.tossademar. com/museu) contains artefacts from an ancient Roman villa nearby and works by artists who stayed at Tossa in the 1930s, including Masson, Benet and – of course – Chagall. Between Tossa and **Lloret de Mar**, the road follows a **clifftop route★★**.

▶ Take the G1 682 N for 22km/13.6mi.

Sant Feliu de Guíxols★

🚌 Sant Feliu de Guíxols

Sheltered from the last spurs of the Serra de les Gavarres, this is one of the most popular locations of this coast. Its seaside boulevard, Passeig de la Mar, is lined with pavement cafés.

The **Església-Monastir de Sant Feliu★** (open for Mass; ☎972 82 15 75) is part of a former Benedictine monastery, whose ruins look giant beside the small village.It has retained its Romanesque facade, known as the **Porta Ferrada★★**, with horseshoe arches dating to pre-Romanesque times. The interior (14C) is Gothic in style.

The lookout by the chapel of Sant Elm commands beautiful **views★★**.

Located on the edge of town, toward Santa Cristina d'Aro, the **Roca de Pedralta★** is one of the largest rocking or 'logan' stones in Europe, set on a wonderful vantage point on the bay.

▶ Head up the coast 4km/2.5mi.

S'Agaro★

Pause, if you wish, in this elegant resort with chalets and luxury villas surrounded by tidy gardens and pine forests. For a scenic walk, trace the sea-wall from Pl. Rosaleda to Platja (beach) de Sa Conca (🚶30min). Diving, the Camino de Ronda offers fine **views★** of the sheer cliffs.

▶ Take the C 253 5.5km/3.4mi N.

Platja d'Aro

The family-friendly beach town with high rises comes alive in the summer; skip it any other time of year.

Cova d'en Daina★

Access the C 31 to Calonge, then take C. Cabanyes.

The secluded snaking road to Gavarres leads to this megalithic tomb. Farther along is the medieval village of La Selva Romanyà.

▶ Take the C 253 5.5km/3.4mi N.

Palamós

This small fishing village has a vibrant marina offering range of leisure and services, making Palamós one of the busiest areas of the Costa Brava.

Museu de la Pesca

Open mid-Jun–mid-Sept 10am–9pm; rest of year Tue–Sat 10am–1.30pm, 3–7pm; Sun & hols 10am–2pm, 4–7pm. €5. ☎972 600 424. www.museudelapesca.org.

This museum takes you on a voyage into the world of fishing and trawls its traditions, particularly those unique to the Costa Brava. The traditional boats collection is a highlight.

② PALAFRUGELL TO THE ILLES MEDES

59km/36.5mi. Allow half a day.

This northern swathe of the Costa Brava is where the scenery is at its most spectacular, particularly around the Cap de Begur.

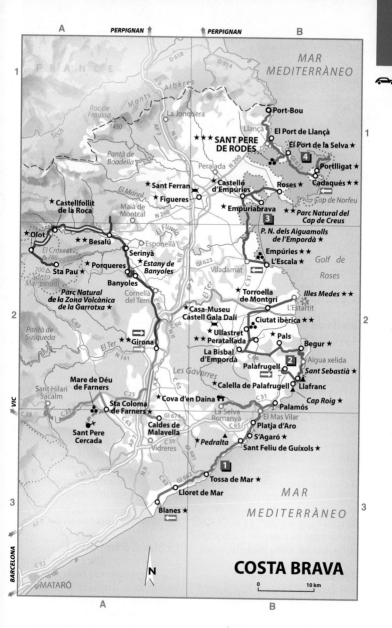

Costa Brava map

PERPIGNAN PERPIGNAN

MAR MEDITERRÀNEO

FRANCE

Monts Albères

Roc de Frausa 1450

La Jonquera

Port-Bou ○

Llançà

El Port de Llançà ○

★★★ **SANT PERE DE RODES**

El Port de la Selva ★ ○

4

Portlligat ★

Peralada

Castelló d'Empúries ★

Roses ★ ○

Cadaqués ★★

Cap de Norfeu

Pantà de Boadella

El Manol

★ Sant Ferran

★ Figueres

★ Empuriabrava

3

★★ Parc Natural del Cap de Creus

★ Castellfollit de la Roca

Maià de Montcal

N 260

P. N. dels Aiguamolls de l'Empordà ★

★ Olot

★★ Besalú

Esponellà

Serinyà

Empúries ★★

L'Escala ★

Golf de Roses

700 △ Sta Pau ★

★ Porqueres

★ Estany de Banyoles

Viladamat

El Croscat △ 786

Parc Natural de la Zona Volcànica de la Garrotxa ★

Banyoles

Cornellà del Terri

Torroella de Montgrí

Illes Medes ★★

Pantà de Susqueda

El Ter

★ Girona

Casa-Museu Castell Gala Dalí

L'Estartit

Ciutat ibèrica ★★

★★ Ullastret

★★ Peratallada

★ Pals

Begur ★

La Bisbal d'Empordà

Palafrugell ○

2

Aigua xelida

Sant Sebastià ★

Les Gavarres

Mare de Déu de Farners

★ Calella de Palafrugell

Llafranc

Cap Roig ★

Sant Hilari Sacalm

Sta Coloma de Farners ★

★ Cova d'en Daina

Palamós ○

Sant Pere Cercada

Caldes de Malavella

La Selva Romanyà

El Mas Vilar

Platja d'Aro

S'Agaró ★

★ Pedralta

Sant Feliu de Guíxols ★

1

Tossa de Mar ★

Lloret de Mar

Blanes ★

MAR MEDITERRÀNEO

COSTA BRAVA

0   10 km

VIC

BARCELONA

MATARÓ

N

Palafrugell

A few miles inland, the town of Palafrugell has a thriving cultural scene, particularly in summer, when it fills with visitors. Restaurants here serve a mean *suquet*, or Catalan fish stew .

In the early 20C, the production of cork made it prosperous.

It is also the birthplace of the prolific writer Josep Pla (1897–1981).

Museu del Suro (Cork Museum)

Placeta del Museu. Open Jul-Aug
Mon-Sat 10am-2pm, 5-8.30pm,
Sun 10am-2pm, rest of year Tue-Fri
10am-1pm, 4-7pm, Sat 10am-2pm,
5-8pm, Sun 10am-2-pm. €3. ℘972 307
825. www.museudelsuro.cat.
This niche museum explains how cork
is made. Perhaps most interesting are
the old utensils used to wash and cut
the cork.

Cala Estreta, Cap Roig near Calella de Palafrugell

▶ 4.5 km/2.7 mi S on the GIV 6546.

Calella de Palafrugell★
🚃Nearest station: Girona (58km)

Traditional fishermen's houses are juxtaposed with modern summer residences in this picturesque fishing port. It is known for its **Festival de Habaneras** (first Saturday in July), when visitors can enjoy Afro-Cuban songs, dances and *cremat* (flambéed coffee with rum).

A road southward leads to the **Jardín Botánic del Cap Roig** (open Apr–Sep 10am–8pm; Oct–Mar 10am–6pm, Jan–Feb Sat–Sun 10am–6pm; €8; ✆972 61 45 82, https://obrasocial.lacaixa.org). These terraced gardens, hewn out of the rock, enjoy wonderful **views★★** of the coast and include over 1 200 plant species laid out along shaded avenues.

Llafranc
2km/1.2 mi from Calella de Palafrugell by the small coastal road leading to Cap de Sant Sebastià, or walk by the GR 12, which runs along the coast (🚶15min). Like Calella de Palafrugell, Llafranc is a harmonious mix of old and new. The marina, which has 140 moorings, is the main attraction, along with a small beach offering many summer activities.

Far de Sant Sebastià★
2km/1.2mi from Llafranc.

Built in 1857, the lighthouse stands on a tiny isthmus surrounded by steep cliffs; the hermitage has a lovely **view★**.

▶ From Calella de Palafrugell, take the GIV 6591 and GIV 6542 11km/6.8mi NE.

Begur★
The town overlooks pretty creeks from an altitude of 200m/656ft above the sea. The castle ruins (16C–17C) offer a fine view of the Cap de Begur.

Pals★★
At the mouth of the Ter river, Pals has a quaint old quarter, **El Pedró**. The vestiges of fortified ramparts enclose ancient houses and winding alleyways, some with covered stairways.

▶ 12km/7.5mi N of Pals on the C 66.

La Bisbal d'Empordà
The capital of the Baix Empordà region (www.visitemporda.com) has been famous for its ceramics for centuries, and a small, vibrant crafts community continues the tradition Along its main streets are dozens of shops selling the distinctive yellow, green and clay-coloured pots, the unmistakable vases and cookware of the Costa Brava.

Castell★
Pl. Castell.
www.hotelcastellemporda.com.

The former residence of the Bishops of Girona is the most remarkable building in La Bisbal, combining Romanesque and Gothic elements. It has recently been converted into a luxury hotel and restaurant.

▶ Back on the C 66, turn left on the C 252, then right on the IM 651.

Peratallada★★

🚌 Nearest station: Flaça (25km)

This fortified village is considered one of the finest medieval ensembles in the **Empordà**. Winding old streets lead to the Plaça Major (main square), where a grand castle-fortress sits, now a luxury hotel. Don't miss the Plaça de les Voltes, with charming porticoes and ancient dwellings, another postcard-worthy snapshot.

The church of Sant Esteve, an austere 13C building situated outside the village, has a bell perforated with a pattern common to the region.

▶ Continue on the IM 651

Ullastret★

This is one of the most picturesque villages in Empordà's hinterland. Its medieval streets are lined with shops where you can buy local ingredients and treats. The Church of Sant Pere, in the centre of the village, is Romanesque. Note the curious Gothic ossuary with carvings of characters and animals.

Ciutat Ibérica

1km E of Ullastret. Open mid-Jun–Sep Tue–Sun, rest of year Wed–Sun; see website for seasonal hours. Closed 25–26 Dec and 1 & 6 Jan. €4; free last Tue Oct–Jun. ℘972 179 058. www.macullastret.cat.

One of Catalunya's most extensive Iberian discoveries is situated near Ullastret on the crest of Mont de Sant Andreu. Tour the remains of a settlement built by in the 5C by the Indiket tribe, which dug canals and a reservoir and lived around a main square. Artefacts such as scripts can be viewed in the Archaeological Museum on the same site.

▶ Continue on the IM 644 and turn right on the IM 643.

Torroella de Montgrí★

Despite a Baroque front, the 14C **Església de Sant Genís** (Pas. de l'Església) is a fine example of Gothic Catalan art. The **castle** on Montaña de Montgrì (🚶1hr on a signposted path among the rocks) is an extraordinary **belvedere★★** with a view to the sea and the Gavarres mountain range.

▶ Take the G1 641 towards the coast.

♙♙ Illes Medes★★

Boat trips around the islands are offered from l'Estartit. 🄸 For info, contact the tourist office; Passeig Marítim, ℘972 75 19 10. www.visitestartit.com. These seven islets and coral reefs are the extension of the calcareous massif of Montgrì. They're popular with lesure divers and ecologists on account of their marine life and ecosystems.

③ GULF OF ROSES

36km/22mi.

The vast majority of this stretch of coastline forms part of the Parc Natural dels Aiguamolls de l'Empordà.

L'Escala★

This resort has sandy beaches and a time-honoured anchovy fishing tradition: You may have even come across the ubiquitous Anxoves l'Escala tins in your local supermarket. Two inlets protect the town's harbour. The Empúries ruins are located to the N.

Empúries★★

Puig i Cadafalch. Check website for seasonal hours. Closed 25, 26 Dec & 1 Jan. €6; free last Tue Oct–Jun. ℘972 77 02 08. www.macempuries.cat.

Greco-Roman Ampurias (Emporion to the Greeks, meaning market) was built on a striking seaside **site★★**. It is still possible to make out the old town (**Paliápolis**), the new town (**Neápolis**) and the Roman town. In the mid-6C BC, the Phoenicians founded Paliápolis, on an offshore island, now joined to the mainland and occupied by the village of Sant Marti d'Empúries. A town began to develop on the shore opposite: Neápolis. As a Roman ally during the Punic Wars, it saw the arrival of an expedition led by Scipio Africanus Major in 218 BC. In 100 BC the Roman town was established to the west. The two centres coexisted until Augustus bestowed Roman citizenship upon the Greeks. The colony suffered barbarian invasions in the 3C. At one time it was a bishopric, as basilica ruins show.

Neápolis – The **Templo de Asclepio** (Aesculapius – god of healing) and a sacred precinct contained altars and statues of the gods. Nearby stood a **watchtower** and drinking water cisterns. The **Templo de Zeus Serapis** (a god associated with the weather and with healing) was surrounded by a colonnade. The **Agora** was the centre of town life; three statues remain. A street from the agora to the sea was bordered on one side by the **stoa** or covered market. Behind it are the ruins of a 6C **palaeo-Christian basilica** with a rounded apse.

Museu Arqueológic d'Empúries – A section of Neápolis is displayed along with models of temples and finds from the excavations.

The Roman Town – Unlike Neápolis, this is a vast, geometrically laid out town, partially excavated, with some restored walls. **House no. 1** (entrance at the back) has an atrium (inner courtyard) with six columns. Around this are residential apartments, the peristyle, or colonnaded court, and the impluvium, or rainwater catchment. The reception rooms are paved in geometric black-and-white mosaic. **House no. 2B** has rooms paved with their original mosaic; one has been reconstituted in clay with its walls resting on stone foundations. The **forum**, a large square lined by porticoes and, to the north and south, respectively, by temples and shops, was the centre of civic life.

A porticoed street led through the city gate to the oval **amphitheatre**, which is still visible.

Castelló d'Empúries★

Situated a short walk from the archaeological site, the former capital of the principality of Empúries (11C–14C) is on a promontory near the coast. The 14C–15C **Basílica de Santa Maria★** is flanked by a typical Catalan belfry. The **portal★★** is a unique example of Gothic art in Catalunya: The tympanum illustrates the Adoration of the Magi, while the Apostles are shown on the jambs. The large central nave is bordered by fine cylindrical pillars. The alabaster **retable★** in the high altar (15C), with conical pinnacles, depicts the Passion. (open 12–2pm, 4–8pm; ℰ972 25 05 19). The village retains buildings from its golden age: the **Ajuntament** (Maritime Commodities Exchange), combining Romanesque and Gothic elements, and the Gothic **Casa Gran**.

▷ Take the C 68 toward the coast.

Empuriabrava★

This luxury residential development features one of the largest marinas in the world.

▷ 9.5km/6mi N on the C 68.

Roses

🚉 Nearest station: Figueres (17km)

Roses, a modern resort and fishing port, may take its name from sailors from Rhodes said to have founded the colony in the 5C.

Its 16C Renaissance **citadel★**, a pentagon with many bastions, was commissioned by Charles V. The Benedictine monastery inside was destroyed by the French during the War of Independence. (Av. de Roses; open Jun & Sep 10am–8pm, Jul-Aug 10am-9pm, rest of year Tue–Sun 10am–6pm; closed 25 Dec, 1, 6 Jan; €5; ℰ972 15 14 66; http://visit. roses.cat/en.)

4 CADAQUÉS TO PORT-BOU

52km/32mi. Allow half a day.

This route traverses the northernmost stretch of the Catalan coast, from the beautiful peninsula of Cap de Creus

(&see p362) reaching Port-Bou at the French border. Begin the drive at Cadaqués (&CADAQUÉS, p361).

El Port de la Selva★

This bay is bathed in golden sunlight at dusk. Traditional white houses stand beside numerous flats and hotels. Fishing is still one of the main activities.

▶ 7km/4.3mi inland from El Port de la Selva on the GI 612.

Monestir de Sant Pere de Rodes★★★

⊙ Leave your car in the car park and proceed on foot for 10min.
Open Jun–Sep 10am–8pm; Oct–May until 5.30pm. Closed 1 & 6 Jan, 25–26 Dec. €6; free last Tue Oct–Jun.
✆972 38 75 59. http://patrimoni.gencat.cat/en/collection/monastery-sant-pere-de-rodes.

This imposing Benedictine monastery stands in a **setting★★** over the Gulf of León and the Cap de Creus peninsula. Begun in the 10C, it was pillaged and abandoned in the 18C. The remarkable **church★★★**, showing pre-Romanesque influence, is an unusual example of architectural harmony for the era. The central nave has barrel vaulting and the two lateral ones, surbased vaulting. They are separated by huge pillars, reinforced with columns on raised bases. Splendid **capitals★**, intricate tracery and acanthus leaves evoke the tradition of Córdoba and Byzantium. The left arm of the transept leads to an upper ambulatory offering an overhead perspective of the central nave.

The 12C **bell tower★★** is Lombardy Gothic.

The coast between El Port de la Selva and Cadaqués features many irregular creeks with crystal-clear waters, accessible only by sea. The road inland offers lovely views of the region.

▶ 20km/12.5mi N on the GIP 6041, then the N 260 motorway.

Port de Llançà

🚎Plaça de la Estación.
Llançà wraps around a bay sheltered from the Mediterranean *tramontana* winds. Its shallow waters are ideal for swimming and splashing.

▶ 10km/6mi N via the N 260.

Port-Bou★

Bordering French Roussillon, this popular holiday spot is also one of Catalunya's main border crossings, especially for rail traffic. (The nucleus of Port-Bou is next to the railway station.) Whether you come in via the N 260 or along the magnificent M 612 coastal route, you can admire some of the steepest cliffs on the Catalan coast and countless pristine coves.

ADDRESSES

🛏 STAY

The **Costa Brava** can be expensive, and in high season, rooms book up fast. For more reasonable prices and better availability, broaden your search to include the hinterland.

⊖⊖🛏 **Hotel La Goleta** – Pintor Terruella 22, Llançà. ✆972 38 01 25. www.hotellagoleta.com. 28 rooms. Close to the port, La Goleta has traditional furnishings and a rooftop terrace. Rooms vary widely in size and price.

⊖⊖🛏 **Hotel Plaça** – Pl. Mercat 22, Sant Feliu de Guíxols. ✆972 32 51 55. www.hotelplaza.org. 19 rooms, ☑€5. A practical, functional choice, the Plaça has pleasant, bright rooms; some overlook a square that's lively on market days. There's a jacuzzi and solarium on the rooftop

⊖⊖🛏 **Hotel Rosa** – Pi i Rallo 19, Begur. ✆972 62 30 15. www.hotel-rosa.com. 21 rooms. Restaurant ⊖⊖🛏. This hotel, in a restored stone house by the church, has a mishmash of traditional and white, beachy furniture. The rooftop terrace and market-cuisine restaurant are highlights.

⊖⊖🛏 **Sant Roc Hotel** – Pl. Atlántic 2, Calella de Palafrugell. ✆972 61 42 50. www.santroc.com. 47 rooms. Restaurant ⊖⊖🛏. Closed mid-Nov–

mid Feb. Set amid pine groves beside the Mediterranean, this property has spacious, old-fashioned rooms and an outdoor restaurant with sea views. There's a small indoor play area for kids. Half-board compulsory in summer.

🛏🍴🛇🛇 **Alàbriga Hotel & Home Suites** – Ctra. de Sant Pol 633, Sant Feliu de Guíxols. ☎872 20 06 00. www.hotelalabriga.com. 28 rooms. In a category all its own, the ultra-luxurious Alàbriga (opened in 2017) has a private beach, a pleasure yacht and butler and private jet service. There are terrific deals in the off season.

🛏🛇🛇 **Hotel Diana** – Plaça de Espanya 6 Tossa de Mar. ☎972 34 18 86. www.hotelesdante.com. 21 rooms. This iconic hotel, housed in a Modernist building by the sea, sees many return guests. The decor may be a bit frumpy, but the service, cleanliness and terrific location make up for any aesthetic foibles.

🍴/**EAT**

🛇🛇🛇 **Can Bolet** – Sant Mateu 6, Lloret de Mar. ☎972 371 237. Closed Sun eve–Mon. Try the squid sautéed with brandy, garlic and parsley at this 60-year-old family restaurant. Set lunch menus are a good value.

🛇🛇🛇 **Portal de la Gallarda** – Pere Estany 14, Mollet de Peralada. Castelló d'Empúries. ☎972 250 152. Closed Tue out of season. The restaurant specialises in grilled fish and is set in a 12C building with a terrace facing the Natural Park.

🛇🛇🛇 **Victoria** – Passeig del Mar 23, Tossa de Mar. ☎972 34 01 66. www. hrvictoriatossa.com. Closed 15 Nov–31 Jan, Tue (Sep–Jun). Mussels and seafood stews are popular at this restaurant with a terrace overlooking the beach. Above, hotel rooms (🛏🛇) have sea views.

🛇🛇🛇 **El Vaixell** – Carrer Castellar 62, Llançà. ☎972 38 02 95. Closed Mon. This family-owned restaurant in its third generation serves good-value 'gastronomic' set menus as well as à la carte dishes like potato-garlic soup and sea urchins still in the shell.

🛇🛇🛇🛇 **Pa i Raïm** – Torres i Jonama 56, Palafrugell. ☎972 30 45 72. www.pairaim. com. Closed Sun eve, Mon–Tue. Settle in for a meal of baroquely presented

modern Mediterranean fare in the family home of writer Josep Pla (♿see p365). Request a terrace table, weather permitting.

CAFE BARS

Grand Café Latino – Passeig d'Agustí Font 18-16, Lloret de Mar. ☎697 431 304. Let loose at this dance bar, frequented by folks roughly ages 30–50, where Latin music and cocktails are king.

Cala Banys – Camí Cala Banys, Lloret de Mar. ☎972 365 515. www.calabanys.es. Perched high on a cliff that plunges into the sea, this outdoor bar with cushy sofas serves great tiki cocktails.

ACTIVITIES

👥 **Nautilus** – Passeig Marítim 23, L'Estartit. ☎972 751 489. www.nautilus.es. Sign up for a tour of the Medes Islands and surrounding coastline aboard a wooden 'pirate' ship or glass-bottom boat, both a hit with kids.

👥 **Creuers Mare Nostrum** – Maranges 3, L'Escala. ☎972 773 797. www.creuers-marenostrum.com. A fleet of 10 glass-bottom boats (including 2 catamarans) tours the coastline, including the Medes Islands.

👥 **Aquabrava** – Ctra. de Cadaqués. 1km/0.5mi from Roses. Jun–mid-Sep 10am–7pm. ☎972 254 344. www. aquabrava.com. This water park is known for its wave pool, sandy beach and tropical vegetation. €32, children up to 1.20m/3ft 6in €20.

Hípica dels Aiguamolls – Rte de Palau Savardera, Castelló d'Empúries. ☎639 787 732. www.haiguamolls.com. Horseriding experiences from 30min to a whole day, plus lessons, are available.

SHOPPING

Carrer de l'Aigüeta – La Bisbal d'Empordà. Painted ceramics are a centuries-old tradition in this town, and you'll find all sorts of objects – plates, pitchers, bowls, you name it - in the shops on this street. Cerámica Bosch is a must.

Figueres★

Figueres, the capital of Alt Empordà county (*comarca*), is birthplace of Surrealist artist Salvador Dalí (1904–89), who also spent his last years here building his extravagant museum. It is an agricultural hub and, in summer, one of Catalunya's premier tourism destinations.

A BIT OF HISTORY

The end of the Spanish Civil War – The last meeting of the Republican Cortes was held here on 1 February 1939. Three days later, Girona fell to the Nationalists and the Republican leaders fled to France.

DALÍ THEATRE-MUSEUM★★

Pl. de Dalí i Gala. Open Mar–Jun & Oct Tue–Sun 9.30am–5.15pm (last admission); Jul–Sep 9am–7.15pm; Nov–Feb Tue–Sun 10.30am–5.15pm. Closed 11, 18 & 25 Dec, 1 Jan. €15.
℘972 67 75 05. www.salvador-dali.org.
Dalí's dream world of folly and caprice may charm or exasperate but never fails to impress. As the artist said, 'The museum cannot be considered as such; it is a gigantic surrealist object, where everything is coherent, where nothing has eluded my design.' To a restored 1850 theatre, which burned in the Civil War, Dalí added an immense glass dome (beneath which he is buried) and patio. Fantasy objects are everywhere you look, from giant egg to , bread rolls to basins and gilt dummies. Note those on the circular **Torre Galatea★**. He gave his eccentricity full rein not only in the exhibits – some of his (less recognisable) canvases are exhibited as well as works by Pitxot and Duchamp – but in the squares around the museum, where figures perch on columns of tyres.

CIUTAT VELLA (OLD TOWN)

Figueres has a pleasant historical centre with attractive squares and alleys. The Rambla is a pleasant street full of outdoor bars and restaurants; it fills with market stalls every Thursday.

Museu de Joguets★

Hotel París, Sant Pere 1. Open Jun–Jul & Sep Mon–Sat 10.30am–7pm, Sun & public hols 10.30am–2.30pm; Oct–May Tue–Fri 10am–6.30pm, Sat 10am–7.30pm, Aug Mon–Sat 10.30am–8pm, Sun & public hols 10.30am–2.30pm. Closed 25–26 Dec, 1 Jan, mid-Jan–mid-Feb. €7.
℘972 50 45 85. www.mjc.cat.
Step into a child's paradise with all manner of toys and stuffed animals from different countries on display.

Museu de l'Empordà

Rambla 2. Open Tue–Sat 11am–8pm (Nov–Apr 7pm), Sun & hols 11am–2pm. Closed 1 & 6 Jan and 25–26 Dec. €4; free with Dalí Museum ticket. ℘972 50 23 05. www.museuemporda.org.
This fresh-feeling collection is devoted to the modern history of the region (the archaeological exhibits have been removed). The 'Country of Cooks' exhibit is a must for foodies.

▶ **Population:** 46 381
Ⓒ **Michelin Map:** 574 F 38 – map 122 Costa Brava. See local map under Costa Brava p359.
🅘 **Info:** Plaça del Sol. ℘972 50 31 55. http://en.visitfigueres.cat.
▶ **Location:** Figueres is located 20km/12.4mi inland, at the heart of the area known as the Ampurdán, at the crossroads of routes leading to the Costa Brava and the French city of Perpignan, 58km/36mi N. 🚆Figueres (AVE).
😊 **Don't Miss:** Everything Dalí, and a trip down memory lane to the Toy Museum.
🕓 **Timing:** One day.

Dalí Teatre-Museu, Figueres

© Turespaña

The World of Dalí

Born in 1904, Dalí is the world's most famous Surrealist artist, even if his 'paranoid-critical' method, based on an ironic vision of reality, resulted in his expulsion from the Surrealist ranks by its founder, André Breton. In his most famous paintings (*The Great Masturbator, The Persistence of Memory, Atomic Leda…*) Dalí expresses his personal world through amorphous forms loaded with sensuality and sexual connotations.

Round the corner from the stunning Teatre Museu in Figueres is the much smaller, oft-overlooked **Dalí Joies** (Jewels) museum, a collection of 37 extravagant jewels plus drawings and paintings that Salvador Dalí designed in his inimitable style (see website for times and prices: www.salvador-dali.org).

A short drive away are also the **Casa-Museu Salvador Dalí**, in the charming fishing village of **Portlligat★★** (&see p362), and the **Casa-Museu Castell Gala Dalí** (&GIRONA, p356) housed in the castle that Dalí gave to his wife, Gala.

EXCURSION

Castell de Sant Ferran★

Open Jul–mid-Sep and Holy Week 10am–8pm; late Oct–late Mar 10.30am–3pm; rest of year 10.30am–6pm. Closed 25 Dec, 1 Jan. €3.50; 2hr guided tours €15. &972 50 60 94. www.castillosanfernando.org.

This mid-18C fortress with a star-shaped perimeter once defended the border with France. Its parade ground alone covered 12 000sq m/14 340sq yds, making it the second largest of its kind in Europe. The **stables★** and **views★** over the Empordà plain are highlights. Guided tours explore the elaborate 'Catedral de Agua' (water cathedral) irrigation system in the bowels of the castle.

ADDRESSES

🏠 STAY

◔◕◔ **Hotel Duràn** – Lasauca 5. &972 50 12 50. www.hotelduran.com. 65 rooms, ⌑ €11. Restaurant◔◕◔◕. This city-centre hotel has large, comfy rooms. Dalí used to dine here.

◔◕◔ **Hotel Empordà** – Av. Salvador Dalí i Domènech. &972 500 562. www.hotelemporda.com. 42 rooms, ⌑ €13. While the hotel is nice enough, the reason to come here is for the restaurant, El Motel (◔◕◔◕), arguably the birthplace of modern Catalan cuisine.

◔◕◔ **Mas Jonquer** – Can Prat. 9.6km/6mi SW of Figueres on the N 260. &972 54 72 54. www.masjonquer.com. 8 rooms. This charming hotel feels more like a country inn, complete with a cosy living room full of books, a tennis court and two outdoor pools. Cycling and horseriding are available. Rooms are simple but comfortable.

◔◕◔◕ **Mas Falgarona** – Avinyonet de Puigventós. 5.4km/3.3mi SW of Figueres on the N 260. &972 54 66 28. www.masfalgarona.com. 11 rooms. This luxury retreat with a restaurant (◔◕◔◕) occupies an old farmhouse (*mas*). Works of modern art grace the walls, Decor is minimalist. There's a quiet garden arched around a pool.

Solsona★★

Solsona is a tranquil town with a noble air and attractive squares. Elegant medieval residences line its gently sloping streets.

SIGHTS
Museu Diocesà i Comarcal★★ (Diocesan and Regional Museum)

Pl. del Palau 1. Open mid-Dec–mid-Mar Fri–Sat 11am–5pm, Sun & hols 10am–2pm; mid-Mar–mid-Dec Wed–Sat 11am–6.30pm (plus Tue Jul–Aug), Sun & hols 10am–2pm. Closed 1 & 6 Jan, 25–26 Dec. €5. ℘973 48 21 01. www.museusolsona.cat.

Romanesque and Gothic paintings★★ in the Palau Episcopal (Episcopal Palace, an 18C Baroque building) are excellent examples of Catalan art.

The frescoes include a painting from the Sant Quirze de Pedret church★★, discovered beneath an overpainting. Executed in an archaic style, it shows God, with arms outstretched, in a circle that represents heaven, surmounted by a phoenix symbolising immortality. Totally different are the thinly outlined 13C paintings from Sant Pau de Caserres★ – in particular, the angels★★ of the Last Judgement.

Known for its altar fronts, the museum has another highlight in La Cena de Santa Constanza★, a realistic Last Supper, by Jaime Ferrer (15C). In the Museu de la Sal (Salt Museum), everything is carved out of rock salt from Cardona.

Catedral★

Pl. de la Catedral. Open Mon–Sat 9am–1pm, 4–8pm, Sun 9am–1pm, 4–6pm. ℘973 48 23 10.

Only the belfry and the apse remain of the Romanesque church; the rest is Gothic with Baroque additions such as the portals and 18C Capella de la Virgen (Lady Chapel). This chapel houses the Mare de Déu del Claustro★, a carved Romanesque Virgin Mary in black stone. After visiting the cathedral, stroll around the rest of the old city, particularly the Plaça Major, framed by medieval houses

- ▶ **Population:** 9 014
- **Michelin Map:** 574 G 3 – Catalunya (Lleida).
- **Info:** Carretera Bassella 1. ℘973 48 23 10. www.solonaturisme.com.
- ▷ **Location:** The capital of the Solsonès region is on the C 1410 road linking Manresa with the C 1313 heading into the Pyrenees. Nearest station: Manresa (48km).
- **Timing:** Avoid Mondays, when musuems are shut.

and porches; the Carrer del Castell, home of the 16C ajuntament; and Plaça de Sant Joan.

EXCURSION
Cardona★

▷ 20km/12.4mi SE along the C 55, at the foot of an imposing castle.

Castillo de Cardona★

This spectacular hilltop fortress, at 589m/1 933ft, dates to the 8C. Of the 11C buildings there remain a truncated tower, the Torre de la Minyona, and the collegiate church, surrounded by Vauban-style walls and bulwarks built in the 17C and 18C. The castle is a Parador commanding a marvellous view★ over the Parc Cultural de Muntanya de Sal ★★ (open Tue–Fri 10am–3pm; descent to mine 11.30am & 1.30pm; Sat–Sun open 10am–6pm with descent to mine every 30min; €12; ℘938 69 24 75; www.cardonaturisme.com), at the heart of which is a salt mine that's been operating since Roman times.

Col·legiata de Sant Vicenç★★

Open Oct–May Tue–Sun 10am–1pm, 3–5pm; Jun–Sep 10am–1pm, 3–7pm. Closed 1, 6 Jan, 25–26 Dec. €3; free Tue. ℘938 68 41 69.

The collegiate church built in 1040 has Lombard features. The groined vaulting in the crypt★ rests on six graceful columns. The Gothic cloisters are 15C.

Pirineos Catalanes★★★

The Catalan Pyrenees form a barrier 230km/143mi long and 100km/62mi wide, stretching from the Vall d'Aran to the Mediterranean with altitudes above 2500m/8202ft. They are deeply cut by isolated valleys, each with its own personality and traditions.

All offer delicious regional cuisine and opportunities for skiing, hunting, fishing, mountain climbing and adventure sports. The area is also great for simply driving around: The tours outlined below can be followed on the map in this section.

ART AND ARCHITECTURE

The Pyrenean villages and valleys of Catalunya denote a unique Roman-esque style of art and architecture.

In the 11C, as the local population was fighting against the Arabs, small village churches were built and painted with entrancing murals graphically depicting Christian doctrine for a largely illiterate population. The movement reached its climax in the Vall de Boí (see p376), a UNESCO World Heritage site.

Michelin Map: 574 D 32, E 32–37 and F 32–37 – Catalunya (Girona, Lleida)

Info: Camprodon: Sant Roc 22; 972 74 00 10; www.vallde camprodon.org.Puigcerdà: Pl. Santa Maria; 972 88 05 42; www.puigcerda.cat. La Seu d'Urgell: Calle Mayor 8; 973 35 15 11. www. turismeseu.com. Tremp: Passeig del Vall; 973 65 34 70; www.ajuntamentdetremp.cat. Vielha: Avda. Libertat 16; 973 64 06 88; www.visitvaldaran.com.

Location: The Pyrenees extend almost unbroken for 230km/143mi from the Mediterranean to the high Aran Valley (2 500m/8 202ft). The last range, the Montes Alberes, plunges into the Mediterranean from 700m/ 2 297ft. Nearest major station: Lleida Pirineus (AVE Barcelona-Madrid line).

Timing: Geography will oblige you to select one or two valleys to explore from the south access.

🚗 DRIVING TOURS

1 VALL DE CAMPRODON

30km/18.6mi. Allow half a day.

Two large valleys lie in the Ripollès area under mountains towering to 3 000m/ 10 000ft.

Camprodon★

Camprodon is at the confluence of the Ritort and Ter rivers, crossed by a 12C humpbacked bridge, **Pont Nou★**.

The community developed around the **Monesteri de Sant Pere**, of which only the 12C **Romanesque church★** remains. The cloisters of **Monasterio de Sant Pere de Camprodon★** (Pl. de Santa Maria) are simple and elegant, all sweeping arches and slender columns. The **museum** houses a collection of embroidered fabric.

Opposite the church on the square stands the 14C former Abbatial Palace. The **medieval bridge★** spans the Ter on the way toward Ripoll.

Leave N via the C 38, and after 3.5km/2mi take the winding Carretera Camprodón-Baget mountain road.

Beget★★

This idyllic mountain village with stone houses enjoys a pleasant **setting★** deep in a valley.

The **San Cristófol church★★** (10C–12C), with Lombard arcatures and a slender lantern-tower, houses the **Majestad de Beget★**, a magnificent Christ carved in the 12C (open 9am–7pm; ask for the keys from Joan Coma, Carrer Bellaire; €1; ✆972 74 01 36).

▶ Continue on the Carretera Camprodon-Baget before taking the C 38 to Molló.

Molló

The 12C Romanesque church has a lovely Catalan belfry. Further along the C 38, at 1 513m/5 000ft, the Col d'Ares marks the Spanish-French border.

② VALL DE RIBES

22km/13.6mi from Ripoll to Vall de Núria. Allow a couple of hours.

The Vall de Ribes is popular with Barceloneses as an easily reached skiing and hiking spot, particularly the Vall de Núria.

Ripoll★

✆972 71 41 42. www.ripoll.cat.
Tucked deep in a valley amid the first Pyrenean cliffs, this small industrial city and commercial centre is considered the 'cradle of Catalonia.' It derives its fame from the great Benedictine monastery of Santa Maria, founded in the 9C by Count Wilfred the Hairy, which, until the 12C, served as a necropolis for the Counts of Barcelona, Besalú, Girona, Ausona and Cerdanya. Ripollès's capital has a medieval core at the confluence of two rivers and a few Modernista houses (Can Codina, Can Dou and Casa Bonada).

Monasterio de Santa Maria★

Pl. de l'Abat Oliba. Open Oct–Mar 10am–1.30pm, 3.30–6pm; Apr–Sep 10am–2pm, 4–7pm; Sun 10am–2pm year round. €5.70. ✆972 70 42 03. www.monestirderipoll.cat.
All that remains of the original monastery are the church portal and cloisters. In 1032, Abbot Oliba consecrated an enlarged **church★**, a jewel of early Romanesque art that was damaged

© mafrmcfa/iStockphoto.com
Beget

over the years. It was rebuilt at the end of the 19C to the original plan.
The **portada★★★**, or portal, is composed of a series of horizontal registers illustrating the glory of god victorious over his enemies (Passage of the Red Sea). The **claustro★** (cloisters) abutting the church dates to the 12–14C.

Museu Etnografic

Opposite the monastery. Open Tue–Sat 10am–1.30pm, 4–6pm (Jul–Aug & Holy Week until 7pm). Sun & hols 10am–2pm. €4; free last Sun. ✆972 70 31 44. www.museuderipoll.org.
The Ethnographic Museum traces the history of the area. Inaugurated in 1920, it contains more than 5 000 pieces, from clothing and ceramics to forges and firearms from the 16–19C.

▶ Take the C 26 NW.

Monasterio de Sant Joan de les Abadesses★★

Open Mon–Sat & hols: Mar–Apr & Oct 10am–2pm, 4–6pm; May–Jun & Sep 10am–2pm, 4–7pm; Jul–Aug 10am–7pm; Nov–Feb Mon–Fri 10am–2pm; Sat & hols 10am–2pm 4–6pm. €3. ✆972 72 23 53. www.monestirsantjoanabadesses.cat.
The monastery was founded in the 9C under the rule of a Benedictine abbess, though it soon shut out women.
With its arches and columns with carved capitals, the church recalls those of southwest France. A 1251 **Descent from the Cross★★** in polychrome wood is in the central apse. In 1426 an unbroken host was purportedly discovered on the

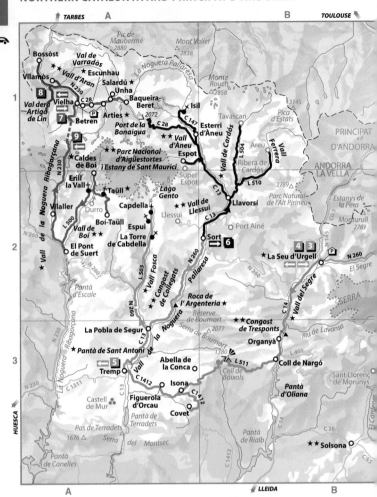

Christ figure's head; it is venerated to this day.

▶ Head N along the N 152 for 17km/10.5mi.

Ribes de Freser

www.vallderibes.cat.
This famous spa stands at the confluence of three rivers and is known for the healing properties of its waters. A rack railway runs to the Vall de Núria.

▶ Continue 7km/4.3mi on N 152 to the Vall de Núria, passing scenic Queralbs and its **rack railway** 🚶‍♂️🚶.

Vall de Núria★

The valley is hemmed in by a rocky amphitheatre stretching from Puigmal to the Sierra de Torreneules. The Virgin of Núria, the patron saint of Pyrenean shepherds, is venerated in a sanctuary in the upper part of the valley.

③ LA CERDANYA★★

145km/90mi from La Seu d'Urgell to La Molina. Allow about 5hr. 🚃Nearest station: Puigcerdà (25km).
The fertile Cerdanya Basin, watered by the River Segre, was formed by subsidence. The northern section, La Cerdagne, was ceded to France under the Treaty of the Pyrenees in 1659. The

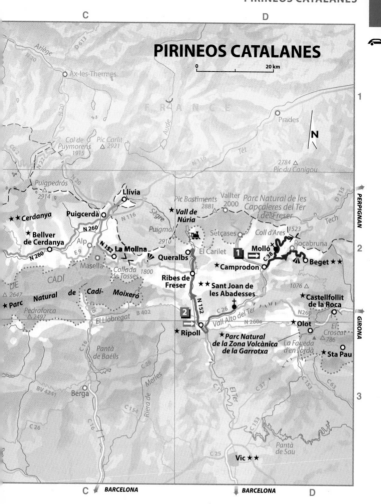

La Seu d'Urgell – Past and Present

Relics discovered at Mt Castellciutat show Bronze Age settlements, but Romans preferred to settle down on the plain, at the confluence of the Segre and Valira rivers. In the 5C, the bishops of Urgell established their Episcopal (or Seu), making way for expansion of the city. Thus, La Seu d'Urgell became the capital of the county, which by the 10C was the most powerful in Catalunya.

Today this lively township – gateway to Andorra, capital of the Alt Urgell region and unofficial capital of the Catalan Pyrenees – has important agriculture, livestock and tourism industries as well as a significant industrial sector. Its dairy products, particularly its cheese, are renowned and protected by their own DOC (designation of origin label).

Due to an historical twist of fate, the Bishop of Urgell (along with the President of France) is bestowed with the title of Co-Prince of Andorra.

Túnel del Cadí facilitates access from Manresa.

From Ribes de Freser to Puigcerdà, the corniche up to the Collado de Toses commands **views**★ of the Segre and its slopes.

▶ 66 km/41mi W on the N 116 then N 152, passing Puigcerdá.

La Seu d'Urgell/Seo de Urgell★

This city of prince-archbishops stands where the Valira, which rises in Andorra, joins the Segre river.

Catedral de Santa Maria★★

Santa Maria. Open Mon–Sat 10am–1.30pm, 4–6pm (Jul–Aug 7pm), Sun & public hols 10am–1.30pm. €3 (incl museum). ✆973 35 32 42. www.cataloniasacra.cat

The cathedral, started in the 12C, shows strong Lombard influence. The central section of the west face, crowned by a small campanile, is typically Italian.

Inside, the nave rises on cruciform pillars, surrounded in French style by engaged columns.

The **cloisters**★ are 13C; the east gallery was rebuilt in 1603 and features granite capitals illustrating humans and animals carved by masons from the Roussillon. The Santa Maria door (southeast corner) opens into the 11C **Església de Sant Miquel**★, the only remaining building of those constructed by St Ermangol. The cathedral houses the **Museu Diocesano**★, which has works of art dating from the 10C to the 18C. The most precious is a beautifully illuminated 11C **Beatus**★★, one of the best-preserved copies of St John's Commentary on the Apocalypse written in the 8C by the priest Beatus of Liébana.

Note the **papyrus**★ belonging to Pope Sylvester II. The crypt contains the 18C funerary urn of St Ermangol.

▶ Follow the N 260 W for 31km/19mi.

Bellver de Cerdanya★

Poised on a rocky crag dominating the Vall del Segre, Bellver de Cerdanya has a fine main square with beautiful balconied stone houses and wooden porches.

▶ 18km/11mi NW on the N 260.

Puigcerdà

The capital of Cerdanya, which developed on a terrace overlooking the River Segre, is one of the most popular holiday resorts of the Pyrenees, with old-fashioned shops, ancient streets and balconied buildings.

▶ Follow signs to Llívia on the D 68.

Llívia

This 12sq km/5sq mi Spanish exclave is in France, 6km/3.7mi from Puigcerdà. Under the Treaty of the Pyrenees, France was granted the Roussillon area plus 33 villages from Cerdanya. Llívia was classed a town, so it remained Spanish. Llívia features Europe's oldest chemist shop, the **Farmacia de Llívia** (mid-Jun–mid-Sep Tue–Fri 10am–8pm, mid-Sep–mid-Jun until 6pm, Sat until 8pm year round, Sun until 2pm year round; €3.50; ✆972 89 63 13; www.llivia.org), which now houses the Museu Municipal.

▶ Ca. Barcelona-Puigcerdà N 152 SE.

La Molina

www.lamolina.cat.

This is one of Catalunya's leading ski resorts. The village of Alp is popular in winter and in summer.

▶ From here you may continue on the E 9 to the Parc Naturel del Cadí-Moixeró.

Parc Natural del Cadí-Moixeró

Information centres in Talló near Bellver de Cerdanya, ✆973 51 08 02 and Bagà (approx. 20 km/12.5mi N of Berga), Centro del Parque ✆93 824 41 51. www.parcsnaturals.gencat.cat/es/cadi

The 413 sq km/160 sq mi park is located between the Cadí and Moixeró mountain ranges, which form a 30km/18.6mi-

Parc Natural del Cadí-Moixeró

long barrier of altitudes of between 900m/2 952ft and 2 647m/8 684ft. Vertical cliffs enclose the deep valleys and canyons, and the vegetation is exceptional: Low temperatures and high humidity favour the proliferation of unusual Mediterranean flora. More than 400km/248.5mi of trails for all levels wind through the park.

④ VALL DEL SEGRE★

73km/45mi. Allow 3hr.

The River Segre forms a huge basin where it flows into the Valira.

Congost de Tresponts★★
The Segre winds through dark rocks *(puzolana)* and pastures. Downstream, the limestone of Ares and Montsec de Tost offers a typically Pyrenean landscape dropping to a cultivated basin, where the river vanishes.

Organyà
www.organya.cat.
This picturesque village has a small medieval centre, its old streets lined with arcades, porches and Gothic mansions. Organyà is renowned for the **Homilies**, the oldest text written in Catalan, from the late 12C.

Pantà d'Oliana★
www.oliana.cat.
The dam is surrounded by grey rocks with lively waterfalls in spring. Even from the road, the sight is quite spectacular.

▶ 6km/3.7mi S on the C 14.

Coll de Nargó
http://collnargo.ddl.net.
This hamlet has one of the most splendid Romanesque churches in Catalunya, **Sant Climent★** (11C), which has a single nave and an apse adorned with Lombard bands. Its sober **bell tower★** is pre-Romanesque. The town also has a curious dinosaur museum, **Dinosfera**, showing fossils found in the area; a 'paleosafari' ensues (Xavier Marot; open 11am–2pm, 5–7pm, Sun until 2pm; €3.50; www.dinosfera.com).

Collado de Bòixols Road★★
Between Coll de Nargó and Tremp, the L 511 follows canyons on slopes clad in pine and holm oak. It continues upward beneath yellow and pink crests, offering lovely **landscapes**, especially from the Collado de Bòixols, and then enters a U-shaped valley, where terraced cultivation extends to the foot of the glacial ridge of Bòixols. The descent into the valley leads to the Conca de Tremp basin.

Abella de la Conca
Blink and you could miss this village, tucked behind the rocky Sarsús summit. Pause to see the Romanesque church of Sant Esteve (11C).

▶ Head back to the L 511 and continue to Isona.

Isona

This ancient Roman city was founded around 100 BC. Isona hosts an interesting museum, mainly devoted to Roman times and palaeontological sites in the area where the remains of dinosaurs have been found (it also organises tours). Its parish church was restored after the civil war of 1936.

▶ Head out of Isona via the C 1412 in the direction of Lleida and turn right for Covet.

Covet

Covet's Esglesia de Santa Maria boasts a beautiful interior. The vaulted nave, is reinforced by supporting arches and columns topped with carved capitals yet the **doorway**★★ is the most remarkable. It features a beautiful carved tympanum and skillfully sculptured arch-based columns. Notice the figurines of angels, musicians, beasts, the characters of the Holy Family and scenes from the book of Genesis.

▶ Continue on the C 1412 towards Tremp.

Figuerola d'Orcau

This small medieval town has interesting streets lined with arcaded houses.

▶ Continue to Tremp.

⑤ VALL DEL NOGUERA PALLARESA

143km/89mi. Allow 1 day, from Tremp to Llavorsí.

Pallars is in the uppermost region of the Catalan Pyrenees. The highest summit is Pica d'Estats (3 145m/10 318ft). To the north is **Pallars Sobirà**, at the heart of the Pyrenees; to the south, **Pallars Jussà** incorporates the vast pre-Pyrenean zone formed by Conca de Tremp. The road follows the bed of the Noguera Pallaresa, and after La Pobla de Segur, cuts across a limestone landscape of remarkable uniformity.

Tremp

In the centre of the Conca de Tremp – a huge basin with lush crops – the village retains its old quarter and three towers from its walls. The **Església de Santa María**★ houses an astonishing 2m/6.5ft-high Gothic statue in polychrome wood: **Santa Maria de Valldeflors**★ (14C). The municipality has a reservoir, the **Pantano de Sant Antoni**★ ≛≛, an ideal spot to fish, canoe/kayak, windsurf, sail and waterski.

▶ 13km/8mi N on the C 13.

La Pobla de Segur

☏ 973 68 00 38. www.pobladesegur.cat.
This popular resort is the only means of access to the Valle de Arán, Alta Ribagorça and Pallars Sobirà.

▶ The C 147 follows the course of the river and the banks of lake Sant Antoni.

Vall Fosca★

This valley is dotted with delightful hamlets including **Torre de Capdella** (www.torredecapdella.org), **Espui** and **Capdella**, each with a Romanesque church. In the upper valley the main attraction is the cobalt-blue glacial lake of **Estany Gento**, visitable via cable car (€12), which sits at 2 141 m/7 024 ft above sea level.

▶ Return to La Pobla de Segur and proceed upwards along the N 260.

Congost de Collegats★★

Eroded by torrents, the red, grey and ochre limestone rocks take on the appearance of spectacular cliffs. Note the **Roca de l'Argentería**★, stalactite-shaped rocks near the Gerri de la Sal.

Sort

www.sortturisme.com.
Kayakers and rafters love this resort for its events held on the Noguera Pallaresa. Sort means 'luck' in Catalan and is consequently a favourite place to buy lottery tickets.

▶ At Rialp, bear left towards Lessui.

Vall de Llessui★★

The road winds way up to the north-west, through a steep granite landscape featuring numerous ravines.

▶ Take the C 13 N to Llavorsí.

⑥ UPPER VALLEY OF THE NOGUERA PALLARESA★

105km/65mi. Allow half a day, from Llavorsí to Port de la Bonaigua.

On this drive through three valleys, mountains dominate a wild landscape.

Llavorsí

This peaceful village sits at the confluence of the Aneu, Cardós and Ferrera basins.

▶ Take the L 504 then turn right on to the L 510 in a NE direction.

Vall Ferrera

http://vallferrera.com.
The easternmost and closest of the three valleys is wedged between high mountains including the Pica d'Estats (3 145m/10 318ft), the highest mountain in Catalunya. ⚑ From here, some beautiful hikes can be taken to Andorra.

▶ Rejoin the L 504 and continue N.

Vall de Cardós★

The Noguera de Cardós River forms the axis of this valley studded with over 20 pretty hamlets.

▶ Return to Llavorsí and take the C 13 towards Baqueira.

Vall d'Aneu★★

www.vallsdaneu.org.
Below the road is the valley of **Espot**, a picturesque village beside a mountain stream, gateway to the Pallars section of a **national park★★** (*see PARC NACIONAL D'AIGÜESTORTES I ESTANY DE SANT MAURICI, p380*). Beyond Esterri d'Aneu the road crosses a breathtak-ing landscape dotted with Romanesque churches such as the **Església de Sant Joan d'Isil★**, glimpsed between summits, and twists up to **Port de la Bonaigua** (2 072m/6 799ft), circled by many peaks.

Esterri d'Àneu

The **Ecomuseu de les Àneu Valls d'Àneu**, occupying a 18C homestead, explains regional life and customs (📞973 626 436; www.ecomuseu.com). After Esterri d'Àneu, the road rises to a dramatic landscape with more Romanesque churches hidden among the peaks.

⑦ LA VALL D'ARAN★★

45km/28mi. Allow half a day, from Vielha to Baqueira Beret.

The **Aran Valley**, in the northwest tip of the Catalan Pyrenees, occupies the upper valley of the Garonne river. Its isolation has helped it to preserve its local traditions and dialect: Aranese is a variation of French Occitan; by law, students in the region have two hours of lessons in Aranese per day. The Vielha Tunnel ended the valley's seclusion in 1948. In recent years the region has seen the creation of several ski resorts.

Vielha

At an altitude of 971m/3 186ft, the capital of the Arán Valley is a holiday resort. Don't miss the 16C and 17C homes in the old town as well as the **Església Parroquial de Sant Miquèu★** with its 14C octagonal tower and 13C Gothic doorway. Inside lies the **Cristo de Mijaran★**, a fragment dating from a 12C Descent from the Cross.

Musèu dera Val d'Aran

Major 28. Open Tue–Sat 10am–1pm, 5–8pm, Sun & hols 10am–1pm. €3. 📞973 641 815. www.cultura.conselharan.org.
In an elegant 16C manor house, this museum introduces visitors to the area's geology, glaciology, history and distinctive dialect.

▶ Leave Vielha to the E on the C 28.

Betren

The **Església de San Esteve★**, built during the transition from Romanesque to Gothic, has archivolts on its **portal★★** decorated with human faces, alluding to the Last Judgement and the Resurrection.

▷ Continue along the C 28 1.3km/1mi to Escunha.

Escunhau

The **Església de San Pedro★** has a 12C **portal★★** bearing an expressive Christ, and capitals adorned with human faces.

▷ Continue along the C 28 3km/2mi to Arties.

Arties★

The Romanesque church here has an apse decorated with scenes illustrating the Last Judgement, heaven and hell.

▷ Continue on C 28 3km/2mi.

Salardú★

Salardú has granite-and-slate houses gathered around the **Església de Sant Andreu★** (12C–13C), whose interior contains 16C **Gothic paintings★★** and a 12C **Christ in Majesty★★**, a stylised 65cm/25in wood statue of remarkable anatomical precision. Note the slender octagonal belfry (15C).

▷ Head N for 1.5km/1mi.

Unha

This hamlet is home to the 12C Romanesque church of Santa Eulàlia. Inside there are vestiges of Romanesque paintings. In the village, the fortified late-16C residence **Çò de Braste** features Renaissance windows and doors.

▷ Return to the C 28 and follow the road W for 9km/5mi.

Baqueira Beret★

www.baqueira.es.
This ski resort, rising from 1 500m/4 900ft to 2 510m/8 230ft, offers excellent lodging and services. It is one of the most popular in Spain.

⑧ VIELHA TO BOSSÒST

52km/32mi. Allow half a day.

Vall de Varrados

The most coveted natural site in this valley is the **Sauth deth Pish waterfall**, which spurts down through a gorge.

▷ From Vielha, take the N230 12km/7.5mi NW.

Vilamòs

This ancient village, suspended on a natural platform 400m/1 300ft above the valley, has traditional architecture and magnificent, unobstructed mountain views. At the far end, a home has been restored to illustrate traditional Aranese life. (Çò de Joanchiquet; open mid-Jun–mid-Sep 11am–2pm, 5–8pm, mid-Sep–mid-Jun Tue–Sun 11am–2pm, 4–7pm; ✆973 64 01 10; www.visitval-daran.com).

▷ On the N 230, head for Bossòst.

Vall de la Artiga de Lin

The Joeu River crosses this valley resplendent with dense pine and beech forest.

Bossòst

The **Església de la Purificació de Maria★★** is the area's best example of Romanesque architecture (12C). Its three apses, in three naves, are adorned with Lombard bands. The colourful north **doorway** features archaic relief work in its tympanum, depicting the Creator surrounded by the Sun, Moon and symbols of the Evangelists.

⑨ LA VALL DE BOÍ★★ AND LA VALL DE LA NOGUERA RIBAGOCANA

58km/36mi. Allow half a day, from Caldes de Boí to Vielha.

Watered by the Noguera de Tor and the Sant Nicolau rivers, this valley is renowned for its cluster of Lombard **Romanesque churches** (11C–12C); they are the finest in the Pyrenees and collectively form a UNESCO World Heritage site. With their slate roofs and irregular masonry, they stand out for their pure, sober lines and for their fine frescoes (several reproductions remain), now in the **Museu d'Art de Catalunya** (ⓒsee *BARCELONA, p343*).

Note the distinctive high silhouette of the belfries, separate but resting against the nave, and the ornamentation of Lombard bands.

Caldes de Boí★

℘973 69 62 10.
www.caldesdeboi.com.
At an altitude of 1 550m/5 084ft, Caldes de Boí is a thermal spa with 37 springs at temperatures between 240°C and 560°C (750°F to 1330°F). Nearby is the ski resort of **Boí-Taüll**.

Taüll★

Taüll is famous for the frescoes of its two early 12C churches. Considered to be masterpieces of Romanesque art, they are exhibited in Barcelona's Museu d'Art de Catalunya.

The village of labyrinthine streets, stone houses and wooden balconies clusters around the **Església de Santa Maria★** (open 10am–7pm, Jul-Aug until 8pm; ℘973 69 40 00), a Romanesque church with three naves separated by cylindrical pillars.

Outside the village is the **Església de Sant Climent★★** (open 10am–2pm, 4–7pm; €1.50; ℘973 69 40 00), with a slender six-storey belfry. A replica of the famous Pantocrator of Taüll is in the apse.

▶ Return to the L 500.

Erill la Vall

In addition to the Romanesque church of Santa Eulàlia, the village has an information centre on Romanesque art, the **Centre del Romànic** (open 9am–2pm,

5–7pm; €5; ℘973 69 6715; www.centreromanic.com).

Vall D'Erill to the Pont de Suert

Continuing along the L 500, your discovery of Romanesque heritage continues with visits to the churches of Sant Felíu de Berruera, and La Nativitat in Durro (2km/1.2mi on the left). After the village of Castelló de Tor, you've crossed into the Vall de Boí.

▶ Take the N 230 on the left to El Pont de Suert.

El Pont de Suert

This area, dotted with attractive hamlets – **Castelló de Tor, Casòs, Malpàs** – retains its rusticity and charm.

▶ Take the N 230 9km/6mi N to Vilaller.

Vilaller

Perched on a rocky outcrop, the village has retained the steep and narrow streets of its ancient heart. In medieval times it was surrounded by walls, whose remains are visible.

▶ Continue on the N 230 and take the the tunnel to Vielha.

ADDRESSES

🏠 STAY

🍴🛏 **Casa Rural La Vall del Cadí** – Ctra Cerc-Tuixent, 1km/.06mi from La Seu d'Urgell, near the Parc Olímpic. ℘973 350 390. www.valldelcadi.com. 7 rooms, ⌑€7.50. This period building has renovated rustic rooms featuring wood with wrought-iron and stone elements.

🍴🛏 **Hostal del Ripollès** – Pl. Nova 11, Ripoll. ℘972 700 215. www.hostal delripolles.com. 8 rooms. Clean (if rather drab) rooms sit above a pleasant restaurant with an outdoor terrace serving Italian and Catalan dishes.

🍴🛏 **Hotel Vall d'Àssua** – Crta. de Llessui, Altron (Vall de la Noguera Pallaresa), 4km/2.5mi NE of Sort. ℘973 621 738.

www.hostalvalldassua.com. 9 rooms. This small hotel has comfortable en suite rooms at a value price. The restaurant's speciality is chargrilled meat.

⊖⊜ **Edelweiss** – Ctra. de Sant Joan 28, Camprodon. ☏972 740 614. www.hoteledelweiss.cat/en. 21 rooms. Expect cosy, tastefully decorated rooms, many of which have balconies. The four-storey building has an attractive stone facade.

⊖⊜ **Mas la Casanova** – Ctra de Ribes de Freser, 3km/1.87mi from the Queralbs in Vall de Ribes. ☏972 198 077. maslacasanova.es. 6 rooms, ⊑ €6.50. Cosy stone cottages dot this homestead in the heart of the Vall de Ribes. Home-cooked meals (on request) are fantastic.

⊖⊜⊜ **Catalunya Park** – Pg. Mauri 9, Ribes de Freser. ☏972 727 198. www.catalunyaparkhotels.com. Open Holy Week and Jul–Sep. 45 rooms. Restaurant ⊖. Expect comfort without pretentiousness at this ideal base for exploring the Vall de Núria. The pool is a plus.

⊖⊜⊜ **Hotel Estel** – Sant Fruitós 39, Berga. ☏938 213 463. www.hotelestel.com. 37 rooms. This friendly hotel, on one of the main avenues into the city, is modern, simple and comfortable.

⊖⊜⊜ **Hotel Segle XX** – Pl. de la Creu.8, Tremp. ☏973 650 000. www.hotelseglexx.com. 48 rooms. Restaurant ⊖⊜. Founded in 1880, this hotel has comfortable updated rooms; the restaurant, serving classic Catalan cuisine, feels more old-fashioned. There's an indoor pool.

⊖⊜⊜ **Hotel Vall de Núria** – Vall de Núria ski resort, Queralbs. ☏972 732 020. www.valldenuria.cat. 75 rooms. This hotel, reachable by rack rail only, has attentive service and a good restaurant serving local dishes. Ski lifts are right out the door, and there's an archery range and kids' play area. Min. stay of two nights.

⊖⊜⊜⊜ **Hotel Calitxó** – Passatge El Serrat, Molló. ☏972 740 386. www.hotelcalitxo.com. 25 rooms ⊑€9. Restaurant ⊖⊜⊜. The elegant Swiss-chalet style property, great for nature enthusiasts, is surrounded by gardens and meadows. Rooms, with light wood accents, have plush furnishings.

⊖⊜⊜⊜ **Hotel La Coma** – Setcases, 10km/6mi N of Comprodon. ☏972 136 074. www.hotellacoma.com.

22 rooms ⊑€10. Restaurant ⊖⊜⊜. This high mountain hotel, popular with skiers, is in an old stone building. Facilities include a spa, indoor pool and gym.

⊖⊜⊜⊜ **Hotel del Lago** – Av. Dr. Piguillem 7, Puigcerdà, Cerdanya. ☏972 881 000. www.hotellago.com. 30 rooms, ⊑ €11. This lakeside family-run hotel, with garden, spa and wellness facilities, is surrounded by a large landscaped area with a pool.

⊖⊜⊜⊜ **Hotel Can Boix** – on the outskirts of Peramola, 17km/10.5mi SW of Coll de Nargó in the Vall del Segre. ☏973 470 266. www.canboix.cat. Closed mid-Jan–mid-Feb and 2 weeks in Nov. 41 rooms, ⊑ €12.40. Restaurant ⊖⊜⊜. Attention to detail is this mountain hotel's strong suit. Rooms combine the warmth of wood with soft-toned furnishings and more modern touches, especially in bathrooms.

⊖⊜⊜⊜ **Parador de La Seu d'Urgell** – Sant Domènec 6, La Seu d'Urgell. ☏902 54 79 79. www.parador.es. 79 rooms, ⊑ €15. Restaurant ⊖⊜⊜. Set around a former Renaissance cloister, this hotel offers modern amenities and minimalist design. The upscale restaurant serves regional dishes.

⊖⊜⊜⊜ **Hotel Spa Riberies** – Camí de Riberies, Llavorsí. ☏973 622 051. www.riberies.com. 34 rooms ⊑€14. Restaurant ⊖⊜⊜. This relaxing hotel offers both contemporary and traditional (attic) rooms and a serene indoor pool. Worth seeking out, the experimental restaurant punches above its weight.

⊖⊜⊜⊜ **Parador de Vielha** – 2.5km/1.5mi S of Vielfa on the N 230. ☏902 54 79 79. www.parador.es. 118 rooms, ⊑ €18. Restaurant ⊖⊜⊜. Enjoy great views over the valley, especially from the circular living area and sprawling pool deck. Spacious rooms boast all the creature comforts.

♡/EAT

Ⓐ In Puigcerdà, typical dishes include *tiró amb naps* (goose with turnips) and rabbit cooked with the famous pears of the region.

⊖⊜ **Cal Teo** – Av. Pau Claris 38, La Seu d'Urgell. ☏973 36 05 35. Closed Sun–Mon eve, Tue. The dependable grill restaurant in the heart of La Seu has delectable flame-licked vegetables topped with melted goat cheese.

◎◎ **Llacs de Cardós** – Vall de Cardós on Ctra Tavascan, Tavascan in the Vall de l'Alt. ☎973 623 178. www.hotellllacsdecardos.com. This rustic mountain hotel restaurant serves hearty local fare; trout is a speciality. Comfortable rooms. (◎◎).

◎◎ **Miscela** – Av. Pau Claris 24, La Seu d'Urgell. ☎973 354 620. www.avenhotel.com. This brightly decorated modern restaurant, great for families, serves traditional dishes as well as pizzas, salads and pastas.

◎◎ **Mikado** – Carrer Pere III 3, Berga. ☎938 212 106. The warm staff and relaxed atmosphere make Mikado a safe bet. Local ingredients are given imaginative flourishes. The weekday set menu (€13.50) will satisfy the most ravenous of appetites.

◎◎◎ **Boixetes de Cal Manel** – on Ctra N 230 at Pont d'Arròs. ☎973 641 168. Closed May, Nov and Mon. In a traditional homestead located outside the village, this restaurant specialises in local cuisine. Its garlicky rabbit *al ajillo* is especially satisfying on snowy days.

◎◎◎ **Restaurant Dachs** – on Ctra de Ripoll at Berga (C 26), 7.5km/4.5mi SW of Ripoll. ☎972 714 425. Open Thu–Sun 10am–6pm. Flavourful meats sourced from the surrounding valley make this restaurant stand out; don't skip the sausage, made in house.

◎◎◎ **Dolcet** – Zulueta 1, Alàs i Cerc, 7km/6mi E of La Seu d'Urgell. ☎973 361 349. Closed Fri, Nov and 15 days in Jun–Jul. This busy roadside restaurant serves Pyrenean classics like braised snails and *trinxat*, a cabbage-and-potato dish akin to bubble and squeak.

◎◎◎ **La Formatgeria de Llívia** – Pla de Ro, Llívia. ☎972 14 62 79. www.laformatgeria.com. Dairy fiends shouldn't miss this French-inflected cheese factory–restaurant hybrid known for its fondue, steak-frites, and foie gras.

◎◎◎ **La Taverna dels Nogueres** – El Pont de Bar, 15km/9mi E de La Seu on the N 260. ☎973 384 020. http://tavernadelsnoguers.com. The fireplace, beamed ceilings and red-checkered tablecloths make this tavern perfect for winter-weather dining.

◎◎◎◎ **La Fonda Xesc** – Pl. Roser 1, Gombrèn, 12.5km/7.5mi NW of Ripoll via the N 152 (towards Puigcerdà) then left on the GI 401. ☎972 730 404. www.fondaxesc.com. Closed Sun eve, Mon, Tue eve, Wed eve, 15 days in Jan and 10 days in Jul. When you can't look at another hearty stew or slab of roast meat, make a beeline for this Michelin-starred restaurant with a fresher, brighter take on the regional cuisine. Above the restaurant there are rooms available (◎◎◎).

◎◎◎◎ **Casa Irene** – Major 4, Arties, in the Vall de l'Alt. ☎973 644 364. www.hotelcasairene.com. Occupying the ground floor of a rustic-chic hotel (◎◎◎◎), this refined yet unfussy restaurant serves internationally inflected Pyrenean cuisine with an extra helping of hospitality.

◎◎◎◎ **Fogony** – Av. Generalitat 45, Sort. ☎973 621 225. www.fogony.com. Closed Sun eve, Mon and 2 weeks in Jan. Innovative takes on Catalan dishes will delight and surprise you here; try the 'Slow Food 0km' menu (◎◎◎) if available. Service is excellent and so are the set-menu lunches (€35).

SPORT AND RECREATION

Tourism-wise, hiking and skiing are the raison d'être of the Pirineos Catalanes. The region has numerous ski resorts, some with large hotels.

The best of these include: **HG Molina** (☎972 89 29 75; www.hghoteles.com), in Girona province, less than two hours from Barcelona, and the **Meliá Royal Tanau Boutique** (☎973 64 44 46; www.melia.com/RoyalTanau) in the resort of **Baqueira-Beret** (Val d'Aran), which has some 153km/95mi of ski runs.

The website www.onthesnow.co.uk provides a useful overview.

SHOPPING

Pastissería Confitería Cosp – Carrer Major 20, Puigcerdà ☎972 88 01 03. The Cosp sisters lure locals and visitors alike to their charming pastry shop (est. 1806), known for its hyperlocal sweet treats like margaritas, almond cookies, and cerdans, hazelnut confections.

Parc Nacional d'Aigüestortes i Estany de Sant Maurici★★

This national park boasts some of the most splendid mountain scenery in Europe. Twisting waterways – *aigües tortes* – burble between mossy meadows and wooded slopes. Glaciers created the harsh beauty of its U-shaped valleys, high mountain lakes and snow-covered peaks. Evergreens include firs and Scots pines; birch and beech trees provide a fiery splash of colour in autumn.

SIGHTS

The park's 14 119ha/34 888 acres, between altitudes of 1 500m/4 921ft and 3 000m/9 842.5ft, are mainly granite and slate, formed in the Paleozoic era when they emerged from the depths of the sea, drawing steep cliffs and deep valleys. Cows graze in the meadows and grouse and partridge squawk in the woods. Wild deer inhabit the higher, less accessible peaks. Both entries – Espot, to the east, and Boí, to the west – have parking areas (driving private vehicles in the park is prohibited). Paths are well signposted.

Make an ℹ️information centre your first stop: **Casa del Parc del Boí** or the **Casa del Parc del Espot** (both open 9am–2pm, 3.30–5.45 pm, exc Sun pm; closed 1 & 6 Jan, 25–26 Dec).

Estany de Sant Maurici (reached by a tarmac road from Espot) is the most accesble and therefore most visited of the 24 lakes in the park. It is surrounded by forest and reflects the peaks of the Sierra dels Encantats.

Hikes

Portarró d'Espot – 🏃 3hr there and back on foot from the Estany de Sant Maurici. The path crosses the Sant Nicolau Valley. At Redó lake, admire the panorama★★.

- **Michelin Map:** 574 E 32–33. Local map, see PIRINEOS CATALANES map, p376–377 – Catalunya (Lleida)
- **Info:** Casa del Parque de Boí: Graieres 2. ℘973 69 61 89; Casa del Parque de Espot: Sant Maurici 5. ℘973 62 40 36. www.gencat.cat/parcs/aiguestortes.
- **Location:** The park is just west of Andorra and south of France. 🚃Nearest station La Poble de Segur (70km).
- **Don't Miss:** A forest walk up to grand panoramas.
- **Timing:** One day incl hikes (longer for nature fiends).

Estany Gran d' Amitges – 🏃 3hr there and back on foot from Sant Maurici lake. Beside the lake, mountain streams form impressive waterfalls. The snow-capped Bassiero (2 887m/9 472 ft) and Saboredo (2 814m/9 232ft) peaks dominate this unique area of high mountains.

Estany Negre – 🏃 5hr there and back on foot from Espot; 4hr from Sant Maurici lake. Cross the stunning Peguera Valley to Estany Negre (Black Lake), hemmed in by awesome summits.

Aigüestortes – Western section.🏃3hr there and back. The entry road leads to Aigüestortes, where a stream winds through rich pastures. Hike to Estany Llong.

ADDRESSES

🛏️STAY

Camping is prohibited but there are 14 mountain refuges. Most are open Jun–Sep and during Holy Week.

Principat d'Andorra★★

Principality of Andorra

This teensy nation in the sky, sandwiched between Spain and France, spans high plateaus and deep valleys cut by charming mountain roads. Once the Bhutan of Europe, in recent decades Andorra has traded in bucolic solitude for urbanisation and a tourism boom. But tradition remains in the terraced slopes planted with tobacco and in religious pilgrimages (notably the famous Catalan *aplec*).

▶ **Population:** 76 965
🕐 **Michelin Map:** 574 E 34-35.
🏢 **Info:** Andorra la Vella: Plaça de la Rotonda. ☎376 750 100. www.visitandorra.com.
◐ **Location:** Between Spain and France, 20km/12.4mi from La Seu d'Urgell. 🚂Nearest Spanish station is Puigcerda (80km) – or L'Hospitalet (France, 3 km).
👪 **Kids:** Museu Nacional de l'Automòbil.
🕐 **Timing:** Spend a day driving through the valleys.
🅿 **Parking:** Forget about parking in Andorra la Vella.
🙂 **Formalities:** The currency is the euro. Visitors need a valid passport; drivers need a current driving licence. There are customs checkpoints on the borders. If calling from Spain, prefix numbers with 00.

ANDORRA TODAY

Andorra is known in Spain for its duty-free shopping in and around the small capital of Andorra la Vella. In fact, an astonishing 8 million visitors a year descend upon the principality, many clutching their credit card.

The main skiing valleys are also busy in season, with some €50 million recently invested in winter infrastructure. By contrast the outlying villages remain largely uncommercialised.

A BIT OF HISTORY

Until 1993 Andorra was a co-principality subject to an unusual political regime dating back to the days of feudalism. The neighbouring rulers, the Bishop of Urgell and the counts of Foix, enjoyed coequal rights and exercised powers over this small territory jointly. Today Andorra is a sovereign state and a full-fledged member of the United Nations.

🚗 DRIVING TOURS

VALL DEU VALIRA D'ORIENT

30km/18.6mi from Pas de la Casa to Andorra la Vella. Allow half a day.

This drive will lead you around Andorra's stunning countryside, slowly easing into the shopping, spa and hotel frenzy of Andorra La Vella.

Pas de la Casa★

Historically a simple frontier post, the highest village in Andorra (2 091m/6 861ft) is the main ski resort of the region.

◐ The road snakes through the mountains before reaching Port d'Envalira, offering great views of Font Negre.

Port d'Envalira★★

🅐 Roads may be snowbound but usually reopen within 24hr.

Envalira boasts the highest altitude of the major Pyrenean passes (2 407m/7 897ft). On the Atlantic-Mediterranean divide, it commands a **panorama★**.

◐ Take the CG-2 in the direction of Canillo, stopping just outside the town.

Església de Sant Joan de Caselles

Av. Sant Joan de Caselles, Canillo.
Ask at the tourist office about times.
☏ +376 753 600.

Below an openwork tower and rows of ornamental windows, this church is one of the best examples of Romanesque architecture in Andorra. Behind the wrought-iron grid of the presbytery stands a painted altarpiece by the master **Canillo** (1525), representing the life and visions of the Apostle St John. The Romanesque **Crucifixion**★ was restored in 1963: A Christ in stucco was placed atop a fresco illustrating the Calvary.

▶ Continue to Canillo.

Canillo

The bell tower of the church set against rocks is the highest in Andorra. At its side is an ossuary, characteristic of early Iberian occupation.

Santuari de Meritxell

Beyond Los Bons pass lies a lovely **site**★ of houses gathered under a ruined castle and the Capella de Sant Romà. Nearby stands the church of Nuestra Señora de Meritxell (open mid-Jul–mid-Sept daily 10am–7pm; rest of year 9am–1pm, 3–7pm, closed Sun eve and Tue; ☏376 85 12 53, www.cultura.ad/per-visitar/monuments), national sanctuary of the principality since 1976.

▶ Continue on the same road to Encamp.

Encamp

This village has two churches: Santa Eulàlia has a tall steeple (23 m/75.5ft), a 14C porch and Baroque altarpieces; Sant Romà de les Bons contains reproductions of Gothic paintings. Encamp also has two worthwhile museums:

Casa Cristo - Museu Etnografic★

Cavallers 2. Open Jul–Aug Tue–Sat 9.30am – 1.30pm, 3–7.30pm, Sun 9.30am–1.30pm; rest of the year 9.30am–1.30pm, 3–6.30pm, Sun 10am–2pm. €3.
☏376 833 551. www.encamp.ad.

Set in a 19C homestead, this museum illustrates what everyday life was once like for a modest agrarian family.

▲▲ Museu Nacional de l'Automòbil★

Av. de Joan Martí, 66. Open May–Oct Tue–Sat 10am–2pm, 3–6pm, Sun 10am–2pm. Dec–Apr Tue–Sat 10am–1pm, 3–8pm. €5. ☏376 83 22 66.

This collection offers over a century of automotive history, with 88 cars, 105 bicycles and 68 motorcycles from classic and vintage marques such as Bugatti, Rolls-Royce, Ferrari and Cadillac.

Estany d'Engolasters (Engolasters Lake)

The Engolasters plateau is a pastured extension of Andorra la Vella used for sports and recreation. The fine Romanesque tower of the church of Sant Miquel rises above the rolling plains.
▲ Climb over the crest among the pine trees at the end of the road and descend on foot to an impressive hydroelectric dam, surrounded by trees, which has raised the waters of the lake (alt 1 616m/5 301ft) some 10m/33ft.

▶ Continue S on the CS 200.

Andorra la Vella

Houses in the capital cluster onto a terrace overlooking the Gran Valira. Streets in the old quarter remain almost intact. The ancient stone building, **Casa de la Vall** (Parliament House; Vall; by 30min guided tour, only May–Oct 10am–2pm, 3–6pm; closed Sun pm & Mon pm; €5; ☏376 82 91 29, www.casadelavall.ad), houses the Consell General de les Valls, both Parliament and courthouse to the small nation. To the east, Andorra la Vella joins Les Escaldes, dominated by **Caldaea** (www.caldea.com), a family-friendly thermal spa with futuristic design.

VALLS DE GRAN VALIRA AND VALIRA DEL NORD

9km/5.5mi from Sant Julia de Loria to La Cortinada to Andorra la Vella. Allow half a day.

This drives takes you through the valleys of Andorra's ski country, but it's beautiful out of season too.

Sant Julia de Loria

Museu del Tabac – Dr. Palau, 17; open Jul–Aug Tue–Sat 9am–6.30pm, Sun 9am–1pm; Sept–Jun Tue–Fri 9am–6pm, Sat until, 6.30pm, Sun 10am–1pm. €7. ℘376 74 15 45. www.museudeltabac.com. This museum occupies a former tobacco factory and explains the whole process, from drying to rolling to packaging, accompanied by a video narrated by former workers.

▷ Continue N on the CS 100, then take the CG 3 toward La Massana.

Gargantas de Sant Antoni

From the bridge over the Vall de Valira de Nord you can see the old bridge used by medieval shepherds on your right.

▷ Go through the Túnel de Sant Antoni on the CG 3.

La Massana

Casa Rull de Sispony★ – C. Major. Open Tue–Sat 10am–2pm, 3–6pm; May–Oct Sun 10am–2pm. €5. ℘376 83 69 19. This 17C homestead reconstructs local everyday life. It belonged to one of the richest families in La Massana, and there are many details to ponder over, particularly in the kitchen.

▷ Continue N on the CG 3.

Ordino

Park by the church in the upper town. Ordino is a quaint village with a maze of charming alleyways. The **Casa d'Areny-Plandolit★** (open same hours as Casa Rull; €5; ℘376 83 97 60, www.cultura.ad/per-visitar/museus) dates to 1676 and belonged to a family that included the village's master ironworker. The metalwork on the balconies, Art Nouveau dining room and ceramic-tiled kitchen are highlights.
Nearby are the **Museu Postal d'Andorra** (Camí de Segudet; open same hours as Casa Rull; €5; ℘376 839 760; www.cultura.ad/per-visitar/museus) and the **Museu de la Miniatura** (Edifici Maragda; ℘376 838 338).

▷ From here continue to La Cortinada to visit the Cal Pal Mola i Serradora (mill and sawmill; ℘376 878173 www.ordino.ad).

Tarragona and Southern Catalunya

With the exception of coastal resorts like Salou, which boasts Port Aventura (Spain's largest theme park), Southern Catalunya, is often overlooked by visitors. Their loss: Its provincial capitals, particularly Tarragona, offer a wealth of cultural interest, from expansive Roman remains to soaring Gothic cathedrals. Its inland towns are every bit as atmospheric as the prettied-up medieval hamlets of the north, but restaurants and hotels are cheaper. The landscape is diverse, taking in wide plains, orchards, wetlands and rolling vineyards (Monsant is one of Spain's most up-and-coming wine regions).

Highlights

1. Tarragona's atmospheric **Medieval Quarter** and **cathedral** (p393)
2. The peaceful **Monastery of Poblet** (p397)
3. Soaking up the sun on the **Costa Daurada** (p401)
4. A day out out with the kids at **Port Aventura** (p401)
5. Getting away from it all in the **Ebro Delta** wetlands (p402)

Little Egret in the Ebro Delta

© Jean-Claude Carton/Biosphoto/Photoshot

Tarragona and the coast

Easily accessible by both car and train, the Costa Daurada takes its name from the long golden beaches that begin south at the Ebro Delta and stretch north almost as far as Sitges. With the exception of Salou, the resorts here are mostly low-key and (again, aside from Salou) geared toward Spanish holidaymakers. Tarragona also has good beaches, but it's understandably better-known for its UNESCO World Heritage recognised Roman archeological ensemble and a magnificent cathedral.

When Barcelona was still a mere trading post, Tarragona (or Tarraco, as it was called) was the Roman capital of Hispania. The Romans built a forum, amphitheatre, sophisticated aqueduct and other infrastructures in this bustling port, many of which can be visited today. By contrast, 10km/6.2mi away is Spain's top-rated theme park, Port Aventura.

Inland and Lleida

The province of Lleida (Lérida in Castilian), on the other hand, had its golden age during the 11 and 12C, when nobles and knights set about making a stronghold of the Catalan plains. The small town of Mont-blanc contains many surviving medieval features, and Poblet and Santes Creus boast two of the finest monasteries in Spain.

The Delta Ebro and Tortosa

Spain's most voluminous river meets the sea at the Delta Ebro, where one of the bloodiest battles of the Spanish Civil War took place. Today people visit to bird-watch, fish or simply laze beside the marshy waters. A good home base for exploring this area is the sleepy town of Tortosa, which feels a world away from the region's main cities and resorts.

Tarragona★★

Tarragona, with its ancient and medieval heritage, is also a modern town with wide avenues and a lively commercial centre. Its gardened seafront promenade skirts the cliffside and surrounds the old city and Palace of Augustus, following the city walls in the shadow of the cathedral. Long a major port, Tarragona also has 15km/9.3mi of beaches that attract summer visitors.

▶ **Population:** 131 300
◔ **Michelin Map:** 574 I 33 – Catalunya (Tarragona)
🗎 **Info:** Major 37. ℘977 25 07 95. www.tarragona turisme.cat.
◗ **Location:** Tarragona is in Cataluña in NE Spain, SW along the coast from Barcelona. 🚆Camp de Tarragona (AVE).
👪 **Kids:** The city's beaches.

ROMAN TARRAGONA★★

Passeig Arqueològic★ (Archaeological Promenade)

Av. Catalunya. Open Holy Week & May–Sep Tue–Sat 9am–9pm. Rest of year Tue–Sat 9am–7pm. Sun & public hols 9am–3pm. Closed 1, 6 Jan, 1 May, 25–26 Dec. €3.30 single attraction, €11.05 all attractions. ℘977 24 57 96. http://museuhistoria.tarragona.cat.

Scipios built Tarragona's walls in the 3C BC on existing Cyclopean bases. They were so massive that they were long thought to have been barbarian or pre-Roman. Medieval inhabitants rebuilt the ramparts; 18C citizens remodelled them but thankfully left many marks of their 2 000 years of history. A garden walk follows the walls.

Museu Nacional Arqueològic de Tarragona★★ (Archaeological Museum)

Tinglado 4, Moll de la Costa. Open Mon–Sat 9.30am–8.30pm (Oct–May until 6pm), Sun & public hols 10am–2pm. €4.50 (incl entry to Necropolis); free last Tue Oct–Jun. ℘977 23 62 09. www.mnat.cat.

With the main Plaça del Rei building closed for renovations, MNAT has temporarily moved a number of key exhibits to its 'Tinglado 4' offshoot in the port. Though it doesn't compare to the full MNAT experience, you can still get a taste of Tarragona's stunning **Roman architecture, mosaics★★** and **Roman sculpture★**.

Capital of Hispania Tarraconensis

The history of Tarragona dates back thousands of years. The imposing ramparts built of enormous Cyclopean blocks of stone indicate that it was founded by peoples from the eastern Mediterranean early in the first millennium BC. In due course it suffered occupation by the Iberians. The Romans, who by 218 BC had control of the larger part of the peninsula, developed Tarraconensis into a major city and overseas capital. Although it could never equal Rome, it enjoyed many of the same privileges as the imperial capital. Augustus, Galba and Hadrian did not disdain to live in it. Conversion to Christianity, often attributed to the gospel of St Paul, brought it appointment as a metropolitan seat, and its dignitaries the primacy of Spain. Its prestige was retained through both the barbarian invasions of the 5C and the defeat of the Moors in the 8C, but it ultimately lost to the ambition of Toledo in the 11C.

Amfiteatre

© cwrgutierrez/iStockphoto.com

Recinte Monumental del Pretori i del Circ Romà★ (Praetorium and Roman Circus)

Pl. del Rey 5. Open Holy Week & Apr–Sep Tue–Sat 9am–9pm. Rest of year Tue–Sat 9am–7.30pm. Sun & public hols 9am–3pm. Closed 1, 6 Jan, 1 May, 25–26 Dec. Prices as Archaeological Promenade. ℘977 24 22 20.

Visit the **vaulted underground galleries★** of a 1C BC tower; then, enjoy the sweeping **view★★** from the top. **Hippolyte's sarcophagus★★**, found virtually intact on the bed of the Mediterranean, bears lively sculptured ornamentation. The vast **Roman Circus** (325m x 115m/1 066ft x 378ft) was designed for chariot races. Only a few terraces, vaults and sections of the facade remain.

Amfiteatre★★

Parque del Miracle. Opening times and prices as Praetorium and Circus. ℘977 24 22 20.

The seaside elliptical amphitheatre is in a naturally sloped **site★**. Bishop Fructuosus and his deacons, Augurius and Eulogius, were martyred here in 259. The Església de Santa Maria del Miracle (church) replaced a Visigothic basilica in the 12C and lies in ruin.

Forum Romà

Opening times and prices as Passeig Arqueològic. ℘977 24 22 20.

The Forum was the core of the Roman city. A few reliefs, pieces of frieze and sections of a street remain.

Museu i Necrópolis Paleocristianas

Av. Ramon y Cajal 80. Open Jun–Sep Tue–Sat 9.30am–1.30, 4–8pm, Sun & public hols 10am–2pm; rest of the year Tue–Sat 9.30am–1.30pm, 3–5.30pm; Sun & public hols 10am–2pm. €4.50 (incl entry to Museu Arqueològic). ℘977 211 175. www.mnat.es.

A 3C–7C burial site with over 2 000 tombs was uncovered here in 1923. A section has been restored for viewing, with many of the remains now in the Archaeological Museum.

MODERNIST HERITAGE

Tarragona's Modernista buildings include a clutch of residential houses along the Rambla Nova; the Mercat Central (1905), southwest of the Rambla Nova; and El Escorxador, the defunct abattoir (1902).

El Serrallo

◗ Southwest of the centre, beyond the railway tracks. Access by bus #2 or # 5 or a 20-minute walk.

This old fishing district, which sprung up in the mid-19C, boasts some of the best restaurants in town, and a famous fish market is held here every day. Made up of a handful of narrow alleys around the church of Sant Pere, El Serrallo comes alive at night and is a great place to people-watch.

 WALKING TOUR

CIUDAD MEDIEVAL

Tarragona's medieval inhabitants integrated the vestiges of the Roman city
into their urban planning.

Plaça de la Font

Dominated by the facade of the **Ajuntament** (city hall) and adorned with
fountains, this pedestrianised square
is Tarragona's main meeting point, a
great place to relax on a café terrace.

▷ Turn right on Carrer de
l'Ajuntament Sant Domènec, then
right again on Carrer Roser.

Plaça del Pallol

Roman remains are hidden under the
Medieval buildings in this peaceful
square. Next to the Antiga Audiència
building (an old courthouse), porches
and large Gothic windows survive as
well as the ruins of the Roman gate to
the provincial forum.

▷ From the plaça, take the exit onto
Carrer dels Cavallers.

Carrer dels Cavallers

As is the case of Barcelona's Carrer de
Montcada (👓see p337), the Carrer dels
Chevaliers was the main artery of medieval Tarragona. It is still lined with a few
mansions that belonged to the wealthi-
est families in the city.

Casa-Museu Castellarnau

Cavallers 14. Open first Sat of the month
only, 9am–3pm.
The Emperor Charles V is said to have
stayed in this wealthy 14C–15C residence. It features a pretty Gothic patio
and fine 18C furniture, though recent
remodelling has left it emptier and with
less charm.

▷ Turn left on the Carrer Major.

Carrer Major

The 'Main Street' of Tarragaona leads
directly to the cathedral's main portal.
Arcades and shops, many historical and

at times with a distinct retro feel, lend
an attrative amabiance.
Arcades on Carrer Merceria (on the
right before you reach Plaça del Seu).
These are the only remnants of the
old medieval market. In summer, the
arcades provide respite from the heat.

▷ Continue to the Plaça de la Seu.

Catedral★★

Pl. de la Seu. Open Mon–Sat mid-Mar–
mid-Jun 10am–7pm, mid-Jun–mid-Sep
until 8pm, mid-Sep–Oct until 7pm;
Nov–Feb Mon–Fri until 5pm, Sat until
7pm. Closed Sun & public hols. €5 (incl
Museum, cloister and treasury). 🖉977
22 69 35. www.catedraldetarragona.com.
Construction began in 1174, on the site
of a mosque that followed a temple to
Jupiter, in transitional Gothic style,
although the side chapels are both
Plateresque and Baroque.

Facade★

A Gothic central section with rose window is flanked by Romanesque sections.
The **main doorway** displays the Last
Judgement, with expressive relief work.
The archivolts are carved with Apostles
and Prophets. On the pier, the Virgin
(13C) receives the Faithful.

Interior★★

Following a Latin cross plan, there are
three naves and a transept. The Romanesque apse has semicircular arches. At
each end of the transept are 14C rose
windows with stained glass. The three
naves are mostly Gothic. The finest work
of art is undoubtedly the **altarpiece of
Santa Tecla★★★** (Capella Mayor, 1430),
closing off the central apse, which is
reached by two Gothic doorways. Santa
Tecla (St Thecla), who was converted by
St Paul and supposedly escaped death
multiple times through divine interven-
tion, is the city's patron saint. This work
by Pere Joan shows a talent for detail,
ornamentation and the picturesque.
To the right of the altar is the 14C **Tomb
of the Infante Don Juan de Aragón★★**,
attributed to an Italian master. The
Capella de la Virgen de Montserrat

(second chapel, left) houses a **retable**★ by Luis Borrassà (15C).

Reliefs★ in the Capella de Santa Tecla (third chapel in the right-hand aisle) recount the saint's life. The **Capella de los Sastres**★★ (to the left of the Capella Major) features intricate ribbed vaulting, a lovely altarpiece and paintings. Sumptuous tapestries are decorated with allegorical motifs.

Claustro★★

The 12C–13C cloisters are unusually large: Each gallery is 45m/148ft long. The arches and geometric decoration are Romanesque, but the vaulting is Gothic, as are the supporting arches. Moorish influence is evident in the *claustra* of geometrically patterned and pierced panels filling the oculi below the arches, the line of multifoil arches at the base of the Cathedral roof and the belfry in one corner, rising 70m/230ft. Inlaid in the west gallery is a *mihrab*-like stone niche, dated 960. A remarkable **Romanesque doorway**★, with a Christ in Majesty, links the cathedral to the cloisters.

Museu Diocesá★★

Pl. de la Seu. Open same hours/ticket as Cathedral.

The capitular outbuildings contain religious vestments, paintings, altarpieces and reliefs. Tapestries in Room III include the 15C Flemish **La Buena Vida**★. In the Capella del Corpus Christi are a richly ornate **monstrance**★ (n°105) and a polychrome alabaster relief work depicting St Jerome (16C).

▶ Retrace your steps to the Carrer Major, then turn left into the Carrer Sant Lorenç.

Antic Hospital★

Coques.

This 12C–14C hospital, now used by the local council, is a surprising mix of styles. It retains its Romanesque facade and doorway.

▶ Backtrack along Carrer de Sant Lorenç.

Museu d'Art Modern

Carrer Santa Anna 8. Open Tue–Fri 10am–8pm, Sat 10am–3pm, 5–8pm, Sun & hols 11am–2pm. Closed 1, 6 Jan, 1 May, 11 Sep, 25–26 Dec. ☏977 235 032. www.dipta.cat/mamt.

Inaugurated in 1991, this museum presents a harmonious collection of *Modernisme*, the Catalan equivalent to Art Nouveau. The local sculptor Julio Antonio (1889–1919), author of the monument to the heroes of 1811 on La Rambla, is well-represented.

EXCURSIONS

Acueducto de Les Ferreres★★

▶ Leave the city along rambla Nova. 4km/2.5mi north of Tarragona you will see the well-preserved two-tier Roman aqueduct on your right, 217m/712ft long. You can walk (🏃30min) through the pines to the base then ascend and safely walk across the top of it in the channel where the water used to flow.

Vil·la Romana de Centcelles★★

▶ 4km/2.5mi NW. Exit the city along Av. Ramon i Cajal. Take the Reus road; bear right after crossing the Francolí. Turn right in Constanti into Centcelles; continue 450m/492yd on an unsurfaced road; turn left just before the village. Open Tue–Sat 10am–1.30pm, 3–4pm (extended hours in summer), Sun & hols 10am–2pm. Closed 1 & 20 Jan , 1 May, 1 Aug, 25–26 Dec. €2.50. ☏977 52 33 74. www.mnat.cat.

Two monumental buildings in a vineyard are faced in pink tiles. They were built in the 4C by a wealthy Roman near his vast summer residence. The first chamber is covered by an immense cupola (diameter: 11m/36ft) decorated with **mosaics**★★ on themes such as the hunt and Daniel in the lion's den. The adjoining chamber has an apse on either side.

Torre de los Escipiones★

▶ Leave Tarragona along Vía Augusta. After 5km/3mi turn left.

The upper and central parts of this square funerary tower (1C) bear reliefs portraying Atis, a Phrygian divinity associated with death rituals (not the Escipion brothers as once thought).

Vil·la Romana de Els Munts★

▶ 12km/7.4mi E along the N 340. Leave Tarragona along Vía Augusta. Open same hours as Villa Romana de Centcelles. Closed 1 & 6 Jan, 1 May, 11 Nov, 25–26 Dec. €2.50. ℘977 65 28 06. www.mnat.cat.

This Roman villa is tucked in Altafulla, a privileged **site★★** gently sloping toward the sea. The L-shaped arcaded passage was flanked by gardens and **baths★** with a complex plan.

Arco de Berà★

▶ Follow Vía Augusta. The arch is situated in the locality of Roda de Berà, 20km/12.4mi along the N 340.

Vía Augusta once passed under this imposing, well-proportioned arch (1C). Its eight grooved pilasters are crowned by Corinthian capitals.

ADDRESSES

🛏 STAY

▭ Hotel Plaça de la Font – Plaça de la Font 26. ℘977 246 134. www.hotelpdelafont.com. 20 rooms. �€3.60. Restaurant▭▭. In an attracive square in the old town, this four-storey hotel and restaurant is an excellent budget option. Public parking nearby.

▭▭▭ Hotel Sercotel Urbis Centre – Pl. Corsini 10. ℘977 24 01 16. www.sercotelhoteles.com. 44 rooms. ⊿€9.50. Restaurant ▭▭▭. Situated near the old city, this comfortable 3-star hotel hotel offers functional rooms with modernised bathrooms. Views over the rooftops make it worth ponying up the extra coin for 'Atic' rooms.

▭▭▭▭ Hotel La Boella – La Canonja, 7.9km/4.9mi SE of Tarragona on the T 11. ℘977 77 15 15. www.laboella.com. 13 rooms. ⊿€14. Restaurant ▭▭▭. A charming, château-like country hotel a short drive from the city centre, La Boella boasts huge gardens and olive groves from which the estate's own

extra virgin oil is produced. There's a smart restaurant with an impressive wine cellar on the grounds as well, ideal for travelling gourmands and oenophiles.

℘/EAT

▭▭ El Llagut– Carrer de Natzaret 10. ℘977 22 89 38. www.elllagut.com Mediterranean-inspired tapas and excellent fish dishes are this rustic-chic restaurant's claim to fame. The prawns are a favourite with regulars.

▭▭▭ Racó de l'Abat – Carrer de l'Abat 2. ℘977 780 371. www.abatrestaurant.com. Call for opening times.An ancient stone abode complete with interior Gothic arches houses this mom-and-pop restaurant (he's manages the front while she cooks in the back). Comforting Catalan dishes like simply grilled fish and local sausages with fried potatoes ensure a constant stream of locals and out-of-towners.

▭▭▭▭ El Terrat – Carrer Pons d'Icart 19. ℘977 24 84 85. Closed Mon eve. www.elterratrestaurant.com. El Terrat, helmed by a 28-year-old chef, proves that a restaurant doesn't need white tablecloths or a suited maître d' to make phenomenally delicious, creative food: Rice and seafood dishes are particularly standout. Fixed-price lunches are a steal at €21.

▭▭▭▭ AQ Restaurant – Carrer de les Coques 7. ℘977 215 954. www.aq-restaurant.com. Closed Sun and Mon. Colourful, in-your-face dishes that resist categorisation are the hallmark of this *nueva cocina* hotspot. The minimalist, streamlined dining room lets the gorgeous food – like Texas-style wagyu beef brisket or stuffed baby artichokes cloaked in brick-red *romesco* sauce – take centre stage.

Montblanc★★

Montblanc rises above rolling vineyards and almond orchards. Within its ancient walls lie narrow cobbled streets, ornate palaces and gorgeous Gothic churches.

▶ **Population:** 7 283
🕭 **Michelin Map:** 574 H 33 – Catalunya (Tarragona)
🅰 **Info:** Antiga Església de Sant Francesc. ✆977 86 17 33. www.montblancmedieval.cat.
◐ **Location:** At the crossroads of the N 240 (Tarragona-Lleida) and the C 240 from Reus (29km/18mi S). 🚃 Montblanc.

SIGHTS

The Ramparts★★

Enquire at 🅰tourist office for opening details, €4. www.montblancmedieval.cat
The ramparts were commissioned by Peter IV of Aragón in the mid-14C. Two thirds of the original walls (1 500m/5 000ft) remain, along with 32 square towers and two of four gates: that of Sant Jordi (S) and Bover (NE).

Església de Santa Maria★★

Pl. de l'Església. Open 11am–1pm daily, Mon–Sat 4–6pm.
This Gothic church overlooking the city has a single nave and radiating chapel. The unfinished facade is Baroque. Inside there's a 17C organ★★, a Gothic altarpiece in polychrome stone (14C) and an elegant silver monstrance.

Museu Comarcal de la Conca de Barberà★ (CIAR i Museu d'Art Frederic Marès de Montblanc)

Pedrera 2. Open Tue–Fri 10am–2pm, 4–7pm, Sat–Sun & hols by appointment. Closed 1 Jan, 25–26 Dec. €2.90. ✆977 860 349. www.mccb.cat.
The ground floor of this dual-themed museum feaures an interpretation centre of local rock art (Centre d'Interpretació de l'Art Rupestre - CIAR) practiced by its first inhabitants.
Up one level you'll find the Marès collection (🕭see Museu Frederic Marès, Barcelona, p331), bequeathed to the city by the sculptor and collector who, between 1945 and 1952, stayed in Montblanc to restore the Royal Tombs of the Poblet Monastery (🕭see p397). The religious paintings and sculptures from the 14C–19C are remarkable, particularly the Early Gothic wooden figurines.

There are several other attractions under the Museu Comarcal's umbrella including the Molins de la Vila, two ancient flour mills 1km/0.6mi out of town toward Prenafeta.

Plaça Mayor

Among the arcades of shops and cafés around the main square, note the town hall (ayuntamiento) and the Gothic-style Casa dels Desclergue.

Església de Sant Miquel★

Pl. de Sant Miquel. Prebooked guided tours. ✆977 86 17 33.
Fronted by a Romanesque facade, this small 13C Gothic church has pure, sober lines. It hosted the Estates General of Catalunya several times in the 14C and 15C. Next to the church stands the **Palau del Castlà**, formerly the residence of the king's representative. A 15C prison is on its ground floor.

Call Judío (Jewish Quarter)

Until 1489, Montblanc was a thriving town with a prosperous Jewish community (*Jueus*). Its golden age was the 14C, when its economic supremacy was reflected in the political arena with several Estates General being held in the town at the instigation of Catalan-Aragonese monarchs. Only the Carrer dels Jueus (Street of Jews) and part of a Gothic house in Plaça dels Àngels remain of the former Jewish district. Another intriguing building is the 14C **Casa Alenyà**, a slender Gothic house.

Monestir Santa Maria de Poblet

© José Fuste Raga/Getty Images

OUTSIDE THE WALLS
Convent i Santuari de la Serra★
Open 8.15am–2pm, 4–6pm (until 7pm May–Oct). Closed Fri am. €4.
This ex-convent of the Order of St Clare stands on a small hill. It houses the venerated **Mare de Déu de la Serra**, an alabaster statue made in the 14C.

Hospital de Santa Magdalena★
Open Aug–mid-Sep 11am–3pm; rest of year 10am–7pm.
The small yet remarkable 15C **cloisters** illustrate the transition between Gothic and Renaissance. The vertical perspective on the ground floor, featuring fluted columns and pointed arches, is broken in the upper section.

EXCURSION
Valls
The prosperous city of Valls is wedged between two tributaries and keeps its medieval character. It's well-known for its *castells*, human towers that soar high in the air, since Catalunya's top troupe, the **Xiquets de Valls**, hail from here. Calçots, local spring onions, are another Valls claims to fame: In season from November to April, they're chargrilled over grapevine embers and served on curved tiles alongside *romesco* sauce, a blend of almonds, tomatoes, garlic and red peppers. Always eaten out of hand, they're messy but delectable. Try them at the **Calçotada** spring onion festival, which takes place on the last Sunday in January.

🚗 DRIVING TOUR
CISTERCIAN ROUTE
90km/56mi. Allow one day
www.larutadelcister.info.

Along this route, visit the most important Cistercian monasteries in Catalunya, founded in the 12C after the 'reconquest' of Catalunya by Ramón Berenguer IV.

▶ Exit Montblanc on the N 240 to l'Espluga de Francolí. From here, follow the T 700 for 4km/2.5mi.

Monestir Santa Maria de Poblet★★★
🚃 Nearest station: Valls 18km (Tarragona, on AVE line 50km). Zona del Monasterio, Vimbodí. Open 10:30am–12.30pm, 3–5.25pm. Closed 1 Jan, 27 Jun, 25–26 Dec. €8 (€12 with Vallbona and Santes Creus monasteries). ☎977 870 089. www.poblet.cat.
The **site★** of one of the largest and best-preserved active Cistercian monasteries is sheltered by the Prades mountains. Founded in the 12C, it blossomed under the protection of the crown of Aragón and was nearly ruined in the mid-19C during an anticlerical uprising.
A 2km/1.2mi-perimeter protected the monastery and its vegetable gardens.

Capella de Sant Jordi★★
The Late Gothic interior of this 15C chapel features broken barrel vaulting. An inner wall with polygonal towers enclosed annexes where visitors

were received. The 15C **Porta Daurada** (Golden Door), named after the gilded bronze sheets that form its covering, was commissioned by Philip II.

Plaça Major★

On this irregular main square stand the **Capella de Santa Caterina** (12C), shops, a hospital for pilgrims and a carpentry workshop. On the right are the ruins of the 16C Abbatial Palace and the **stone cross** erected by Abbey Guimerà, also 16C. A third wall (608m/1 995ft long, 11m/36ft high and 2m/6.5ft thick), built by Peter the Ceremonious, surrounds the monastery proper, fortified by 13 towers. On the right stands the **Baroque facade of the church**, built around 1670 and flanked, 50 years later, by heavily ornate windows. Pleasing in itself, it breaks with the overall austerity.

Porta Reial★

This is the gateway to the conventual buildings, appearing somewhat like the entrance to a fortress.

Palau del Rei Martí★

Beyond the door, to the right, a narrow staircase rises to this 14C Gothic palace. Its rooms are bright thanks to pointed bay windows.

Locutorio

Originally a dormitory for converts, this room became a wine press. The 14C vaulting rests on the walls. Note the Gothic **cellar** and concert hall.

Claustro★★

The size of these cloisters (40 x 35m/ 131 x 115ft) and their sober lines indicate the monastery's importance. The south gallery (c. 1200) and huge lavabo or **templete★**, with its marble fountain and 30 taps, are Romanesque; the other galleries, built a century later, have floral motif tracery and scrollwork adorning the **capitals★**. The **kitchen** (cocina) and the huge **monk's refectory** (refectorio de los monjes), both built around 1200 and still in use, open onto the cloisters. The **library** (biblioteca) – the former scriptorium – is crowned by ogival

vaulting on 13C columns. The 13C **chapter house★★** (sala capitular), through a Romanesque doorway, has four octagonal columns and palm-shaped vaulting.

Església★★

The light, airy church is typically Cistercian: It has pure lines, broken barrel vaulting and unadorned capitals. The windows and wide arches dividing the nave join in a large eave. The church incorporated numerous altars for its growing community; the apse was ringed by an ambulatory and radiating chapels, a feature more commonly found in Benedictine churches.

The **royal pantheon★★** (panteó reial), the church's most original feature, has immense yet shallow arches spanning the transepts, surmounted by the royal tombs. These were constructed using alabaster ca. 1350.

The **retable★★** (retablo) at the **high altar** (altar mayor) is a monumental marble Renaissance altarpiece carved by Damián Forment in 1527: Figures in four superimposed registers glorify Christ and the Virgin.

In the narthex, an opening added in 1275, is the Renaissance **altar of the Holy Sepulchre**.

Wide stairs lead from the transept to the dormitory. Massive central arches support the ridge roof above the 87m/285ft-long **Dormitorio gallery**.

▶ Leave Poblet on the T 232 towards Maldà, and take the road to Vallbona.

Monestir de Vallbona de les Monges★★

🚊 Nearest station: Lleida on AVE line (55km). C. Mayor. Visit by guided tour only (45min); see website for guided tour times on the hour in Spanish or Catalan (usually Mon–Fri 10.30am–6pm, Sat-Sun 12–6pm). Closed 1 & 6 Jan, Good Friday, 25 Dec. €7 (€12 with Poblet and Santes Creus monasteries). ✆973 33 02 66. www.monestirvallbona.cat.

The **Monestir de Santa Maria** was founded in 1157 by the hermit Ramón de Vallbona and became a Cistercian community for women.

Església★★

Built chiefly in the 13C and the 14C, this church is a fine example of transitional Gothic. The interior is simple and surprisingly light thanks to two octagonal lantern towers: One (13C) lies above the transept crossing; the other (14C) overlooks the centre of the nave. The church contains the beautiful tombs of Queen Violante of Hungary, wife of James I the Conqueror of Aragón, and her daughter, as well as a huge polychrome Virgin from the 15C.

Cloisters★

The east and west galleries are Romanesque (12C–13C). The 14C Gothic north wing features attractive capitals with plant motifs. In the south gallery (15C), note the 12C statue of Nuestra Señora del Claustro (of the Cloisters).

▶ Head toward Rocallaura then toward Montblanc along the C 240 to link up with the AP 2. Turn onto the TP 2002 at exit 11.

Monestir de Santes Creus★★★

🚉Nearest station: Valls 18km (Tarragona on AVE line 33km). Pl. Jaume el Just, Aiguamurcia. 46km/29mi SE of Vallbona. Guided tours (2hr). Open Tue–Sun & hol Mons 10am–5.30pm (until 7pm Jun–Sep). €5.50 (€12 with Vallbona and Santes Creus monasteries; free last Tue Oct–Jun. ☎977 63 83 29. www.mhcat.cat.

The monastery was founded in the 12C by monks from Toulouse. Its plan is similar to that of Poblet, with three perimeter walls. A Baroque gateway leads to the courtyard where the monastic buildings, enhanced with fine *sgraffiti*, now serve as shops and private residences. To the right is the abbatial palace, with its attractive patio, now the town hall; at the end stands the 12C–13C church.

Gran Claustro★★★

Construction began in 1313 on the site of earlier ('great') cloisters. The ornamentation on capitals and bands illustrates Gothic motifs ranging from plants to animals to mythological and satiri-

cal creatures. The Puerta Real, or Royal Gate, on the south side opens onto cloisters with Gothic bays with lively carvings – note Eve shown emerging from Adam's rib and the fine tracery of the arches (1350–1430). In contrast, the transitional style of the **lavabo** appears almost clumsy. Carved noble tombs fill the niches.

The **chapter house★★** (sala capitular) is an elegant hall. Stairs next to the chapter house lead to the 12C **dormitory** (dormitorio), a gallery divided by diaphragm arches supporting a timber roof, now used as a concert hall.

Església★★

The church (1174) closely follows the Cistercian pattern of a flat east end and overall austerity. The lantern (14C), stained glass and apsidal **rose window** relieve the bareness. Ribbed vaults rest on pillars that extend back along the walls and end in unusual consoles. Gothic canopies at the transept openings shelter the **royal tombs★★**: on the north side (c. 1295), that of **Pere the Great** (III of Aragón, II of Barcelona) and on the south (14C), that of his son, **Jaime II**, the Just, and his queen, **Blanche d'Anjou**. The Plateresque decoration below the crowned recumbent figures in Cistercian habits was added in the 16C.

Claustro Viejo

These 17C 'old cloisters' occupy the site of former ones dating to the 12C. The design is simple with a small central fountain and a few cypresses in the close. Leading off are the kitchens, refectory and **royal palace** (note the 14C **patio★**).

ADDRESSES

🛏 STAY

⊖ **Fonda dels Àngels** – Pl. Els Àngels 1. ☎977 86 01 73. www.fonda delsangels.com. ⊡€6. Simple rooms in a bay-windowed Gothic house are above a small dining room (😋😋).

Lleida★

Lleida (Lérida in Castilian), an ancient citadel, was stormed by the legions of Caesar and held by the Moors from the 8C–12C. The Arab fortress, the Zuda, sited like an acropolis, was savaged by artillery fire in 1812 and 1936. The glacis has been converted into gardens. Lleida is an important fruit-growing centre.

▶ **Population:** 137 735
🜨 **Michelin Map:** 574 H 31 – Catalunya (Lleida)
🗊 **Info:** Major 31a. ℘973 700 319. www.turismedelleida.cat.
◖ **Location:** Lleida is linked to Barcelona by the AP 2 motorway, the Pyrenees by the C 1313 and N 240 and Huesca via the N 240. 🚃Lleida Pirineus (AVE).
🅿 **Parking:** Space is limited in the old quarter.
☺ **Don't Miss:** A walk up to the Suda for commanding views of city and plain.

SIGHTS
LA SEU VELLA★★★ (OLD CATHEDRAL)

Arrive via the lift from Plaça de Sant Joan. Cathedral: Open May–Sep Tue–Sat 10am–7.30pm. Oct–Mar Tue–Fri 10am–1.30pm, 3–5.30pm, Sat 10am–5.30pm. Sun & hols 10am–3pm. Suda (Castle area): Open slightly different times; see website. Closed 1 & 6 Jan, 25–26 Dec. €6, cathedral and suda; €3 Suda only; free first Tue. ℘973 23 06 53. www.turoseuvella.cat.

The Cathedral **site★** dominates the city from inside the walls. It was built between 1203 and 1278 over a mosque; the octagonal belfry was added in the 14C. Philip V converted the military fortification that surrounds the site into a garrison fortress in 1707, now known as the **Castillo del Rey o Suda** (Castle of the King or Suda – the latter is an Arabic word meaning closed urban area).

Església★★

The **capitals★** of this transitional-style church are varied and detailed. Moorish influences show in the exterior decoration. The extremely delicate style of carving, reminiscent of Moorish stuccowork, has come to be known as the Romanesque School of Lleida. It is seen throughout the region, in particular on the superb **portal★★** of the Església de **Agramunt** (52km/32.3mi NE).

Claustro★★

The cloisters' 14C galleries are remarkable for the size of the bays and the artistry of the stone tracery. The Gothic style shows Moorish influence in the plant motifs on the **capitals★**. There is a fine view from the south gallery. In the southwest corner stands the Gothic **bell tower★★**, 60m/197ft high. Along Carrer Major are three major monuments: The 13C **Palau de la Paeria** is now the town hall (ajuntament; open Mon–Sat 11am–2pm, 5–8pm, Sun 11am–2pm; ℘973 70 03 00), with a fine **facade★**. The old **Hospital de Santa Maria** (Jun–Sep Tue–Fri 10am–2pm, 6–9pm; Sat 11am–2pm, 7–9pm; Sun 11am–2pm; Oct–May Tue–Fri until 8.30pm; Sat 12–2pm, 5.30–8.30pm; Sun 12–2pm) is now the Institut d'Estudis Ilerdencs cultural centre with a **patio★** showing Renaissance influence. The 18C **Seu Nova** (New Cathedral; open 9am–1pm, 5–7pm; www.cataloniasacra.cat) was built 1761–81.

Museu de Lleida i Diocesà Comarcal

Jaume I el Conqueridor 1. Open Tue–Thu & Sat 10am–2pm, 5–7pm (4–6pm Oct-May), Sat, Sun & hols year-round 10am–2pm . Closed 1 & 6 Jan, Good Fri, Easter Mon, 25–26 Dec. €5; free first Tue, 2 Feb, 11 & 18 May, 11 Sept, 30 Nov. ℘973 28 30 75. www.museudelleida.cat. The collection chronicles the history of the region, from the Bronze Age to the Islamic era to the Christian repossession and beyond.

La Costa Daurada★★

The Golden Coast unfurls along the shores of the province of Tarragona with sun-drenched beaches offering calm, shallow waters. Tourist resorts here tend to cater to local and Northern European package holidaymakers, in contrast to the more upmarket Costa Brava. High-rise hotels blight the otherwise harmonious landscape, but there are plenty of unspoilt corners if you know where to look.

- ⚙ **Michelin Map:** 574 I-K31-34.
- ▣ **Info:** Xalet Torremar, Pg. Jaume I, Salou. ℘977 350 102. www.costadaurada.info.
- ◐ **Location:** A 150km/93mi stretch of coast in Tarragona province. 🚌Port Aventura.
- 👪 **Kids:** Days on the beach, at a water park or at Port Aventura.

SIGHTS

Coastal Towns

The Costa Daurada is easily reached via the train line between Barcelona and Tarragona, making it a great day-trip or overnight beach getaway. The best locales are **Altafulla**, with its long stretch of unspoilt sand and impressive Roman Villa; **Els Munts**; and **Cambrils**. These resorts, as well as Calafell, Torr-dembarra and Coma-Ruga, are popular with Spanish holidaymakers. **El Vendrell** was the birthplace of the famed cellist Pau Casals, and you can visit his former home (Casa-Natal Pau Casals, (www.elvendrellturistic.com). The area's most famous son is Gaudí, born in Reus, celebrated at the **Gaudí Centre** (www.gaudicentre.cat).

👪 Port Aventura★★

◐ 10km/6.2mi SW towards Salou. See website for seasonal hours. From €48 (special rates for combination and multi-day tickets). Parking €12. ℘902 20 22 20. www.portaventuraworld.com.

The sprawling Universal Studios Port Aventura amusement park is divided into five geographical zones, each with characteristic rides, performances, shops etc. Little tykes love the Ses-ame Street-themed SésamoAventura area. **Mediterrània** is a coastal town; in **Polynesia★**, a path winds through tropical vegetation; **China★★** is the heart of the park, evoking (albeit ste-reotypically) the magic and mystery of a millenary civilisation.

The newest addition, inspired by the great Temple of Angkor Wat, is **Angkor** featuring the longest theme park boat ride, in Europe. A star attraction is **Dragon Khan★★★**, with eight gigantic loops. **Mexico★★** spans Mayan ruins, colonial Mexico, Mariachi music and Mexican cuisine. In the **Far West★★** (Wild West) town of **Penitence**, visitors can play the lead role in a western or dance in the saloon. Adjacent is the excellent **Caribe Aquatic Park** (open mid-May–Sep; see website for schedule; from €29), with a Caribbean island theme.

Salou★

◐ 10km/6.2mi SW. 🚌Salou.

This is the principal resort on the Costa Dorada, popular with British and German tourists. Aside from Port Aventura (⚙see above), the most popular day off the beach is at **Aquopolis Costa Dorada** 👪 water park and dolphinarium (La Pineda; open mid-May–mid-Sep; from €18.90; see website for schedules and discounts; ℘977 033 448; www.costa-dorada.aquopolis.es). Salou merges west into the attractive little fishing port of **Cambrils**, renowned for its restaurants.

Tortosa★

Tortosa, for centuries the last waypoint before the sea, once guarded the region's only bridge. From the Castillo de la Suda, now a Parador, you can enjoy a fine view of the Ebro and its valley. Tortosa's artistic endowment ranges from Gothic monuments to fine examples of Modernism.

▸ **Population:** 33 510
◉ **Michelin Map:** 574 J 31.
▯ **Info:** Rambla Felip Pedrell 3.
   ℰ977 44 96 48.
   www.tortosaturisme.cat.
◖ **Location:** 14km/8.7mi
   off the coastal motor-
   way 90km/56mi south of
   Tarragona. ▦Tortosa.

SIGHTS

Catedral★★

Croera. Open Tue–Sat 10am–2pm, 4–7pm (10am–1.30pm, 4–6.30pm mid-Oct–Mar), Sun 11–2pm. €4.50.
ℰ977 44 61 10.

The Cathedral was built in pure Gothic style even though construction, begun in 1347, continued for 200 years. The 18C Baroque **facade★** is lavishly decorated: capitals with plant motifs, curved columns and outstanding reliefs.

In Catalan tradition the lines of the **interior★★** are plain, the high arches divided into two tiers only in the nave. The retable at the high altar has a large 14C wood **polyptych★** illustrating the Life of Christ and the Virgin Mary. Another interesting work is the 15C **altarpiece of the Transfiguration★**. Two stone 15C **pulpits★** in the nave are carved with low reliefs: On the left are the Evangelists; on the right, Saints Gregory, Jerome, Ambrose and Augustine.

Built in Baroque style between 1642 and 1725, the **Capella de Nuestra Señora de la Cinta★** (Chapel of Our Lady of the Sash) is decorated with paintings and local jasper and marble; at its centre is the sash of Our Lady (services of special veneration: first week in September). The stone **font** is said to have stood in the garden of the antipope Benedict XIII, Pedro de Luna, and bears his arms.

Palau Episcopal★

Croera 9. Open Mon–Fri 10am-2pm.
Closed public hols & Aug.
ℰ977 44 96 48.

The 14C Catalan patio of this Bishop's Palace, built in the 13C–14C, is known for its straight flight of steps and arcaded gallery. On the upper floor, the **Gothic chapel★** has ogive vaulting in which the ribs descend to figured bosses.

Reials Col·legis de Tortosa★

Sant Domènec 12. Open Tue–Sat 10am–1.30pm, 4.30–7.30pm (3.30–6.30pm Apr–Oct), Sun 11am–1.30pm.
€3; free last Sun. ℰ977 44 46 68.

In 1564 Emperor Charles V commissioned this lovely Renaissance ensemble. The **Colegio de Sant Lluís★** at one time educated newly converted Muslims. The oblong **patio★★** is curiously decorated with characters in a wide range of expressions and attitudes. The Renaissance facade of the **Colegio de Sant Jordi y de Sant Domingo** bears a Latin inscription (*Domus Sapientiae*, House of Knowledge). The adjacent **Església de Sant Domènec** was built in the 16C and once formed part of the Reales Colegios.

EXCURSION

Parque Natural del Delta del Ebro★★ (Ebro Delta Nature Reserve)

◖ 25km/15.5mi E. of Tortosa.

This vast delta (www.deltebre.net), a swampy stretch of alluvium deposits dumped by the Ebro, now acts as a bird reserve. **Boat trips** between the main settlement of Deltebre and the river mouth are available (ℰ977 480 128; www.creuersdeltaebre.com).

Aragón

One of Spain's least-known and least-visited regions, Aragón is over twice the size of Wales or New Jersey but about as sparsely populated as the Shetland Islands or Vermont. Half of its 1.3 million denizens pile into its only city, Zaragoza (👍see Rural Flight sidebar, p404). The very name Aragón evokes images of a romantic, medieval past: Its kingdom once held sway in Barcelona, Valencia and as far afield as Sardinia. The Crown of Aragón disbanded after its union with Castile and, by the early 18C, was already settling into its sleepy provincial role. Today it is largely a destination for hikers and nature lovers.

Zaragoza and Central Aragón

Say it with us: *tha-ra-go-tha*. The tongue-twisting capital of Aragón, whose name supposedly derives from the Roman colony of Caesar Augusta, is a lived-in city virtually untouched by tourism.

At first sight it's unprepossessing with traffic-laden streets and unsightly modern buildings, but a jaunt through the typically Spanish old town *(casco viejo)* will make you reconsider.

Outside the capital, much of central Aragón is flat and featureless. The main source of livelihood is farming, around Huesca, and stock-raising, in the valleys. Huesca, the quiet capital of Upper Aragón, has an appealing medieval core. Nearby Barbastro boasts fine 16C architecture and makes a good base for exploring the Central Pyrenees and far-flung villages like Roda de Isábena.

Northern Aragón

The northernmost part of Aragón abuts the French border and is known as the Aragonese Pyrenees (Pirineos Aragoneses). The highlight along this stretch is the Parque Nacional de Ordesa y Monte Perdido; the Ordesa Canyon is one of Spain's natural wonders and Europe's riposte to the Grand Canyon in the US. Nearby, the Monasterio de San Juan de la Peña occupies an awe-inspiring location beneath overhanging rock.

Southern Aragón

The clay hills bordering the Ebro Basin in Bajo Aragón (Lower Aragón) around Daroca and Alcañiz are planted with vineyards and olive groves. Brick villages and ochre-coloured houses merge with the tawny-hued and deeply scored hillsides. The jewel of

Highlights

1 The sheer size and various styles of the cathedral, La Seo, **Zaragoza** (p404)

2 Magnificent Mudéjar towers and other architecture in **Teruel** (p409)

3 The location of **Monasterio de San Juan de la Peña** (p415)

4 Trekking amid breathtaking scenery in the **Parque Nacional de Ordesa** (p417)

5 Crossing the **Valle de Pineta** in the Aragonese Pyrenees (p420)

Bajo (Lower) Aragón is Teruel, declared a UNESCO World Heritage site on account of its rich Mudéjar (Christian-Moorish) architecture.

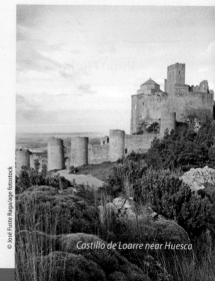

© José Fuste Raga/age fotostock

Castillo de Loarre near Huesca

Zaragoza★★

The domes of the Basílica del Pilar, the leading Marian shrine in Spain, dominate Zaragoza, on the right bank of the River Ebro. The city, rebuilt after the 19C War of Independence, combines historic monuments with bustling modern boulevards. It's a college town and religious centre.

- ▶ **Population:** 663 023
- 🕭 **Michelin Map:** 54 H 27 (town plan).
- 🗊 **Info:** Ntra. Sra. del Pilar. ✆902 142 008. www.turismodezaragoza.es.
- ◖ **Location:** Zaragoza is in NE Spain in a fertile pocket watered by the Aragón canal and the Ebro, Gállego, Jalón and Huerva rivers. 🚄Zaragoza (AVE).

THE CITY TODAY

The legacy of Zaragoza's successful Expo 2008 is a much more visitor-friendly city. The most notable addition is the Parque del Agua, a development along the Ebro of outdoor bars and restaurants, urban beaches and bike lanes. Since then, mew hotels, better infrastructure (within the city and connecting it to the rest of Spain) and improvements in tourist facilities have also been beneficial.

A BIT OF HISTORY

Caesaraugusta-Sarakusta – The town of Salduba, at the confluence of the Ebro and its tributaries, became Roman Caesaraugusta in 25 BC. On 2 January AD 40, the Virgin supposedly appeared to St James and left him the pillar around which the **Basílica de Nuestra Señora del Pilar** was later built. The Uncounted Martyrs of the 3C,

persecuted by Diocletian, are interred in the crypt of **Santa Engracia**.

The city's Roman past is explored in four **Caesaraugusta museums**: **Museo del Teatro de Caesaraugusta** (Theatre Museum, San Jorge 12; ✆976 72 60 75); **Museo de las Termas Públicas** (Public Baths Museum, San Juan y San Pedro; ✆976 72 14 23); **Museo del Foro de Caesaraugusta** (Forum Museum, pl. la Seo 2; ✆976 72 12 21); and **Museo del Puerto Fluvial de Caesaraugusta** (River Port Museum, pl. San Bruno 8; ✆976 72 12 07). All sites open Tue–Sat 10am–2pm, 5–9pm, Sun 10am–2.30pm. €3 each or €7 combined ticket, free first Sun; www.zaragoza.es/ciudad/museos.

The city's Islamic era, which renamed the city Sarakusta, lasted four centuries. The **Aljafería** (🕭 see Sights), a palace built by the first Benihud monarch of an 11C taifa kingdom, is a unique example of Hispano-Muslim art.

Capital of Aragón – The Aragón kings freed Zaragoza from the Moors and proclaimed it capital. The city retained its autonomy and prospered. It protected its Muslim masons, who embellished the apse of **La Seo** (Cathedral, 🕭 see Sights, p405), the **San Pablo** (San Pablo 42) and **Magdalena** (pl. Magdalena) churches in Mudéjar style. Houses with elegant patios and *artesonado* ceilings reflect prosperity in the 16C.

Two heroic sieges – Zaragoza resisted a siege by Napoleon's army in the sum-

Rural Flight

Between 2000 and 2019, Zaragoza's population grew by 13%, which seems like good news – except, in the same period, 77% of counties in Aragón saw a decline in population. In 37 of its towns, more than half of the residents are over 65. These sobering stats raise questions about the future of rural Aragón: When the older Aragoneses are gone, who will take their place? .

Basílica de Nuestra Señora del Pilar by the Ebro

mer of 1808, and exultant Zaragozans sang 'The Virgin of Pilar will never be French'. Alas, General Lannes laid siege again, and by 1809, 54 000 – around half of the city – had died. The shrapnel-pitted **Puerta del Carmen** (Carmen Gate; Av. César Augusto) still bears witness.

SIGHTS
La Seo★★

Pl. de la Seo. Open summer Mon–Thu 10am–6pm, 8-8.30pm, Fri 10am–6pm, Sat 10am-12pm, 1–8.30pm, Sun 10-11.30am, 1.30am–8.30pm; winter Mon–Fri 10am–2pm, 4–6.30pm, Sat 10am–12.30pm, 4–6.30pm, Sun 10–12pm, 4–6.30pm. €4 (incl museums). ℘976 29 12 31.

Not to be confused with the Basilica, the Cathedral of Zaragoza, La Seo, is of remarkable size and includes a panoply of styles from Mudéjar to Churrigueresque, although it is basically Gothic. The belfry was added in the 17C and the Baroque facade in the 18C. View the Mudéjar **east end** from calle del Sepulcro. The interior has five aisles of equal height. Above the high altar is a Gothic **retable★**, with a predella carved by the Catalan Pere Johan, and shree central panels of the Ascension, Epiphany and Transfiguration sculpted by Hans of Swabia (the stance and modelling of the faces and robes strike a German note). The **surrounding wall of the chancel** *(trascoro)* and some of the side chapels were adorned in the 16C with carved figures, evidence of the vitality of Renaissance Spanish sculpture. Other chapels, ornamented in the 18C, show Churrigueresque exuberance. One exception is the **Parroquieta**, a Gothic chapel with a Burgundian-influenced 14C tomb and a Moorish **cupola★** in polychrome wood with stalactites and strapwork (15C).

Museo Capitular★

In the sacristy. Exhibited are paintings, an enamel triptych and church plate including silver reliquaries, chalices and an enormous processional monstrance made of 24 000 pieces.

Museo de Tapices★★

An outstanding collection of Gothic hangings, woven in Arras and Brussels.

La Lonja★

Pl. del Pilar. Open only during exhibitions, usually Tue–Sat 10am–2pm, 5–9pm, Sun & public hols 10am–2.30pm. ℘976 39 72 39.

Zaragoza, like many other Spanish trading centres, founded a commercial exchange during the 16C. These buildings, in a style between Gothic and Plateresque, represent some of the finest civil architecture in Spain. The vast hall is divided in three by tall columns, their shafts ornamented with a band of grotesques. Coats of arms supported by cherubim mark the start of the ribs, which open into star

vaulting. The **ayuntamiento** (town hall; Pl. del Pilar 18) has been rebuilt in traditional Aragón style with ornate eaves. Two modern bronzes stand at the entrance.

Basílica de Nuestra Señora del Pilar★

Open 6.45am–8.30pm (9.30pm Sun). 🖉976 39 74 97. www.basilicadelpilar.es. Successive sanctuaries on this site have enshrined the miraculous pillar (pilar) above which the Virgin appeared. The present building, Zaragoza's second cathedral, was designed by Francisco Herrera the Younger in about 1677.

A buttressed quadrilateral, it is lit by a central dome. The cupolas, with small lantern towers, whose ornamental tiles reflect in the Ebro, were added by Ventura Rodríguez in the 18C. Inside, some of the frescoes decorating the cupolas were painted by Goya as a young man. The **Capilla de la Virgen** (Lady Chapel) by Ventura Rodríguez is virtually a miniature church. It contains, in a niche on the right, the pillar and a Gothic wood statue of the Virgin. The Virgin's mantle is changed every day except on the 2nd of the month (the Apparition was on 2 January), and the 12th of the month (for the Día de la Hispanidad, 12 October). Pilgrims kiss the pillar through an opening at the rear. The **high altar** is surmounted by a **retable★** by Damián Forment of which the predella is outstanding. The **coro** is closed by a high grille and adorned with Plateresque stalls.

Museo Pilarista★

Open Mon-Fri 10am-2pm, 4-8pm, Sat 10am-2pm. €2. 🖉976 299 564. On display are sketches made by Goya, González, Velázquez and Bayeu for the cupolas of Our Lady of the Pillar, a model by Ventura Rodríguez, and some of the jewels that adorn the Virgin during the Pilar festivals. Among old ivory pieces are an 11C hunting horn and a Moorish jewellery box.

Palacio de la Aljafería★

Av. de Madrid. Open Apr–mid-Oct daily 10am–2pm, 4.30–8pm; mid-Oct–Mar 10am–2pm, 4–6.30pm, Sun 10am–2pm. Guided tours in English Jul–Aug at 10am and 5pm. Last admission 30mins before closing. €5; free Sun. 🖉976 28 96 83. It's a rare treat to find such magnificent Moorish architecture in this part of Spain. Built in the 11C by the Benihud family, the Aljafería, a Moorish palace, was modified by the Aragonese kings (14C) and Catholic Monarchs (15C) before being taken over by the Inquisition and later converted into a barracks.

It centres on a rectangular patio bordered by porticoes with delicate tracery and carved capitals.

The **musallah**, the mosque of the emirs, is restored with *mihrab* and multifoil arches and floral decoration.

The first floor and the staircase are in the Flamboyant Gothic of the Catholic Monarchs. Only the ornate **ceiling★**, its cells divided by geometric interlacing and decorated with fir cones, remains of the throne room.

Museo Goya – Collección Ibercaja★

Calle Espoz y Mina 23. Open Mon–Sat Mar–Oct 10am–8pm, Nov–Feb 10am–2pm, 4–8pm, Sun 10am–2pm. Closed 1 & 6 Jan, 25 Dec. €6; free second Sun, 29 Jan, 5 Mar, 23 Apr, 18 May. 🖉976 397 387. http://museogoya.ibercaja.es. This museum, fruit of a collection gathered by the historian José Camón Aznar (1898–1979), consists of a plethora of paintings from the 15–20C exhibited in the Casa Alguilar, a sumptuous Renaissance palace. An entire section is devoted to drawings and prints by Goya, from the famous *Los Caprichos* to *The Disasters of War* and the *Tauromaquia* (Bullfighting) series.

Executed at the turn of the 18–19C, these works were a creative breakaway for Goya as he began exploring controversial social subjects in his painting.

Museo Pablo Gargallo★

San Felipe Pl 3. Open Tue–Sat
10am–2pm, 5–9pm, Sun 10am–2.30pm.
€4; free first Sun, 29 Jan, 18 May, 12 Oct.
℘976 72 49 23.

The Condes de Argillo palace plays
host to this delightful and surprising
museum dedicated to the great
Aragonese sculptor Pablo Gargallo
(1881–1934). A friend of Picasso and
Juan Gris, Gargallo divided his time
between Barcelona and Paris and
worked mainly in metals (copper, iron,
lead etc.), focussing on the human body
in a figurative style.

The museum also includes drawings,
documents, his working tools and a
timeline, all of which help place this
little-known artist in context among
his contemporaries.

Museo de Zaragoza★

Pl. de los Sitios 6. Open Tue–Sat
10am–2pm, 5–8pm, Sun 10am–2pm.
℘976 22 21 81.
www.museodezaragoza.es.

Founded in 1848 to house artworks
from defunct convents and monasteries, this grand museum has gone on to
extend its collection to archaeological
remains from the city's Iberian origins
and to fine art, including several Goyas.

Centro de Historias★

Pl. San Agustín 2. Open Tue–Sat
10am–2pm, 5–9pm, Sun 10am–2.30pm.
℘976 72 18 85.

Housed in a former convent, this
museum thematically traces Zaragoza's
history with special emphasis on trade. It
hosts temporary art exhibitions.

IAACC Pablo Serrano

Po. María Agustín 20. Open Tue–Sat
10am–2, 5–9pm, Sun 10am–2pm.
℘976 28 06 60. www.iaacc.es.

This institute of contemporary art and
culture, named after a local sculptor, has
a wide range of exhibits including those
relating to architecture and design.

CaixaForum

Av. de José Anselmo Clavé 4. Open
10am–8pm. €4 for exhibitions. ℘976 76
82 00. https://obrasocial.lacaixa.es.

Opened in 2014, this cultural centre
hosts exhibitions on the themes of art
and science.

EXCURSIONS

Fuendetodos
Casa Natal de Goya

↻ 45km/28mi SW along the N 330; after
21km/13mi, bear left onto the Z 100. Open
Tue–Sun & public hols 11am–2pm,
4–7pm. Closed 1 Jan, 24, 25, 31 Dec. €3.
℘976 14 38 30.
www.fundacionfuendetodosgoya.org.

It was in a modest house in this village
– now the **Casa Natal de Goya y Museo
del Grabado** – that the great painter
Francisco Goya y Lucientes was born in
1746. There is a display of his etchings
next door.

Tarazona

↻ 21km/13mi SW on the N 121.

Tarazona was once the residence of the
kings of Aragón. The royal mansion,
now the **Palacio Episcopal** (Episcopal
Palace; Rúa Alta de Bécquer; open Sat–
Sun & public hols 11.30am–2.30pm,
4.30–8.30pm; ℘976 64 28 61), is in a
quarter with narrow streets overlooking
the quays of the River Queiles.

Catedral de Tarazona

C. Gutiérrez de Córdoba. Open Apr–mid-
Sep Tue–Sat 11am–2pm, 4–7pm, (Sun
until 6pm). See website calendar for
winter schedule. €4, incl museum. ℘976
64 02 71. www.catedraldetarazona.es.

The Cathedral was largely rebuilt in the
15C and 16C. Its mix of styles includes
Aragón Mudéjar in the belfry tower
and lantern, Renaissance in the portal
and, in the **second chapel★** as you walk
left round the ambulatory, delicately
carved Gothic **tombs** of the two Calvil-
los cardinals from Avignon. The **Mudéjar
cloisters** have bays filled with 16C
Moorish plasterwork tracery.

Monasterio de Veruela★★

► 39km/24mi S from Tudela. From Tarazona (17km/10.5mi), take the N 122 toward Zaragoza, then bear right onto the Z 373. Open Apr–Sep Wed–Mon 10.30am–8pm; Oct–Mar Wed–Mon 10.30am–6pm. ℘976 64 90 25. www. monasteriodeveruela.blogspot.com.
Cistercian monks from France founded a fortified monastery in the mid-12C. The 19C Sevillian poet **Bécquer** stayed here while writing *Letters from My Cell*, in which he described the Aragón countryside.

Iglesia★★

The church, built in the transitional period between Romanesque and Gothic, has a sober facade with a single oculus, a band of blind arcades lacking a baseline and a doorway decorated with friezes, billets and capitals. Inside, vault groins are pointed over the nave; they're horseshoe-shaped elsewhere.

Claustro★

The cloisters are ornate Gothic. At ground level the brackets are carved with the heads of men and beasts; above are three Platresque galleries. In the **Sala Capitular★** (chapter house), in pure Cistercian style, are the tombs of the first 15 abbots.

Daroca★

► At the crossroads of the N 234 and N330, close to Calatayud (40km/25mi N); Zaragoza (85km/53mi NE); Teruel (96km/59.6mi S).
Daroca's battlemented walls★, originally with 100 towers and gateways, lie between two ridges. **Puerta Baja** (Lower Gate) is flanked by square towers.

Colegiata de Santa María

Pl. de España 8. Open Tue–Sun 8am–1pm, 5.30–6.30pm. €3. ℘976 80 07 32.
This Romanesque collegiate church, a repository for the holy cloths, was modified in the 15C and 16C.
Beside the belfry is a Flamboyant Gothic portal. The late Gothic nave includes a Renaissance cupola above the transept crossing. The **south chapels** are partly faced with 16C *azulejos*. To the right of the entrance is a 15C **altarpiece★** in multicoloured alabaster believed to have been carved in England. The 15C **Capilla de los Corporales★** (Chapel of the Holy Relics) is on the site of the original Romanesque apse. The altar includes a shrine enclosing the holy altar cloths. Statues in delightful poses are carved of multicoloured alabaster. The painted Gothic **retable★** is dedicated to St Michael.

Museo Parroquial★

Pl. de España. Open Tue–Sun 11am–1pm, 6–8pm. €3. ℘976 80 07 61.
Holdings include **chasubles**, local gold and silver plate and two rare (if damaged) 13C panels and **altarpieces** to St Peter (14C) and St Martin (15C).

Monasterio de Piedra★★

Monastery: open 10am–1pm, 3–5pm. €8.50. Park & waterfalls: open Apr–Sep 9am–7pm, Oct–Mar 9am–6pm. €16. ℘976 87 07 00.
www.monasteriopiedra.com.
Hidden in a fold of this arid plateau is an oasis fed by the River Piedra. Approach the monastery via Ateca, across a parched landscape above the Tranquera Reservoir and past the village of Nuévalos. The site was discovered by Cistercian monks, who had a knack for putting down roots in pleasant surroundings. Monks from the Abbey of Poblet in Tarragona established a monastery in 1194. It was rebuilt several times; recently, some buildings have been reconstructed to incorporate a spa hotel, but the main part of the abbey is open to visitors. Here you can not only appreciate the Cistercian architecture but also a **Museum of Wine**, an exhibition on chocolate-making and a **Carriage Museum**.
The monastery park's **waterfalls and cascades★★** burble beside the footpath through the forest (🄰follow red signposts to go, blue to return). The paths, steps and tunnels laid out last century by **Juan Federico Muntadas**, have transformed an impenetrable forest into a popular park.

The first fall is the **Cola de Caballo** (Horse's Tail), a cascade of 53m/174ft. You come on it again at the end of your walk if you descend steep and slippery steps into the **Cueva Iris** (Iris Grotto). **Baño de Diana** (Diana's Bath) and **Lago del Espejo** (Mirror Lake) are nearby.

ADDRESSES

🛏 STAY

🛏 **Be Hostel Zaragoza** – Predicadores 70. 📞976 282 043. 29 rooms. 🍽€5. www.behostels.com/zaragoza. In a 15C palace near the river, this rambunctious hostel has double rooms as well as dorms. There is a kitchen. Ask about the free guided tours and live music.

🛏 **Be Hostel Zaragoza** – Predicadores 70. 📞976 282 043. 29 rooms. 🍽€5. www.behostels.com/zaragoza. In a 15C palace near the river, this rambunctious hostel has double rooms as well as dorms. There is a kitchen. Ask about the free guided tours and live music.

🛏🛏🛏 **Hotel Alfonso Zaragoza** – C. del Coso 15. 📞876 54 11 18. www. hotelalfonsozaragoza.com. 120 rooms. 🍽€12. The wrap-around rooftop pooldeck is this hotel's crown jewel, but the bright rooms with blond wood accents are perfectly pleasant.

🍴/EAT

🛏🛏 **Bodegas Almau** – Estébanes 10. 📞976 299 834. www.bodegasalmau.es. Wash inventive tapas down with local Garnacha at this bar, whose a tiled interior dates to 1870.

🛏🛏🛏 **Casa Lac** – Mártires 12. 📞976 396 196. www.restaurantecasalac.com. This 'El Tubo' district restaurant is one of the oldest in Spain. Vegetables from the proprietary garden feature prominently.

Teruel★

Teruel may be the butt of many a Spanish joke about country bumpkins, but locals get the last laugh: The city brims with time-warpy charm and is recognised as a UNESCO World Heritage site for its ensemble of Mudéjar architecture.

▶ **Population:** 35 691
◔ **Michelin Map:** 574 K 26.
🛈 **Info:** Pl. Amantes 6. 📞978 62 41 05. www.turismo.teruel.es.
◖ **Location:** Teruel is at 916m/ 3 005ft directly east of Madrid on the Turia river. 🚌Teruel.

SIGHTS

Plaza del Torico, the heart of the town, is lined with Rococo-style houses. It is named for a small statue of a bull calf.

Torre de San Martín★
Pl. del Perá Prado.
The most central of the four Mudéjar towers in Teruel actually consists of two, one embedded within the other. Note the lovely green-and-white ceramic embellishment.

Casa de la Comunidad – Museo Provincial★
Pl. Fray Anselmo Polanco 3. Open Tue–Fri & public hols 10am–2pm, 4–7pm, Sat–Sun 10am–2pm. Closed 1 Jan, 1 May, 24, 25, 31 Dec. 📞978 60 01 50. http://museo.deteruel.es.

The museum, in a Renaissance mansion, displays ethnological and archaeological collections including tools and everyday objects. Note the reconstitution of a forge and the 15C Gothic door knocker. The first floor is given over to ceramics, for which Teruel has been renowned since the 13C. The upper floors contain objects from many time periods: prehistory (the Iron Age sword from Alcorisa), the Iberian age, the Roman period (a catapult), and from the Islamic era (11C incense burner).

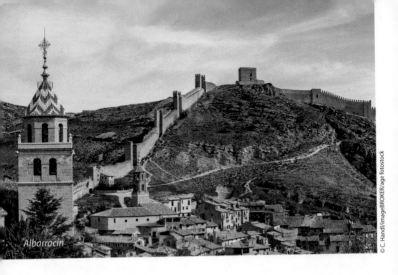

Albarracín

© C. Handl/imageBROKER/age fotostock

Catedral de Santa María de Mediavilla

Pl. de la Catedral. Open Jun–Oct Mon–Sat 11am–2pm, 4–8pm, Sun 4–8pm; Nov–May Mon–Sat 11am–2pm, 4–7pm, Sun 4–7pm. €3. ℘978 61 80 16.

The cathedral, originating in the 13C (tower), was enlarged in the 16C and 17C. The late-13C **artesonado ceiling★**, once hidden beneath star vaulting, is a precious example of Mudéjar art. Its beams and consoles are painted with decorative motifs, people at court and hunting scenes. In the north transept is a 15C **altarpiece** of the Coronation of the Virgin.

Iglesia de San Pedro & Mausoleo de los Amantes

Matías Abad. Open daily 10am–2pm, 4–8pm, Sun 10am–8pm . €10, mausoleum only, €4. ℘978 618 398. www.amantesdeteruel.es.

The church, with a stunning star-spangled ceiling, retains a Mudéjar tower and east end. The adjoining **Mausoleo de los Amantes** (The Mausoleum of the Lovers) houses the town's very own 13C Romeo and Juliet – *Juan (Diego) Martinez de Marcilla and Isabel de Segura*. The deceased are depicted in a 20C alabaster relief by Juan de Ávalos.

EXCURSIONS
Albarracín★

◗ 38km/23.6mi W along the N 234 and A 1512.

Hidden in the Sierra de **Albarracín**, this pink-tinged medieval city has an exceptional **site★**, on a cliff above the Guadalaviar river. The ramparts rising behind the town were built by the Moors in the 10C and restored by the Christians in the 14C.

Caves in the surrounding sierra contain **rock engravings** from the Upper Palaeolithic era such as the sites at Callejón del Plou and Cueva del Navaza (5km/3mi SE towards Bezas and Valdecuenca).

Alcañiz

◗ 49km/92mi NE of Teruel along the N 420 and N 211.

Alcañiz, set in olive groves, is the capital of Lower Aragón. The region is famous for its Holy Week ceremonies.

Two memorable facades meet on the **Plaza de España★**: the tall Catalan Gothic arcade of the **Lonja**, once a market, and the Renaissance town hall *(ayuntamiento)*. Both are crowned by an Aragón gallery with overhanging eaves. Vertical lines and a Baroque **portal★** mark the collegiate **Colegiata de Santa María la Mayor** (open daily 9am–1pm, 4–7pm), rebuilt in the 18C. Massive columns with composite capitals rise to a projecting cornice. The hilltop **Castillo de los Calatravos** (open 10am-7pm, ℘ 978 83 12 13; www.alcaniz.es) was the local seat of the Order of Calatrava in the 12C. The part used as a Parador dates to the 18C. Note the Gothic chapel, with its aisle of equilateral arches, and in the keep, 14C wall paintings.

Huesca★

The tranquillity of Huesca, capital of Alto Aragón (Upper Aragón), belies its turbulent past. The old town huddles around the top of a promontory crowned by an imposing cathedral.

A BIT OF HISTORY

Huesca has been a capital of a Roman state, a stronghold for the Moors (until its reconquest by **Pedro I of Aragón** in 1096) and capital of Aragón until 1118. In Spanish, when something is 'ringing like the bell of Huesca', it means a dire event is about to ensue. In the 12C, King **Ramiro II** summoned his truculent nobles to watch the casting of a bell – and promptly had them beheaded.

SIGHTS

OLD QUARTER
Catedral★

Pl. de la Catedral 4. Open Mon–Fri 10am–1.30pm, 4–6pm, Sat 10am–1.30pm. €4 (incl museum and tower). ☏974 23 10 99.
The 13C Gothic facade is divided unusually by a gallery and an Aragonese carved wood overhang. A gable encloses a rose window and the portal covings with weathered statues. On the tympanum are the Magi and Christ before Mary Magdalene.
The alabaster **altarpiece★★** dates to 1533. In this masterpiece by Damián Forment, three scenes of the Crucifixion appear in high relief in the middle of Flamboyant canopy and frieze decoration. Facing the Cathedral, the town hall is a tastefully decorated town house.

Museo de Huesca★

Pl. Universidad 1. Open Tue–Sat 10am–2pm, 5–8pm, Sun & public hols 10am–2pm. Closed 1 & 6 Jan, 24–25, 31 Dec. ☏974 22 05 86.
www.museodehuesca.es
This museum is set in the old university, built in 1690 around a fine octagonal patio incorporating parts of the royal palace (the site of the notorious 'bell' massacre). The collection includes prehistoric artefacts and **Aragonese primitive paintings★**, several by the Maestro de Sigena (16C).

Iglesia de San Pedro el Viejo★

Pl. de San Pedro. Open Mon–Sat 10am–1.30pm, 4–6pm; Sun 11am–12pm, 1–2 pm. €2.50. ☏974 22 23 87.
The 11C monastery's **cloisters★**, with their historiated capitals, are a jewel of Romanesque sculpture in Aragón. The tympanum of the cloister doorway has an atypical Adoration of the Magi with emphasis on movement. A Romanesque chapel holds the tombs of kings Ramiro II and Alfonso I, the Battler.

CDAN – Fundación Beulas

Av. Doctor Artero, by bus from Coso Bajo and Alto, on the Zaragoza/Pamplona road. Open Thu–Fri 6–9pm, Sat 11am–2pm, 6–9pm (Nov–Mar afternoons 5–8pm); Sun & hols 11am–2pm. €5. ☏974 23 98 93.
www.cdan.es
Huesca's Centro de Arte and Naturaleza was founded by local artist José Beulas as a space dedicated to contemporary art in a serene setting. Its temporary exhibitions are perhaps its strongest suit.

▶ **Population:** 52 463
◔ **Michelin Map:** 574 F 28.
▯ **Info:** Pl. Luis López Allué. ☏974 29 21 70. www.huescaturismo.com.
◖ **Location:** Huesca is 72km/44.7mi N of Zaragoza, 91km/56.5mi S of Jaca and 123km/76.4mi NW of Lleida, along the E 7 motorway. It is a good base for excursions into the Pyrenees. ▭Huesca (AVE).
◷ **Timing:** 2hr for the town.

Rock formations of Los Mallos de Riglos

© santirf/iStockphoto.com

EXCURSION

Monasterio de Monte Aragón

▶ 5km/3mi E along the N 240.
This monastery was originally a fortress built by 11C king Sancho Ramírez.

🚗 DRIVING TOUR

SIERRA DE LOARRE – LOS MALLOS DE RIGLOS

100km/62mi NW. Allow half a day.
♿ See Pirineos Aragoneses map p421.

▶ Leave Huesca on the
A 132 toward Pamplona.
After 12.5km/7.5mi, just beyond Esquedas, take the A 1206 right.

Bolea

The main church **altarpiece** is a superb example of 15C Hispano-Flemish art.

▶ Follow the road to Loarre; before the village, follow signs to the castle.

Castillo de Loarre★★

Open Nov–Feb Tue–Sun 11am–5.30pm; mid-Jun–mid-Sep daily 10am–8pm; rest of the year daily 10am–7pm. Closed 1 Jan, 25 Dec. €5. Guided tours €7. ☎974 34 21 61. www.castillodeloarre.es.
In the 11C, Sancho Ramírez, King of Aragón and Navarra, had this picture-book fortress built; today it is the best-preserved Romanesque castle in Europe. At an altitude of 1 100m/3 609ft, the walls, flanked by round tow-

ers, command a vast **panorama★★** of the Ebro Basin. After wandering the keep and covered stairway, view the 12C church; note the harmonious capitals.

▶ Take the A 206 9.5km/6mi to Ayerbe.

Los Mallos de Riglos★★

The Río Gállego is banked by reddish crumbling cliffs. **Los Mallos** are a formation of rose pudding-stone, eroded into sugar loaf forms. The most dramatic group (to the right) dominates the village of **Riglos**.

▶ Return to the A 132, and after 1.5km/1mi, bear left toward Agüero.

Agüero

The village is set against the spectacular background of **Los Mallos**. Before Agüero, a road leads (right) to the Romanesque **Iglesia de Santiago**.

ADDRESSES

🏠 STAY

🛏️ **Masía La Torre** – 50km/31mi SE of Teruel, Mora de Rubielos. ☎978 80 63 12. www.masialatorre.es. 11 rooms. ⊡ €10. Minimalist décor makes this converted stone house in the countryside all the more peaceful. The owners are set to open a second, higher-end hotel in 2020.

Barbastro

Barbastro's architecture bears witness to its 16C importance. Today it's the capital of the pioneering Somontano wine region and a good base for Pyrenees excursions.

- ▶ **Population:** 17 020
- ⦿ **Michelin Map:** 574 F 30 – Aragón (Huesca).
- 🛈 **Info:** Avenida de la Merced 64. ℘974 30 83 50. www.barbastro.org; www.turismosomontano.es.
- ◖ **Location:** Barbastro is at the end of two Pyrenean valleys, one leading to Parque de Ordesa, the other to the Maladeta range, via the Congosto de Ventamillo canyon. 🚃 Nearest station: Huesca (51km, AVE).

SIGHTS
Catedral★
San José de Calasanz.

Museo Diocesano – Open Tue–Sat 10am–1pm and Jun–Sep 5–8pm, Oct–Apr 4–7pm. €5, incl cathedral. ℘974 31 55 81. www.museodiocesano.es. The cathedral takes in three aisles beneath gilded vaulting supported by slender columns. The predella on the high altar **retable** is an important work by Damián Forment. Several side chapels are Churrigueresque; the first on the left holds an early-16C retable.

Complejo de San Julián y Santa Lucía
Av. de la Merced.

The former Hospital de San Julián houses the tourist office, a wine shop and a **museum** dedicated to the excellent Somontano appellation. Opposite, the 16C Renaissance church of San Julián houses the **Centro de Interpretación del Somontano★** (open Mon–Sat 10am–2pm, 4–7.30pm, Sun 10am–2pm Jul–Aug; €2; ℘974 30 83 50; www. rutadelvinosomanto.com), highlighting the area from the visitor's perspective.

EXCURSIONS
Alquézar★
◖ 23km/14mi NW on the A 1232, following the Río Vero.
Alquézar is easily one of Spain's most postcard-worthy towns. Its dramatic, isolated **setting★★**, amid red earth, appears to cling to a rocky promontory in a loop of the river.

Old Quarter
The medieval old quarter is a maze of uneven streets lined by houses adorned with rounded stone doorways and coats of arms. The arcaded main square is enchanting.

Colegiata★ – Walls and a church (rebuilt in 1530) were added in the 12C to the now-ruined Moorish **alcázar**, for which the city takes its name. A Romanesque Christ dates to the 12C. **Cañon de Río Vero★** – 🚶Allow a day to walk up, and in some places wade or swim, this spectacular canyon, or hike only to the Roman bridge at Villacantal (2hr round trip) for an bird's-eye view and to see impressive ochre and grey walls.

Alquézar

© Jorgefontestad/iStockphoto.com

🚗 DRIVING TOUR

THROUGH THE RIBAGORZA

85km/53mi. Allow one day.
👣See Pirineos Aragoneses map, p421.

Follow the Esera and Isábena rivers, through the historic county of Ribagorza in the pre-Pyrenees of Aragón.

▶ Leave Barbastro on the N 123; after 16km/10mi go right onto the A 2211.

Santuario de Torreciudad

Open Jul–Aug 10am–2pm (Sun from 9.30am), 4–6.30pm; slightly reduced hours rest of the year (check website).
📞974 30 40 25. www.torreciudad.org.
In 1804, an 11C Romanesque statue of Our Lady of Torreciudad was placed in a small shrine and locally venerated. In 1975 a pilgrimage church was built under the auspices of José María Escrivá de Balaguer, founder of Opus Dei (1928). Before the brick buildings, a vast esplanade affords beautiful **views**★ of the Pyrenees and the El Grado dam. The statue of Our Lady of Torreciudad is in the lower part of the altarpiece.

▶ From Torreciudad, return to the A 2211, heading towards La Puebla de Castro, then take the N 123ª.

Graus

The village huddles around the frescoed **Plaza de España**, lined by old houses decorated with frescoes, carved beams and brick galleries. The cliffside 16C **Santuario de la Virgen de la Peña**★★ has a Renaissance doorway and single aisle.

▶ The A 1605 crosses the Esera river.

Roda de Isábena★

26.5km/16.5mi from Graus.
This picturesque village is on an escarpment in a beautiful mountain **setting**★. Construction of the **cathedral**★ (guided tours (30min) €2.50; reserve in advance; 📞974 54 45 35), the smallest in Spain, began in the 11C. Most of the interior, basilical with three aisles, was built in the 12C.
In the central **crypt** is the **tomb of San Ramón**★★, with interesting polychrome low reliefs. A 13C fresco adorns a chapel off the cloisters.

▶ Continue 16km/10mi N on A 1605.

Monasterio de Santa María de Obarra
Only the 10C–11C church, built by Lombard masters, remains of this monastery. A 12C hermitage stands beside it.

ADDRESSES

🛏 STAY

🪙🍽 **Hospedería de Roda de Isábena** – Pl de la Catedral, Roda de Isábena. 📞974 54 45 54. www.hospederia-rdi. com. 10 rooms. 🛏€7.50. This medieval building overlooking the cathedral has clean rooms at budget prices. The rear balconies offer magnificent views.

🪙🪙🍽 **Hotel El Mudayyan** – Nueva 18, Teruel. 📞978 62 30 42. www. elmudayyan.com. 28 rooms. 🛏€5.90. In the heart of the old town, this three-star hotel has bright, updated rooms as well as a cafe and Moroccan-style tearoom. Underground are a series of medieval tunnels, which can be visited.

🍴 EAT

🪙🍽 **Hospedería de la Catedral** – Pl Pons Sorolla, Roda de Isábena. 📞974 54 45 45. www.hospederia-rdi.com. Closed Sun eve, Nov, 20–26 Dec. This restaurant occupies the former refectory of the monastery. It is decorated with reproductions of paintings by Velázquez and furniture from the same period as well as original 14C frescoes on one wall. Fried trout and bean stew (*pochas*) are specialities.

🪙🪙🍽 **Restaurante San Ramón del Somontano** – C. Academia Cerbuna 2, Barbastro. 📞974 31 43 04. www. hotelsanramonsomontano.com. The city's best-loved restaurant serves a menu hinging on local ingredients like Somontano pink tomatoes, black truffle and foraged mushrooms, all accompanied by wines from the region.

Jaca★

Jaca, the 'pearl of the Pyrenees', stands strategically at their feet, under the Peña de Oroel. It was an important stop on the Camino de Santiago and became the capital of Aragón in the 9C.

- ▶ **Population:** 12 813
- ⚅ **Michelin Map:** 574 E 28.
- 🗊 **Info:** Plaza de San Pedro nº 11–13. ℰ974 36 00 98. www.jaca.com/turismo.htm.
- ◗ **Location:** Jaca is off the A 23, from Huesca to El Puerto de Somport, and the N 240, to Pamplona (111km/69mi NW). 🚞Jaca.

SIGHTS
Catedral★

Open 12–2pm, 4–7pm. ℰ974 35 63 78. www.diocesisdejaca.org. Free self-guided; €2.50 guided.

Spain's oldest Romanesque cathedral, dating to the 11C, influenced craftsmen who worked on churches along the pilgrim route to Santiago de Compostela. Note the **historiated capitals★** of the south porch and great detail in the south doorway figures. Gothic vaulting covers unusually wide aisles. The apse and side chapels are decorated with sculpture, but the cupola on squinches over the transept crossing has retained its simplicity.

Museo Diocesano (Diocesan Museum)

Pl. de San Pedro. Open Sep–Jun Mon–Fri 10am–1.30pm, 4–7pm (Sat until 8pm), Sun 10am–1.30 pm. Jul–Aug Tue–Sun 10am–1.30pm, 4–8pm, €6. ℰ974 35 63 78. www.diocesisdejaca.org

The cloisters and adjoining halls contain Romanesque and Gothic **wall paintings★** from village churches in the area, and Romanesque paintings.

Castillo de San Pedro

Av. del Primer Viernes de Mayo. See website for opening times. €5 castle, €4 toy soldier museum, €8 both; ℰ974 35 71 57. www.ciudadeladejaca.es.

Built in 1595 during the reign of Philip II as part of a network of castles and towers to guard the French border, this massive star-shaped citadel is an outstanding example of 16C military architecture and has been declared a National Monument. Surrounded by a moat, the fortress has a perfect pentagonal plan, with defensive bulwarks

at each vertex. Inside, the **Museo de Miniaturas Militares** (www.museominiaturasjaca.es) has over 32 000 military figurines.

🚗DRIVING TOURS

1⃞ MONASTERIO DE SAN JUAN DE LA PEÑA★★

25km/15.5mi. Allow half a day. Take the N 240 from Jaca. After 11km/6.8mi, turn off toward Santa Cruz de la Serós.

Santa Cruz de la Serós★

Pl. Mayor. Open 10am–2pm. Also Nov–Feb Sat 10am–5pm, Mar–May & Sep–Oct 3.30–7pm, Jun–Aug 3–8pm. €7; €8.50 incl Monasterio de San Juan de la Peña (⚅below); €12 all areas, see website for details. Closed 1 Jan, 25 Dec. ℰ974 35 51 19. www.monasteriosanjuan.com.

This 10C convent, endowed by nobles and princesses, was abandoned in the 16C. Only the **Romanesque church★**, surrounded by small Aragonese houses, remains. The stout belfry, crowned by an octagonal turret, abuts the lantern. The portal recalls Jaca Cathedral.

◗ Beyond Santa Cruz de la Serós, the road winds through the sierra.

Monasterio de San Juan de la Peña★★

Same hours as Santa Cruz de Seros. €7, or combined ticket (⚅ above). ℰ974 35 51 19. www.monasteriosanjuan.com.

The most striking feature of this monastery is its **setting★★** in a hollow

Capitals of the cloisters, Monasterio de San Juan de la Peña

© Jose Fuste Raga/age fotostock

beneath overhanging rocks. The monastery was chosen as a pantheon for the kings and nobles of Aragón and Navarra and expanded in the 12C.

The oldest features can be seen on the lower storey, where the Lower Church dates to the early Mozarabic monastery. The **Sala de Concilios** (Council Chamber) was built by King Sancho Garcés ca. 922.

The 11C–14C **Panteón de Nobles Aragoneses** are niches with coats of arms, sacred monograms bearing crosses with four roses, the emblem of Iñigo Arista, founder of the Kingdom of Navarra.

The late 11C **Iglesia Alta** (Upper Church) comprises a single aisle, while the three apsidal chapels with blind arcades are hollowed out of the cliff. The **Panteón de Reyes** (Royal Pantheon) opens off the north wall. The 12C **cloisters★★**, between precipice and cliff, are accessed by a Mozarabic door. Only two galleries and fragments of another remain. The **capitals★★** exhibit a personal style and use of symbolism that would influence sculpture in the region for years. There are two interpretation centres: one dedicated to the monastery, the other to the Kingdom of Aragon.

2 VALLE DE HECHO AND VALLE DE ANSÓ★

114km/71mi (146km/91mi with the detour to Zuriza). Allow one day.

The lost-in-time twin valleys of Hecho and Ansó played an important role during the so-called Reconquista. Self-sustaining for centuries, they have retained an archaic economic structure based on sheep farming and agrarian activities. Grey stone mountain homes with distinctive, conical chimneys are clustered together in pretty hamlets in order to provide protection against the harsh winters. The inhabitants of both valleys speak a distinct dialect, and their ancient culture and traditional dress are celebrated with charming festivals that attract more locals than tourists.

▶ Leave Jaca on the N 240. In Puente la Reina de Jaca, go right on the A 176.

The road follows the Aragón Subordán. The traditional houses of **Hecho★** (www.hecho.es) have stone doorways, many with coats of arms.

The **Museo de Arte Contemporáneo** *al aire libre*, by the tourist office, shows sculpture in the open. There is also the **Museo Etnológico Casa Mazo** (open Jul–mid-Sept 10.30am–1.30pm, 6–9pm; €1; ℘974 37 50 02, www. museosaspeecho.com). 2km/1.2mi to the north in Siresa is the 11C **Iglesia de San Pedro★★**, once part of a monastery. The **altarpieces★** are principally 15C (open 11am–1pm, 3–5pm; summer 11am–1pm, 5–8pm; €1.50).

▶ The road continues through a narrow valley toward Selva de Oza. Return to Hecho and go right on the A 17 and right again to Ansó.

Surrounded by a dramatic alpine landscape, the sleepy village of **Ansó** consists of traditional mountain homes clustered around the village church. Inside is the **Museo del Traje Ansotano**, which focusses on traditional costumes of the area (call for opening times; €2;

☏ 974 370 250; www.aspejacetania.
com). After taking a stroll around the
village, head to Zuriza (16km/10mi
away) at the bottom of the valley which
opens out on to a large field dominated
by mountains. By following the course
of the Veral River via the 1602, you'll
come across the 500m/1640ft-long
Foz de Biniés (Biniés Gorge) enclosed
by two natural stone arches.

▶ Take the N 240 back to Jaca.

③ TOUR THROUGH SERRABLO

20km/19.5mi. Allow half a day.

This excursion follows the Río Gállego
and includes extraordinary 10C and 11C
Mozarabic churches.

▶ Leave Jaca on the A 23 E towards
Sabiñánigo.

Museo de Dibujo
(Sketch Museum)

In Larrés, 18km/11mi E of Jaca off the A
23. Open Jul-Aug 10am-2pm, 4.30-
8.30pm, Sep-Jun 10am-1.30pm, 4-7pm.
€4. ☏ 974 48 29 81.
www.serrablo.org/museodibujo.
This sketch museum, set in the 14C Castillo de Larrés, displays works by Martín
Chirino, Salvador Dalí and others. A section covers graphic humour.

Mozarabic churches

The churches of the Serrablo region are
small and rectangular with a semicir-
cular apse. The most impressive are in
Orós Bajo, San Martín de Oliván, **San
Juan de Busa**★ (with unfinished apse),
San Pedro de Lárrede★ and Satué.

Museo Ángel Oresanz y Artes
de Serrablo★

San Nicolás 1, Sabiñánigo. In Puente de
Sabiñánigo, S of the town centre.
Open Tue–Sun 10.30am–1.30pm
also Sep–Jun 3–6.30pm and Jul–Aug
5–8.30pm. Closed 1 Jan, 25 Jul, 25 Dec.
€2. ☏ 974 48 42 61.
www.museo-orensanz-serrablo.
blogspot.com.es.
The major ethnographic collection in
the Huescan Pyrenees is in a wonderful ancient traditional Serrablan house.

▶ From here you can continue to the
Graganta del Escalar and Carretera del
Portalet (◒ see p421).

EXCURSION
Parque Nacional de Ordesa y
Monte Perdido★★★

◒ 61km/38mi E of Jaca in the central
Pyrenees (with its twin on the French
side). Largely inaccessible in cold-
weather months. Approach from Torla
to the W or from Ainsa to the SE. www.

ordesa.net. 🚆Nearest station: Jaca (61km).

The most pristine, awe-inspiring area of the Pyrenees, Ordesa National Park has majestic mountains, tumbling waterfalls, crystalline streams and a valley that cuts through vast, layered limestone folds. Escarpments rise nearly 1 000m/3 280ft in grey and ochre strata, streaked in spring with cascades of snowmelt. Monte Perdido peaks at 3 355m/11 004ft. Growing up the lower slopes are pines, larches, firs – some 25m/82ft tall – and a carpet of box, hawthorn and service trees.

Walks

A viewpoint on the entry road offers a general panorama. A second point, near the road's end, overlooks the 60m/197ft-high **Cascada de Tamborrotera**.

👁 The rest of the park may only be visited on foot. The best route for inexperienced walkers is the shaded path along the base of the canyon. (🚶 Allow a day from the car park to the end of the canyon and back). The following walks are for experienced, well-equipped hikers.

Circuito del Circo de Soaso
(Soaso Cirque Route)
🚶 Start from the Cadiera hut beyond the car park; 7hr. The walk to the valley floor is easy. The second part, via the Cola de Caballo (Horse's Tail), is only recommended to well-equipped hikers in good shape (steep climbs).

This walk provides the best and most complete tour of the Ordesa Valley. From the Circo de Soaso path, view several waterfalls including the **Gradas de Soaso**, or Soaso Steps, and the 70m/230ft-high **Cola de Caballo**. The path continues along the **Faja de Pelay** overlooking the canyon to a depth of 2 000m/6 550ft at the foot of the Sierra de Cutas.

Continue on the **Senda de los Cazadores** (Huntsman's Path) for a wonderful view of the canyon. The best panorama is from the **Mirador de Calcilarruego**. The path back to the hut drops almost 1 000m/3 281ft.

Circo de Cotatuero
(Cotatuero Cirque)
🚶 Start from the restaurant; 4hr.
On the park's northern border are the **Cotatuero** and the **Copos de Lana** waterfalls, each some 250m/820ft high.

Circo de Carriata
🚶 From the Centro de Información; 4hr.
The *clavijas* (mountaineering peg track), not suitable for those with a fear of heights, is a rewarding and picturesque challenge. A long hike is possible to Monte Perdido via the Goriz refuge, or to the Cirque de Gavarnie in France via the Brecha de Rolando (Roland Gap) (ask at the Centro de Información).

Cañón de Añisclo★★★

Access from Escalona village on the Bielsa-Ainsa road – a 13km/8mi drive.
In this brushstroke-like landscape, pine trees cling to limestone walls.

Walk to Ripareta
🚶 Start from the San Urbez bridge. 5hr there and back.
A wide, well-defined path follows the enclosed Río Vellos down to its confluence with the Pardina.

ADDRESSES

🛏 STAY

🍴🛏 **Conde Aznar** – Po. de la Constitución 3, Jaca. 📞974 36 10 50. www.condeaznar.com. 34 rooms. 🍽€8. This cosy hotel in a shady setting is decorated with antique furniture.

🛏🛏🛏 **Parador de Bielsa** – 14km/8.5mi from Biesal in the Pineta Valley via the HU-V-6402. 📞902 54 79 79. www.parador.es. 39 rooms. Closed Feb–mid-Mar. 🍽€16. Pamper yourself at this riverside luxury lodge whose restaurant serves in Pyrenean cuisine.

🍽 EAT

🍴 **Bodegas Langa** – Pl. San Pedro, Jaca. www.bodegaslanga.es. 📞974 36 04 94. A Jaca institution, this bar serves cheeses, charcuterie and regional tapas on barrels fashioned into tables, alongside its own excellent wines.

Pirineos Aragoneses★★

The central Pyrenees, in the north of Huesca province, include the highest peaks: Aneto (3 404m/11 165ft), Posets (3 371m/11 060ft) and Monte Perdido (3 355m/11 004ft). The foothills are often ravined with sparse vegetation. At the heart of the massif, accessible up the river courses, valleys lead to mountain cirques you can explore on foot.

A BIT OF HISTORY

Structure and relief – Vast longitudinal bands are clear in this region. The **axis of Palaeozoic terrain** comprises the Maladeta, Posets, Vignemale and Balaïtous massifs, where there are remains of Quaternary glaciers.

In the **Pre-Pyrenees** (Monte Perdido), deep **Mesozoic limestone** is eroded in the canyons, gorges and cirques of the upper valleys. The limestone area, which extends in broken mountain chains to the Ebro Basin, is divided at Jaca by the long depression of the River Aragón. Many hills are bare of vegetation in a blue marl landscape like that around the **Yesa Reservoir**.

Life in the valleys – The upper valleys of the Kingdom of Aragón developed self-contained communities. Folk traditions are still followed, and native costume is worn on special occasions. Emigration has led to the abandonment of a number of villages. Tourism is a major economic activity. Winter resorts include Candanchú, Astún, Canfranc, Panticosa, El Formigal and Benasque.

🚗 DRIVING TOURS

1 FROM AINSA TO BENASQUE

121km/75mi. Allow half a day.

Ainsa★

🚉 Nearest station: Jaca (71km).
Ainsa, one of the prettiest towns in the Pyrenees, stands on a promontory still

---

🦶 **Michelin Map:** 574 D 28-32, E 29-32 and F 30-31 – Aragón (Huesca)

🅱 **Info:** Avenida Ordesa 5, Ainsa. 🖉974 50 07 67. www.pirineos.com.

🅲 **Location:** From Pamplona/Iruña follow the N 240 to Jaca (111km/69mi SE); from Huesca the N 330 to Jaca (91km/57mi N); from Barbastro the N 123 and the A 138 to Ainsa (52km/32.5mi N).

😊 **Don't Miss:** Spectacular canyons.

---

girded by a wall at the juncture of the River Cinca and River Ara. In the 11C it was the capital of the kingdom of Sobrarbe.

Its arcaded **Plaza Mayor★★** in the upper town, under the tower of a Romanesque church, is a gem of Aragonese architecture. The contemporary **Museo de Oficios y Artes Tradicionales★** (Pl. San Salvador 5; open Jul–Aug 10.30am–2pm, 5.30–9.30pm, Sep–Jun Sat–Sun 11am–2pm, 4.30–7pm; €3; 🖉974 51 00 75, www.villadeainsa.com) is an arts and crafts museum.

🔽 N 260. At Morillo de Liena, head N.

Campo

👫 **Museo de los Juegos Tradicionales** (park near the tourist office, on the N 260, and walk up; open Tue–Sat 11am–2pm, 5–8pm, Sun 11am–2pm; €2; 🖉974 55 01 36). This museum displays ingenious handmade toys and bygone games from the region's rural areas.

🔽 11km/7mi further on is Siera.

Seira

The **Museo de Electricidad** (in the tourist office; Tue–Fri 12–2pm; 🖉974 55 31 31, www.seira.es) covers the development of the town's electric plant, with turbines, transformers, ammeters etc.

Congosto de Ventamillo★★

This 3km/1.8mi defile has sheer lime-stone rock walls.

▷ Take the N 260 to Castejón de Sos, a paragliding centre, then the A 139. The road goes through Villanova, which has two 11C churches

Valle de Benasque★

Benasque (1 138m/3 734ft) lies in an open valley, lush and green, in the shadow of the Maladeta massif, a base for walkers, climbers (ascending the Aneto) and skiers (Cerler, 5km/3mi). Streets are lined with old mansions. **Anciles**, 1.6km/1mi away, is known for its attractive houses. 15km/9.3mi further north, before the road ends, a turn-off leads to the Hospital de Benasque (www.llanosdelhospital.com), a spa-hotel departure point for excursions into Parque Natural Posets-Maladeta.

② NORTH OF AINSA

50km/31mi to Gistaín.

▷ From Ainsa take the A 138 toward Escalona and Bielsa. At Labuerda, take the San Vicente de Labuerda turning.

San Vincente de Labuerda

3km/1.2mi from Labuerda. Open in summer; rest of year, ask for the key at the local bar.

Via a narrow and occasion-ally steep road, you arrive at this small 12C church, set apart from the vil-lage. Enter through an *esconjuradero* (small stone shelter). Inside is a late-15C Gothic altarpiece. From the church, a walk of 40 mins leads to the hermitage of San Visorio, a French saint whose relics are preserved in the church. From there,

the view extends over the valley of the Cinca.

▷ Take the A 138 towards Bielsa.

In **Escalona**, turn left into the **Cañón de Añisclo★★★** (see p418) or con-tinue on the A 138 through dramatic landscape up to the **Desfiladero de las Devotas★★**.

▷ Take the A 138 and bear right at Salinas de Sin.

Valle de Gistaín★

In this valley, also known as the Valle de Chistau, are some of the most pictur-esque villages in the Pyrenees including **Plan**, **San Juan de Plan** and **Gistaín**.

▷ Following the A 138 N will take you to Biesla and the Vall de Pineta.

Bielsa and Valle de Pineta

19km/11.8mi NW of Plan, along A 138. From the pleasant village of Bielsa, a narrow road climbs the valley of the Cinca River, traversing the impressive landscapes of the **Valle de Pineta★★** to the Parador de Bielsa, nestled in a stunning glacial cirque.

Ordesa Valley, Parque Nacional de Ordesa y Monte Perdido

③ FROM AINSA TO BIESCAS

81km/51mi. Allow about 3hr.

Between **Boltaña** (16C church; www.boltana.es) and **Fiscal** (medieval tower; www.aytofiscal.es), the river course reveals underlying strata. Beyond Broto, the Mondarruego massif (alt 2 848m/9 341ft), closing the Ordesa Valley, backs a **landscape★★** in which the slate-roofed village of **Torla★** lies on the western slope of the Ara Valley. The church, Iglesia de San Salvador, houses 18C altar-

pieces. The castle-abbey in Torla has an **ethnographic museum** (for information, call town hall; €1; ✆974 48 63 78). Broto, Torla and Fiscal are good bases from which to explore the **Parque Nacional de Ordesa y Monte Perdido ★★★** (♿see p417).

④ THE PORTALET ROAD

52km/32.3mi. Allow about 2hr.

The **Tena** Valley beyond Biescas widens out into the vast Búbal reservoir.

▶ A short distance before Escarilla, bear right onto HU 610 for Panticosa.

Garganta del Escalar★★ (Escalar Gorge)

The sun rarely penetrates this gorge. The road cuts down the west slope by ramps and hairpin bends to an austere mountain cirque, the setting for the **Balneario de Panticosa★** (✆974 48 71 61; www.panticosa.com), a spa resort with six sulphurous springs and a charming 19C air.

▶ Return to Escarilla and continue to the Portalet Pass.

Sallent de Gállego, at 1 305m/4 281ft, hosts a summer music festival and is renowned for trout fishing and mountaineering. **Formigal** (alt 1 480m/4 856ft), further on, is a ski resort.

Carretera del Portalet
Alt 1 794m/5 886ft.
The pass lies between Portalet peak and Aneu summit to the west. The view extends to the Aneu cirque and Pic du Midi d'Ossau in France (alt 2 884m/9 462ft).

5 FROM BIESCAS TO THE PUERTO DE SOMPORT

58km/36mi. Allow about 2hr.

▶ Continue S on the N 260 to Sabiñánigo – from here it is possible to follow the tour through the Serrablo (🧭 see JACA p4) – then take the N330 to Jaca (🧭 see JACA) and continue north.

The **Cueva de las Güixas**, (www.turismo villanua.net) a cave in Villanúa, has 300m/330yd of galleries. Canfranc is best known for its huge, long abandoned **international railway station★★** (www.canfranc.es) that once linked Spain with France. An extraordinary example of early 20C architecture, still awaiting redevelopment, it was used during the filming of Doctor Zhivago. In August 2019 Canfranc greenlighted the €4 million construction of a cable car connecting the railway station to the **Ip glacial lake★** (*ibón*), also reachable via a steep hike from the town (🔺6hr round trip).
The **Puerto de Somport★★** (alt 1 632m/ 5 354ft), beside the Somport tunnel, is the only pass in the Central Pyrenees that remains snow free all year.
Candanchú (www.candanchu.com) is the region's best-known ski resort (1km/0.6mi away). The mound to the right of the monument has a fine **pano-rama★★**.

ADDRESSES

🛏 STAY

🍽🛏 **Hotel Dos Ríos** – Av. Central 2, Aínsa. 𝄞974 50 09 61. www.hoteldos rios.com. 18 rooms. ⊡ €7.90. Located in the lower part of the resort beside the road, this two-star hotel offers well-kept recently refurbished rooms.

🛏🛏🛏 **Los Arcos** – Pl. Mayor 23, Aínsa. 𝄞974 50 00 16. www.hotellos arcosainsa.com. 7 rooms. ⊡ €7. This romantic getaway has rooms with stone walls and wooden beams plus modern bathrooms and cushy furniture.

🛏🛏🛏 **Hotel & Spa Peña Montañesa** – 2km/0.75mi S of Labuerda on the 138 road. 𝄞974 51 00 51. www.hotel penamontanesa.com. 49 rooms. ⊡ €8. Expect an upscale lodge with freshly mowed lawns, two pools and a sauna and hammam, ideal on chilly nights.

🛏🛏🛏 **Barceló Monastario de Boltaña** – 6km/4mi NE from Aínsa on the N 260. 𝄞974 50 80 00. www. monasteriodeboltana.es. 130 rooms. ⊡ €16. Post up in a 17C monastery at this cosy, well-furnished hotel with spacious rooms and indoor and outdoor pools.

🍴 EAT

🍽 **El Portal** – C. Portal de Bajo 5, Aínsa. 𝄞974 50 03 53. Opposite the Plaza Mayor, this restaurant has a pretty terrace that affords a view of the river and serves simple *cocina de mercado*.

🍽🍽🍽 **Bodegón de Mallacán** – Pl. Mayor 6, Aínsa. 𝄞974 500 977. www. posadareal.com. Tuck into typical Pyrenean cuisine featuring game and wild mushrooms. There's a good-value lunch menu and rooms (🍽🍽) for those wishing to stay.

🍽🍽🍽 **Callizo** – Pl. Mayor, Aínsa. 𝄞974 50 03 85. www.restaurantecallizo.es. Much-loved and recently renovated, Callizo specialises in traditional Aragonese dishes. Set menus are available at varying price points. The ever-enthusiastic waitstaff are known to give impromptu tableside history lessons.

La Comunitat Valenciana and La Región de Murcia

The eastern coastal strip of Valencia, Alicante and Murcia comprises the lesser-known Costa del Azahar (Orange Blossom Coast), the hugely popular Costa Blanca (White Coast) and the Costa Cálida (Warm Coast). The beaches and dunes are mostly low-lying with offshore sandbars, pools and lagoons. The climate is Mediterranean but drier than average; little rain falls except in autumn, when rivers sometimes jump their banks. The millennial vegetation – a mix of scrubland, pinewoods, grapevines and olive, almond and carob trees – has been supplanted in many parts by *huertas* (irrigated industrial farms), citrus orchards and market gardens. There are palm groves around Elche/Elx and Orihuela in the south, and rice is grown in swampy areas. That said, the powerhouse of the region's economy is, of course, tourism.

Alicante and Costa Blanca

Alicante province is expat and package-holiday territory. The coastal landscape is blighted by huge swathes of building projects. Its most (in)famous resort is Benidorm, which – shockingly – has the most skyscrapers per capita on earth. Popular since the 1960s, it's all about pure, hedonistic holiday pleasure (get your culture elsewhere) with beautiful (man-made) beaches, budget accommodation and nearby theme parks. By contrast, the towns of Alicante/Alacant and Elche/Elx feel far more lived-in. Inland, the parched, stony Sierra Serella provides a different perspective.

Murcia

In the hot, flat region of Murcia, visitors tend to flock around the tourist beach developments of the Costa Cálida and particularly the Mar Menor, which is Spain's largest natural lake and the most expansive salty lagoon in Mediterranean Europe. A cultural oasis in the eye of the tourist tornado, Murcia city remains true to its roots.

Valencia and Costa del Azahar

Valencia city has always had a fascinating old town, popular beaches and excellent food (it is famous as the home of paella). More recently La Ciudad de las Artes y las Ciencias – a high-profile museum-arts complex – has cemented it on the international tourist circuit. The burgeoning neighbourhood of Ruzafa is popular with artsy and alternative types.

Highlights

1 Scraping a paella pan clean in **El Palmar** (p437)

2 Strolling the futuristic **Ciutat de les Arts i les Ciències** (p432)

3 Exploring the old quarter of postcard-perfect **Peñíscola** (p435)

4 Sheltering from the heat in Elche's sprawling **Palm Grove** (p434)

5 Looking out from Castillo de Santa Bárbara, **Alicante** (p441)

North of Valencia, the Costa del Azahar is a favourite among Spanish holidaymakers who like their resorts low key. Its jewel is Peñíscola (Spain's answer to Mont St-Michel). Inland, the rugged mountain region of El Maestrazgo has beguiling, little-known villages, while Xàtiva boasts an impressive ensemble of medieval architecture.

Peñíscola

© Isidoro Ruiz Haro/age fotostock

Valencia★★

Spain's third-largest city, Valencia is unprepossessing at first glance with workaday high-rises at its outer limits. But venture into its core, and you'll find palm-lined avenues, fortified gateways, trendy restaurants, quaint shops and Gothic houses. This is a city reborn, thanks to 21C urban puilding projects (many by Valencia-born Santiago Calatrava), and a city in the making, with burgeoning *barris* like Russafa leading the charge. Main beaches are reachable by tram.

THE CITY TODAY

In the last decade, Valencia has become a popular city break to rank almost alongside Barcelona. Like its Catalan cousin, it too has turned its face back to the sea with its beach – and particularly its port area – revitalised since hosting the America's Cup in 2007. Today the city is one of Spain's leading art, dining and nightlife destinations.

A BIT OF HISTORY

2 000 years of history – Founded by the Greeks in 138 BC, the city passed into the hands of Carthaginians, Romans, Visigoths and Moors before being briefly reconquered in 1094 by **El Cid** and taken definitively in 1238 by James the Conqueror. Valencia then prospered, experiencing a silk renaissance in the 17C. The city subsequently sided with Charles of Austria in the War of the Spanish Succession and lost its privileges. Ever tenacious, in 1808 it rose against the French and in 1939 was the last Republican redoubt.

Art in Valencia – Valencia flourished economically and artistically in the 15C, as seen in the Gothic architecture of palaces, the cathedral and the Lonja (exchange). Among its painters were **Luis Dalmau**, who developed a Hispano-Flemish style; **Jaime Baço** (**Jacomart**); **Juan Reixach**; and the **Osonas**, father and son. Notable 15C decorative arts were ironwork, gold-

- ▶ **Population:** 789 004
- ◔ **Michelin Map:** 577 N 28 (town plan) or 574 N 28.
- 🛈 **Info:** Pl. de la Reina 19. ✆963 15 39 31. www.visitvalencia.com
- ◖ **Location:** Valencia is the main city of the Levante. 🚆Valencia (AVE). Metro, 30 mins, connects airport to city centre.
- 🅿 **Parking:** Don't bank on finding a park in the old town.
- ✆ **Don't Miss:** A walk in the old town and the Ciutat de les Arts i les Ciències.
- 🕐 **Timing:** Start with unmissable modern architecture (Santiago Calatrava's City of Arts and Sciences and the convention centre) and Sir Norman Foster's Turia bridge, or with the heritage section of the city.
- 👪 **Kids:** L'Oceanogràfic is one of the world's great aquariums.

and silversmithing and ceramics (◔see Museo Nacional de Cerámica in Sights, p422). **The Valencia huerta and Albufera** – The Roman irrigation system around Valencia was improved by the Moors. Today its orchards and farms fill fruit bowls across Europe. South of Valencia lies a vast lagoon, the **Parque Natural de La Albufera** (◔see p437).

👣 WALKING TOUR

1️⃣ CIUDAD VIEJA★ (OLD TOWN)

Allow 3hr. Follow route on town plan. Start at El Miguelete, the bell tower of the cathedral.

El Miguelete★

Pl. de la Reina. Open Mon–Fri 10am–7.30pm (until 6.30pm Nov–Mar); Sat 10am–7pm; Sun 10am–1pm, 5.30–

Cathedral

7pm. €2. ☎963 91 81 27.
www.museocatedralvalencia.com.
'Little Michael' is the main bell of this
octagonal Gothic tower dating to 1418.
Climb to the top for a view of the cathedral and the city's roofscape.

Catedral★

Pl. de la Reina. Open Jun-Sep daily
10am–6.30pm (from 2pm Sun). Rest of
the year 10am–5.30pm (Sun 2–5.30pm).
Closed Sun Nov–Mar. €8 (including
museum). ☎963 91 81 27.
www.museocatedralvalencia.com.
Work on the cathedral began in 1262,
though most of the building is 14C–15C
Gothic. The slender early-18C west
face imitates Italian Baroque style; the
Assumption on the pediment is by Vergara and Esteve.
The south door is Romanesque and the
north, the **Portada de los Apóstoles**
(Apostles' Door), Gothic, decorated with
time-worn sculptures. A statue of the
Virgin and Child on the tympanum is
surrounded by music-playing cherubim.
Inside, light filters through the alabaster
windows in the Flamboyant Gothic **lantern**. The **retable** in the capilla mayor
(chancel), by Fernando de Llanos and
Yáñez de la Almedina (early 16C) and
influenced by Leonardo, illustrates
the Lives of Christ and the Virgin. In
the ambulatory, a Renaissance portico
protects an alabaster relief of the Resurrection (1510). Opposite is the 15C
Late Gothic Virgen del Coro (Chancel
Virgin), also in alabaster. In a chapel is
a Baroque Cristo de la Buena Muerte
(Christ of Good Death).

Capilla del Santo Cáliz or Sala Capitular★ (Chapel of the Holy Grail or Chapter House)

Last chapel along the north aisle.
This chapel has elegant star vaulting
and, behind the altar, 12 alabaster low
reliefs. In the centre, a magnificent 1C
carnelian agate cup is said to be the
Holy Grail, brought to Spain in the 3C.
The **museum** (same hours as cathedral)
beyond contains a sizable body of work
from the Valencian painter Juan de
Juanes (1523–79).

▶ Leave through the main entrance
and cross Correjería to Pl. de la Reina.

L'Almoina

Pl. Décimo Junio Bruto. Open Mon–Sat
10am–7pm, Sun & hols 10am–2pm.
☎962 08 41 73. €2; free Sun & hols.
Archaeological excavations uncovered
these Roman and Visigothic remains. An
underground tour lets you discover the
substructure of ancient Valencia including vestiges of the Visigothic cathedral.

▶ Cross Correjería again and follow
C. de la Bachilla to Pl. de la Amoina.

Casa del Punt de Gantxo

Plaza de la Almoina.
The facade of this building, by Manuel
Peris Ferrando, has unusual decorative
elements. Against a background of coloured ceramic decorated with foliage
stand pilasters whose capitals are made
with plant motifs (branches and flowers). These ornaments are reminiscent

of those that were used in the 15C to decorate the Lonja (&see p424).

▶ Return to C. de la Bachilla and turn left.

Museo de la Ciudad

Pl del Arzobispo 3. Open Mon–Sat 10am–7pm, Sun & hols 10am–2pm. €2; free Sun. ℘962 08 41 26.

Situated inside the palace of the Marquis de Campo (18C–19C), this

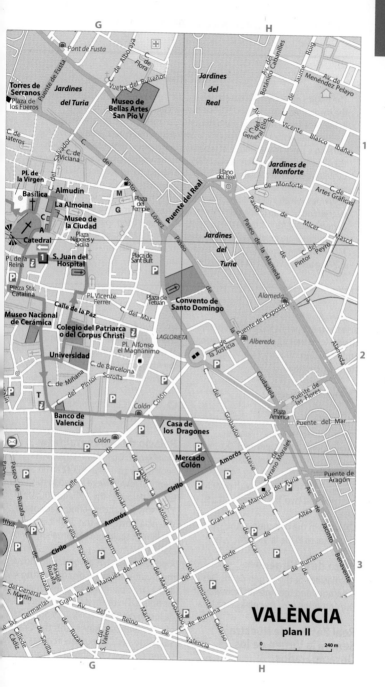

museum displays the municipal art collections. Exhibits are varied, from 14–15C ivory carvings to old weights and measures.

Cripta Arqueológica de la Cárcel de San Vicente

Pl. del Arzobispo 1.
Open Mon–Sat 9.30am–7pm, Sun & hols 10am–3pm. €2, free Sun & hols.
℘ 962 084 573.

Las Fallas

The origins of this festival date to the Middle Ages when on St Joseph's Day, the carpenters' brotherhood burned their accumulated wood shavings in bonfires known as **fallas** (from the Latin *fax*: torch). The name became synonymous with a festival for which, over time, objects were made solely for burning – particularly effigies of less popular members of the community. In the 17C single effigies were replaced by pasteboard groups or floats produced by neighbourhoods: Rivalry is such that the figures today are fantastic in size, artistry and satirical implication. Prizes are awarded during the general festivities, which include fireworks, processions, bullfights etc. before everything goes up in the *cremá* (fires) on the evening of 19 March. Figures (*ninots*) dating from 1934 to the present, which have been spared from the bonfires, are on display in the **Museo Fallero** (Pl. Monteolivete 4; open Mon–Sat 10am–7pm, Sun & hols 10am–2pm; closed 1 & 6 Jan, 1 May, 25 Dec; €2; free Sun; ℘963 52 54 78; www.fallas.com).

Visit the remains of a Visigothic funerary chapel with four finely worked screens and a 6C burial, plus two Visigothic stone sarcophagi.

◉ Cross C. Almudín.

Almudín
Pl. San Luis Bertrán. Open Tue–Sat 10am–2pm, 4.30-8.30pm (mid-Oct–mid-Mar until 6pm), Sun & hols 10am–3pm. €2; free Sun & hols. ℘963 52 54 78.
This is a 14C–16C granary with primitive frescoes and two 19C *azulejos* altars.

◉ Head in the direction of the cathedral to Pl. de la Virgen.

Plaza de la Virgen★
The Basilica of the Virgen de los Desamparados and the Apostle Doorway of the Cathedral face this pleasant plaza.

Real Basílica de Nuestra Señora la Virgen de los Desamparados
Pl. de la Virgen, s/n. Open: Basilica, daily 7am–2pm, 4.30–9pm. Free. Open: Museu Mariano, Mon & Thu 11am–2pm; Sat 10.30am–2pm, 5–8pm; Sun 10.30am–2pm. ℘ 963 91 92 14. www.basilicadesamparados.org.
This late-17C church is linked to the apse of the cathedral by a Renaissance arch. The floor plan is oval. Beneath the painted cupola is the venerated statue of the patron of Valencia, the Virgin of the Abandoned (*desamparados*), which receives a steady flow of devotees.

◉ Go to C. Caballeros, on the west of the Plaza.

Palacio de la Generalitat★
Caballeros 2. Open Mon–Fri 9am–2pm, bookings required. ℘963 42 46 36.
Identical towers were added to this 15C Gothic palace in the 17C and 20C. Until 1707 this was the meeting place of the Valencia Cortes. In the Gothic patio is Benlliure's sculpture of Dante's Inferno (1900).
A golden salon has a wonderful gilded multicoloured **artesonado ceiling★** and a large painting of the Tribunal de las Aguas. On the first floor are the Sala de los Reyes (Royal Hall), with portraits of the Valencian kings, and the Gran Salón de las Cortes Valencianas, or Grand Council Chamber. The *azulejos*, frieze and coffered ceiling are 16C. The rear facade and the Palau de la Batlia (provincial administration) look onto the **Plaza de Manises**.

◉ From P. Manises take C. Serranos and walk to the end.

Torres de Serranos★

Pl. Fueros. Open Mon–Sat 9.30am–7pm, Sun & hols 10am–2pm. €2; free Sun. ℘963 91 90 70.

These fairytale towers guarding one of the city entrances are a superb example of late-14C military architecture. Climb to the top for great views.

▶ Return to P. de Manises.

Calle Caballeros

The most important street of the old city runs from Plaza de la Virgen into the colourful Carmen district. Some houses have Gothic patios.

Iglesia de San Nicolás de Bari

Caballeros 35. Open Tue–Fri 10.30am–7.30pm, Sat until 6.30pm, Sun 1–7pm, Jul–Sep Tue–Fri 10.30am–9pm, Sat until 7.30pm, Sun 11.30am–9pm. €7. ℘963 91 33 17. www.sannicolasvalencia.com.

This is one of Valencia's oldest churches, built Churrigueresque style with an altarpiece by Juan de Juanes (to the left) and, by the baptismal font, *Calvary* by Osona the Elder.

▶ Continue to Pl. del Esparto, then follow C. de Quart to the end.

Torres de Quart

Av. Guillem de Castro.

These 15C towers were damaged in the 19C by Napoleon's cannons.

▶ From Pl. del Esparto, take C. Bolsería.

La Lonja★★ (Silk Exchange)

Pl. del Mercado. Open Mon–Sat 10am–7pm, Sun & hols 10am–2pm. €2; free Sun & hols. ℘962 08 41 53.

This 15C Flamboyant Gothic building, designated a UNESCO World Heritage centre, replaced an earlier exchange outgrown by prosperous merchants. The left wing, separated from the entrance by a tower, is crowned by a gallery with a medallion frieze. The old commercial **silk hall★★** is lofty, with ogival arches supported on slender, elegantly cabled columns; the bays are filled with delicate tracery.

Iglesia de Santa Catalina

Pl. de Santa Catalina. Open 10.30am–2.30pm, 5.30–7.30pm. €2 (incl tower). ℘963 91 77 13.

The church is notable for its 17C **Baroque belfry★**. Climb the tower for a close-up view. The church interior is sober Gothic.

Plaza Redonda

A passage on the right leads to this curious little 19C circular plaza.

▶ Out on C. Pere Compte, cross C. San Vicente Martyr, then immediately turn right on C. Abadía San Martín.

Palacio del Marqués de Dos Aguas★★

Rinconada García Sanchiz 6. Open Tue–Sat 10am–2pm, 4–8pm, Sun & public hols 10am–2pm. Closed 1 Jan, 1 May, 24–25 & 31 Dec. €3; free Sat pm, Sun. ℘963 51 63 92. www.mecd.gob.es/mnceramica.

The **Museo Nacional de Cerámica y de las Artes Suntuarias González Martí★★** (National Museum of Ceramics and Decorative Art) is housed in what is perhaps the most stunning Baroque building in all of Spain. Its 18C marble portal was once covered by paintings. On the **ground floor** is the richly decorated **carriage★** of the Marquis of Dos Aguas (1753). Rooms on the **first floor** include the Chinese salon, *fumoir* and chapel.

The **ceramic collection** on the **second floor** includes Moorish ceramics (the basis of the craft in Spain), green and black porcelain and later pieces from Málaga, Murcia and Manises. Christian ceramics of the 13C and 14C evidence continuity from the Moorish tradition. Outstanding are green and manganese ceramics from **Paterna** (6km/3.7mi N of Valencia). The golden age of ceramics in **Manises** (8km/5mi N of Valencia) is represented by lovely pieces as well.

The **Real Fábrica de Alcora**, established in 1727, became the centre of innovation in Spain, spreading the Louis XIV, Classic and Baroque styles. Pieces from 19C **Manises** evidence later styles that spread through southern and eastern Spain. There is also a Valencian kitchen with 18C and 19C tiles.

▶ Take C. Poeta Querol and turn left on C. Salva.

Colegio del Patriarca o del Corpus Christi★ (Patriarch or Corpus Christi College)

Nave 1. Only prebooked guided tours (55 mins) Mon–Fri 10am–1pm, 5–6pm; Sat 10am–1pm. Open 11am–1.30pm. €7. ☏692 49 17 69.

This ex-seminary dates to the 16C. The **church** (enter left door) is one of the few Renaissance churches in Spain with frescoes; on the lower wall sections are Manises tiles. The seminary is built around a harmonious patio decorated with Talavera *azulejo* friezes.

The small **museum** of 15C–17C art includes paintings by Juan de Juanes, a **triptych of the Passion★** by Dirk Bouts, a 14C Byzantine crucifix from the Monastery of Athos, a 13C Romanesque *Christ* and a portrait of the founder, Ribera, by Ribalta, plus paintings by Ribalta, Morales and El Greco. In the same plaza is the **Universidad** (University; www.uv.es).

▶ Return to C. Juan de la Ribera, cross C. de la Paz, right on C. Medines.

Iglesia de San Juan del Hospital ★ (Church of St John of the Hospital)

Trinquete de Caballeros 5 (access through courtyard). Open Mon–Sat 9.30am–1.30pm, 5–9pm; (Mon–Fri also 6.45–7.45am); Sun 11am–2pm, 5–9pm. €2 optional donation ☏963 92 29 65. www.sanjuandelhospital.es.

This early-13C Gothic church consists of a single nave with pointed barrel vault. In the first chapel are 13C murals. There is also a museum.

▶▶ WALKING TOUR

② MODERNIST VALENCIA★

Allow 1.5hr from the Mercado Central to Plaza de la Reina. ♿ Follow the route on the town plan.

Valencia's economic boom at the end of the 19C created the need for new neighbourhoods and a partial remodelling of the historic district. The bourgeoisie, local administrative powers and financial movers and shakers seized the opportunity to flaunt their wealth by building spectacular edifices. This architectural movement adopted the *modernista* style in the early years of the 20C, before returning to a more conformist approach.

Mercado Central★

Pl. Ciudad de Brujas. Open Mon–Sat 7am–3pm. ☏963 82 91 00. www.mercadocentralvalencia.es.

Dating to 1928, the enormous metal-and-glass Central Market is a glorious example of *modernista* architecture. It is busiest in the mornings when the stalls are bursting with fish and local produce. Luckily it hasn't yet become a froufrou gastro-emporium like so many other traditional Spanish markets (*hola*, Mercado de San Miguel and La Boqueria).

▶ Head S to the Pl. del Ayuntamiento.

Plaza del Ayuntamiento

This vast square is Valencia's nerve centre. A flower market makes it welcomingly colourful. The building that holds the town hall (*ayuntamiento*), was built in 1915 and has a colossal facade with two corner towers topped with domes, and a grandiose entrance with a portico and campanile.

The main post office (**Correos** at the corner of Calle Correos) sits opposite. Inaugurated in 1923, its is distinguished by a dome decorated with neoclassical garlands of flowers and ribbons. North of these stand two **neo-Gothic buildings** with colourful facades.

The World's Largest Food Fight

The town of **Buñol** (40km/25mi W of Valencia off the A 3), numbering some 10 000 inhabitants, lies in a tranquil fold of the Sierra de Las Cabrillas. At the end of every August, it swells beyond all proportion for the celebration of one of the most famous festivals in Spain, **La Tomatina** (www.tomatina.es). First, a week-long festival of parades honours the town's patron, San Luis Bertràn. Then, on Wednesday at 10am, the crowds are challenged to snatch a ham placed on a greasy pole. The feat achieved, the firing of water cannons marks the release of a hundred metric tons of tomatoes and one hour of chaotic tomato throwing. Legend has it that this helter-skelter celebration began when a food fight among the town's youths broke out in 1945. It has now become one of the defining images of Spanish fiestas.

Avenida Marqués de Sotelo

Many buildings along this avenue feature detailed facades and a wide range of decorative elements including monumental gates, towers, terraces, steeples and pediments.

▷ Walk to C. de Xativa.

Estación del Norte★

This landmark *modernista* railway station was built by Demetrio Ribes between 1909 and 1917. Echoing the architecture of the Austrian Secession (note its geometric structure), the station also pays homage to local culture and imagery: Ceramic relief friezes depict orange trees and mosaic murals scenes of Valencian agrarian life. The lobby has a riot of decorative details: columns, lamp posts, gold mosaics and more.

Next to the station, the **Plaza de Toros** (bullring), built in the mid-19C, is one of the most picturesque and important in Spain.

▷ Pass the P. de Toros, then turn right on C. Ruzafa and left on C. Cirilo Amorós.

Calle de Cirilio Amorós

This road passes through the El Pla del Remei residential neighbourhood, which developed in the late 19C–20C. It now hosts chic designer and fashion boutiques, clustered around the Mercado Colón. At no. 26, notice the beautiful bay windows incorporating elements of Gothic architecture such as a rosette, and at no. 27, a door and balcony in Art Nouveau style. At no. 29 the **Casa Ferrer** was built in 1908 by Vicente Ferrer Pérez in an Art Deco style. It features stylised rose motifs and ceramic disk-like elements on a chequerboard background raised above a triglyph.

▷ Continue along C. de Cirilo Amorós.

Mercado Colón★

C. Jorge Juan, 19. Open 7:30am–3am.
℘963 37 11 01

The brick, metal and glass building from 1913 is the work of Francisco Mora y Belenguer. The main facade draws on Valencia's artistic traditions with aged stone, colourful mosaics depicting harvest scenes, shiny ceramics and stained glass. It houses an upmarket selection of shops, bars and trendy restaurants.

▷ Turn left on C. Conde Salvatierra de Älava then left on C. de Sorni.

Casa de los Dragónes

At the corner of C. de Sorni and C. Jorge Juan, the Casa del Dragón owes its name to the sculptures that adorn its facade. Built in 1901 by Jose Manuel Cortina, it incorporates Gothic-inspired elements.

▷ Cross C. Colon and continue to C. Don Juan de Austria.

Banco de Valencia

At the intersection of C. Pintor Sorolla, this building is in a pretty neo-Baroque style with yellows and pinks, curved

THE AMERICA'S CUP

Like Barcelona, Valencia latched onto an international event as a catalyst for change. Coincidentally Valencia won the bid to host the 32nd America's Cup – the world's most prestigious sailing event – against Barcelona, and as with Barcelona's triumphal 1992 Olympics, the shoreline was a major beneficiary. British architect David Chipperfield created an arresting headquarters there for the event, and a spate of chic bars, restaurants and hotels soon sprung up. Transport to the area also improved: It's now served by metro, tram and wide avenues with bike lanes. As always, progress came at a price. As gentrification continues apace, some mourn that the erstwhile charm of El Cabayal – Valencia's old maritime neighbourhood – is forever lost.

balconies, ornate windows and other charming decorative details.

▶ From C. Poeta Querol turn right at the Teatro Reial. Continue on C. Marqués de Dos Aguas and turn left on C. de la Paz.

Calle de la Paz

This street has many historic buildings. At the far end, in the Plaza de la Reina, La Isla de Cuba, a former retail complex, was designed by the architect Lucas García Cardona in 1896. Here he blends classicism with new techniques (note the use of cast-iron columns). The decoration is heaviest on the upper frieze, where you can see ceramic panels of ancient Greek dancers in blue and pink.

AVANT-GARDE VALENCIA

🏛🚶 Ciutat de les Arts i les Ciències★★★

♿ Buy tickets online in advance to skip lines and to score possible discounts.

€38.20 (all three venues, valid 3 days; see website for individual venue prices); public areas are free. Parking €2.30 per hour. ✆961 97 46 86. www.cac.es.
The City of Arts and Sciences is a city within a city, an expansive culture and leisure complex consisting of a series of otherworldly, avant-garde, blindingly white buildings positioned around reflecting pools. The complex is the brainchild ofrenowned Valencian-born architect Santiago Calatrava.

🏛🚶 L'Oceanogràfic★★

Open mid-Jul–Aug 10–12am, rest of year generally 10am–6pm; see website for further seasonal hours. €30.70.
The largest aquarium in Europe is set around a lake and joined by gardens and tunnels. The exhibits focus on marine life in the Mediterranean, the Arctic and the Antarctic (with plenty of penguins) and the oceans, the highlight being a 30m/100ft aquarium-tunnel with sharks and rays. The dolphin enclosure hosts performances all day.
L'Umbracle★ – White parabolic arches shelter this pleasant palm garden on a terrace facing the Museu de las Ciencias.

Museu de las Ciencias ★★

Open Jul–first week Sep 10am–9pm; rest of year generally 10am–6pm; see website for further seasonal hours. €8.
The largest interactive Science Museum in Europe is set in a building that evokes the skeleton of a giant sea creature. Inside is a hands-on encounter with the human genome plus 'space' travel, astronomy and more.

L'Hemisfèric★

Open daily year-round. Shows usually 11am–6pm (Fri–Sun 8pm) See website for programme. €8.
The unusual Calatrava design symbolises a human eye, open to the world; appropriately it houses a planetarium and IMAX cinema projecting onto a concave screen of 900 sq m.
Palau de les Arts Reina Sofía (✆961 97 58 00; www.lesarts.com) – The four halls here host classical and modern opera, music, theatre and dance.

ADDITIONAL SIGHTS

Museo de Bellas Artes★

San Pío V 9.

Open Tue–Sun 10am–8pm. Closed 1 Jan, Good Friday, 25 Dec. ℘963 87 03 00. www.museobellasartesvalencia.gva.es.
This fine arts museum is in an 18–19C collegiate church and seminary, and a contemporary extension, near the Jardines del Real (Royal Gardens).

The collection is notable for its **Valencian Primitives★★** with outstanding altarpieces, while the Renaissance period is represented by Macip and Juan de Juanes. Other outstanding works include *St Bartholomew* by Luca Giordanom, *St John the Baptist* by El Greco, an impressive *St Sebastian* by Ribera and a self-portrait by Velázquez. Goya's mastery of portraits is shown in his paintings of Francisco Bayeu and Joaquina Candado.

Jardines del Real (Royal Gardens)

San Pío V.

Open daily 7.30am–sunset
The city's biggest park, which contains a small zoo ♟♟, is close to the pleasant **Jardín de Monforte**. The **Puente del Real** (Royal Bridge) across the **Jardín del Turia** is 16C.

Instituto Valenciano de Arte Moderno (IVAM)

Guillem de Castro 118.

Open Tue–Sun 10am–7pm (Fri until 9pm). €6; free Fri 7.30-9pm.
℘963 17 66 00. www.ivam.es.
This modern building houses more than 7 000 works of contemporary art on rotating display and boasts the largest collection of the works of sculptor **Julio González** (1876–1942).

Jardín Botánico de la Universidad (Botanical Garden)

C. Quart 80.

Open 10am–sunset. €2.50.
℘963 15 68 00. www.jardibotanic.org.
Valencia was one of the first Spanish cities to embrace the public garden: These opened in 1802.

Convento de Santo Domingo

Pl. de Tetuán 22. Group visits only.
Highlights of this building include a courtyard, the Capilla de los Reyes chapel and a front gate designed by King Philipe II.

Museo Valenciano de la Ilustración y la Modernidad MUVIM (Museum of Illustration and Modernity)

C. Guillén de Castro 8.

Open Tue–Sat 10am–2pm, 4–8pm, Sun & hols 10am–8pm. €2, free Sat & Sun.
℘963 883 730. www.muvim.es.
The pleasing contemporary building by Guillermo Vázquez Consuegra provides the backdrop for numerous fascinating art exhibitions. The permanent 'Adventure of Thought' traces five centuries of social and intellectual history in Europe.

Museo de la Historia★

C. Valencia 42.

Open Tue–Sat 10am–7pm, Sun & hols 10am–2pm. €2; free Sun & public hols.
℘963 70 11 05. www.mhv.valencia.es.
In a restored 19C waterworks, this museum tells the story of Valencia from its beginnings to the end of the 20C with evocative, dramatised audio-visual presentations.

ADDRESSES

🛏 STAY

⊜⊜ Hostal Antigua Morellana – C. d'en Bou 2. ℘963 91 57 73. www.hostalam.com. 18 rooms. Close to the Lonja and main market, this family-run hotel offers comfortable and bright rooms with views of the picturesque Carmen district.

⊜⊜ Hotel Alkazar – C. Mosén Fernandes 1. ℘963 51 55 51. www.hotelalkazar.es. 17 rooms. ⊒€4. Smart, modern, recently refurbished rooms offer good value in the heart of town. The walls are thin, so pack earplugs.

⊜⊜ Hostal Venecia – Pl. Ayuntamiento (enter through Llop 5). ℘963 52 42 67. www.hotelvenecia.com. 66 rooms. ⊒€6.90. The building is outstanding, with balconies facing the plaza del Ayuntamiento. Rooms are attractively furnished in contemporary style.

🛏🛏🛏🛏 **Hotel Vincci Palace** – La Paz 42. 🕿962 062 377. www.vinccihoteles.com. 76 rooms. ⛶€13.20. From the dependable Vincci name comes this comfortable if slightly dated hotel five minutes from the cathedral.

🛏🛏🛏🛏 **Caro Hotel** – Carrer de l'Almirall 14. 🕿963 05 90 00. www.carohotel.com. 26 rooms. ⛶€22. This sleek, understated newcomer keeps the frescoed ceilings of the former palace it occupies, but its furnishings – think dark-wood panelling and sheeny marble – ooze high-design minimalism.

♈/ EAT

🍽 **Tasca Ángel** – Púrísima 1 (adjacent to Plaza Ibáñez). 🕿963 91 78 35. Closed Sun. One bite of the house speciality, grilled sardines, and you'll understand why this bar has been in business since 1946.

🍽🍽 **Kuzina** – Salvador 5. 🕿960 01 35 54. www.kuzinavlc.com. Closed Tue. Greek cuisine meets Spanish tapas in this tiny central restaurant that's popular with a young crowd. Reservations are a must.

🍽🍽🍽 **Casa Montes** – Pl. Obispo Amigó 5. 🕿963 85 50 25. Open Tue–Sun for lunch, Wed–Sat for dinner. Good -value Mediterranean market cuisine and good service have earned this spot a regular local crowd.

🍽🍽🍽 **Sagardi** – San Vicente Mártir 6. 🕿963 91 06 68. www.sagardi.com. This Basque restaurant with two working cider barrels and a tapas bar makes for a fun, rambunctious evening.

🍽🍽🍽🍽 **Baobab** – Gran Via del Marqués del Túria 73. 🕿961 67 66 75. www.baobabgastronomia.com. Valencia's golden-boy chef Raúl Aleixandre, of (now-shuttered) Vinícolas fame, is back with this envelope-pushing Mediterranean restaurant that, despite opening in 2018, is already famous for its perfectly executed rice dishes and *buñuelos de bacalao* (cod fritters).

TAPAS

Bar La Pilareta – Moro Zeit 13. 🕿963 91 04 97. www.barlapilareta.es. Founded in 1917, Pilareta is synonymous with *clóchinas* (tiny mussels), which locals devour standing at the marble bar.

Mercado de San Valero – Gran Via de les Germanies, 21. 🕿960 71 23 40. www.mercadosanvalero.com. Tapas-crawl through this uber-trendy 'street food' market that opened in 2018: You've got 10 internationally inflected stalls (plus a wine bar) to choose from.

CAFÉS

Retrogusto Coffeemates – Mercat Central. 🕿637 95 92 70. Retrogusto brought world-class third-wave coffee to Valencia. Baristas weigh every last bean for precise, highly complex pulls.

NIGHTLIFE

Calle Caballeros – This is the hub of Valencia's nightlife, especially between the Pl de la Virgen and Pl Tossal.

Café de las Horas – Conde de Almodóvar 1. 🕿963 91 73 36. www.cafedelashoras.com. You'll feel like a million bucks sipping a *gin-tónic* at this gaudy café with kitsch 19C decor.

Café Negrito – Pl. Negrito 1. 🕿665 13 05 28. Open from 4pm. This artists' café, on a small square in the old town, is a popular meeting place for cocktails.

SHOPPING

Lladró Boutique – Poeta Querol 9. 🕿963 51 16 25. www.lladro.com. Closed Sun. Splurge on Llandó's world-famous ceramics on its home turf.

Mercadillo de la Plaza Redonda – Open Mon–Sat 10am–8pm, Sun 8am–2pm. The Sunday open-air flea market is the best time to go.

Turrones Ramos – Sombrerería 11. 🕿963 92 33 98. www.turronesramos.com. This shop has sold hand-made *turrón* (nougat) since 1890.

FESTIVALS

In addition to **Las Fallas** (🕯*see sidebar p42*), Valencia has a solemn **Corpus Christi** procession and a festival of the **Virgen de los Desamparados**, (second Sun May; www.basilicadesamparados.org).

Costa del Azahar

Backed by mountains, the sunny 'Orange Blossom' Coast is one of Spain's major tourist centres, marked by high-rise blocks and hotels along sandy beaches and orange groves. A number of small towns and villages preserve old quarters brimming with history.

- ♿ **Michelin Map:** 577 K 31, L 30, M 29, N 28–29, O 28–29.
- 🅸 **Info:** Castelló de la Plana: Plaza de la Hierba; ℘964 35 86 88. Gandía: Paseo Marítimo Neptuno; ℘962 84 24 07. Peñíscola: Paseo Marítimo; ℘964 48 02 08. www.castellon-costaazahar.com.
- ▶ **Location:** Costa del Azahar stretches along the Mediterranean coast in eastern Spain from Valencia. The AP 7 Autopista connects the beaches.
- 👪 **Kids:** Beaches and Cuevas de San José.

🚗 DRIVING TOUR

FROM VINARÒS TO CASTELLÓ
72km/45mi.

▶ Follow either the N 340 or the AP 7 toll motorway.

The northern coast of the province of Castelló is separated from the interior by the Maestrazgo mountains, recalling knights from the Templar and Montesa orders who controlled this area during the Middle Ages. Large resorts include Peñíscola and Benicàssim.

Vinaròs
🚉Vinaròs.

Vinaròs has the 16C **Iglesia de Nuestra Señora de la Asunción** (pl. Parroquial; ℘964 45 19 33), and a pleasant promenade close to the fishing port.

Peñíscola★★
🚉Nearest station: Benicarló-Peñíscola (5km).

The **old quarter★**, surrounded by walls, sits on a small rocky peninsula in the shadow of an imposing fortress. Its sandy beaches extend to either side. A small **fishing port** is still active.

Castillo Peñíscola★
Castillo. Open Holy Week–15 Oct 9.30am–9.30pm; 16 Oct–Holy Week 10.30am–5.30pm. Closed 1 & 6 Jan, 7 & 9 Sep, 9 Oct, 25 Dec. €5. ℘964 48 00 21.

Built by Templars in the early 14C, the castle was subsequently modified by Pope Luna, whose coat of arms, featuring a crescent moon in allusion to his name, can be seen on a gate. Grouped around the parade ground are the vast church, with pointed vaulting, and a free-standing tower. The castle featured in the famous 1961 Hollywood movie, *El Cid*.

The terrace offers a **panorama★** of the village and coastline. The castle is a fitting spot for events such as the Festival of Baroque and Ancient Music, in the first fortnight of August. The coastal road passes through an arid landscape. The resort of Alcossebre, popular with Spanish families, stands between Peñíscola and Benicàssim.

Benicàssim
🚉Benicàssim.

This is the other major tourist centre in the province of Castelló, separated from the interior by the **Desierto de las Palmas** (Palm Desert), which has suffered badly from fire in the past few years. Benicàssim has excellent beaches, lined by villas and apartments. It hosts one of Europe's top pop and electronic music festivals every July (FIB; www.fiberfib.com), attended by 170 000 fans a year. The quieter town of Oropesa is located to the north.

A Legendary Siege

Sagunto has a heroic place in Spain's bloody history. In 218 BC the Carthaginian general **Hannibal** besieged Sagunto, then a small seaport allied to Rome, for a period of eight months. Seeing only one alternative to surrender, the local inhabitants lit a huge fire into which all the women, children, sick and elderly flung themselves. Meanwhile, the macho soldiers made a suicidal sortie against the enemy. The event marked the beginning of the Second Punic War. Five years later, Scipio Africanus Major rebuilt the city, which became an important Roman town.

Castelló de la Plana

🚌 Pintor Oliet 2.

A mere 15km/9mi separate Benicàssim from the port of Castelló, whose origins date to the 13C. On the main square is the **Catedral de Santa María** (Arcipreste Balaguer 1; open Mon–Sat 8–12.45am, 5–8.45pm; Sun 8.30–1.45am, 6–8.45pm; ☎964 22 34 63, www.concatedral.com), rebuilt after the Spanish Civil War; the octagonal bell tower is late 16C.
The town hall (ayuntamiento) is from the late 17C. Other sights include paintings attributed to Zurbarán in the Convento de las Madres Capuchinas and the Museo Provincial de Bellas Artes (Av. Hermanos Bou 28; open Tue–Sat 10am–2pm, 4–8pm, Sun & public hols 10am–2pm; ☎964 72 75 00; www.culturalcas.com/va/museu/bellas-artes), featuring prehistoric objects, canvases and ceramics.

FROM CASTELLÓ TO VALENCIA

69km/43mi. 22km/14mi NW on the CV 10 and CV 160.

Vilafamés★★

🚌 Nearest station:
Castelló de la Plana (27km).
Vilafamés is an attractive town of Moorish origin with whitewashed houses and artists' workshops extending below the ruins of a castle.

Museu d'Art Contemporani Vicente Aguilera Cerni ★

Diputació 20. Open Tue–Sun 10am–2pm, 4–6.30pm; €3. ☎964 32 91 52. www.macvac.es.
Works by Miró, Barjola, Serrano, Genovés, Chillida and Grupo Crónica are on display in a 15C palace.

▶ Return to Castelló; continue along the A 7 for 25km/15mi to Vall d'Uxo.

👥 Coves de Sant Josep

In Vall d'Uxo, follow signs to the caves (45min guided tours 10am–1pm, 3.30–5.30pm; Nov-Feb 10am–2pm. Closed 1 & 6 Jan, 25 Dec; €10; ☎964 69 05 76; www.covesdesantjosep.es). An underground river hollowed out these caves at the foot of the Parque Natural de la Sierra de Espadán. Tours by boat cover some 1.2km/0.75mi.

▶ Continue for 20km/12.4mi along the CV 230, then follow the N 234.

Segorbe

🚌 Explanada Estación 2.
Visit the **cathedral museum** (Pl. de San Cristóbal; open Tue–Sun 11am–1.30pm, exc during Mass; closed 1 Jan, Good Fri, 25 Dec; ☎964 71 10 14, www.catedraldesegorbe.es), which contains a large **collection of altarpieces** painted by the **Valencia School★**. There are several paintings by **Vicente Macip** (d. 1545), who was influenced by the Italian Renaissance style. Other works include a 15C marble Madonna by Donatello.

▶ Continue along the N 234 toward the coast.

Sagunt/Sagunto★

🚃Vía Férrea. 🎧'A Legendary Siege' sidebar above.
Historic Sagunto sits at the foot of a hill occupied by the ruins of a castle and Roman theatre.

Castillo & Teatro Romano de Sagunto

C. del Castillo, access via the old Jewish quarter. Open Apr–Oct Tue–Sat 10am–8pm, Sun & public hols 10am–2pm; Nov–Mar Tue–Sat 10am–6pm, Sun & public hols 10am–2pm. Closed 1 Jan, Good Fri, 25 Dec. 🕾962 65 58 59. www.turismo.sagunto.es.
The 1C **theatre**, restored and still in use, with fine acoustics, was built into the hillside by the Romans. The **Acropolis** consists of the ruins and remains of ramparts, temples and houses built by Iberians, Phoenicians, Carthaginians, Romans, Visigoths and Moors. Buildings to the west date to the War of Independence, when the French general Suchet besieged the town. The **view★** encompasses the town, countryside and sea.

Valencia 🎧See VALENCIA

VALENCIA TO XÀTIVA
122km/76mi.

▶ Leave Valencia along the coast road S.

Parque Natural de La Albufera

Centro de Interpretación del Racó de l'Olla. Ctra. El Palmar. Open 9am–2pm. Closed 1 & 6 Jan, 19 Mar, 24–25 & 31 Dec. 🕾963 86 80 50. www.albufera.com.
This vast body of water (*albufera*, 'small sea' in Arabic) south of Valencia is the largest freshwater lagoon in Spain, separated from the sea by an offshore bar, the Dehesa, that has been planted with rice since the 13C. Its eels appear on typical menus in restaurants in **El Palmar** (to the south) which also serve Valencia's signature dish, **paella**.

▶ Continue along the CV 500.

Cullera

www.culleraturismo.com.
This resort lies at the mouth of the River Júcar; its bay is demarcated to the north by a lighthouse, the Faro de Cullera. In the town are remains of a 13C castle.

▶ Head 27km/17mi S along the N 332.

Gandia

🚃Parc de L'estacio.
Gandia is at the centre of a *huerta* which produces large quantities of oranges. A high-rise-laden resort, Platja de Gandia, stretches from the harbour along a 3km/1.8mi-long sandy **beach**. There's a tranquil, family-orientated area and another section popular with college kids, thanks to famous nightclubs like the Coco Loco. (The fact that a TV show called *Gandía Shore*, modelled after *Jersey Shore*, was filmed here should tell you something about the type of nightlife you can expect).

Palacio Ducal dels Borja Gandia

C. del Duc Alfons El Vell 1. Open Mon–Sat 10am–1.30pm, 3–6.30pm (Apr–Sep 4–7.30pm). Sun & hols 10am–1.30pm. €6. 🕾962 87 14 65. www.palauducal.com.
The mansion in which St Francis Borja was born, now a Jesuit college, underwent considerable modification between the 16C and 18C. Only the patio remains Gothic in appearance and is typical of those along this coast. **The Colegiata de Santa María** (6–8pm; free; 🕾962 87 19 51), a collegiate church in nearby Plaza Mayor, was built in the 14C–15C and expanded in the 16C. It is one of the finest Gothic structures in Valencia province.

▶ Head inland along the CV 60.
Before Palomar, bear right on the A 7.

Xàtiva

🚃Xàtiva/Játiva.
www.xativaturismo.com
Known as 'the town of the thousand fountains', Xàtiva stands in a plain covered with a Mediterranean landscape of vineyards, orchards and cypress trees. The town was the birthplace of

two members of the Borja family who became popes, Calixtus III (1455–58) and Alexander VI, and, in 1591, of the painter **José Ribera**. The 16C **colegiata** (collegiate church; Pl. Calixto III; open Tue–Sun 10.30am–1pm; ℰ 962 28 14 81; www.xativa.es), modified in the 18C, faces the former **Hospital Royal**, which has an ornate Gothic-Plateresque facade.

Museo de l'Almodí

Corretgeria 46. Open 16 Sep–14 Jun Tue–Fri 10am–2pm, 4–6pm, Sat–Sun 10am–2pm; 15 Jun–15 Sep Tue–Fri 9.30am–2.30pm, Sat–Sun 10am–2.30pm €2.40; free Sun. ℰ962 27 65 97.
The Almudin, a Renaissance-style granary with a Gothic facade, houses fine Moorish-era artefacts along with gold and silverwork and paintings. An 11C **Moorish fountain** (pila) of pink marble is exceptional for its depiction of human figures, extremely rare in Islamic art.

Ermita de Sant Feliu

◯ On the castle road. Open Nov–Mar Mon–Sat 10am–1pm, 3–6pm, Sun & public hols 10am–1pm; Apr–Oct Mon–Sat 10am–1pm, 4–7pm, Sun & public hols 10am–1pm. ℰ962 27 33 46.
Built on the flank of the hill, this chapel contains a group of 15C–16C Valencian primitives. At the entrance, note the white marble **stoup★**.

Castillo

Subida al Castillo. Open Tue–Sun Apr–Sep 10am–7pm; Oct–Mar 10am–6pm. Closed 1 Jan, 25 Dec. €3.80. ℰ962 27 42 74.
With 30 towers and four fortified gates, this enormous castle is a mix of an Iberian-Roman fortress and a later Arab castle. Cascading down from the castle are the walls, which until the 10C enclosed the Roman city. A second wall was added later, which took in what today is the historic quarter.

ADDRESSES

🛏 STAY

🛏🛏🛏 **Hotel Mare Nostrum** – Molino 4, Peñíscola. ℰ964 48 16 26. www. hotelmarenostrum.net. 24 rooms. At the foot of the citadel near the beach, this small hotel has rooms with magnificent views. Breakfast is served on the rooftop terrace facing the old city.

🛏🛏🛏 **Albatros** – Clot de la Mota 11, Platja de Gandia. ℰ982 84 56 00. www. hotel-albatros.com. 46 rooms. ⊆€8. Set 300 metres from the beach, this hotel offers simple rooms and a small pool.

🛏🛏🛏 **Hostería del Mar** – Av. Papa Luna 18, Peñíscola. ℰ902 48 06 00. www.hosteriadelmar.net. 86 rooms. This updated beachside hotel has terracotta roofs and a grass-fringed courtyard pool. The restaurant specialises in fish and rice dishes as well as grilled meats.

🛏🛏🛏 **Hotel Mont Sant** – Ctra de Castillo, Xàtiva. ℰ962 27 50 81. www. mont-sant.com. 15 rooms. Restaurant 🛏🛏. Set amid a lush garden, this boutique hotel has rooms decorated with antiques as well as a modern, chalet-style annexe. The pool is shaded by orange trees and the Moorish city wall.

🛏🛏🛏 **El Jardin Vertical** – Nou 15, Vilafamés. ℰ964 32 99 38. www.eljardin vertical.com. 9 rooms. High in the village, this casa rural occupies a 17C mansion built over five levels. Rooms are cosy; some have fireplaces. Breakfast is served on a terrace with views to the horizon.

🍴 EAT

🍴🍴 **Casa La Abuela** – Reina 17, Xàtiva. ℰ962 27 05 25. www.casalaabuela xativa.es. Closed Tue eve & Sun eve. This acclaimed restaurant has specialised in rice dishes for 65 years.

🍴🍴 **Cervecería Casa Isidro** – Carrer de Formentera 50, Platja de Gandia. ℰ616 67 62 45. Cheap and cheerful, Casa Isidro serves textbook-perfect fried calamari, ensaladilla rusa and – importantly – a hefty free tapa with every drink.

🍴🍴 **El Peñón** – Santos Mártires 22, Peñíscola. ℰ964 48 07 16. www. elpenyon.es. The Peñón is a friendly old-town restaurant with attractive decor and a killer *fideuà*, the vermicelli 'paella' that was invented in these parts.

Morella

Morella has an amazing site★: 14C ramparts, punctuated by towers, form a mile-long girdle round a 1 004m/3 294ft hill, which the town ascends in tiers to castle ruins.

SIGHTS

A stroll around Morella's concentric streets reveals eye-catching mansions and religious buildings. The Iglesia de San Miguel houses a small Temps de Dinosaures **museum** (Tue–Sun 11am–2pm, 4–6pm, until 7pm Apr–Oct; €2; ℘964 17 31 17).

Iglesia de Santa María la Mayor★

Placeta de la Iglesia. Open Jul–Aug 11am–2pm, 4–7pm; Sep–Jun Tue–Sat 11–2pm, 4–6pm. Museum €1.50. ℘964 16 07 93.

One of the most interesting Gothic churches in the Levante has two fine portals and a raised Renaissance *coro* featuring a spiral staircase carved with biblical scenes. The small **museum** has a beautiful Valencian *Descent from the Cross* and a 14C Madonna by Sassoferrato.

Castillo

Pl. San Francisco. Open May–Oct 11am–7pm, Nov–Apr 11am–5pm. €3.50. ℘964 17 30 32.

On the way up are superb **views★** of the town, the ruins of the Convento de San Francisco with its Gothic cloisters, the 14C–15C aqueduct and the mountains.

EXCURSIONS

Santuario de la Balma

◐ 25km/15.5mi NW along the CV 14. Open 10am–5pm (Sun until 7pm). ℘964 17 70 95. www.zoritadelmaestrazgo.es. This unusual Marian sanctuary is where the Virgin supposedly appeared.

Mirambel

◐ 30km/19mi W on the CS 840. Bear left after 11km/7mi. This small, well-preserved mountain village retains its medieval character.

▶ **Population:** 2 794
◔ **Michelin Map:** 577 K 29.
🛈 **Info:** Pl. de San Miguel ℘964 17 30 32. www.en.morellaturistica.com.
◖ **Location:** In the Maestrazgo of Valencia, linked to the coast by the N 232 to Peñíscola (78km/49mi) and Castelló de la Plana (98km/61mi). 🚂Nearest station: Benicarló-Peñíscola (73km).

Vallivana

◐ 24km/15mi SE via the N 232. On the road down to Vinaròs, Morella and the Costa del Azahar, a few houses and a chapel make up this small village. The shrine houses a statue of the Virgin who, according to legend, stopped the plague in Morella in 1672.

Sant Mateu★

◐ 40km/25mi SE on the N 232 then right on the CV 132i. In the historic capital of the Maestrazgo region, the **Iglesia de Sant Mateu/ Arciprestal★** (open by guided tour only Tue–Sun; see website for times; €1.50; ℘964 41 66 58, www.santmateu.com) is one of the most remarkable Gothic sanctuaries in Valencia. It is reached by a 13C Romanesque portal, though the rest of the building dates to the 14C. Only the **chapel of San Clemente** was rebuilt in the 18C.

ADDRESSES

🍴 STAY

⊜⊜⊜ **El Hotel del Pastor** – San Julián 12, Morella. ℘964 16 10 16. www.hoteldelpastor.com. 12 rooms. Restaurant ⊜⊜⊜. This small, family-run establishment, with a lovely stone facade and traditional, has rooms outfitted with traditional Casatilian wood furniture. The restaurant serves local cuisine.

Alicante/ Alacant★

The Greeks called Alicante *Akra Leuka* (white citadel) and the Romans named it *Lucentum* (city of light). Today it buzzes as the cosmopolitan gateway to the Costa Blanca. Happily, most of its monuments are free.

WALKING TOUR

OLD TOWN
Follow the route on the map.

Explanada de España★
The most pleasant promenade in the region, running past the marina, is shaded by magnificent palms. Sunday concerts are held on the bandstand.

Catedral de San Nicolás
Pl. Abad Penalva. Open Mon–Fri 7.30am–1.30, 5.30–8pm, Sat–Sun from 8.30am. ℘965 21 26 62. www.concatedralalicante.com.
The 17C building on the site of a mosque – the city was only reconquered in 1296 – has a well-proportioned cupola, 45m/148ft high, over a Herreran nave. On calle Labradores, with its terraces, are the 18C Palacio Maisonnave, no. 9 (now the Municipal Archives; open Mon–Fri Sep–Jun 9am–2pm; Jul–Aug 9am–1.30pm), and an 18C mansion, no. 14, now a cultural centre.

Ayuntamiento (Town Hall)
Pl. del Ayuntamiento 1. Open Mon–Fri 9am–2pm. ℘965 14 91 00. www.alicante-ayto.es.
Visit the Rococo chapel of this imposing, golden, stone-balconied 18C palace with *azulejos* from Manises and reception rooms with blue silk hangings.

Museo de Bellas Artes Gravina★
C. Gravina, 13. Open Tue–Sat 10am–8pm Sun 10am–2pm. Jul–Aug Tue–Sat 11am–9pm, Sun 11am–3pm. ℘965 14 67 80. www.mubag.org.

▶ **Population:** 331 577
Michelin Map: 577 Q 28 (town plan) – map 123 COSTA BLANCA.
Info: Rambla Méndez Núñez 41, ℘965 20 00 00. www.alicanteturismo.com.
Location: Alicante is midway down Spain's Mediterranean coast, 110km/69mi from Cartagena. ▭Alicante; bus service from Alicante airport).
Don't Miss: A stroll along the Explanada by the harbour.
Timing: Start with a view from the Castillo de Santa Bárbara.
Kids: Castillo de Santa Bárbara.

The permanent collection occupies the first level of two 17C and 18C mansions. Decorative art objects of note include three intricate sideboards from the 16–17C. In the paintings section, notice the beautiful *Calvary,* by Rodrigo de Osona (late 15C), and *Saint John, Saint Joseph and Child,* by **Cristobal Llorens** (16C). A view of Alicante by Vincente Suarez Ordóñez shows what the city was like in the early 19C.

Iglesia de Santa María
Pl. de Santa María. Open 12–1pm, 6–7.30pm. ℘965 21 60 26.
Formerly a mosque, the church was altered in the 17C when Churrigueresque decoration was added. Its 8C Baroque façade★ has wreathed columns, pillars and breaks in its cornices. Note the graceful Renaissance marble fonts and a painting of John the Baptist and John the Apostle by Rodrigo de Osuna the Younger.

Museo de Arte Contemporáneo de Alicante★
Pl. de Santa María 3. Open Tue–Sat 10am–8pm, Sun & hols 10am–2pm. ℘965 21 31 56. www.maca-alicante.es.
Opened in 2011, the MACA's most prized pieces, mostly 20C painting and sculp-

ture, were donated by sculptor Eugenio Sempere. There's a rotation of temporary exhibitions of varying quality. Famous artists' works represented here include Miró, Picasso, Gargallo, Tàpies Dalí, Vasarely, Braque, Chagall and Kandinsky.

👥 Castillo de Santa Bárbara

Frente Playa Postiguet.

🚠 Ascend by lift and walk down, either all the way (good views) or to the halfway stop. Guided tours Mon–Sat. Open 10am– 8pm (Apr–Sep 10pm). Guided tour €2.70. ☎965 14 71 60. www.castillodesantabarbara.com.

This Moorish fortress atop Benacantil hill dates to the 9C, though outbuildings were raised in the 16C. The Revellín del Bon Repós rampart was built in the 18C. The Philip II hall is a worthy highlight. The Plaza de la Torreta is surrounded by the oldest buildings. A platform commands a fine **view**★ of the harbour and town. The 16C section is at the halfway stop on the lift; the 17C perimeter is lower down. A footpath leads to the medieval streets and tiny squares of working-class Santa Cruz.

SIGHT

MARQ (Museo Arqueológico Provincial de Alicante)★★

Pl. Doctor Gómez Ulla. Open Tue–Sat 10am–7pm (Sat until 8.30pm), Sun & public hols 10am–2pm. Jul & Aug 10am–2pm, 6-10pm. €3. ☎965 14 90 00. www.marqalicante.com.

MARQ makes archaeology accessible to all with a riveting presentation focussed on the ancients of the area. The museum is organised into large halls (Prehistory, Iberian, Roman, Middle Ages and Modern) around a space devoted to archaeology itself. Here you can get right into excavations in a cave, a church and an underwater site.

EXCURSIONS

ELCHE/ELX★

🚗 24km/15mi SW. 🚉 Pl. del Parc 3. ☎966 65 81 96. www.visitelche.com. 🚆Elche Parque.

El Palmeral, Elche/Elx
©Turespaña

Elche (Elx in Valencian) hugs the Vinalopó river. The **Dama de Elche** (4C BC), a masterpiece of Iberian art now in the Museo Arqueológico de Madrid, was discovered in **La Alcudia** (2km/1.2mi S). **El Misteri** d'Elx is a medieval verse drama with an all-male cast that recounts the Dormition, Assumption and Coronation of the Virgin. It is on UNESCO's Oral and Intangible Heritage of Humanity list (played in the Basílica de Santa María; Aug, Oct and Nov; www.misteridelx.com).

El Palmeral (Palm Grove) ★★ (Porta de la Morera 49; open 10am–sunset) – The groves, planted by the Phoenicians and expanded by the Arabs, are the largest in Europe, with more than 200 000 trees, and are a UNESCO World Heritage site. The palms flourish with the aid of a remarkable irrigation system. Female trees produce dates, and the fronds from the male trees are used in Palm Sunday processions and handicrafts.

Huerto del Cura★★ (open from 10am; see website for closing times; €5; ☎966 61 00 11; http://jardin.huertodelcura.com) – This delightful garden of Mediterranean and subtropical plants lies under magnificent palm trees; one, with seven trunks, is said to be nearly two centuries old.

Parque Municipal★ (Pas. de l'Estació) – A well-tended garden with palm trees. **Museo Arqueológico y de Historia de Elche (MAHE)** (Diagonal del Palau; open Mon–Sat 10am–6pm, Sun & hols 10am–3pm; €3; ☎966 65 82 03) – The museum is in the Moorish Palacio de Altamira.

The archaeological section traces Elche from its origins to the Visigothic era. Notable are ceramics from the Iberian period and the *Venus of Illicis*, a carved white marble Roman sculpture.

Basílica de Santa María (Pl. Congreso Eucarístico; open 7am– 1pm, 5.30–9pm; tower €2; ℘965 45 15 40) – This monumental 17C–18C Baroque basilica with a beautiful portal by Nicolás de Bussi is the setting for the annual mystery play. View the palm groves from the tower. Nearby are the 17C–18C Almohad tower, **La Calahorra** (Uberna 14), and the Baños árabes.

Baños Árabes (Pas. de Santa Llucía 13; access through a side door of the Convento de la Merced; open Tue–Sat 10am–2pm, 3–6pm, Sun & public hols 10am–2pm; €1; ℘965 45 28 87) – An exhibition inside the arched underground galleries details the culture of the Arabic baths in the 12C.

La Alcudia: archaeological site and museum (Ctra Dolores; 2km/1.2mi S; open Tue–Sat 10am–6pm; €5; ℘966 61 15 06, www.laalcudia.ua.es) – The remains and a museum reveal the story of this city from the Neolithic period to its decline in Visigoth times.

🚗 DRIVING TOUR

INLAND THROUGH ALICANTE
176km/110mi N.

▷ Take the N 340 in San Juan, then the Alcoi road and then turn right.

Cuevas de Canalobre
Guided tours (45min) Holy Week & Jul–Aug 10.30am–7.30pm, Sep–Jun Mon–Fri 10.30am–4.50pm, Sat–Sun until 5.50pm. Closed 1 Jan, Mon after Easter Mon, 25 Dec. €7. ℘965 69 92 50. www.turismobusot.com.
These caves are 700m/2 296.5ft up Mount Cabezón de Oro and take their name from their spectacular candelabra (*canalobre*)-like formations.

▷ Return to the N 340 through groves of fig and carob trees.

Jijona/Xixona
Every Spaniard knows this village's name for its *turrón*, a nougat confection, typically made of almonds, honey, sugar and egg white that's eaten primarily during the holiday season.
You can visit – and roll out of – the **Turrón Museum** and factory (El Lobo; Ctra Jijona-Busot; open: museum, Jan–mid-Jul Mon–Sat 10am–1pm, 4–5.30pm; mid Jul–Sept Mon–Sat 10am–1pm, 3.30–6.30pm; factory usually operates mid-Jun–mid Dec, see operations from a viewing gallery in the museum; €1.50 low season, €3 high season; ℘965 61 07 12; www.museodelturron.com).
Beyond Jijona the road twists up through almond terraces to the **Puerto de la Carrasqueta★** (1 024m/3 360ft), a pass with a view toward Alicante.

Alcoy/Alcoi
🚌Plaza Estación.
Alcoy is an industrial town in a mountain setting. Every year, between 22 and 24 April, the **Moors and Christians★** (Moros y Cristianos) **festival** (www.alcoi. org) celebrates a vital Christian victory in 1276. It is the biggest, most colourful and noisiest of Spain's many Moors and Christians events.

▷ Take the CV 795 to Barxell, then follow the CV 794.

Bocairent
🚌Camino de la Estación, Ontiyent 10km/7mi N. www.bocairent.org.
The church in this hilltop market village has a **Museo Parroquial** (Parish Museum; Abadía 36; 45min guided tours by appointment only; €3; ℘962 90 50 62) with works by **Juan de Juanes** (1523–79) – who died here – and his school.

▷ Take the CV 81.

Villena

🚌Ronda de la Estación.

The spectacularly located **Castillo de la Atalaya** (guided tours every hour Tue–Sun 11am–1pm, Tue–Sat & public hols also 4–5pm; €3; 📞965 80 38 04, www.turismovillena.com), of Arabic origin, dominates its former feudal domain. Among its owners have been famed men of letters: **Don Juan Manuel** in the 14C and the poet prince, **Henry of Aragon** (**Marqués de Villena**, 1384–1434). The original castle keep survives, with circular towers in the corners, and large 15C Homenaje (homage) towers. There are fine views from the walls.

Iglesia Arcedianal de Santiago (Pl. de Santiago; visit by guided tour only, from the tourist office every 30min Tue–Sat 11am–2pm exc Fri, 1–2pm; Sun & public hols 11.30am–1pm; €1; 📞965 81 39 19, www.turismovillena.com) – This Gothic-Renaissance church (14C–17C) with a bell tower stands near the town hall. **Spiral pillars★** support Gothic vaults and a Renaissance-style baptismal font.

Museo Arqueológico (Archaeological Museum) – (Pl. de Santiago 1; open Tue–Fri 10am–2pm, Sat–Sun & public hols 11am–2pm; closed 1 Jan, 25 Dec; €2; 📞965 80 11 50; www.museovillena.com) – Housed in the town hall (Palacio Municipal) with a fine Renaissance facade and patio, this museum displays solid gold from the Bronze Age (1500–1000 BC). The outstanding **Villena Treasure★★** includes jewellery and gourds decorated with sea urchin shell patterns.

ADDRESSES

☎ STAY

🛏🛏 **La Milagrosa Bed & Breakfast** – Villavieja 8, Alicante. 📞965 21 69 18. www.lamilagrosa.eu. 20 rooms. This basic *pensión* has bright rooms; some overlook the Plaza de Santa María. There's a garden-terrace upstairs.

🛏🛏 **Hostal Les Monges Palace** – San Agustín 4, Alicante. 📞965 21 50 46. www.lesmonges.es. 28 rooms. ☕€6. A prime location in the old town makes this bright hotel blending old and new a safe bet. Note the marble staircase and large mirrors and windows, vestiges from the original 18C building.

🛏🛏🛏 **Eurostars Mediterránea Plaza** – Pl. de Ayuntamiento 6, Alicante. 📞965 21 0188. www.eurostarshotels.com. 49 rooms. ☕€8. Located in the historical centre, the streamlined Eurostars has all the creature comforts you expect from an international chain.

₯/EAT

🍴🍴🍴 **La Taberna del Gourmet** – San Fernando 10, Alicante. 📞965 20 42 33. www.latabernadelgourmet.com.

Always bustling, this tavern serves elegant mains at dinner and relaxed tapas at lunch. On your way out, snap up local ingredients from the on-site gourmet shop.

🍴🍴🍴🍴 **Nou Manolín** – Villegas 3. Alicante. 📞965 20 03 68. www.noumanolin.com. This Alicante institution, modern with a rustic feel, serves refined seafood dishes.

🍴🍴🍴🍴 **La Ereta** – Parque de La Ereta. 📞965 14 32 50. www.laereta.es. On a hillside between the castle and the city, La Ereta has large windows overlooking Alicante. Expect gorgeously presented refined local dishes.

TAPAS

El Cantó – Alemania 26. 📞965 92 56 50. Hand-cut *jamón* and *gambas al ajillo* are terrific here.

Cervecería Sento Rambla – Gerona 1. 📞646 93 22 13. Well-made salads, sandwiches and tapas keep this place hopping at breakfast, lunch and dinner.

NIGHTLIFE

Barrio del Carmen – After 11pm on weekends, Alicante's old quarter is transformed into one huge disco.

Puerto de Alicante – This is the place to be on summer nights.

Costa Blanca★

The 'White Coast' stretches south from Valencia to Murcia. It's mosly flat and sandy, with occasional highlands where the sierras drop to the sea. A hot climate, low rainfall, dazzling light, long beaches and turquoise waters attract vast numbers of tourists fleeing cooler climes.

- **Michelin Map:** 577 P 29–30, Q 29–30 – Communitat Valenciana (Alicante/Alacant), Murcia.
- **Info:** Altea: Plaza José María Planelles, ℘965 84 41 14. Benidorm: Plaza de Canalejos 1, ℘96 585 13 11. Denia: Dr. Manuel Lattur 1, ℘966 42 23 67. www.costablanca.org.
- **Location:** Costa Blanca towns are linked by the N 332 and the AP 7 toll motorway.
- **Don't Miss:** Guadalest.
- **Kids:** Tierra Mítica amusement park.

🚗 DRIVING TOUR

DENIA TO GUADALEST
115km/71mi. Allow 2 days.

Dénia
🚃Denia.
www.denia.net.
The former Greek colony became Roman *Dianium*. Denia today is a fishing harbour, toy manufacturing centre and seaside resort. In the fortress (€3, including museum; ℘966 42 06 56) above town is an archaeological museum. The coast south of here is steep, rocky and forested.

Cap de Sant Antoni★
Near the lighthouse on this headland, a last foothill of the Sierra del Mongó, is a **view**★ toward Xàbia and the Cabo de la Nao headland.

Xàbia★
The attractive old quarter is on the hill around a fortified 14C Gothic church. The modern part is set around the harbour, the excellent beach, and Parador.

Cap de la Nau★
The climb affords views over Xàbia at the foot of the Sierra del Mongó then enters thick pinewoods where villas stand in clearings. Cap de la Nau is an eastern extension of the Sierras Béticas (Baetic Cordillera) that continues under the sea to reappear as the island of Ibiza. There is a beautiful **view**★ south from the point down the coast to the Penyal d'Ifac. Sea caves (approached by boat) and charming creeks such as **La Gra-** nadella (south) and **Cala Blanca** (north) are excellent for diving.

Calp
The **Penyal d'Ifac**★, a rocky outcrop 332m/1 089ft high, is the setting of Calp (Calpe in Castilian). A path leads to the top of the Penyal (🚶 1hr) with views of the coast , salt pans, mountain chains and, northwards, a stretch reaching Cap de la Nau.
The Sierra de Bernia road twists and turns before crossing the spectacular Barranco de Mascarat (Mascarat Ravine) in the hinterland to Cabo de la Nao.

Altea
Altea's white walls, rose-coloured roofs and glazed blue tile domes rise in tiers up a hillside overlooking the sea, a symphony of colour and reflected light below the Sierra de Bernia. A walk through the alleys to the church, and then the view from the square over the village and beyond to the Penyal d'Ifac, will reveal the attraction of so many painters towards Altea.

Benidorm
🚃Benidorm.
The excellent climate, cheap packaged holidays from Britain and Germany and

two immense beaches (the Levante and the Poniente) that curve around either side of a small rock promontory define this village-cum-tourism megalith. From the Balcón del Mediterraneo lookout, there are fine **views**★ of the beaches and sea. The oft-overlooked old quarter stands behind the point, close to the blue-domed church.

♣♣ Terra Mítica

3km/2mi from Benidorm. Exit 65 A of the AP 7. Open second wk Apr–Oct 10.30am–8pm/midnight; see website for full schedule. €39; next day free. ✆902 02 02 20. www.terramiticapark.com.

This excellent theme park inspired by Egypt, Greece, Rome and Iberia has attractions and shows for visitors of all ages and tastes.

Main attractions – In 'Ancient Egypt', enter the Pyramid of Terror, or descend the Cataracts of the Nile on a bracing white-water roller-coaster ride. In 'Greece', emulate Theseus in the Labyrinth of the Minotaur, or experience the sensation of falling down a waterfall in the Fury of Triton. The Magnus Colossus in Rome is a spectacular wooden roller coaster. In the Flight of the Phoenix, enjoy the excitement of a free fall from 54m/177ft, or battle against currents and whirlpools in the Rapids of Argos.

▷ Take the CV 70 to Callosa d'En Sarrià, then head along the CV 755 to Alcoi.

On the drive inland, you pass through small valleys teeming with all sorts of fruit trees including citrus and medlars. The picturesque village of **Polop** stretches up a hillside. Beyond, the landscape becomes more arid but the views more extensive and the mountains more magnificent.

Guadalest★

Guadalest rises above terraced valleys of olive and almond trees and perches on a limestone escarpment of the Sierra de Aitana. The **site**★ is breathtaking. The village, forced halfway up a ridge of rock, is a stronghold accessible only

through an archway cut into stone. Walk round the **Castillo de San José** (Iglesia 2; open 10am–8pm; closed 1 Jan, 25 Dec; €4; ✆965 88 52 98), where ruins remain of fortifications wrecked by an earthquake in 1744. The splendid view takes in the Guadalest reservoir with its reflections of surrounding mountain crests, the amazing site of the old village and, in the distance, the sea.

ADDRESSES

☜ STAY

◐▣ **Hostal L'Ánfora** – Expl. Cervantes 8, Dénia. ✆966 43 01 01. www.hostal lanfora.com. 20 rooms. This small building with its distinctive terracotta facade is located at the fishing port. Although small and basic, the rooms are bright and clean with views of the local fishing fleet.

◐▣▣ **Hostal Triskel** – Sor María Gallart 3. Xàbia. ✆966 46 21 91. www.hostal-triskel.com. 5 rooms. ⊐€5. In the heart of the historic district in a beautiful building, Triskel has individualised rooms with antiques, terracotta floor tiles, porcelain switches and retro phones.

⦿/EAT

◐▣▣ **Oustau de Altea** – Mayor 5, Altea. ✆965 842 078. www.oustau.es. In a brightly decorated, quaint house in the old town, this restaurant specialises in French-Mediterranean cuisine. Try to snag a terrace table.

◐▣▣▣ **Villa Venecia** – Pl. Sant Jaumé, Benidorm. ✆965 855 466. www. hotelvillavenecia.com. White-tablecloth Mediterranean fare is served in the waterside dining roomm or on the terrace of this five-star hotel (◐▣▣▣).

TAPAS

La Cava Aragonesa – Pl. de la Constitución (also entry on Callejón Santo Domingo), Benidorm Old Town. ✆966 80 12 06. www.lacavaaragonesa.es. This typically Spanish restaurant and tapas bar, with its cured hams hanging from the ceiling, is a godsend in this gastronomically challenged resort.

Murcia★

Murcia, an historic but also booming university town, lies along the Segura in a fertile market-gardening area *(huerta)* known for its plethora of golf courses.

A BIT OF HISTORY

Murcia, founded in the reign of Abd ar-Rahman II in 825 as Madina Mursiya, was reconquered by the Spanish in 1266. Up to the 18C, it prospered from agriculture and silk weaving.

SIGHTS

Catedral★

Pl. Cardenal Belluga. Open Sep-Jun Mon-Sat 7am-1pm, 5-8pm, Sun 7am-1pm, 6.30-8pm, Jul-Aug Mon-Fri 7am-1pm, 6.30-8pm, Sat & Sun 7am-1.15pm, 6.30-9pm. ℘968 21 63 44.

The original 14C cathedral is camouflaged beneath Renaissance and Baroque additions. The **facade**★, with an arrangement of columns and curves,

Star vaulting, Capilla de los Vélez, Catedral

© F. Monheim/B. Opitz/age fotostock

▶ **Population:** 442 123
◔ **Michelin Map:** 123. Costa Blanca.
🄸 **Info:** Plaza Cardenal Belluga. ℘968 35 87 49. www.murciaturistica.es.
◖ **Location:** 50km/31mi from the coast. 🚃Murcia del Carmen.

is a brilliant example of Baroque. The impressive belfry, 95m/311ft in height, was completed by Ventura Rodríguez in the 18C. The interior, beyond the entry cupola, is preponderantly Gothic, apart from the 16C **Capilla de los Junterones** (fourth south chapel), which has rich Renaissance decoration.

The **Capilla de los Vélez**★ (off the ambulatory) is sumptuous Late Gothic with splendid star vaulting and wall decoration with Renaissance and Mudéjar motifs. The sacristy, approached through successive Plateresque doors (beautiful panels on the first), is covered by an unusual radiating dome. The walls are richly panelled with Plateresque carving below and Baroque above.

Museo Salzillo★

Pl. San Agustín 3. Open mid-Jun–mid-Sep Mon–Fri 10am–2pm. Rest of year Mon–Sat 10am–5pm, Sun & public hols 11am–2pm. Closed 1, 6 Jan, Holy Week, 1 May, 9 Jun, 6, 25 Dec. €5. ℘968 29 18 93. www.museosalzillo.es.

The museum possesses Salzillo's masterpieces including the eight polychrome wood sculptures of **pasos** carried in the Good Friday procession during Holy Week, kept in side chapels off the nave of the Church of Jesus. The deep emotion on the faces is impressive. The museum also contains vivid terracotta pieces used to create scenes from the life of Jesus.

Palacio Episcopal★

Pl. del Cardenal Belluga.

Built between 1748 and 1768, this palace shows a clear influence of Italian Baroque. The two-level patio has medallions embossed with figures of bishops in the pediments of the windows, and the courtyard is decorated with many carved coats of arms. This leads to the grand staircase topped with a cupola. Don't miss the circular chapel.

Museo de Bellas Artes – MuBAM★

C. Obispo Frutos 8–12. Open Sep–Jun Tue–Sat 10am–2pm, 5–8pm (Sat from 11am), Sun & hols 11am–2pm. Jul–Aug Tue–Fri 10am–2pm, Sat–Sun 11am–2pm. ℘968 23 93 46.
www.museosdemurcia.com.
On the ground floor is an altarpiece by Juan de Vitoria (16C) representing Calvary and the Martyrdom of Santiago. On the first floor, which is devoted to the Golden Age, is *St Jerome* (1613), attributed to José de Ribera. In the same room is a beautiful Crucifixion by Murillo (1670) and, by the same artist, a moving Ecce Homo★.

Museo Santa Clara★★

Po. Alfonso X El Sabio 1. Open Tue–Sat 10am–1pm, 4–6.30pm, Sun & hols 10am–1pm; Jul–Aug Tue–Sun 10am–1pm. Free. ℘968 27 23 98.
www.murciaturistica.es.
This monastery was founded in the 14C on the site of an Almohad palace that had not been completely destroyed. The Gothic cloister was built around the central basin of the Arabian palace. The garden beds have been replanted with species in accordance with the original flora. Behind the magnificent arcades of the cloister stands a portico★ with three richly decorated arches, which gave access to one of the main halls of the palace.
Excavations have unearthed the oldest remains including traces of a courtyard belonging to a 12C Almoravid palace. In the centre stand the remains of a colonnaded pavilion, in which is preserved a fragment of 12C painting representing a flutist★. The museum★ maintains a collection held by the community of the convent of Santa Clara. Note a Christ on the Cross★★ (1770), by Francisco Salzillo. Carved life size, the piece shows exceptional balance and features a serene face.

EXCURSIONS

Orihuela★

◗ 24km/15mi NE on the A 7. 🚆Orihuela Intermodal. www.orihuelaturistica.es
This peaceful town, with its many churches, lies along the Segura, which provides water for market gardens *(huertas)* and for the local palm grove. For centuries, Orihuela was a university town. The house of the early-20C poet and dramatist Miguel Hernández is now a museum (Miguel Hernández 73; open Jun–Sep Tue–Sat 10am–2pm, 5–8pm; Oct–May Tue–Sat 10am–2pm, 4–7pm; Sun & public hols 10am–2pm year-round; closed 1, 6 Jan, 25 Dec; ℘965 30 63 27; www.miguelhernandezvirtual.es).

Catedral del Salvador★

C. Mayor. Open Tue–Fri 10.30am–2pm, 4–6.30pm, Sat 10.30am–2pm. €2. ℘966 74 36 27.
Constructed in the 14C–16C, the cathedral has a Renaissance north doorway. The interior has three cruciform Gothic naves, an ambulatory and unusual vaulting with spiral ribs.
The stalls of the choir are carved in Baroque style. There are notable Renaissance grilles around the choir and presbytery. The Museo de la Catedral houses a *Temptation of St Thomas Aquinas* by Velázquez, a *Christ* by Morales and a *Mary Magdalene* by Ribera.
The Palacio del Obispo on calle Ramón y Cajal behind the cathedral has a magnificent 18C patio.

Colegio de Santo Domingo

Adolfo Clavarana (north of the city). Open Tue–Sat 10am–2pm, 5–9pm, winter 9.30am–1.30pm, 4–7pm Sun & hols year-round 10am–2pm. Closed 1, 6 Jan, 17 Jul, 25 Dec. €2. ℘965 30 02 40. www.cdsantodomingo.com.
This monumental building (16C–18C), formerly the university, started in Renaissance style and morphed into Baroque. The long college facade con-

ceals two sober cloisters (17C–18C). The 18C **church**★ is covered with murals and exuberant stucco mouldings.

Museo de la Muralla

Río. Open Tue–Sat 10am–2pm, 4–7pm (5–8pm in summer), Sun & public hols 10am–2pm. ✆965 30 46 98.

Go below street level to the remains of the city wall and dwellings and baths from the Moorish era, then back up to a Gothic palace and Baroque building. The **Iglesia de Santiago** (Pl. de Santiago 2; open Tue–Fri 10am–2pm, 4–6.30pm, Sat 10am–2pm; ✆965 30 46 45), near the town hall, is Gothic with a Renaissance transept and apse. It was founded by the Catholic Monarchs whose yoke-and-arrow emblems, together with a statue of St James, are on the Gothic portal. Inside, note statues attributed to Salzillo in the side chapels.

Santuario de la Fuensanta (La Fuensanta Shrine)

◗ 7km/4.3mi S. Follow the signs from Puente Viejo.

From the shrine of the Virgen de la Fuensanta, patron saint of Murcia, enjoy fine **views** of the town and outlying *huertas*.

Cartagena

◗ 62km/39mi SE along the N 301.
🚂Cartagena.

In 223 BC this bay settlement was captured by the Carthaginians; it was subsequently colonised by the Romans as *Cartago Nova*. Philip II fortified the surrounding hilltops, and Charles III built the Arsenal. The city is known for its dramatic Holy Week processions.

Near the Plaza del Ayuntamiento is an early **submarine** invented by native son Isaac Peral in 1888. From the top of the **Castillo de la Concepción** (C. Gisbert) there is a **view** of the harbour and the ruins of the former Romanesque cathedral of Santa María la Vieja.

Today the city is getting a second look by many Spaniards seeking a side of culture with their sunny holiday. **Cala Cortina**, a wild, hidden-gem beach outside the city, is reason enough to visit.

Museo Teatro Romano★★

Pl. del Ayuntamiento. Open May–Sep Tue–Sat 10am–8pm (Oct–Apr until 6pm). Sun 10am–2pm. €6. ✆968 504 802. www.teatroromanocartagena.org.

After touring the remains of this restored Roman theatre, travel through a 'Corridor of History' from the city's origins to the present.

Castillo de la Concepción★

Open Jul–mid-Sep daily 10am–8pm, Apr–Jun and mid-Sep–Oct Tue–Sun until 7pm, Nov–Mar Tue–Sun until 5.30pm. €3.50. ✆968 500 093.

This hilltop castle not only gives great viwes over the city but also has an exhibit on Cartagena's history. There is a lift for those who don't fancy the walk.

Museo Arqueológico Municipal★

Ramón y Cajal 45. Open May–Sep Tue–Fri 10am–2pm, 5–8pm; Sun 11am–2pm. ✆968 128 968. www.mueoarqueologicocartagena.es.

Built on a Roman burial ground (which you can see), this museum gives a good introduction to the history of the city. Highlights include a Roman tiled floor and a sculpture of a child's head dating to 1AD.

ARQUA - Museo Nacional de Arqueología Subacuática★★

Po. del Muelle Alfonso XII 22. Open Tue–Sat 10am–8pm (mid-Apr–mid-Oct 9pm). Sun & public hols 10am–3pm. €3; free Sat (from 2pm), Sun. ✆968 12 11 66. http://museoarqua.mcu.es.

This museum displays underwater finds, notably Phoenician, Punic and Roman amphorae. Maps and models of vessels (galleys, biremes and triremes) illustrate seafaring in times past.

Museo Naval★

Muelle de Alfonso XII. Open mid-Jun–Sep Tue–Fri 9am–2pm, rest of year Tue–Sat 10am–1.30pm, 4.30–7.30pm; Sun 10am–2pm. €3; ✆968 12 71 38.

Housed in an 18th-century arsenal, this museum gives an overview of Cartagena's role as a crucial naval port. Highlights include an exhibition on Isaac Peral, the man who invented the submarine.

Mar Menor

◯ At La Manga: 81km/51mi SE via the N 301 and MU 312 and 33km/21mi from Cartagena.

The Mar Menor, or Little Sea, is a lagoon separated from the open Mediterranean by **La Manga**, a sand bar 500m/1 640ft wide that extends from the eastern end of the Cabo de Palos headland. Gilthead bream, mullet and king prawns are fished from its shallow salt basin.

La Manga del Mar Menor is a large, elongated sports-oriented seaside resort with futuristic tower blocks stretching for miles.

In **Santiago de la Ribera**, where there is no natural beach, pontoons with changing cabins line the seafront.

Alcantarilla

◯ 9km/5.6mi W on the N 340.

The **Museo Etnológico de la Huerta** (Av. Príncipe; open Tue–Fri 9am–7pm/8pm in summer; Sat 10am–2pm, 4–7.30pm; Sun 10am–2pm; closed Aug; ℘968 893 866, www.alcantarilla.es) is dedicated to local **agriculture and irrigation**. Among the orange trees are white rustic dwellings (barracas) and a **noria**, a giant waterwheel devised for irrigation by the Moors.

Lorca★

◯ 67km/42mi SW along the N 340-E 12.
🚂Alameda de Menchirón.

Lorca lies in an irrigated valley at the foot of a hill crowned by a **castle**, the **Fortaleza del Sol** 👫 (open daily 10.30am until dusk; €6 ℘902 40 00 47; www.lorcatallerdeltiempo.es), where visitors can step back into the Middle Ages with interactive exhibits.

The main sights are the **Plaza de España**, surrounded by the Baroque facades of the **ayuntamiento** (town hall); the **Juzgado** (Law Courts), embellished with a corner sculpture; the **Colegiata de San Patricio** (℘968 46 99 66), a collegiate church built in the 16C and 18C; and the **Palacio de Guevara★★** (open Tue–Sat 10am–1pm, 5.30–7.30pm; Sun

10.30am–2pm; ℘902 40 00 47; www.lorcatallerdeltiempo.es). Its late 17C doorway, although in poor condition, is a fine example of Baroque.

Caravaca de la Cruz★

◯ 70km/44mi W along the C 415.
🛈 Las Monjas 17. ℘968 70 24 24.
www.turismocaravaca.org.

This attractive town is topped by its castle of Muslim origin, which was extended in the 15C by the Knights Templars. Within the compound the **Santuario de la Santa Cruz** is an impressive Baroque monument. The town below retains superb Renaissance architecture, the jewel in the crown being the **Iglesia de San Salvador**.

ADDRESSES

🛏 **STAY**

◒◒ **Hotel Arco de San Juan** – Pl. Ceballos 10, Murcia. ℘968 21 04 55. www.arcossanjuan.com. 97 rooms. Restaurant ◒◒◒. Stylish, contemporary rooms lie behind the neoclassical facade of this three-star hotel near the cathedral. The restaraurant, Los Churrascos, serves regional cuisine with a modern touch.

◒◒ **NH Cartagena** – Real 2, Cartagena. ℘968 12 09 08. www.nh-hotels.com. 100 rooms. Next to the sea and a short walk from the port, this modern hotel has chic rooms, some with balconies, and a gastrobar serving tapas and cocktails.

🍽**EAT**

◒ **Restaurante Casa Corro** – Av. Dr García Rogel 23, Orihuela. ℘965 30 29 63. www.restaurantecasacorro.com. Hearty regional cuisine is on the menu at this century-old restaurant. House specialities include cocido (stew) and roast goat. There are eight simple rooms overhead (◒).

◒◒ **Bodega La Fuente** – C. Jara 27, Cartagena. ℘868 04 73 22. Yes, they really salt-cure their own anchovies at this legendary corner restaurant that also happens to make sigh-worthy crêpes.

Balearic Islands

The Balearics evoke summer sunshine and frenetic nightlife, but they have a fascinating history and culture. You'd be forgiven for thinking there isn't an unspoilt corner left here – the islands heave with tourists – but happily, over 40% of the nature in the archipelago is protected by law.

Highlights

The **Balearic archipelago** lies off Spain's Levante, in the Mediterranean, and covers 5 000sq km/1 900sq mi. It includes three large islands, **Mallorca, Menorca and Ibiza**, each with a distinctive character; two smaller inhabited isles, Formentera and Cabrera; and a smatteirng of uninhabited islets. The three large islands have airports, and inter-island ferries link them together. **Palma,** the capital of **Mallorca** and the only *city* city in the archipelago, is also the administrative seat of the Balearic Autonomous Community. Many locals speak a Balearic dialect of Catalan, though all speak Castilian with with ease.

The Balearics took off as **holiday islands** in the 1950s with Mallorca in the vanguard of mass tourism. Initially a fashionable 'jet-set' destination, *Majorca* (as it was then known in English) by the 1980s became synonymous with the worst excesses of holiday commercialisation. To reverse the scourge, the island rebranded itself, demolishing old hotels and launching marketing campaigns to lure visitors inland. Today mass tourism continues, but the island attracts enough fashionable, culture-hungry visitors to support a growing cohort of designer hotels, *agroturismos* and fine-dining restaurants. Palma, once a mere waypoint for most tourists, is now a bona fide city-break destination.

Ibiza was put through a similar mass-tourism ringer. A sleepy bohemian oasis in the 60s and 70s known for its back-to-the-landers and art communes, it succumbed to the mass tourism boom and was never the same again – just ask any local over 65. But idyllic rural pockets still exist away from the noisy centres, especially the farther inland you venture. Ibiza's thrilling, anything-goes club scene remains as relevant as ever and keeps the island feeling young.

Menorca is the quietest of the main islands, all quiet sandy beaches, storied medieval sites and natural attractions. Its tranquility and exclusive feel draw a stream of well-heeled families, couples and solo travellers from Northern Europe

Formentera is where Balearic islanders go to get away from it all. Cruise ships aren't allowed to dock here, meaning its (protected) beaches are far less jammed.

Across the archipelago, the best deals are had in the off season, between October and May, when it often feels like you have the islands to yourself.

Cala Salada, Ibiza

© Jon Arnold Images/hemis.fr

Mallorca★★★

Mallorca, the largest and by far most visited of the Balearic Islands, is a holiday playground for Northern Europeans, particularly Brits and Germans. The dramatic, steep cliff landscapes of the north, indented with coves, contrast with the beaches of the gentle south with their crystalline turquoise waters. Remember: For every slab-like seaside resort you come across, there are innumerable picturesque villages in the interior lying in wait – you just have to find them.

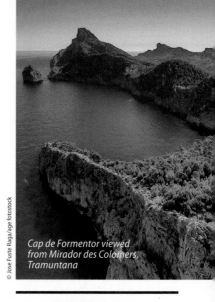

Cap de Formentor viewed from Mirador des Colomers, Tramuntana

© Jose Fuste Raga/age fotostock

LANDSCAPE AND TRADITION

The **Serra de Tramuntana** in the north-west rises in limstone crests of which the highest is **Puig Major** (1 445m/4 740ft), parallel to the coast.

In fact, the island's jagged mountains are high enough to block winds from the mainland. Pines, junipers and holm oaks cover the slopes, interspersed with Mallorca's characteristic olive trees. Terraces of vegetables and fruit trees surround hillside villages. The central plain, **Es Pla**, is divided by low walls through meadows and fig and almond orchards. Market towns, with outlying windmills to pump water, retain their medieval street plan. The **Serra de Levant** to the east is hollowed out into countless secret caves.

A BIT OF HISTORY

A Short-lived kingdom (1262–1349) – James I (Jaume I) of Aragón recaptured Mallorca from the Moors in 1229 and 30 years later united Mallorca-Baleares, Roussillon and Montpellier under a kingdom the he bequeathed to his son, James II. He and his successor, Sancho, founded new Catalan towns. Pedro IV seized the archipelago in 1343 to reunite it with Aragón. A merchant navy was established, bringing prosperity, and a school of cartography rapidly became famous.

- ▶ **Population:** 894 897
- ⚅ **Michelin Map:**
  579 –Baleares.
- 🛈 **Info:** Palma: Plaza de la Reina. ✆902 40 47 04 www.illesbalears.travel Airport: ✆ 971 78 95 56
- 👥 **Kids:** Marineland; Palma Aquarium.

Mallorcan Primitives (14–15C) – Gothic Mallorcan painting, characterised by a gentleness of expression, was open to external influences: the so-called **Master of Privileges** (Maestro de los Privilegios) showed a Sienese preference for miniaturisation and warm colours; later, **Joan Daurer** and

GETTING THERE

BY AIR – From the mainland, the Balearic Islands are served by Iberia (www.iberia.com), Vueling (www.vueling.com), Air Europa (www.air-europa.com) and a handful of other airlines.

BY SEA – Trasmediterránea (www.trasmediterranea.es) and Baleària (www.balearia.com) run regular ferries from the mainland and between the islands.

the **Maestro de Obispo Galiana** were inspired by Catalan painting.

Artists of the 15C included **Gabriel Moger**, **Miguel de Alcanyis** and **Martí Torner**, who studied in Valencia. The **Maestro de Predelas** is distinguishable by his attention to detail, **Rafael Moger** by his realism. **Pedro (Pere) Nisart** and **Alonso de Sedano** introduced the Flemish style (see Museo de Mallorca, p455).

Famous Mallorcans and visitors – **Ramón Llull** (1232–1315) personified the cosmopolitan 13C outlook of Mallorca. He learned languages and studied philosophy, theology and alchemy, and was beatified. **Fray Junípero Serra** (1713–84) founded missions in California. He was beatified in 1988. Among the foreign artists to visit in the 19C were **Frédéric Chopin** and **George Sand**. **Robert Graves** (1895–1985), the English poet and author, lived here from 1929. The Austrian archduke **Ludwig Salvator** (1847–1915) compiled the most detailed study of the archipelago and was patron to the French speleologist E A Martel.

ADDRESSES: PALMA

STAY

Hostal Ritzi – Apuntadores 6. 971 71 46 10. 18 rooms. This simple guesthouse offers traditional white-washed rooms with checkered-tile floors along with a warm welcome.

Hotel Born – Sant Jaume 3. 971 71 29 42. www.hotelborn.com. 36 rooms. The Ibizan-style patio is the highlight of this hotel in a 16C palace. Some rooms have four-poster beds.

Santa Clara Urban Hotel & Spa – Sant Alonso 16. 971 72 92 31. www.santaclarahotel.es. 20 rooms. €15. This nobleman's townhouse has is now a boutique hotel and spa with clean, minimalist décor and stripped-down stone walls. The rooftop terrace has a superb view.

Hotel San Lorenzo – San Lorenzo 14. 971 72 82 00. www.hotelsanlorenzo.com. 9 rooms. Kick back in a 17C mansion with wrought-iron

balconies and genial staff. Rooms are bright (if slightly outdated), and there's a pool and garden.

Sant Francesc Hotel Singular – Pl. de Sant Francesc 5. 971 49 50 00. www.hotelsantfrancesc.com. 42 rooms. Behold Palma's luxury makeover: Impeccable design and a spa-like atmosphere throughout make this converted palace one of the most stunning, head-turning hotels in the country. Tasting menus at Quadrat ( ) are worth the splurge.

EAT

Bar Bosch – Pl. del Rei Joan Carles I, 6. 971 72 22 28. www.barbosch.es. This legendary bar (est 1936) has dependably good sandwiches, breakfasts and tapas and a terrace overlooking the Passeig del Born.

Cafè Es Pes de Sa Palla –Pl. of Pes de sa Palla. 971 72 25 05. www.cafesbotiga.amadipesment.org. Closed Sun. Managed by a local association for people with learning difficulties, this café is blissfully removed from the touristy old city. The vegetable-heavy menu is a welcome reprieve from greasy tapas.

La Bodeguilla – Sant Jaume 1. 971 71 82 74. www.la-bodeguilla.com. This sleek wine-focussed restaurant has an adjoining wine shop. Start things off with ice-cold oysters and a glass of cava.

Forn de San Joan – S. Joan 4. 971 72 84 22. www.forndesantjoan. com. Good cocktails and experimental tapas are a wham-bam combination, as this hotspot goes to show.

Patrón Lunares – Fábrica 30. 971 577 154. www.patronlunares.com. Closed Mon. Resembling a traditional fishermen's cantine, this hip Santa Catalina restaurant is known for its seafood and Sunday brunch.

Marc Fosh – Missió 7-A. 971 720 114. www.marcfosh.com. Closed Sun. Treat yourself to a Michelin-starred meal using pristine local ingredients in the heart of the old town.

Palma de Mallorca★★

Palma wraps around a wide bay, its residential quarters flanking either side of the historic centre. The old harbour, bordered by Passeig Sagrera, serves passenger and merchant ships; the new harbour at the southern tip of El Terreno accommodates the largest liners. Bahía de Palma, the bay, is shielded from north and west winds by the highest peak on Mallorca, Puig Major, lending it a mild climate all year. To the west, hotels stand along the indented Bendinat shoreline where there is little sand, except at Palmanova and Magaluf. The coast to the east is less sheltered but has long stretches of fine sand dotted with resorts like Can Pastilla, Ses Meravelles and S'Arenal.

- ▶ **Population:** 400 578.
- ⚙ **Michelin Map:** pp450–451.
- ⓘ **Info:** Airport: ✆971 78 95 56. Plaza de la Reina: ✆971 173 990. Parc de la Mar: ✆902 102 365. www.palmademallorca.es. 🚃Palma de Mallorca. Narrow gauge & local service.
- ◐ **Location:** Palma is located on the southwest coast of of the island of Mallorca.
- 👥 **Kids:** The Spanish Village (Poble Espanyol).
- 🕐 **Timing:** Allow a good half day to see the main sites of the city.

A BIT OF HISTORY

'Ciutat de Mallorca' – Palma was known by this name after its liberation on 31 December 1229. Trade links were forged with the mainland, Africa and northern Europe; Jews and Genoese arrived and put down roots. James II and his successors endowed the city with splendid Gothic buildings. Aragonese expansion to Naples and Sicily enabled Palma to extend its commerce. **Palma's old mansions** – In the 15–16C, Palma's aristocrats favoured the Italian style, building residences with stone facades relieved by windows with Renaissance decoration. In the 18C a distinctive Mallorcan style of home appeared, with an inner court of massive marble columns, wide shallow arches and a high and graceful loggia.
Modern Palma – Palma is home to much of the island's year-round population and one of the most popular cities in Spain to visit. Tourists congregate around **El Terreno** – especially in plaza Gomila – and **Cala Major** quarters in the west of town, but the native heart of the city remains the **Passeig des Born.** Shops sell pearls, glassware and leather in the old town east of El Born, on pedestrian streets around Plaça Major and along Avinguda Jaume III.

BARRIO DE LA CATEDRAL★
HISTORIC CENTRE
Catedral★★

Pl. Almoina. Open Apr–May and Oct Mon–Fri 10am–5.15pm, Sat 10am–2.15pm; Jun–Sep Mon–Fri 10am–6.15pm, Sat 10am–2.15pm; rest of the year Mon–Fri 10am–3.15pm, Sat 10am–2.15pm. €12 incl museum. ✆902 02 24 45. www.catedraldemallorca.org.
Palma's cathedral is downright stunning. Its buttresses, surmounted by pinnacles, rise above the sea, mere steps from its entrance. The Santanyí limestone of its walls changes colour according to the time of day: ochre, golden or pink. Begun in the early 14C, it is one of the great late-Gothic constructions.
The west face was rebuilt in neo-Gothic style in the 19C after an earthquake; its 16C Renaissance portal remains intact. The south door, the **Portada del Mirador** (Viewpoint Doorway), overlooks the sea, its delicate Gothic decoration dating to the 15C. Statues of St Peter and St Paul on either side prove that Sagrera, architect of the Llotja (Exchange), was a talented sculptor.

Cathedral viewed from the port

The **interior** is large and light, measuring 121m x 55m (397ft x 180ft) and 44m/144ft to the top of the vaulting. Slender octagonal pillars divide the nave from the aisles. The Capilla Mayor or Real (Royal Chapel) contains an enormous wrought-iron baldaquin by Gaudí (1912) with Renaissance choir stalls on either side. Tombs of the kings of Mallorca, James II and Jaume III, lie in the Capilla de la Trinidad (Trinity Chapel).

Museo de la Seu

Almoina house, next to the cathedral bell tower. Open same hours as cathedral. 902 02 24 45.
In the Gothic chapter house is the Santa Eulàlia altarpiece by the Maestro de los Privilegios (1335). In the oval Baroque chapter house are reliquaries including one of the 'True Cross'.

Palacio Real de La Almudaina

Open Tue–Sun 10am–6pm (Apr–Sep until 8pm). €7; free for EU citizens Wed & Thu 3–6pm Oct–Mar and 5–8pm Apr–Sep and for all 18 May & 12 Oct. 914 54 87 00. www.patrimonionacional.es.
This fortress of the Córdoba caliphate was converted in the 14–15C into a royal palace. Today, as a residence of the King of Spain, several rooms have been restored and furnished with Flemish tapestries and paintings. In the courtyard, note the carved eaves and the doorway of the Iglesia de Santa Ana (St Anne's Church), a rare Romanesque structure in the Balearics.

Ayuntamiento

Pl. Cort 1.
Carved wooden eaves overhang the 17C facade of the town hall.

Iglesia de Santa Eulàlia

Pl. Santa Eulàlia 2. Open Mon–Sat 9am–10.30am, 5–8pm. 971 71 46 25.
The tall nave of this 13–15C church is unusually bare for the Gothic period. In the first chapel off the south aisle is a 15C altarpiece. Between Santa Eulàlia and Sant Francesc, at no. 2 Carrer Savellà, is the 18C **Can Vivot**, its beautiful patio decorated with marble columns.

Basilica de Sant Francesc

Pl. Sant Francesc 7. Open Mon–Sat 10am–2.30pm, 3–6pm. €5. 971 71 26 95.
The facade of this 13–14C church, rebuilt in the late 17C, has an immense Plateresque rose window and a Baroque portal with a carved tympanum by Francisco Herrera. The first apsidal chapel on the left contains the tomb of Ramón Llull. The **cloisters★** *(claustro)* date to 1286.

Casa Marqués del Palmer

Sol 7.
In Carrer del Sol stands Casa Marqués del Palmer (Can Catlar), a mansion built in 1556 in stone now blackened by age. Renaissance decoration around the upper-floor windows mellows the austerity of Gothic walls. The upper gallery, under deep eaves, is a replica of that on

the Llotja. The old Jewish quarter, **La Portella**, lies close against the town wall.

Museo de Mallorca

Portella 5. Open Tue–Fri 10am–6pm, Sat 11am–2pm. €2.50. ✆971 17 78 38. http://museudemallorca.caib.es.

The ground floor displays Muslim capitals, *artesonado* ceilings and ceramics. The **Fine Arts**★ section displays Mallorcan Gothic paintings. Works from the early 14C show clear Italian influence. Catalan works begin to appear after 1349 when Mallorca was annexed by Aragón: The *Crucifixion* by Ramón Destorrents, interesting for its composition and expression, was to influence other paintings. Francesch Comes, one of the most prestigious of the early 15C painters, is represented here by his **St George**★ (room 3), remarkable for the depth and detail of the landscape.

Baños Árabes★

Can Serra 7. Open 9am–7pm. €2. ✆637 046 534.

These Moorish baths, the only relic from the caliphate, feature small circular windows and a classical dome on 12 columns with rudimentary capitals.

Museu Diocesà (Diocesan Museum)

Mirador 5. Open 10am–2pm. €3; free with cathedral ticket. ✆971 72 38 60.

Among the many Gothic works is Pere Nisart's outstanding **St George**★ (1568) which shows the saint slaying the dragon against a backdrop of 16C Palma.

WEST OF EL BORN

Museu Fundación Juan March★

Sant Miguel 11. Open Mon–Fri 10am–6.30 pm, Sat 10.30am–2pm. Closed 25 Dec, 1 Jan. ✆971 71 35 15. www.march.es/arte/palma.

This 18C mansion has a **permanent collection**★ of contemporary Spanish art.

Baños Árabes
© Jacques Sierpinski/hemis.fr

Fundació Palma Espai d'Art - Casal Solleric

Passeig des Born 27. Open Tue–Sat 11am–2pm, 3.30–8.30pm, Sun & public hols 11am–2.30pm. ✆971 72 20 92. https://casalsolleric.palma.cat.

The 18C Palau Solleric, overlooking the Born, is completed by an elegant loggia. A narrow covered way leads to the most idyllic **patio**★ in Palma, along with a double staircase with delicate ironwork. The building stages a dynamic programme of temporary exhibitions of contemporary art.

Casa Berga

Pl. Mercat 12.

This 1712 mansion is the Palacio de Justicia (Law Courts). The facade is encumbered with stone balconies, but the vast inner courtyard is typically Mallorcan.

Sa Llotja (La Lonja)★

Passeig Sagrera. Open during exhibitions only: Tue–Sat 11am–2pm, 5–9pm, Sun 11am–2pm. ✆971 71 17 05.

Guillermo Sagrera designed this 15C commodities exchange. The Llotja's military features are only for appearances, to distract the eye from the buttresses and austerity of the walls. The interior is elegant with pointed arches on spiral fluted columns.

Fundació Pilar i Joan Miró

© Rubén Perdomo/Fundació Pilar i Joan Miró

Antiguo Consulado del Mar (Former Maritime Consulate)

Passeig Sagrera. ℰ971 71 60 92.
The early-17C building with a Renaissance balcony was the meeting place of the Tribunal de Comercio Marítimo (Merchant Shipping Tribunal). Today it houses the regional administration.

Es Baluard Museu d'Art Modern i Contemporani de Palma (Museum of Modern and Contemporary Art of Palma)

Pl. Porta Santa Catalina 10. Open Tue–Sat 10am–8pm, Sun 10am–3pm. Closed 1 Jan, 25 Dec. €6; €4 temp exhibition only; Fri by donation (minimum €0.10).
ℰ971 90 82 00. www.esbaluard.org.
Occupying part of a medieval fortress, Mallorca's newest major gallery occupies a stunning angular white concrete-and-glass building. The permanent collection includes Mediterranean landscapes by Joaquín Sorolla, Santiago Rusiñol and Joan Miró; ceramics by Picasso; drawings by Chagall, Toulouse-Lautrec, and Barceló; and a Miró gallery. Top-notch temporary exhibitions feature international artists.

OUTSIDE THE CENTRE
Castell de Bellver★

Camilo José Cela 17. Open Tue-Sat 10am-7pm (Oct-Mar until 6pm), Sun 10am-3pm. €4; free Sun. ℰ971 73 50 65. www.castelldebellver.palma.cat.
The castle, built by the Mallorcan kings of the 14C as a summer residence, served as a prison until 1915. The round buildings and circular perimeter and court are highly original; a free-standing keep dominates all. On display are Roman statues and finds from excavations in Pollença. Enjoy the **panorama★★** of the bay from the terrace.

Fundació Pilar i Joan Miró (Pilar and Joan Miró Foundation).

Joan de Saridakis 29. Open Tue–Sat 10am–6pm (mid-May–mid-Sep 7pm), Sun & hols 10am–3pm. Closed 1 Sep & 25 Dec. €7.50; free Sat 3–6pm, first Sun 10am–3pm. ℰ971 70 14 20. www.miromallorca.com.
This museum is the legacy of Joan Miró, who worked here from 1956 until his death in 1983. The museum and exhibition spaces are set around his studio.

EXCURSIONS
👥 Palma Aquarium

Manuela De Los Herreros i Sora 21. Open Apr–Oct 9.30am–6. 30pm. Nov–Mar Mon–Fri 10am–3.30pm, Sat–Sun & hols 10am–5.30pm. Ticket office closes 1hr 30min before park. €25.50. ℰ902 70 29 02. www.palmaaquarium.com.
Located near the airport, but in lovely grounds, this spectacular aquarium is one of the finest in Europe. It sprawls over 50 different viewing areas containing some 8 000 specimens of 700 species – from seahorses to sharks – plucked from the Mediterranean and more exotic waters.

👥 Marineland

C. Garcilaso de la Vega 9, Costa d'en Blanes. Open Apr–Oct 9.30am–6pm (ticket office closes 4.30pm). €26 (online discounts available). ℰ971 67 51 25. www.marineland.es.

This huge dolphinarium is rated among the best in Europe and also includes Californian Sea Lions. Other attractions include an exotic birds show, an aquarium with penguins and sharks, a tropical bird house and aviary and a children's water park.

🚗 DRIVING TOUR

③ SOUTH SIDE OF THE TRAMUNTANA RANGE

75km/46.5 mi. Allow 3hr.

▶ Leave Palma on the Ma 13 heading NE toward Alcúdia. **See map pp458–459.**

Inca

31km/19mi from Palma. 🚂Inca.

This sizeable market town prospered during the wine-making boom, but was virtually abandoned during the phylloxera vine epidemic of the late 19C – hence the number of *bodegas* (cellars), that have been converted into cafés and restaurants – with the notable exception of **Bodegas Munar**, where you can taste small-production wines made the traditional way (Ctra. Inca–Sineu; ℘971 50 27 23; by appointment only; from €10).

The present prosperity of Inca is due to the leather industry in general and footwear in particular, and many famous Spanish have a presence here. Every Thursday the biggest **market** on the island takes place at Inca featuring lots of authentic (and plenty of faux) leather items.

Note the Església de Santa Maria la Major and the Església de Sant Domingo, both Baroque.

👥 Coves de Campanet

15km/9mi along the Ma 13 and 4km/2mi along a secondary, signposted road. Guided tours (45min) 10am–6.30pm. €15. ℘971 51 61 30.
www.covesdecampanet.com.
About half of these caves along the 1.3km/0.8mi-long path have ceased

formation. In the waterlogged area, the most common features are straight and delicate stalactites.

▶ The road crosses countryside bristling with windmills.

Muro

The **Museu Etnologic de Mallorca** (Ethnological Museum; Major 15; open Tue–Sat 10am–3pm, Thu also 5–8pm; closed Aug ℘971 86 06 47), set in a large 17C noble residence, displays exhibits on traditional furniture, dress, farming and island trades.

▶ Return to the Ma 13 and follow it to Alcúdia.

Alcúdia

Alcúdia, encircled by 14C ramparts, guards the promontory dividing the bays of Pollença and Alcúdia. Two gates (**Puerta del Muelle** to the harbour and the **Puerta de San Sebastián** across town) from early walls were incorporated into 14C ramparts. The streets in the shadow of the walls have a palpable medieval air.

2km/1.2mi south is the site of Roman **Pollentia**, founded in the 2C BC. Only the theatre ruins remain.

Museo Monográfico de Pollentia

Sant Jaume 30, Alcúdia. Open Tue–Fri 10am-3.30pm, Sat & Sun 10.30am-1.30pm. Closed holidays. €4, incl admission to Roman City remains. ℘971 54 70 04.
www.alcudiamallorca.com.
A chapel in Alcúdia's old quarter houses statues, oil lamps, bronzes and jewellery from the ancient city of Pollentia.

Port d'Alcúdia

2km/1.2mi E.

The port of Alcúdia overlooks a vast bay that has become a full-fledged resort built up with hotels. A beach stretches to the south as far as Can Picafort. The nearby marsh of S'Albufera (open 9am–5pm, Apr–Sep until 6pm; pick up a permit from the Visitor Centre before 4pm; ℘971 89 22 50) is a nature reserve.

Tramuntana★★★

The rocky western coast of Mallorca is one of the island's highlights. Here, mountains plunge into deep turquoise waters. This sharp contrast is tempered by the presence of abundant Mediterranean vegetation in some places and acres of orchards in others. The beaches are a delight, especially north of Pollensa and Alcúdia and east of the dramatic Cap de Formentor, known locally as the 'meeting point of the winds'.

⌖ **Michelin Map:** 579 I-M 4-6.

🛈 **Info:** Po. Pere Ventayol, Alcúdia. ☎971 54 90 22. www.sierradetramuntana.net.

▶ **Location:** Between Palma and Alcúdia, along the western coast, 157km/98mi (55km/34mi inland).

👪 **Kids:** Discovering all the secret *calas* (coves) and beaches.

◷ **Timing:** At least two days to explore.

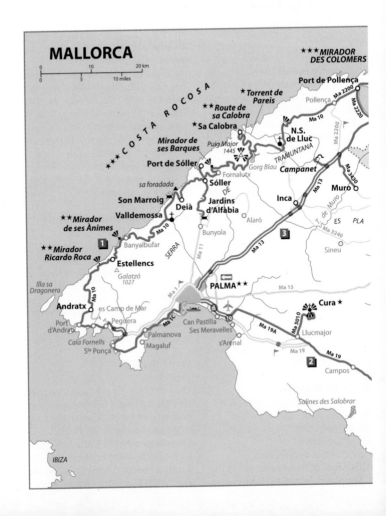

🚗 DRIVING TOUR

1 COSTA ROCOSA

264km/165mi. Allow 2 days. Leave Palma along Passeig Sagrera. Palma to Alcúdia.

Mallorca's west coast is dominated by the limestone Serra de Tramuntana, rising to 1 445m/4 740ft at Puig Major. In the south, around Estellencs and Banyalbufar, slopes are terraced into *marjades* of olives, almonds and vines.

Port d'Andratx★

32km/18.6mi W of Palma.
The small fishing port is now also used by pleasure craft. The clifftop C 710 from Andratx to Sóller is scenic★★★.

Mirador Ricardo Roca★★

18km/11.2mi NE of Port d'Andratx.
The **view** from this lookout drops sheer to tiny coves lapped by the limpid sea.

▶ Follow the M 10.

Estellencs

This pretty village is surrounded by stone terraces covered with almond and apricot trees.

▶ Continue along the M 10.

Mirador de Ses Ànimes★★

The **panorama** from the watchtower stretches south from the Isla de Dragonera and north to Port de Sóller.

Real Cartuja de Valldemossa (Valldemossa Royal Carthusian Monastery) & Palacio Rey Sancho

Pl. de la Cartuja, Valldemossa.
45km/28mi NE of Port d'Andratx.
Open Mon–Sat from 9.30am.
Monastery closes Dec–Jan 3pm, Feb & Nov 5pm, Mar & Oct 5.30pm, rest of year 6.30pm. Sun 10am–1pm. Palace closes 10–15 mins later. Closed Sun Dec & Jan, 1 Jan, 25 Dec. €9.50 plus €4 Chopin cell. Chopin cell free with online purchase. ℘971 612 986.
www.cartoixadevalldemossa.com.
The monastery was made famous by the visit George Sand and Chopin paid in the winter of 1838–39. The cell (celda) in which Chopin stayed is open to visitors (extra charge), and Chopin piano recitals (15min) occur at regular intervals during the day. Sand made his stay famous by invoking the countryside in *A Winter in Majorca*. Adjacent to the monastery is the royal palace built by King Jaume (Sancho) II in the early 14C for his asthmatic son.
Valldemossa is one of the prettiest villages on Mallorca, but time your visit early or late in the day to avoid the coach parties.

Son Marroig

Ctra de Valldemossa-Deià. 7km/4.3mi N of Valldemossa. Open Mon–Sat 10am–6pm (Apr–Sep 9.30am-6.30pm). €4. ℘971 63 91 58. www.sonmarroig.com. The former residence of Archduke Ludwig Salvator displays archaeological finds and Mallorcan furniture.

Deià

4km/2.5mi E of Son Marroig. Another honeypot Mallorcan village, Deià is tucked among the Tramuntana hills. It has maintained its character despite the hordes of visitors it receives. Writer and poet Robert Graves lived here from 1929, on and off, until his death in 1985, and is buried in Deià Cemetery. His house is open to visitors (open Apr–Oct Mon–Fri 10am–5pm, Sat until 3pm; Nov–Mar Mon–Fri 9am–4pm, Sat 9am–2pm; €7; ℘971 636 185; www.lacasaderobertgraves.org).

Sóller

11km/6.8mi NE of Deiá. 🚆Sóller. www.visitsoller.com
The cream-coloured 19C houses of Sóller spread out in a quiet valley. The vintage wooden narrow-gauge **Tren de Sóller★★** (€32 return to Palma; ℘971 75 20 51; www.trendesoller.com) has been juddering along the 27km/17 miles from Palma to Sóller since 1913. In spring, it passes through pink blossoming almond and cherry groves. It's taken almost exclusively by tourists. Visit the **Can Prunera Museu Modernista** (Lluna 86–90; open Mar–Oct daily 10.30am-6.30pm, Nov–Feb Tue–Sun until 6pm; €5, free second Sun in May, 18 May, 24 Aug; ℘971 638 973; www.canprunera.com), a restored Modernist house.

Port de Sóller

5km/3mi N of Sóller. Bus no. 211 links the port to Sóller.
Port de Sóller, on an almost circular bay where pleasure boats bob, is the major resort of the west coast. Its seaside promenade has buskers and great people-watching.

▶ C 711 from Sóller to Alfàbia.

Jardines de Alfàbia

Open Nov & mid-Feb–Mar Mon–Fri 9.30am–5.30pm, Sat 9.30am–1.30pm, rest of year Mon–Sat 9.30am–6.30pm. €7.50; winter €5.50 (discounts on website). ℘971 61 31 23. www.jardinesdealfabia.com.
Only the *artesonado* ceiling over the porch remains from a 14C Moorish residence. Follow the path through the gardens to the **library** for a taste of a traditional seigniorial residence.

▶ Return to Sóller. Take the narrow mountain road via the picturesque villages of Biniaraix and Fornalutx, then follow the C 710.

Mirador de Ses Barques

From this viewpoint there is a **panorama** of Port de Sóller. The road heads through a long tunnel before following the upper valley of the Pareis.

▶ After skirting the Gorg Blau reservoir, take the Sa Calobra road.

Sa Calobra road★★★

This road plunges 900m/2 953ft in 14km/8.7mi through steep rocks.

Sa Calobra★

Near the village is the mouth of the **Pareis river★**, its clear water pouring over round white shingle.

▶ Return to the C 710.

1km/0.6mi north of the Sa Calobra fork, a small **mirador★** (lookout;, alt 664m/2 178ft) gives a good view over the cleft hollowed out by the Pareis.

Monasterio de Nuestra Sra de Lluc

Open (museum) Sun–Fri 10am–2pm. €4. ℘971 87 15 25. www.lluc.net.
The monastery dates to the 13C when a young shepherd found a statue of the Virgin. *La Moreneta*, the dark stone statue, is patron of Mallorca.

Port de Pollença

This large resort has a perfect **setting★** in a vast sheltered bay between the Cabo

Formentor headland to the north and Cabo del Pinar to the south.

Cabo de Formentor road★
Take in spectacular views as it twists upward. The **Mirador des Colomer ★★★** (access via stepped path) overlooks rock

promontories. The **Platja de Formentor** is a sheltered beach. The grand Hotel Formentor was once famous for its casino and millionaire guests.
The road continues through a tunnel and a steep and arid landscape. **Cabo de Formentor★** has a lighthouse.

La Costa de las Calas★★

The east coast of Mallorca is renowned for its string of *calas* – (coves), and also caves (*cuevas*). Formed through thousands of years of erosion and of varying sizes, they provide sheltered swimming spots and fascinating natural formations.

🚗 DRIVING TOUR

② EAST COAST COVES AND CAVES★★

From Artà to Palma
165km/102.5mi. Allow 1 day.
♿ See map pp458–459.

Artà
The high rock site is crowned by the Iglesia de Sant Salvador and the ruins of an ancient fortress.

▶ Continue along the C 715.

Capdepera
Access the fortress by car, along narrow streets, or on foot, up steps. The remains of a 14C fortress give Capdepera an angular silhouette of crenellated walls and square towers.

Cala Rajada
3km/1.8mi NE of Capdepera.
Cala Rajada is a delightful fishing village and pleasure-boat harbour.

▶ Return to Capdepera and follow the signs to the Coves d'Artà.

♿ **Michelin Map:** 579.
O5-8 and pp458–459.

🛈 **Info:** Plaza del Convent 3, Manacor. ℘662 350 891.

👥 Coves d'Artà★★★
Open Apr–Oct 10am–6pm (Jul–Sep until 7pm); rest of year 10am–5pm. €15.
℘971 84 12 93. www.cuevasdearta.com.
Largely hollowed out by the sea, inside these caves are the Dantesque **Reina de las Columnas** (Queen of Columns), the **Sala del Infierno** (Chamber of Hell) and a fantastical **Sala de las Banderas.**

▶ Return to the PM 404; bear left. At Portocristo, take the Manacor road; turn shortly for the Coves dels Hams.

👥 Coves dels Hams
Guided tours (45min) year-round daily 10am–5pm (Nov–Mar until 4pm). €21.
℘971 82 09 88. www.cuevas-hams.com.
As the caves meet the sea the water level in several pools rises and falls with the Mediterranean tide.

▶ Return to Portocristo, bear right.

👥 Coves del Drach★★★
Guided tours (1hr on the hour) mid-Mar–Oct 10am–5pm; rest of the year 10.45am, 12pm, 2pm, 3.30pm. €16. ℘971 82 07 53.
www.cuevasdeldrach.com.
Four succeeding chambers cover 2km/1.2mi. The cave **roofs**, are amazing, glittering with countless sharply pointed stalactites. In the caves, Lake Martel is one of the largest subterranean lakes in the world, (177m by 30m). A boat takes you on the lake, and there are daily classical music performances.

▷ Continue toward Santanyí then right onto the PM 401.

Monasterio de Sant Salvador★

Open 8am–9pm. ☎971 51 52 60.
www.santsalvadorhotel.com.
The monastery, on a rise 500m/1 640ft above the plain (☺ tight hairpin bends), commands a wide **panorama★★**.
It was founded in the 14C. In the church, behind the Baroque high altar, is a **Virgin and Child**; in the south chapels are **Nativities** and a multicoloured 14C stone **altarpiece** carved with the Passion. There's a hotel and restaurant.

▷ Return to the Santanyí road.

Secondary roads lead to resorts built up in the creeks along the coast, namely **Cala d'Or**; **Cala Figuera★**, which has remained a quiet fishing village; and, in a lovely narrow bay, **Cala Santanyí★**.

▷ From Santanyí follow the C 717 towards Palma. In Llucmajor, bear right onto the PM 501.

Santuario de Cura★

Open 10am–5pm, summer 10am–6pm.
☎971 12 02 60. www.santuaridecura.com.
The road climbs to the monastery whose buildings have been restored and modernised by the Franciscans. These include the 17C **church**, Sala de Gramática (Grammar Room), a small **museum** and bar/restaurant. From the terrace on the west side there is a **panorama★★**.

▷ Continue W on C 717 to Palma.

Menorca★★

Menorca, with an area of 669sq km/258sq mi, has managed to avoid the rampant development that has blighted its neighbours, and its coastline is dotted with sandy coves of crystal-clear water, excellent for diving. The island is also famous for its prehistoric monuments.

LANDSCAPE AND TRADITION

Menorca's highest point, Monte Toro, 358m/1 175ft, is in the north of the island, known as the Tramuntana, where there are outcrops of dark slate rock. Along the coast, these ancient, eroded cliffs have been cut into a saw's edge of *rías* (inlets) and deep coves. South of the Maó-Ciutadella line, the Migjorn limestone platform forms cliffs along the coast. Vegetation is typically Mediterranean: slender pines, gnarled wild olive trees, heather and aromatic herbs such as rosemary, chamomile and thyme. Drystone walls divide fields punctuated by gates of twisted olive branches.

▶ **Population:** 93 759
◔ **Michelin Map:** 579.
▯ **Info:** Mahón: Plaça Constitució. ☎971 36 37 90. Cuitadella: Plaça des Born. ☎971 484 155. Menorca Call Centre: ☎902 92 90 15/50. www.menorca.es.
▷ **Location:** Menorca is the Balearic island farthest from the mainland.

Megalithic monuments – In the second millennium BC, the cavernous nature of the Menorcan countryside offered shelter for both the living and the dead. Some of the caves, such as **Calascoves**, are even decorated. At the same time, **talayots** began to appear (over 200 have been identified). These great cones of stones were used perhaps as a funeral chamber or for forming the base for a wooden house. Other ancient monuments include **taulas**, consisting of two huge stone blocks placed atop each other in the shape of a T, possibly serving as altars, and **navetas**, which resemble upturned boats and contain funeral chambers.

☺ A locally available map shows the monument sites: Mapa Arqueológico de Menorca, by J Mascaró Pasarius.

Architecture – The walls and even the roofs of Menorcan houses are brightly whitewashed. Low dividing walls have a white band along the top. Tiles are used for roofing, chimneys and guttering. Houses face south, their fronts characterised by wide, open bays. Northern walls, exposed to fierce *tramontana* winds, have small windows. English influence on architecture is evident: Many houses in towns have sash windows, and some mansions are in the Palladian style of 18C Britain.

The fields around Ciutadella are scattered with *barracas*, curious stone constructions with false ceilings, which served as shepherds' huts.

A BIT OF HISTORY

Prehistoric peoples left monuments throughout the island. Menorca was colonised by the Romans, conquered by Vandals in 427 and came under Islamic control in 903. In the 13C, Alfonso III of Aragón invaded, made Ciutadella capital and encouraged people from Catalunya and Aragón to settle.

In the 16C, Barbary pirates left Maó and Ciutadella in virtual ruin.

In 1713, Menorca, which had begun to prosper through trade in the late 17C, was ceded to the English crown by the Treaty of Utrecht. Maó became England's stronghold in the Mediterranean. Apart from a short period of French rule from 1756 to 1763, the island remained throughout the 18C under the British. The first road, between Maó and Ciutadella, still exists (north of the C 1); it's called Camino Kane for a British governor. At the beginning of the 19C, Menorca was restored to Spain.

The island's economy has gradually been orientated toward the leather industry and jewellery-making, while cattle raising provides the island with its well-known cheeses – but tourism, of course, is the major money maker.

SIGHTS
CIUTADELLA★

In the Middle Ages, Ciutadella (Ciudadela in Castilian), citadel and capital of Menorca, was ringed with walls. The fortified aspect of the city becomes evident when viewed from the harbour. Sacked by Turkish pirates in the 16C, 3,495 of its denizens sold into slavery in Constantinople, it was partly rebuilt in the late 17C and 18C.

The **Midsummer's Day festivities**, or **Fiestas de San Juan** (24 Jun), are celebrated in traditional fashion. On the preceding Sunday, a man representing John the Baptist, dressed in skins and carrying a lamb, runs to the sound of *fabiols* (flutes) and *tambourins*. On 24–25 June, over 100 horsemen take part in jousting tournaments and processions.

Barrio Antiguo (Old Quarter)

Plaza del Born, the ex-parade ground, is flanked by the eclectic 19C **ayuntamiento** (town hall) and the early-19C **Palacio de Torre-Saura**, a palace with side loggias. An obelisk commemorates resistance against the Turks in the 16C.

Castell de Sant Nicolau

Passeig Maritim. Open summer 10am–1pm, 5–9pm. Winter: call for times. ✆ 971 38 10 50.

This castle, complete with moat and drawbridge, was built in the late 17C, before the British occupation, to defend the port. Its entrance bears the emblem of the Crown of Aragón, and the ground floor was used for storing food, weapons and ammunition.

A spiral staircase near the front door provides access to the upper floor and tower.

Catedral

Pl. de la Catedral. Open May–Oct Mon –Sat 10am–4pm, Nov–Apr 8am–1pm, 5–9pm. €6. ✆ 971 38 03 43. www.bisbatdemenorca.com.

The late-14C fortified church retains a minaret from Islamic days. The single aisle is ogival and the apse pentagonal. View the Baroque doorway from calle del Rosario. At the end of the

A British base

Menorca was ceded to Britain by the Treaty of Utrecht in 1713, and the British made Maó (Mahon) their Mediterranean economic base for the next 70 years. The city is built on a cliff at the edge of a deep harbour. This combination facilitated the protection of both harbour and city for centuries from the greed of other European powers. Situated at the crossroads of maritime routes between Southern Europe and North Africa, Menorca held a strategic position – and benefited from it.

Several companies tours of the harbour. Departures generally leave between 10am and 3.30pm and head south toward the Costa de Ses Voltes.

street, turn left on Calle del Santísimo. **Palacio Saura** has a Baroque facade with a cornice. **Palacio Martorell** across the street is more sober. Take Calle del Obispo Vila, passing the Claustro de Socorro (Socorro Cloisters) and the Iglesia de Santo Cristo (Church of the Holy Christ) to the main street, which leads to **Plaza de España** and the arcaded **carrer de Ses Voltes**.

Puerto (Harbour)

The ramp approach to the harbour, which serves pleasure craft, is along a former counterscarp. Quayside cafés and restaurants bustle with life. The esplanade, Plaça de Sant Joan, the centre for Midsummer's Day festivities, is bordered by boat shelters hollowed out of rock. The area comes alive at night.

EXCURSIONS
Lithica – Pedreres de s'Hostal

❍ 1km/0.8mi from Ciutadella on the Me 1. Camí Vell 1. Open May–Sep Mon–Sat 9.30am–2.30pm, 4.30pm–sunset. Sun 9.30am–2.30pm. Rest of year 9.30am–2.30pm. €6, free Nov–Apr. ✆971 48 15 78, www.lithica.es.

This unusual attraction is situated in sandstone quarries that are being reclaimed by nature. Plants, greenery and sculptures have been artfully placed between the labyrinthine formations of the mined sandstone. In the summer, music, dance, cinema, arts and environmentally focussed events are staged here.

Naveta d'Es Tudons

❍ 5km/3mi E of Ciutadella.
The most striking megalithic funerary monument on the island is shaped like an upturned ship and is constructed from boulders.

Cala Santandria

❍ 3km/1.8mi S of Ciutadella.
This small, sheltered beach in an inlet is a local resort popular with locals.

Arenal de Son Saura, Cala en Turqueta, Cala Macarella

❍ SE of Ciutadella. **Son Saura:** 12km/7.4mi via Torre Saura; **Turqueta:** 12km/7.4mi via Sant Joanet; **Macarella:** 14km/8.7mi via Sant Joan Gran.
The three often-packed beaches are set in snug, unspoilt inlets fringed by pines. Arrive early, or late, in summer.

Maó/Mahón★★

❍ 45km/28mi E of Ciutadella on Me 1.
Maó's **site**★ is most striking when approached from the sea: It sits atop a cliff in the curve of a deep, 5km/3mi-long natural harbour, one of the most scenic in Europe. Maó was endowed with Palladian-style mansions during English occupation. On the north side of the port is the Finca de San Antonio – the Golden Farm – where Admiral Nelson put the finishing touches on his book, *Sketches of My Life* (October 1799). Most of Maó's shops are between **Plaza del Ejército**, a large, lively square lined with cafés and restaurants, and the quieter **Plaza de España,** with its two churches: **Santa María**, with a Baroque organ, and **Carmen**, the Carmelite church, whose cloisters now hold the municipal market. Mahón also gave its name to mayonnaise!

Museo de Menorca

Av. de Guardia. Open Jun–Sep Tue–Sat 10am–2pm, 6–8.30pm, Sun 10am–2pm; Oct–May Mon–Fri 10am–6pm, Sat–Sun 10am–2pm. ℘971 35 09 55. www.museudemenorca.com.

The museum is in a former Franciscan monastery. Rooms around a sober 18C cloister display prehistoric and other objects relating to Menorcan history. A room is dedicated to talayot culture.

Puerto (Harbour)★

Walk down the steep ramp from Carrer de Ses Voltes, cut by a majestic flight of steps, and follow the quay to the north side. Take in the classic view of the town lining the clifftop.

La Rada★ (Roadstead)

On the south side are coves and villages, among them Cala Figuera with its fishing harbour and restaurants. **Es Castell** was an English garrison named Georgetown. It has a grid plan, with a parade ground at its centre.

The islands in the harbour include Lazareto and Cuarentena; the latter was a quarantine hospital for sailors. A road follows the northern shore to the lighthouse affording views of Maó.

Talayot de Trepucó

◗ 1km/0.6mi S of Maó.

This megalithic site is famous for its 4.80m/16ft *taula*.

Sant Lluís

◗ 4km/2.5mi S.

This town with narrow streets was founded by the French. Small resorts have grown up nearby at **Alcaufar** and **Binibèquer Vell**, a new village modelled after a traditional old fishing hamlet. It's popular with island visitors.

Es Grau

◗ 8km/5mi N.

Beside the attractive white village with its long beach is a vast lagoon, **Albufera de es Grau**, 2km/1.2mi long and 400m/437yd wide. Birds – and birdwatchers – flock here.

Cala en Porter

◗ 12km/7.4mi W.

Promontories protect a narrow estuary lined by a sandy beach. Houses perch upon the left cliff. Troglodyte dwellings, the **Coves d'en Xoroi** (www.covadenxoroi.com), are now a see-and-be-seen chill-out bar overlooking the sea.

Mercadal

◗ 19km/11.8mi NW of Cala en Porter.

Mercadal, a village of brilliantly whitewashed houses halfway between Maó and Ciutadella, is where roads to the coast meet on the north–south axis.

Monte Toro

◗ 3.5km/2mi along a narrow road.

On a clear day, the **view**★★ from the church-crowned summit (358m/1 175ft) is of the entire island.

Fornells★

◗ 8.5km/5.3mi N on the C 723.

Fornells, another fishing village of whitewashed houses, is arched around a palm-fringed marina at the mouth of a deep inlet surrounded by moors.

Cap de Cavalleria

◗ 12km/7.4mi N along the PM 722.

The drive to the cape, the island's northernmost point, is through windswept moorland dotted with elegant country houses. The **view** from the lighthouse is of a rocky, indented coast reminiscent of the Atlantic.

Cala (Santa) Galdana

◗ 16km/10mi SW via Ferreries.

This otherwise idyllic sandy cove has been marred by large hotels.

🏃 You can walk to the cove from **the Algendar ravine** (on leaving Ferreries, take the track left towards Ciutadella; 3hr there and back).

Within walking distance of Cala Galdana are the Caribbean-esque **white-sand coves** of Cala Mitjana, Cala Turqueta, Cala Macarella and Cala Trébaluger. They're busy in peak season. Small boats service these beaches from Cala Galdana and Cala n'Bosch.

Ibiza★

Ibiza (Eivissa in Balearic Catalan), covering 572sq km/221sq mi, is renowned for nightlife and visiting hedonists, yet parts of the island – especially in the north – remain an agrarian paradise. There are stunning beaches, hidden coves and old villages with narrow streets and whitewashed houses; together, they forge a personality that is uniquely *Ibicenco*.

LANDSCAPE & TRADITION

Ibiza, the **Isla Blanca** (White Island), 72.4km/45mi southwest of Mallorca, is 41km/25mi in length. Dazzling white houses, flat roof terraces, tortuous alleys and an atmosphere similar to that of a Greek island are all part of Ibiza's magic. It is mountainous, with little space for cultivation. Among pines and junipers on the hillsides stand the cube-shaped houses of many small villages. The notched shore appears untamed; promontories are marked by rocks out to sea, some as high as the limestone needle known as **Vedrá★** (almost 400m/1 300ft).

Traditional architecture – The typical Ibizan cottage, or **casament**, now found largely inland, is made up of several white cubes with few windows. Arcaded porches provide shade and a cool crop storage.

Country churches are equally plain with gleaming white exteriors and dark interiors. Their facades are surmounted by narrow bell gables pierced by wide porches. Fortified churches once provided shelter from pirates in Sant Carles, Sant Joan, Sant Jordi and Sant Miquel.

Folklore and traditional costume – Ibiza's folklore lives on. Elderly women still wear the traditional long gathered skirt and dark shawl. At festivals the costume is brightened with fine gold filigree necklaces called **emprendades**. Dances are performed to the accompaniment of flute, tambourine and castanets.

▶ **Population:** 144 659
◔ **Michelin Map:** 579.
🄵 **Info:** Eivissa: Plaça de la Catedral. ☎971 397 600. www.turismo.eivissa.es.
◖ **Location:** Ibiza is the closest island to the Spanish mainland (83km/52mi).

A BIT OF HISTORY

In the 10C BC, Phoenicians made the island a staging-post for ships loaded with ores; in the 7C BC, Carthage founded a colony; and under the Romans the capital grew and prospered.

EIVISSA/IBIZA (TOWN)★

Eivissa's colourful beauty and impressive **site★★** are best appreciated from the sea; alternatively, take the **Talamanca** road and look back (3km/1.8mi NE). The town, built on a hill, consists of an old quarter ringed by walls, the lively Marina district near the harbour and, farther out, residential and shopping areas. Along the shore are large hotels.

UPPER TOWN★ (DALT VILA)

Allow 1hr30min.

The Dalt Vila, enclosed by the 16C walls built under Emperor Charles V, is the heart of the old city and retains a rustic, medieval character. There remain many noble houses with vast patios and Gothic windows. Enter the quarter through the **Porta de ses Taules**, a gateway emblazoned with Aragón's crest. Continue by car up a steep slope to the cathedral square, or stroll the meandering streets among shops and art galleries.

Catedral

Pl. de la Catedral. Open Tue–Sun 10am–2pm, 5–8pm (Jul–Aug 6–9pm). ☎971 31 27 73.

The Cathedral's massive 13C belfry, which resembles a keep, dominates the town. The nave was rebuilt in the 17C. An ancient bastion behind the east end affords a **panoramic view★**.

Museo Arqueológico de Ibiza y Formentera★

Vía Romana 31. Open Apr–Sep Tue–Sun 10am–2pm, 6:30–9pm (Sun am only); Jan–Mar Tue–Sun 9:30am–3pm, Sun 10am–2pm. €2.40. ☏971 30 17 71. www.maef.es.

The most impressive exhibits are its Punic art, which developed around the Mediterranean from the 7C BC to 3C AD. Particularly impressive are the ex-votos discovered on Ibiza and Formentera, predominantly from excavations at Illa Plana and the Es Cuiram cave. The cave is believed to have been a temple to the goddess **Tanit**, who was venerated from the 5–2C BC. Also worthy of note are the polychrome moulded glass and Punic, Roman and Moorish ceramics.

Museo Puget

C. Mayor 18. Open Apr–Sep Tue–Fri 10am–2pm, 5–8pm, Sat–Sun 10am–2pm; Oct–Mar Tue–Fri 10am–4.30pm, Sat–Sun 10am–2pm. ☏971 39 21 37.

Situated in Can Comasema, a noble-man's house, this museum exhibits 130 watercolours, drawings and paintings by **Narcís Puget Viñas** (1874–1960) and his son, Narcís Puget Riquer (1916–83). They are an interesting testimony to the customs and habits of Ibizans in the last century and the landscapes of the island.

LOWER TOWN
Necrópolis Puig des Molins★

Vía Romana 31. Open Apr–Sep Tue–Sat 10am–2pm, 6.30–9pm, Sun 10am–2pm; Oct–Mar Tue–Sat 9.30am–3pm, Sun 10am–2pm. Closed public hols. €2.40. ☏971 30 17 71. www.maef.es.

The Puig des Molins hillside necropolis was a burial ground for the Phoenicians from the 7C BC and for the Romans until the 1C AD. There is a model of the site; some of the hypogea (funer-ary chambers), of which over 3 000 have been discovered, may be visited. The objects displayed were found in the tombs and include everyday and ritual items. The outstanding, partly coloured, 5C BC **bust of the goddess Tanit★**, a

Punic version of the Phoenician Astarte, typifies Greek beauty. A second bust is more Carthaginian.

La Marina

The Marina district near the market and harbour, with its restaurants, bars and shops, stands in lively contrast to the quieter Dalt Vila.

Sa Penya★

This former fishermen's quarter, now the centre of Ibiza's nightlife, is built on a narrow rock promontory at the har-bour mouth. White cubic houses over-lap in picturesque chaos, completely blocking streets and forcing bypasses via steps cut out of the rock.

SANT ANTONI DE PORTMANY/ SAN ANTONIO ABA

Sant Antoni, with its vast, curved bay, has been extensively developed. The old quarter, hidden behind modern apartment blocks, centres on a fortified 14C church rebuilt in the 16C. There is a large pleasure boat harbour. Several coves and creeks are within easy reach.

EXCURSIONS
Cala Gració

▶ 2km/1.2mi N.
This is a picturesque, accessible, shel-tered creek.

Cala Salada

▶ 5km/3mi N.
The road descends through pines to another secluded cala.

Port des Torrent & Cala Bassa

▶ 5km/3mi SW.
Port des Torrent is all rocks; Cala Bassa a long, pine-edged beach. Rocks are smooth and separate and just above or just below the water line, providing per-fect underwater swimming conditions.

Cala Vedella

▶ 15km/9.3mi S.
A road skirts the shoreline through pine trees between the beaches of Cala Tarida (rather built-up), Es Molí

(unspoilt) and Cala Vedella in its enclosed creek. You can return to Sant Antoni along a mountain road cut into the cliffs as far as Sant Josep.

Santa Eulària Des Riu/ Santa Eulàlia Del Río

Santa Eulària des Riu, in a fertile plain watered by Ibiza's only river, is a large seaside resort. Nearby beaches such as **Es Canar** have also been developed.

Puig de Missa★

❍ Bear right off the Eivissa/Ibiza road 50m/55yd after the petrol station (on the left).

This minute, fortified town crowning the hilltop provides a remarkable over-view of the island's traditional peasant architecture; in times of danger, the church (16C) served as a refuge.

Portinatx★

❍ 27km/17mi N on the PM 810, PM 811 and C 733.

The road passes through **Sant Carles**, which has a fine church and is a depar-ture point for quiet local beaches. It descends to the vast **Sant Vicent** creek (cala) with its sandy beach and, oppo-site, the Isla de Togomago, then crosses a landscape covered in pines. The last section threads between holm oaks and almond trees looking down on **Cala Xarraca**. Paradisiacal calas make **Cala de Portinatx** one of the island's most attractive areas.

ADDRESSES

🏠 STAY

😊 **Hostal Las Nieves** – Joan d'Austria 18, Eivissa. 📞971 19 03 19. www. hostalibiza.com.com. 20 rooms. Ten minutes' walk from the old town, this simple, bare-bones hostal has clean white rooms. There is also a roof terrace. No aircon or lift.

😊😊 **Hotel Rural Es Cucons** – Santa Agnès de Corona. 1km/0.6mi along Corona, Camí des Plà de Corona. 📞971 80 55 01. www.escucons.com. 15 rooms. Restaurant 😊😊😊.

Closed Nov–Mar. What was once an Ibizan farmstead is now a rustic-chic architectural jewel with modern digs and a pool overlooking the hills.

😊😊😊 **Vara de Rey** – Paseo Vara de Rey 7, Eivissa. 📞971 30 13 76. www. hibiza.com. 11 rooms. In the old town, this high-ceilinged mansion offers comfortable stays in cosy, old-fashioned rooms, all with balconies or terraces.

😊😊😊😊 **Atzaró** – Diseminado P 12, Sta Eulàlia. 6km/3.7mi from Sta Eulàlia beach. 📞971 33 88 38. www.atzaro. com. 24 rooms. An exclusive (and expensive) agroturismo frequented by celebrities, Atzaró has two locavore restaurants, a spa, and rustic yet sumptuous rooms, many with private swimming pools.

😊😊😊😊 **MiM Ibiza** – C. de Carles Roman Ferrer 8, Eivissa. 📞971 30 19 02. www.hotelmimibiza.com. 52 rooms. Finally, a high-end hotel in Eivissa Town with some design sense: Situated just 50m/164ft from the beach, MiM is an adults-only property with high-ceilinged rooms and Art Deco interiors.

🍴 EAT

Typical Ibizan desserts include flaó, a tart made of creamy cheese flavoured with mint and (sometimes) anise, and greixonera, a 'bread' pudding made from leftover ensaimadas (a Balearic pastry) to which milk, eggs and cinnamon are added.

😊 **Croissant Show** – Pl. de la Constitució 2, Eivissa. 📞971 31 76 65. Grab a quick coffee and (ultra-flaky) croissant here before embarking on the climb to the old city.

😊 **Peixet** – Pl. de Sa Tertúlia 4. 📞971 31 10 25, Eivissa. This casual bar in the Sa Penya district makes a mean Greixonera.

😊😊😊 **Re.Art** – Carrer de Castella 9, Eivissa. 📞871 03 65 75. www.reart.es. Closed Sun. Experimental tapas with an Asian flair are on the menu at this new gastrobar with an open kitchen.

😊😊😊😊 **Ca n'Alfredo** – Vara de Rey 16, Eivissa. 📞971 311 274. www. canalfredo.com. Closed Mon. This well-loved dining room on the northern edge of the old town serves terrific seafood and rice dishes.

Formentera

Formentera, the smallest main island in the archipelago (84sq km/32sq mi), has quintessential Mediterranean scenery and beaches lapped by crystal-clear water. Come here to unplug and decompress.

LANDSCAPE & TRADITION

Formentera takes in two islets and a sandy isthmus and clocks in at 14km/8.7mi long. The western islet holds the tiny capital (Sant Francesc), passenger port, salt pans, Cabo de Barbaria lighthouse and a dry open expanse where cereals, figs, almonds and a few scraggly vines grow. The island's 192m/630ft mountain rises from the **Mola** promontory on the eastern islet, where rock cliffs and sand dunes alternate along the shore. Access to Formentera is exclusively by sea, and the best way to explore is by bicycle.

A BIT OF HISTORY

Formentera's inhabitants arrived comparatively recently, the island having been abandoned in the Middle Ages due to marauding Barbary pirates and only repopulated at the end of the 17C. Most of the present population consists of fishermen and farmers, who ship figs and fish to Ibiza and salt to Barcelona.

SIGHTS

The Beaches

White sandy beaches with clear water are the island's main attraction: There's not much more to do than relax. Long beaches stretch along either side of the isthmus, the rocky Tramuntana to the north and the sheltered, sandy Migjorn to the south. Smaller beaches include Es Pujòls (the most developed), Illetes and Cala Saona.

Cala Savina/La Savina

Your landing point is in the main harbour. A few white houses stand between two big lagoons. Salt marshes glisten in the distance on the left.

▶ **Population:** 10 365
🕐 **Michelin Map:** 579.
🛈 **Info:** Sant Francesc: Plaça de la Constitució 1. La Savina: Calpe ℘971 32 20 57 (both). www.formentera.es.
▶ **Location:** Formentera lies 7km/4.3mi south of Ibiza at its nearest point.

Island of the Sargantana

The symbol of Formentera is the sargantana, a lizard that is found almost exclusively on the 'Pine Islands' (Ibiza, Formentera and their islets). Larger than their reptilian cousins on the peninsula, they eat insects and pollen. Their shimmering skins are shaded in whites, blues and greens.

Sant Francesc (San Francisco Javier)

▶ 3km/1.8mi SE of Savina.
The tiny capital is arranged around the 18C church-fortress, in front of which an arts and crafts market takes place most days.

El Pilar de la Mola

▶ 14km/8.7mi SE of Sant Francesc.
The hamlet at the centre of the Mola promontory has this geometrically designed church which is similar to those on Ibiza, only smaller.

Far de la Mola

▶ 2km/1.2mi SE of Pilar de la Mola.
The lighthouse overlooks an impressive cliff. There is a monument to Jules Verne who mentioned this spot in *Off on a Comet* (1877).

Andalucía and the Canary Islands

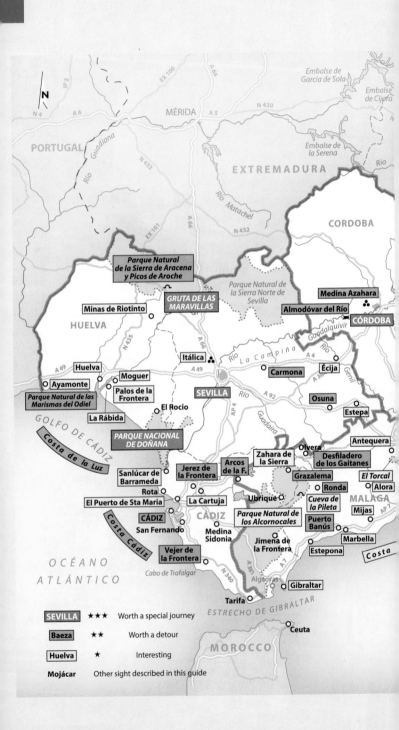

Embalse de
Garcia de Sola

Embalse
de Cijara

MÉRIDA

PORTUGAL

EXTREMADURA

Embalse de
la Serena

CORDOBA

Parque Natural
de la Sierra de Aracena
y Picos de Aroche

Parque Natural de
la Sierra Norte de
Sevilla

Medina Azahara

GRUTA DE LAS
MARAVILLAS

Almodóvar del Río

CÓRDOBA

Minas de Riotinto

HUELVA

Guadalquivir

Itálica

La Campiña

Huelva

Moguer

Carmona

Écija

Ayamonte

Palos de la
Frontera

SEVILLA

Parque Natural de las
Marismas del Odiel

La Rábida

El Rocio

Osuna

Estepa

GOLFO DE CÁDIZ

Costa de la Luz

PARQUE NACIONAL
DE DOÑANA

Antequera

Zahara de
la Sierra

Olvera

Desfiladero
de los Gaitanes

Arcos
de la F.

El Torcal

Sanlúcar de
Barrameda

Jerez de
la Frontera

Grazalema

Ronda

Alora

MÁLAGA

Rota

Ubrique

Cueva de
la Pileta

Mijas

El Puerto de Sta Maria

La Cartuja

CÁDIZ

CÁDIZ

San Fernando

Costa Cádiz

Medina
Sidonia

Parque Natural de
los Alcornocales

Puerto
Banús

Marbella

Jimena de
la Frontera

Estepona

Costa

OCÉANO
ATLÁNTICO

Vejer de
la Frontera

Cabo de Trafalgar

Algeciras

Gibraltar

Tarifa

ESTRECHO DE GIBRALTAR

Ceuta

MOROCCO

SEVILLA	★★★	Worth a special journey
Baeza	★★	Worth a detour
Huelva	★	Interesting
Mojácar		Other sight described in this guide

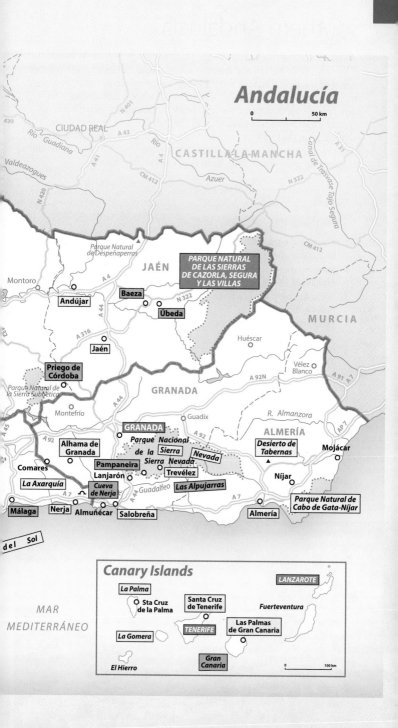

Southern Andalucía

Andalucía is the Spain of postcards: a land of olive groves, sunny beach resorts, brick-red soil and dazzling white villages. But its southern reaches transcend the typical images and stereotypes propogated by travel brochures and Washington Irving's *Tales of the Alhambra*. Sure, this is ground zero for flamenco, bullfighting, gazpacho and sherry, but the area is seeing a cultural renaissance with museum-packed cities like Málaga – with its new Centre Pompidou – at the forefront. Summer is the most popular time to visit, but winter vacationers are treated to temperate weather and short lines in the cities and plenty of snow in the Sierra Nevada, a major ski destination.

Highlights

1 A stroll in the splendid gardens of Granada's **Generalife** (p480)

2 Stunning scenery of the **Alpujarras** (p484)

3 **Málaga**'s unexpected cultural riches in its museums (p489)

4 Extraordinary rock formations in the **Sierra del Torcal** (p493)

5 Contemplating *Death in the Afternoon* in the Bullring of **Ronda** (p494)

Southern Andalucía

The revamped port city of Málaga is the gateway to Málaga Province and the Costa del Sol, Spain's frenetic holiday playground. A few miles inland lie some of Spain's prettiest **pueblos blancos** (white villages) and quintessentially Andalucían towns such as Antequera and Ronda, the home of bull-fighting.

Southeast Andalucía

Granada is the crown jewel of this region with its gorgeous natural setting and, in the Alhambra, one of the greatest Moorish palaces ever built. Despite its apeal to tourism, the city has an earthy atmosphere and more than its share of attractions.

Towering above the city is the snow-capped Sierra Nevada. In spring and fall, it's quite possible to ski here in the morning and sunbathe on the beach in the afternoon, perhaps on the sands of the Almería coastline, the latest of Spain's costas to be fashionably developed for sun-starved Northern Europeans. Despite getting little rain, the area's fertile plain (*vega*) produces a cornucopia of fruit and vegetables – even if you can't see them beneath the swathes of protective plastic sheeting.

Zahara de la Sierra, one of the Pueblos Blancos

© Jose Peral/age fotostock

Granada★★★

Granada enjoys a glorious setting★★★ on the fertile *vega* overlooked by three hills and the majestic peaks of the Sierra Nevada. It's guarded by the breathtaking Alhambra, one of the most magnificent monuments ever created and, for many, the highlight of Spain.

THE CITY TODAY

Today Granada is a teeming maze of cobblestoned streets that empty onto plazas and miradores (viewponts), where locals and tourists rub shoulders in sardine-can tapas bars and sing along to buskers playing flamenco guitar. In June 2019 the first fast train (AVE) arrived, facilitating travel to and from the city from Madrid and Barcelona .

A BIT OF HISTORY

Granada gained importance in the 11C as Córdoba declined. It became capital of the Almoravids, who were ousted a century later by the Almohads. In the 13C, Muslims from Córdoba fleeing Christian persecution settled, enriching the city. In 1238, the new **Nasrid** ruler, Mohammed ibn Nasr, submitted to the authority of Ferdinand III, ensuring peace, and the kingdom flourished. **The fall of Granada** – The taifa (kingdom) of Granada was the last Islamic stronghold of the Peninsula, but by 2 January 1492, after a six-month siege by the Catholic Monarchs, the city fell. Boabdil, the last Nasrid king, went into exile. As he looked back at his forfeited city, his mother is said to have scolded him: 'You weep like a woman for what you could not hold as a man'.
Granada flourished again in the Renaissance, but its fortunes suffered during the ruthless suppression of the Las Alpujarras revolt in 1570.
Modern Granada – The peaceful, green old quarters east of **Plaza Nueva**, on the Alhambra and Albaicín hills, contrast with the noisy, bustling lower town and the pedestrian quarter around the

▶ **Population:** 233 764
◔ **Michelin Map:** 578 U 19 (town plan) map 124 Costa del Sol.
🛈 **Info:** Central Tourist Office: Pl. del Carmen. ℘ 958 24 82 80. Info points: Alhambra; Carrera del Darro 16. www.granadatur.com.
▶ **Location:** Granada is in southern Andalucía, separated from the sea by the Sierra Nevada. The A 44 and other highways link with major cities in the region. 🚆Granada (AVE).
🅿 **Parking:** Space is limited in the Albaicín; there is visitor parking at the Alhambra.
☻ **Don't Miss:** The Alhambra.
🧍 **Kids:** Parque de las Ciencias or a flamenco performance in the caves of Sacromonte.

Cathedral between **Gran Vía de Colón** and **Calle de los Reyes Católicos**.

THE ALHAMBRA AND GENERALIFE★★★

Real de la Alhambra. Open Apr–mid-Oct 8.30am–8pm; mid-Oct–Mar 8.30am–6pm. Night visits Apr–mid-Oct Tue–Sat 10–11.30pm; mid-Oct–Mar Fri–Sat 8–9.30pm. Closed 1 Jan, 25 Dec. €14 general ticket incl Generalife gardens specifying entry time to the Nasrid Palaces; €7 Generalife only; €5 night visit to Generalife *or* Nasrid Palaces; €17 general Alhambra plus Fundación Rodríguez-Acosta (◔see below).
☺ **Because of stringent caps on visitor numbers, advance booking – preferably months out – is essential.** If tickets are sold out, check the website daily as occasional cancellations free up tickets, or book an official private tour via the website (these get a special allotment). ℘958 02 79 71. www.tickets.alhambra-patronato.es.
Nasrid architecture was the last desperate expression of a civilisation in

Patio de los Leones, Palacios Nazaríes, the Alhambra

© Manfred Gottschalk/Getty Images

decline. Nasrid princes built hastily for the moment: Beneath fabulous decoration lie ill-assorted bricks and rubble, so it is surprising how little time has diminished this masterpiece.

Decoration was the main concern. Walls and ceilings everywhere reveal an art without equal. **Stuccowork** is worked in patterns in a low relief of flat planes to catch the light; another type of decoration was made by cutting away layers of plaster to form stalactites (mocárabes). This type of ornament, painted and even gilded, covered capitals, cornice mouldings, arches, pendentives and entire cupolas.

Ceramic tiles provided geometric decoration for walls: **alicatados** formed a colourful marquetry, with lines of arabesque motifs making star designs; **azulejos** gave colour, different hues separated by a thin raised fillet or a black line (**cuerda seca**). **Calligraphy** employed elegant Andalucían cursive; the more decorative Cufic was reserved for religious aphorisms in scrollwork.

The Alhambra★★★

See map p479.

The Calat Alhambra (Red Castle) is one of the most remarkable fortresses ever built. It commands views of the town, the Sacromonte heights, hillsides and the gardens of the Albaicín. Enter through the Puerta de Las Granadas (Pomegranate Gateway) built by Emperor Charles V; a paved footpath then leads through the **shrubbery★**.

Palacios Nazaríes★★★ (Nasrid Palace)

The 14C Nasrid Palace was built around the Patio de los Arrayanes and Patio de los Leones. Its richness and originality defy description. In the **Mexuar**, used for government and judicial administration, a frieze of azulejos and an epigraphic border cover the walls.

An oratory stands at one end. Cross the **Patio del Cuarto Dorado**. The south wall, protected by a remarkable carved wood cornice, exemplifies Granada art: Windows are surrounded by panels covered with every variety of stucco and tile decoration. The **Cuarto Dorado** (Golden Room) has tiled panelling, fine stuccowork and a wooden ceiling. The delightful **view★** extends over the Albaicín.

Adjoining is the oblong **Patio de los Arrayanes** (Myrtle Courtyard). A pool banked by myrtles reflects the **Torre de Comares** (Comares Tower), which contrasts with slender porticoes that give onto the **Sala de la Barca** (from barakha, benediction) and the **Salón de Embajadores** (Hall of Ambassadors), an audience chamber with a magnificent domed cedar ceiling.

At the heart of a second palace stands the **Patio de los Leones** (Lion Courtyard) built by Mohammed V. Twelve rough stone lions support a low fountain, which was restored and returned to its former glory in 2012. Arcades of slender columns lead to the main state apartments. The **Sala de los Abencerrajes** (named for the family massacred here) has a splendid star-shaped **mocárabe** cupola.

The vaulting at the end of the **Sala de los Reyes** (Kings' Chamber) is atypically painted to illustrate pastimes of Moorish and Christian princes – possibly done after the so-called Reconquista. The **Sala de las Dos Hermanas** (Hall of the Two Sisters), named for two marble slabs in the pavement, is renowned for honeycomb cupola vaulting.

Beyond are the resplendent **Sala de los Ajimeces** and the **Mirador de Lindaraja**. Past a room once occupied by Washington Irving is a gallery with views of the Albaicín. Descend to the Patio de la Reja.

▶ Cross the Patio de Lindaraja to the Partal Gardens.

Gardens and perimeter towers★★

The terraced Jardines del Partal descend to the 14C porticoed **Torre de las Damas** (Ladies' Tower). The Torre de Mihrab (right) is a former oratory. The Torre de la Cautiva and Torre de las Infantas (Captive's and Infantas' towers) are sumptuously decorated inside.

▶ Enter the Palacio de Carlos V.

Palacio de Carlos V★★ (Emperor Charles V's Palace)

In 1526, Pedro Machuca was commissioned to design a palace to be financed by a tax on the Moors. The 1568 uprising delayed construction. It is one of the most successful Renaissance creations in Spain. Although in comparison with the Nasrid Palaces the building may appear dull, its grandeur shines through in its Classical proportions and central circular patio.

Museo de la Alhambra★

Palacio de Carlos V. Open Apr–mid-Oct Wed–Sat 8.30am–8pm (until 6pm mid-Oct–Mar), Sun & Tue 8.30am–2.30pm. Closed 1 Jan, 25 Dec. ☏958 02 79 00. This museum is devoted to Hispano-Moorish art: ceramics, woodcarvings, panels and more. Outstanding are the famous 14C **blue** (or **gazelle**) **amphora★** and the Pila de Almanzor, decorated with lions and deer.

Museo de Bellas Artes (Fine Arts Museum)

Palacio de Carlos V. Open mid-Oct–Mar Tue–Sat 9am–6pm (Apr–Jun & Sep until 8pm, Jul–Sep until 3.30pm), Sun 9am–3pm. ☏958 56 35 08. Religious sculpture and paintings of the 16–18C predominate: works by Diego de Siloé, Pedro de Mena, Vicente Carducho and Alonso Cano, plus a magnificent still life, **Thistle and Carrots★★**, by Juan Sánchez Cotán.

Alcazaba★

The two towers of this austere fortress on the Plaza de los Aljibes (Cistern Court) date to the 13C. The Torre de la Vela (Watchtower) commands a fine **panorama★★** of the palace, gardens, Sacromonte and the Sierra Nevada.

Puerta de la Justicia★

The massive Justice Gateway is built into a tower in the outer walls. On the facade, a strip of delightful 16C azulejos bears an image of the Virgin and Child.

The Generalife★★

The **water gardens** are one of the most enjoyable parts of the 14C Generalife, the summer palace. The Patio de los Cipreses (Cypress Alley) and Patio de las Adelfas (Oleander), questionable replicas of the original gardens, lead in. The nucleus is the **Patio de la Acequia** (Canal Court), a pool with fountains with a pavilion at either end and a mirador in the middle.

The pavilion to the rear contains the Sala Regia, with fine stuccowork.

The upper gardens contain the famous **escalera del agua**, or water staircase.

CATHEDRAL QUARTER
Capilla Real★★ (Chapel Royal)

Oficios 3. Open Mon–Sat 10.15am–6.30pm, Sun 11am–6.30pm. Closed 1 Jan, Good Friday, 25 Dec. €5. Free Sun. ☏958 22 78 48. www.capillarealgranada.com.

The **Catholic Monarchs** commissioned this Isabelline Gothic chapel by Enrique Egas. To enter (by the south door), cross the courtyard of the old **Lonja** (Exchange), also by Egas. The south

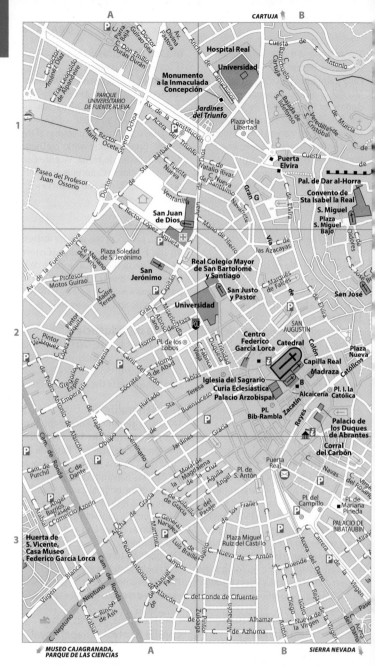

front has a Renaissance facade of super-imposed arcades with turned columns. Every decoration of the Isabelline style is seen inside: ribbed vaulting, coats of arms, the yoke and fasces (revived in 1934 by the Falange), monograms and the eagle of St John. In the chancel, closed by a gilded **screen★★★** by Master Bartolomé, are the **mausoleums★★★** of the Catholic Monarchs on the right, and of Philip the Handsome and Juana the Mad, the parents of Charles V, on the left. The first was carved by Fancelli in Genoa in 1517, and the second, magnificent in scale and workmanship, by Bartolomé Ordóñez (the sarcophagi

MURCIA ALMERÍA C   D

GRANADA

0   200 m

N

EL SACROMONTE

SACROMONTE

Museo Cuevas
del Sacromonte

Arco de
las Pesas

El Salvador

S. NICOLÁS

MIRADOR DE
SAN NICOLÁS

Casa del
Chapiz

Casa-Museo
Max Moreau

ALBAICÍN

Palacio de
los Córdova

Darro

Convento de
Sta Catalina
de Zafra

Paseo
del Padre
Manjón

Museo
Arqueológico

Casa de
Porras

Casa de Zafra
El Bañuelo

del

San Pedro

ALHAMBRA

MIRADOR

Carrera

PUENTE
DEL CADÍ

Torre de
Comares

PALACIOS
NAZARÍES

Generalife

Sta Ana y
San Gil

Alcazaba

TORRE DE LAS DAMAS
TORRE DEL MIHRAB

TORRE DE LA
VELA

Puerta
del Vino

Jardines
del Partal

Real
Chancillería

PUERTA DE
LAS GRANADAS

Pta de la
Justicia

Palacio de Carlos V

TORRE DE LA CAUTIVA

Torres Bermejas

Pilar de
Carlos V

TORRE DE
LAS INFANTAS

Museo Sefardí

Fundación
Rodríguez-
Acosta

PARADOR

Museo-Casa
de los Tiros

Paseo del Generalife

Paseo del
Generalife

Pl. de
Carlos Cano

REALEJO

Santo
Domingo

CAMPO DEL
PRINCIPE

Auditorio
Manuel de Falla

Casa-Museo
Manuel de Falla

CUARTO REAL
SANTO DOMINGO

Carmen de
los Mártires

C   D

are in the crypt). Note he high altar
retable★ (1520) by Felipe Vigarny.
The lower register of the predella
depicts the siege of Granada and the
baptism of the Moriscos.

Sacristía-Museo

Among objects on display are **Queen
Isabel's sceptre and crown, King
Ferdinand's sword** and outstanding
paintings★★ by Flemish (Rogier Van
der Weyden), Italian (Perugino, Botticelli) and Spanish (Bartolomé Bermejo,
Pedro Berruguete) artists.

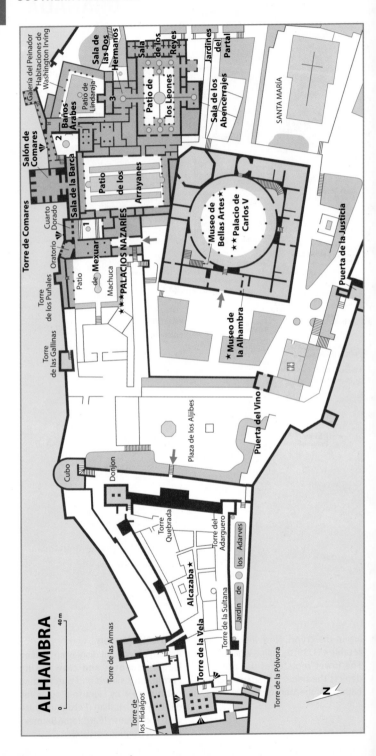

ALHAMBRA

0   40 m

N

Torre de los Hidalgos
Torre de las Armas
Torre de las Gallinas
Torre de los Puñales
Torre de Comares
Galería del Peinador
Habitaciones de Washington Irving
Sala de las Dos Hermanos
Sala de los Reyes
Jardines del Partal
SANTA MARÍA

Salón de Comares
Baños Árabes
Patio de Lindaraja
3
Patio de los Leones
Sala de los Abencerrajes

2
Sala de la Barca
Cuarto Dorado
Oratorio
1
Patio de los Arrayanes

★★★ PALACIOS NAZARÍES

Cubo
Donjón
Machuca
Patio
de Mexuar

Museo de Bellas Artes ★
★★ Palacio de Carlos V

Puerta de la Justicia

★ Museo de la Alhambra

Plaza de los Aljibes

Puerta del Vino

Torre Quebrada
Torre del Adarguero
Torre del Adarves

Alcazaba ★

Jardín de los Adarves

Torre de la Sultana
Torre de la Vela
Torre de la Pólvora

480

The Alambra and Albaicín viewed from Sacromonte

The central section of the Triptych of the Passion was painted by the Fleming Dirk Bouts. Two sculptures of the Catholic Monarchs at prayer are by Felipe Vigarny. Opposite are the 18C Baroque-style former **town hall (ayuntamiento)**. Just below is the **Centro de Arte José Guerrero**, dedicated to modern art and especially the work of Granada's José Guerrero (1914–91) (Oficios 8; open Tue–Sat 10.30am–2pm, 4.30–9pm, Sun & public hols 10.30am–2pm; closed 1 Jan, 25 Dec; ✆ 958 22 01 09; www.centroguerrero.org).

Catedral★

Gran Vía de Colón 5. Open Mon–Sat 10am–6.30pm; Sun 3–6pm. €5; free Sun. ✆958 22 29 59. www.catedraldegranada.com.
Construction started in 1518. Diego de Siloé introduced the Renaissance style to the design of Enrique Egas. The facade (1667) is by Alonso Cano. The **Capilla Mayor★** is surprising. Siloé designed a rotunda circled by an ambulatory, cleverly linked to the basilica. The rotunda combines superimposed orders, the uppermost with paintings by Alonso Cano of the Life of the Virgin and beautiful 16C stained glass. Marking the rotunda entrance are figures of the Catholic Monarchs by Pedro de Mena and, in a medallion by Alonso Cano, Adam and Eve.
The **organ★** from about 1750 is by Leonardo of Ávila. The finely carved Isabelline doorway in the south transept is the original **north portal★** of the older Capilla Real.

Alcaicería

This area, with craft and souvenir shops, was the silk market in Moorish times.

Corral del Carbón

Mariana Pineda. Open 15 Sep–Apr 10am-5pm, May–15 Sep 9.30am-2.30pm, 5-8.30pm. €5, incl El Bañuelo, Palacio de Dar al-Horra & Horno de Oro; free Sun.
This 14C former Moorish storehouse has an arched doorway with *alfiz* surround and panels of *sebka* decoration.

ALBAICÍN★★

This quarter covers a slope facing the Alhambra. The Moors lived here after the Catholic Monarchs took the city. Alleys are lined by white-walled houses. Walls enclose luxuriant gardens of cármenes (town houses). Go to the **Iglesia de San Nicolás** (Plaza de San Nicolás) at sunset, for an awe-inspiring **view★★★** of the Alhambra and Generalife. The Sierra Nevada, beyond, looks spectacular under snow in winter.

Baños Árabes★ (El Bañuelo)

Car. del Darro 31. Hours & price as Corral de Carbón, ✆958 02 79 71.
The 11C baths, with star-pierced vaulting, are the best-preserved in Spain, though you wouldn't know it from the lack of information provided. They were in operation until the 16C.

Monasterio de San Jerónimo★

Rector López Argüeta. Open 10am-1.30pm daily, winter 3–6:30pm, summer 4–7:30pm. €4. ✆958 27 93 37.

Sacristy, Monasterio de la Cartuja

© sedmak/iStockphoto.com

This 16C monastery was principally designed by Diego de Siloé. Plateresque and Renaissance doorways lead to harmonious cloisters. The **church★★**, with the tomb of Gonzalo Fernández de Córdoba, the Gran Capitán, has a Renaissance apse and superb coffers and vaulting adorned with saints, angels and animals. The **retable★★** is a jewel of the Granadine School. The paintings are from the 18C.

Basílica de San Juan de Dios★

San Juan de Dios 19. Open Mon–Sat 10am–1pm, 4–7pm; Sun 4–7pm. €5. ℘958 27 57 00.
The Baroque Church of St John of God is noted for its richness and stylistic uniformity. Behind a massive Churrigueresque altarpiece of gilded wood is a lavish *camarín* with the funerary urn of **San Juan de Dios**, founder of the Order of Knights Hospitallers. Put a few *céntimos* in the donation box to illuminate the gilded wall of the altar.

Monasterio de la Cartuja★

Po. de la Cartuja. Open Apr–Oct 10am–1pm, 4–8pm; Nov–Mar 10am–1pm, 3–6pm. €5. ℘958 16 19 32.
Go in through the cloisters. The church is exuberantly decorated with Baroque stucco. At the back of the apse is the early-18C Sancta Sanctorum, a camarín decorated with multi-hued marble; beneath the cupola, painted in false relief, a marble Sagrario contains the Tabernacle.

The outstanding Late Baroque **sacristy★★** (1727–64) is called the Christian Alhambra for its intricate stuccowork. The door and cedarwood furnishings, inlaid with tortoiseshell, mother-of-pearl and silver, are by a Carthusian monk, José Manuel Vásquez.

♠♣ Parque de las Ciencias★

Av. de la Ciencia. Open Tue–Sat 10am–7pm; Sun & public hols 10am–3pm. Closed 1 Jan, 1 May, 25 Dec. €7, addl €2.50 planetarium. ℘958 13 19 00. www.parqueciencias.com.
This science park includes an interactive museum, planetarium, observatory and tropical butterfly collection.

Sacromonte

The hillside opposite the Generalife is the Romani quarter, where (touristy) flamenco performances that vary in quality are given in caves. At the end of Camino del Sacromonte is the 17C–18C abbey for which the hill is named. Inside is the Museo Cuevas (Cave Museum) del Sacromonte interpretation centre and ethnographic museum (Barranco de los Negros; open mid-Mar–mid-Oct 10am–8pm, until 6pm in winter; €5; ℘958 21 51 20; www.sacromonte-granada.com), detailing local Romani life past and present.

Hospital Real

Cuesta del Hospicio.
The royal hospital, now the university rectorate, was founded by the Catholic

Monarchs. The plan, similar to those in Toledo and Santiago de Compostela, is of a cross within a square. Four Plateresque windows adorn the facade.

Fundación Rodríguez-Acosta★
Callejón Niños del Rollo 8.
Open mid-Mar–mid-Oct 10am–6.30pm (until 4.30pm rest of year). €5. Combined ticket with Alhambra €17. ℘958 227 497. www.fundacionrodriguezacosta.com.
Below the Alhambra, this extraordinary modernist complex, cascading down the hillside, was built between 1914 and 1928 and is a National Monument. It comprises the studio and library of acclaimed painter José María Rodríguez-Acosta (1886–1941) and the collection of archaeologist Manuel Gómez-Moreno (1870–1970).
Gómez-Moreno's personal collection includes Romanesque and Gothic pieces and canvases by Zurbarán, Ribera, Alonso Cano and others as well as Aztec and Chinese artefacts.
A guided 50-min tour also takes in the splendid terraced gardens offering panoramic views, caves and underground galleries.

Carmen de los Mártires
Po. de los Mártires.
Open Mon–Fri 10am–2pm, 6–8pm (4–6pm mid-Oct–Mar), Sat–Sun & public hols 10am–8pm (until 6pm mid-Oct–Mar). ℘958 22 79 53.
The romantic terraced gardens★ of this Carmelite monastery on the Alhambra hill are embellished with fountains and sculptures.

OTHER SIGHTS
Museo Sefardí
Placeta Berrocal 5.
Open Mar-Oct Tue-Sat 9.30am-7.30pm, Nov-Feb 9.30am-6pm, Sun 10am-3pm. €5. ℘925 22 36 65.
www.museosefardidegranada.es.
This charming house in the Realejo area, formerly Granata al-Yahud, offers an abridged version of the story of the city's once-vibrant and influential Jewish population, banished in 1492.

Huerta de San Vicente – Casa-Museo Federico García Lorca
Virgen Blanca. Open Tue-Sun; see website for seasonal hours. Guided vists every 45min from 10am. €3; free Wed exc hols. ℘958 258 466.
www.huertadesanvicente.com.
On the southwest outskirts of Granada is the house where Lorca (◐ see Fuente Vaqueros) wrote many of his best-known works. It is surrounded by a public park with a children's play area and outdoor cafés.

EXCURSIONS
Fuente Vaqueros
Federico García Lorca, poet and dramatist, was born 20km/12.4mi from Granada, in this village in 1898.
The Museo Casa Natal (birthplace museum) offers admirers an insight into his life. (Poeta Federico García Lorca, nº 4; open by guided tour only on the hour Tue–Sun Oct–Mar 10am–1pm, 4pm & 5pm; Apr–Jun 10am–1pm, 5pm & 6pm; Jul–Sep 10am–2pm; closed Sun pm; €1.80; ℘958 51 64 53; www.patronatogarcialorca.org.)

SIERRA NEVADA★★
The Sierra Nevada between the Costa del Sol and Granada is massive, beautiful, and often snow-capped. There is skiing at Solynieve, with over 60km/37mi of slopes, 45 runs and 20 ski lifts. Lodging is at Pradollano.
Vehicular access to the national park is restricted; the best way to tour is on foot. The most interesting routes are the ascents to the Laguna de la Yeguas, Mulhacén (3 482m/11 424ft) and Veleta (3 394m/11 132ft). Contact El Dornajo Visitor Centre (Ctra de Granada a Sierra Nevada/A-395, km. 23; open Wed–Sun mid-Apr–Jun 9.30am-2.30pm, 4.30-7.30pm; ℘958 34 06 25).

Alhama de Granada★
◖ 60km/37mi SW on the A 92 and A 335.
Alhama de Granada is a village of whitewashed houses and narrow streets above a deep gorge, dominated by the

The Alpujarran Uprising

In 1499 the Arabs who did not wish to leave Spain were forced to renounce their religion and to convert to Christianity. In 1566 Philip II forbade these converts (*moriscos*) from their language and traditional dress, which sparked a serious uprising, especially in Las Alpujarras where the Moriscos proclaimed as king Fernando de Córdoba under the name Abén Humeya. In 1571 Philip II sent in the army under Don Juan of Austria, who crushed the rebellion. Unrest remained, at least according to the Crown, and in 1609 Philip III ordered the expulsion of all Moriscos (who numbered about 275 000) from Spain.

Iglesia de la Encarnación★, a well-proportioned church built of golden stone. The stunning **view★** from the belvedere behind the Iglesia del Carmen encompasses the canyon of the Alhama River. Baths on the outskirts date to the Roman period. A Moorish **cistern★** survives.

🚗 DRIVING TOUR

THE ALPUJARRAS★★
90km/56mi. Allow one day.

This isolated region stretches across the southern slopes of the Sierra Nevada.

From Lanjarón to Valor
The High Alpujarras encompass the valley of the Guadalfeo river. Houses typically have a flat roof terrace, or *terrao*.

Lanjarón
This resort is famous for its medicinal mineral water (Lanjarón is a major bottled-water brand) and spa. The 16C castle affords fine valley views.

▶ 9km/5.6mi from Lanjarón, before Órgiva, take the GR 421, a narrow mountain road.

Pampaneira★★
Of all the villages in the **Poqueira Valley★★**, Pampaneira best preserves its traditional architecture, including the 17C Iglesia de Santa Cruz.
Bubión, a centre of Morisco resistance in 1569, is 5km/3mi further along. In **Capileira** is the **Museo de Artes y Costumbres Populares**, a museum re-creating 19C Alpujarran life through its popular arts and customs (📞958 76 30 51, www.capileira.es).

▶ Return to the GR 421. The road enters the **Trevélez Valley★**.

Trevélez★
Trevélez, the highest municipality in Spain (1 600m/5,248ft), is famous for its cured hams and dried sausages. Behind the village rises the **Mulhacén**, continental Spain's highest peak (3 482m/11 424ft). Beyond Trevélez, the valley opens and the verdant landscape gives way to drier terrain planted with the occasional vineyard. **Yegen** owes its fame to the Englishman Gerald Brenan, author of *South from Granada*.
Abén Humeya (☞see The Alpujarran Uprising, above) was born and lived in Válor, the next village after Yegen. Its 16C church, like many in the region, is built in Mudéjar style.

ADDRESSES

🛏 STAY

🍴 **Hotel Los Tilos** – Pl. de Bib Rambla 4. 📞958 26 67 12. www.hotellostilos.com. 30 rooms. ⌑€7. This basic, modern hotel fronts onto a pretty square filled with flower stalls, adjacent to the cathedral. Request a room with plaza views.

🍴 **Hotel Maciá Plaza** – Pl. Nueva 5. 📞958 22 75 36. www.maciaplaza.com. 44 rooms. ⌑€7. At the foot of the Alhambra, this cheerful hotel has simple rooms with gaudy patterned accents.

⊖⊜⊜ **Hotel América** – Real de la Alhambra 53. ℘958 22 74 71. www. hotelamericagranada.com. 16 rooms. ⊏€8.50. Restaurant ⊖⊜. Closed Dec–Feb. The charming central patio is the main selling point of this family-run hotel wihin the Alhambra complex.

⊖⊜⊜⊜ **Hotel Casa 1800 Granada** – C. Benalua 11.℘958 21 07 00. www. hotelcasa1800granada.com. 25 rooms. ⊏€11.50. Take a walk on Granada's Moorish side at this 16C palace–cum– luxury hotel with painted artesonado ceilings and Alhambra views. Breakfasts, taken in the traditional Andalucían patio (fountains, ivy, azulejos) are heavenly.

⊗/ EAT

⊖⊜⊜ **El Mercader** – Imprenta 2. ℘633 79 04 40. The husband-and-wife team behind El Mercader serves fresh, quirky renditions of Andalucían classics. Vegetarian and gluten-free options abound. There's a good selection of local wines.

⊖⊜⊜ **Las Tinajas** – C. Martínez Campos 17. ℘958 25 43 93. www. restaurantelastinajas.com. A gorgeous traditional Andalucían dining room (carved-wood furniture, ironed tablecloths, framed memorabilia) sets the scene for soul-satisfying comfort-food meals served with panache. Things are less buttoned-down in the bar.

⊖⊜⊜ **Chikito** – Pl. Campillo 9. ℘958 22 33 64. www.restaurantechikito.com. Perennially packed, Chikito is synonymous with hand-sliced jamón a good home cooking. Lorca was a regular in the 30s.

⊖⊜⊜⊜ **Mirador de Morayma** – Pianista García Carrillo 2. ℘958 22 48 12. www.miradordemorayma.com. Closed Sun July–Aug, Sun eve rest of year. Hotel Rural's restaurant in the Albaicín has one of the best settings of any in the city (and maybe Spain): directly across from the Alhambra. Expect updated *Graníano* cuisine, private-label wines and the occasional flamenco show.

TAPAS

Bodegas Castañeda – Almireceros 1. ℘958 21 54 64. This old bodega with hundreds of bottles on display serves terrific budget-friendly tapas samplers.

Casa Enrique – Acera del Darro 8. ℘958 25 50 08. Closed Sun and half of Aug. Stop into this 19C cubby for some *vino*.

La Trastienda – Pl. Cuchilleros 11. ℘958 22 69 65. Closed Aug. Head down the steps into this former grocery store, which has retained its 19C counter, to tuck into charcuterie plates.

CAFÉS

La Fontana – Carrera del Darro 19. ℘958 22 77 59. Housed in an old residence at the foot of the Alhambra and Albaicín hills, this antique-adorned café is a fine place for a quiet drink.

Teterías – Calderería Nueva. Calle Calderería Nueva, between the city centre and the Albaicín, is a typical ex-Moorish quarter street. It's lined with cosy *teterías*, or Arab-style tea houses, of which **Kasbah** (no 4) is a fine example. Some offer hookah service.

BARS & NIGHTLIFE

El Camborio – Camino de Sacromonte 47. ℘692 80 24 24. Open Thu–Sat. Party in a cave– four, in this case –at this nightclub that's been pumping for over 30 years. Take a taxi as it is located in a slightly seedy district.

Paripe– Calle Moras 1 ℘629 42 38 55. This relaxed cocktail bar attracts the post-work crowd, and the party continues with lively music playing until 3am.

Tic Tac – Calle Horno de Haza 19. ℘958 29 63 66. Students, locals and out-of-towners intermingle at this pocket-size gay bar that's welcome to all. A catchy pop soundtrack keeps the party going until 4am on weekends.

Taller de Arte Vimaambi – Cuesta de San Gregorio 30. ℘958 22 73 34. www.vimaambi.com. Open Thu–Sat. This arts centre in the Albaicín hosts regular flamenco performances by up-and-coming artists.

FIESTAS

The city's religious festivals are lively, colourful events, especially those held during Holy Week and on Corpus Christi. There's also an annual **music and dance festival** (www.granadafestival. org) in June and July held in the stunning Generalife gardens.

Almería

Almería is a swathe of white between the Mediterranean and a fortress-crowned hill. Its hot dry climate – hills shelter it from winds – has helped make it a tourist hotspot. Life bustles in the city centre on the tree-lined Paseo de Almería. Another oasis, Parque de Nicolás Salmerón, stretches along the harbour. Houses in La Chanca, the fishermen's quarter, are hewn into rock.

▶ **Population:** 194 952
◔ **Michelin Map:** 124 Costa del Sol.
🯅 **Info:** Plaza de la Constitución. 𝒫950 21 05 38. www.turismodealmeria.org.
▶ **Location:** Almería lies on the southern coast on the Mediterranean. 🚍 Almería.
◉ **Don't Miss:** The Alcazaba of Almería, the Moorish castle that overlooks the city.
🕐 **Timing:** Take a half day.
👪 **Kids:** Visit the Wild West at Oasys theme park.

A BIT OF HISTORY

The city was founded by Emir and Caliph of Córdoba Abd ar-Rahman III in 955 and played an important role in the 11C when it was the capital of a taifa kingdom. It was captured by Alfonso VII in 1147, but upon his death ten years later, it fell back into Moorish hands. Almería was part of the Nasrid kingdom of Granada until 1489, when it was reconquered.

In the last third of the 20C, the development of advanced agricultural techniques and the opening-up of modern infrastructures placed this provincial capital at the forefront of Span's year-round fruit and vegetable cultivation.

SIGHTS

Alcazaba★

Open mid-Sep–Mar Tue–Sat 9am– 6pm. Apr–mid-Jun Tue–Sat 9am–8pm. Jun–mid-Sep Tue–Sun 9am–3pm. 𝒫950 80 10 08.

Abd ar-Rahman III ordered this fortress built in the 10C. Almotacín added a splendid palace, enlarged by the Catholic Monarchs, whose crenellated ochre walls dominate Almería. A section of old ramparts links the fort to San Cristóbal hill, once crowned by a castle. Attractive **gardens** are laid out in the first walled enclosure where rivulets spring from fountains. The bell in the Muro de la Vela, a wall separating the enclosures, once warned of pirates. In the third enclosure, the keep (Torre del Homenaje), with incredibly thick walls, looks down on the Christian *alcázar*. The **view★** from the battlements takes in the town, surrounding hills and sea.

Catedral★

Pl. de la Catedral. Open daily; see website for seasonal hours. €5 (incl museum). 𝒫950 23 48 48.

The cathedral was built in 1524 and fortified against raids by Barbary pirates. It has two **portals★** and, at the east end, a **carved sunburst★**. The high altar and pulpits of inlaid marble and jasper are 18C, the choir stalls are from 1560 and the *jasper trascoro* with three alabaster statues is 18C. A chapel in the ambulatory houses a statue of the Cristo de la Escucha.

Aljibes de Jayrán

C. Tenor Iribarne. Open Tue–Sun 10am –2pm and Fri–Sat Jun–Sep 6–9pm, Oct–May 5–8pm. 𝒫950 27 30 39.

Take a peek inside the Moorish water cisterns that once supplied the city.

Museo de Almería

Ctra de Ronda 91. Open mid-Jun–mid-Sep Tue–Sun 9am–3.30pm, mid-Sep–mid-Jun Tue–Sat 9am–8.30pm, Sun 9am–3.30pm. 𝒫950 10 04 09. www.museosdeandalucia.es.

Museum exhibits cover prehistory through the Islamic era with pieces from sites in the province, notably of the El Argar and Los Millares cultures.

🚗 DRIVING TOUR

THE EAST COAST★

240km/150mi. Take the airport road and turn right after 14.5km/9mi.

Parque Natural de Cabo de Gata-Níjar★★

📞950 38 02 99. Oficina de Turismo de San José. Av. San José 27. Níjar. www.cabodegata-nijar.com.

South of the volcanic Cabo de Gata mountains, past the Acosta salt flats, this park is a haven of wild, unspoilt beaches. The lighthouse faces Mermaid Reef, popular for fishing.

On the other side of the mountain is the small summer resort of San José with two beautiful beaches: los **Genoveses★** and the nudist beach of **Monsul★** (2km/1.2mi from the centre of the town). Ask locally for directions to Cala Rajá and Cala de Entremedio, two quieter beaches.

▶ Take the AL 12; turn at Venta del Probe.

Agua Amarga

Agua Amarga is a pleasant seaside village with an attractive beach and a good café at Bar La Plaza.

▶ Follow the coast road to Mojácar (32km/20mi). The road twists upwards, offering views of the coast, a 17C fortified tower and a 13–14C Moorish watchtower.

Mojácar★

The village stands on a splendid **site★** on an outcrop with **views** of the coast (2km/1.2mi away) and a plain broken by odd rock formations. The steep, narrow village streets are clearly Moorish.

▶ Follow the AL 12 back towards Almería, turning off at Níjar.

Níjar

This one-time Arab village carries on the craft of weaving jarapas (blankets) using strips of material called trapos.

Tabernas

55km/34mi along the N 370.

The dunes stretching from Benahadux to Tabernas have been used countless times as film locations, from *El Cid*, *Lawrence of Arabia* and Sergio Leone's Spaghetti Westerns right up to an episode of *Dr Who* with Matt Smith. **Oasys/ Mini Hollywood** is a desert theme park (Ctra Nacional 340, km. 464, Tabernas open Holy Week–Oct 10am–sunset, rest of year weekends only 10am– 6pm; see website for full hours and events; €22.90; 📞902 533 532; www. oasysparquetematico.com) that brings to life some of the movie magic with Wild West shows in a mock-up town complete with a saloon and Can-Can dancers. Less congruous is the park zoo, which includes a cactus garden and parrot shows as well as an 'African Savannah' with giraffes, lions, white rhinos, ostriches, gazelles, warthogs and hyenas. Pack your swimming costume for a dip in the park's pool.

Beyond Tabernas, the land is red and barren, and pottery-making is the main occupation. **Sorbas** has a singular and vertiginous **setting★**. Its houses cling to a cliff encircled by a river.

ADDRESSES

🏨 STAY

🍽🍽 **Hotel Costasol** – Po. de Almería 58. 📞950 23 40 11. www.hotelcostasol.com. 55 rooms. 🛏€6.70. The Costasol is set on Almería's busiest shopping street. Rrooms are bright, modern, large and comfy; some have balconies.

🍽🍽🍽 **Las Salinas de Cabo de Gata** – Brrda. Almadraba de Monteleva, Cabo de Gata. 📞950 37 01 03. www. hoteldelassalinas.amhotel.com. 20 rooms. Restaurant 🍽🍽🍽. The hotel's tranquil location in Parque Natural de Cabo de Gata makes it an ideal base from which to enjoy excursions into the outlying countryside.

Málaga★

Founded by Phoenicians, Málaga became a Roman colony and later the main port of Moorish Granada. Today, it is the gateway to the tourist-laden Costa del Sol but retains characteristic old houses and gardens that reflect its importance as a 19C port. Beaches stretch eastwards from La Malagueta, at one end of the Paseo Marítimo, to El Palo (5km/3mi E), a former fishing quarter.

▶ **Population:** 569 005
◔ **Michelin Map:** 578 and 124.
🗈 **Info:** Pl. de la Marina 11.
   ℘951 92 92 50.
   www.malagaturismo.com.
◗ **Location:** Málaga is 59km/ 37mi E of Marbella and 124km/77mi SW of Granada, set at the mouth of the Guadalmedina and on the Mediterranean.
   🚃Málaga (AVE).
🅿 **Parking:** Not in old quarter.
👁 **Don't Miss:** Alcazaba; Museo Carmen Thyssen Málaga; Centre Pompidou Málaga; Colección Ifergan.

THE CITY TODAY

Málaga used to be a gritty rundown port city that most visitors would skip over on their way to the beach resorts of the Costa del Sol. Today, however, you might call it Andalucía's cultural capital thanks to its slew of art galleries, museums, upscale restaurants and refurbished harbour. Malagá's transformation was solidified in 2015 with the opening of the only Centre Pompidou outside of France.

Plaza de la Merced is the city hub, while in spring and summer the action shifts to the beaches, particularly to Pedregalejo, on the edge of town.

SIGHTS

Museo Picasso Málaga★

San Agustín 8. Open Jul–Aug 10am–8pm, Mar–Jun and Sep–Oct until 7pm, Nov–Feb until 6pm. Closed 1 & 6 Jan, 25 Dec. €8; free last two hours of Sun. ℘952 12 76 00. www.museopicassomalaga.org.

The 16C Palacio de Buenavista houses lesser-known oils, sketches, engravings, sculptures and ceramics by Málaga's most famous native son, Picasso, drawn from the collections of Christine and Bernard Ruiz-Picasso, the artist's daughter-in-law and grandson.

Among the paintings are *Bust of Woman with Arms Crossed Behind Head* (1939), *Woman in an Armchair* (1946) and *Jacqueline Seated* (1954). There is also a library and archive. Temporary exhibitions (additional charge) of other artists' work are held.

Alcazaba★★

Alcazabilla 2. Take the lift from C. Guillén Sotelo, behind the Town Hall. Open Apr–Oct 9am–8pm, Nov–Mar 9am–6pm. €3.50; €5.50 incl Castillo de Gibralfaro. ℘952 93 29 87.

The ruins of a **Roman theatre** line the approach to this 11C Moorish fortress on the sea, the largest of its kind in Europe. Inside the final gateway are Moorish gardens. There is a **view★** of the harbour and city from the ramparts. The former Nasrid palace is within. Higher up is the **Castillo de Gibralfaro★** (same opening times as the Alcazaba), which houses a museum and the city's Parador.

Catedral★

C. Molina Lario. Open Mon–Fri 10am–6pm, Sat 10am–5pm (Sun & pub hols mass only). €6 ea Catedral and Cubiertas; €10 combined ticket. ℘952 22 03 45.

Construction over a massive former mosque spanned three centuries (16C–18C), but the south tower was never completed, hence the cathedral's nickname, 'la manquita' (the one-armed little lady) . **Oven vaulting★** covers the aisles. Classically ordered Corinthian columns, entablatures and cornices stalls★ bear figures by Pedro de Mena that show the influence of Alonso Cano. Overhead are 4 500 organ pipes. There is an early-15C carved and painted Gothic retable★ in the ambulatory. The 18C Palacio Episcopal (Episcopal Palace) on the square, in Baroque style, has a marble facade. El Sagrario, an unusual 16C rectangular church in the cathedral gardens, features a north portal★ in Isabelline Gothic style. The 18C interior is Baroque, with a Mannerist altarpiece★★. Since 2016 visitors can take a guided rooftop (cubiertas) tour★, perfect at sunset.

Fundación Picasso/Museo-Casa Natal Pablo Picasso

Pl. de la Merced 15. Open 9.30am–8pm. Closed 1 Jan, 25 Dec & Tue Nov–Mar. €3, addl €1 for exhibitions; free Sun after 4pm. ✆951 92 66 60. http://fundacionpicasso.malaga.eu. This mid-15C building on the Plaza de la Merced shows a number of Picasso's drawings as well as photos and ceramics.

Museo Unicaja de Artes y Costumbres Populares★ (Unicaja Museum of Popular Arts and Customs)

Pasillo de Santa Isabel 10. Open Mon–Fri 10am–5pm, Sat 10am–3pm. Closed public holidays. €4. ✆952 21 71 37. www.museoartespopulares.com. This charming, rustic folk museum, housed in a 17C inn, displays numerous interesting objects from the 18C and 19C that were used in the home, on the farm or at sea. There are also costumes.

Santuario de la Virgen de la Victoria★

Pl. del Santuario. Guided tours (45min) Tue–Fri, Sun 10am–12pm, 4.30–7pm, Sat 10am–12pm. ✆951 92 66 20. The sanctuary was founded by the Catholic Monarchs. The church is dominated by a large 17C altarpiece at the centre of which stands the camarín★★, a Baroque masterpiece covered by stuccowork and presided over by a fine 15C German Virgin and Child.

Centro de Arte Contemporáneo de Málaga

C. Alemania. Open Tue–Sun 10am–8pm; late Jun–second wk Sep 10am–2pm, 5–9pm. Closed 1 Jan, 25 Dec. ✆952 12 00 55. www.cacmalaga.org. The old wholesale market, a Rationalist building by Luis Gutiérrez Soto (1939), is a modern art centre with rotating exhibitions.

Museo Carmen Thyssen Málaga

C. Compañía 10. Tue–Sun 10am–8pm. Closed 1 Jan, 25 Dec. €10, incl temporary exhibitions; free Sun after 5pm. ✆902 303 131. www.carmenthyssenmalaga.org. The stately 16C Palacio de Villalón is the setting for 230 hand-picked works of art from the collection of Baroness Carmen von Thyssen-Bornemisza. The paintings concentrate on 19C Spanish artists with works by Julio Romero de Torres, Joaquim Sorolla and Ignacio Zuloaga among the most famous.

Centre Pompidou Málaga★★

Puerto de Málaga, Pasaje Dr. Carnillo Casaux. Open Wed–Mon mid-Jun–mid-Sep 11am–10pm, mid-Sep–mid-Jun 9.30am–8pm. Closed 1 Jan and 25 Dec. €9 incl temporary exhibitions; free Sun after 4pm. ✆951 92 62 00. www.centrepompidou-malaga.eu. Opened in 2015, this outpost of the Centre Pompidou Paris is housed in 'El Cubo', a pop-up white 'cube', in the city's revitalised port area. There are works by Picasso, Magritte and Kahlo in the permanent exhibition, and three temporary modern art exhibitions are held each year.

Centre Pompidou Málaga★★

Puerto de Málaga, Pasaje Dr. Carnillo Casaux. Open Wed–Mon mid-Jun–mid-Sep 11am–10pm, mid-Sep–mid-Jun 9.30am–8pm. Closed 1 Jan and 25 Dec. €9 incl temporary exhibitions; free Sun after 4pm. ✆951 92 62 00. www.centrepompidou-malaga.eu. Opened in 2015, this outpost of the Centre Pompidou Paris is housed in 'El Cubo', a pop-up white 'cube', in the city's revitalised port area. There are works by Picasso, Magritte and Kahlo in the permanent exhibition, and three temporary modern art exhibitions are held each year.

Ifergan Collection★

C. Sebastián Souvirón 9. Open Mon–Fri 10am–7pm. Closed second half Aug, 1 & 7 Jan, 25 Dec. €10. ☏951 93 73 41. www.ifergan-collection.com.

The world's premier compilation of Phoenician art can be found in this private gallery that quietly opened in 2018. The exhibit, which includes specimens from all the great civilisations, culminates in a backlit chamber lined with dozens of religious idols recovered from a Phoenician ship that sank over two millennia ago, perhaps on its way to Málaga.

Mercado de Atarazanas

Atarazanas 10. Open Mon–Sat 8am–2pm. Closed 1 Jan, 25 Dec. ☏951 92 60 10.

The recently refurbished traditional food market sells the finest local ingredients: olives, sardines, mangoes etc.

Beaches

Málaga's favourite strand is the Pedregalejo beach northeast of the city, where nightlife rages and the famous Malagueño sardine barbecues are an attraction year round. The sardines are cooked on stakes (*espetos*) inclined over coals so the juice runs down into the sand instead of dripping into the fire and creating a conflagration. The beaches west of Málaga proceed from (the unsightly) La Malagueta to San Andrés, La Misericordia, Guadalmar, Los Álamos, Playamar La Carihuela and Torremolinos, each with lifeguards, rentable lounge chairs and blue-flag ratings.

EXCURSION
Jardín Botánico Histórico Finca de la Concepción★

◐ Ctra de las Pedrizas, 7km/4.3mi N. Open Tue–Sat Oct–Easter 9.30am–4.30pm. Easter–Sep 9.30am–7.30pm. €5.20. ☏951 92 61 80. http://laconcepcion.malaga.eu.

Stroll through this delightful jungle, planted with some 300 tropical and subtropical species and dotted with streams, waterfalls and Roman ruins.

🚗 DRIVING TOURS

AXARQUÍA★

This tiny, little-known area is blanketed with almond and olive trees and wheat fields. Bordered to the west by the Sierra de Málaga and to the east by the Sierras de Tejeda and Almijara, the Axarquía falls south to the Costa del Sol. Mudéjar bell towers rise over ex-Moorish warrens and villages built by locals fleeing the attacks of Barbary pirates. The Axarquía was also ground zero for the Moorish uprising that followed the end of the so-called Reconquistat.

Comares

About 40km/25mi from Rincón de la Victoria toward Benagalbón (45min).

Comares, accessible via a snaking but scenic road, is know as 'the balcony of the Axarquía'. On a hilltop, the town overlooks the entire region and has magical sunsets. A marked route guides you through the streets of this village of Moorish origins: Follow the ceramic tiles set into the pavement. (🏃 Several long-range hiking trails also originate in the main square.) On the walk, you'll come across the Mudéjar **Iglesia de Nuestra Señora de la Encarnación**, built on the footprint of the former mosque. **Plaza de los Verdiales**, named for the typical regional dances of Málaga, leads into a street through two exposed-brick Moorish arches. From the ruins of the **Moorish castle**, the view over the rooftops and the mountains is memorable. Comares was a strategic military prize. Omar ibn Hafsun was based here during his revolt against the Ummayyads. Don't miss the **cemetery★** featuring a typical burial style: Rocky soil necessitated the construction of tombs. The oldest are to the right of the entrance.

Northen Axarquía

Allow half a day.

The narrow roads leading to **Alfarnate** (via Riogordo) cross fruit and olive orchards. More than the village itself, the countryside around Alfarnate is what merits the detour: This rough terrain is a result of the proximity of the mountains and the ensemble of Mediterranean scrub and oak trees. ⊼Three marked hikes depart from the village.

The most spectacular leads to the summit of the **Pico de Vilo** (1 415m/4 600ft), from which a 360° view looks over the Sierra Nevada, Maroma peak, Viñuela lake and the sea (moderately difficult 4hr round trip). After resting up at the Venta, you can descend to the south through olive-oil producing **Periana** and **Viñuela** (a large dammed lake). En route, to the east, is the impressive **Ventas de Zafarraya**, a breach carved through the Sierra de Almijara back to Alhama de Granada.

The Nerja Road

S of Viñuela, the scenic MA 4106 and MA 4105 connect several adorable villages. **Salares**, built next to a roaring brook and spanned by a Roman bridge, is filled with sleepy once-Moorish streets. Don't miss the brick-and-tile bell tower/**minaret** from the Almohade era. On the far side of the bridge, follow the marked path (⊼ easy 3hr, 6km/4mi loop) that winds along the flank of the mountain through orange, walnut and cherry groves. The bell tower/minaret of **Archez** is a Mudéjar gem, with motifs in brick *sekba* in its main body.

The largest village of the Axarquía, Competa (23km/14mi from Nerja and 60km/37mi from Málaga) has a lovely old nucleus as well as real tourist infrastructure. Sweet **Málaga wine**, for sale everywhere, is celebrated with a fiesta on 15 August. Another of many post-card-perfect white villages above the coast is **Frigiliana**, beautifully restored but rather overrun by tourists. It boasts pretty streets, the ruins of a castle and a sugar cane manufacturer installed in a former palace. Frigiliana is connected to Nerja (6km/4mi) by a bus.

ADDRESSES

🛏 STAY

😑😑😑 **Hotel Castilla y Guerrero** – Córdoba 7. ℰ952 21 86 35. www.hotel castillaguerrero.com. 46 rooms. ⊑€4.50. Plain but comfortable and well situated, this budget hotel has spacious rooms and genial staff. Go up the stairs to check in.

😑😑😑 **Hotel Don Curro** – Sancha de Lara 7. ℰ952 22 72 00. www. hoteldoncurro.com. 118 rooms Restaurant 😑😑😑. This high-rise hotel is in the centre of town and features simple, clean (if fusty) digs and a games room that's always full.

℣ EAT

😑😑 **El Chinitas** – Moreno Monroy 4–6. ℰ952 21 09 72. www.elchinitas.com. Ceramic murals, photos and pictures of popular personalities and artists make this one of the most characterful restaurants in Málaga. The terrace on a pedestrianised street is pleasant, and there are dining areas on three floors.

😑😑😑 **El Trillo**– C. de Don Juan Diaz 4. ℰ952 60 39 20. www.trillomalaga.com. The outdoor tables at this upscale Andalucían tavern afford terrific people-watching in the old town. The tomato salad topped with tuna *ventresca* (oil-cured belly) is heavenly, as is the *rabo de toro* (stewed oxtail).

TAPAS

La Mesonera – C. Gómez Pallete 11. ℰ609 93 36 45. This sardine-can bar fills up with performers before and after performances at the Teatro Cervantes opposite. Celebrity sightings or not, cound on delectable tapas and a typically Andalucían atmosphere.

Lo Güeno Mesón – C. Marín García 9. ℰ952 22 30 48. www.logueno.es. Over 75 choices, from sautéed wild mushrooms to venison stew to saucy snails, are on this casual spot's menu.

Antigua Casa de Guardia – Alameda 18. ℰ952 21 46 80. www. antiguacasadeguardia.net. Málaga's oldest bar (est.1840), lined with wine barrels, oozes old-world character.

CAFÉS

Café Central – Pl. de la Constitución 11. ℘952 22 49 72. www.cafecentral malaga.com. One of Málaga's most legendary and long-standing coffee houses has a fine terrace on the square and a bustling tea room. There are no coldbrews or flat whites here – just the traditional stuff.

Casa Aránda – Herrería del Rey 3. ℘952 22 28 12. www.casa-aranda.net This lively, atmospheric café (est 1932) is the perfect place for meeting friends over *chocolate con churros*.

NIGHTLIFE

El Pimpi – Granada 62. ℘952 22 89 90. www.elpimpi.com. Málaga's most famous restaurant, with barrels signed by Picasso and other celebrities, is an atmospheric spot to have some Málaga wine and tapas. The food, while nothing to write home about, gets the job done.

Puerta Oscura – Molina Lario 5. ℘952 22 19 00. www.puertaoscura malaga.com. Unwind here with a coffee or a cocktail while you listen to chamber music. The setting is classically elegant, intimate and refined.

Kelipe, Centro de Arte Flamenco – C. Muro de Puerta Nueva 10. ℘692 82 98 85. www.kelipe.net. Thu–Sat show starts 9pm. Reservations essential (English spoken). An intimate 19C palace is the setting for the best and most authentic flamenco show in town.

Antequera★

Set against the backdrop of the Sierra del Torcal, an extraordinary range of eroded rock formations, blindingly white Antequera overlooks a fertile plain with the silhouette of the Peña de los Enamorados ("the lovers' cliff") in the distance. There, according to local legend, an Arab princess and a young Christian threw themselves to their death to avoid capture by the soldiers sent by the girl's father. The town's cobblestone alleys, grilled windows and fine churches are quintessential Andalucía.

- ▶ **Population:** 41 154
- ⚲ **Michelin Map:** 578 U 16.
- ▤ **Info:** Plaza de San Sebastián 7. ℘952 70 25 05 www.turismo.antequera.es.
- ◗ **Location:** Antequera lies in southern Andalucía, inland from the Costa del Sol. Antequera (AVE) - Antequera-Santa Ana (18km).
- ⦿ **Don't Miss:** Ancient dolmens (burial chambers).
- ⦿ **Kids:** Unusual rock formations in the Parque Natural de El Torcal.

A BIT OF HISTORY

Antequera, at the geological centre of Andalucía, has for millennia been a crossroads between Málaga, Córdoba, Granada and Sevilla, much fought over by Castilian and Nasrid troops. Its strategic position brought important artistic and religious treasures and many monuments, particularly after the Reconquest by Ferdinand of Castile in 1410.

SIGHTS

Alcazaba★★

Open 10am–6pm. Closed 1 & 6 Jan, 25 Dec. €6 incl Real Colegiata de Santa María. ℘952 70 07 37.

This was the first fortress taken by the Christians during the 'reconquest' of the kingdom of Granada (1410), but it was soon lost again. Today its walls shelter a pleasant garden and its towers offer a fine **view★** over Antequera.

Antequera with the Alcazaba

Real Colegiata de Santa María La Mayor★

Pl. de Santa María. Open Mon–Sat 10am-7pm; mid-Sep–Mar Mon–Sat 10.30am-5.30pm; Sun 10.30am-3pm. €6 incl Alcazaba. ℘952 70 07 37.

Access to this defunct church, at the foot of the castle gardens, is by the 16C **Arco de los Gigantes** (Arch of Giants). Built in 1514, it has one of the earliest Renaissance facades in Andalucía. The adjacent observation point looks out on 1C Roman baths.

Iglesia del Carmen★

Pl. del Carmen. Open Tue–Fri 11.30am–1.30pm, 4.30–5.45pm, Sat–Sun & pub hols 11.30am–2pm. €1.50.

The central nave of the church boasts a Mudéjar *artesonado* ceiling and a magnificent Churrigueresque altarpiece.

Museo de la Ciudad de Antequera

Palacio de Nájera, Pl. del Coso Viejo. Open Tue–Fri 9.30am–2pm, 4.30–6.30pm, Sat 9.30am–2pm, 4–7pm, Sun 10am–2pm. Mid-Jun–mid-Sep same morning hours, afternoons Tue–Fri 7–9pm, Sat 6–9pm. Closed public hols. €; free Sun for EU citizens. ℘952 70 83 00.

The town's main museum, set in a 17C palace, exhibits archaeological pieces. The most outstanding item is the **Ephebus of Antequera★**, a 1C bronze Roman sculpture.

EXCURSION

Parque Natural de El Torcal★

▶ 14km/8.7mi SE. Take the C 3310 toward Villanueva de la Concepción; Centro de Recepción/Visitantes 'El Torcal' (signposted) open Apr–Sep 10am–7pm (5pm rest of year). ℘952 24 33 24. www.torcaldeantequera.com.

The park, spread over 12ha/30 acres, has some of Spain's most unusual natural scenery, in eroded karst. Learn about its geological history in the Interpretation Centre, have a coffee on the cafe terrace overlooking the rocky landscape, then strike out along one of the two signposted paths (🚶 1hr or 3hr).

Note to stargazers: The centre also includes an observatory.

🚗 DRIVING TOURS

MENGA & VIERA DOLMENS★

Ctra de Málaga 5. To the left of the Antequera exit on the A 354, toward Granada. Open Jun–mid-Sep Tue–Sun 9am–3pm; Apr–May Tue–Sat 9am–7.30pm, Sun until 3pm; mid-Sep–Mar Tue–Sat 9am–5.30pm, Sun until 3.30pm. ℘952 71 22 06.

Dating to 2 500–2 200 BC, these dolmens are enormous funerary chambers beneath stone slabs and are one of Spain's newest UNESCO sites. Menga, the older and larger, is oblong, divided by pillars supporting stone slabs.

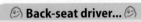

😊 Back-seat driver... 😊

Given the dangerous nature of the ravine, we recommend that you go no further than the metal bridge high above the El Chorro gorge.

▷ Continue along the A 354 and turn left onto the N 331.

Dolmen de El Romeral★

Cerro Romeral. Antigua CN 232 toward Córdoba. Open same times as Menga & Viera.

This is the most recent chamber (1800 BC), consisting of small flat stones laid to create a trapezoidal section.

TOUR TO THE DESFILADERO DE LOS GAITANES★★

50km/31mi SW.

This protected area in the Subbética mountain range includes the spectacular Gaitaines Gorge, through which the River Guardalhorce flows. Golden eagles nest in the peaks.

▷ Take the A 343 to Álora.

After the Abdajalís Valley, the road zigzags through mountain scenery up to **Álora★**, a village of twisting alleyways overlooking the Guadalhorce river.

▷ Take the MA 444 from Álora. Leave your car at the El Chorro campsite. Continue on foot along a tarmac track (🚶 30min there and back) up to a metal bridge with canyon views.

FROM ANTEQUERA TO MÁLAGA★

62km/39mi S by the A 45, C 356, C 345.
These roads afford stunning **views★★** beyond the Puerto del León (Lion Pass, 960m/3 150ft) to Málaga and the sea.

Ronda★★

Ronda stands in a spectacular natural site★★★ above a deep ravine. Its isolation and legends of local highwaymen made it a place of pilgrimage for writers and poets beginning in the 19C Romantic period. Erich Maria Remarque and Ernest Hemingway were 20C Ronda regulars, each seduced by the clifftop houses, historic bullring and vertiginous gorge.

▸ **Population:** 33 978
👁 **Michelin Map:** 578 V 14.
🛈 **Info:** Paseo de Blas Infante. ☎952 18 71 19. www.turismoderonda.es.
▷ **Location:** 60km/37mi inland and over the mountains from Marbella. 🚃Ronda.

SIGHTS

Museo Municipal★

Pl. Mondragón. Open spring & summer Mon–Fri 10am–7pm, Sat–Sun & hols 10am–3pm. Fall & winter Mon–Fri 10am–6pm. Closed 1 & 6 Jan, Good Fri, 25 Dec. €4. ☎952 87 08 18. www.museoderonda.es.

The museum's charming **Mudéjar patio★★** has the remains of azulejos and stucco work between its arches. The collection includes the natural habitats of the Serranía de Ronda, plus historical and ethnographic sections.

Plaza de Toros: Museo Taurino★

Virgen de la Paz. Open 10am; 6–8pm seasonally. €8, bullring and museum. ☎952 87 41 32. www.rmcr.org.

Dating to 1785 and with a capacity for 6 000, the bullring (👁see Cradle of Bullfighting, p496) is aesthetically stunning,

Ronda with the Puente Nuevo

regardless of your views on bullfighting. Enter through an elegant gateway. Traditional Corridas Goyescas, fights in period costumes, are held annually. The museum contains sumptuous costumes and mementos of Ronda matadors.

Casa del Rey Moro

Cuesta de Santo Domingo. Open Oct–Apr 10am–8pm, May–Sep 10am–9:30pm. €7. ☏617 61 08 08. www.casadelreymoro.org.

Though the house (not built by a 'Moorish King' but rather an 18C nobleman) is closed, you can visit the impressive Moorish steps, known as **La Mina**, which descend to the river. The **gardens★** were laid out in 1912 by French landscapist **Jean-Claude Forestier**, who also designed María Luisa Park in Sevilla.

Museo del Bandolero

C. Armiñán 65. Open winter & autumn 11am–7pm, spring & summer 11am–8.30pm. €3.75. ☏952 87 77 85. www.museobandolero.com.

The Serranía de Ronda range was once frequented by bandits, brigands and outlaws. This museum provides insight into these legendary figures.

ꙮ WALKING TOUR

The River Guadalevín divides Ronda into two parts connected by the 18C Puente Nuevo, offering a **view★** of the El Tajo ravine: to the south, the **Ciudad**,

the old quarter and, to the north, the **Mercadillo** old market area. The Camino de los Molinos road provides views★ of the cliffs and the ravine.

LA CIUDAD★★

Guided tours (2hr) from Puente Nuevo. The old walled town, a vestige of the Islamic era (until 1485), is a picturesque quarter of alleys and whitewashed houses with wrought-iron balconies.

▶ Cross the bridge and follow Santo Domingo, passing the 18C neo-Mudéjar Casa del Rey Moro.

Palacio del Marqués de Salvatierra

This small mansion is graced with an exceptional Renaissance **portal★★** and a wrought-iron balcony decorated with pre-Columbian-inspired statues.

▶ From the Arco de Felipe V, by the Puente Viejo, a stone path leads to the Baños Árabes.

Baños Árabes★

Molino. Open Mon–Fri 10am–6pm (until 7pm spring & summer), Sat–Sun 10am–3pm. Closed 1 & 6 Jan, 24 Dec. €3.50. ☏952 18 71 19.

Built at the end of the 13C in the artisans' and tanners' district, the Moorish baths comprise three rooms topped with barrel vaults and illuminated by star-shaped skylights, or *lunettes*.

Cradle of Bullfighting

Ronda is synonymous with bullfighting. Francisco Romero, who was born here in 1700, penned the rules of the 'sport', which until then had been a free-for-all display of audacity and agility. He became the father of modern bullfighting by his introduction of the artistic work with the small cape, or *muleta*. His son Juan introduced the *cuadrilla*, or supporting cast, and his grandson, Pedro Romero (1754–1839), became one of Spain's greatest bullfighters. He founded the Ronda School, known for artistic classicism, strict observance of the rules, and for the *estocada recibiendo*, in which the matador holds his ground and allows the charging bull to impale himself on the sword, considered the most dangerous and 'beautiful' kill.

▶ Follow a stone staircase parallel to the walls, then pass through a 13C gateway, the Puerta de la Acijara.

Minarete de San Sebastián★

This graceful minaret is the only one remaining from a 14C Nasrid mosque. A horseshoe arch frames the door.

Iglesia de Santa María la Mayor★

Pl. de la Duquesa de Parcent. Open Mon–Sat 10am–8pm; Sun 10am–12.30pm, 2–8pm. €4.50. ☎952 87 22 46. www.turismoderonda.es.
The Collegiate Church of St Mary was built over the town's main mosque. Today, only a 13C horseshoe arch, decorated with *atauriques* and calligraphic motifs, and a minaret remain from the original building. The interior is divided into three distinct architectural styles: Gothic (aisles), Plateresque (high altar) and Baroque (choir stalls).

▶ Continue along Manuel Montero.

Palacio de Mondragón

Two Mudéjar towers crown the Renaissance facade of the palace, now the **Museo de la Ciudad** (see p493).

EXCURSIONS

Cuevas de San Antón/Ermita Rupestre de la Virgen de la Cabeza★

▶ 2.7km/1.7mi on the A 369 Algeciras. Opening times vary; enquire at the ℹ️tourist office. €3.
This 9C Mozarabic monastery was excavated out of rock. The frescoes in the church were painted in the 18C. The **views★★** of Ronda are impressive.

Ruinas de Acinipo

▶ 19km/11.8mi along the A 376 toward Sevilla. Hours posted monthly on Facbeook page. ☎952 187 119. www.facebook.com/acinipoenclavearqueologico.
Known as Ronda la Vieja, the ruins of Acinipo retain a 1C AD theatre, with part of the stage and terraces.

Cueva de la Pileta★

▶ 20km/12.4mi SW. Take the A 376 toward Sevilla, then the MA 555 toward Benaoján. Bear onto the MA 561. Guided 1hr tours 10am–1pm, 4–5pm (6pm Apr–Sep). €10. ☎687 13 33 38. www.cuevadelapileta.org.
A hidden gem, the cave has over 2km/1.2mi of galleries. Red and black wall paintings predate those of Altamira (see page 517), with figurative motifs from the Palaeolithic era (20 000 BC) and symbolic art and Neolithic animal drawings (goats, panthers, etc) from 4 000 BC.

Ronda to San Pedro de Alcántara★★

▶ 49km/30mi SE on the C 339. About 1hr.
For 20km/12.4mi the road crosses a bare mountain landscape; it then climbs steeply into a **corniche★★** above the Guadalmedina valley. The route is deserted; there's not a single village.

🚗 DRIVING TOURS

RONDA TO ALGECIRAS★
118km/71mi SW on the C 341, C 3331 and A 7. About 3hr.

The road climbs to overlook the Genal Valley, then winds around the foot of **Jimena de la Frontera** (🚌 Juan de Dios 17), perched on a hill, and crosses the **Parque Natural de los Alcornocales★**, one of the largest cork oak forests in Spain.
After 22km/13mi, a narrow road leads (right) to **Castellar de la Frontera★**, a village of flower-filled alleyways huddled within the castle grounds.

Pueblos Blancos★★
To the west of Ronda, in often curiously shaped mountains, are the remains of the pinsapos forest of pines dating to the beginning of the Quaternary era. The beauty of the countryside is set off by delightful white towns (pueblos blancos), characteristically perched on rocky crags or stretched along escarpments, their houses dominated by a ruined castle or a church.

FROM RONDA TO ARCOS DE LA FRONTERA
By the northern route; 130km/81mi. About 4hr.

▶ Take the MA 428 toward Arriate, then continue on the CA 4211.

Setenil de las Bodegas★
This village in the gorge of the Guadalporcún river contains a number of troglodyte dwellings built into the rock. Also of interest are the **tourist office** (Villa 2; 📞659 54 66 26; www.setenil.com), in an impressive building with a handsome 16C **artesonado ceiling**; the keep *(torre del homenaje)*; and the Iglesia de la Encarnación.

▶ Travel 16km/10mi NW.

Olvera
Olvera enjoys an impressive hillside **site★★** amid olive groves, crowned by the keep of its triangular-shaped **castle** and the Iglesia de la Encarnación (Pl. de la Iglesia; open Tue–Sun 11am–1pm; €2 with museum; 📞956 12 08 16, www.turismolvera.es). Olvera is renowned for its fruity, multilayered olive oils.

▶ Take the A 384 for Algodonales; turn right onto the CA 531.

Zahara de la Sierra★
The village enjoys an extraordinary hilltop **setting★★**. Zahara was a defensive enclave for the Nasrids, later for Christians. The outlines of the 12C **castle** and 18C Baroque **Iglesia de Santa María de Mesa** stand out.

▶ Return to the A 382 and continue towards Villamartín.

Villamartín
The **Alberite dolmen** (📞956 733 396), a 20m/65ft gallery formed by stone slabs dating to around 4 000 BC, is currently in an unforgivable state of neglect but can be visited 4km/2.4mi to the south. If no one is there, climb around the fence to get a closer look (you didn't hear it from us).

Bornos
The Plaza del Ayuntamiento is fronted by the **Castillo-Palacio de los Ribera★** (Pl. Alcalde José González; 📞956 72 82 64), home to the tourist office. Inside are a Renaissance-style **patio** and 16C garden. Also on the square is the Gothic late-15C **Iglesia de Santo Domingo**.

Espera
10km/6.2mi NW of Bornos via CA 402
This village on a small outcrop is dominated by the ruins of a Moorish castle, the **Castillo de Fatetar** (📞956 72 00 11).

Arcos de la Frontera★★
Arcos has a remarkable **site★★** atop a crag enclosed by a loop in the Guadalete river. The old town huddles against formidable crenellated castle walls and those of the two churches.
🅿 Park below the village in Plaza de Andalucía. Ascend the Cuesta de Belén,

The Adoration of Orson and Papa

Ronda's romantic landscape and link to bullfighting inspired both Ernest 'Papa' Hemingway and Orson Welles, who now have paseos named in their honour. In *Death in the Afternoon* (1932), Hemingway states that Ronda 'is where you should go if you ever go to Spain on a honeymoon'. Welles's ashes are interred in the nearby farm of El Recreo (on the estate of Antonio Ordóñez, whom Hemingway wrote about in *The Dangerous Summer*). In Welles' own words 'A man is not from where he is born, but where he chooses to die'.

a hill that connects modern Arcos with the medieval town. Note the 15C Gothic-Mudéjar **facade★** of the **Palacio del Conde del Águila**.

▷ Continue to the right along Calle Nueva to Plaza del Cabildo.

Plaza del Cabildo

Overhanging the precipice, one side of the plaza boasts a **view★** that extends to a bend in the Guadalete. On the plaza are the town hall (ayuntamiento), Parador (ex-palace), and castle (closed).

Basilica de Santa María★

Pl. del Cabildo. Open Mon–Sat 10am–8pm, Sun 10am–12.30pm, 2-8pm. Closed 1 & 6 Jan, 25 Dec. €4.50. ℘952 87 22 46.

This church was built around 1530. The **west facade★** is Plateresque. Don't miss the 17C **altarpiece** of the Ascension of the Virgin. A charming maze of alleys leads to the other side of the cliff, where the Capilla de la Misericordia, the Palacio del Mayorazgo and the **Iglesia de San Pedro** can be seen.

Iglesia de San Pedro

San Pedro. Open Mon–Sat 10am–1pm, 4–7pm, Sun 10am–1.30pm.

This church dates to the early 15C and boasts a facade crowned by an impressive Neoclassical bell tower.

ARCOS DE LA FRONTERA TO RONDA

102km/61mi – about 3hr. ▭ Nearest station: Jerez de la Frontera (36km).

Leave Arcos on the A 372 toward **El Bosque**. The Parque Natural Sierra de Grazalema visitor centre is here (Av. Diputación; ℘956 72 70 29).

▷ Leave El Bosque on the A 373.

Ubrique

The **road★** enters the heart of the Sierra de Grazalema. Beyond the **Plaza del Ayuntamiento** is the 18C parish church of **Nuestra Señora de la O**.

▷ From Ubrique, continue 10km/ 6.2mi E along the A 374.

Villaluenga del Rosario

This village is the highest in Cádiz province. Its irregularly shaped **bullring** (Plaza de Toros; Calle Real 19; ℘956 46 00 01) is built on top of a rock.

▷ Head 15km/9.3mi NE on the A 374.

Grazalema★★

Grazalema, one of Andalucía's most charming villages, is shockingly the wettest place in Spain. It retains its Moorish layout as well as the tower of the **Iglesia de San Juan** (José M Jiménez; ℘956 13 20 10). The 18C **Iglesia de la Aurora** (Pl. de España 8) is adorned with an unusual fountain. Grazalema is famous for its white-and-brown woollen blankets.

▷ Return to Ronda on the A 372.

Costa del Sol★

Sheltered by the Sierra Nevada,
Spain´s 'Sun Coast' enjoys mild
winters and hot summers.
Millions of visitors flock to its sandy
beaches, quaint towns and villages
and a variety of leisure activities.
In summer, the beaches are packed
and the parties rage until dawn.

🚗 DRIVING TOURS

TOUR OF THE WESTERN COASTLINE★★

From Estepona to Málaga
139km/86mi. Allow one day.

Estepona★
🚃 Nearest station: Fuengirola 40km
east or San Roque-La Linea 40km west.
The **old quarter★** retains its Andalucían
charm. Its attractions are the **Plaza de
las Flores**, the ruins of the castle and
the 18C **Iglesia de los Remedios** (Pl.
San Francisco).

In the hills above Estepona is **Selwo
Aventura Park** 🧒🧑 (open third week
Feb–Jan; check website for seasonal
hours and discounts; €25.90, car park
€4; ℘952 577 773; www.selwo.es), a
safari park with rhinos, giraffes, zebras,
lions and tigers roaming in large enclosures.

Casares★, 24km/15mi inland along the
A 377 and MA 539, is a much-photo-
graphed whitewashed town of Moorish
origin with a warren of narrow streets.
The village appears to cling to a rock in
the Sierra de Crestenilla.

San Pedro de Alcántara
22km/14mi E of Estepona, off E 15.
Archaeological sites close to the beach
include **Las Bóvedas** (thermal baths
dating to the 3C AD) and the palaeo-
Christian basilica of Vega del Mar
(1hr45min guided tours; book ahead:
℘ 952 82 50 35; for a description of the
road from Ronda, ⏾ see RONDA, p494).

🌐 **Michelin Map:** 578
V16-22, W 14-15-16.

ℹ **Info:** Estepona: Plaza de
Flores; ℘952 80 20 02.
Marbella: Glorieta de la
Fontanilla; ℘952 768 760.
Nerja: Carmen 1; ℘952 52
15 31. Salobreña: Plaza de
Goya; ℘958 61 03 14.
www.visitcostadelsol.com.

▶ **Location:** The Costa del Sol
stretches from the Strait of
Gibraltar to east of Almería.

🅿 **Parking:** You'll have to make
a few go-rounds in beach
towns, so plan ahead.

🧒🧑 **Kids:** Selwo Aventura Park,
Selwo Marina Dolphinarium.

Puerto Banús★★
4km/2.5mi E of San Pedro along A 7.
This chichi marina attracts some of the
world's most luxurious sailing craft. Its
many restaurants, bars and boutiques
are popular on summer evenings.

Marbella★★
8km/5mi E of Puerto Banús along N 340.
🚃 Nearest station: Fuengirola 30km.
The long-established capital of the
Costa del Sol is still an international
jet-set destination. Whitewashed
old buildings stand beside shops,
bars and restaurants within a maze
of streets and lanes in the **old quar-
ter★**.The enchanting **Plaza de los
Naranjos★**, named for its sweet-
scented orange trees, is bounded by
the 16C town hall, 17C Casa del Corregidor and a small 15C chapel, the
Ermita de Nuestro Señor Santiago.
Other sights in the old quarter are the
17C Iglesia de Santa María de la Encarnación and the **Museo del Grabado
Español Contemporáneo★** (open Mon
& Sat 9am-2pm, Tue-Fri 9am–7pm; €3;
℘952 76 57 41; www.mgec.es) devoted
to contemporary prints, set in a 16C former hospital.
Marbella also has a marina, luxury
accommodations, excellent beaches, a

long promenade, designer boutiques, health spas and golf courses – a veritable summer camp for well-heeled travellers of all ages.

Fuengirola

35km/22mi E of Marbella off E 15.

The Castillo de Sohail, of Moorish origin, dominates this large resort. The remains of Roman baths and villas are in the Santa Fe district.

▶ Head N for 9km/5.6mi to Mijas.

Mijas★

🚆 Nearest station: Fuengirola 8km

Views★ from this picturesque white-washed town in the sierra encompass much of the coast. Stroll the narrow, winding streets dotted with tiny squares and charming nooks. Highlights are sections of the old Moorish wall and the 16C Iglesia de la Inmaculada Concepción, crowned by a Mudéjar tower. Shops display Andalucían arts and crafts (pottery, basketwork and textiles). Mijas also has an unusual miniatures museum, the **Carromato de Max** (Avenida del Compás; open daily 10am–8pm, until 10pm in summer and 6pm Nov–Easter; €3; Tourist Office; 🖉952 58 90 34, www.mijas.es).

Benalmádena

8km/5mi E of Mijas along A 7.

🚆Benalmadena-Arroyo de la Miel.

Benalmádena stands several kilometres inland from the resort of Benalmádena Costa. Its main historical sights are several 16C watchtowers and the **Museo de Arte Precolombino Felipe Orlando** (Museum of Pre-Columbian Art; Av. Juan Luis Peralta 43; open Tue–Sat 9.30am–1.30pm, 5–7pm, 6–8pm in summer; Sun & hols 10am–2pm; closed 1 & 6 Jan, Good Fri, 1 May, 24–25 & 31 Dec; 🖉952 44 85 93), one of the most important collections of its kind in Spain.

The village is also now famous for its **teléferico★** (cable car; see website for schedule; €16.50 return; www.teleferi-cobenalmadena.com), which flies up to the summit of the Sierra Calamorro offering unrivalled views of the Costa del Sol, the Sierra Nevada and even Gibraltar and the African Coast.

The folks behind Selvo Aventura Park run the **Selwo Marina Dolphinarium** 👥 (open third wk Feb–Jan 6 10am–late; see website for discounts and seasonal hours; €22; parking €4; 🖉952 57 77 73; www.selwomarina.es). In addition to dolphin performances, it puts on snake handling acts, sea lion spectacles, exotic bird shows and more .

Torremolinos

12km/7.4mi NE of Benalmádena, off E 15. www.torremolinos.es.

The promenade and the long beach are the main attractions of this one-time fishing village that's now a huge resort.

Málaga★ 🖉See MÁLAGA

17km/10.5mi NE from Torremolinos off A 7. 🚆Málaga.

TOUR OF THE EASTERN COASTLINE★

From Málaga to Almería

204km/127mi. Allow one day.

This picturesque coast is punctuated by the ruins of torres de vigía, medieval watchtowers built to ward off attacks by Barbary pirates.

Nerja★

53km/33mi E of Málaga along E 15.

🚆 Nearest station: Malaga 67km.

Nerja, a medium-sized resort, overlooks the Mediterranean from the top of a promontory. The **Balcón de Europa★** is a mirador offering views of the dramatic coastline and, on clear days, glimpses of North Africa.

👥 Cueva de Nerja★★

4.5km/2.7mi E along the Motril road. Open Sep–Jun 9:30am–3pm; Jul–Aug 9:30am–6pm Closed 1 Jan, 15 May. €11.75. 🖉952 52 95 20. www.thenerjacaves.com.

Paintings, weapons, jewels and bones were found in this huge cave, indicating Palaeolithic habitation. Its size and stalactites and stalagmites are impressive and include the world's largest stalagmite, standing at 105ft (32m) tall. An annual festival of music and dance is held in the Sala de la Cascada (Cascade Chamber) in July.

THE ROAD FROM NERJA TO LA HERRADURA★

The scenic road snakes along a mountainside with delightful **views★★**.

Almuñécar

23km/14mi E of Nerja along N 340.
Bananas, medlars, pomegranates and mangoes are grown on the small alluvial plain (hoya) behind this resort.
The **Cueva de los Siete Palacios** houses an archaeological museum (open Tue–Sat 10am–1.30pm, 4–6.30pm, Sun 10am–1pm; €2.35; ℘958 838 623, www.turismoalmunecar.es). Visit the ruined **Castillo de San Miguel** with the same ticket (same times and contact details).

Salobreña★

13km/8mi E of Almuñécar along E 15.
www.ayto-salobrena.es
Salobreña, perhaps the the prettiest town on this coast, spreads across a hill, a white blanket punctuated by purple splashes of bougainvillea. The Castillo de Salobreña (open 10am–2pm, afternoon times vary; €4, free Mon pm; ℘958 61 03 14), an imposing Moorish **fortress** converted into a palatial residence by Nasrid kings in the 14C, stands guard over the town.

THE ROAD FROM CALAHONDA TO CASTELL DE FERRO★

The road hugs the rocky coast, offering mountain and sea views. After Balanegra the N 340 turns inland through an immense sweep of greenhouses around El Ejido, where flowers, vegetables and tropical fruit are grown.

Almería ௹See ALMERÍA

ADDRESSES

🛏 STAY

ALMUÑÉCAR

🛏🍴 **Hotel Casablanca** – Pl.San Cristóbal 4. ℘958 63 55 75. www.hotel casablancaalmunecar.com. 35 rooms. ⊑€4.50. Restaurant 🛏🍴. The Casablanca sits behind the two main beaches and has Moorish decor.

BENALMÁDENA

🛏🍴 **Hotel La Fonda** – Santo Domingo 7. ℘952 56 90 47. www. lafondabenalmadena.com 28 rooms. ⊑€12. Restaurant 🛏🍴. In the newer part of town but with a backdrop of the Sierra de Castillejos, this hotel has spacious rooms, sea views and an indoor pool.

ESTEPONA

🛏 **Hotel Boutique Al-Ana** – Tamesis 16. ℘952 92 85 75. www. al-anamarbella.com. 9 rooms. The sea is a 10-minute stroll from this eensy canary-yellow hotel. Rooms have private patios, and the communal gardens and pool are charming.

MARBELLA

🛏🍴 **Hotel La Morada Más Hermosa** – Montenebros 16. ℘952 92 44 67. www.lamoradamashermosa.com. 8 rooms. ⊑€9. You'll find this hotel on a plant-bedecked alley in the old part of town. Settle into rooms appointed in a colonial Andalucían style.

🛏🍴 **Nobu Hotel Marbella** – Bulevar Príncipe Alfonso von Hohenlohe. ℘952 77 85 85. www. marbella.nobuhotels.com.81 rooms. Restaurant 🛏🍴. Steps from the beach on Marbella's Golden Mile, Nobu is the ultimate luxury hotel, with minimalist Japanese design, world-class dining (omasake, *por favor*) and over-the-top amenities like boat excursions, golf and on-demand tennis lessons.

🛏🍴 **Marbella Club** – Bulevar Príncipe Alfonso von Hohenlohe. ℘952 82 22 11. www.marbellaclub.com. 121 rooms. ⊑€36. Three restaurants 🛏🍴. This is one of the best – and most expensive – hotels along coast, surrounded by a manicured garden planted with palm trees. Bungalows here frequently host the rich and famous.

NERJA

⊖ **Hostal San Miguel** – San Miguel 36. ✆952 52 18 86. 13 rooms. ☕€3.50. Set in a restored town house near the centre, this hostel has modest but comfortable rooms. There's a bar–coffee shop and a top-floor terrace with a pool and sea and mountain views.

⊖⊖ **Hostal Marissal** – Pas. Balcón de Europa 3. ✆952 52 01 99. www.hostalmarissal.com. 22 rooms. Restaurant⊖⊖. What the hotel lacks in updated design (floral duvets? seriously?) it makes up for with a superb location, next to the Balcón de Europa lookout point.

OJÉN

⊖ **Refugio de Juanar** – Sierra Blanca. ✆952 88 10 00. www.juanar.com. 26 rooms. ☕€8.80. This charming hotel located in the middle of a game reserve is a peaceful alternative to the beaches. Rooms are spacious with country-style furnishings.

EAT

MARBELLA

⊖ **Churrería Ramón** –Pl. de los Naranjos 8. ✆952 77 85 46. www.churreriaramon.es. Always-hot churros dipped in porridge-thick hot chocolate in the main square – need we say more?.

⊖⊖ **El Balcón de la Virgen** – Remedios 2. ✆952 77 60 92. www.elbalcondelavirgen.com. Closed Jan, 1–15 Feb. On an attractive street lined by a succession of restaurant terraces, this restaurant serves internationally inflected Andalucían cuisine.

⊖⊖⊖ **Casa de la Era** – 1km/0.6mi N. ✆952 77 06 25. www.casadelaera.com. See website or call for opening times. In a chalet-style house, this restaurant with a cheerily decorated dinign room (red tablecloths, potted plants) affords mountain views and serves Andalucían and Moroccan dishes.

MIJAS

⊖⊖⊖ **La Alcazaba de Mijas** – Pl. de la Constitución. ✆952 59 02 53. www.restaurantelaalcazabamijas.com. Closed Sat and Feb. Reservations recommended. Squarely on the Arab walls of Mijas with fine vistas and careful decoration, La Alcazaba serves simple Andalucían fare in a Mozarabic dining room. The catch of the day is always a safe bet.

⊖⊖⊖ **El Olivar** – Av. Virgen de la Peña, edificio El Rosario. ✆952 48 61 96. www.restaurantemesonelolivar.com. Closed Feb, Sat. This country restaurant offers ierra views through its large windows and blissfully unobstructed ones from its terrace.

OJÉN

⊖⊖ **Restaurante El Tunel** – Calle la Carrera 44. ✆662 38 83 87. Closed Tue. Reservations recommended. Hefty portions of good, simply prepared Andalucían food (plus pastas and pizzas) make this restaurant the most popular in town.

TAPAS

The pedestrianised district of **La Carihuela**, alongside the beach, is the original and most attractive part of Torremolinos, with dozens of bars, restaurants, hotels and shops. Two of the best restaurants are **Restaurante Juan** (Pas. Marítimo 28; ✆952 38 56 56, www.restaurantejuan.es), which has been specialising in seafood for more than 30 years, and **La Jábega** (Mar 17; ✆952 38 47 65; www.chiringuitolajabega.com), overlooking the promenade.

SHOPPING

Marbella is one of the best places for shopping on the Costa del Sol with all the top names in international fashion represented. Most of the big-box stores are concentrated in Puerto Banús, where there is also an impressive nucleus of designer boutiques, and in the centre of Marbella, particularly along **Avenida Ricardo Soriano** and **Calle Ramón y Cajal**. The best indoor shopping centre on the Costa del Sol is also here.

Markets are an important feature of life on the Costa del Sol. The one in Marbella takes place on **Saturday mornings** next to the Nueva Andalucía bullring (Pl. de Toros) near Puerto Banús.

Northern Andalucía

Northern Andalucía begins south of the Despeñaperros Pass, the spectacular natural barrier separating the *meseta,* or tableland of Castilla, and the Guadalquivir Valley. The Guadalquivir river is the thread that connects much of Andalucía, from its headwaters in the Sierra de Cazorla to the estuary at Sanlúcar de Barrameda. The river that launched ships to the New World in the late 15C passes through the olive groves of Jaén and Úbeda and on to the urban yet laid-back hubs of Córdoba and Sevilla, two of the 'three sisters'(including Granada) that developed into the most important cities in southern Spain.

Córdoba

Córdoba was the Manhattan of the 9C, the city where the three cultures that defined the Iberian Peninsula – Christian, Muslim and Jewish – lived in harmony for a brief but fruitful interlude during the reign of King Abderraman III. Seneca, Averroes, Lucan and Maimonides all called Córdoba home at one time or another, and the city celebrates its intellectual pedigree with monuments and museums such as the Torre de Calahorra, where a facsimile of Alfonso X El Sabio – the great Christian warrior, king, musician and poet – debates the Muslim and Judaic philosophies of Maimonides and Averroes. The Realist painter Julio Romero de Torres is 'modern' Córdoba's favourite son, a multi-talented artist known for his dashing figure and flamenco *cante jondo* performances as well as his sensual, symbolic canvases.

Northern Andalucía today

Jaén province is the most overlooked part of Andalucía, which is a boon to independent travellers as its dramatic scenery, magnificent castles and historic Paradors make it perfect for off-the-grid touring with little in the way of tourist fripperies. Baeza and Úbeda are two of Andalucía's architectural treasures; either make a good base. In addition to killer olive oil, Jaén is famous for its cathedral and Moorish baths. Beyond it, a driving excursion or walk in the hills of the Sierras de Cazorla, Spain's largest nature reserve, is a zen-filled treat.

Highlights

1 Walking between the 856 columns of the Mezquita in **Cordóba** (p495)

2 Baroque and Moorish jewels in **Priego de Córdoba** (p503)

3 Exploring Rennaissance **Baeza**, olive oil central (p504)

4 Hiking or driving the dramatic **Parque Natural de las Sierras de Cazorla, Segura y Las Villas** (p508)

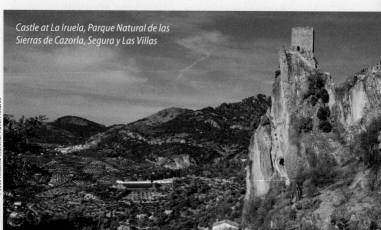

Castle at La Iruela, Parque Natural de las Sierras de Cazorla, Segura y Las Villas

© José Antonio Moreno/Travel Pictures

Córdoba★★★

Córdoba owes its fame to the legacy of the Roman, Islamic, Jewish and Christian civilisations that have endowed its rich and varied history. The Mezquita, the city's most precious jewel, dominates the old section whose narrow, whitewashed streets and charming small squares are embellished with wrought-iron grilles and flower-filled patios.

THE CITY TODAY

The city is on the same well-trodden Moorish Spain sightseeing trail as Seville and Granada, but due to its distance from the coast and smaller size it receives fewer visitors. Córdoba is not just a preserved tourist theme park: Beyond the medieval core lies a lively, modern and sophisticated centre with buzzing bars and nightlife.

A BIT OF HISTORY

The Roman city – Córdoba was the birthplace of **Seneca the Rhetorician** (55 BC–AD 39) and his son **Seneca the Philosopher** (4 BC–AD 65). A noted early bishop was **Hossius** (257–359), counsellor to Emperor Constantine. Of Roman Córdoba only the mausoleum in the Jardines de la Victoria, a ruined 1C temple, and the bridge linking the old section with the Torre de la Calahorra remain.

The Córdoba Caliphate – Emirs from Damascus established themselves in Córdoba as early as 719.

In 756 **Abd ar-Rahman I**, sole survivor of the **Umayyads**, founded the dynasty that was to rule Muslim Spain for three centuries. In 929 **Abd ar-Rahman III** proclaimed himself Caliph of Córdoba. In the 10C a university was founded. Christians, Jews and Muslims lived side by side and enriched one another intellectually and culturally. On the accession of the feeble **Hisham II** in 976, power fell into the hands of the ruthless **Al-Mansur** (the Victorious). Al-Andalus fragmented into warring kingdoms, the **reinos de taifas**. Córdoba became part of the Kingdom of Sevilla in 1070.

▶ **Population:** 326 262
🕭 **Michelin Map:** 578 S 15.
🗟 Info: Calle Rey Heredia, 22.
　　☎957 20 17 74.
　　www.turismodecordoba.org.
◑ **Location:** Córdoba hugs the Guadalquivir river in Andalucía, between ranchland and olive country. The A4 highway runs to Écija (52km/32mi SW) and Sevilla (143km/89mi SW). 🚃Córdoba (AVE).
🅿 **Parking:** Park outside the old city and walk Córdoba's lanes and alleys.
🕲 **Don't Miss:** The Mezquita.
🕑 **Timing:** See the Mezquita, followed by the Jewish quarter. Cross the Roman bridge.

Through the upheaval, intellectual life never waned. **Averroes**, physicist, astrologer, mathematician and doctor, brought the learnings of Aristotle to the West. The Jew **Maimonides** (1135–1204) was famed in medicine, theology and philosophy, but fled persecution. 'Reconquered' in 1236, Córdoba declined until the 16C, when its tooled leatherwork became fashionable.

SIGHTS
THE MEZQUITA AND THE JUDERÍA★★★
Mezquita-Catedral★★★ (Mosque-Cathedral)

C. Cardenal Herrero 1. Visita Diurna (day visits): Mon–Sat 10am–6pm (Mar–Oct until 7pm), Sun & public hols 8.30–11.30am, 3–6pm (Mar–Oct until 7pm). €10. Free Mon–Sat (excl hols) 8.30–9.30am for individual silent visits. Visita Nocturna (night visits): see website for seasonal hours. €18. ☎957 47 05 12. www.mezquita-catedraldecordoba.es.

The Mezquita

The traditional Muslim crenellated square encloses the Patio de los Naranjos (Orange Tree Court) with a **Basin of**

© sorincolac/iStockphoto.com

Mezquita

Al-Mansur (1) for ritual ablution, a hall for prayer and a minaret.

The first Muslims in Córdoba shared the Visigothic church of St Vincent with the Christians. Soon Abd ar-Rahman I (731–788) purchased part of the site. He razed the church and around the year 780 began the construction of a splendid mosque with 11 aisles, each opening onto the Patio de los Naranjos. Marble pillars and Roman and Visigothic stone were reused. The mosque was architecturally innovative in its superimposition of two tiers of arches to add height and spaciousness.

In 848 Abd ar-Rahman II had the mosque extended to the present-day Capilla de Villaviciosa (Villaviciosa Chapel). In 961 El Hakam II built the mihrab, and in 987, Al-Mansur added eight aisles (with red-brick floors). After the 'Reconquista', Christians built chapels in the west nave including the 17C **Capilla de la Purísima Concepción (2)**, completely covered with marble.

Interior

Enter via the Puerta de las Palmas. The interior is a forest of columns (about 850) and striped horseshoe arches. The

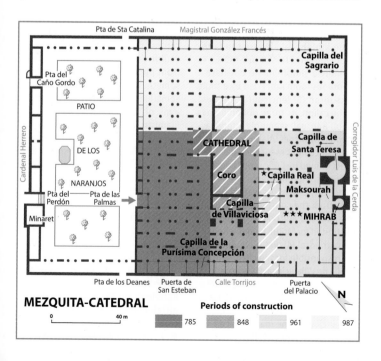

MEZQUITA-CATEDRAL

0 — 40 m

Periods of construction

785   848   961   987

The Sephardic Jews

Of indescribable importance to Spain's development are the **Sefardíes,** whose cultural richness is still palpable in **juderías** (old Jewish quarters) and synagogues despite there being hardly any (40 000, by some estimates) Jews in Spain today. Historically the main Jewish towns on the Peninsula were Córdoba, Toledo and Granada, though there were Jewish quarters across Spain.

The Sephardic Jews (**Sepharad** is the Hebrew word for Spain) came to the Iberian Peninsula in Antiquity around the same time as the Greeks and Phoenicians. In the 8C, during the Berber invasions, they welcomed the Muslims, who regarded the Jews as sympathetic allies. The Moors often made them the 'middle men' in negotiatons with the Christians. As merchants, bankers, craftsmen, doctors and scholars, Jews played a key economic role and made major contributions to culture and science. Some became famous, like the Torah scholar Maimonides of Córdoba (1135–1204). The Jews were particularly prosperous under the Caliphate of Córdoba (929–1031), but persecution by the Almohads led them to head north to cities like Toledo and Girona. There they would be persecuted, and sometimes killed, by Christians during the Reconquista. A royal decree forced Jews to wear a piece of red or yellow cloth.

The Alhambra Decree expelling all non-Catholics from Spain was proclaimed in 1492 by the Catholic Monarchs. Some chose to convert; others (known as **Marranos**), though having publicly converted, continued practising their Jewish faith in hiding. The Inquisition was established In 1478 for the purpose of identifying and punishing so-called crypto-Jews. Most of Spain's Jewish community fled to other parts of the Mediterranean.Today Sephardic Jews account for up to 20 per cent of the world's Jewish population. A handful have kept their language, Ladino, derived from 15C Castilian.

wide main aisle off the doorway has a beautiful *artesonado* ceiling. It leads to the **kiblah** wall, where the faithful prayed, and to the **mihrab★★★**, normally a simple niche but here a sumptuous room preceded by a triple **maksourah (3)** (enclosure) reserved for the caliph. Its three ribbed domes rest on unusual, seemngly interweaving multifoil arches. Alabaster plaques, ornate stucco arabesques and palm-leaf motifs framed by Cufic script add awe-inspiring sumptuousness.

In the 13C, Christians walled off the aisles from the court. A few columns were removed, and pointed arches were substituted for Moorish ones when the first **cathedral (4)** was built. Alfonso X was responsible for the chancel in the **Capilla de Villaviciosa** or **Lucernario (5)** and built the **Capilla Real★ (6)**, decorated in the 13C with Mudéjar stucco. Chapels were built in the western nave including the marble-faced 17C **Purísima Concepción (2).**

Catedral

In the 16C, the canons cut away the centre of the mosque to erect loftier vaulting. Emperor Charles V was far from pleased: 'You have destroyed something unique,' he said, 'to build something commonplace'. The roof is a mix of 16C and 17C styles (Hispano-Flemish, Renaissance and Baroque). Additional enrichments are the Baroque **choir stalls★★ (8)** by Pedro Duque Cornejo (c. 1750) and two **pulpits★★ (7)** of marble, jasper and mahogany.

Tesoro

The treasury in the **Capilla del Cardenal** (Cardinal's Chapel) **(9)**, built by the Baroque architect Francisco Hurtado Izquierdo, includes a large 16C **monstrance★** by E Arfe and an exceptional Baroque Christ in ivory.

Exterior features include the **minaret**, enveloped by a 17C Baroque tower. Giving onto the street is the 14C Mudéjar **Puerta del Perdón** (Pardon Doorway) faced with bronze. Further on is the small chapel of the **Virgen de los Faroles** (Virgin of the Lanterns) **(10)**.

Judería★★
(Old Jewish Quarter)
NW of the Mezquita.

Narrow streets, flower-draped walls, cool patios, and lively nightlife characterise the quarter from which Jews were expelled.

Sinagoga
C. Judíos20. Open mid Sep–mid Jun Tue–Sat 9am–8.30pm, Sun until 3.30pm, mid Jun–mid Sep 9am–3pm. €0.30; free for EU citizens. ℘957 20 29 28.

This early-14C synagogue is a small square room with a balcony for the women. The upper walls are covered in Mudéjar stucco. Look close and you can make out some Hebrew lettering.

Casa de Sefarad★
Judíos. Open Mon–Sat 11am–6pm, Sun 11am–2pm. €4. ℘957 421 404. www.casadesefarad.es.

This cultural centre is devoted to Spain's Sephardic Jews. Five rooms spread around a central patio show the daily life of the medieval Jewish community; other rooms evoke the history of the Cordoban Jewish quarter and its festivities, traditions and music. Occasional concerts are held in the patio.

Nearby is the **Zoco Municipal** (souk; open 10am–8pm), where craftspeople work around a large patio, a setting for flamenco dancing in summer.

Palacio de Viana★★
Pl. de Don Gome 2. Guided tours (1hr) Sept–Jun Tue–Sat 10am–7pm, Sun & hols 10am–3pm. Jul–Aug Tue–Sun 9am–3pm. €8 (€5 patios only, no tour). ℘957 49 67 41. www.palaciodeviana.com.

This fine example of 14C–19C Cordoban civil architecture has 12 patios and an attractive garden that's outstanding even in a city already famous for its beautiful patios.

On the ground floor are collections of porcelain, 17C–19C side-arms and tapestries. The staircase to the first floor

has a cedar Mudéjar *artesonado* ceiling. Overall highlights include the Cordoban leather room; tapestries made in the royal workshops from cartoons by Goya; the library; and the main room with a rich artesonado ceiling and tapestries illustrating the Trojan War and Spanish tales.

Museo Arqueológico★★
Pl. Jerónimo Páez. Open mid-Jun–mid-Sept Tue–Sun 9am–3pm; mid-Sept–mid-Jun Tue–Sat 9am–8pm, Sun 9am–3pm. €1.50; free for EU citizens. ℘957 35 55 17.

The archaeological museum is in the 16C Palacio de los Páez, a palace designed by Hernán Ruiz. Displayed here are prehistoric Iberian objects, Visigothic remains and, of particular note, the **Roman collection★** (reliefs, capitals, sarcophagi and mosaics).

There are also Islamic ceramics, capitals and the outstanding 10C **stag★** (*cervatillo*) from Medina Azahara (◔see Excursions).

Alcázar de los Reyes
Cristianos★
Caballerizas Reales. Open Tue–Sat 8.30am–8pm (mid Jun–mid Sep 8.30am–3pm), Sun 8.30am–2.30pm. €4.50, €7 incl evening light show, see website for details; free Tue–Thu (excl hols) 8.30–9.30am. ℘957 20 17 16. www.alcazardelosreyescristianos. cordoba.es.

This 14C complex, later expanded, retains attractive Moorish patios with ornamental basins and pools; baths; rooms with Roman **mosaics★** and a 3C **sarcophagus★**. The towers afford garden and city **views**. The **gardens★**, in Arabic style, are terraced and refreshed with pools and fountains. In the evenings the grounds, fountains and buildings are transformed into a spectacular show by ingenious, lighting projection and sound techniques.

Posada del Potro - Centro
Flamenco Fosforito
Pl. del Potro. Open Tue–Sat 8.30am –7.30pm, Sun 9.30am-2.30pm.

Entrance of Yafar's house, Medina Azahara

℘957 47 68 29. www.centroflamenco
fosforito.cordoba.es.com.
In a 15C inn mentioned in Cervantes'
Don Quixote, this cultural centre specialises in the study and interpretation of
Andalucían flamenco. A museum traces
the history of the art from its origins to
the present day. There are often lunchtime musical performances.

Museo de Bellas Artes
(Fine Art Museum)
Plaza del Potro. Open mid-Jun–mid-Sept
Tue–Sun 9am–3pm; mid–Sept–mid-Jun
Tue–Sat 9am–8pm, Sun and hols 9am
–3pm. €1.50, free for EU citizens. ℘957
103 659. www.museosdeandalucia.es.
This museum in a former hospital
specialises in art from the Córdoba
area from the Middle Ages to the 20C.

Iglesias Fernandinas★
The celebratory refinement of the 14
parish churches built soon after the
reconquest by Ferdinand in 1236 can
still be seen today, particularly in **Santa
Marina** (Pl. del Conde de Priego), **San
Miguel** (Pl. de San Miguel) and **San Lorenzo** (Pl. de San Lorenzo). Constructed
in a primitive Gothic style, they show
a sober beauty in purely structural
elements. The single trumpet-shaped
doorways are the only lighter aspect
of the architecture.

Palacio de la Merced★
Pl. de Colón.
The provincial Parliament building is the
former Convento de la Merced, built in
the 18C. The facade is graced by a white
marble Baroque doorway. Inside are a
patio, staircase and church.

Museo Torre de la Calahorra
Puente Romano. Open Oct–Apr
10am–6pm, May–Sep 10am–2pm,
4.30–8.30pm €4.50. ℘957 29 39 29.
www.torrecalahorra.com.
In the 14C Moorish fortress a museum
traces the caliphate using audioguides
and video (55 min, addl €3). There is also
a fine **model★** of the mosque as it was
in the 13C.

El Cristo de los Faroles
The Calvary surrounded by lanterns
(*faroles*) in **Plaza de Capuchinos★** is
known throughout Spain.

EXCURSIONS
Medina Azahara★★
▶ Leave Córdoba on the A 431 (W of
plan). After 8km/5mi bear right. Open
Tue–Sat: mid-Sep–Mar 9am–6.30pm;
Apr–mid-Jun 9am–8.30pm; mid-Jun–
mid-Sep 9am–3.30pm. Sun & public hols
9am–3.30pm. €1.50; free for EU citizens.
℘957 35 28 74.
www.museosdeandalucia.es.
One of Spain's newest UNESCO World
Heritage sites (added in 2018), this
sumptuous 10C city built by Abd ar-
Rahman III has three tiers – a mosque
below, gardens and public areas in the
middle and an *alcázar* above. It was
intended to be the capital of a new
province of the Caliphate of Cordoba
but was sacked by Berbers in 1013.
Today only ruins remain. The archaeo-

logical complex includes the visitor centre and Musuem of Madinat Al-Zahra. The **Abd ar-Rahman III room** features magnificent carved stone work.

Castillo de Almodóvar del Río★★

▶ 25km/15mi W along the A 431. Open Sep–Jun Mon–Fri 11am–2.30pm, 4–7pm, Sat–Sun 11am–7pm (until 8pm Apr–Sep). Jul–Aug Mon–Fri 10am–3pm (Thu 7pm–12am), Sat 10–12am, Sun & hols 10am–6pm. Closed 25 Dec, 1 Jan. €9; guided and dramatised tours available. ℘957 63 40 55. www.castillodealmodovar.com.

This imposing 14C eight-towered Gothic **castle** dominates town and countryside. It was a filming location in *Game of Thrones*. Stroll the path linking the parapet, parade ground and towers.

Andújar★

▶ 76km/47mi E along the A 4. Andújar retains many 15–16C houses and churches. On the last Sunday of April, a popular *romería* (pilgrimage) is held to the Santuario de la Virgen de la Cabeza (32km/20mi N on the J 5010), set in the **Parque Natural de la Sierra de Andújar★**, with pasture and ravines.

Iglesia de Santa María

Pl. Santa María. ℘953 50 01 39. The 15C–17C Church of St Mary holds El Greco's *Christ in the Garden of Olives*★★, set in a chapel enclosed by a fine **grille**★ by Master Bartolomé.

An *Assumption of the Virgin* by Pacheco is in the north apsidal chapel.

ADDRESSES

🛏 STAY

⊖ **Hostal La Milagrosa** – C. Rey Heredia 12. ℘957 47 33 17. www.lamilagrosahostal.es. 8 rooms. Near the Mezquita, this basic hostel wraps around a plant lined Cordoban patio.

⊖⊜ **Hotel Casa de los Azulejos** – C. Fernando Colón 5. ℘957 47 00 00. www.casadelosazulejos.com. 8 rooms. This charming hotel is a traditional Andalucían house with a colonial

flavour. Notable features include an interior garden with plants and large rooms with period furnishings, iron headboards, original floors and colourful baths.

⊖⊜⊜ **Hotel Viento 10** – C. Ronquillo Briceño 10. ℘957 76 49 60. www.hotelviento10.es. 7 rooms. ☲€7. Viento 10, opened in 2015, manages to be both affordable and exclusive-feeling with its stark-white rooms centred around a Mudéjar patio supported by original sandstone columns. The owner, Gerardo Holgado, happened upon the building on a stroll in 2005, and the rest is history. He receives every guest personally.

⊖⊜⊜ **Hotel González** – Manríquez 3. ℘957 47 98 19. www.hotel-gonzalez.com. 16 rooms. ☲€9. Restaurant⊖⊜⊜. The rooms in this 16C palace (near the Mezquita, Judería and Alcázar) are spacious and well-appointed. The Moorish-inspired patio is used as a cafe area.

⊖⊜⊜ **Hotel Hacienda Posada de Vallina** – C. del Corregidor Luis de la Cerda 83. ℘957 49 87 50. www.hhposadadevallina.es. 24 rooms. ☲€5. Expect elegance and comfort at this small hotel in a tastefully restored Cordoban house; windows look out onto the Mezquita. There's a pleasant cafe area.

🍽 EAT

Córdoba does full justice to Andalucía's tapas tradition with boisterous bars offering a wide selection of local specialities such as *salmorejo* (a local extra-thick gazpacho variant), *flamenquines* (fried chicken roulades filled with ham and cheese), *rabo de toro* (braised oxtail) and *embutidos* (sausage).

⊖⊜ **El Rincón de Carmen** – Romero 4. ℘957 29 10 55. Closed Mon in low season and Sun in high season. The patio provides an escape from the frenzied tourist activity in the Judería. The seared tuna and fried eggplant are excellent, and there's an above-average wine list.

⊖⊜⊜ **Almudaina** – Pl. Campo Santo de los Mártires 1. ℘957 47 43 42. www.restaurantealmudaina.com. Closed Sun eve. This sumptuously

Fiesta de los Patios de Córdoba

© Marcelino Ramírez/age fotostock

decorated restaurant near the Alcázar has dining on two levels around a covered patio. Expect upmarket renditions of Cordoban classics.

Casa Palacio Bandolero – Torrijos 6. ☏957 47 64 91. Set in a gorgeous building opposite the Mezquita, this rustic-chic tavern is a popular place with locals and out-of-towners. Homemade local cuisine and tapas are served at the bar, in the medieval-style dining room or on the flower-decked patio, all washed down by local wine.

TAPAS

Bodega Guzman – C. de los Judíos 7. Local Montilla-Moriles sherries and vermouths are poured straight from the barrel. Bullfighting memorabilia decorates the bar.

Casa Pepe de la Judería –Romero 1. ☏957 20 07 44. www.restaurante casapepedelajuderia.com. Reservations recommended. This taberna opened in 1928 and boasts original fittings updated with stylish modern furnishings. Set around an attractive patio, it offers outstanding tapas. If you haven't tried *flamenquines* yet, get them here.

Taberna Salinas – Tundidores 3. ☏957 48 01 35. www.tabernasalinas.com. Closed Aug, Sun. Open for over a century, this welcoming bar consists of a counter, small patio, two rooms decorated with azulejos and photos of celebrities. The *salmorejo* is terrific.

Taberna San Miguel-Casa El Pisto – Pl. San Miguel 1. ☏957 47 01 66. www. casaelpisto.com. Closed Sun and Aug. Founded in 1886, Taberna San Miguel has delectable fried anchovies and slow-cooked *pisto*, Spain's answer to ratatouille topped witha sunny egg.

BARS / CAFÉS

Café Málaga – Málaga 3. ☏957 47 41 07. Open from 4pm. This quiet café with classical décor and cushy seating near Plaza de las Tendillas is great for a quiet drink.

NIGHTLIFE

Tablao El Cardenal – C. Torrijos 10. ☏691 217 922. www.tablaocardenal.es. Prepare to be blown away by fantastic flamenco acts in this converted 16C courtyard. Reservations are a must.

SHOPPING

The city's traditional craftwork includes embossed leather and cordovans (horse-hide shoes), plus gold and silver filigree. Another good buy are the local Jerez-style wines and brandies from **Montilla-Moriles**, just south of town.

FESTIVALS

Festival of the Crosses (Cruces de Mayo) (www.turismodecordoba.org). At the beginning of **May**, the central squares of the city (San Basilio, Santa Marina and San Augustín) are adorned with over 80 large crosses made of flowers, with a prize for the best.

Also in early May, Córdoba is famous for its glorious **Patios** (www.patios.cordoba.es), when many private residences open their courtyards to the public for intimate, unofficial tours. As with the Crosses, many compete in the 'Concurso de Patios Cordobeses' for the title of town's best patio. Ask at the tourist office for a map, or simply browse the old town, particularly on and around Calle San Basilio, looking out for Patio signs.

The ever-popular **Feria** is held at the end of the month with the usual Andalucían equestrian events, fireworks, flamenco and revelries.

Jaén

Jaén, which many travellers whiz past on their way from Madrid to the Costa del Sol, is well-worth a stop: Its castle is stunning, its olive oils divine and its food scene virtually unscathed by international chains.Its heritage includes Moorish remains and Renaissance buildings, many designed by Andrés de Vandelvira, the architect synonymous with Úbeda (p515).

▶ **Population:** 113 457
Michelin Map: 578 S 18.
Info: Calle Maestra 8. 953 19 04 55. www.turjaen.org.
Location: Jaen is at the base of the Sierra de Jabalcuz. The A 44 heads south to Granada (94km/59mi S) past the Parque Natural de la Sierra Mágina. Jaén (AVE).
Timing: One or two days .

SIGHTS

Catedral★★

Pl. Santa María. Open Mon–Fri 10am –2pm, 5–8pm (Sat 7pm). Sun 10am– noon. €5 incl sacristry & museum. 953 23 42 33. www.catedraldejaen.org.

The 16-17C cathedral looms over the historical centre. It was built by **Andrés de Vandelvira**, master of Andalucían Baroque. The facade, with statues, bal- conies and pilasters, is palatial.

The triple-nave **interior★★** is crowned by fine ribbed vaulting and an imposing cupola above the transept. Behind the Renaissance altarpiece, with its Gothic image of the **Virgen de la Antigua★**, a chapel holds the **Reliquía del Santo Rostro★**, said to be the cloth used by St Veronica to wipe Christ's face. The **choir stalls★★** are carved in the Berruguete style. The sacristy, also by Vandelvira, houses a **museum** with two canvases by Ribera, a Flemish Virgin and Child, a large bronze candelabra by Master Bartolomé and miniature choir books.

Baños Árabes★★

Pl. de Santa Luisa de Marillac. Open Tue– Sat & hols 9am–10pm, Sun 9am–3pm. Closed 1 & 6 Jan, 24–25 & 31 Dec. 953 24 80 68. www.bañosarabesjaen.es.

These Moorish baths are the largest in Spain (470sq m/5 059sq ft). They lie beneath the 16C **Palacio de Villardom- pardo**, which now contains a cultural centre as well as museums of naive art and local arts and traditions. The baths are restored to their 11C appearance.

Castillo de Santa Catalina★

Ctra del Neveral 5. Open Tue–Sat 10am–2pm also mid-May–mid-Oct 5–9pm and mid-Oct–mid May 3.30– 7.30pm. €3.50. 902 54 79 79.

On a ridge to the west of Jaén stands the Castillo de Santa Catalina (Castillo de Jaén), built during a period of Arab rule in the early 13C. It was captured in 1246 by Ferdinand III and extended to hold out against the repeated attacks by the Moors over the next two hundred years. The castle was rebuilt and extended to form the Parador (www.parador.es), but you can visit the castle separately. There is a magnificent 360° panorama from here.

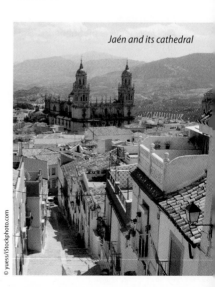

Jaén and its cathedral

© yuess/iStockphoto.com

Priego de Córdoba★★

This capital of Cordoban Baroque flourished with the silk industry in the 18C. Its fountains, churches and delightful old Moorish quarter come as a pleasant surprise in this isolated part of Andalucía. Enquire at the tourist office about the €5 combination ticket to many of the below sights.

▸ **Population:** 22 585
   Michelin Map: 578 T 17.
   Info: Pl. de la Constitución. ✆957 70 06 25. www.turismodepriego.com
▸ **Location:** Priego is on a plain in the Subbética Cordobesa range, away from major road and rail links. ▭Nearest station: Jaén (67km).

SIGHTS

Fuentes del Rey y de la Salud★★ (Fountains of the King and of Health)

At the end of C. del Río.

The older fountain, the **Fuente de la Salud**, is a 16C Mannerist masterpiece. The more lavish **Fuente del Rey** was completed at the beginning of the 19C; its dimensions and rich design evoke Baroque palace gardens, and 139 jets spout water from masks. The central display represents Neptune's chariot.

Barrio de la Villa★★

This charming quarter, dating to Moorish times, has narrow, winding streets and flower-decked houses.

El Adarve★

Take in views over the Subbética range to the north.

Parroquia de la Asunción★ (Parish Church of the Assumption)

Abad Palomino. Open for Mass Mon–Tue & Thu–Sat 7.15–8pm, Sun 11.15am–12pm. This 16C church was remodelled in Baroque style in the 18C. The presbytery is dominated by a carved and painted 16C Mannerist **altarpiece**.

El Sagrario★★

Open Tue–Sun 11.30am–2pm. €2. ✆957 70 06 25.

The chapel, which opens on to the Nave del Evangelio, is a bona fide triumph of Andalucían Baroque. An antechamber

Plasterwork decoration, El Sagrario

© PacoLozano/iStockphoto.com

leads into an octagonal space. Light plays on the scene; intensified by white walls and ceiling, it shimmers over the extensive and lavish **yeserías★★★** (plasterwork decoration), creating a magical atmosphere. In spite of excessive adornment, the effect is one of delicacy.

From the Paseo del Abad Palomino, view the remains of a Moorish **fortress** (open Mon–Fri 10am–2pm, 4–7pm, Sat 11.30am–1.30pm, 5–7pm, Sun 11.30am–1.30pm; €1.15), modified in the 13–14C. Priego has numerous churches: the charming Rococo **Iglesia de las Angustias**; the **Aurora**, with a fine portal; and **San Pedro**, adorned with interesting statues. Don't miss the 16C **royal abattoir★** (Carnicerías Reales, San Luis; open daily, enquire at tourist office for seasonal hours; €1.50), now an exhibition centre.

Baeza★★

This Renaissance gem with golden stonework overlooking the fertile valleys of the Guadalquivir and its tributary, the Guadalimar, stands over an undulating landscape. Along with Úbeda, 9km/5mi away, Baeza is an exceptional urban ensemble, designated a UNESCO World Heritage site. It lies at the heart of a region for which olive oil is basically religion. The quiet historical centre is perfect for a stroll.

▶ **Population:** 15 902
 Michelin Map: 578 S 19.
 Info: Plaza del Pópulo.
   𝒫953 77 99 82.
   http://turismo.baeza.net.
 Location: With nearby Úbeda, Baeza is in the green centre of Jaén province, near the Parque Natural de Cazorla (to the east). ▭Nearest station: Linares Baeza (16km)
 Don't Miss: The heritage plazas.
 Timing: Take half a day for the old quarter.

SIGHTS
MONUMENTAL CENTRE★★★
Plaza del Pópulo★

In the small, irregular square is the **Fuente de los Leones** (Lion Fountain), built with fragments from Cástulo. The Renaissance building to the left, bearing the coat of arms of Charles V, was surprisingly the **carnicería** (abattoir). The **Casa del Pópulo** (now the tourist office) at the end of the square has Plateresque windows and medallions. Six doors once opened on six notaries' offices; court hearings were held upstairs. A balcony projects onto the **Puerta de Jaén**, which, along with the Villalar arch, honoured Charles V. The Jaén gate marked the emperor's visit on his way to Sevilla to marry Isabel of Portugal in 1526.

The **Arco de Villalar** was erected in submission to the king after his victory, in 1521, over the revolting Comuneros, whom the town had supported.

Plaza de Santa María★

The walls of the 17C **Seminario de San Felipe Neri** bear 'graffiti' painted using bull's blood upon graduation. Behind the **Fuente de Santa María**, an arch adorned with atlantes, is the Gothic facade of the **Casas Consistoriales Altas**, with the coats of arms of Juana the Mad and Philip the Fair. Also in the plaza is the **Iglesia de San Andrés**, notable for the **Gothic paintings★** in the sacristy.

Catedral★

Pl. de Santa María. Museum open Mon–Fri 10.30am–2pm, 4–7pm. Sat 10.30am–7pm, Sun 10.30am–6pm. €4. 𝒫953 74 41 57.

The **interior★★** was remodelled by Vandelvira and his acolytes in the 16C. The outstanding Capilla Dorada (Gold Chapel) bears Italianate relief; St James' chapel has a fine Antique setting and St Joseph's is flanked by caryatids. The sacristy door has scrollwork and angels' heads. A monumental iron grille by Bartolomé closes the first bay in the nave, and a pulpit of painted metal (1580) is in the transept. In the **Capilla del Sagrario**, to one end on the right, is a Baroque silver monstrance carried in procession on the feast of Corpus Christi.

In the cloisters are four Mudéjar chapels with *atauriques*, inscribed in Arabic.

Palacio de Jabalquinto★

Pl. de Santa Cruz. Open Mon–Fri 9am–2pm. Closed public hols. 𝒫953 74 27 75.

The palace facade★★, in perfect Flamboyant-Gothic style, is best seen in the morning when the sun accentuates the decoration of windows and pinnacles. The **patio** (ca. 1600) is more sober, with a monumental Baroque stairway

Capital of Olive Oil

'An olive grove opens and closes like a fan', wrote Federico García Lorca. They stretch as far as the eye can see across the undulating expanse around Jaén, Spain's leading producer of olives with 66 million trees and an annual harvest of 3.2 million tonnes (about 45% of national production). The principal olive variety here is the slightly acidic **picual**. The province of Jaén has three **Denominación de Origen** zones: Sierras de Segura, de Cazorla and Mágina.

---

guarded by two lions. Opposite is the Romanesque **Iglesia de Santa Cruz**, built immediately after the town's reconquest, with a Gothic chapel and wall paintings in the apse.

Antigua Universidad

Conde de Romanones.
Now a secondary school, the seat of the university was built between 1568 and 1593 and functioned until the 19C. Past the plain facade is an elegant Renaissance patio (open Tue–Sun 10am–2pm, 4–7pm).

Plaza del Mercado Viejo (Plaza de la Constitución)

This busy square is lined with bars and cafés. Fronting it are the **Antigua Alhóndiga** (former grain and cereals market), with a porticoed facade (1554), and the **Casas Consistoriales Bajas** (1703), whose gallery is used by officials to view celebrations.

Ayuntamiento★ (Town Hall)

Pasaje Cardenal Benavides 10.
The old law courts and prison building has a Plateresque facade and ornate balconies.

Ruinas de San Francisco

San Francisco.
Only the vast transept, apse and majestic stone altarpieces remain of the 16C church that once stood here. It is now an auditorium.

Palacio de Los Salcedo (Palace of the Counts of Garcíez)

C. San Pedro 18.
Gothic windows and a Plateresque patio adorn this early-16C palace, now a hotel. Along the street is the **Iglesia de San Pablo**, with a Renaissance facade.

EXCURSION

Museo de la Cultura del Olivio★

◗ On the Jaén road 9km/5.5mi SW of Baeza, turn right toward Complejo la Laguna (1km/.06mi). Puente del Obispo town. Open 10.30am–1.30pm, spring 4.30-7pm, summer 5.30-8pm, autumn 4.30-7pm, winter 4-6.30pm. €4.50. Enquire about guided tours in English.
℘953 76 51 42.
www.museodelaculturadelolivo.com.
This excellent museum on olive culture occupies the premises of a former press. From the botanical garden, which displays different kinds of olives, to the magnificent bodega, where deep barrels stand in rows under vaulted ceilings, to the powerful wooden olive presses, the secrets of Jaén's green gold are revealed – deliciously. 2.5km/1.5mi away, **Laguna Grande** is a protected natural area reached by crossing several beautiful olive groves.

ADDRESSES

🏠 STAY

🛏🛏🛏 **Puerta de la Luna** – Canónigo Melgares Raya 7. ℘953 74 70 19. www.hotelpuertadelaluna.com. 44 rooms. ⊑€14.50. Restaurant 🍽🍽🍽. This restored 16C palace by the cathedral blends modern creature comforts with old-world tranquillity. Outside is a cypress-fringed pool.

Úbeda★★

Set amid olive groves, Úbeda is one of Andalucía's architectural treasures. It flourished in the 16C, when palaces, churches and fine squares were built under the patronage of monied dignitaries.

BARRIO ANTIGUO★★
(OLD QUARTER)
Allow one day.

Plaza Vázquez de Molina★★

The square is lined with historic buildings such as the **Palacio del Deán Ortega**, now a Parador.

Palacio de las Cadenas★
(Palace of Chains)

Pl. Vázquez de Molina. Open Mon–Fri 8am–2.30pm. ☎953 75 04 40.
Now the **ayuntamiento** (town hall) and historical archive, this mansion is named for the chains round the forecourt.
It was designed in 1562 by Vandelvira, also responsible for the Jaén Cathedral. The majestic **facade★★**, relieved by bays and pilasters, is decorated with caryatids and atlantes.
The Renaissance patio is enchanting. On the upper floor is the Archivo Histórico Municipal, with views of the square.

Basílica de Santa María de los Reales Alcázares★

Pl. Vázquez de Molina. Open May–Aug Mon–Sat 10am–2pm, 5–8pm; Sun 11am–2pm, 5–8pm; see website for rest of year. €4. ☎953 756 583.
www.santamariadeubeda.es.
The church was built in the 13C on the site of a mosque and damaged in the Civil War. Note the harmonious facade, the main doo, the late-16C Puerta de la Consolada (left side) and the 16C Renaissance cloisters. Several **chapels★** are adorned with sculptures and profuse decoration and enclosed by impressive **grilles★**, most the work of Master Bartolomé.

▶ **Population:** 34 602
⚙ **Michelin Map:** 578 R 19.
🔋 **Info:** Calle Baja del Marqués 4 (Palacio Marqués de Contadero). ☎953 77 92 04. www.turismoubeda.com.
◐ **Location:** Úbeda is south of Madrid, between the Guadalquivir and Guadalimar rivers. 🚆Nearest station: Linares Baeza (27km).
👁 **Don't Miss:** The Renaissance ensemble of the city centre.

Capilla de El Salvador★★

Pl. Vázquez de Molina. Open Mon–Sat 9.30am–2pm, Sun 11.30am–2pm (until 3pm Oct–Mar), Apr–May 4.30pm–6.30pm (Sun until 7.30pm), Jun–Sep 5–7pm (Sun 8pm), Oct–Mar 4–6pm (Sun 7pm). €5. ☎609 27 99 05. http://en.fundacionmedinaceli.org/monumentos/capilla.
Diego de Siloé designed this sumptuous church in 1536. Its facade is ornamented with Renaissance motifs.
The **interior★★** is almost theatrical: the single nave, closed by a monumental grille, has vaulting outlined in blue and gold. The Capilla Mayor (chancel) forms a kind of rotunda. A huge 16C altarpiece includes a baldaquin with a sculpture by Berruguete of the Transfiguration. The **sacristy★★**, by Vandelvira, is ornamented with coffered decoration, caryatids and atlantes with all the splendour of the Italian Renaissance style.

Casa de los Salvajes
(House of the Savages)

C. Ventaja.
On the facade, two savages in animal skins support a bishop's crest.

Iglesia de San Pablo★

Pl. Primero de Mayo. Open for Mass Mon–Sat 7.30–8.30pm, Sun & public hols 11.30am–1pm.
The church has a Gothic west door and Isabelline **south door** (1511). The Capilla de las Calaveras (Skull Chapel) was

Antiguo Hospital de Santiago

© Lucas Vallecillos/age fotostock

designed by Vandelvira. The Isabelline Capilla de las Mercedes is enclosed by an extraordinary **grille★★** – note the imaginative depiction of Adam and Eve.

Palacio del Torrente

Pl. Primero de Mayo.

This Early Renaissance palace has a monumental gate flanked by twisted columns.

Casa Mudéjar/Museo Arqueológico

C. Cervantes 6. Open mid-Jun–mid-Sep Tue–Sun 9am–3.30pm; mid-Sep–mid-Jun Tue–Sat 9am–8.30pm, Sun & hols 9am–3.30pm. Closed 1 & 6 Jan, 1 May, 24–25 & 31 Dec. €1.50, free for EU citizens. ℘953 10 86 23.

In this restored 14C Mudéjar house is the **Museo Arqueológico** displaying local finds.

Palacio del Conde de Guadiana

C. Real. The early-17C Palace of the Count of Guadiana is crowned by a fine **tower★**.

Palacio de la Vela de los Cobos

Juan Montilla. ℘953 75 00 34.

The palace's facade is late 18C. A Renaissance appearance bears witness to the long survival of this style in Úbeda.

Palacio del Marqués del Contadero (Palace of the Marquis of Contadero)

Baja del Marqués 4. Open Mon–Fri 9am–3.30pm, Sat–Sun 9.30am–3pm. ℘953 77 92 04.

The late-18C facade, crowned by a gallery, is also Renaissance in style.

Antiguo Hospital de Santiago

Av. Cristo Rey. Open daily 7am–2.30pm, 5–10pm. Closed Sun in Jul and Sat–Sun in Aug.

This 'Andalusian Escorial' is probably Vandelvira's most accomplished work. Its sober facade provides a marked contrast to its interior. Don't miss its chapel.

ADDRESSES

🛏 STAY

😑😑 **Hotel Zenit El Postigo** – Postigo 5. ℘953 75 00 00. http://elpostigo. zenithoteles.com. 26 rooms. ☑€6. The outdoor splash pool in a stone-walled courtyard is the highlight of this simple, value-orientated hotel.

😑😑😑😑 **Palacio de la Rambla** – Pl. del Marqués 1. ℘953 75 01 96. www.palaciodelarambla.com. 8 rooms. Closed mid-Jul–early Aug. This welcoming 16C palace with a Renaissance patio has traditional rooms with carved-wood furnishings.

🍴 EAT

😑😑😑 **Mesón Gabino** – Fuente Seca. ℘953 75 75 53. Closed Mon eve. Set in the fortress walls, this atmospheric restaurant specialises in grilled meats and regional dishes. Set menus are also available.

😑😑😑 **Asador de Santiago** – av Cristo Rey 4. ℘953 75 04 63. www.asadordesantiago.com. Don't be put off by the tawdry decor: This grill restaurant uses top-quality ingredients on its contemporary Andalucían menu.

Parque Natural de las Sierras de Cazorla, Segura y Las Villas★★★

Spain's largest nature reserve extends over 214 300ha/529 535 acres at an altitude of between 600m/1 968ft and 2 017m/6 616ft. Steep cliffs, deep gorges and a complex of rivers and streams, including the source of the Guadalquivir, make up this park. The dense, scrubby mountain vegetation is similar to that of Mediterranean regions. Deer, mountain goats, wild boar, golden eagles, griffon vultures and osprey abound.

🕭 **Michelin Map:** 578 S 20-21-22 R 20-21-22 Q 21-22.

🔃 **Info:** Ctra del Tranco, Km48.3, Torre del Vinagre. Coto-Rios ℘953 71 30 17. www.sierrasde cazorlaseguraylasvillas.es

▶ **Location:** The park lies in southeastern Spain, east of Úbeda. 🚉Nearest station: Linares Baeza (113km).

🕑 **Timing:** Allow a full day at least for the park.

🚗 DRIVING TOURS

🚐 Before exploring the park, visit one of the **information offices** at Torre del Vinagre, Cazorla, Segura de la Sierra, or Siles (🕭see website above for details). Mountain-bikers, horse-riders and hikers can follow the extensive network of forest tracks and marked footpaths.

FROM TÍSCAR TO THE EMBALSE DEL TRANCO DE BEAS
92km/57mi. Allow one day.

Tíscar★
The **Santuario de Tíscar** (open Oct–May 11.30am–12.30pm; Jun–Sep 11am–2pm, 6–8pm) occupies a scenic mountain nook. Below this place of pilgrimage is the impressive **Cueva del Agua★**, a cave formation that you can walk through where a torrent of water emerges from between the rocks.

▶ Follow the C 323 as far as Quesada.

Quesada
The village sits on the Cerro de la Magdalena hill, amid olive groves. A **museum** is dedicated to Quesada-born Expressionist painter Rafael Zabaleta (1907–60) (Pl. Cesáreo Rodríguez Aguilera; open Wed–Sat Mar–Oct 10am–2pm, 5–8pm; Nov–Apr 10am–2pm, 4–7pm; Sun & pub hols 10am–2.30pm; closed 1 Jan, 25 Dec; €4; ℘953 73 42 60; www.museo-zabaleta.blogspot.com). The Cañada de las Fuentes, a ravine on the outskirts, is the **source of the Guadalquivir river** (access via a track off the A 315, to the N of Quesada). Wall paintings from the Palaeolithic era can be viewed in Cerro Vitar and in the Cueva del Encajero, a short distance from the town.

▶ Take the A 315 towards Peal de Becerro, then bear right on the A 319.

Cazorla★
Cazorla occupies an outstanding **site★** below the Peña de los Halcones, dominated by the **Castillo de la Yedra** (Camino del Castillo; open mid-Jun–mid-Sep Tue–Sun 9am–3pm, mid-Sep–mid-Jun Tue–Sat 9am–8.30pm; Sun 10am–3pm. €1.50; free for EU citizens; ℘953 10 14 02), its whitewashed houses adorned with balconies. At the centre of the plaza de Santa María stands a Renaissance fountain. The ruins of the Iglesia de Santa María (Pl. Santa María), by Vandelvira, are used as an auditorium.

▶ Head 1.5km/1mi NE along the A 319; turn right at a signposted junction.

La Iruela

The remains of a Templar castle offer views★★ (Camino del Castillo; free) of the Guadalquivir Valley. The Iglesia (church) de Santo Domingo was designed by Vandelvira.

THE ROAD FROM LA IRUELA TO THE TRANCO RESERVOIR★

The first 17km/10.5mi stretch provides spectacular views★★. The Parador de El Adelantado is 8km/5mi along a branch road up through pine forests.

▶ Follow the A 319 along the river.

Torre del Vinagre

Carretera del Tranco, A 319. Open 10am–2pm, 4–7pm (Jul–Aug 5–8pm). Closed 25 Dec. ℘953 71 30 17.
This is the park's main information centre, including a hunting museum as well as a botanical garden with species native to the park. Several routes start here. Game reserve **Parque Cinegético de Collado del Almendral**, 15km/9.3mi along the A 319, has lookouts for viewing deer, mouflons and mountain goats.

Embalse del Tranco de Beas

⚠ Several camping areas and hotels are close to this reservoir. Water sports are available. The islands in the reservoir are Isla de Cabeza la Viña and **Isla de Bujaraiza**, the latter with ruins of a Moorish castle. Both are seen from the **Mirador Rodríguez de la Fuente** viewpoint.

SANTIAGO-PONTONES TO SILES

80km/50mi. Allow half a day.

Santiago-Pontones

This municipality includes scattered mountain villages, the 9 000-year-old **Cueva del Nacimiento** and the **Cuevas de Engalbo**, with impressive wall art.

▶ From Pontones, go NW on the A 317.

Hornos

Fortress remains rise above a steep cliff affording views★ of the reservoir and Guadalquivir Valley.

▶ Take the A 317, then bear right to Segura de la Sierra at a junction.

Segura de la Sierra★

www.sierradesegura.com.
This picturesque village, birthplace of the 15C poet Jorge Manrique, is at an altitude of 1 240m/4 067ft in the shelter of its Mudéjar **castle★** (open Wed–Sun 10.30am–2pm, 4–7pm; €4.50; ℘953 48 21 73) with its sweeping **panorama★★** of the Sierra de Segura. Note that it's an 88-step climb to the top. Also worth a look is the **town hall**'s Plateresque doorway, the **parish church** (for its delicate polychrome statue of the Virgin Mary and a recumbent Christ attributed to Gregorio Hernández) and the **Moorish baths** (baños árabes).

▶ Follow the JV 7020 to Orcera.

Orcera

The Iglesia de Nuestra Señora de la Asunción, with its sober Renaissance portal, and the Fuente de los Chorros, a 15C fountain, can be seen in the main square. Vestiges of the former Moorish fortress are on the outskirts of Orcera.

▶ Continue along the JV 7020 beyond Benatae, then take the JV 7021.

Siles

The village retains part of its old walls. Nearby is Las Acebeas nature reserve.

ADDRESSES

☺ STAY

☺☺ **Molino La Fárraga** – Camino de la Hoz. ℘953 72 12 49. www.molinolafarraga.com. 8 rooms. Closed 15 Dec–15 Feb. This ex-18C olive oil mill has old-fashioned rooms, well-kept gardens and a swimming pool with castle views.

♀/ EAT

CAZORLA

☺☺☺ **Mesón Don Chema** – Escaleras del Mercado 2. ℘953 71 05 29. Venison, wild boar and other game are this old-fashioned restaurant's speciality.

Western Andalucía

S easide Cádiz is Europe's oldest city, oozing millennia of history, while Huelva's uplands are prime jamón country, blanketed in ancient Mediterranean forest. These provinces draw a mostly Spanish crowd, save for the odd off-the-beaten-path type or surfer at Costa de la Luz.

Sevilla might be Spain's most crowd-pleasing city, thanks to its phenomenal nightlife, sigh-worthy architecture at every turn and palpable sense of *alegría*. A walk along the Gualdalquivir, past age-old monuments, impassioned buskers and strolling couples, is one of the country's great simple pleasures.

You can't talk about Jerez de la Frontera without mentioning its storied sherry bodegas and dazzling Andalucían horsemanship, both of which are integral to the greater region's identity and a major tourist draw.

Cádiz: Birthplace of Tapas

Tapas were supposedly invented at a tavern in Cádiz (still open, by the way) called El Chato del Ventorrillo. The story goes that on a junket to Andalucía, Alfonso XIII stopped into the bar for a tipple. It was muggy out, so the barman, thinking on his feet, draped the rim of the sherry glass with some jamón, lest a gnat spoil His Highness's sipping. The king found the idea so ingenious that he ordered another round "con tapa" – with a covering – and the rest is history. Fact or fiction, Cádiz, and western Andalucía overall, has truly phenomenal tapas, the product of the area's proximity to both the sea and hog country.

Highlights

1 Dazzling white sands on the **Costa de la Luz** (p533)

2 Spotting flamingos in the **Parque Nacional de Doñana** (p535)

3 Enjoying a tipple in a sherry bodega in **Jerez** (p537)

4 **Sevilla** during Semana Santa, a sober yet opulent affair (p520)

5 Cheeky Barbary apes on a tour of the Rock of **Gibraltar** (p547)

The Rolls-Royce of hams

La dehesa ('the pasture') is a sprawling expanse of scrubby Mediterranean forest, an ancient ecosystem maintained by and for the free-range Ibérico pig, a direct descendant of the *sus mediterraneus* boar that roamed Iberia's wild forests of yore. Traditionally, these black pigs eat only acorns for the final three months of their lives, lending their marbled meat an exceptionally nutty, grassy taste and aroma. One taste is a potential prosciutto-ruiner.

Feria del Caballo,
Jerez de la Frontera

Sevilla★★★

Sevilla, set in the plain of the Guadalquivir, is capital of Andalucía and Spain's fourth-largest city. To savour its many moods, wander the narrow streets of old quarters like Santa Cruz and Triana, or find a shady tree to read under in one of the parks. If you haven't seen live flamenco yet, this is the place to do it: Every interpretation imaginable is performed in the city's bars, concert halls and tablaos.

THE CITY TODAY

If Spain had a beauty contest for its cities, or a contest for the most Spanish city in Spain, Sevilla would probably win both. It boasts more monumental set pieces and more pretty, unspoilt corners than any other Andalucían city. It also claims the best tapas, the best nightlife and the best *ferias*, and is a stronghold for bullfighting and flamenco. Come here in spring when the orange blossom is in full fragrance, but avoid the heat of high summer.

A BIT OF HISTORY

Sevilla is summed up on the Puerta de Jerez (Jerez Gate): 'Hercules built me; Caesar surrounded me with walls and towers; the King Saint reconquered me'. Sevilla was chief city of Roman Baetica and capital of the Visigothic kingdom

▶ **Population:** 690 000
⚲ **Michelin Map:** 578 T 11-12 (town plan).
🛈 **Info:** Plaza del Triunfo, ☏954 21 00 05. www.visitasevilla.es.
⊙ **Location:** Sevilla, in southwest Spain, has motorways and dual carriageways to Huelva (92km/57mi W), Jerez de la Frontera (90km/56mi SW), Cádiz (123km/77mi SW) and Córdoba (143km/89mi NE). 🚄Sevilla Santa Justa (AVE).
🅿 **Parking:** In the city centre, but watch out for restricted areas.
☺ **Don't Miss:** The Giralda and the Alcázar.
🕐 **Timing:** Take at least a day for the marvels of central Sevilla, then enjoy quarters such as Santa Cruz, Triana and La Macarena and sites nearby.
👥 **Kids:** Isla Mágica warrants at least a day.

before Toledo. In 712 the first Berber invasions ensued; in the 11C, it became capital of a kingdom that prospered under the Almohads. **Sultan Yacoub al-Mansur** (1184–99), builder of the Giralda, defeated the Christians at Alar-

---

A Tradition of Fiestas

The great festivals, when vast crowds flock to the city from all over Spain and overseas, reveal the provincial capital in many guises. During **Semana Santa**, or **Holy Week**, pasos processions are organised nightly in each city quarter by rival brotherhoods. **Pasos** are great litters sumptuously bejewelled and garlanded with flowers on which are mounted religious, polychrome wood statues; these constructions are borne through the crowd on the shoulders of between 25 and 60 men. Accompanying the statues are penitents, hidden beneath tall pointed hoods; from time to time a voice is raised in a **saeta**, an improvised religious lament. During the **April Fair or Feria**, which began life in the middle of the 19C as an animal fair, the city becomes a fairground with horse and carriage parades. The women in ruffled dresses and the men in full Andalucían costume ride up to specially erected canvas pavilions to dance **sevillanas**.

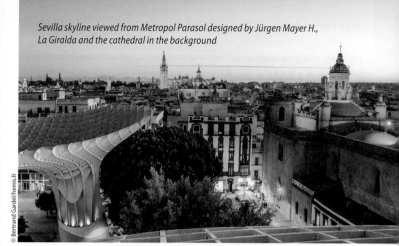

Sevilla skyline viewed from Metropol Parasol designed by Jürgen Mayer H., La Giralda and the cathedral in the background

© Bertrand Gardel/hemis.fr

cos in 1195. On 19 November 1248, **King Ferdinand III of Castilla** took the city from the Moors. 'New World' discoveries brought new prosperity. By 1503, Isabel the Catholic had created the **Casa de Contratación,** or Exchange, to control trade with America. The monopoly lasted until 1717.

Art and architecture in Sevilla – The northern ramparts, the Alcázar walls, the **Torre del Oro** (Golden Tower) and the Giralda were built by the Moors. The ubiquitous **Mudéjar style**, at the intersection of Moorish and Christian traditions, is a testimony to the lasting influence of the Islamic era following the expulsion of the Muslims.

Golden Age painters of the **Seville School** corresponded to three reigns: under Philip III (1598–1621), **Roelas** and **Pacheco**; under Philip IV (1621–65), **Herrera the Elder** and Zurbarán (1598–1664) and under Charles II (1665–1700), **Murillo** (1617–82), who created radiant Immaculate Conceptions and evocative everyday scenes. The best work of **Valdés Leal** (1622–90) can be seen in the Hospital de la Caridad. **Diego Velázquez** (1599–1660) was born in Sevilla. Many statues are the work of 17C sculptor **Martínez Montañés**. Well known are the *Cristo del Gran Poder* (Christ of Great Power) by **Juan de Mesa** and the *Cachorro* by Francisco Antonio Gijón in the **Capilla del Patrocinio** (Calle Castilla). The **Macarena Virgin** is the most venerated religious figure in Sevilla.

THE GIRALDA AND CATHEDRAL★★★

Av. de la Constitución. Allow 1hr 30min. Open Mon 11am–3:30pm, Tue–Sat 11am–5pm, Sun 2:30–6pm; see website for Jul–Aug and Holy Week hours. Closed 1 & 6 Jan, 20 & 22 Mar, 26 & 30 May, 15 Aug, 8 & 25 Dec. €9 incl both sites. ℘902 099 692. www.catedraldesevilla.es.

La Giralda★★★

When this bell tower was built as a minaret in the 12C, its 98m/322ft it resembled the Koutoubia in Marrakesh. It's hard to imagine how imposing it must have looked at the time against low-lying houses and farmland. The top storey and Renaissance lantern were added in the 16C. Typically Almohad, it creates grandeur in harmony with the ideal of simplicity. A gently sloping ramp (accessible from inside the cathedral) leads to the top (70m/230ft) for excellent **views★★★**.

Cathedral★★★

Sevilla's cathedral is the third largest in Europe after St Peter's in Rome and St Paul's in London. When its construction began in 1401, members of the cathedral chapter are said to have declared 'Let us build a cathedral so immense that everyone, on beholding it, will take us for madmen'.

The Late Gothic cathedral shows Renaissance influence. Its main portals are modern, but the Puerta de la Natividad (Nativity Doorway) and Puerta del

GETTING FROM A TO B

Airport – Seville Airport, 8km/5mi in the direction of Madrid on the N IV motorway, (*℘*954 44 90 00; www.aena.es). The 'EA' bus line services the airport to and from the railway station and city centre.

Trains – Estación de Santa Justa. The high-speed AVE departs from this station. It takes 45min to reach Córdoba and 2hr 15min for Madrid. For information and bookings, call *℘*912 320 320 or visit www.renfe.com.

Inter-city buses – Sevilla has two bus stations: Estación Pl. de Armas *℘*954 90 80 40 and Estación del Prado de San Sebastián *℘*955 479 290.

Rideshare – Blablacar is an affordable and environmentally sound way to get around within Andalucía and beyond. The app is a cinch to use. www.blablacar.com.

Taxis – Radio Taxi. *℘*954 57 11 11. www.radiotaxidesevilla.es.

Ride-hailing apps – Uber and Cabify operate in Sevilla.

SIGHTSEEING

Publications – Monthly bilingual publications *Welcome Olé* and *The Tourist* are available at major hotels and monuments. **TheLocal.es** and **TheOlivePress.es** are popular anglophone news websites. Sevilla's Department of Culture publishes a monthly brochure listing cultural events. *El Giraldillo*, a monthly Spanish-language publication covering the region, lists fairs, exhibitions, showtimes and more. www.elgirhoy.com.

Horse-drawn carriages – Horse-drawn carriages are everywhere, though the treatment of the animals has been brought into question recently. Carriages can normally be hired at Cathedral, Torre del Oro and in María Luisa park.

Boat trips on the Guadalquivir – Boat trips lasting 1hr during the day and 1hr 30min at night depart every half-hour from the Torre del Oro. Ask at the tourist office for details.

Bautismo (Baptism Doorway), right and left of the west door, show beautiful sculptures by Mercadente de Bretaña (c. 1460). Miguel Perrin (1520) made full use of Renaissance perspective in the tympana of the Puerta de los Palos and Puerta de las Campanillas (east end doorways).

▶ Enter via Puerta de San Cristóbal.

The **interior** is striking. Massive columns appear slender because they are so tall. Flamboyant Gothic vaulting rises a whopping 56m/184ft above the transept crossing. A **mirror** on the floor affords a striking view.

Capilla Mayor (Chancel)

Plateresque **grilles★★** (1518–33) precede an immense Flemish **altarpiece★★★**, profusely carved with scenes from the life of Christ and gleaming with gold leaf (1482–1525).

Tesoro (Treasury)

The **Sacristía de los Cálices** (Chalice Sacristy) contains canvases by Goya (*Santa Justa* and *Santa Rufina*), Valdés Leal, Murillo and Zurbarán, and a triptych by Alejo Fernández.

In the 16C **Sacristía Mayor** are a Renaissance **monstrance** by Juan de Arfe, 3.9m/13ft in height and weighing 475kg/1 045lb, and paintings by Zurbarán, Murillo and Lucas Jordán.

Capilla Real★★ (Chapel Royal)

A Renaissance dome is decorated with carved busts. On either side are the tombs of Alfonso X of Castilla (d. 1284) and his mother, Beatrice of Swabia. On the high altar is the robed **Virgen de los Reyes**, patron of Sevilla, given by St Louis of France to St Ferdinand of Spain, who is buried in a silver gilt shrine below.

Patio de los Naranjos (Orange Tree Court) – This patio served as the ablutions area in the original mosque.
Exit by the **Puerta del Perdón**, an Almohad arch decorated with stucco and two statues by Miguel Perrin.

AROUND THE CATHEDRAL
Real Alcázar★★★
Patio de Banderas. Open Oct–Mar 9.30am–5pm. Apr–Sep 9.30am–7pm; see website for details of Night Visits. Closed 1 & 6 Jan, Good Fri, 25 Dec & official ceremonies. general €11.50; Cuarto Real addl €4.50; night visits from €13.
℘954 50 23 24. www.alcazarsevilla.org.
All that remains of the 12C Almohad Alcázar are the **Patio de Yeso** (Patio of Plaster), a courtyard wall and the baths. In the 13C, Alfonso X built a palace, known today as **Charles V's rooms**. Peter I (1350–69) erected the nucleus of the present building, known as **Peter the Cruel's Palace**, in 1362, using masons from Granada. It is one of the purest examples of the Mudéjar style.

Baños de María de Padilla★★★ (María de Padilla's Baths)
The old baths, named after the mistress of King Peter I, are beneath the Patio del Crucero. They were built in the 12–13C and contain a **cistern** and gothic nave.

Cuarto Real Alto
An 30min guided tour (fee) grants access to the King and Queen of Spain's official residence in Sevilla. Rooms have *artesonado* ceilings and contain 19C furniture and clocks, 18C tapestries and French lamps. Note the **Capilla de los Reyes Católicos** (Chapel of the Catholic Monarchs) – an exquisite oratory with a ceramic font, by Nicola Pisano – and the Mudéjar **Sala de Audiencias**.

Cuarto del Almirante (Admiral's Apartments)
Right side, the Patio de la Montería.
In the Sala de Audiencias (Audience Chamber) the **Virgin of the Navigators★** altarpiece (1531–36) is by Alejo Fernández.

© Lucas Vallecillos/age fotostock

Detail of the decoration, Salón de Embajadores, Palacio de Pedro el Cruel

Palacio de Pedro el Cruel★★★ (Palace of Peter the Cruel)
A passage leads to the **Patio de las Doncellas** (Court of the Maidens), a Moorish arched patio with florid plasterwork; the upper storey was added in the 16C. An elevated round arch leads to the **Dormitorio de los Reyes Moros** (Bedroom of the Moorish Kings), two rooms decorated with blue-toned stucco and a magnificent *artesonado* ceiling. Through a small room is the **Patio de las Muñecas** (Dolls' Court) with Granada-type decoration. The gallery on the upper floor dates to the 19C. The Catholic Monarchs' bedroom leads to the **Salón de Felipe II** (Philip II Salon), the **Arco de los Pavones** (Peacock Arch) and the **Salón de Embajadores** (Ambassadors Hall), the most sumptuous room, with a 15C gilded cedarwood **cupola★★★**. The **Sala del Techo de Carlos V** (Charles V Room), the former chapel, has a gorgeous ceiling.

WEST OF THE CATHEDRAL
Museo de Bellas Artes★★★ (Fine Arts Museum)
Pl. del Museo 9. Open mid-June–mid-Sep Tue–Sun & public hols 9am–3pm. Mid-Sep–mid-Jun Tue–Sat 9am–8.30pm, Sun & public hols 9am–3pm. Closed 1 & 6 Jan, 1 May, 24–25 & 31 Dec. €1.50; free for EU citizens. Advance booking recommended. ℘955 54 29 42.
www.museodebellasartesdesevilla.es.

This is Spain's second-best Fine Arts museum (after the Prado). It's housed in the Convento de la Merced (Merced Friary), built in the 17C by Juan de Oviedo around three beautiful patios.

Sala I contains medieval art. **Room II** is dedicated to Renaissance art, with a fine sculpture of *St Jerome* by Pietro Torrigiani, a contemporary of Michelangelo.

Two portraits of *A Lady and a Gentleman* by Pedro Pacheco are the highlight in **Room III**.

In **Room V★★★**, walls decorated with paintings by the 18C artist Domingo Martínez lead to outstanding work by Murillo and a Zurbarán masterpiece, *The Apotheosis of St Thomas Aquinas* (in the nave), with skilful play of light and shade. **Murillo**'s monumental *Immaculate Conception,* with its energetic movement, is in the transept. To the right of the transept is a benevolent *Virgen de la Servilleta* (note the effect of the Child approaching).

Upper Floor: Room VI displays a collection of saints. **Room VIII** is devoted to Baroque artist Valdés Leal. European Baroque is represented in **Room IX**. **Room X★★** includes works of **Zurbarán**. In *Christ on the Cross*, the body of Christ appears as if sculpted. His *St Hugh and Carthusian Monks at Table* displays errors in perspective.

In the inner room, look up to admire the ceiling. **Room XI** holds **Goya**'s *Portrait of Canon José Duato.*

Metropol Parasol★

Pl. de la Encarnación. Rooftop open 9.30am–11pm (Fri–Sat until 11.30pm). €3 incl beverage. 955 47 15 80. www.setasdesevilla.com.

This gasp-inducing 100ft/30m-high landmark building was unveiled in 2011. Its official name comes from the shade it offers, though its mushroom-like appearance cemented its nickname among Sevillanos as Las Setas. Covering 18 000 square meters, it is said to be the world's largest wooden structure. Beneath it sit an archeological site, farmers market, multiple bars and restaurants. On the roof there is a restaurant, viewing gallery and a winding, undulating walkway. Lines are notoriously long here; off times are best.

Iglesia de San Luis de los Franceses★

San Luis 37. Open Tue–Sun 10am–2pm, 4–8pm (Jul–Aug 10am–2pm, 6–10pm). €4. 954 55 02 07.

This recently restored church, by Leonardo de Figueroa, is one of the best examples of the Sevillan Baroque. The exuberant **interior★★** is a mix of outstanding murals, sumptuous *retables* and fine *azulejos*. The crypt was closed for renovation as of September 2019.

Monasterio de Santa Paula★

Santa Paula 11. Shop open Tue–Sun 10am–1pm, 5–6.30pm. Museum Tue–Sun 10am–1pm. Closed for certain religious ceremonies. €4. 954 53 63 30. www.santapaula.es.

This functioning convent (ring the bell to enter) sells nun-made jams and chestnut butter. The church's breathtaking **portal★** (1504) is adorned with ceramics. Despite its mix of styles, the overall effect is harmonious. **Inside★**, the nave is covered by a 17C roof and the chancel by a frescoed Gothic vault. The **museum★** (entrance through no. 11 on the plaza) has works by Ribera, Pedro de Mena, Alonso de Cana and others. The gilded **Capilla de San José★** gleams at night.

Palacio de la Condesa de Lebrija★

Cuna 8. Open Sep–Jun Mon–Fri 10.30am–7.30pm. Sat 10am–2pm, 4–6pm. Sun 10am–2pm. Jul–Aug Mon–Fri 9am–3pm, Sat 10am–2pm. €12. 954 22 78 02. www.palaciodelebrija.com.

This noble home is decorated with **Roman mosaics★** (from Itálica), Mudéjar *artesonado* ceilings, 16C–17C *azulejos* and a sumptuous **stairway★**.

Iglesia del Salvador★

Pl. del Salvador. Open Mon–Sat & public hols 11am (9.30 hols)–5.30pm, 7.30–9pm. Sun 12–1.30pm, 3–7pm, 7.30–9pm. €3 donation. 954 59 54 05.

This 17C–18C church has some of the city's most impressive 18C **Baroque retables★★**.

Ayuntamiento
(Town Hall)
Pl. Nueva 1. Prebooked guided tours Mon–Thu 7pm & 8pm, Sat 10am. €4. ℘902 55 93 86.
The attractive **east facade★** (1527–34) is Renaissance in style and adorned with delicate scrollwork.

Basílica de la Macarena★
Bécquer 1–3. Open Mon–Sun 9.30am–2pm, 6–8pm (5–9pm Oct–mid-Apr). Closed 1 & 6 Jan, 1 May, 24, 25, 31 Dec. €5 museum, Basilica free. ℘954 90 18 00.
Home to Sevilla's most beloved icon, La Virgen de la Esperanza Macarena, the basilica is also the hub of a vibrant working-class neighbourhood.
Built in 1949 by Aurelio Gómez Millán, the neo-Baroque basilica contains the most universally admired Marian image in Sevilla. Sculpted in the 17C by Luisa Roldán, La Macarena is named for the Puerta de la Macarena, an entrance through the city walls built by Roman centurion Macarius Ena in the 2C AD. Her face, glistening with glass tears, is acclaimed as the most beautiful of all. Coveted by the Romani and by bullfighters, La Macarena's Holy Week appearance is one of the celebration's most emotional moments.

Iglesia de la Magdalena★
C. San Pablo 10. Open Mon–Sat 7.45am–1.30pm, 6.30–9pm, Sun 8.45am–2pm, 6.30–9pm. Closed 1 & 6 Jan, 1 May, 24–25 & 31 Dec. ℘954 22 96 03.
This monolith between Plaza Nueva and the Museo de Bellas Artes contains important artistic treasures. From the Mudéjar **Capilla de la Quinta Angustia** (Chapel of the Fifth Anguish) to the 1709 Baroque section by architect Leonardo de Figueroa, it's a rambling jumble of cupolas and domes filled with art. Zurbarán's *Santo Domingo de Soria* and the Lucas Valdés frescoes *Alegoría del triunfo de la fé* (*Allegory of the Triumph of Faith*) are works to look out for.

▶ Cross the Patio de la Montería and go down a vaulted passage (right).

Palacio Gótico or Salones de Carlos V (Gothic Palace or Charles V's Rooms)
The palace, which was built in the reign of Alfonso X, houses magnificent **tapestries★★** from the Real Fábrica de Tapices illustrating Charles V's conquest of Tunis in 1535.

Jardines★
Continue to the Mercurio pool and 17C **Galería del Grutesco★** to view the picturesque Moorish gardens. The most enchanting parts are **Charles V's pavilion**, the maze and the English garden. The silhouette of the Giralda rises above the **Patio de Banderas** (Flag Court), bordered by elegant facades.

Hospital de la Caridad★
(Hospital of Charity)
Temprado 3. Open Mon–Sun 10am-7.30pm, Sun 1-2.30pm. €5. ℘954 22 32 32. www.santa-caridad.es.
The hospital was founded in 1625. Great Sevillan artists decorated the **church★★**. Valdés Leal illustrated Death with a striking sense of the macabre. Murillo showed Charity in *The Miracle of the Loaves and Fishes*, *Moses Smiting Water from the Rock*, *St John of God* and *St Isabel of Hungary Caring for the Sick*. Pedro Roldan's **Entombment★★** adorns the high altar.

Archivo General de Indias
(Archives of the Indies)
Av. de la Constitución 3. Open Mon–Sat 9.30am-5pm, Sun 10am-2pm. ℘954 50 05 28. www.mcu.es/archivos/MC/AGI.
The 16C building, designed as an exchange (*lonja*) by Juan de Herrera, houses priceless documents on the Americas at the time of the Conquest, including maps and charts.

© LucVi/iStockphoto.com

EAST OF THE CATHEDRAL

Parque de María Luisa★★

The vast semicircular **Plaza de España★★** of this 19C park remains from the 1929 Ibero-American Exhibition. Each ceramic bench represents a province of Spain, with motifs, azulejos and images illustrative of each.

Museo Arqueológico★

Pl. de América. Open mid-Jun–mid-Sep Tue–Sun & public hols 9am–3.30pm, mid-Sep–mid-Jun Tue–Sat 9am–8pm, Sun & public hols 9am–3pm. Closed 1 & 6 Jan, 1 May, 24–25 & 31 Dec. €1.50; free for EU citizens. ℘955 12 06 32.

The archaeological museum is in a palace on Plaza de América. The 7C–6C BC **Carambolo Treasure★** includes a statue with a Phoenician inscription. In the **Roman section★** are statues and mosaics from Itálica (ℭsee Excursions).

BARRIO DE SANTA CRUZ★★★
(SANTA CRUZ QUARTER)

The former Jewish quarter is replete with alleys, wrought-iron grilles and flower-filled patios. It is delightful in the evenings when cafés and restaurants overflow into the squares.

Casa de Pilatos★★
(Pilate's House)

Pl. de Pilatos 1. Open Apr–Oct 9am–7pm; Nov–Mar 9am–6pm. €12, €10 ground floor only. ℘954 22 52 98. www.fundacionmedinaceli.org/monumentos/pilatos.

The large Mudéjar patio of this 15C–16C palace displays stuccowork and magnificent lustre **azulejos★★**. *Artesonado* ceilings; the chapel, with Gothic vaulting and *azulejo* and stucco decoration; and a remarkable wood **dome★** over the grand **staircase★★** illustrate the vitality of the Mudéjar style during the Renaissance. The gardens are open to the public.

Hospital de los Venerables★

Pl. de los Venerables 8. Open 10am–2pm, 4–8pm. Closed 1 Jan, 25 Mar, 25 Dec. €5.50; free Sun pm. ℘954 56 26 96. www.focus.abengoa.es.

This building, in lively Plaza de los Venerables, is one of the best examples of 17C Sevillan Baroque. Its fine **church★** is covered with frescoes by Valdés Leal and his son Lucas Valdés.

Museo del Baile Flamenco

Manuel Rojas Marcos 3. Open 10am–7pm (flamenco performance 7–8pm, 8.45–9.45pm in summer). Closed 1 & 6 Jan, 1 May, 24, 25, 31 Dec. €10 museo, €22 performance, €26 combined. ℘954 34 03 11. www.museodelbaileflamenco.com.

Learn all about the art of flamenco at this well-presented museum. **Cristina Hoyos**, one of the great *bailaoras*, founded it as an introduction for tourists and flamenco beginners as well as a repository of flamenco history for aficionados and professionals. Catch heart-pounding, foot-stomping shows here.

Iglesia de Santa María la Blanca★

Santa María la Blanca 5. ℘954 21 50 40. In the **interior★** of this former synagogue, exuberant Baroque ceilings are balanced by pink marble columns.

👥 ISLA DE LA CARTUJA
Isla Mágica★

Open Holy Week– first weekend Nov;
see website for seasonal hours and
discounts. €28. ✆902 16 17 16.
www.islamagica.es.

This major theme park takes visitors
around Seville, Spain, the 'New World',
Eldorado, Amazonia and the Mayan civilization. Rides vary from gentle carou-
sels to the latest white-knuckle roller
coasters and water rides, 3D films and
simulators, and there are live shows in
most areas. The fun doesn't stop after
dark, so consider overnighting here, to
see the fireworks-and-laser extrava-
ganza on the lake.

There is a waterpark in the complex
as well, **Aqua Mágica** (open only to Isla
Mágica ticket holders, same season, see
website for dates and times; €9).

Centro Andaluz de Arte Contemporáneo

Av. de Américo Vespucio 2. Open Tue
–Sat 11am–9pm, Sun 11am–3.30pm.
Closed 1 & 6 Jan, 3 Apr, 1 May, 12 Oct, 2
Nov, 7, 24, 25 & 31 Dec. €3.01; free Tue–
Fri 5–9pm, Sat. ✆955 03 70 70.
www.caac.es.

This contemporary art museum is in the
former La Cartuja monastery; some **convent buildings★** remain. The collection
includes art from 1957 onwards.

ADDITIONAL SIGHTS
Barrio de Triana★

Triana is Sevilla's classic Bohemian
neighbourhood (think sailors, Romani
people, bullfighters and flamenco
dancers) on the west bank of the Guadalquivir river. Though most of its original working-class denizens have been
displaced by gentrification, the barrio
has retained its locals-only, rough-and-
ready feel. The Santa Ana church, food
produce market and **Capilla de los Mar-
ineros** are important sights, along with
the Capilla de la Estrella and the Iglesia de San Jacinto. Calle Alfarería is the
ceramics centre of Sevilla, while Calle
Betis along the edge of the Guaqalquivir
is lined with taverns and restaurants.

Casa Anselma on Calle Pagés del Corro
is a popular flamenco jam session that
starts up around midnight.

Also here, on the waterfront, is the
Pabellón de la Navegación (open May–
Oct Tue–Sat 10am–8.30pm, Sun until
3pm; Nov–Apr Tue–Sat 10am–7.30pm,
Sun until 3pm; €4.90; ✆954 04 31 11),
a museum dedicated to Spanish sailing
and discovery. The ticket grants access
to the top of the 65m **Torre Schindler**,
with panormanic views.

EXCURSIONS
Ruinas de Itálica★

▶ Av. de Extremadura 2, Santiponce.
9km/6mi NW on the N 630. Open
mid-Jun–mid-Sep Tue–Sun 9am–3pm.
Apr–mid-Jun Tue–Sat 9am–8m, Sun
9am–3pm. Mid-Sep–Mar Tue–Sat
9am–6pm, Sun 9am–3pm. €1.50;
no charge for EU citizens. ✆600 14 17 67.
This **Roman town** was the birthplace of
emperors Hadrian and Trajan. Mosaics
of birds and Neptune are in their original sites. The **Anfiteatro** (amphitheatre),
seating 25 000, was one of the largest
in the empire.

Carmona★★

▶ 40km/25mi W along the A 4.
Carmona, with its heritage buildings,
overlooks the River Corbones.
🅿 Park in the lower part of town.

Old Town★

Note the **Baroque tower★** of the **Iglesia de San Pedro★** (Arco de la Carne),
a church with a sumptuous sacrarium
chapel (Capilla del Sagrario) and, farther
along, the **Convento de la Concepción**
with cloisters and a Mudéjar church.
Through the **Puerta de Sevilla★** is the
17C–18C **Iglesia de San Bartolomé**
(Prim 29). The capilla mayor in the
Mudéjar church of **San Felipe★** (San
Felipe) is covered with 16C ceramics.
The Baroque **town hall** (ayuntami-
ento), facing **Plaza de San Fernando**
(entrance on Calle de El Salvador), has a
Roman mosaic. Next door, the 17C–19C
Iglesia del Salvador is adorned with a
Churrigueresque altarpiece (open Mon,
Thu, Fri 11am–2pm, 4–6pm, Sat–Sun

The Legendary *Jamón*

The free-range, Ibérico black pig stores monounsaturated fats from acorns in marbled layers in its muscle tissue. Not only are these acorn-based oleic acids relatively healthy, but their flavours and aromas, after two years of ageing, are so complex, nutty, earthy and floral that the world's top chefs can't get enough of it. The fat in best (black-tagged) *jamón ibérico de bellota* (purebred Ibérico pig fed exclusively on acorns – up to 10kg/22lb a day) liquefies at room temperature, so it literally melts in your mouth.

11am–2pm; €4, free with Cathedral ticket; ℘954 14 12 70). The 15C Gothic **Iglesia de Santa María la Mayor★** is nearby: A monumental **Plateresque altarpiece★** illustrates the Passion. The **Convento de las Descalzas★** is a stunning example of 18C Sevillan Baroque. The Mudéjar church of the **Convento de Santa Clara** contains paintings by Valdés Leal.

The **Alcázar de Arriba** (Upper Fortress), a Roman structure, offers terrific **views★**. It is now a Parador.

Necrópolis Romana★

Av. de Jorge Bonsor 9, Carmona. ♿Access to the Roman necropolis is indicated along the road to Sevilla. Open mid-Jun–mid-Sep Tue–Sun 9am–3pm. Apr–mid-Jun Tue–Sat 9am–8pm, Sun until 3pm. Mid-Sep–Mar Tue–Sat 9am–6pm, Sun & pub hols 9am–3pm. €1.50, free for EU citizens. ℘600 14 36 32.

Of more than 300 1C tombs, mausoleums and crematoria, the most interesting are the large **Tumba del Elefante** and even bigger **Tumba de Servilia**.

Aracena★

www.aracena.es.

Aracena rises in tiers up a hillside, crowned by the remains of a Templars castle, its whitewashed houses adorned with ornate grilles. No trip to Aracena is complete without trying the exquisite *pata negra* cured ham.

👥 Gruta de las Maravillas (Cave of Wonders) ★★★

Pozo de la Nieve. 45min guided tours 10am–1.30pm, 3–6pm. Closed 24, 25, 31 Dec & 6 Jan. €10; advance booking recommended. ℘663 93 78 76.

Rivers below the castle formed vast caves with limpid pools. Formations include draperies and pipes coloured by iron and copper oxide and brilliant white calcite crystal as in the **Salón de la Cristalería de Dios★★** (God's Crystal Chamber). Here also is the local **Museo del Jamón** (open 10.45am–2.30pm, 3.45–7pm; €3.50), dedicated to Iberian pigs and their delicious ham.

Castillo e Iglesia del Mayor Dolor

Open Sept–Jun 10am–5.30pm, Jul–Aug 10am–7pm.

The 9C castle was built over an Almohad fortress. Note the decoration on the north side of the tower next to the church, similar to that of the Giralda in Sevilla.

Parque Natural de la Sierra de Aracena y Picos de Aroche★★

www.marcaparquenatural.com.

The cool forests of this remote, little-visited park are punctuated by slender peaks and unspoilt villages such as whitewashed **Alájar★** and **Almonaster la Real★**, concealed amid chestnut, eucalyptus, cork and holm oak. The latter has a rare intact **mosque★** (open Sat–Sun & public hols 11am–7pm). Nearby, **Jabugo** is justifiably famous for its delicious cured hams.

👥 Parque Minero de Riotinto★★

🚃Nearest station La Palma del Condado 55km (Seville 86km). Open daily; see website for seasonal hours. €24 incl train ride, mine and museum. ℘959 59 00 25.

www.parquemineroderiotinto.es.

The mining tradition of this area dates to antiquity. Learn about this history on aboard a 19C train that goes through the spectacular open-cast Peña de Hierro mines of **Corta Atalaya**★★★ and **Cerro Colorado**★★ and to the source of the Río Tinto (the Red River), which gives this area its name. The refurbished **House no 21**, dating from 1895, gives you an idea of what daily life would have been like for the workers and managers (many of whom were British), at the mine.

ADDRESSES

🏨 STAY

During Holy Week and the Feria, prices often double or triple. If you're planning to stay in the city for these events, book as far ahead as possible and check rates carefully.

⊖ **Hotel Londres** – San Pedro Mártir 1. ✆954 212 896. www.hotel-londres-sevilla.com. 22 rooms. ⊡€12. This centrally located hotel has basic but tastefully furnished rooms, some with balconies overlooking the street.

⊖ **Reyes Catolicos** –Gravina 57. ✆954 21 12 00. www.hotelreyescatolicos.info. 29 rooms. ⊡€8. Restaurant ⊖⊜. Centrally located by the Plaza de Armas and the Isla Mágica theme park, this budget hotel has well-equipped (if bland) rooms.

⊖⊜⊠ **Hotel Amadeus Sevilla & La Musica** – Farnesio 6. ✆954 50 14 43. www.hotelamadeussevilla.com. 30 rooms. ⊡€8.50. A family of musicians converted two typical Sevillan houses in the heart of the Santa Cruz district into a delightful hotel. The decor enhances the buildings' original architectural features. There is a lovely roof terrace, a piano for guests and concerts in the courtyard.

⊖⊜⊠⊠ **Hotel Las Casas de la Judería** – C. de Santa María La Blanca 5. ✆954 41 51 50. www.lascasasdelajuderiasevilla.com. 116 rooms. Restaurant ⊖⊜⊠⊠. Set in the old Jewish quarter, this refined hotel comprises 27 former houses adorned with with Roman statues and pedestals, jugs and antique and original furniture. Courtyards, gardens and a pool are nice pluses.

⊖⊜⊠⊠ **Hotel Casa 1800 Sevilla** – C. Rodrigo Caro 6. ✆954 56 18 00. www.hotelcasa1800sevilla.com. 33 rooms. ⊡€11.50. Finally, a luxury hotel with traditional Andalucían furnishings that doesn't feel forced or kitsch. Casa 1800 blends modernity and tradition seamlessly in rooms with original 19C parquet, gilded headboards, gauzy drapes and exposed-brick walls.

⊖⊜⊠⊠ **Hotel Alfonso XIII** – San Fernando 2. ✆954 91 70 00. www.marriott.com. 151 rooms. ⊡€30. Built in 1928 in neo-Mudéjar style, the Alfonso XIII is one of Sevilla's most luxurious and famous hotels. An excellent location opposite the gardens of the Alcázar is part of its allure.

ARACENA

⊖⊖ **Hotel Los Castaños** – Av. de Huelva 5. ✆959 12 63 00. www.loscastanoshotel.com. 30 rooms. ⊡€8.80. This simply furnished Andalucían-style building is in the centre of town. Accommodation is comfortable and well maintained if outdated. Some rooms face a large inner patio. The hotel also has a fine restaurant.

🍴 EAT

⊖⊜⊠ **Corral del Agua** – Callejón del Agua 6. ✆954 22 48 41. www.corraldelagua.es. Closed Sun. It doesn't get much more romantic than a white-tablecloth dinner in the tree-shaded courtyard illuminated by twinkling candles. Seafood and braised meat dishes are excellent here (skip the rice).

⊖⊜⊠ **Az-Zait** – Pl. de San Lorenzo 1. ✆954 90 64 75. www.az-zait.es. Expect showy, colourful reinterpretations of Andalucían classics here. The tasting menu is a steal.

⊖⊜⊠⊠ **Ispal** – Pl. San Sebastián 1. ✆955 54 71 27. www.restauranteispal.com. Sun eve, Mon. One of the hottest tables in town is at this experimental restaurant with a cosy, modern dining room serving '100% Sevillano' locavore tasting menus.

⊖⊜⊠⊠ **Taberna del Alabardero** – Zaragoza 20. ✆954 50 27 21. www.tabernadelalabardero.es. Closed Aug.

This 19C mansion houses a true-blue old-school fine dining restaurant, the kind with chandeliers, tabletop lamps and billowy curtains. There's no dry ice or blowtorches in the dining room here – just upscale Andalucían cuisine executed to the T.

ARACENA

⊜⊜⊜ **José Vicente** – Av. Andalucía 53. ✆959 12 84 55. Call to check opening times. Sublime yet unpretentious, José Vicente uses the finest local produce, and it shows in this award-winning restaurant. Spring for the cep mushrooms when in season.

TAPAS

Bar Europa – Siete Revueltas 35 (Pl. del Pan) ✆954 21 79 08. www.bareuropa. info. Step into an old-fashioned bar that's retained its Belle-Epoque feel, and stick around for a sudsy pint and well-priced *molletes* (mini sandwiches).

Bodeguita Romero – Harinas 10. ✆954 22 95 56. www.bodeguita-romero.com. Closed Sun pm, Mon and half of Aug. Post up at the U-shaped bar and get the *pringá*, a soft, warm breadroll stuffed with a dribbly rubble of bacon, chorizo and blood sausage.

Bodega San José – Adriano 10. ✆954 22 41 05. Close to the Maestranza bullring, this no-frills bodega with a sawdust-covered floor is frequented by sherry-sipping bullfighting aficionados.

La Giralda – Mateos Gago 1. ✆954 22 82 50. Built into what was once a Moorish bath, this pocket-size bar is known for its *solomillo* (filet) *al whisky*.

El Rinconcillo – Gerona 40 y Alhóndiga 2. ✆954 22 31 83. www. elrinconcillo.es. Closed 3 weeks Jul–Aug. One The bar that made *espinacas con garbanzos* (chickpeas and spinach) famous, El Rinconcillo has been chalking tabs on the wooden bar since 1670 (though the decor is mostly 19C).

CAFÉS

Confitería La Campana – Sierpes 1. ✆954 22 35 70. www.confiteriala campana.com. One of Sevilla's classic *cafeterías* has Modernist decor and delectable homemade pastries.

NIGHTLIFE

Maquila – Delgado 4. ✆955 18 23 20. www.levies18.com. Gobble down some of Sevilla's most delectable *nueva cocina* tapas between local microbrews at this craft beer bar. The mussels are excellent.

Paseo de las Delicias – This avenue is lined with buzzing music bars that attract a local crowd. Two worth seeking out are Líbano (www. kioscolibano.com) and Bilindo (www. terrazabilindo.com).

ENTERTAINMENT

La Carbonería – Levíes 18 (Pl. de las Mercaderías). ✆954 56 37 49. www. levies18.com. Decent flamenco in Sevilla *for free*? It sounds too good to be true, and that's why this casual bar is packed to the gills night in, night out. Just skip the food and so-so sangría. .

Casa Anselma – Pagés del Corro 49. ✆954 21 28 89. Spontaneous flamenco 11.30pm–4am. Triana's most famous (and infamous) diva, Anselma is the bouncer, MC and occasional performer in this rollicking late-night tablao.

El Patio Sevillano – Po. de Cristóbal Colón 11 A. ✆954 21 41 20. www. elpatiosevillano.com. This classic flamenco club is less touristy than most.

Tablao El Arenal – Rodó 7 (Arenal). ✆954 21 64 92. www.tablaoelarenal.com. Savour flamenco in its purest form here.

SHOPPING

Antique lovers should wander the historic centre of the city, particularly the Santa Cruz district. The **Jueves** (Thursday) is a weekly small market held on Calle Feria. Sevilla has a rich **arts and crafts** tradition. Potters can still be found in the Santa Cruz and **Triana** districts (in the latter on calle Alfarería). The La Cartuja factory is heir to this tradition, which dates to Islamic and Roman times. Other products from Sevilla include inlaid woodwork, shawls, fans, wrought iron, harnesses, guitars and castanets.

Osuna★★

This elegant town in the Sevillan countryside retains a beautiful monumental centre★ from its past as a ducal seat of the house of Osuna, one of the most powerful on the Iberian Peninsula.

TOWN CENTRE

Mainly around Pl. del Duque and Pl. España.

Osuna's streets are lined with Baroque mansions and palaces ★★ whose thick, copper-nailed doors belie fine grilles and leafy green patios. Of particular note are **Calle San Pedro**★ (Cilla del Cabildo, Palacio de los Marqueses de la Gomera), the Antigua Audencia (former Law Courts), the Palacio de los Cepeda, the former Palacio de Puente Hermoso, several fine churches (e.g., Santo Domingo, La Compañía) and the **belfry of the Iglesia de la Merced**★, built by the same architect as the **Cilla del Cabildo**.

SIGHTS

Zona Monumental★

Follow signs to Centro Ciudad (town centre) and Zona Monumental.

Colegiata (Museo de Arte Sacro)★

Pl. de la Encarnación. Open Tue–Sun 10am–1.30pm, 3.30–6.30pm (4–7pm May–Sep; closed Sun pm Jul & Aug). Prebooked guided tour €5.
℘954 81 04 44.
This 16C Renaissance-style collegiate church houses five **paintings**★★ by **José (Jusepe) de Ribera 'El Españoleto'** (1591–1652), including *The Expiration of Christ*, in the side chapel off the Nave del Evangelio. The remainder are exhibited in the sacristy.

Panteón Ducal★★ (Ducal Pantheon)

The pantheon was built in Plateresque style in 1545 for the Dukes of Osuna. It is approached by a delightful patio.

- **Population:** 17 622
- **Michelin Map:** 578 U 14.
- **Info:** Sevilla 37. ℘954 81 57 32. www.osuna.es.
- **Location:** Osuna rises to the south of the Guadalquivir Basin, near the A 92 highway linking Granada (160km/100mi E) with Sevilla. 🚌Osuna.
- **Don't Miss:** Heritage buildings untouched by time.

The chapel (1545) stands below the Colegiata's main altar and is crowned by a blue-and-gold polychrome coffered ceiling, now blackened by candle smoke. Another crypt, built in 1901, holds the tombs of the most important dukes. Nearby stand the 16C **former university** (Antigua Universidad) and the 17C **Monasterio de la Encarnación**★ (Cuesta de San Antón 15; open same hours as Colegiata; €3.50; ℘954 81 11 21), in which the highlight is the magnificent **dado**★ of 17C Sevillan *azulejos* in the patio. The nuns here make and sell addictive biscuits and pastries.

On the descent into the town centre, note the 12–13C Torre del Agua, a former defensive tower now a small **archaeological museum** (Pl. de la Duquesa; open same hours as Colegiata; €3.50; ℘954 81 12 07).

EXCURSIONS

Écija★

🡒 34km/21mi N along the A 351. www.turismoecija.com.
Spain's 'frying pan' (it gets deathly hot here in summer) lies in the Guadalquivir depression and is renowned for its lofty Baroque belfries decorated with ceramic tiles such as the 18C **Torre de San Juan**★ (Pl. de San Juan; park car in Pl. de España; open Tue–Sat 10am–1pm, 4.30–5.30pm, Sun 10am–1pm; €2).

Osuna with the Colegiata

© Stuart Black/age fotostock

The **ayuntamiento** (town hall) has two **Roman mosaic floors★** and a *camera obscura* (a precursor to the modern camera) that offers a peculiar perspectives of the city (Pl. de España 1; open 10am–1.30pm; €4; ☎955 90 02 40).

Écija has several attractive small squares bounded by houses adorned with decorative columns and coats of arms. Along the streets adjoining Avenida Miguel de Cervantes are several old palaces with fine **facades★**.

The 18C Baroque **Palacio de Benamejí** houses the tourist office and the Museo Histórico Municipal (Cánovas del Castillo; open Oct–May Tue–Fri 10am–1.30pm, 4.30–6.30pm, Sat 10am–2pm, 5.30–8pm, Sun & public hols 10am–3pm; Jun–Sep Tue–Fri 10am–2.30pm, Sat 10am–2pm, 8–10pm, Sun & public hols 10am–3pm; ☎954 83 04 31, www.museo.ecija.es). Note too the concave, frescoed **Palacio de Peñaflor** (Emilio Castelar 26), its portal built on columns, and the Plateresque **Palacio de Valdehermoso** (Emilio Castelar 37).

Several churches are noteworthy; **Los Descalzos** stands out for its exuberant **interior★**.

Santa María (Pl. de Santa María; open Mon–Sat 9.30am–1.30pm, 5.30–8.30pm, Sun 9.30am–1.30pm; ☎954 83 04 30, www.iglesiadesantamaria.org), boasts an impressive tower.

The Convento de los Santísima Trinidad y Purísima Concepción, better known as 'Las Marroquíes', also has a lofty **bell tower★**; its crumbly *marroquíes* biscuits are produced and sold by the nuns.

The **Iglesia de Santiago★** retains the Mudéjar windows of an earlier building and a Gothic **retable★** at the high altar illustrating the Passion and the Resurrection.

The Iglesia de Santa Cruz houses the **Museo de Arte Sacro** (sacred art museum) with 16–19C works. (Pl. Virgen del Valle; open Mon–Fri 9am–1pm, 4–7.30pm, Sat 5–7.30pm, Sun 10am–1pm, 6–8pm; ☎954 83 06 13).

Estepa★

◐ 25km/15mi E of Osuna. 🚃Nearest station Huelva (52km).

In 206 BC, this town commit collective suicide in the face of a Roman invasion. In the 19C, Washington Irving chronicled the Spanish and Moorish *bandoleros* who plagued Estepa. Today it is a peaceful labyrinth of narrow streets known for its killer *mantecados* and *polvorones*, local biscuits made with lard. The Baroque **Iglesia de Nuestra Señora del Carmen** is Estepa's best monument, while the Iglesia de San Sebastián and Palacio de los Marqueses de Cerverales are further examples of Andalucían rural architecture.

Cerro de San Cristóbal offers memorable panoramas of Estepa's towers, such as the **Torre de la Victoria★** rising from the plaza of the same name, and rolling countryside, *la campiña*, beyond.

Costa de la Luz★

The southwestern coast in the provinces of Huelva and Cádiz is edged with wide, grass-fringed beaches intersected by the mouths of major rivers: the Guadiana, Tinto and Guadalquivir. Several resorts interrupt the dazzling white sand and translucent skies that make this the 'Coast of Light'.

Michelin Map: 578 U 7-8-9-10, V 10, W 10-11, X 11-12-13 – Andalucía (Huelva, Cádiz)

Info: El Puerto de Santa María: Palacio de Aranibar, Plaza del Castillo; ℘956 483 715. Huelva: Fernando El Católico, 14; ℘959 25 74 67. Sanlúcar de Barrameda: Calzada Duquesa Isabel; ℘956 36 61 10. Tarifa: Paseo de la Alameda; ℘956 68 09 93. www.andalucia.org.

Location: From Ayamonte, at the mouth of the Guadiana,

🚗 DRIVING TOURS

THE HUELVA COAST★
Ayamonte to the Parque Nacional de Doñana – 135km/84mi. Alow one day.

Ayamonte★
This fishing port at the mouth of the Guadiana is a lively border town of cobbled streets and whitewashed and brightly coloured houses. In the old quarter are the 16C colonial-style Iglesia de las Angustias; Convento de San Francisco, with its elegant bell tower and magnificent *artesonado* work; and 13C Iglesia del Salvador.

Boat service is available to Vila Real de Santo António in Portugal. Coastal resorts between Ayamonte and Huelva include **Isla Canela, Isla Cristina** (www.islacristina.org), **La Antilla** (www.lepe.es) and **Punta Umbría** (www.ayto-puntaumbria.es). This area also includes the marshland of the **Marismas del Río Piedras y Flecha de El Rompido★**, the Portil lagoon and the Enebrales de Punta Umbría, a landscape dominated by juniper trees.

Huelva★
🚃Huelva.

In the 15–16C, the estuary formed by the Tinto and Odiel rivers saw the departure of numerous expeditions to the 'New World', notably those led by Columbus. A large monument to those explorers, the **Monumento a Colón** (1929), stands near the harbour at Punta del Sebo.

In Huelva, see the unusual **Barrio Reina Victoria★**, an English-style district named after Queen Victoria; the **Catedral de La Merced** (Pl. de la Merced; ℘959 24 30 36), with its Renaissance facade and sculpture of the Virgen de la Cinta, the town's patron saint, by Martínez Montañés; paintings by Zurbarán in the **Iglesia de la Concepción**; and the **Museo de Huelva** (Alameda Sundheim 13; open mid-Jun–mid-Sep Tue–Sun 9am–3pm; mid-Sep–mid-Jun Tue–Sat 9am–8pm, Sun 9am–3pm; €1.50, free for EU citizens; ℘959 65 04 24).

Paraje Natural de las Marismas del Odiel★★
2km/1.2mi SE. Exit Huelva along Av. Tomás Domínguez. Anastasio Senra Visitor Centre, Ctra. del Dique Juan Carlos I. 🖐 Book activities. ℘959 52 43 34/35.

This marshland (marisma) of outstanding beauty, at the mouth of the Tinto and Odiel rivers is a **World Biosphere Reserve**. It provides a habitat for over 200 bird species and can only be visited by boat including spoonbills, flamingos and loons.

La Rábida★
10km/6.2mi SE of Huelva off N 442.
🚃Nearest station Huelva (10km).

In 1484, the Prior of the **Monasterio de Santa María** (Camino del Monasterio; open Nov–Mar Tue–Sat 10am–1pm, 4–6.15pm, Apr–Oct Tue–Sat 10am–

1pm, 4–7pm. €3.50; ℘959 35 04 11, www.monasteriodelarabida.com), Juan Pérez, believed Columbus's claim that the world was round and acted as an intermediary to obtain the support of the Catholic Monarchs.

The **church★** preserves old frescoes, wooden *artesonado* work and the delicate 14C alabaster statue of the **Virgen de los Milagros★** (Virgin of Miracles), in front of which Columbus is said to have prayed prior to setting sail. A small room displays a **mapamundi★**, by Juan de la Cosa, that outlined the coast of America for the first time.

Full-scale replicas of Columbus's three caravels are moored at the **Muelle de las Carabelas★** (open mid-Sep–mid-Jun Tue–Sun 9.30am–7.30pm, mid-Jun–mid-Sep Tue–Sun 10am–9pm; €3.60; ℘959 53 05 97), a modern dock and museum on the Tinto Estuary.

Palos de la Frontera★

13km/8mi SE of Huelva by A 5026.
🚃Nearest station Huelva 13 km
www.palosfrontera.com.

This seafaring town on the left bank of the Río Tinto was the birthplace of the Pinzón brothers, who sailed with Columbus. The **Casa-Museo de Martín Alonso Pinzón** (open Mon–Fri 10am–2pm; €1; ℘959 10 00 41) and the *azulejos* dotted around the town provide a reminder of the first voyage. The 15C **Iglesia de San Jorge** is fronted by an intriguing Gothic-Mudéjar doorway.

Moguer★

20km/12.4mi NE of Huelva off A 494.
Expeditions to lands unknown left from this tranquil town, with elegant houses. The verses of **Juan Ramón Jiménez** (1881–1958), Moguer's most illustrious son and winner of the Nobel Prize for Literature in 1956, adorn *azulejo* panelling dotted around the town centre. His home is a museum, the **Casa-Museo Juan Ramón Jiménez★** (Juán Ramón Jimenez 10; open by guided tour every hr, Tue–Sun 10am-2pm, also Tue–Sat 5–8pm; €3.50; ℘959 37 21 48, www.fundacion-jrj.es).

The **town hall** (ayuntamiento) has a fine Renaissance **facade★**. Head along the pedestrianised **Calle Andalucía★** to see interesting buildings such as the Archivo Histórico Municipal and Biblioteca Iberoamericana and the 15C Convento de San Francisco, with its Mannerist cloisters, Baroque altarpiece and lofty belfry. The **tower★** of the Iglesia de **Nuestra Señora de la Granada** recalls the Giralda in Sevilla.

Convento de Santa Clara★

Guided tours (40min) each hr Tue–Sat 10.30am–12.30pm, 5.30–6.30pm. Sun 10.30am, 11.30am. Closed public hols. €3.50. ℘959 37 01 07.
www.monasteriodesantaclara.com.

The church of this Gothic-Mudéjar monastery houses the Renaissance-style marble **tombs of the Portocarrero family★**, noteworthy **tombs★** at the high altar and exceptional 14C **Nasrid-Mudéjar choir stalls★★**.

▶ Return to the C 442, which follows the coast.

Parque Nacional de Doñana★

🚃Nearest station Huelva 64 km.
El Acebuche visitor centre: Pl. Acebuchal 22, El Rocío, Carretera A-483, km. 37,5; ℘959 43 96 27.
www.andalucia.org/es/espacios-naturales/parque-nacional/donana.

At the crossroads between Europe and Africa and the Atlantic and the Mediterranean, the Doñana – Spain's largest wildlife reserve with a protected area of 73 000ha/180 387 acres – is a pit stop for thousands of African and European migratory birds. The **salt marshes** are the larger part of the park and are the ideal habitat for birds that migrate to Europe over the winter. **Sand dunes** are grouped in formation parallel to the Atlantic and advance inland at a rate of 6m/19.6ft per year. The stabilised sands or **cotos** are dry, undulating areas covered with heather, rockrose, rosemary and thyme and trees such as cork oak and pine. The Doñana is home to lynx, wild boar, deer and a wide variety of birds including Spanish imperial

Horseracing on the beach of Sanlúcar de Barrameda

© Thomas Dressler/age fotostock

eagles, flamingos, herons, wild ducks and coots.

Because of the park's fragile ecology, entry to the **Doñana** is rigorously regulated. The El Acebuche visitor centre coordinates all park activities (book jeep tours in advance with the cooperative Marismas del Rocío tours; two visits per day Tue–Sun at 8.30am and 3pm/5pm May–mid-Sep; €30 ℘959 430 432; www.donanavisitas.es). Itineraries vary according to the time of year.

Walking tours depart from the El Acebuche and other information centres, where details on the level of difficulty and duration are available. Excursions are also available on horseback or by horse-drawn carriage (enquire at visitor centre).

El Rocío
65km/40.4mi E of Huelva, along A 483.

This small village is famous as the site of the **Santuario de Nuestra Señora del Rocío** (Sanctuary of the Virgin of the Dew; ℘959 44 24 25), to which Spain's most popular religious pilgrimage (*romería*) is made during Whitsun weekend every year.

CÁDIZ COAST★
From Sanlúcar de Barrameda to Tarifa 160km/99.4mi. Allow one day.

Sanlúcar de Barrameda★
🚃 Nearest station El Puerto de Santa María 24km

The fishing port of Sanlúcar, at the mouth of the Guadalquivir, is the hometown of *manzanilla*, a dry sherry

matured like *fino* that has a distinct briny flavour thanks to the sea air and particular microclimate. The bodegas (wine cellars) are in the old quarter on the hill around the massive **Castillo de Santiago** (Cava de Castillo).

The **Iglesia de Nuestra Señora de la O** (Pl. de la Paz) nearby has a fine Mudéjar **doorway★★** and a 16C **Mudéjar artesonado ceiling★**. The **Palacio de Orleans y Borbón** (Cuesta de Belén), a 19C palace built in neo-Moorish style, is now Sanlúcar's town hall and tourist office. Note its **covachas★**, a mysterious series of five ogee arches decorated with Gothic tracery. The lower town has two main churches: the **Iglesia de la Trinidad** (Pl. de San Roque), with its magnificent 15C Mudéjar **artesonado★★**, and the **Iglesia de Santo Domingo**, with the noble proportions of a Renaissance building.

The **Centro de Visitantes Fábrica de Hielo** (open 9am–7pm, until later in summer; ℘956 38 65 77), a visitor centre in an old ice factory located in Bajo de Guía (near the mouth of the Guadalquivir), provides information on the Parque Nacional de Doñana across the river. Park excursions also depart from here.

Rota
23km/14mi S of Sanlúcar off A 491.

The **old town★** inside the ramparts is laid out around the **Castillo de la Luna** (Av. Mancomunidad Bajo Guadalquivir 3; ℘956 84 63 45) and the **Iglesia de Nuestra Señora de la O★** (Luis Vázquez 2; ℘956 81 00 84). Rota is known for

Windsurfers, Playa de Bolonia near Tarifa

© Robert Harding/hemis.fr

beaches including the **Playa de la Costilla★**. A 24 sq km/9.2 sq mi Spanish naval station completely funded by the United States is on the outskirts of the town. As a place where warships refuel on their way to the Middle East, it often sees antiwar protests.

El Puerto de Santa María★
See p544.
24km/15mi SE of Sanlúcar, off A 491.
El Puerto de Santa María.
This harbour town in the bay of Cádiz played a prominent role in early trade with the 'New World'. Today, fishing, sherry exports and tourism drive its economy.

Cádiz★★ See CÁDIZ, p541.
52km/32mi S of Sanlúcar.
South of Cádiz, there are good beaches at **La Barrosa★★**, Chiclana de la Frontera and **Conil de la Frontera** (**Playa de la Fontanilla** and **Playa de los Bateles**).

Vejer de la Frontera★
57km/35mi SE of Cádiz along E 5.
Nearest station Cadiz (57km).
Vejer, perched on a crag, is one of the prettiest white villages of Andalucía. The best approach is along the hillside road from the south.
The **Iglesia del Divino Salvador,** a mix of Romanesque and Gothic, has a three-aisle **interior★**. The road on to Tarifa runs through the Baetic foothills. The **Parque Natural La Breña y Marismas de Barbate★** (Barbate, Puerto Pesquero; 956 45 97 80), has vertiginous cliffs and tranquil coves such as the

Cala de los Caños de Meca★★, some 10km/6mi from Vejer.

Ruinas Romanas de Baelo Claudia★
Open Tue–Sun from 9am–6pm (Apr–mid-Jun until 8pm, mid-Jun–mid-Sep until 3pm). €1.50; free for EU citizens. Guided tours available. 956 10 67 97.
Mere steps inland from **Playa de Bolonia★★**, a favourite beach for its climable sand dune, lie the remains of the textbook Roman city of Baelo Claudia. It dates to the 2C BC, when a salting factory specialising in the production of *garum* (a pungent sauce made from fermented fish) was established here. Vestiges of the basilica, forum and theatre are visble.

Tarifa
105km/65mi S of Cádiz, along E 5.
Nearest station: Algeciras (23km).
Spain's breezy southernmost point is a hotspot for windsurfing and kitesurfing, especially in the inlets of **Los Lances** and **Valdevaqueros**.
The **Castillo de Guzmán el Bueno,** dominates the town. It was taken by the Christians in 1292 and commanded by Guzmán el Bueno, who famously chose to accept the execution of his own sons, captured by the Moors, rather than surrender the town back to them.

ADDRESSES

STAY
 Hotel Convento de San Francisco – La Plazuela, Vejer de la

Frontera. ☎956 45 10 01. www.tugasa. com. 25 rooms. Restaurant ⊖⊜⊜. This former 17C convent is situated in Vejer's old quarter. Although soberly decorated, the rooms are pleasant, with high ceilings and exposed stone walls and beams.

⊖⊜⊜ **Hotel Copacabana Tarifa Beach** – Playa de Valdevaqueros Los Porro, 12 ☎956 681 709 www.copacabanatarifa. com. 26 rooms. Set on Valdevaqueros Beach, this middle-of-the-road, tropical-themed hotel offers great views of the Moroccan coast and the dunes of Punta Paloma Beach. It's a fine spot to post up for a few nights while spending most of your time in the water.

⊖⊜⊜⊜ **Hotel Toruño** – Pl. del Acebuchal 22, El Rocío. ☎959 44 23 23. www.toruno.es. 31 rooms. At the edge of Parque Nacional de Doñana, this enormous white 'guesthouse' blends perfectly into the village of El Rocío. Some rooms have lovely marsh views, and the hotel offers several Doñana exploration packages. Beware, prices soar during the pilgrimage of El Rocio.

⊖⊜⊜⊜ **Posada de Palacio** – Caballeros 11, Sanlúcar de Barrameda. ☎956 36 48 40. www.posadadepalacio. com. 34 rooms. ⊇€7. This family-run hotel is in a lovely 18C mansion opposite the town hall in the upper section of Sanlúcar. The rooms, laid out around an attractive patio, are simply yet tastefully decorated with patterned duvets and art on the walls.

⏍ EAT

⊖ **Churrería Rábida** – Rábida 8, Huelva. Closed Sun. Get your *chocolate con churros* fix at the best churrería around.

⊖⊜⊜ **Casa Bigote** – Bajo de Guía 10, Sanlúcar de Barrameda. ☎956 36 26 96. www.restaurantecasabigote.com. Closed Sun. This old tavern in the river district of Bajo Guía has become a gastronomic landmark. Run by the same family for the past 50 years, it's acclaimed for its sweet, juicy prawns.

⊖⊜⊜ **Trafalgar** – Pl. de España 31, Vejer de la Frontera. ☎956 44 76 38. www.restaurantetrafalgar.com. Snag a terrace table at this smart restaurant to try colourfully presented Andalucían tapas with an international bent.

⊖⊜⊜ **La Casona** – Pedro Cortes 6, Tarifa. ☎956 68 25 23. La Casona has an easy-going, family-friendly appeal but takes is Moroccan-Mediterranean food seriously. Save room for the homemade desserts.

Jerez de la Frontera★★

Jerez looks out at fertile countryside. A scruffy, provincial capital, it springs into life at fiesta time, sharing its traditions of wine, horsemanship and flamenco.

THE CITY TODAY

Modern Jerez was built around 150 years ago on its Anglo-Spanish sherry wealth and has an aristocratic, rather staid air. Few visitors stay overnight – there's an inexplicable dearth of great hotels – but those who do can enjoy real-deal flamenco (the town has a siz-able Romani population) and the elec-tric energy of *tabancos*, Jerez's famous down-home taverns.

▶ **Population:** 212 879
⦿ **Michelin Map:** 578 V 11.
▤ **Info:** Pl. del Arenal, Edificio Los Arcos. ☎956 34 17 11. www.turismojerez.com.
▶ **Location:** Jerez is in the Andalucían countryside, 35km/22mi from the provincial capital Cádiz and 90km/56mi from Sevilla. ▭Jerez de la Frontera. Train to city from Jerez airport 9mins
⦿ **Don't Miss:** A bodega tour.
⦿ **Timing:** Take several hours to stroll the town's historic quarters, stopping off at at least one bodega or tabanco.

A BIT OF HISTORY

Jerez was one of the first towns to be founded by the Moors on the Iberian Peninsula. A number of vestiges remain from their 'Sahrish' including sections of the old walls, the fortress *(alcazaba)* and a mosque. In 1264, Jerez was conquered by the troops of Alfonso X and became a settlement of strategic importance as well as a leading commercial centre. The economic resurgence experienced by the province of Cádiz in the 18C left its mark on Jerez, with the construction of fine Baroque buildings and its famous wine cellars, some of which can still be seen and toured today.

SIGHTS

Bodegas Domecq

Madre de Dios. Prebooked guided tours only. From €8. ✆670 09 99 90. www.migueldomecq.com.

A visit to the oldest Jerez bodega includes storehouses where a host of celebrities have signed their names.

Bodegas González Byass (Tío Pepe)

Manuel María González 12. Guided tours in English Jun–Oct Mon–Sat 12pm, 1pm, 2pm, 5.15pm (Nov–May last visit at 5pm); Sun 12pm, 1pm, 2pm. Book ahead. From €15 (incl two wine tastes). ✆902 44 00 77. www.bodegastiopepe.com.

The region's most famous storehouse is the spectacular La Concha bodega, designed by Gustave Eiffel in 1862.

Palacio del Tiempo★

Cervantes 3. Prebooked guided tours Mon–Fri 9.30am–1.15pm. Closed 24–25, 31 Dec. €6. ✆956 18 21 00. www.museosdelaatalaya.com.

Santa María de Gracia	B
Palacio del Marqués de Bertemati	C
Museo Arqueológico	E
Palacio de Riquelme	F

JEREZ DE LA FRONTERA

0 300 m

CÁDIZ, BODEGA WILLIAMS & HUMBERT

This clock museum, housed in the 19C Palacete de la Atalaya, exhibits over 280 18–19C timepieces in perfect working order.

Real Escuela Andaluza del Arte Ecuestre★

Av. Duque de Abrantes. Guided 30min tour incl facilities and training sessions. See website for tour and show schedules. Closed public holidays. From €6.50 for tours; shows from €21. ℘956 31 96 35. www.realescuela.org.

This foundation, set in a 19C mansion by Charles Garnier, is dedicated to the equestrian arts. It has two museums. A **show★★** in the arena is the highlight (call to confirm showtimes).

Museo Arqueológico de Jerez

Pl. del Mercado. Open mid-Sep–mid-Jun Tue–Fri 10am–2pm, 4–7pm, Sat–Sun & public hols 10am–2pm; mid-Jun– mid-Sep Tue–Fri 9am–2.30pm. Sat–Sun 10am–2.30pm €5; free first Sun.

The most memorable exhibit in the archaeological museum is a **Greek helmet★**.

 WALKING TOUR

THE OLD TOWN

Plaza del Mercado

The medieval market is now a tranquil square bordered by the **Palacio Riquelme**, with an imposing Renaissance facade; the 15C **Iglesia de San Mateo**; and the **Museo Arqueológico**.

▷ Take Cabezas to the **Iglesia de San Lucas,** then Ánimas de Lucas, Plaza de Orbaneja and San Juan.

Iglesia de San Juan de los Caballeros★

Pl. de San Juan.
This medieval church has a 14C **polygonal apse★** topped by a ribbed cupola with jagged decoration.

▷ Take Francos, then Canto to Plaza de Ponce de León.

Note the fine **Plateresque window★★** on one of the corners.

▷ Go along Juana de Dios Lacoste, cross Francos, then follow Compañía.

Iglesia de San Marcos

Pl. de San Marcos.
This late-15C church has a beautiful 16C **star vault**. The apse is hidden by a 16C polygonal **altarpiece★** showing strong Flemish influence.

▷ From the square, Tonería leads to Plaza de Plateros.

Plaza de Plateros

The **Torre de Atalaya**, a 15C tower, is adorned with Gothic windows.

▷ Head down José Luis Díez.

Plaza de la Asunción★

The Renaissance facade of the **Casa del Cabildo★★** (1575) is adorned with grotesque figures. The Gothic **Iglesia de San Dionisio** (℘956 34 29 40) shows Mudéjar influence.

▷ Continue along José Luis Díez.

Plaza del Arroyo

The **Palacio del Marqués de Bertemati★** has fine Baroque balconies.

▷ Continue on José Luis Díez and on to Plaza del Arroyo, turn left at del Encarnación, then right at Manuel María González.

Catedral★★

Pl. de la Encarnación. Open Mon– Sat 10am–6.30pm. €6. ℘956 16 90 59. www.catedraldejerez.es.

This monumental cathedral with five aisles combines Renaissance and Baroque features. The cupola bears basreliefs of the Evangelists. The annual wine harvest festival is held in front of the cathedral.

▷ Return to Manuel María González and head NE. Turn right at Plaza Monti, left at Armas and right at Plaza del Arenal.

Alcázar★

Alameda Vieja. Open Jul–Sep Mon–Fri 10am–5.30pm, Sat–Sun 9.30am–2.30pm; rest of year Mon–Sat 9.30am–2.30pm. Closed 1, 6 Jan, 25 Dec. €7 (incl camera obscura). ☎956 14 99 55.

From this 12C Almohad fortress, enjoy an excellent **view★★** of the cathedral. Enter by the **Puerta de la Ciudad** (City Gateway). The prayer room in the **mosque★★**, located within the walls of the Alcázar, is covered by an **octagonal cupola**. A **camera obscura** in the **Palacio de Villavicencio** provides a unique view of Jerez via its mirrors and lenses.

▷ Head NE along Plaza del Arenal towards Caballeros, turn right at San Miguel and bear left towards the church.

Iglesia de San Miguel★★

Pl. de San Miguel.
Construction began in Gothic style in the late 16C; the Baroque tower dates to two centuries later.
The older San José facade is a fine example of the Hispano-Flemish style. The Renaissance **altarpiece★** is by Martínez Montañés.

EXCURSIONS

La Cartuja★

▷ Carrera de Jerez a Algeciras, 6km/3.5mi SE. Gardens and patio are open Tue–Sat 7am–7am. Closed public hols. ☎956 15 64 65. www.turismojerez.com.
This Carthusian monastery, founded in 1477, has a Greco-Roman portal attributed to Andrés de Ribera. The Flamboyant Gothic church has a richly decorated Baroque **facade★★★**.

▲⁑ La Cartuja Stud Farm★ (Yeguada de la Cartuja)

▷ At the Finca Fuente del Suero, 6.5km/4mi from Jerez on the Medina Sidonia road. Guided tours. Sat show (11am–1.30pm incl visit) from €16; see website for full schedule and prices. ☎956 16 28 09.
www.yeguadacartuja.com.
In the 16C, the local Carthusian monastery crossed Andalucían, Neapolitan and German breeds, creating the famous **Cartujana** breed. Visitors to this stud farm get a close look at their famous descendant.

ADDRESSES

🛏 STAY

⊖⊖ Hotel Doña Blanca –
Bodegas 11. ☎956 34 87 61. www.hoteldonablanca.com. 30 rooms. ⊡€7. This laid-back hotel in an attractive Andalucían-style building has a central location. Bedrooms are newly renovated, bright and spacious.

⊖⊖⊖⊖ Hotel Villa Jerez –
Av. Cruz Roja 7. ☎956 15 31 00. www.hotelvillajerezdelafrontera.spainhotels.it. 18 rooms. ⊡€13. An elegant, well-appointed boutique hotel in a sea of outdated big-box brands, the Villa Jerez has an outdoor pool, fabulous breakfasts, and spacious rooms.

🍽 EAT

⊖⊖ Atuvera –
Ramón de Cala 13. ☎675 54 85 84. www.atuvera.apartamentosjerez.com. Off Plaza Arenal, Atuvera is a haven in the centre of the city. In summer, tables spill out into the street and brim with beautifully plated tapas and local craft beers.

TAPAS

Bodega Las Botas – Santo Domingo 13. ☎665 21 63 42. Closed Sun. Removed from the tourist fray, this locals-only spot serves textbook renditions of classics like garlicky mushroom caps, fried calamari and marinated anchovies, all in a rustic, barrel-lined barroom.

Juanito – Pescadería Vieja 8–10. ☎956 33 48 38. www.bar-juanito.com. Closed during Jerez fair. This Jerez classic, on a pedestrianised street lined with outdoor terraces, has been in business for over 50 years, thanks to killer tapas like braised artichokes and butterflied fried anchovies.

NIGHTLIFE

Bereber – Cabezas 10. $\mathcal{C}$605 94 75 77. Reservations recommended. Bereber, in a Moorish palace, is Jerez's most iconic nightspot. Its spaces (café, bar, dance floors in wine cellars and restaurant with flamenco) are decorated playfully in Arabian and Andalucían style.

ENTERTAINMENT

The **Teatro Villamarta** (Pl. Romero Martínez; $\mathcal{C}$956 14 96 85; www.jerez.es) offers theatre and music acts including, flamenco. The city's best-known flamenco club (*peña*) is **Peña Tío José de Paula** (Merced 11; $\mathcal{C}$956 32 01 96).

LEISURE

Baños Árabes Hammam Andalusí – Salvador 6. $\mathcal{C}$956 34 90 66. www. hammamandalusi.com. Baths 10am–10pm in 2hr sessions (reservation essential). From €27. These re-created Moorish baths transport visitors to Islamic Spain. The terrace and tea house look out to the Cathedral.

FIESTAS

In **early May** there's horse racing, dressage and carriage competitions at the **Feria del Caballo** (Horse Fair), but most attendees are there to drink, dance in the *casetas* and have fun. Unlike Sevilla's feria, with its many VIP booths, Jerez's is open to all. www.jerez. es/especiales/feria.

In **September** the **Fiesta de la Vendimia** (Wine Harvest Festival; sometimes held outside Jerez) has a cavalcade and a bevy of cultural events;

Cante Jondo (literally 'deep song'; a vocal style of flamenco) is alive and kicking in Jerez, a town that produced such famous singers as **Antonio Chacón** (1869–1929) and **Manuel Torres (1878–1933)**.

Cádiz★★

Surrounded by water on three sides, Cádiz has attracted mariners for over 3 000 years. It is also one of Andalucía's most delightful capitals, with charming squares, narrow alleyways and a quiet air broken only by the exuberant Carnival, the best in peninsular Spain. It's no surprise, then, that *The New York Times* **chose Cádiz as one of its '52 Places to Go in 2019'.**

THE CITY TODAY

Despite being flanked by gorgeous beaches, Cádiz hasn't succumbed to over-commercialisation. In summer, Spanish holidaymakers and, to a lesser degree, cruise ship day-trippers make up most of its visitors. At other times of year its fishing and shipbuilding ports make it a hive of activity with all

▶ **Population:** 124 892
Michelin Map: 578 W 11.
Info: Paseo de Canalejas. $\mathcal{C}$956 241 001. www.cadizturismo.com.
Location: This coastal city is positioned with the Atlantic to the south and west, the Bahía de Cádiz to the north and east. Cadiz (AVE).
Parking: It's difficult in the old quarter.
Don't Miss: A wander within the walls.

nationalities passing through. Start your stay with a stroll along the sea before burrowing inland to explore the cobbled streets lined with boutiques and seafood restaurants.

A BIT OF HISTORY

Oldest city in Europe – Cádiz was founded by the Phoenicians in 1100 BC, making it the oldest continually inhabited city on the continent. It was conquered by the Romans in 206 BC and in turn by the Visigoths and Moors. Alfonso X conquered the city in 1262. During the 16C, Cádiz was attacked by English corsairs and partially destroyed by the Earl of Essex in 1596.

In the 18C, Cádiz became a great port. **Constitution of Cádiz** – During the French siege of 1812, patriots convened the Cortes to pen one of the world's first liberal constitutions, which defended freedom of the press, free enterprise and abolished feudalism. A threat to the monarchy's totalitarian reign, it was abolished by Ferdinand VII in 1814. **Watchtowers** – Between the 16C and 18C, merchants in Cádiz built over 160 towers to monitor their ships. A handful remain (see Torre Tavira, p542).

The Migrant Crisis

On 30 August 2019, the *Open Arms* rescue ship delivered 15 refugees to Cádiz's port. The vessel had been bobbing for nearly a month at high sea as European leaders squabbled over who would take the migrants, ominously echoing the case of the *MS St. Louis*, which carried some 900 Jews fleeing Nazi Germany for the Western Hemisphere and was tragically turned back to Europe.

The coast near Cádiz has long seen the landing of *pateras* (dinghies) overflowing with migrants, but arrivals have skyrocketed since the onset of the European refugee crisis. With thousands dying at sea each year, it remains to be seen whether Spain will step up to the plate in any meaningful way.

SIGHTS

Iglesia de Santa Cruz (Catedral Vieja)★

Pl. Fray Féliz. Open Tue–Fri 9.45am–12.45pm, 5.30–7pm (5.30–6.30pm Sat); Sun 10am–12.30pm, 5.30–6.30pm. ☎956 28 77 04.
The old cathedral was rebuilt after the 1596 sacking by the Earl of Essex. Note the robust Tuscan columns. The church museum (**Museo Catedralicio**) is next door (see next entry).

Museo y Archivos Catedralicio★

Pl. Fray Félix. Open 10am–4pm. €7 incl Catedral Nueva & Torre del Reloj. ☎956 28 66 20. www.catedraldecadiz.com.
Abutting the old cathedral, this museum in the Casa de la Contaduría has a 16C **Mudéjar patio**★ and holds liturgical objects and art like the 16C **Custodia del Cogollo**★, a gold-plated monstrance attributed to Enrique Arfe, and the 18C **Custodia del Millón**.

Catedral Nueva★★

Pl. de la Catedral. Open Mon–Sat 10am–7pm, Sun 2-7pm. €7 incl Museo Catedralicio & Torre del Reloj. ☎956 28 61 54. www.catedraldecadiz.com.
Work on the new cathedral began in 1722 and lasted over a century. The result is Baroque with the occasional Neoclassical feature. The **facade**★ is flanked by two lofty towers. The triple-aisle interior is surprisingly light and airy. The crypt holds the remains of *Gaditano* composer **Manuel de Falla** (1876–1946). You can also ascend the cathedral Torre de Poniente tower.

Oratorio de la Santa Cueva★

Rosario. Open Tue–Sat 10.30am–2pm, 5.30–8.30pm (Jul–Aug; no Sat) 4.30–8pm (Sep–Jun); Sun 10am–1pm. €4. ☎956 22 22 62.
Three **canvases**★★ in this elliptical oratory were painted by Goya in 1795.

Museo de Cádiz★

Pl. de Mina. Open mid-Jun–mid-Sep Tue–Sun 9am–3pm, mid-Sep–mid-Jun Tue–Sat 9am–8pm, Sun 9am–3pm.

Cádiz viewed from Catedral Nueva

© digicomphoto/iStockphoto.com

Closed 1 & 6 Jan, 1 May, 24–25 & 31 Dec. €1.50; free for EU citizens.
𝒫856 105 023.

The city's museum is in a mid-19C Neoclassical palace. The collection includes vases, oil lamps and jewellery including two 5C BC Greek **anthropoidal sarcophagi**★★ based on Egyptian models. Paintings include nine **panels**★ by Zurbarán from the Carthusian monastery in Jerez.

♨ Torre Tavira★

Marqués del Real Tesoro 10. Open May–Sep 10am–8pm (until 6pm Oct–Apr). €6.
𝒫956 21 29 10. www.torretavira.com.
This 18C watchtower houses the very first **camera obscura** in Spain. Rooftop views seen from the illuminated table are popular with kids and adults alike.

Oratorio de San Felipe Neri

Santa Inés. Open: Oratorio: Tue–Sat 10am–2pm, Tue–Fri 4.30–8pm, Sun 10am–1pm. Interpretation Centre: Tue–Sun 11am–1.45pm. €4 for oratorio.
𝒫956 807 018.
The Cortes declared the Constitution of Cádiz in 1812 in this elliptical Baroque church. The **Immaculate Conception** was painted by Murillo in 1680 just before his death.

Museo de las Cortes de Cádiz

Open Tue–Fri 9am–6pm, Sat–Sun 9am–2pm. Closed public hols.
𝒫956 22 17 88.
The museum's main exhibit is a **model**★ of Cádiz in the reign of Charles III.

Playa de la Caleta★

Could this charming beach facing the ocean have been the site of the first Phoenician landing in the 11C BC? In any case, La Caleta was Cádiz's natural port for many years. The location is surprisingly serene for an urban beach, with a small spa protected from Atlantic by the long breakwater leading out to the **Castillo de San Sebastián**. The other extremity of the beach is **Castillo de Santa Catalina**, where, in season, there are musical performances (Po. Antonio Burgos; open Mar–Oct 11am–8.30pm, Nov–Feb until 7pm; 𝒫956 226 333).

▰ WALKING TOUR

AROUND SANTA MARÍA AND THE PÓPULO DISTRICT

Plaza de San Juan de Dios

This 16C square is the most popular in the city. On one side stands the Neoclassical facade of the 1799 **town hall** *(ayuntamiento)*, by Torcuato Benjumeda, beside the Baroque tower of the Iglesia de San Juan de Dios. The tourist office is in another Neoclassical building.

▷ Take Sopranis, to the left of the Iglesia de San Juan de Dios.

Calle Sopranis

The street contains some of the best Baroque civil architecture in Cádiz, particularly the houses at nos. 9, 10 and 17. At the end of the street, note

The Order of Alcántara

The Knights of San Juan de Pereiro became the Order of Alcántara when they were entrusted with the defence of the town in 1218. Like the other orders of chivalry in Spain, it aimed to regain the country from the Moors. Each order, founded as a military unit under the command of a master, lived in a community under Cistercian rule. These religious militias, always prepared for combat and capable of withstanding long sieges, played a major role in the so-called Reconquista. The order is the oldest of its kind in Spain.

---

the 19C iron-and-brick former **tobacco factory** and the **Convento de Santo Domingo** (open 10am–1pm, 6.30–9.30pm).

▶ Continue along Plocia as far as Concepción Arenal.

Cárcel Real★

Concepción Arenal.
The 1792 royal jail, by Torcuato Benjumeda, is one of the most important Baroque civil buildings in Andalucía. The facade with triumphal-arch entry bears the escutcheon of the monarchy. It houses the city's law courts.

Iglesia de Santa María

Santa María.
The spire on the belfry of this 17C Mannerist church is adorned with *azulejos*.

▶ Continue along Santa María, past the 18C Casa Lasquetty (left); cross Félix Soto toward the 13C Arco de los Blancos.

Casa del Almirante

Pl. de San Martín. Closed to the public. The outstanding feature of this 17C Baroque palace is the double-section Italian marble **doorway★★**.

Iglesia de Santa Cruz (Catedral Vieja)★ and Catedral★★ (&see above)

FROM PLAZA SAN JUAN DE DIOS TO THE CATHEDRAL

▶ Follow Nueva to Pl. San Juan de Dios. Turn left on Cristóbal Colón.

Casa de las Cadenas

This Baroque mansion has a Genoese marble **doorway★**.

▶ Continue along Cristóbal Colón and Cobos streets to Pl. de la Candelaria; return to Nueva. Past Pl. de San Agustín, take Rosario to the Oratorio de la Santa Cueva (&see Sights).

Plaza de San Francisco

This charming plaza, under the Baroque tower of the Iglesia de San Francisco, is lined with lively bars and cafés.

Plaza de Mina★★

Once the kitchen garden of the Convento de San Francisco, this verdant square is imbued with a colonial feel. Fine examples of Isabelline buildings around the square include the **Museo de Cádiz** (&see Sights).

▶ Head down Calle de San José to the Oratorio de San Felipe Neri. The oratory stands alongside the Museo de las Cortes de Cádiz (&see Sights).

Hospital de Mujeres★

Hospital de Mujeres. Closed for renovation. ℘956 22 36 47.
This Baroque building is planned around two patios linked by an extraordinary Imperial-style **stairway★★**. The Vía Crucis in the patio is created from 18C Triana *azulejos*.

▶ Continue to the Torre Tavira (&see Sights) on Sacramento.

Plaza de las Flores

Flower and plant stalls, cafés and shops contribute to the electric atmosphere in one of the city's favourite squares.

◯ Return to Pl. de la Catedral.

EXCURSIONS

El Puerto de Santa María

El Puerto de Santa María.

On the northern shore of the bay facing Cádiz (23km/14mi), El Puerto de Santa María is heavily frequented by tourists but pleasant in the off season.

Columbus set sail twice from the docks of El Puerto de Santa María, and the town subsequently prospered thanks to the plundering of the American colonies. The town is one of the three points making up the **sherry triangle**, with Jerez and Sanlúcar de Barrameda. The old town is on the west bank of the Guadalete, known as **La Ribera del Marisco** (seafood coast). Avenida de la Bejamar runs along the river and borders the historic centre.

Plaza de las Galeras Reales

At the edge of the Guadalete, on the spot where royal galleys used to dock, stands this bustling square. Restaurant seating spills out around the square, and Calle Luna, the main shopping street, leads to the Tourist Office and Plaza de España.

Iglesia Mayor Prioral

Plaza de España. Open Mon–Fri 10am–12.30pm, 5–7.30pm, Sat 10am–12pm, 6–7.30pm, Sun 8.30am–1.45pm, 6.30–9pm. €1. ☎956 85 17 16. www.iglesiamayorialelpuerto.com.

Consecrated in 1493 and rebuilt many times sinc, this church stands next to Plaza de España. The **Portada del Sol** (17C), with both Plateresque and Baroque elements, is the main treasure, though it's in need of restoration.

Fundación Rafael Alberti

C. Santo Domingo, 25. Open mid Sep-Jun Tue-Fri 10am-2pm, Sat-Sun 11am-2pm, Jul–mid-Sep open Tue–Fri (see website for hours), Sat–Sun 11am-2pm. €4. ☎956 85 07 11. www.rafaelalberti.es.

Painter, poet and communist, Rafael Alberti (1902–99) was born in this house. He was part of the literary 'Generation of 1927', a movement that included, among others, Federico García Lorca and Antonio and Miguel Machado. Alberti's alphabet work, unifying poetry and calligraphy, is on display, demonstrating his commitment to the cause of social justice throughout Spain's turbulent 20C.

Castillo de San Marcos★

This castle was built by Alfonso X on the site of a mosque, of which the *mihrab* is visible. The conquering Christians enlarged the building, converting it into a fortified church.

Las Bodegas

The *bodegas* (wineries) are almost all open to the public by guided tour (usually Mon–Sat), with prior booking. All finish with a tasting. For more information on visiting, call the bodegas directly or enquire at the tourist office. **Bodegas Barbadillo** (Luis de Eguilaz 11; open 10am-3pm; ☎956 38 55 11, www.barbadillo.com) is a good place to try a glass of local manzanilla sherry.

Bodegas Osborne (Bodega de Mora, C. de Los Moros; call for schedule and prices; ☎956 86 91 00, www.bodegas-osborne.com) is famous for its black bull silhouette found along highways across Spain. Originally created in order to elude a ban on roadside billboards, the iconic figures are now classified, and protected, as national monuments.

San Fernando

◯ 9km/5.5mi SE along the CA 33. ☎956 94 42 26.

This town has been a naval base since the 18C. The main monuments – the town hall, Iglesia del Carmen and Museo Histórico Municipal – have Royal *(Real)* grants. Seek out the Neoclassical **Real Instituto y Observatorio de la Armada** (Cecilio Pujazón; 1hr guided tours; ☎956 545 099) from 1753.

Medina Sidonia★

44km/27mi E on CA 33, A 48 and A 390. C. San Juan. ☎956 41 24 04. www.medinasidonia.es.

The **Iglesia Mayor Santa María la Coronada★** (Pl. de la Iglesia Mayor); a 15C Gothic church, holds an exquisite Plateresque **altarpiece★** by Juan Bautista Vázquez el Viejo. The **Torre de Doña Blanca**, a tower next to the church, provides access to the remains of the alcázar and the old quarter with its 16C houses. The descent to the modern town passes under the Arco de la Pastora, to reach the **Conjunto Arqueológico Romano**, a Roman complex with 30m/98ft of underground galleries from the 1C. (Espíritu Santo 3; Open 10.30am–2pm, 5.30–7.30pm, Apr–Jun 8pm; Jul–Oct 5–9.30pm; €4; ☎956 41 24 04). The **cardo maximus** was the main street in Roman days. On the Plaza de España lies the 18C Neoclassical **town hall**.

ADDRESSES

STAY

Hostal Fantoni – Flamenco 5. ☎956 28 27 04. www.hostalfantoni.es 12 rooms. Closed Dec–mid-Feb. No breakfast. This clean, bare-bones hostel is in the centre of town. Request a room with a (smart ensuite) bathroom facing the pedestrianised lane.

Hotel Las Cortes de Cádiz – San Francisco 9. ☎956 22 04 89. www.hotellascortes.com. 36 rooms. €8.80. Rooms in this 19C home in the old quarter are newly renovated and well-equipped, set around a covered patio. There's a rooftop terrace.

Hotel de Francia y París – Pl. de San Francisco 6. ☎956 21 23 19. www.hotelfrancia.com. 57 rooms. €6. The early 20C hotel with pleasant, updated rooms fronts an attractive small square in the centre of the city.

EAT

El Faro – San Félix 15. ☎902 21 10 68. www.elfarodecadiz.com. This old-fashioned restaurant and tapas bar serves Andalucían comfort food with seafood taking centre stage. If you haven't tried the Gaditano speciality *tortillitas de camarón* (shrimp fritters) yet, now's the time.

TAPAS

Aurelio – Zorrilla 1. ☎956 04 64 46. Closed Mon in Aug–Jun. Get to this fantastic seafood bar early, or risk waiting outside. The fried anchovies are divine.

Casa Manteca – Corralón de los Carros 66. ☎956 21 36 03. Closed Mon. The most legendary tavern in town, Casa Manteca serves Ibérico ham and charcuterie on wax paper. Tallies are chalked on the wooden counter.

Ultramar&Nos – Enrique de Las Marinas 2. ☎856 07 69 46. www.ultramarynos.com. You're in seafood lover's heaven, as the name suggests. The classics are all here, plus fusion tapas like ceviche.

BARS / CAFÉS

Café de Levante – Rosario 35. ☎956 22 02 27. www.cafedelevantecadiz.com. Unwind in this quiet, modern café on one of the old quarter's iconic streets.

La Cava – Antonio López 16. ☎956 21 18 66. www.flamencolacava.com. Closed Jan–Feb. Show and drink €25 (shows Apr–Nov Tue, Thu & Sat 9.30pm). This intimate tavern puts on flamenco interpreted by young artists.

FESTIVALS

Carnaval de Cádiz – www.carnavaldecadiz.com. Early Feb. The carnival on the week before Ash Wednesday is without doubt the most famous and lively in peninsular Spain. It's famed for uniformed ***chirigotas*** (comedy groups), and poet-dramatic ***comparsas***.

NIGHTLIFE

Gran Teatro Falla – Pl. Falla. ☎956 22 08 34. Named after composer Manuel de Falla (1876–1946), this theatre hosts events year round. The **cultural centres** – **El Palillero** (Pl. Palillero; ☎956 22 65 16), **El Bidón** (Alcalde Juan de Dios Molina 23; ☎956 26 15 02), and **Sala Central La Lechera** (Pl. Argüelles 2; ☎956 22 06 28) host exhibitions, workshops etc, and flamenco at the **Baluarte de la Candelaria** (Alameda Marqués de Comillas; ☎956 808 472).

© Bernd Haak/Fotolia.com

Upper Rock of Gibraltar

Gibraltar★

One of the last outposts of the British Empire and a self-governing British Overseas Territory, the towering bulk of Gibraltar is impressive and distinctive, visible for miles. For many visitors, the first contact with Gibraltar is likely to be the unusual experience of driving across an aircraft landing strip to cross into the territory!

▶ **Population:** 34 571
Ⓒ **Michelin Map:** 578 X 13.
🗐 **Info:** 13 John Mackintosh Square. ℘+350 200 45000; www.visitgibraltar.gi.
◖ **Location:** The SW tip of Spain, 24km/15mi from North Africa. 🚃 Nearest station San Roque-La Linea 15km.
🅰 **Don't Miss:** Top of the Rock.
👪 **Kids:** The Apes' Den; dolphin spotting.

A BIT OF GEOGRAPHY

The **Rock of Gibraltar★** is a monolith of Jurassic limestone that forms a craggy promontory connected with mainland Spain to the north and stretching south into the Strait. It covers some 6.5km/2.5sq mi (4.5km/3mi long and 1.4km/0.9mi at its widest), rising to 423m/1 388ft at Mount Misery.
The east face of the Rock drops sheer into the sea, while the less-steep west face has been partially reclaimed at the water's edge by the town.

A BIT OF HISTORY

Archaeological discoveries on Gibraltar testify to 100 000 years of human occupation, by Carthaginians, Phoenicians and even Neanderthals.
The Rock of Gibraltar, considered by the Ancient Greeks to be one of the **Pillars of Hercules**, was transformed into an Islamic citadel after the Berber invasions under **Tarik-ibn-Zeyad** in AD 711. Jebel Tarik (Tarik's Mountain, hence Gibraltar) was the site of a castle, now in ruins but still known as the Moorish Castle.
Gibraltar was conquered by the Christians on 20 August 1462. During the War of Spanish Succession, Anglo-Dutch naval forces, under **Admiral Rooke**, captured the Rock in 1704. Gibraltar was ceded to Britain in the Treaty of Utrecht in 1713, and the citadel guarding the Strait of Gibraltar has remained in British hands ever since. In the **Great Siege of 1779–83**, the garrison resisted Spanish and French efforts to starve or bomb them into submission. The old city of Gibraltar was destroyed, but the

Rock lived up to its reputation of being impregnable. Gibraltar became a British Crown Colony in 1830.

In 1967, Gibraltar's inhabitants voted resoundingly to retain their connection with Britain, by 12 138 votes to 44, in a referendum. In 1969, Spain closed the border and maintained a blockade until 1985. Even today it is not unusual for Spanish customs to delay vehicles.

With its people descended from a variety of races, religions and cultures, their identity shaped by years of resisting sieges, Gibraltar is an example of a harmonious, multicultural society.

The territory is a free port, and trade is based on transit and refuelling; the economy is based on financial services and tourism.

The naval and commercial ports, as well as the town with its mixture of English- and Spanish-style houses, pubs and shops, lie against the west face of the Rock. Examples of Moorish architecture can still to be seen, even in the cathedral, which has the ground plan of a mosque.

Though Gibraltar voted overwhelmingly to remain in the European Union, it will cease to be part of the European Union upon the implementation of **Brexit**. It remains to be seen what effect the legislation will have on border policies between the territory and Spain.

SIGHTS
Tour of the Rock★

Open 9.30am–5.45pm. Cable car 9.30am–7.15pm (Nov–Mar 5.15pm). From €25 incl return trip and Nature Reserve (Apes' Den, Great Siege Tunnels, St Michael's Cave and Moorish Castle) ℘+350 200 12700. www.gibraltar-rock-tours.com (official Rock Tour by taxi).

The Top of the Rock can be reached on foot, by cable car and in official tour vehicles (☺ private cars are not allowed on the Upper Rock). Go down Queensway and follow the signs to Upper Rock, a **nature reserve** and home to a number of Gibraltar's historical sites. The road leads first to **St Michael's Cave★**, (www.gibraltarinfo.gi), once inhabited by Neolithic humans, which features illuminated stalactites and stalagmites. From here it is possible to walk to the Top of the Rock (⚐1hr there and back), where there are excellent **views★★** of both sides of the rock and of the Spanish and North African coasts. The road continues to the **Apes' Den** 👥, home of the famous Barbary Apes. Don't miss the fascinating story of the **Great Siege Tunnels★**, excavated in 1779 to mount guns on the north face of the Rock, creating a defence system still impressive for its ingenuity. A military heritage centre is housed in Princess Caroline's Battery. There are ruins of the **Moorish Castle** and the northern defences dominating the hillside.

Barbary Macaques

The origin of the apes, one of Gibraltar's best-known attractions, is unknown. When it looked as if they could go extinct in 1942, Churchill sent in reinforcements. The ape colony has since flourished – there are currently some 300 of them. They are renowned for their highly inquisitive natures – and occasional mischievousness (watch your rucksack!). The apes, in reality tailless monkeys, are the mascots of the Gibraltar Regiment.

©David Stanley/iStockphoto.com

PRACTICALITIES

Customs and other formalities:
Gibraltar is a British Overseas Territory. The border is open 24hr a day. Visitors must be in possession of a valid passport. Holders of UK passports and citizens of other EU countries do not need a visa. Other nationalities should check visa requirements with a British consulate, high commission or embassy. Gibraltar is a VAT-free shopping area.

Travel and accommodation:
There are daily scheduled flights from London Heathrow, Gatwick, Luton and Manchester and a daily ▰▰▰ ferry service to Tangier, Morocco (www.directferries.co.uk). Regular flights also operate to and from Málaga and Jerez. There are many hotels but no campsites.

Money matters: The currency is the Gibraltar pound, on a par with sterling.

The Euro and credit cards are widely accepted.

Language: The official language is English, but most people speak some Spanish. The local dialect, Llanito, mixes the two.

Time: Gibraltar is on European time (one hour ahead of GMT).

Motoring: Driving is on the right. Drivers must have a current licence, vehicle registration documents, evidence of insurance and nationality plates.

Telephoning: The international code for Gibraltar is 350 (from Spain, omit this and dial 9567 before the five-digit local number).

Tourist information: Tourist information in the UK is available from: Gibraltar Government Office, 150 Strand, London WC2R 1JA. ✆0207 836 0777. www.visitgibraltar.gi.

Gibraltar Museum

18/20 Bomb House Ln. Open Mon–Fri 10am–6pm, Sat 10am–2pm (last entry 30min before closing). £5. ✆350 200 74289. www.gibmuseum.gi.

The museum covers local military and natural history. It also houses the well-preserved **Moorish Baths**.

The **Alameda Gardens** display stunning plants including Canary Islands dragon trees, cacti, succulents and Mediterranean vegetation. Gibraltar is home to some 600 species of flowering plant, which flourish in the subtropical climate, with a few unique to the Rock such as the national flower, the Gibraltar Candytuft.

If you are interested in seeing more examples of Gibraltar's plant and bird life, take the **Mediterranean Steps**, leading from Jews' Gate (good view of the other Pillar of Hercules and Jebel Musa in Morocco) round the south of the Rock and up the east face of the Rock to the summit (⏱ 3hr from Jews' Gate, steep in parts; wear good boots).

STRAITS OF GIBRALTAR

Michelin map 578 X 1, Gibraltar: British Overseas Territory. The A 7 motorway links the southernmost part of Spain to the Costa del Sol.

The Straits, the gateway to the Mediterranean just 14km/9mi wide, have always played a strategic role. The Bay of Algeciras is surrounded by Algeciras and La Línea de la Concepción, and the British outpost of Gibraltar.

TOURING THE STRAITS

Fourteen species of cetaceans – whales, dolphins and porpoises – swim in the Straits, and **whale ▰▰- and dolphin-watching cruises** are popular, sailing from Gibraltar, Algeciras, La Línea and Tarifa. Reputable operators include Dolphin Safari (✆350 200 71914; www.dolphinsafari.gi), Turmares Tarifa (✆956 68 07 41; www.turmares.com) and Whale Watch (✆670 79 66 50; www.whalewatchtarifa.net). The probability of seeing these beautiful creatures is 90–95%;

Mountains in Morocco across the Straits of Gibraltar viewed from near Tarifa

© Guillermo Perales Gonzalez/iStockphoto.com

and some operators will refund your money in the event of a 'no-show'.

While boats for larger groups may provide underwater viewing areas, small, fast boats provide more thrills as they race along with the dolphins swimming in their wake and criss-crossing the bows. The 21km/13mi of road linking Tarifa to Algeciras provides stunning views★★★ of the North African coast. The best viewpoint is at the Mirador del Estrecho, 8km/5mi from Tarifa.

Tarifa
&See COSTA DE LA LUZ

Algeciras
Berbers arrived in al-Yazirat-al-jadra (Green Island, now joined to the mainland) in 711 and remained until 1344.

Neanderthal Man or Gibraltar Woman?

Eight years before the discovery in 1856 of a 60 000-year-old skeleton in the Neander Tal (Valley), east of Düsseldorf, Germany, a skull of the same age, thought to be that of a woman, was discovered on Gibraltar. However, delays in publicising the Gibraltar findings meant that Gibraltar Woman didn't gain the fame of Neanderthal Man.

The Bahía de Algeciras is a safe anchorage and strategic vantage point overlooking the Straits.

Algeciras is Spain's busiest passenger port with crossings to Tangier and **Ceuta** several times a day. The main sights of interest are the Plaza Alta, the hub of the town, fronted by two churches – the 18C **Iglesia de Nuestra Señora de la Palma**, and the Baroque Iglesia de Nuestra Señora de la Aurora – and the **Museo Municipal** (Ortega y Gasset; open late Oct–Mar Mon–Fri 9am–2pm, 5–7pm; Sat 10am–2pm; Apr–late Oct Mon–Fri 9am–2pm; closed public hols; *956 57 06 72), displaying exhibits on the **Siege of Algeciras** (1342–44).

ACROSS THE STRAITS
Ceuta
Michelin map 742 folds 5 and 10 – North Africa. Population 84 726.
Trasmediterránea operates services between Algeciras and Ceuta (also Algeciras and Tangier). Journey time: 40min. *902 45 46 45.
www.trasmediterranea.es.
Ceuta occupies a strategic position, monitoring the Straits of Gibraltar. With its European architecture, it is situated on a narrow isthmus on the coast of North Africa. The closest African port to Europe, Ceuta was conquered by the Portuguese in 1415 and passed to Spain in 1580.

Museo del Revellín

Po. de Revellín 30. Open Tue–Sat 11am–2pm, 5–9pm. Public hols 11am–2pm. ℘956 511 770. www.ceuta.es/museos.

This museum houses a white marble Roman sarcophagus, Punic and Roman amphorae, a collection of coins and old weapons and ceramic ware.

Parque Marítimo del Mediterráneo

Compañía del Mar. Open 11am–8.30pm exc Thu Sep–May. From €3.50. ℘956 51 74 91. www.ceutasi.com.

Palm trees, exotic plants, swimming pools, lakes, waterfalls and sculptures were integrated by the great Lanzarote landscape artist, César Manrique, to create this leisure park on 56ha/138 acres facing the sea. Several restaurants, a nightclub and a casino operate inside the fort, which dominates the park. A cinema complex is in the Poblado Marinero.

Other places of interest are the **Iglesia de Nuestra Señora de África** (Church of Our Lady of Africa; Pl. de África; ℘956 51 17 23), housing the statue of the town's patron saint; the 18C **Catedral** (Pl. de África; open Tue–Sun 9am–1.30pm, 6.15–7.15pm; ℘956 51 77 71); and **Foso de San Felipe** (open 11am–7pm; ℘956 51 17 70), the Portuguese fort where San Juan de Dios, founder of the Order of the Hospitallers of St John, worked in 1530.

Monte Hacho★

Best visited in the morning.

Calle Independencia and Calle Recintor Sur, parallel to the seafront, lead to the foot of Monte Hacho, which has a citadel at its summit. The corniche road encircling the peninsula offers beautiful **views** of the Western Rif coastline to the south and of the Spanish coast and the Rock of Gibraltar to the north.

◗ Before reaching the lighthouse (no entry), bear left.

Ermita de San Antonio

♿ Leave your car in the car park.

The wide flight of steps leads to a charming square fronted by the 16C Capilla de San Antonio (Chapel of St Anthony). The imposing **Fortaleza de Hacho** (Ctra. de Circunvalación del Monte Hacho; prebooked guided tours available; ℘956 51 16 21) stands atop a hill nearby.

From here there is a splendid **view★★** of the town, port and coastline.

ADDRESSES

🏨 STAY

🛏 **Emile Youth Hostel** – 25 Line Wall Road. ℘+350 200 51106. www.emilehostel.net. 100m/110yd from Casemates Square, Gibraltar's only hostel has 42 beds in single, double and triple rooms.

🛏 **Cannon Hotel** – 9 Cannon Ln. ℘+350 200 51711. www.cannonhotel.gi. 18 rooms. Rates at the best budget hotel on the Rock include a full English breakfast.

🛏🛏🛏 **Hotel Bristol** – 8 Cathedral Sq. ℘+350 200 76800. www.bristolhotel.gi. 60 rooms. ⊡£6. With a pool and subtropical garden, the Bristol is a breath of fresh air in this busy enclave.

🛏🛏🛏🛏 **Sunborn Gibraltar** – 35 Ocean Village Promenade. ℘+350 200 16000. www.sunborngibraltar.com. 189 rooms. Sunborn occupies a moored five-star yacht with luxury rooms to match. There's a casino, outdoor pool and five restaurants and bars.

🍽 EAT

🍴 **The Venture Inn** – 2 Lynch's Ln, Gibraltar. ℘350 200 75776. Get your fish-and-chips fix at this Irish pub and sports bar.

🍴🍴🍴 **Cafe Rojo** – 54 Irish Town. ℘+350 200 51738. You'll find good modern Mediterranean cuisine here.

🍴🍴🍴🍴 **Parador de Ceuta** – Pl. Nuestra Señora de África 15, Ceuta ℘956 51 49 40. www.parador.es. Pop into the Parador's dining area with lush tropical plants and exposed beams. The cooking is Andaucían with Arab influences.

The Canary Islands

The Canary Islands – seven in total with six smaller isles – lie between 100km/62mi and 300km/186.4mi off the northwest coast of Africa. Ferries and puddle jumpers connect the islands, though (unlike in Greece) there is no 'island-hopping' culture. The Canaries are filled with contrasts: The landscape can go from rainforest-like to arid in a matter of miles, and large, empty swathes of nature brush up agianst big-box resorts. The one constant is the temperature, which hovers around 24°C/75°F year round, making the islands one of Europe's most popular holiday destinations.

Highlights

1 Exploring the **Parque Nacional del Teide** on Tenerife (p553)
2 An evening stroll along the Paseo Cornisa, **Las Palmas** (p561)
3 The early-morning sun on the **Playa de las Canteras** (p564)
4 Getting lost in the sand dunes of **Maspalomas** beach (p567)
5 Hiking the **Valle de Hermigua** on the island of La Gomera (p574)

Volcanic creation

The islands were thrust up from the Atlantic seabed by volcanic eruptions. La Gomera and Gran Canaria have a conic silhouette, and most of the islands are hilly and end in steep cliffs. Crowning Tenerife, Pico del Teide at 3 718m/ 12 195ft is the highest point in Spain.La Palma rises to 2 426m/7 959ft and because of its relatively small area is said to be the steepest island in the world. It features the world's largest *caldera* (volcanic crater) too. Here, as elsewhere in the archipelago, lava, slag fields and cinder cones form what is known as *malpaís*, most extensive and most spectacular on Lanzarote where huge areas resemble a moonscape. When the Spanish Conquistadores landed, they found a native Stone Age population known as the **Guanches**, who lived in caves, practised trepanning and mummified their dead. The Guanches had little chance against the invaders and were decimated, not least as a result of illnesses introduced inadvertently by the Spaniards to which they had no natural resistance. By the end of the century the islands were taken and most Guanches were either dead or had assimilated into the new order.

The Fortunate Islands

Ancient mariners nicknamed the archipelago The Fortunate Islands on account of their year-round warm climate: the coastal temperature rarely drops below 18°C/65°F. The weather varies, however, between the north and south of the larger islands, most notably on Tenerife and Gran Canaria. This has encouraged sun-and-fun resorts (such as Playa de las Américas and Playa del Inglés) to develop in the south, where there's next to no rain. By contrast, the northern coasts of Tenerife and Gran Canaria respectively can be (relatively) chilly and wet in winter and as a result have been less commercialised for the holiday trade.

Tenerife★★★

The snow-capped silhouette of El Teide, the highest peak in Spain, is the symbol of this island; Tenerife meant 'snow-covered mountain' in Guanche. At its foot, the spectacular Las Cañadas crater is a testament to Tenerife's violent volcanic past. Year-round sun draws package tourists and families to the man-made resorts of the south, while colonial architecture and natural beauty lure culture-seeking visitors north.

▶ **Population:** 920 253

▤ **Info:** Santa Cruz de Tenerife: Plaza de España. ℘922 892 903; Puerto de la Cruz: Puerto Viejo. ℘922 38 60 00. www.webtenerife.co.uk.

◑ **Location:** Tenerife is the largest of the Canary Islands, with an area of 2 036sq km/786sq mi.

👤👤 **Kids:** Loro Parque, Lago Martiánez, Siam Park, Parque Ecológico de las Aguilas del Teide, Aqualand.

PARQUE NACIONAL DEL TEIDE★★★

Clouds often enshroud Mount Teide and the superb panoramas from its viewpoints.

☺Wear comfortable shoes and bring a light jacket and rainwear: Weather can change dramatically without notice.

La Esperanza Approach★

The road climbs to the crest that divides the island's north and south.

Pinar de la Esperanza★

The road runs for several miles through this extensive pinewood. In a clearing at **Las Raíces**, an obelisk commemorates the rebellion in July 1936 against the Republican government by Francisco Franco, who was stationed here.

Miradores★★

Admire the stark contrast between the lush north coast and the aridity of the Güímar Valley from the roadside belvederes (*miradores*).

After La Crucita, the road enters a high-mountain landscape. The Astronomical Observatory at Izaña is visible (left).

El Portillo

Alt 2 030m/6 660ft. This pass is the gateway to the extraordinary geological world of the Las Cañadas crater.

Parque Nacional del Teide★★★

The El Portillo visitor centre (open 9am–4pm; ℘922 35 60 00; www. webtenerife.com) has exhibits on

GETTING TO THE CANARY ISLANDS

BY AIR – Each island has an airport (Tenerife has two), offering easy, rapid access to the Spanish mainland and the rest of Europe. Several inter-island routes operate throughout the year. The hub airports are on **Tenerife** and **Gran Canaria.** www.aena-aero puertos.es. **Iberia** (℘901 111 500, www.iberia.com); **easyJet** (www. easyjet.com); **Air Europa** (℘971 57 55 27, www.air-europa.com) and **Vueling** (℘807 300 745, www.vueling.com)

fly from the mainland, among others; **Binter Canarias** operate many inter-island flights (℘902 39 13 92, www. bintercanarias.com).

BY SEA – From mainland Spain, a two-day boat trip leaves from Cádiz and travels to Santa Cruz de Tenerife and Las Palmas de Gran Canaria. Ferry, jet-foil and hydrofoil services travel between the islands, though distances, cost and timetables do not encourage 'island-hopping'.

Trasmediterránea ℘902 45 46 45, www.trasmediterranea.es.

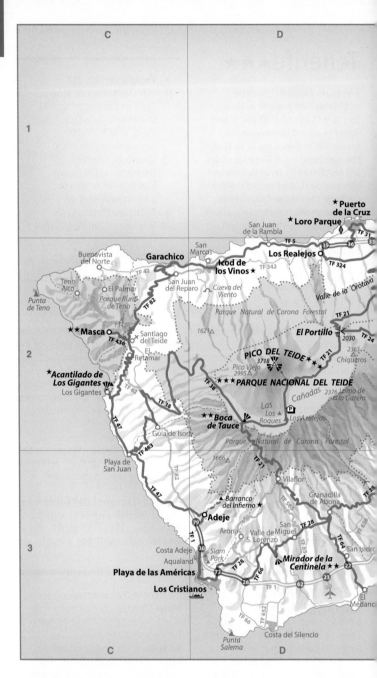

volcanism and information on trails and the park's flora and fauna. The Cañada Blanca visitor centre next to the Parador is under renovation.

About 350m/1 150ft below the summit lies Las Cañadas plateau, a spectacular crater, over 2 000m/6 560ft across, that imploded before El Teide was created. El Teide's peak rises from its northern side. In the centre of the park, opposite the Parador, are **Los Roques**, a spectacular outcrop of lava boulders laid bare by erosion. Another geological feature is **Los Azulejos**, spectacularly flecked

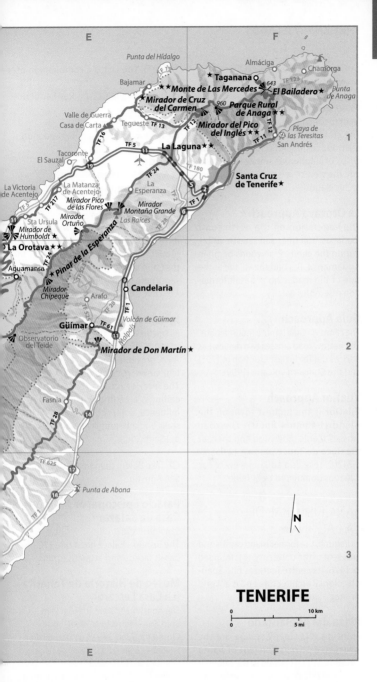

TENERIFE

0   10 km
0   5 mi

boulders covered with copper oxide
that glint blue-green in the sun.

Pico del Teide★★★

🚠 Ascent by **cable car** from La Rambleta
(2 356m/7 728ft); not suitable for those
with respiratory or heart problems

(the cable car climbs 1 199m/3 932ft
in 10min). Open 9am–4pm, weather
permitting. Closed 1 Jan, 25 Dec. €27
return (online rate); reserve in advance.
𝄞 922 01 04 45. www.volcanoteide.com.
🥾 Experienced hikers who wish to walk
to the very top (along the Telesfero Bravo

path) must apply for a permit (free) at www.reservasparquesnacionales.es. From the cable-car dropoff (3 555m/11 660ft), a steep 30min walk across scree leads to the summit.

The crater at the summit is 25m/82ft deep and 50m/164ft across, swathed in wisps of sulphurous smoke. On a clear day, the view covers the whole Canaries archipelago.

La Orotava Approach★

The vegetation on the north coast (bananas, fruit trees and vines) is visible during the climb. Pinewoods begin in **Aguamansa**. Beyond the village at the side of the road, a huge basalt forma-tion resembles a daisy.

Guía Approach

The climb via Guía is more mountainous. The narrow road crosses two defiles, Las Narices del Teide (last eruption in 1798) and the Chinyero volcano (1909).

Vilaflor Approach

Vilaflor is the highest town on the island (1 466m/4 806ft). The road crosses scenic pinewood and then, at the **Boca de Tauce pass★★** (2 055m/ 6 742ft), reveals a striking view of Las Cañadas dominated by El Teide.

SAN CRISTÓBAL DE LA LAGUNA★

La Laguna, the former island capital and now seat of the university, was founded in 1496. Its centre features fine Span-ish colonial architecture and is a World Heritage site.

Plaza del Adelantado

Fronting this sleepy square are the seven-nun-strong **Convent of Santa Catalina**, which opened to the public in 2019 and retains its original upper gal-lery (open 9:30am–12:30pm, 4–5:30pm; www. monasteriodominicaslalaguna. es); the 17C **Palacio de Nava** with stone facade, reminiscent of the Bishop's Palace; and the **ayuntamiento**, with its Neoclassical facade (Obispo Rey Redondo 1; open Mon–Fri 10am–

1.30pm). The last is a combination of several buildings. The 16C and 18C portals on calle Obispo Rey Redondo are impressive.

▶ Follow Calle Obispo Rey Redondo.

Catedral

Pl. Fray Albino. Open Mon–Fri 10am–8pm; Sat 10am–12:30pm, 2–5pm. €5. ☎902 00 31 21. www.lalagunacatedral.com.
The Neoclassical facade was erected in 1819; the nave and four aisles were rebuilt in neo-Gothic style in 1905. In the Capilla de los Remedios (right tran-sept), note the retable, a 16C Virgin and 17C Flemish panels.

Iglesia de la Concepción★

Pl. Doctor Olivera. Open 10am–5pm. €2. ☎922 25 91 30.
A 17C grey tuff-stone tower, with excel-lent views, rises over this 16C church. The interior retains several Mudéjar ceilings, a ceiling with Portuguese influence, a Baroque pulpit and choir stalls and a beaten-silver altar (Capilla del Santísimo).

▶ Take Belén, then head down San Agustín.

Palacio Episcopal or Antigua Casa de Salazar

San Agustín 28.
The Bishop's Palace has a rare 17C blue basalt facade and attractive patio.

Museo de Historia de Tenerife (La Casa Lercaro)

San Agustín 22. Open Tue–Sat 9am– 8pm. Sun–Mon & hols 10am–5pm. Closed 1 & 6 Jan, 24–25, 31 Dec. €5; free Fri–Sat 4–8pm. ☎922 82 59 49. www.museosdetenerife.org.
In the late-16C **Casa Lercaro**, with its fine patio, exhibits provide an overview of the island's history from the 15C.

SANTA CRUZ DE TENERIFE★

The capital began as a port serving La Laguna. An oil refinery, tobacco fac-tory and other industries operate here

Playa de las Teresitas near San Andrés, Pico del Teide in the background

© Chris Hepburn/iStockphoto.com

– it's not the prettiest city. From the harbour breakwater there is a **view★** of the stepped semicircle of high-rise buildings against the back-drop of the Pico del Teide.

The Guimera Theatre, the oldest theatre in the Canaries, inaugurated in 1851; the space-age, blindingly white **Auditorio de Tenerife★**, designed by Santiago Calatrava; and the **Tenerife Espacio de las Artes (TEA)**, a sleek arts complex designed by Herzog & de Meuron and Virgilio Gutiérrez speak to the city's cultural pulse.

Santa Cruz is also famous for its **Carnival** (last week Feb), arguably the most colourful and certainly the largest in Spain.

Iglesia de la Concepción

Tomás Pérez. Open 9am–1pm, 4.30–8pm. ℘922 33 01 87.
A few houses with balconies around this 16C–18C church (fine Baroque retables) are all that remains of the old city.

Museo de la Naturaleza y el Hombre★ (Museum of Nature and Man)

Fuente Morales. Open Tue–Sat 9am–8pm. Sun–Mon & hols 10am–5pm. Closed 1 & 6 Jan, Carnival Tue, 24–25, 31 Dec. €5; free Fri–Sat 4–8pm. ℘922 53 58 16. www.museosdetenerife.org.
The Hospital Civil, a Neoclassical building, now houses archaeology and natural science collections. The highlight is the room with **Guanche mummies★**.

Palacio de Carta

Pl. de la Candelaria.
This 18C palace on Plaza de la Candelaria, now a bank, retains its delightful wooden arches, galleries and patio.

Iglesia de San Francisco

San Francisco 13. Open for Mass. ℘922 24 45 62.
This 17C–18C church is typical of Canarian churches from this era: naves with wooden roofs and cylindrical pillars.

Parque Municipal García Sanabria★

This alluring tropical and Mediterranean garden is a respite from the often busy city centre.

Centro de Interpretación Castillo de San Cristóbal

Pl. de España. Open Mon–Sat 10am–6pm. ℘922 28 56 05. www.museosdetenerife.org.
Nelson lost both the battle and his right arm when attacking this castle on 24 July 1797. The star exhibit is the cannon ('El Tigre') that repulsed him.

🕴🕴 Parque Marítimo César Manrique★

Av. Constitución 5. Open 10am–6pm. €2.50. ℘922 22 93 68. www.maritimosantacruz.com.
This seaside lido, designed by the late, great Lanzarote artist César Manrique, combines volcanic rock, island vegetation and turquoise water.

PUERTO DE LA CRUZ★

Puerto de la Cruz was the first major resort on the island and remains the main destination on the north coast. It has black beaches, dozens of souvenir shops and dillapidated high-rises. It attracts an older clientele than the south but is still lively, particularly at Carnival time. The old town, between the Plaza de la Iglesia and Plaza del Charco, preserves a handful of 17C and 18C balconied houses and, unlike the other resorts on the island, has a genuine Canarian atmosphere. East of town, the **Mirador de Humboldt★★** offers a view of the town and the verdant sweep of the **Orotava Valley** running from the slopes of Mount Teide down to the sea.

♣♣ Costa Martiánez★

Av. de Colon. Open 10am–5pm. Closed fortnight in May. €5.50. ✆922 37 05 72. www.ociocostamartianez.com.
This distinctive landmark lido (aka the Lido or Lago Martiánez, famous for its fountains, is another César Manrique stunner with vernacular architecture and local geological features. The **Casino Taoro** is inside the Costa Martiánez complex.

Playa Jardín★

This black-sand beach is surrounded by gardens designed by César Manrique. The **Castillo de San Felipe** (✆922 38 36 63), a watchtower now used for cultural functions, can be seen at its eastern end.

♣♣ Loro Parque (Parrot Park)★

Av. Loro Parque. Open 8.30am–6.45pm; last admission at 4pm. €38; incl Siam Park €66. ✆922 37 38 41. www.loroparque.com.
The advertising for this mega-park is inescapable; indeed, it's the island's most popular attraction barring Mount Teide. Loro Parque is one of the finest animal and marine theme parks in the world and features a dolphinarium, killer whale shows, sea lions, a penguinarium, a large aquarium, tigers, gorillas, chimps and one of the world's finest collections of birds, all set in lush

grounds. Kinderlandia is a mini-'African' theme park for little ones.

LA OROTAVA★★

This ancient town is arranged in terraces at the foot of Mount Teide. It boasts elegant balconied mansions and is famous for its Corpus Christi festival.

Plaza de la Constitución

The square is fronted by the 17C Baroque church of San Agustín and the Liceo Taoro cultural centre.

Iglesia de la Concepción

Tomás Pérez. Open 9am–1pm, 4.30–8pm. ✆922 33 01 87.
The 18C church has a Baroque facade. Visit the treasury.

Calle de San Francisco★

This street has some of the most charming balconied houses on the island.

La Casa de los Balcones y del Turista

San Francisco 3 & 4. *Casa de los Balcones (no. 3):* open 8.30am–6.30pm; *Casa del Turista (no. 4):* open 9am–6.30pm. €5 museum. ✆922 33 06 29. www.casa-balcones.com.
These abutting 17C houses feature delightful patios, a handicraft shop and a small museum displaying the inside of a local bourgeois house

Museo de Artesanía Iberoamericana

Tomás Zerolo 34. Open Mon–Fri 10am–3pm, 5–7pm, Sat 9am–1pm. €2. ✆922 334 013. www.artenerife.com.
Set in the ex-Convento de San Benito Abad (17C) the museum contains Spanish and Latin American handicrafts.

Jardín de Aclimatación de la Orotava★★

Retama 2. Open Apr–Sep 9am–7pm; Oct–Mar 9am–6pm. Closed 1 Jan, Good Fri, 24 & 25 Dec. €3. ✆922 922 981. www.icia.es.
This 2ha/5 acre botanical garden, created in the 18C, contains trees and flowers from the Canary Islands and

elsewhere, some of which are over 200 years old.

EXCURSIONS

MONTE DE LAS MERCEDES★★

⊙ Round trip of 49km/30mi from La Laguna. Allow 3hr.
The Anaga headland traps clouds from the north; tree laurel, giant heather and *fayas*, a local species, flourish.

Mirador de Cruz del Carmen★

See the La Laguna Valley from this viewpoint in the **Parque Rural de Anaga★★** (Cruz del Carmen visitor centre open 9.30am–3pm, until 4pm in winter; ☎922 63 35 76).

Mirador del Pico del Inglés★★

A marvellous panorama spreads from the 1 024m/3 360ft peak of the Anaga headland to distant Pico del Teide.

El Bailadero★

The road crossing this pass commands views in both directions.

Taganana★

This back-in-time coastal village is surrounded by **panoramas★★**. Visit the **Iglesia Parroquial de Nuestra Señora de Las Nieves** for its Hispano-Flemish altarpiece (Pl. de la Virgen de las Nieves; open 10am–7pm; no visits during religious services; ☎922 59 01 86).

Icod de los Vinos

⊙ On the N coast of the island, 60km/37mi W of Santa Cruz de Tenerife via the TF 5.
The heart and hub of Tenerife's wine district, the peaceful town of Icod de los Vinos, 26km/16mi west of Puerto de la Cruz, is a patchwork of charming squares surrounded by elegant colonial houses with their characteristic Canarian pine balconies. The Casa Museo del Vino (Plaza de la Pila 4) offers Canary Island wines and cheese tasting.
The most famous feature of the village is its 3 000-year-old **Dragon Tree**, towering 17m/57ft over the shore. The

Dracaeno draco, or dragon tree, is the official symbol of the Canary Islands; the Guanche civilization worshipped these trees as sources of wisdom and fertility, using the sap, which is red like blood, in healing ceremonies.

🚗 DRIVING TOUR

TOUR OF THE ISLAND

310km/194mi.
⏱See pp554–555 for map.

Garachico

Set on a stretch of rocky coast with natural pools, Garachico was the finest harbour on the north coast until 1706, when a lava slick, still visible, destroyed most of the old town. Its 16C Castillo de San Miguel (Av. de Tomé Cano; open for temporary exhibitions; €1; ☎922 83 00 00) was the most notable survivor and is now home to a museum. The Iglesia de San Francisco also dates to the 16C; the 17C Convento de Santo Domingo houses a museum of contemporary art.

Masca★★

The 'Machu Picchu of the Canaries' is set on a narrow ridge that plunges into a valley of dramatic rock formations.

Los Gigantes★

The Teno mountain range ends in black cliffs called Los Gigantes, 'the giants', for their 400m/1 300ft vertical drop.

Adeje

Near here is the **Barranco del Infierno (Hell Canyon)★**, popular with walkers.

Playa de las Américas

This sprawling man-made resort is the most popular destination on the island. It features beaches of black sand, several family attractions on its outskirts and a raucous nightlife. Neighbouring **Los Cristianos** is a busy port (ferries depart to La Gomera; www.fredolsen. es) that has been subsumed into the tourist sprawl.

🚗 ▶ Follow the TF 28 in the Valle de San Lorenzo.

Mirador de la Centinela★
Like a sentinel, the viewpoint on a rocky projection commands a vast area.

▶ Return to the inland road.

Mirador de Don Martín★
The belvedere provides a view of the Güímar rift valley and its plantations.

Güímar
Recharge in this bustling coastal town.

Candelaria
Pilgrimages in mid-August end at the town's **basílica** (Pl. de la Basílica; ℰ922 50 01 00) housing a statue of the Virgin.

ADDRESSES

🏠 STAY

🛏🛏🛏 **Hotel Monopol** – Quintana 15, Puerto de la Cruz. ℰ922 38 46 11. www.monopoltf.com. 92 rooms. Restaurant 🍽🍽. This four-storey whitewashed building adorned with wooden balconies stands in a pedestrianised street in a lively shopping district near the seafront. Comfortable if outdated rooms are arranged around a Canarian-style patio.

🛏🛏🛏 **Finca Salamanca** – Ctra. Puertito, Sureste 1.5km/1mi Güímar. ℰ922 51 45 30. www.hotel-finca salamanca.com. 20 rooms. Restaurant 🍽🍽🍽. Set among the avocado trees of a former plantation estate, this newly renovated property offers comfortable lodging in modern, minimalist rooms.

🛏🛏🛏 **Hotel Aguere** – Obispo Rey Redondo (Calle Carrera) 55, La Laguna. ℰ922 31 40 36. www.hotelaguere. es. 23 rooms. Rooms look out onto a large seigneurial patio in this good-value, traditionally decorated hotel. Bathrooms could use renovating.

🛏🛏🛏 **Hotel Rural Victoria** – Hermano Apolinar 8, La Orotava. ℰ922 33 16 83. www.hotelruralvictoria.com. 14 rooms. Restaurant 🍽🍽🍽. Stay in a traditional balconied Canarian country house with comfort-food cooking to match.

🛏🛏🛏 **Senderos de Abona** – La Iglesia 5, Granadilla de Abona. ℰ922 77 02 00. 17 rooms. Restaurant 🍽🍽. This *hotel rural* has a dozy atmosphere, with serene patios, gardens and a splash pool.

🛏🛏🛏🛏 **Hacienda de las Cuatro Ventanas** – C. Playa del Socorro, Los Realejos. ℰ660 86 66 78. www. haciendacuatroventanas.com. 6 villas. Seclusion-seeking celebs and travellers who want nothing to do with Tenerife's big-box resorts hole up in this ultra-modern luxury hacienda – think infinity pools, stone villas and views over banana groves to the ocean.

🛏🛏🛏🛏 **Hotel San Roque** – Esteban de Ponte 32, Garachico. ℰ922 13 34 35. www.hotelsanroque.com. 32 rooms. Restaurant 🍽🍽🍽🍽. This exclusive-feeling designer hotel with a spa is tucked away on a cobbled street. The owner is an art collector, and the property could pass as a museum.

🍽 EAT

🍽 **Bar Baku** – Centro Comercial Terra Nova, Av. de España 25, Costa Adeje. ℰ662 02 80 96. A Caucasus-themed restaurant serving Armenian stuffed grape leaves, Georgian khinkali (soup dumplings) and Russian pelmeni is an unlikely – and welcome – find in this resort area known for middling cuisine.

🍽🍽 **Totem** – Av. Jose Antonio Tavio 4, Santa Cruz. ℰ922 78 58 49. This cosy, if slightly kitsch, dining room fills up with locals dining on well-portioned seafood platters, pizzas and pastas.

🍽🍽🍽 **Solana** – Pérez de Rozas 15, Santa Cruz. ℰ922 24 37 80. www. solanarestaurante.es. Closed Sun, Mon, Aug 7–31. Minimalist decor and fresh, contemporary cooking with local produce make this restaurant stand out.

🍽🍽🍽 **Los Limoneros** – Los Naranjeros, Crtra General del Norte 447, Tacoronte. ℰ922 63 66 37. Closed Sun dinner. One of the area's established favourites offers refined traditional Spanish cuisine.

Gran Canaria★★

Gran Canaria is often described as a continent in miniature on account of its diverse landscapes. Almost half of its area is a UNESCO Biosphere Reserve. From the Pozo de las Nieves (1 949m/6 393ft) at its centre, ravines fan out in all directions. The mountain barrier divides the wetter landscapes of the north and west from extensive semi-desert areas in the south (forest fires forced the evacuation of 9 000 people in August 2019). The north and west coast are steep and rocky; on the accessible south coast are long golden sand beaches and throbbing man-made resorts. Las Palmas is the most cosmopolitan, culture-focussed city in the archipelago.

▸ **Population:** 857 702
ℹ **Info:** Las Palmas: Parque de Santa Catalina. ✆928 44 68 24; Playa del Inglés: Avenida España (Yumbo Centre). ✆928 77 15 50. www.grancanaria.com.
◗ **Location:** Gran Canaria, the third-largest Canary Island (area: 560sq km/602sq mi), is between Tenerife and Fuerteventura.

LAS PALMAS DE GRAN CANARIA★

Las Palmas de Gran Canaria, founded in a palm grove in 1478, is the biggest city in the Canaries and one of Spain's major ports. It was the most fashionable resort on the island for decades but over the past 30 years or so lost its position to the burgeoning resorts of the sunnier south – and the city is probably better for it. Culturally, Las Palmas is the most interesting place to stay on Gran Canaria. The old city, **Vegueta**, dates to the Conquest; with Triana it forms the historic centre. **Puerto de la Luz** and **Las Palmas** compose the tourist district, flanked by the harbour and Alcaraveneras beach in the east and Las Canteras beach in the west.

Vegueta–Triana★
Allow 2hr.

Plaza de Santa Ana
The palm-bordered square is presided over by the town hall (1842) on one side, and the **cathedral** (open Mon–Fri 10am–4.30pm, Sat 10am–1.30pm; €1.50; ✆928 33 14 30) on the other. The latter, begun in the 16C, is the most venerated religious monument in the island chain.

To the side are the Bishop's Palace (Palacio Episcopal, 17C), with an *alfiz*-decorated portal showing Mudéjar influence; the Renaissance-style Casa del Regente; and the Archivo Histórico Provincial (archives). During the Corpus Christi procession, the square is carpeted with flowers and coloured sawdust and salt in beautiful patterns.

Museo Diocesano de Arte Sacro
Entrance on Pl. Espíritu Santo.
Hours and price as cathedral.
✆928 31 49 89.
The museum of sacred art, in buildings around the 16C Patio de los Naranjos, contains 16C–19C engravings and gold and silverwork. In the chapterhouse is a mosaic from Manises (Valencia).

Casa de Colón★
Colón 1. Open Mon–Sat 10am–6pm, Sun & hols 10am–3pm. Closed 1 Jan, 24–25 & 31 Dec. €4; free first weekend of month. ✆928 31 23 73.
www.casadecolon.com.
The palace of the island's first governors, where Columbus stayed in 1502, houses a museum. Maps and instruments evoke Columbus' expeditions. Note the fine *artesonado* ceilings. On the upper floor are 16–19C paintings. The **Iglesia de San Antonio Abad** (Pl. San Antonio Abad 4), on the site where Columbus attended Mass, has a fine Baroque interior.

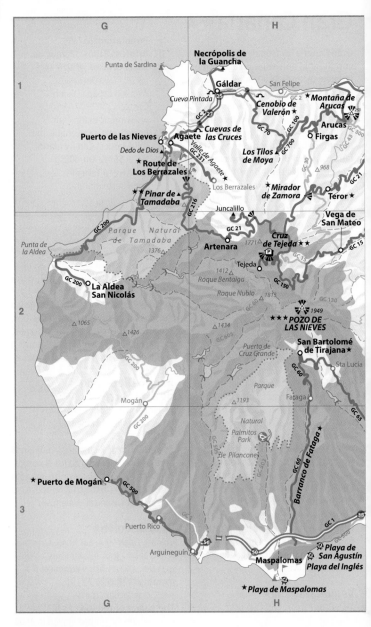

Centro Atlántico de Arte Moderno

Balcones 9–11. Open Tue–Sat 10am–9pm, Sun 10am–2pm. Closed pub hols. €5; free Wed 6–9pm, ℘902 31 18 00. www.caam.net.

Along **Calle de los Balcones,** in one of several 18C buildings with fine door-ways, this modern gallery displays works by 20C artists from the islands, the Spanish mainland and abroad.

Museo Canario★

Doctor Verneau 2. Open Mon–Fri 10am–8pm, Sat–Sun & public hols 10am–2pm. Closed 1 Jan, 25 Dec. €5;

Canaria and whose purpose remains a mystery; and a re-creation of Gáldar's Cueva Pintada (see p565).

Adjacent are the picturesque plazas of **Espíritu Santo** and **Santo Domingo**.

Casa-Museo Pérez Galdós

Cano 2 & 6. Open Tue–Sun & pub hols 10am–6pm (7pm Jul–Sep). Closed 1 Jan, 24–25 & 31 Dec. €3; free first Sat–Sun of month. 928 36 69 76. www.casamuseoperezgaldos.com. Manuscripts, photographs and objects belonging to Pérez Galdós (1843–1920), the leading literary figure in 19C Spain, are displayed in the house where he was born.

Parque de San Telmo

Calle Mayor de Triana, leading from this park, is the main street in the old town. The small **Iglesia de San Bernardo** is full of character with its Baroque altars and paintings. An unusual Modernist kiosk stands in a corner of the park.

MODERN TOWN

Allow 2hr.

 Drive along avenida Marítima del Norte, skirting the town.

Parque Doramas

In this park are the Santa Catalina Hotel with its casino and the **Pueblo Canario**, an idyllicised re-creation of a Canary Island village, cofounded by the Las Palmas-born Modernist painter Néstor de la Torre (1887–1938; open Tue–Sat 10am–8pm, Sun 10.30am–2.30pm; closed 1 Jan, Holy Thu, Good Fri, 25 Dec; €4; 928 24 51 35). Regular folklore shows and festivals are held here. There are crafts shops, a bodega and the **Museo Néstor** (open Tue–Sat 10am–7pm, Sun & public hols 10.30am–2.30pm; €4; 928 24 51 35).

Parque Santa Catalina

By the port, in **Puerto de la Luz**, the Parque Santa Catalina is home to the Museo Elder de la Ciencia y Tecnología, with its interactive stations, 3D cinema, science show and planetarium (Science

GRAN CANARIA

free Mon & Wed 5–8pm. 928 33 68 00. www.elmuseocanario.com.

This collection of artefacts from pre-Hispanic culture includes mummies, idols and skins. Don't miss the collection of **Guanche skulls★**, some of which have been trepanned; the terracotta seals (*pintaderas*), found only on Gran

Columbus and the Canaries

But for the Canary Islands, Christoper Columbus (1451–1506) may never have reached America. His persistence in trying to convince the sovereigns of Portugal, England, France and Castile of the existence of a westerly passage to Asia is well known. Eventually Ferdinand and Isabella of Castile provided three ships – the **Niña**, the **Pinta** and the **Santa María** – for an expedition to the Indies. Colombus (Colón in Spanish) set sail westward from Palos in August 1492 but was forced to dock in Las Palmas and La Gomera for repairs to the **Pinta**. On 12 October 1492 he spied land and set foot on the American continent – well, on the Caribbean island of San Salvador. On his three subsequent voyages, he landed at Las Palmas de Gran Canaria or on La Gomera before going on to 'discover' the rest of the Antilles (1493), the Orinoco delta (1498) and the shores of Honduras (1502).

and Technology Museum; open Tue–Sun 10am–8pm; €6; ✆ 828 011 828; www.museoelder.org).

The bustling surrounding streets are lined with casual restaurants and bars and cheap electronics shops.

Playa de las Canteras★

This stunning 3.5km/2mi beach is sheltered by a line of rocks offshore and backed by a pleasant promenade with restaurants and cafés. At its south-eastern end, the landmark **Auditorio Alfredo Kraus** (www.auditorioteatro-laspalmasgc.es), built in 1997, hosts an opera season. It is the site of the Canaries Music Festival (www.festivaldecanarias.com), held annually Jan–Feb.

Castillo de la Luz

Juan Rejón. Open Mon–Sat 10am–7pm, Sun until 2pm. €4. ✆ 928 463 162.
This 16C fort is home to the foundation of local sculptor Martin Chirino.

🚗 DRIVING TOURS

THE NORTH COAST

LAS PALMAS TO LA ALDEA DE SAN NICOLÁS

128km/79mi. Allow 1 day.
🚗 See map pp562–563.

▷ Leave Las Palmas on the GC 2, heading W. Take exit 8.

Arucas

Arucas is the third-largest town on the island. A narrow road leads up **Montaña de Arucas**, shaped like a sugar loaf, offering a **panorama★** to Las Palmas de Gran Canaria. The black-rock church below pops against the white houses.

▷ Take the C 813. At Buenlugar, 6km/3.7mi beyond Arucas, turn left.

Firgas

This is the source of the archipelago's most popular sparkling mineral water. The village's Paseo de Gran Canaria pays a picturesque homage to the island's communities, dedicating to each a series of azulejo plaques and benches.

▷ Return to the main road.

Los Tilos de Moya

Los Tilos is a protected area with a wood of wild laurel trees.

▷ At Guía, turn right to join the C 810. Head toward Las Palmas, then turn off to Cenobio de Valerón.

Cenobio de Valerón★

Cuesta de Silva, Santa María de Guía. Open Tue–Sun: Oct–Mar 10am–5pm, Apr–Sep 10am–6pm. Closed 1, 5 & 6 Jan, 1 May, 24–25 & 31 Dec. €3. ✆ 618 60 78 96. www.cenobiodevaleron.com.
Cenobio means convent, and tradition has it that here daughters of the nobil-

ity dwelt until they were wed, watched over by protective priests and priestesses. The truth is, this honeycomb of caves hewn out of tufa was merely an ancient granary. Visitors can enter the caves, above which Guanche chiefs met in council (*tagoror*).

▷ Return to the C 810 and head toward Gáldar.

Gáldar

The Guanche king held his court (*guanarteme*) at the foot of Mount Gáldar. The **Museo y Parque Arqueológico Cueva Pintada** (Audiencia 2; open mid-Jun–mid-Sep Tue–Sat 10.30am–7.30pm, Sun & hols 11am–7pm; mid-Sep–mid-Jun Tue–Sat 10am–6pm, Sun & hols 11am–6pm; last tour 90min before closing, booking required; closed 1, 5 & 6 Jan, 1 May, 24–25 & 31 Dec; €6; free first weekend of month; ℘928 89 54 89; www.cuevapintada.com), is devoted to the island's most important ancient discovery, the '**Painted Cave**'★, of Guanche origin. Guanche objects excavated nearby are also displayed, and the cave is viewed behind glass to protect it from visitors' body heat and humidity.

Necrópolis de la Guancha

2km/1.2mi N of Gáldar on coast.
Excavations brought to light the knee-high remains of a Guanche settlement including a necropolis of circular constructions of great blocks of lava and a large burial mound.

▷ Return to Gáldar; take the C 810 S.

Cuevas de las Cruces

Halfway between Gáldar and Agaete.
These are attractive caves in the tufa.

Agaete

The recently opened **Maipés archaeological park**★ (open Oct–Mar Tue–Sun 10am–5pm, Apr–Sep Tue–Sun 10am–6pm; ℘928 171 177; €3; www.maipesdeagaete.com) contains 700 Ancient Canarian burial mounds, some dating back over 1 300 years.

On 4 August the village celebrates the popular **Fiesta de la Rama**.

Los Berrazales Road★

SE of Agaete.
The road follows the verdant **Agaete Valley**★ sheltered by mountains.

Puerto de las Nieves

1.3km/0.8mi W of Agaete.
From the quay of this fishing harbour there's a view of what remains of the **Finger of God** (*Dedo de Dios*), a heavily eroded pointed rock. The village hermitage (**ermita**) contains a 15C Flemish triptych by Joos van Clave (visits by prior arrangement; ℘928 55 43 82).

La Aldea de San Nicolás

A spectacular road follows cliffs and crosses several ravines to La Aldea de San Nicolás, a village in a fertile basin growing sugar cane and tomatoes.

THE CENTRE OF THE ISLAND

156km/97mi. Allow 1 day.
⌚See map pp562–563.

▷ Leave Las Palmas on the GC 110, heading S.

Tafira

A holiday resort favoured by islanders, the town is the site of a university.

Jardín Canario★

Camino del Palmeral.
Open 9am–6pm. ℘928 21 95 80.
www.jardincanario.org.
The largest botanical garden in Spain (27ha/67 acres) is devoted to Canarian flora, with more than 500 species.

▷ In Monte Lentiscal turn left.

Mirador de Bandama★★

A road leads to the summit of Bandama (569m/1 867ft) and a superb view of the enormous Caldera de la Bandama, a crater with its eruption formations intact. The **panorama** takes in Tafira, the Montaña de Arucas and Las Palmas to the north and the crater, Real Club de Golf (the oldest course in Spain) and

Maspalomas dunes

© Oliver Hoffmann/iStockphoto.com

Telde to the south. In the caldera are old incised drawings.

▶ Return to the C 811.

Santa Brígida
This village sits close to a ravine planted with palms. A plant and flower market is held on weekends. The Casa del Vino de Gran Canaria sells wines (Calvo Sotelo 26; open Mon–Fri 10am–2pm; ✆928 64 42 45; www.museosdelvino.es).

Vega de San Mateo
A fruit and vegetable market is held here Saturdays and Sundays.

▶ Continue along the C 811 for 6km/3.7mi, then bear left.

Pozo de las Nieves★★★
From the summit (1 949m/6 394ft), which is sometimes snowy, there's a great **panorama★★★** of the island. On a clear day you can see Mount Teide.

Cruz de Tejeda★★
NW of Pozo de las Nieves.
Near the Parador at the top of the pass (1 450m/4 757ft) lies the village of **Tejeda** in a huge volcanic basin. It's known for its almond pastries. Out of the chaotic landscape rise the peaks of Roque Bentaiga and **Roque Nublo★★**, multistorey rocks venerated by the indigenous people.

▶ Bear W to Artenara along the GC 110.

The drive includes **views★** of the troglodyte village of **Juncalillo**.

Artenara
This village is the highest on the island (1 230m/4 035ft). In the enchanting **Ermita de la Cuevita**, a hermitage dug into the rock, is a statue of the Virgin with Child. The **panorama★** is impressive. From the edge of the village, there is a **view★** of Roque Bentayga.

Pinar de Tamadaba★★
The road passes through Canary pines extending to the edge of a cliff that drops sheer to the sea.

▶ Continue to the end of a tarred road, to the ⚠ Zona de Acampada, then park and walk 200m/220yd.

On a clear day, the **view★★** of Agaete, Gáldar and the coast, with the Pico del Teide on the horizon, is superb.

▶ Return by the same road and turn left onto the GC 110 toward Valleseco.

Mirador de Zamora★
Just north of Valleseco there is an attractive **view★** of Teror.

Teror
Teror has fine mansions with wooden balconies. The 18C **Basílica de Nuestra Señora del Pino** houses a statue of Our Lady of the Pine Tree, the island's patron, who is said to have appeared here on 8 September 1481 (Pl. Nuestra Señora del Pino; open Mon 1–8.30pm, Tue–Fri 9am–1pm, 3–8.30pm, Sat 9am–8.30pm, Sun 7.30am–7.30pm; ✆928 63 01 18). Thousands gather on the anniversary to present gifts and join in worship. On Sunday morning a lively market is held where you'll find nuns selling handmade sweets.

THE SOUTH COAST

LAS PALMAS TO MASPALOMAS
59km/37mi. Allow about 2hr.
▣ See map pp562–563.

◯ Leave Las Palmas along the GC 1, then take exit 8 (Telde).

Telde

This was a Guanche kingdom. In the lower town is the 15C **Iglesia de San Juan Bautista** (Párroco Morales 2; ☎ 922 76 81 25), a church rebuilt in the 17C and 18C that has a 16C Flemish retable.

◯ Take Calle Inés Chimida. Follow C 813 towards Ingenio. Beyond the junction with the C 816 turn left after some cottages into a rough track; the last 250m/270yd is on foot.

Yacimiento Arqueológico de Cuatro Puertas★

6km/3.7mi S of Telde. No formal visiting hours. ☎928 13 90 50.

The cave, which has four openings (*cuatro puertas*), is where the indigenous council (*tagoror*) met. The east face of the mountain is riddled with caves where the Guanche embalmed their dead.

Maspalomas/Playa del Inglés/ Playa de San Agustín

This is one of Spain's largest resort areas, a sprawl of apartments *urbanizaciones* and *centros commerciales* spread along the sandy coastline. Maspalomas has developed around its spectacular dunes and **beach★** and are part of a 400ha/990-acre protected zone including a palm grove and lighthouse. Playa del Inglés and Maspalomas are favourite haunts of the island's large contingent of gay (mostly male) holidaymakers.

Puerto de Mogán★

38km/24mi NW.

This is a picturesque man-made resort in typical Canarian style, built around an attractive marina.

San Bartolomé de Tirajana★

48km/30mi N on the GC 520.

The way up passes through the **Barranco de Fataga★★**, a scenic ravine. San Bartolomé is set in a green mountain cirque.

ADDRESSES

☜ STAY

◉◉ **Aloe Canteras** – Sagasta 98, Las Palmas. ☎928 46 49 07. 42 rooms. ☲€9. Steps from the beach, this budget option has plain, streamlined rooms.

◉◉◉ **Hotel Escuela Santa Brígida** – Real de Coello 2. ☎928 47 84 00. www.hecansa.com. 40 rooms. In a century-old building, the hotel has a tropical garden and rooms with brightly painted walls and wood furnishings, plus a good restaurant (◉◉◉).

◉◉◉ **Casa de Los Camellos** – Progreso 12, Agüimes. ☎928 78 50 03. www.hecansa.com. 12 rooms. Restaurant ◉◉◉. This quaint, welcoming *hotel rural* in the old part of Agüimes is cosy and rustic with plant-shaded patios and spacious bedrooms with beamed ceilings.

◉◉◉ **Hotel Rural El Refugio** – Cruz de Tejeda. ☎928 66 65 13. www.hotel ruralelrefugio.com. 10 rooms. ☲€8. Restaurant ◉◉◉. Deep in the interior, this boutique lodge is set amid lush vegetation. Bedrooms feel snug with period furniture and plentiful art.

◉◉◉◉ **Lopesan Baobab Resort** – Calle Mar Adriático 1, Maspalomas. ☎928 15 44 00. www.lopesan.com. 677 rooms. ☲€11. Restaurants ◉◉◉◉. When all you want is to is swan around a resort with fabulous modern rooms and multiple pools and restaurants, you've found the right place.

♈/EAT

◉◉ **El Arrosar** – Salvador Cuyás 10, Las Palmas. ☎928 27 26 45. Savour perfectly cooked paellas and rice dishes at sebsible prices here.

◉◉ **Casa Osmunda** – Subida Mirador de La Concepcion 2, Las Palmas. ☎922 41 26 35. This pretty cellar restaurant has fresh, non-greasy dishes and a wine list that punches above its weight.

◉◉◉ **Deliciosa Marta** – Pérez Galdós 23, Las Palmas. ☎928 37 08 82. Minimalist decor (think white tablecloths, blond woods and exposed stone walls) set the tone at one of Gran Canaria's top *nueva cocina* restaurants.

Lanzarote★★★

Lanzarote, designated a Biosphere Reserve, is unlike any other place on earth. With an area of 846sq km/326sq mi, its lava-black landscape is dotted with oases of bright green vegetation and dazzling white houses. Unlike many areas of Gran Canaria and Tenerife, it has largely retained a vernacular style and identity: There are few high-rise hotels, no advertising boards or pylons nor many of the other unsightly capitalist accretions. The island owes much of its current state of conservation to César Manrique (1919–92), the Lanzarote-born activist, architect and artist extraordinaire. Wherever you go on Lanzarote, you won't be far from his works or his philosophy.

LANDSCAPE & TRADITION

In 1730, a series of eruptions occurred in the area now known as the **Montañas del Fuego** (Mountains of Fire). These lasted six years and covered one third of the island in lava. In 1824 a new volcano, Tinguatón, engulfed farms and houses. Today Lanzarote's lava fields (*malpaís*) are pitted with over 100 craters. In **La Geria** wine country, where black volcanic pebbles (*lapilli*) are plentiful, vines are protected by low semicircular walls – creating one of the most stunning viticultural landscapes on earth. The grapes produce excellent (mostly white Malvasía) wines with a distinctly floral bouquet.

A BIT OF HISTORY

From the 14C to the present – Lanzarote owes its name to Lanceloto Malocello from Genoa, who landed in the 14C. In 1401 the Normans **Gadifer de la Salle** and **Jean de Bethencourt** captured the island for the King of Castile. Lanzarote was a base for expeditions against the other islands and became prey to marauding slavers.

▶ **Population:** 146 134

▤ **Info:** Arrecife: Parque José Ramírez Cerdá. ℘620 26 47 03. Puerto del Carmen: Av. de Las Playas, ℘928 51 33 51. www.turismolanzarote.com.

◐ **Location:** 100km/62mi off the coast of North Africa.

SIGHTS
Arrecife

This historically strategic port and modern-day island capital was originally defended by the **Castillo de San Gabriel** (open Tue–Fri, 10am–1pm, 4–7pm; Sat 10am–1pm; ℘928 81 17 62; €1.80), built in the 16C on an islet linked to the town by bridges.

Recently given a makeover by the island authorities, Arrecife has good shopping and a pleasant beach and promenade. On its picturesque lagoon, Charco de San Ginés, local fisherman moor their small boats.

The 18C **Castillo de San José,** restored by César Manrique, houses the **Museo Internacional de Arte Contemporáneo** (MIAC, Carretera de Naos; open 10am–8pm; €4; ℘901 20 03 00, www.centrosturisticos.com).

West of Arrecife via the LZ-2, the former house of Portuguese Nobel Laureate José Saramago has been converted into a museum (C. Los Topes 2; open Mon–Sat 10am–2.30pm, last admission 1.30pm; €8; ℘928 83 30 53; http://acasajosesaramago.com).

🚗 DRIVING TOURS

Each tour departs from Arrecife.

THE CENTRE OF THE ISLAND
62km/39mi through the centre.

Fundación César Manrique★
Taro de Tahíche, Villa de Teguise. Open 10am–6pm. Closed 1 Jan. €8; €15 incl Casa-Museo Manrique (◐see p571). ℘928 84 31 38. www.fcmanrique.org.

The foundation devoted to the greatest modern Lanzaroteño is in a eye-popping house that sits atop five volcanic bubbles. César Manrique lived here to explore and demonstrate the bond between architecture and nature.

Monumento al Campesino

This monument near **Mozaga**, by César Manrique, marks the centre of the island and pays homage to the peasant farmers of Lanzarote.

Next to it is the **Casa-Museo del Campesino** (open 10am–6pm; ℘928 52 01 36), in a characteristic peasant house, with an excellent restaurant (lunchtime only).

Museo Agrícola El Patio★

Echeyde 18, Tiagua. Open Mon–Fri 10am–5pm, Sat 10am–2pm. €5. ℘928 52 91 34.

Enjoy exhibits of rural life on the island and a wine tasting (included in ticket).

La Geria★★

La Geria lies between Yaiza and Mozaga in a black-lava wasteland pockmarked with craters where vines grow a bright green. The village is a wine centre.

Museo del Vino El Grifo

El Islote 121, San Bartolomé. Open 10.30am–6pm. Guided tours Mon–Fri 11am & 3pm, Sat–Sun 11am. From €5 incl one taste. ℘928 52 49 51. www.elgrifo.com.

This 18C bodega is the oldest in the Canaries and hosts a museum of traditional winemaking. There's a tranquil, well-kept cactus garden out back.

Los Bermejos

Camino a Los Bermejos 7, San Bartolomé. Open Mon–Fri 8am–3pm. €5 for three tastes. ℘928 52 24 63. www.losbermejos.com.

The New York Times' wine critic, Eric Asimov, rightly raved about Los Bermejos' wines, which are probably the best on the island if not in the archipelago.

THE SOUTH OF THE ISLAND
Round-trip of 124km/77mi from Arrecife.

Parque Nacional de Timanfaya★★★
Tours by coach or camel only (guided).
Open 9am–5pm (until 6pm Jul–Sep).
⊘ To avoid summer crowds, aim to arrive
9am–10.30 or 3–5pm. €9. ✆928 118 042
(Visitor Centre, Mancha Blanca, Tinajo).
www.parquesnacionalesdecanarias.com.
This range of volcanic cones, which
emerged in the 1730–36 eruptions,
is a martian blur of reds, browns and
blacks. It is the major attraction on the
island. The **Montañas de Fuego** form
the centre of this massif.
Coaches follow the 14km/8.7mi **Ruta de
los Volcanes**. Fortunately for the environment and unfortunately for visitors,
there's no getting off the bus or walking.
Through the window, take in views of an
immense lava field stretching to the sea.
Camels, once common beasts of bur-
den on Lanzarote, wait by the road (at
the **Echadero dos Camellos**) 5km/3mi
north of Yaiza to provide a swaying,
bumpy (and abbreviated) ride up the
mountainside, from where there is a
good view of the next crater. Although
the volcanoes have not erupted since
1736, their fires burn and bubble still.
Case in point: At the visitor centre,
park rangers drop twigs into a shallow hole that immediately catch fire
and pour water into a pipe to produce
a plume of steam. The subsoil temperature (140°C/284°F at 10cm/4in,
over 400°C/752°F at 6m/19.6ft) is hot
enough for meat to be cooked over it
at the (otherwise so-so) volcano-top El
Diablo restaurant.

Los Hervideros
In the caverns at the end of the tongue
of lava, the sea boils (*hervir*: to boil) in
an endlessly fascinating spectacle. It is
at its liveliest on a windy day.

El Golfo★★
A lagoon is filled with vivid emerald-
green water; a steep cliff of pitted black
rock forms an impressive backdrop. Terrific seafood restaurants line the shore.

Salinas de Janubio★
Deep blue seawater entering a crater is
harvested to leave gleaming white pyra-
mids of salt in square salinas (salt pans).

Playa Blanca
This pleasant resort, though built up,
retains some of its old character, with
a promenade between old fishermen's
houses and the main beach.

Punta del Papagayo★
This (Rubicón) region is where Bethencourt settled. The only trace is the
Castillo de las Coloradas, a tower on
the cliff edge. Dusty roads lead from
Playa Blanca to the protected **Reserva
Natural de los Ajaches** (open 9am–7pm;
€4 vehicle fee; ✆928 17 34 52), which
in turn empties out onto the isolated,
largely uncommercialised white-sand
Papagayo beaches★★, the finest on the
island. From here there are fine **views★**
of Playa Blanca and Fuerteventura.

THE NORTH OF THE ISLAND
Round trip of 77km/47mi from
Arrecife. About half a day.

Jardín de Cactus★
Ctra General del Norte, Guatiza.
Open daily 10am (9am Jul–Sept)–
5.45pm. €5.80. ✆928 52 93 97.
www.centrosturisticos.com.
This stunning cactus garden, landscaped by Manrique, artfully displays
4 500 cacti of 450 species (both local
and exotic) on terraces in an old quarry.

Cueva de los Verdes★★★
Haría. 1hr guided tours 10am–6pm (until
7pm Jul–Sep); last admission 1hr before
closing. €9.50. ✆901 20 03 00.
www.centrosturisticos.com.
At the foot of the Corona Volcano are
volcanic galleries where the Guanches
took refuge from marauding pirates.
There are 2km/1mi of illuminated passages at different levels; the tour ends
with an amazing trompe l'oeil.

Jameos del Agua★★

Carretera de Órzola, Haría.
Open 10am–6.30pm; also Tue, Fri–Sat 7.30pm–2am. €9.50 (Tue, Fri & Sat eves addl charge for entertainment).
℘901 20 03 00.

A *jameo* is a cavity formed when the top of a volcanic tube collapses. César Manrique turned two into an extraordinary fantasy grotto regarded by many as his masterwork. Curiously, a lagoon in the cave is the habitat of a minute, blind albino millenary crab, only found here. The **Casa de los Volcanes** on the upper level is an excellent exhibition and important international study centre on vulcanism. On Tuesay and Saturday nights the Jameos del Agua transform into an intimate, stylish leisure complex with a restaurant, bar, DJs and concerts.

Mirador del Río★★

Carretera del Norte, Ye.
Open 10am–5.45pm (until 6.45pm Jul–Sep). €4.75. ℘928 52 65 48.

At the north end of the island stands a steep isolated headland, **Riscos de Famara**. The belvedere commands a stunning **panorama★★** across the azure waters of the **El Río** strait to **La Graciosa★★** island (pop. 734) and its neighbouring uninhabited islets; below are salt pans. A **passenger ferry** (Órzola to La Graciosa, 25min: see website for schedule; €26 round trip; ℘928 596 107; www.lineasromero.com) operates between Órzola and La Graciosa.

Haría

From afar Haría resembles a North African village, set in a lush valley replete with palm trees. The best view is from the **Mirador de Haría★**, some 5km/3mi south. Also here is the **Casa-Museo César Manrique** (open daily 10.30am–2.30pm; €10 or €15 combined with Fundación Manrique, see p569; ℘928 84 31 38; www.fcmanrique.org), the high-design bachelor pad where the painter lived and worked during his final years. His studio remains as it was the day he died in a tragic auto accident.

Teguise★★

Inland Teguise, the former capital, is a beautifully restored and wonderfully atmospheric town with some of the finest colonial buildings in the archipelago. Several have been tastefully converted to restaurants, bars and shops.

Teguise is most famous nowadays for its **Sunday Market** (9am–2pm), which draws coaches from all over the island. Overlooking town, and commanding a wonderful view, is the **Castillo de Santa Bárbara,** built in the 16C on the Guanapay volcano. It houses the **Museo del Pirateria** (open 10am–4pm; €3; ℘928 84 50 01; www.museodelapirateria.com), which tells the story of piracy in the Canaries.

ADDRESSES

STAY

€€€ Caserío de Mozaga – Calle Malva 8, Mozaga. ℘928 52 00 60. www.caseriodemozaga.com. 8 rooms. €10.70. The best hotel deals to be had on Lanzarote are inland, and this restored 18C farmhouse smack in the centre of the island is no exception. The farm-to-table restaurant is exceptional.

€€€€ Iberostar Selection Lanzarote Park – Av. Archipiélago 7, Playa Blanca. ℘928 51 70 48. www.iberostar.com. 388 rooms. All the amenities you expect of a five-star international resort chain are here: a spa, 24hr gym, multiple pools and restaurants etc. There are adults-only sections and several types of packages.

EAT

€€€ Amura – Po. Marítimo, Puerto Calero. ℘928 51 31 81. www.restauranteamura.com. Expect refined, prettily plated Canarian cuisine at this marina-side restaurant.

€€€ La Cañada – César Manrique 3, Puerto del Carmen. ℘928 51 04 15. Call it Canarian soul food: The dishes served at La Cañada are simple, hearty and soul-satisfying. The dayboat fish is always sublime.

Fuerteventura

Fuerteventura has a captivating elemental beauty thanks to its bare, largely flat landscape of white-sand beaches lapped with turquoise water. Strong winds and a calm sea on the east coast make the island ideal for sailing, diving, fishing and, in particular, kitesurfing and windsurfing.

▶ **Population:** 115 333

Info: Corralejo: Avenida Marítima 2. ☎928 86 62 35. www.fuerteventura turismo.com.

Location: 100km/62mi NW of the coast of Africa. Immediately N is Lanzarote.

Kids: Oasis Wildlife Park.

LANDSCAPE AND CLIMATE

Arid Fuerteventura is dotted with bare crests and extinct volcanoes. It was described as a 'skeletal island' by its most famous native, the poet and writer **Miguel de Unamuno**, exiled here in 1924. The harsh terrain is only suitable for grazing goats, which far outnumber humans. Villages are marked by palm trees and windmills.

Fuerteventura's climate is basically African. Sand, blown across the sea from the Sahara, formed its southern isthmus, El Jable, famous for its beaches.

🚗 DRIVING TOUR

NORTH TO SOUTH

Corralejo★

This quaint one-time fishing village, the island's main tourist resort, is at the northern tip of the island beyond the *malpaís*. Crystal-clear water and white-dune **beaches** define the Parque Natural Dunas de Corralejo and the Isla de Lobos, a Robinson Crusoe island, accessible by ferry. Lanzarote is visible north.

▶ Leave Corralejo along the FV 101.

La Oliva

The **Centro de Arte Casa Mané** (open Mon–Fri 10am–5pm, Sat 10am–2pm; ☎928 86 82 33, www.centrodeartecanario.com) is the island's best art gallery, devoted to Canarian art. Opposite stands the landmark **Casa de Coroneles**, a grand 18C house. Once the residence of the governor of the island, it is now an arts and cultural centre (open Tue–Sat 10am–6pm; €3, free 18 & 30 May; ☎928 868 280; www.lacasadeloscoroneles.org).

▶ Continue on the FV 10, passing the Guanche's sacred Mount Tindaya on your right. Just before you turn right onto the FV 207, look for the large hillside statue of Miguel de Unamuno. Pass through Tefía.

Ecomuseo de la Alcogida

La Alcogida, Tefía. Open Tue–Sat 10am–5.30pm. €5. ☎928 17 54 34. www.artesaniaymuseosdefuerte ventura.org.

This is the island's most engaging museum, depicting rural country life around 50 to 100 years ago, scattered among seven houses and farms (as of 2019, about half were closed for reasons unknown).

Betancuria★

This pretty valley settlement, no bigger than a small village, was once the capital, founded in 1404 by island conqueror Jean de Bethencourt.

It retains a ruined Franciscan monastery and an ancient **cathedral**, with white walls and a picturesque wooden balcony, now called the **Iglesia de Santa María la Antigua**. The baptistery contains an interesting crucifix; the sacristy has a fine panelled ceiling.

On the south side, a small **Museo Arqueológico** displays Guanche artefacts (Roberto Roldán; open Tue–Sat 10am–6pm; closed public holidays; €2; ☎928 878 241).

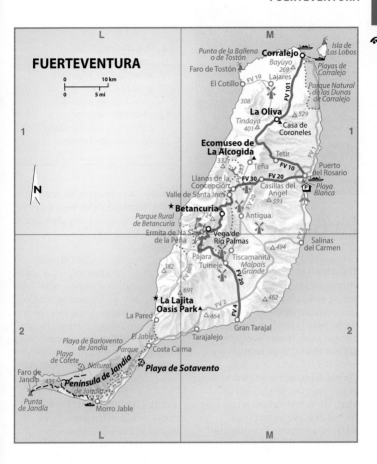

The road south provides an attractive contrast between the wide horizon of bare rose-tinted peaks and the village of **Vega de Río Palmas** nestling in its green valley-oasis.

◗ Head SW along the FV 617, turn left onto the FV2 coast road, then NE for a short distance.

♣♣ Oasis Wildlife Fuerteventura★

Ctra General de Jandia, La Lajita. Open 9am–6pm. €35 (€12 camel ride).
℘928 161 102.
www.fuerteventuraoasispark.com.
Located at the gateway to the Jandía Peninsula, Oasis Park is indeed an oasis of botanical gardens and exotic animals amid the parched southern landscape.

The zoo includes over 200 species of birds and hundreds of small animals and is famous for its camel rides (common on the island until the mid-20C). There are also shows featuring sea lions, birds of prey and crocodiles.

◗ Head back SW on the FV2.

Península de Jandía

The leeward (southern) side of this protected southernmost part of the island is famous for magnificent beaches★★. They are largely uncommercialised, though a number of low-key resorts popular with German visitors have cropped up over the last three decades. Jandía is the main centre for windsurfing and kitesurfing; world championships are staged here.

Valle Gran Rey

La Gomera★

La Gomera, with an area of 378sq km/146sq mi, is ideal for visitors seeking peace, contact with nature and outdoor activities. The round island rises from coastal cliffs, cut by deep ravines, to a *meseta* with a single peak, Mount Garajonay (1 487m/4 880ft). Black beaches are reminders of volcanic activity, as are the dramatic basalt cliffs known as Los Órganos, only visible by boat. The fertile red soil is carefully husbanded into picturesque terraces, a feature of the island.

SIGHTS

San Sebastián de la Gomera

Christopher Columbus stayed here during his first voyage. His route can be traced, down the main street from the corner house where he took on water (ask to see the well, el pozo, in the patio), past the **Iglesia de la Asunción** (Medio; ℘922 87 03 03) where he heard Mass, to the **Casa de la Aguada**, a small house located before the post office, where he is said to have slept.

🚗 DRIVING TOUR

15km/9.3mi.

▶ Leave San Sebastián de la Gomera on the TF 711.

▶ **Population:** 21 525
🈯 **Info:** Calle Real 32, San Sebastián de La Gomera. ℘922 14 15 12. www.lagomera.travel.
◖ **Location:** La Gomera is a 35min ferry ride from Los Cristianos on Tenerife.

The road emerges from the first tunnel in the **Hermigua Valley★★** amid white houses, palms and banana plantations.

Agulo★

19km/11.8m NW from San Sebastián.

This small villages enjoys a sigh-worthy seaside location with Tenerife clearly visible on the horizon. In the **Las Rosas** restaurant (in the eponymous village), there are demonstrations of *El Silbo*, the unique whistling language invented by the islanders in order to communicate with each other across Gomera's many ravines.

Parque Nacional Garajonay★★

Juego de Bolas visitor centre. Open 9.30am–4.30pm. Guided walking tours on Sat by prior arrangement. ℘922 80 09 93.

This national park is covered by laurels, traces of the Tertiary era, and giant heathers, punctuated by rocks. Mist caused by trade winds lends an air of mystery.

Valle Gran Rey★★

55km/34mi from San Sebastián de la Gomera on the TF 713.

The road climbs the slopes to the south; the climb to the central *meseta* in the park is less steep. There are a handful of small roadside villages, including **Chipude**, famous for pottery. Drive through **Arure**, and after the bridge there is a fine **panorama★** of Taguluche. The highlight is the **Barranco del Valle Gran Rey★★**, the most spectacular ravine on the island.

El Hierro

This remote, windswept island, just 278sq km/107sq mi, sees few visitors – and that's precisely its allure. Those who make the trip are rewarded with fertile farmland, spectacular cliffs plunging into the sea, volcanic cones, laurel-carpeted lava fields and some of the most pristine diving on the planet.

▶ **Population:** 10 675
▪ **Info:** Calle Dr Quintero 4, Valverde. ℰ922 55 03 02. www.elhierro.travel.
◔ **Location:** El Hierro is in the far southwest of the archipelago. Ferries run to neighbouring islands (ℰ902 100 107; www.fredolsen.es).

SIGHTS

Tamaduste

◔ 8km/5mi NE.

A large sandbank by the small seaside resort forms a lagoon.

El Golfo★★

◔ 8km/5mi W.

There is a fine view★★ of El Golfo from the **Mirador de La Peña**. The rim of a crater is covered with laurels and giant heather; the level floor is cultivated. La Fuga de Gorreta, near the Salmor rocks (NE), is the habitat of a primeval lizard.

TOUR THROUGH LA DEHESA

◔ 105km/65mi. Head S from Valverde along the TF 912. The excursions below depart from Valverde, the capital of the island, at an altitude of 571m/1 873ft.

Tiñor – Pyramid-shaped formations of ash among fertile fields denote this area. Until 1610, when it was blown down, a Garoé tree was venerated by natives.

Sabinosa – A spa-hotel treats skin and digestive diseases.

La Dehesa – A track 3 km/1.8mi farther on crosses the arid La Dehesa region and provides extensive **views★** of the south coast, where the fiery red earth, pitted with craters, slopes to the sea.

Punta de Orchilla – Orchilla Point was the zero meridian before Greenwich. Beyond the lighthouse are sabine trees, ancient conifers with wildly gnarled trunks found only on El Hierro.

Ermita de Nuestra Señora de los Reyes – In this hermitage is a statue of the Virgen de Los Reyes, patron saint of the island. Every four years since 1741, it is carried in procession to Valverde

Restaurant at Mirador de La Peña

© Franck Guiziou/hemis.fr

(Bajada Virgen de los Reyes). It will next take place on the first Saturday of July in 2021.

El Pinar – An aromatic **pine forest**★ extends across this central region of the island. The shaded picnic area at **Hoya del Morcillo** offers a respite from the bright Canary Island sunlight.

With barbecue pits, picnic tables, toilets, a football pitch and a playground for children, this is also a convenient ⚠ campsite for hikes through the mountainous, wooded wilderness at the heart of the El Hierro. Camping permits must be obtained in advance in Valverde (𝒫 922 55 00 17).

ADDRESSES

🛏 STAY

😊🍽🍽🍽 **Parador de El Hierro** – Las Playas. 𝒫 922 55 80 36. www.parador.es. 45 rooms. 🍴€18. Restaurant 😊🍽🍽🍽. In the Las Playas beach district 20km/ 12.5mi SW of Valverde, this restful Parador built on a ledge of volcanic rock has panoramic views, handsome colonial furnishings and a restaurant specialising in island dishes such as local fish with periwinkles.

🍴 EAT

😊🍽 **La Higuera de Abuela** – Valverde 38900. 𝒫 922 55 10 26. In Echedo, 5km/3mi north east of Valverde, this yellow-walled tavern serves simply prepared meats and seafood.

La Palma★

With a surface area of 706sq km/272sq mi and its highest peak rising to 2 426m/7 962ft, La Palma has the highest average altitude of any island on earth. Rain is more abundant here than in the rest of the Canaries, resulting in numerous streams and springs. Its nickname is 'Beautiful Island' or 'Green Island' because of its woods of laurel and pine and miles of banana plantations. La Palma has distanced itself from major tourist development and appeals to nature-lovers, walkers and those seeking peace and quiet.

A BIT OF HISTORY

The Caldera de Taburiente, a huge mountain arch curiously shaped like a crater, spreads over 10km/6.2mi. A chain of peaks, Las Cumbres, extends south; ravines produce an indented coastline. In the mountains, rainwater is collected to irrigate the lower terraces.

▸ **Population:** 83 159
🛈 **Info:** Plaza de la Constitución, Santa Cruz de la Palma. 𝒫 922 41 21 06. www.visitlapalma.es.
◖ **Location:** La Palma is located in the far northwest of the archipelago.

SIGHTS
SANTA CRUZ DE LA PALMA

The administrative centre was founded in 1493 by the conquistador Alonso Fernández de Lugo. In the 16C, with rising sugar exports and the expansion of the naval yards, Santa Cruz was one of the Spanish Empire's major ports (third only to Sevilla and Antwerp) and prey to pirates; now it is a peaceful city where elegant facades line the seafront. Its most famous native is Manolo Blahnik. At Playa de Los Cancajos (5km/3mi S) the beach and rocks are black.

Plaza de España

Several buildings date to the Renaissance. The 16C **Iglesia de El Salvador** has ceilings with **artesonado orna-**

ment★; the sacristy has Gothic vaulting. Opposite stand the 16C town hall and houses in colonial style. Walk uphill to the delightful **Plaza de Santo Domingo**.

Next to a college stands the **chapel** of a former monastery with beautiful Baroque altars. ⊗ To visit the chapel, ask for the keys at the Iglesia de El Salvador, ℘922 41 32 50.

🚗 DRIVING TOURS

Both tours suggested below depart from Santa Cruz de la Palma.

THE NORTH OF THE ISLAND

Observatorio Roque de los Muchachos★★★

36km/22.3mi NW of Santa Cruz de la Palma. Allow 1hr45min for the ascent.

Laurel bushes and pine trees line the winding road that offers extensive views as it climbs to the **astrophysical observatory**, at 2 432m/7 981ft, including the William Herschel Telescope, one of the largest in the world with a 4.2m/13.7ft mirror (guided tours at 9.30am & 11.30am by prior arrangement; see website for schedule and application form; €9; ℘922 405 500; www.iac.es). From the Roque de los Muchachos a fantastic **panorama★★★** encompasses the caldera, Los Llanos de Aridane, the islands of El Hierro and La Gomera and Mount Teide.

Punta Cumplida

36km/22.3mi N.

There are fine views of the coast from the cliff road, which crosses deep ravines *(barrancos)* in the Los Tilos Biosphere Reserve. Note the impressive number of craters.

La Galga

(15km/9.3mi N off LP 1) – North of the village, after the tunnel, the road crosses a steep and well-wooded **ravine★**.

San Andrés

(22km/13.6mi N off LP 1) – In the church is an intricate Mudéjar ceiling in the chancel.

Charco Azul – Take a dip in natural seawater pools.

Puerto Espíndola – Wander a fishing village where boats are drawn up onto a single beach in a breach in the cliff face.

Punta Cumplida – Walk round the lighthouse to see waves breaking on basalt rock piles. The attractive Fajana swimming pools are north of here.

Los Sauces

(2km/1.2mi W of San Andrés) – This is the main agricultural centre in the north of the island.

Los Tiles★

Detour up Agua Ravine to the lime tree forest. **Los Tiles Interpretation and Investigation Centre** (open Mon-Sun 9am-5pm; ℘922 45 12 46) explains the flora in the reserve.

THE CENTRE AND SOUTH OF THE ISLAND

Vía Los Llanos and Fuencaliente

190km/118mi. Head N out of Santa Cruz. After the ravine, take the first left.

On the seafront of Santa Cruz stands the **Castillo de Santa Catalina**, built to fend off pirate raiders in the 17C.

In the **Barco de la Virgen** (*the Virgin's Boat*), a curious cement reproduction of Columbus's Santa María, is a small **naval museum** (Pérez Galdós 18; ℘922 41 17 87). The road passes the **Fuerte de la Virgen**, a 16C fortress.

Las Nieves

At the foot of Pico de las Nieves, shaded by laurel trees, the **Real Santuario de Nuestra Señora de las Nieves** houses the statue of the island's patron saint. Every five years (the next will be in 2020), it is the centrepiece of a grand parade.

La Concepción★

The summit of the Caldereta commands a **bird's-eye view★** of Santa

Cruz de la Palma, the harbour and the mountains.

▶ Take the TF 812 westwards.

Parque Nacional de la Caldera de Taburiente★★★

4km/2.5mi W of the tunnel on the right is the **Centro de Visitantes** (Ctra. General de Padrón 47, El Paso; ☎922 922 280); info on marked footpaths.

▶ Ahead, turn right for La Cumbrecita.

The **Cumbrecita Pass** (1 833m/6 014ft) and the **Lomo de las Chozas Pass** (1km/0.6mi farther) provide a splendid **panorama★★★** of the Caldera de Taburiente, dotted with Canary pines and crowned by rose-tinted peaks.

Los Llanos de Aridane

The island's second-largest town is tucked amid banana and avocado trees.

El Time★★

The top of El Time cliff affords a remarkable **panorama★★** of the Aridane plain,

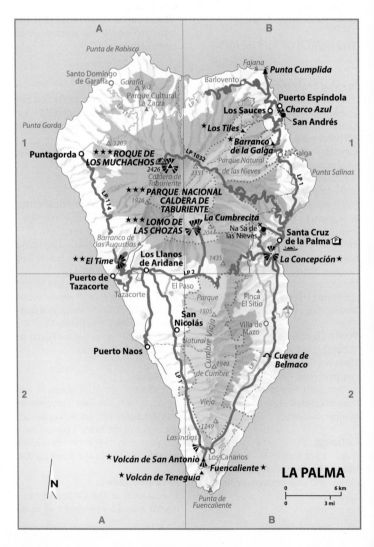

LA PALMA

a sea of banana palms, and of the Barranco de las Angustias, a rock fissure which is the only outlet for the Caldera de Taburiente.

Puntagorda
This fine landscape is particularly breathtaking in spring, when the almond trees are in bloom.

▶ Return to El Time.

Puerto de Tazacorte
Alonso Fernández de Lugo landed in this small harbour in 1492. In 1585, Francis Drake raided the town on his way to the Caribbean. Nicknamed 'París chiquito' (little Paris), the small beach is popular on Sundays.

Puerto Naos
Descend through lava fields from the 1949 eruption and then through the lush avocado and banana plantations irrigated by La Caldera de Taburiente, to the Puerto with its wide beach of black volcanic sand.

San Nicolás
The lava stream from the Nambroque volcano cut the village in two in 1949.

Fuencaliente de la Palma★
Before reaching Fuencaliente, look back from the Mirador de las Indias for a **glimpse★** of the coast through the pines. A hot water spring disappeared during the eruption of **San Antonio volcano★** in 1677. Circle the volcano to see the craters of **Teneguía volcano★**, which appeared in October 1971, and

the lava stream that separated the lighthouse from the village.

Cueva de Belmaco
5km/3mi from the airport fork.
Enter the cave of Guanche king Belamaco. At the back of the cave are rocks with inscriptions.

ADDRESSES

🛏 STAY
🛏 **Pensión La Cubana** – Calle O'Daly 24. ☎922 41 13 54. 6 rooms. www.cubana-pension.com This tiny pension in a traditional townhouse ten minutes from the beach offers is a terrific budget option.

🛏🛏🛏 **Parador de la Palma** – Crtra. El Zumacal. ☎922 43 58 28. www.parador.es. 78 rooms. ⊠€18. Restaurant 🍽🍽🍽. The views from this promontory on the San Antonio to Breña Alta road 6km/4 mi SE of town are extraordinary. Public spaces are open and ample, and guest rooms are spacious.

ⴼ/EAT
🍽🍽🍽 **La Placeta** – Placeta de Borrero 1, Santa Cruz. ☎922 41 52 73. www.restaurantelaplaceta.com. Closed Sun, Aug. Set in an 18C mansion among balconied houses, this bistro-restaurant serves everything from club sandwiches to seared cuttlefish .

🍽🍽🍽 **Parrilla Las Nieves** – Pl. de las Nieves 2, Santa Cruz. ☎922 41 66 00. Closed Thu. Cooking over coals is the speciality at this no-frills, tile-floored tavern. Roast rabbit and goat are favourites.

INDEX

INDEX

INDEX

INDEX

INDEX

INDEX

INDEX

INDEX

INDEX

🛏️ STAY

🍽️ EAT

Thematic Maps

Maps and Plans

	Sight	Seaside resort	Winter sports resort	Spa
Worth a special journey	★★★	🏖🏖🏖	❄❄❄	⚕⚕⚕
Worth a detour	★★	🏖🏖	❄❄	⚕⚕
Interesting	★	🏖	❄	⚕

Additional symbols

🛈		Tourist information
═══ ═══		Motorway or other primary route
❶	❶	Junction: complete, limited
═══ ═══		Pedestrian street
⊏═══⊐		Unsuitable for traffic, street subject to restrictions
▥▥▥	----	Steps – Footpath
🚂	🚃	Train station – Auto-train station
🚌	S.N.C.F.	Coach (bus) station
┄┄┄		Tram
Ⓜ		Metro, underground
P/R		Park-and-Ride
♿		Access for the disabled
✉		Post office
☎		Telephone
✉		Covered market
⊹✕⊹		Barracks
△		Drawbridge
∪		Quarry
✗		Mine
Ⓑ	Ⓕ	Car ferry (river or lake)
🚢		Ferry service: cars and passengers
⛴		Foot passengers only
③		Access route number common to Michelin maps and town plans
Bert (R.)...		Main shopping street
AZ B		Map co-ordinates

Selected monuments and sights

◉━━▶		Tour - Departure point
⛪ ✝		Catholic church
⛪ ✝		Protestant church, other temple
✡ ☪		Synagogue - Mosque
▬		Building
■		Statue, small building
✝		Calvary, wayside cross
◎		Fountain
━●━■▶		Rampart - Tower - Gate
⋈		Château, castle, historic house
∴		Ruins
∪		Dam
✿		Factory, power plant
✩		Fort
∩		Cave
▣		Troglodyte dwelling
⛩		Prehistoric site
▼		Viewing table
Ⓦ		Viewpoint
▲		Other place of interest

603

Useful Words and Phrases

The following phrases denote translations between English and **Castilian**, the official language of Spain and better known as Spanish in the wider world. Yet there are also four other languages officially recognised in various regions of Spain: **Catalan** (Catalonia, Valencia and the Balearics); **Basque** (Basque Country); **Galician** (Galicia); and **Aranès** (northwest Catalonia). These languages are widespread in these areas and many inhabitants see Castilian as their second language.

COMMON WORDS

	Translation
Agreed	De acuerdo
Excuse me	Perdone
Good morning	Buenos días
Good afternoon	Buenas tardes
Goodbye	Hasta luego, Adiós
How are You?	¿Qué tal?
I don't understand	No entiendo
Madam, Mrs	Señora
Miss	Señorita
OK	Vale
Please	Por favor
Sir, Mr; You	Señor; Usted
Thank you (very much)	(Muchas) Gracias
Yes, No	Sí, No

CORRESPONDENCE

	Translation
Letter	Carta
Postbox	Buzón
Postcard	(Tarjeta) Postal
Post Office	Correos
Stamp	Sello
Telephone	Teléfono
Telephone Call	Llamada
Tobacco Shop	Estanco, Tabaquería

FOOD AND DRINK

	Translation
Apple	Manzana
Anchovies	Boquerones
Banana	Plátano
Beef	Vaca/buey
Beer	Cerveza
(Black) pepper	Pimienta (Negra)
Bread	Pan
Butter	Mantequilla
Café solo	Black coffee
Cheese	Queso
Coffee with hot milk	Café con leche
Cream	Crema
Dessert	Postre
Egg	Huevo
Fish	Pescados

Garlic	Ajo
Ham	Jamón
Ice cream	Helado
I'm allergic to...	Tengo alergia a...
Lactose	Lactosa
Lemon	Limón
Meat	Carne
Meatballs	Albóndigas
Mejillones	Mussels
Milk	Leche
Mushrooms	Setas/hongos
Nut(s)	Nuez (Nueces)
Oil, Olives	Aceite, Aceitunas
Omelette	Tortilla
Onion	Cebolla
Orange	Naranja
Potatoes	Patatas
Pork	Cerdo
Prawns	Gambas
Red wine	Vino tinto
Rice	Arroz
Salad	Ensalada
Salad of diced vegetables in mayonaise	Ensalada Rusa
Salt	Sal
Sausages	Salchichas
Seafood, shellfish	Mariscos
Sparkling/still water	Agua con/sin gas
Soup	Potaje
Soya	Soja
Sugar	Azúcar
Vegetables	Legumbres
Vegetarian	Vegetariano/a
Wheat	Trigo
White/rosé wine	Vino blanco/rosado

NUMBERS

	Translation
0	cero
1	uno/una
2	dos
3	tres
4	cuatro
5	cinco
6	seis
7	siete
8	ocho
9	nueve
10	diez
20	veinte
50	cincuenta
100	cien
1 000	mil

ON THE ROAD, IN TOWN

	Translation
After, Beyond	Después de
Beware, Take care	Cuidado
Car	Coche, Auto
Danger, Dangerous	Peligro, Peligroso
On the right	A la derecha
On the left	A la izquierda
Petrol, Gasoline	Gasolina
Roadworks	Obras

OUT AND ABOUT

Also See architectural terms in the Introduction.

	Translation
Artificial Lake	Pantano
Audience, Court	Audiencia

Avenue, Promenade	Paseo		Island, Isle	Isla
Beautiful	Hermoso/a		Keep	Torreón
Belfry	Campanario		Lake	Lago
Belvedere, Viewpoint, Lookout Point	Mirador		Light	Luz
			Main Road	Carretera
Bridge	Puente		Main Square	Plaza Mayor
Bullring	Plaza de Toros		Main street	Calle Mayor
Cape, Headland	Cabo		May one visit...?	¿Se puede visitar...?
Carved Wood	Talla		Monastery	Monasterio
Castle	Castillo		Moorish architectural style under Christian rule	Mudéjar
Cave, Grotto	Cueva, Gruta, Cava			
Cavern, Grotto	Gruta		Mosque	Mezquita
Chapel	Capilla		Mount, Mountain	Monte
Ceiling	Techo		Muslim Palace	Alcázar
Century	Siglo		Museum	Museo
Church	Iglesia		No Entry, Not allowed	Prohibido el paso
Church	Santuario			
College, Colegiata Church	Colegio, Collegiate		Open, Closed	Abierto, Cerrado
			Outskirts	Alrededores
Cloisters	Claustro		Pass, High Pass	Collado
Convent	Convento		Pass, Harbour, Port	Puerto
Cross	Cruz		Picture	Cuadro
Dam	Presa		Portal, Porch	Pórtico
Defile, Cleft	Desfiladero		Porter, Caretaker	Guarda, Conserje
Door, Gate, Entrance	Puerta		Property, Domain	Finca
Entrance, Exit	Entrada, Salida		Quarter	Barrio
Estuary	Ría		Religious Statue/ Sculpture Imágen	
Excavations	Excavaciones		Reservoir, Dam	Embalse
Exuberant early baroque style named for the Churriguera brothers	Churrigueresco		River, Stream	Río
			Road, Track	Camino
			(Royal) Palace	Palacio (Real)
			Source, Birthplace	Nacimiento
Fountain	Fuente		Spa	Balneario
Gorges	Gargantas		Square	Plaza
Guide	Guía		Stained-glass window	Vidriera
Gully, Ravine	Barranco		Station	Estación
Hermitage, Chapel	Ermita		Storey, Stairs, Steps	Piso, Escalera
High Pass, Pass	Collado/Alto		Street	Calle
House	Casa			

GETTING BY IN SPAIN'S OTHER LANGUAGES

English	Aranès	Basque	Catalan	Galician
good morning/hello	bon dia/ola/adiu	egun on/kaixo	bon dia	boas días/ola
good evening	bona tarde	gabon	bona nit	boas noites
please	se vos platz	mesedez	per favor	por favor
thank you	gràcies/mercès	eskerrik asko	gràcies	grazas
today	auè	gaur	avui	hoxe
left	ara esquèra	ezker	esquerre(a)	esquerda
right	ara dreta	eskuin	dret(a)	dereita
open	obert	ireki	obert(a)	aberto
closed	tancat	hertsi	tancat	pechado
toilet	comuns	komuna	servies	servizos

Tapestries	Tapices
Tower, Belfry	Torre
Town, City	Ciudad
Town Hall	Ayuntamiento
Town Hall	Casa Consistorial
Treasury, Treasure	Tesoro
Vegetable/Market Garden	Huerto, Huerta
Vaulting	Boveda
Village, Market Town	Pueblo
Vineyard	Viña
View, Panorama	Vista
Wait!	Espere
Where is...?	¿Dónde está...?
Wine Cellar/store	Bodega

SHOPPING

	Translation
How much?	¿Cuánto (vale)?
(Too) Expensive	(Demasiado) Caro
A Lot, Little	Mucho, Poco
More, Less	Más, Menos
Big, Small	Grande, Pequeño
Credit Card	Tarjeta de Crédito
Receipt	Recibo

TIME

	Translation
Today	Hoy
Tomorrow	Mañana
What time?	¿A qué hora?
When?	¿Cuándo?
Yesterday	Ayer

THE GREEN GUIDE **SPAIN**

Editorial Director	Cynthia Clayton Ochterbeck
Editor	Sophie Friedman
Principal Writers	Benjamin Kemper, Paul Murphy
Production Manager	Natasha George
Cartography	Peter Wrenn
Picture Editor	Yoshimi Kanazawa
Interior Design	Natasha George, Jonathan P. Gilbert
Layout	Natasha George
Cover Design	Chris Bell, Christelle Le Déan
Contact Us	Michelin Travel and Lifestyle North America One Parkway South Greenville, SC 29615 USA travel.lifestyle@us.michelin.com
	Michelin Travel Partner Hannay House 39 Clarendon Road Watford, Herts WD17 1JA UK ✆01923 205240 travelpubsales@uk.michelin.com www.viamichelin.co.uk
Special Sales	For information regarding bulk sales, customized editions and premium sales, please contact us at: travel.lifestyle@us.michelin.com

**YOUR OPINION IS ESSENTIAL
TO IMPROVING OUR PRODUCTS**

*Help us by answering the
questionnaire on our website:*
satisfaction.michelin.com

Michelin Travel Partner

Société par actions simplifiées au capital de 15 044 940 EUR
27 cours de l'Ile Seguin - 92100 Boulogne Billancourt (France)
R.C.S. Nanterre 433 677 721

© Michelin Travel Partner
ISBN 978-2-067243-08-8
Printed: October 2019
Printed and bound in France : Imprimerie CHIRAT, 42540 Saint-Just-la-Pendue - N° 201910.0423

Metro
1 Pinar de Chamartín/Valdecarros
2 Las Rosas/Cuatro Caminos
3 Villaverde Alto/Moncloa
4 Argüelles/Pinar de Chamartín
5 Alameda de Osuna/Casa de Campo
6 Circular
7 Hospital del Henares/Pitis
8 Nuevos Ministerios/Aeropuerto
9 Mirasierra/Arganda del Rey
10 Hospital Infanta Sofía/Puerta del Sur
11 Plaza Elíptica/La Fortuna
12 MetroSur
R Ópera/Príncipe Pío

Cercanías
C2 Guadalajara/Alcalá/Atocha/Chamartín
C3 Chamartín/Sol/Atocha/Aranjuez
C3a Pinto/San Martín de la Vega
C4 Parla/Atocha/Sol/Chamartín/
    Alcobendas-San Sebastián de los Reyes
    Colmenar Viejo
C5 Móstoles-El Soto/Atocha/Fuenlabrada/Humanes
C7 Alcalá de Henares/Atocha/Chamartín/Príncipe Pío/
    Atocha/Chamartín/Fuente de la Mora
C8 Atocha/Chamartín/Villalba
    Villalba/El Escorial
    Villalba/Cercedilla
C9 Cercedilla/Cotos
C10 Villalba/Príncipe Pío/Atocha/
    Chamartín/Fuente de la Mora

Metro Ligero
1 Pinar de Chamartín/Las Tablas
2 Colonia Jardín/Estación de Aravaca
3 Colonia Jardín/Puerta de Boadilla